ORIENTALIST JONES

ORIENTALIST JONES

SIR WILLIAM JONES, POET,
LAWYER, AND LINGUIST,
1746–1794

MICHAEL J. FRANKLIN

OXFORD
UNIVERSITY PRESS

OXFORD
UNIVERSITY PRESS

Great Clarendon Street, Oxford OX2 6DP

Oxford University Press is a department of the University of Oxford.
It furthers the University's objective of excellence in research, scholarship,
and education by publishing worldwide in

Oxford New York

Auckland Cape Town Dar es Salaam Hong Kong Karachi
Kuala Lumpur Madrid Melbourne Mexico City Nairobi
New Delhi Shanghai Taipei Toronto

With offices in

Argentina Austria Brazil Chile Czech Republic France Greece
Guatemala Hungary Italy Japan Poland Portugal Singapore
South Korea Switzerland Thailand Turkey Ukraine Vietnam

Oxford is a registered trade mark of Oxford University Press
in the UK and in certain other countries

Published in the United States
by Oxford University Press Inc., New York

© Michael J. Franklin 2011

The moral rights of the author have been asserted
Database right Oxford University Press (maker)

First published 2011

All rights reserved. No part of this publication may be reproduced,
stored in a retrieval system, or transmitted, in any form or by any means,
without the prior permission in writing of Oxford University Press,
or as expressly permitted by law, or under terms agreed with the appropriate
reprographics rights organization. Enquiries concerning reproduction
outside the scope of the above should be sent to the Rights Department,
Oxford University Press, at the address above

You must not circulate this book in any other binding or cover
and you must impose the same condition on any acquirer

British Library Cataloguing in Publication Data

Data available

Library of Congress Cataloging in Publication Data

Data available

Typeset by SPI Publisher Services, Pondicherry, India
Printed in Great Britain
on acid-free paper by
MPG Books Group, Bodmin and King's Lynn

ISBN 978–0–19–953200–1

1 3 5 7 9 10 8 6 4 2

For Caroline, Beatriz and Geraint, Céline and Ieuan

Contents

Preface	viii
List of Illustrations	xi
1. Claiming Kin in Calcutta: Jones Discovers the Indo-European Family of Languages	1
2. 'Persian' Jones, London Welshman, Surveys his Roots	43
3. 'Druid' Jones on the Carmarthen Circuit: Radicalization and Recreation on the Celtic Fringe	90
4. Impressive Patrons and Impressing Mariners	124
5. Republican Jones and the 'Poetry of Politics': Fragments of Liberty	163
6. Knowing India: Asiatic Researches/Recreations	205
7. Europe Falls in Love with Śakuntalā	251
8. Life and Death in Calcutta: A Courtroom View of the Ethics of Empire	287
9. 'Indo-Persian' Jones and Indian Pluralism	333
Select Bibliography	362
Index	375

Preface

> '*the gay dunce sits pining for a partner, while Jones the Orientalist leads up the ball*'
> (Hester Lynch Thrale Piozzi)

To write on a polymath is to be constantly reminded of one's own inadequacies. So, if any wise Sanskritist, postcolonialist, shiny new or scuffed old historicist—indeed any expert in any of the diverse fields of scholarship which Sir William Jones opened up—detects deficiencies in what follows, her/his characterization of this biographer as a 'gay dunce' will not be one that has not frequently occurred to the biographer himself. As he sits before his screen, on which global knowledge is instantly available, he is pining only for a more capacious brain, rather than an invitation to the intellectuals' ball.

Nevertheless, to write on Jones has been an unexpurgated joy, facilitated, I gratefully add, by the Arts and Humanities Research Council. Jones remains an immensely attractive figure and all the qualities that engaged his friends are reflected in his poetry, his personal letters, and his scholarly discourse. If something of this emerges in the following pages I shall have achieved much. Above all, completing this book has been a learning process. Dr Thomas Barnard, dean of Derry, poetically outlining the self-improvement available from fellow Turk's Head Club members, wrote: 'Jones teach me modesty and Greek'—I'd settle for sensibility and Sanskrit. I share Jones's delight in the sensuousness of India, her rich multifariousness and vibrant cultural mingling. I was drawn to research him by an Indo-European love of fragrant spices and Kashmiri curry, the mysticism of India's music, and the classical precision of her dance. In return Jones taught me to appreciate the exquisite delicacy of Indo-Persian poetry and the sophisticated beauties of Kālidāsa and Jayadeva.

As I sit writing this in the air-conditioned comfort of the Fales Library in Washington Square, an autograph manuscript written in the relentless heat of Calcutta lies on the table before me. Outlining Sir William Jones's 'Literary Projects', it lists 'Odes in Four Books: I. Celtick; II. Saxon; III. Norman; IV. Teutonick. Object: to praise great *Warriours*, *Patriots*, and *Statesmen* who have flourished in Britain, and to recommend them as objects of imitation by *Englishmen*'. Beneath are recorded his plans for:

Hymns in Four Books

I Indian	European
II Persian	Asiatick
III Arabian	African
IV Hyperborean	American

Object: to recommend universal toleration by showing that all nations, even those esteemed the most idolatrous, agree in the essentials of religion, a belief in one God, Creator and preserver, and in a future state of rewards and punishments.   (New York, Fales Library, Jones MSS: 1: 20)

With the United Nations summit meeting here in New York to consider 'the promise of the Millennium Declaration for a better world', the need for great 'statesmen' and for 'universal toleration' has never been more urgent. The wisdom and visionary projects of an eighteenth-century polymath still have much to say to a twenty-first-century world.

My debt to Garland Cannon—who donated Parcel 698 of Jones's papers to the Fales Library—must also be acknowledged, for his scrupulous editing of Jones's letters, not to mention his valuable biography and troops of articles. It was both an honour and a pleasure to collaborate on a jointly authored article with Garland via email and the cheery offices of Texas A & M University librarian Hal Hall in 2005. If it was Jones's passion for India that infected Caroline and myself with a corresponding enthusiasm, our thanks are to Professors Malabika Sarkar, Ramakanta Chakrabarty, Gulfishan Khan, Ali Fatihi, Abdul Kidwai, Shobhana Bhattacharji, Shyamala Narayan, and Surya Pandey, who made our trips to Kolkata, Aligarh, New Delhi, and Vāranāsī so valuable and memorable. I also record my special appreciation of the kind generosity of Professor Thomas Curley who allowed me to borrow his microfilms of the Hyde and Chambers Papers. Tom let me hear, admittedly via the court interpreters, the voices of ordinary Indian men and women, Hindu, Muslim, Zoroastrian, Sikh, and Christian, relaying the details of their interconnected lives.

Electronic resources, everything from Eighteenth-Century Collections Online to dear young Google Books, are revolutionizing research and it would be churlish not to acknowledge my gratitude. The ability to search text digitally and instantaneously provides the scholar with more precious time to consult manuscripts which, one day, will also be scanned. In writing this biography I have used the printed materials and manuscript resources of the Asiatic Society, Kolkata, the British Library; the National Library of Wales, Aberystwyth; the Bodleian Library, Oxford, Cambridge University Library, the New York Public Library; the National Archives of India, New Delhi; the Beinecke Library at New Haven; the Royal Asiatic Society, London, and the university libraries of Swansea, Cardiff, and Aberystwyth. I am grateful for the helpful efficiency of the library staff at all these institutions.

The help and advice of other scholars in a variety of disciplines is also thankfully acknowledged, including that of Charles Allen, Mohsen Ashtiany, Imre Bangha, Anna Livia Beelaert, Connie Bobroff, Huw Bowen, Ken Bryant, Pratik Chakrabarti, Ceri Davies, John Drew, Elizabeth Eger, Tim Fulford, Geert Jan van Gelder, Saeed Ghahremani, Jack Hawley, Fritz-Gregor Herrmann, Bill Johnson, G.M. Kapur, Nigel Leask, Parvin Loloi, P.J. Marshall, Miles Ogborn, Paola Orsatti, Glyn Parry, Frances Pritchett, Geoff Quilley, Rosane and Ludo Rocher, William Rothwell, Dinkar Sitaram, Adam Talib, Anthony Tedeschi, and David Trotter. I should also like to express my gratitude to my editor, Luciana O'Flaherty, not least for her patience and adaptability, and to her Oxford University Press colleagues, Matthew Cotton and Deborah Protheroe, for their tireless assistance. Penultimate but not least, my thanks are to my Romantic Orientalism students who continually inspire me with their fresh and perceptive insights. As ever, my deepest debt is to Caroline, my wisest, and very best choice of, partner.

Mike Franklin
21 September 2010

List of Illustrations

1. New Court House and Chandpal Ghaut, aquatint with etching, coloured by Thomas Daniell, 1787. (© The British Library Board, c. 13602–84) — 17
2. View of the Ghats at Benares, 1787, by William Hodges. (© John Hammond Royal Academy of Arts, London) — 26
3. Statue of Jones by John Bacon, in St Paul's Cathedral, 1799. (Conway Library, The Courtauld Institute of Art, London) — 41
4. William Jones (1675–1749), mathematician and father of Jones, by William Hogarth, oil on canvas, 1740 (© National Portrait Gallery, London) — 50
5. Sir William Jones as a boy, by Sir Joshua Reynolds, oil on canvas, c.1753. (The Asiatic Society, Kolkata) — 52
6. *Philosophical Transactions of the Royal Society*, 46 (London, 1752), 468–9 — 53
7. Sir William Jones, by Sir Joshua Reynolds, oil on canvas, 1769. (From the Collection at Althorp) — 68
8. Sir William Jones, attributed to James Northcote, oil on canvas, c.1772. (Amgueddfa Genedlaethol Cymru National Museum of Wales, Cardiff) — 99
9. Kilgarren Castle, South Wales, print by William Elliott after Richard Wilson, 1775. (© The Trustees of the British Museum) — 105
10. Sir William Jones, by Robert Home, oil on canvas, c.1785 (The Asiatic Society, Kolkata) — 218
11. Drawing of Anna Maria Jones from Sir William Jones's notebook. (Collection of English Drawings, James Marshall and Marie–Louise Osborn Collection, Beinecke Rare Book and Manuscript Library, Yale University) — 243
12. Letter from Jones to 2nd Earl Spencer, Crishna-nagar, 1–11 September 1787. (© The British Library Board, Add MS 75978) — 254–55
13. 'Radha and Krishna Exchange Clothes', opaque watercolour and gold on paper, Himachal Pradesh, Kangra. c.1800. (Los Angeles County Museum of Art © 2009 Museum Associates/ LACMA/Act Resource NY/Scala, Florence) — 282

14. Anna Maria Jones, drawings: a) 'Fight between Buffalo and tiger', 4 March 1785; b) 'Pandit Ramalochan',15 Oct. 1785 ; c) 'Ch'hátiyána/ Septaparna, or Seven-leaved', pen-and-ink and watercolour. (Royal Asiatic Society of Great Britain and Ireland)   314–16
15. Sir William Jones, aged 47, by Arthur William Devis, oil on canvas, 1793. (© The British Library Board, Foster 890)   322
16. Equestrian portrait of Dara Shikoh as a young man, by Chitarman, gouache, *c.*1640. (Royal Asiatic Society of Great Britain and Ireland)   344

1

Claiming Kin in Calcutta: Jones Discovers the Indo-European Family of Languages

Sir William Jones had made it! The *arriviste* had arrived even before he set out. Relaxing aboard the neat new 24-gun *Crocodile* frigate as it sailed past Spithead before a long-awaited brisk southeasterly, he could savour the sweet taste of success. The wind had changed in more ways than one. It was 12 April 1783, a bright fresh Saturday afternoon, he was a youthful 36 and, with Anna Maria, his wife of four days, he was on his way to India.

The dizzying whirl of the last month or so was at last settling down. The chaos had begun on 4 March when the papers had announced his appointment as a judge of 'his Majesty's supreme court of judicature at Fort William in Bengal', with an amazing salary of £6,000 per annum, ten times his earnings as a successful barrister. The following weeks had been a blur of social and professional engagements: resigning his Oxford fellowship and his post as Commissioner for Bankruptcy; attending an endless succession of farewell parties; packing books and East India requisites for the long passage to Calcutta. At the king's levee of 20 March Mr Justice Jones was knighted Sir William.

On Tuesday 8 April Anna Maria and William were expected at the celebrated bluestocking Elizabeth Vesey's literary gathering in Bolton Street, Piccadilly, but a message arrived in their stead: they were at that moment being married by special licence. The company agreed, 'it was so romantic', even the stolid Samuel Johnson was affected; and the staunchly evangelical 'Saint' Hannah More saw that 'banishment' to pagan Hindostan would be welcomed by the loving couple:

They will now be completely banished, but as they will be banished together, they do not think it a hardship. May God bless them, and may his stupendous learning be sanctified![1]

Anna's father, the radical bishop of St Asaph, Jonathan Shipley, was saddened to think he might never look upon his daughter again, but Hannah More comforts him that 'she goes with what she best loves,—an advantage with which few women set out to India'. At the centre of a hurried round of congratulations and preparations, the couple were excited, full of optimism. Jones had been impatiently waiting to be appointed since early 1778—five long years. Now he had the job and the title and the girl all at once, together with the prospect of a five months' honeymoon as they voyaged to Bengal.

Among the many treasured letters of congratulation was one from a close friend of both bride and groom, the United States minister plenipotentiary to the court of France, Benjamin Franklin, enclosing a proof of the Libertas Americana medal. As Jones examined the medal, bearing the Horatian motto he had recommended to Franklin: 'Non Sine Diis Animosus Infans' ('Not without divine help is the child courageous'), he recalled his enthusiasm for American revolutionary courage. American friends in Paris and London had encouraged him to become a legislator of the infant republic beside the James River in Virginia, but he was destined to accomplish revolutionary changes on the wider banks of the Hugli.

It was barely a year since Jones composed, at Franklin's house in Passy, *The Principles of Government* (1782), radically reminding the people of their legal right to bear arms in the resistance of despotic royal power. By a supreme irony, while the high sheriff of Flintshire, Thomas Fitzmaurice, was prosecuting William Shipley, dean of St Asaph and Jones's future brother-in-law, for reprinting this 'seditious, treasonable, and diabolical' tract at Wrexham in January 1783, Fitzmaurice's brother, Prime Minister Lord Shelburne, was recommending Jones to the king for the Indian judgeship.

Jones's radicalism long delayed his India appointment, but now he could safely relish the ironies—as rich as the madeira they would take on board at Funchal. He reassured Anna that her brother was in no danger since there was no precedent for indicting a theoretical essay on government. But the lawyer could appreciate the uniqueness of the situation whereby a Supreme

---

1. *Memoirs of the Life and Correspondence of Mrs Hannah More*, ed. William Roberts, 4 vols (London, 1835), 1: 167.

Court judge was appointed and knighted while his pamphlet was the subject of a seditious libel prosecution. Publishing *The Principles of Government* displayed Jones's principles. His belief in universal manhood suffrage, popular education, parliamentary reform, and co-operative association anticipates the works of Thomas Paine and William Godwin. Jones was proud to think he had made no compromises to gain a judge's long robes.

But there were other, less attractive, ironies. This radical intellectual, instinctively resentful of unconstitutional power, was now a colonial administrator. Jones, with all his loathing of odious despots, was sailing eastwards to serve a despotic regime. The supporter of American revolt against British imperial rule was a key functionary in what was shortly to become the biggest empire ever, governing roughly a quarter of the world's population. How does a lawyer who values liberty above all end up part of a global machine of world subjugation?

Yet, in a sense, there was a consistency here. Jones had always maintained that despotic government should not necessarily be seen as an Oriental preserve. British India was ruled by a peculiarly British despotism modelled upon enlightened Mughal governance. Jones, who had published on Islamic property law, knew he might help continue that tradition.

The pursuit of happiness for Jones necessitated a situation where the pursuit of knowledge meshed with the pursuit of wealth. India fulfilled those essential requirements, but there were dangers—of climate and corruption. Franklin had added to his congratulations 'Wishes that you may return from that corrupting Country, with a great deal of Money honestly acquir'd, and with full as much Virtue as you carry out with you.' Ten years in Bengal would enable Jones to re-create himself as a country gentleman and independent MP, free from party and from patronage.

So, was William Jones any different from the 'nabobs' who saw in India a means of making a fast fortune and were despised on their return for their new money and their erosion of class boundaries? The influential *European Magazine* announced its opinion:

> His residence in that country may be considered as fortunate for the advancement of knowledge. There he will have an opportunity of enquiring, with great advantage, into the manners, customs, and literature of the Asiatic nations: and the humanity of his disposition will, in proportion to the sphere of his authority and influence, be a blessing to the natives of Indostan.
>
> (*European Magazine*, 4 December 1783, 445)

In truth, it was all about enquiring and acquiring—acquiring more than mere money. The *Bengal Annual* came closest to the mark when, having praised his 'disinterested love of literature', it added, 'It may be said that, he was not altogether disinterested, and that his object was fame.'[2]

For speeches in favour of universal suffrage and support of the Americans he had been branded 'Republican' Jones by many establishment figures. Had he left his principles on the Portsmouth quayside? India was not America, Jones would argue: 'I shall certainly not preach democracy to the Indians, who must and will be governed by absolute power.'[3] That Indians should be ruled by their own laws was a species of enfranchisement, and Jones's key project would be an exhaustive digest of Hindu and Muslim law.

So the republican at home morphed into the enlightened despot abroad, but Jones had not abandoned radicalism—revolutionary ideas were soon to come from Bengal. But let's not rush things: the passage to India, even in a trim frigate like the *Crocodile*, took at least five months. The sea was in his blood. As a young man, his father, 'Longitude' Jones, voyaged to the West Indies. His mother taught him the use of a sextant and many of his shipboard letters provide precise bearings in minutes and seconds.

As they sailed between the emerald Azores and the mouth of the Tagus, Jones was studying Persian and law, and delighting in 'the sweet society and conversation of Anna Maria'. Those very qualities were being sorely missed by her father. On 24 April he wrote—almost Lear-like—to Franklin:

> I do not mean to depreciate the rest; but She had more of that domestick kindness and attention which You know how to value and which an old Man wants and delights in. And tho' Sir Wm Jones is a worthy and indeed a superior Man; yet so total a Separation with only a bare distant possibility of meeting again is as deeply and as tenderly affecting, if I can judge truely of my own feelings, as her Death itself would have been.[4]

But this was no tragedy; as in Nahum Tate's 'improved' adaptation of *King Lear*, Shipley's Cordelia had married her Edgar. On May Day they anchored at Madeira and, having braved the surf on landing, were soon sketching the island from the flower-filled terrace of Consul Charles Murray's elegant

---

2. *The Bengal Annual; A Literary Keepsake for MDCCCXXX*, ed. David Lester Richardson (Calcutta, 1830), p. 9.
3. *The Letters of Sir William Jones*, ed. Garland Cannon, 2 vols (Oxford, 1970), 2: 616; henceforth '*Letters*'.
4. Letter from Bishop Jonathan Shipley to Franklin, 24 April 1783, *The Papers of Benjamin Franklin*, available at http://www.franklinpapers.org/franklin/ (accessed 3 March 2011).

quinta. They were supremely happy, but Jones did not forget his affection for his young Welsh friend Arthur Pritchard, also newly married. Jones had encouraged Pritchard to take passage to India, together with his own new bride, to be his legal secretary. With characteristic thoughtfulness, Jones writes from Funchal on 2 May instructing Arthur to wait upon Laurence Sulivan, Chairman of the East India Company Court of Directors, General John Caillaud, commander-in-chief under Clive, and Robert Orme, historian of India, for assistance and advice.

Mid-May saw Anna and William enjoying guavas and musk melons at Porto Praia on St Iago, the largest of the Cape Verde islands. Jones rode with John Williamson, the *Crocodile*'s master, through the perfumed tamarind and citrus groves into the mountains. Anna wanted to accompany them, but Jones, thinking it too hot for her, 'exerted his *Authority*'. 'I should be quite afraid for Sir William', she wrote to her cousin Georgiana, Duchess of Devonshire, 'but he is such a Salamander he is never hurt by heat'.[5] Despite their long engagement, they were obviously still learning much about each other. Sir William, as she habitually called him, could certainly be rather domineering, but she was quite wrong about his tolerance for heat. In Calcutta, Sūrya, the Hindu sun god, was the deity he feared most.

On 28 July, having rounded the Cape of Good Hope, 'our eyes were delighted with a prospect so beautiful, that neither a painter nor a poet could perfectly represent it [...] the sun rising in full splendour on the island of *Mayata*'.[6] The frigate was passing Mayotte, in the Comoros archipelago, lying between Madagascar and Africa. 'Oriental' Jones was at last in the Indian Ocean.

They had arrived at the beautiful island of Hinzuan or Johanna, now Nzwani or Anjouan, 'Lat.12°. 10ʹ. 47″. S. Long. 44°. 25ʹ. 5″. E.'. Anchoring in the pellucid waters of the bay, the *Crocodile* was surrounded by canoes and the natives presented letters of recommendation from Englishmen: 'We had *Lords*, *Dukes*, and *Princes* on board, soliciting our custom, and importuning us for presents [...] they justly imagined, that those ridiculous titles would serve as marks of distinction, and, by attracting notice, procure for them something substantial' (*Works*, 4: 271). The regular watering stops of East Indiamen rendered Mutsamudu town a fascinating example of global

---

5. Chatsworth, Devonshire Collection, Family Papers, Letter of 15 May 1783.
6. 'Remarks on the Island of Hinzuan or Johanna', *The Works of Sir William Jones*, ed. Anna Maria Jones, 13 vols (London, 1807), 4: 269–313; 270; henceforth *Works*.

integration. Anjouan's position on international trade routes between southern Arabia and western India afforded an object lesson in cultural hybridity, populated as it was by Arabs, African mainlanders, Creoles, Malayo-Indonesian peoples, and Shirazi Persians.

Jones is delighted with Anjouan, exploring with Williamson its verdant forests and waterfalls tumbling into the sea. 'I have seen many a mountain of stupendous height in Wales and Switzerland, but never saw one before, round the bosom of which clouds were almost continually rolling, while its green summit rose flourishing above them.' Subsequently, accompanied by an islander, 'my friend Tumuni', Jones spends two days amongst the abundant variety of flowers and birds in the spiced air of 'this magnificent garden', intoxicated by vibrant colours and the exotic scents of trees, 'spangled with white blossoms equal in fragrance to orange-flowers: my guide called them *Monongos*'. Its loveliness far 'surpassed *Ermenonville* or *Blenheim*, or any other imitations of nature', this 'little island twelve degrees to the south of the Line' outstripped St Iago or even the delights of Merionethshire.

He enjoys conversing with the inhabitants, tasting more exciting curries than he had ever found in London. Cultural exchange is supplemented by exchange of gifts. Jones presents the ruler, Shaikh Ahmed, with a beautiful Koran, and 'a very handsome dress of blue silk with golden flowers' he had worn at a Ranelagh masquerade. In response to the Shaikh's question as to why a justice who professes peace should wear a sword, Jones expounds his theory of patriot self-reliance: 'I was a man before I was a magistrate; and, if it should ever happen, that law could not protect me, I must protect myself.' On Jones's departure Shaikh Ahmed saluted him with his whole ordnance, a single cannon: 'I waved my hat, and said *Allar Acbar*.'

Jones's amazement at the governor's brother Alwi's questions regarding American independence and European politics, or his surprise at Shaikh Ahmed's 'enlargement of mind' and commercial sophistication in suggesting trade between Anjouan and Bombay, demonstrate he still has many preconceptions to abandon. As aspiring botanist, Jones identifies a plant of which he had only read in Arabic poems, henna, and discovers that its 'dark orange-scarlet' dye is used to decorate the hands and nails and not, as he had thought, as a rouge for the cheeks. But there are perplexing elements.

His narrative frequently undermines prejudice, establishing a humane relativism: '[I]f the women of rank at *Paris,* or those in *London* who wish to imitate them, be inclined to call the *Arabs* barbarians; let them view their own head-dresses and cheeks in a glass, and, if they have left no room for blushes, be inwardly at least ashamed of their censure.' Yet 'Linguist' Jones reveals a philistinic anti-East African prejudice: Shaikh Ahmed's gift to Williamson of 'a hymn in *Arabic* letters, but in the language of *Mombaza*, which was mixed with *Arabic* [. . .] hardly deserved examination, since the study of languages has little intrinsic value, and is only useful as the instrument of real knowledge, which we can scarce expect from the poets of the *Mozambique*' (p. 285).

He visits his first mosque, impressing the natives by reading out the Arabic moral sentences above the gateway: 'wealth [is given us] to be liberally bestowed, not avariciously hoarded; and learning, to produce good actions, not empty disputes', sterling advice for any would-be nabob or Calcutta bencher. Less gratifying is his first sight of a haram, 'two or three miserable creatures', with the favourite, standing behind a coarse curtain, showing only her ankles loaded with silver rings, 'glittering fetters rather than ornaments': 'a rational being would have preferred the condition of a wild beast, exposed to perils and hunger in a forest, to the splendid misery of being wife or mistress to *Salim*' (*Works*, 4: 277–8).

Shocked at being offered a little African boy in return for one of his illuminated Korans, Jones treats the Arab rulers to an anti-slavery lecture. Alwi insists such children were the unfortunate victims of tribal war and African poverty: '[I]f we buy them, they will live: if they become valuable servants, they will live comfortably; but, if they are not sold, they must die miserably.' Jones's response reveals a weighty forensic logic:

> There may be such cases; but you fallaciously draw a general conclusion from a few particular instances; and this is the very fallacy, which, on a thousand other occasions, deludes mankind. It is not to be doubted, that a constant and gainful traffick in human creatures foments war, in which captives are always made, and keeps up that perpetual enmity. (*Works*, 4: 290)

Jones adopts a high moral tone as he speaks of disposing of slaves 'with as much indifference as if you were selling cattle', but he makes no mention of the slave plantations owned by his friend Paradise in Virginia, or by his brother-in-law Shipley in St Kitt's and Nevis. Jones himself was to have servants, openly bought as slaves, in Calcutta; it was another half century before the British would begin to dismantle their own extensive and lucrative slave trade. Game, set, and moral match to Alwi of Anjouan.

They set sail early in August northeast by east for Bengal, and one memorable evening Jones, 'on inspecting the observations of the day', realized he was surrounded by amazing Asiatic potential:

> India lay before us, and Persia on our left, whilst a breeze from Arabia blew nearly on our stern. A situation so pleasing in itself, and to me so new, could not fail to awaken a train of reflexions in a mind, which had early been accustomed to contemplate with delight the eventful histories and agreeable fictions of this eastern world.   (*Works*, 3: 1–2)

His meditation is no passive, perfumed Oriental idyll out of the *Arabian Nights*. If it belongs to romance and sensuality, then it is the romance of knowledge and a clear-sighted lust for its emancipatory power. What is taking shape in the brain of this intellectual explorer is a prodigiously energetic, inspired, and inspiring research programme of subcontinental proportions. Jones's response to the artistic, scientific, and historical potential of 'the vast regions of Asia' is profoundly visionary, but this is balanced by an eminently practical awareness of the difficulties inherent in transforming vision into functioning reality.

On 2 September the *Crocodile* anchored in Madras Roads and, longing to make their first Indian landfall, the couple entrust their lives to skilful Massoulah boatmen who navigate their flexible buoyant craft through the thundering surf to beach safely on the white sand opposite the sea-gate of Fort St George. Jones knew about chunam, the oyster-shell lime and sea-sand mixture, with which mansions and public buildings were plastered, but nothing had prepared them for the blindingly dazzling whiteness or the intense heat of the enormous orange-red sun. They are surrounded by a bewildering confusion of humanity—some virtually naked, some enveloped in muslin—horses, livestock, rickshaws, camels, cacophony, chaos. It is exhilarating, terrifying, and incomprehensible as Jones's classical Persian and attempts at Hindi are met with blank stares. Feeling like griffins, as newly arrived Europeans were labelled, they ensconce themselves within a palanquin, draw down the venetian blinds against the sun, and are borne off to Government House.

They were welcomed by Lord George Macartney, a handsome, accomplished, and engaging host. With the personal support of Lord Sandwich at the Admiralty, he was the first non-EIC servant to be appointed to the £15,000 per annum post of governor of Madras. They talked of campaigns against the French and against Haidar Ali of Mysore and the threat posed by Haidar's heir, Tipū Sultan; Macartney was pleased to hear from Anna news of friends in Ireland.

A few days later they sailed up the coast, Williamson taking advantage of the tail-end of the southwest monsoon winds. Arriving in mid-September in Balasore Roads, they awaited a pilot to take them up the Hugli, a western distributary of the Ganges. Jones used the opportunity to notify Chief Justice Elijah Impey of his imminent arrival and to buy a pipe of claret for 200 rupees (£25). The last leg of their long journey proved frustrating as they won their way against the impetuous current of the mighty river. Once they were rewarded with a glimpse of a tiger emerging from a jungle thicket to drink. The huge variety of river traffic fascinated them: junks from the Maldives, Arab dhows, local fishing-boats, elegant budgerows, and country barges overloaded with paddy-straw like floating haystacks.

On nearing Garden Reach, they begin to understand why Calcutta was called the 'City of Palaces'. Along the river bank were verdant well-tended gardens stretching down to the water's edge, each surrounding an elegant villa or mansion. Anna is delighted with these charming residences, little knowing that she would spend the happiest years of her life here in a garden house in Ariśnagar on the banks of the Hugli. At last, beyond a sudden bend in the river, they glimpse, through a forest of ships' masts, the lofty white neoclassical mansions of this 'modern capital of the East', its splendour bolstered by the extensive ramparts of Fort William in the foreground. As they pass the impressive fortress, both the size and the architectural detail of Calcutta's magnificent public and private buildings could be discerned. The first professional landscape artist to visit India, William Hodges, whose patron was Governor-General Warren Hastings, described the financially segregated 'White Town' two years earlier:

> The streets are broad; the line of buildings surrounding two sides of the esplanade of the fort, is magnificent; and it adds greatly to the superb appearance, that the houses are detached from each other, and insulated in a great space. The buildings are all on a large scale, from the necessity of having a free circulation of air, in a climate the heat of which is extreme. The general approach to the houses is by a flight of steps, with great projecting porticoes, or surrounded by colonades or arcades, which give them the appearance of Grecian temples; and indeed every house may be considered as a temple dedicated to hospitality.[7]

For Hodges the city has a classical grandeur: for a Bengali—albeit a pro-British one—his first sight of Calcutta evokes a verse idyll, which takes him beyond the 'exquisite workmanship' of English and Chinese architecture

---

7. *Travels in India* (1793), reprinted in *The European Discovery of India: Key Indological Sources of Romanticism*, ed. Michael J. Franklin, 6 vols (London, 2001), 3: 15.

and luxury goods to a celestial plane mirrored in the 'moon-like radiance' of its 'truthful and well-behaved' inhabitants:

> Wonderful is the City of Calcutta in Bengal;
> For it is a model of China and England.
> Its buildings please the heart and the soul,
> And tower to the height of the air.
> A master-hand has wrought such workmanship in it,
> That everything is apaint [sic] and everything beautiful.
> [...]
> People, whilst promenading in gardens,
> Like wandering stars, meet each other in their walks.
> Such a city in the country of the Bengalis,
> No one had seen, no one had heard of.[8]

The intense commercial activity that funded all this opulence was everywhere apparent; subsequently the Joneses visited custom-house wharf at the old fort with its enormous warehouses of muslins, sugar, silk, saltpetre, opium, indigo, pepper, rice, civet, and gum lac. To the accompaniment of a 21-gun salute, the *Crocodile* cast anchor at Chandpal Ghat on 25 September. Sir William and Lady Jones came ashore amidst lavish ceremonial on the governor-general's barge, disembarking at the end of Esplanade Row, where an immense number of people waited to greet them.

The couple were exhausted, but Sir Robert Chambers, Jones's Oxford and club friend and now colleague, had kindly made available his palatial home. He had hoped to welcome them but, beset by grief concerning the wreck of the *Grosvenor* in which his 6-year-old son Thomas had been sailing to England, Chambers had departed upriver to Banaras with his exquisitely beautiful wife Frances. He could not bring himself to break the dreadful news. This lent a sad note to the Joneses' arrival after their safe and enjoyable passage but, as they recovered their energies, the grandeur of the Palladian mansion overlooking the river and the attentions of scores of devoted servants enabled them to enjoy a second honeymoon, this time on dry land. While taking tea they could observe the beauty of the Hugli, with 'the sweet little *Crocodile* riding almost under my window'. Chambers had provided Jones with the key to his library, but when Anna could prise

---

8. Ghulām Hussain Salim Zaidpuri, *Riyazu-s-Salatin* (1788), trans. Abdus Salam (Calcutta, 1902), 34–5.

him away from Persian manuscripts, the house was superbly located for their sorties into the otherness of Calcutta.

Some extracts from Anna's 'exceedingly entertaining journal'—subsequently thrown on the fire by a stupid relative—provide a flavour of their first impressions as they acclimatized to Calcutta's onslaught upon the senses:

> 25 October 1783
>
> We are still at Sir Robert Chambers's & hear of no house that will suit us. Calcutta is unlike any town you ever saw, a great number of fine large houses quite detach'd from each other, with courts round each house which makes them very airy, & has nothing of the closeness of a Town. It stands upon very dry ground & being upon the river you have continually cooling breezes. [...]
>
> The weather is still too hot to stir out after eight in the morning till half an hour after five & then it so soon grows dark we can see but little of the country, however we air an hour or two, by the light of the moon or the *Mausalgies* or Torch bearers—of which we have four. I have walked this morning before breakfast. I think what strikes me most in this country is the number of living creatures with which the Air, Earth, & Water swarm, 'tis inconceivable to those who have not witness'd it themselves. I never saw a farmyard so full of Cocks & Hens as this town is of Ravens, Eagles, Crows, & all sorts of Birds of prey, & of an evening such troops of Jackalls & wild Dogs come howling in search of food, & of infinite use all animals of this class are in a country where every thing so soon turns putrid that the numbers of Dead bodies left unburied, & the quantity of Meat that is every day dress'd more than is eat would soon breed a plague, were they not carried off by these animals of prey. The fire flies or flying Glow-worms have a beautiful and extraordinary effect in a dark night. They remind me of Trees of Emeralds & flowers of diamonds you read of in the Arabian tales, they keep chiefly amongst trees & hedges where they swarm in such quantities as to make the leaves and branches very visible—if you want to know what it is o'clock you make one of your attendants catch one of these flies & shut it in the glass of your watch, it shows you the hours distinctly.[9]

Anna captures a sense of teeming life and the physical dangers of Indian corruption, naturally remedied by the beautiful kites, which still circle the skies of a very different Kolkata. The juxtaposition of the putrefying heat and their magical moonlit walks through illuminated trees, of Oriental romance and prosaic practicality—if you want to know the time, ask (for)

---

9. BL, Add. MSS 75,735 Althorp Papers.

a glow-worm—reveal her talents as an engaging travel writer. Her narrative also has the power to disturb. The matter-of-fact fashion in which she mentions unburied bodies in the streets reminds us that the anchor-chains of East Indiamen riding in the Hugli were regularly fouled by the corpses of those whose families could not afford the wood for a funeral pyre. Fabulous wealth and unbelievable poverty dwarfed even the extremes encountered in London. In the 'abundant garden' of Bengal at the height of the 1769–70 famine five hundred people a day starved at Murshidabad. While Jones regrets 'unavoidable' inroads into his parsimonious plan to save at least half his salary: 'Anna rides a prancing steed every morning, and I have just given an hundred & twenty five pounds for a strong riding horse, and two hundred for four bay coach-horses', a skilled Murshidabad silk-weaver might be lucky enough to earn three or four rupees a month.

The next day, Sunday, 26 October, was spent at Hastings's house at Alipore. They had been invited for breakfast at seven, but feeling insufficiently strong for such an early hour, they had arrived at one o'clock:

> Mr Hastings has two Garden Houses within a hundred yards of each other in a very pleasant lawn, as pretty as an entire flat can be. We found Zophani drawing one of the Elephants pictures & Mr Hastings standing by him. A magnificent Palankeen was waiting to carry me to the other House where Mrs Hastings was sitting in her bed chamber in a very elegant Eastern dress & a Turban, she had been very ill, & is in so bad a state of health that she goes to England in Decr as the last resource. We look'd over some Drawings of views in India till Dinner. We sat down 20 in one room which was so large and airy that tho' we had a great dinner, I have not din'd so cool since I came here. Sir Thomas Mills sat next to me, & from his knowing every Lady in England I had a very pleasant chat with him. Mr Hastings sat at the upper end of the table, Sr Willm on one side of him, I on the other & Mrs Hastings next to Sir Willm. I like Mr Hastings better & better every time I see him, he has great natural politeness & attention with much agreeable knowledge & a thousand little anecdotes & stories which he relates vastly well. After dinner the whole party broke up, & I was shown into an elegant apartment—a little dressing room with every possible convenience for washing &c., a bedroom with a silver bedstead & very fine muslin furniture, where I slept for an hour. When we made our appearance again we saw three large Elephants richly caparison'd. Mr Hastings desir'd I would go with him upon one, Sir W^m & Capt. Williamson on another, Mr Smoult & Zophani on the 3rd. Thus mounted & escorted by a troop of horse & a little Thousand of Foot with Chasse Manches, we set out & took an airing of 4 or 5 miles, & found Mrs Hastings & tea ready for us in the other house, where there was Tea, Chess, Chat & Cards

till supper at nine. Soon after ten, we return'd home lighted by our six *Mausalgies*, four carrying Flambeaux, & two, large branches with night lights in each. (BL, Add. MSS 75,735 Althorp Papers)

Returning to the Esplanade, this time by the light of candle-lit branches, Anna and William discussed their Sunday entertainment—elephant rides, Mughal cuisine, a troop of horse, scores of sepoys (Indian soldiers under British command)—could this be the plain-living, unostentatious governor-general of whom they had been told? The two men had immediately hit it off, however, and Jones concluded that Dr Johnson, who had sent Hastings Jones's *Persian Grammar*, was justified in describing him as 'something new, a Governor of Bengal who patronises learning'. Jones was eager to visit the Calcutta Madrasah established by Hastings in 1781—originally at his own expense—to train young Muslims as administrators of the revenue and judiciary. Hastings was delighted that, at long last, the arrival of this eminent Orientalist would further advance his judicial plan to 'found the authority of the British Government in Bengal on its ancient laws'.

Anna was most taken by the attentions of the Hastings couple to personal hygiene; according to the sale advertisement, the upper-roomed house at Alipore boasted 'a complete bathing-house containing two rooms finished with Madras chunam'. Not the least of what the British learned in a land where water was essential to the ritual ablutions of both Hindu and Muslim, were substantially higher standards of personal cleanliness. Such transculturation frequently led to what was functional in the colony becoming fashionable in the metropole, from bathing to the use of cool Indian muslins. Both Anna and William soon followed the Alipore example of adopting Indian dress at home. But, though the application of water was undoubtedly healthy, its consumption was not. Jones, the dedicated water-drinker who generally diluted his wine, was unaware of the pathogenic bacteria it contained.

Anna had enjoyed looking at Hodges's sketches in the company of her namesake, born Anna Maria Apollonia Chapuset; always plain Marian to her devoted husband, although plain she most definitely was not. William had heard about their romance aboard the *Duke of Grafton* in 1769 en route to Madras; Hastings a 37-year-old widower had been nursed back to health by the Baroness von Imhoff, as she was then. On becoming governor of Bengal in 1772, they had met again in Calcutta, and there had been much speculation, and more gossip, about whether they had lived together during her lengthy divorce proceedings before their marriage in the summer of 1777. Might that be the reason for the two adjacent Alipore garden houses, they wondered.

It was good to see Johan Joseph Zoffany again. Jones had dined with him at Sir Joshua Reynolds in Leicester Fields and they both admired the talent of this first-rate portrait painter whom George III had nominated to the Royal Academy. Zoffany specialized in life-size groups, but this was his first elephant portrait. Having neglected to obtain the necessary permissions from the Company, the 50-year-old artist had gamely signed on as a midshipman on the *Lord Macartney*, arriving at Calcutta only ten days before the Joneses. As a protégé of Sir Joseph Banks, Zoffany had been engaged to accompany him on Cook's second voyage, but the *Resolution*'s accommodation proving inadequate for Banks's entourage—including a mistress disguised as a manservant—Banks had withdrawn both himself and Zoffany from the expedition. William Hodges took Zoffany's place, and here in Calcutta, Hodges recommended the deserting midshipman to Hastings. It was indeed a small world.

Zoffany told them of his warm welcome at Chinsura, 18 miles upriver, by Lady Chambers, daughter of sculptor Joseph Wilton; he presented her with a half-length portrait of her 9-year-old daughter, Frances Maria, in London for her education. Sir Thomas Mills, who amused Anna, had been receiver-general at Quebec, and rumours persisted concerning his personal receipts. Like Zoffany, he enjoyed the friendship of David Garrick and Reynolds, but he was a man of notoriety rather than talent. It might seem puzzling that he should be a house guest of Hastings, but all is explained by Horace Walpole's description of Mills: 'a noisy Fellow, who lived at a vast Expense without any visible means; but was supposed to be a natural Son of Lord Mansfield'.[10] As the protégé of the chief justice of the King's Bench, Mills had come to India to repair his fortune, and Hastings needed to respect the wishes of his friend Mansfield who had written so supportively, a month earlier:

> [T]he Fate of Empires has often, & generally does, depend upon One Man. We lost the West Indies for want of such a Man & had it not been for you, we should have lost the East.[11]

---

10. *Satirical Poems Published Anonymously by William Mason with Notes by Horace Walpole*, ed. Paget Toynbee (Oxford, 1926), 117.
11. BL, Add. MSS 29,160, Letter of Mansfield to Hastings, 27 September 1783.

Much of what Hastings doggedly achieved in dismantling the powerful Indian confederacy in the Carnatic was in the face of his authority being contested by the Supreme Council in Calcutta or his diplomacy being obstinately disregarded by Lord Macartney in Madras. At the time of the Joneses' visit, he was also beset by insubordination at Lucknow, and fears that the chain of granaries he had planned along the Ganges might not be constructed in time to avert threatened famine in Bihar. Anna allows us to see 'the saviour of British empire in India' exercising artistic and political patronage during some rare moments of relaxation at Alipore.

The couple were enjoying themselves. 'Sir William is the happiest of Men', Anna writes home, 'He meets with so many People to converse with in his beloved Oriental Languages', but she confides to her father that; '[T]ho' as well receivd as possible, She cannot help complaining that She finds a most mortifying difference between the Society She left, especially that of the Women, and that which She now lives in.'[12] There were few women of style in Calcutta at this period. Anna relished the company of Mary Impey whose fascinating menagerie and pioneering interest in the birds of India, their habitat and local names, inspired the Joneses' studies in natural history. Together they examined the superbly detailed paintings that Mary commissioned from the brilliant Muslim artist Sheikh Zayn al-Din and his Hindu colleagues, Bhavani Das and Ram Das. Zoffany's painting of the Impeys on their verandah, in which their daughter dances in the graceful north Indian fashion to the accompaniment of strolling musicians, watched by her parents, siblings, servants, and ayahs, and flanked by a classical column of the portico and a luxuriant exotic tree, captures both the colonial integration and the congenial intimacy of their home life.

Sadly, the Impeys departed for England on the 3 December. Also returning in the *Worcester* was William Hodges, to whom the Joneses had only recently been introduced. The following month the delicate Marian Hastings sailed homeward on the *Atlas* for her health. Calcutta was deprived of its brightest ornament and, as a sorrowing Hastings immersed himself in work, Anna lamented another lost friend. On the Chambers' return from Banaras, the Joneses attempted to alleviate the parents' grief at the loss of their son, and the elegant young Lady Chambers gradually resumed her prominent place in Calcutta social life. Her diary for 1784 records visits with

---

12. Letter of 1784 from Shipley to Franklin; The Papers of Benjamin Franklin, available online at http://www.franklinpapers.org/franklin/ (accessed 3 March 2011).

Anna Maria, Mrs Mary Hyde, daughter of the Revd Lord Francis Seymour, and wife of Jones's colleague, an excellent harpsichordist and singer; Mrs Helena Halhed, née Ribaut, daughter of the Dutch governor of Chinsura, and wife of Jones's friend; Mrs Emma Bristow, née Wrangham, fêted actress and theatre manger; and Mrs Sophia Plowden, pioneering collector of Hindustani songs.[13] Music—both western and Indian—and music-making was a central focus of this dynamic circle, to which should be added the names of Margaret Fowke, who travelled with the Chambers to join her brother Francis at Banaras, and Lady Benedicta, the wife of Advocate-General Sir John Day. All were enthusiastic musicians and some were amateur musicologists. Cultivated Indians were invited to performances of western music and they reciprocated. Attuned to such interesting female companionship, whose enthusiasm infected their husbands, Anna's hankerings after aristocratic society diminished. Her own husband, like Hastings, who 'sings the Hindostannie Airs perfectly well',[14] Johnson, and Wilkins, was profoundly interested in both the theory and the practice of Indian music. Anna was pleased that this leisure pursuit, like botany, was one they might share.

While Anna luxuriates in bed—'I got up at Eleven for I am uncommonly lazy'—her early-rising husband settles into a busy regime, consulting 'with Arabs and Persians in the morning, Hindus in the evening', and mastering the orders of the Supreme Court. The new court house, in an impressive Palladian range of buildings, was conveniently situated at the western end of the Esplanade. Jones took the oaths of Office and Allegiance on Wednesday, 22 October, the first day of the fourth term of 1783, and, assuming his seat as Junior Judge, was immediately plunged into the busy schedule of court business.

Throughout the summer of 1783, Chambers's absence meant that Sir Elijah Impey and Mr Justice Hyde shared the burden of the causes. Now, briefly, there were three judges on the bench, but John Hyde, though physically robust, was by no means immune to the dangers of 'Jungle Fever', emanating from nearby undrained malarial swamps. Impey, fluent in Persian and Urdu, had been inspecting the *diwani adalats* (district civil

---

13. BL, APAC, MSS Eur. A 172, Diary of Lady Frances Chambers, dated 1784.
14. Letter of 28 July 1785 from Joseph Fowke to Lady Clive, cited in Ian Woodfield, *Music of the Raj: A Social and Economic History of Music in Late Eighteenth-century Anglo-Indian Society* (Oxford, 2000), 175.

1. New Court House and Chandpal Ghaut, coloured etching by Thomas Daniell. (British Library)

courts), but upon learning he had assumed—at Hastings's suggestion—the presidency of the *sadr diwani adalat* (chief civil court) in tandem with his chief justiceship, the Commons had decided to recall him. Consequently Jones was shortly alone on the bench, working, as he wrote to Althorp on 2 December, from six in the morning till ten at night:

> The Chief Justice leaves us to-morrow; Chambers is at Benares: Hyde in the country; the governor and council do not act as magistrates; and there are no others. All the *police* and *judicial* power, therefore, of this settlement, where at least half a million of natives reside, are in my hands: I tremble at the power, which I possess; but should tremble more, if I did not know myself.
>
> (*Letters*, 2: 623–4)

His self-reliance is rooted in self-knowledge, of which he is as proud as the Elizabethan Welsh Middle Templar and poet, Sir John Davies, who chose *Nosce Teipsum* for the title of his major philosophical poem. But Jones is not content to obey Pope's injunction: 'Know then thyself, presume not God to scan,/The proper study of mankind is Man'. Absorption in ancient cultures leads to fascinated investigation of the gods of India. The muse of poetry is now recalled in the service of the Hindu pantheon. With the help of new friends such as Charles Wilkins, the first Englishman to master Sanskrit, and Richard Johnson, a patron of Indian poets, artists, and musicians, and in consultation with their pandits, he began work on a projected series of eighteen 'Hymns to Hindu Deities'.

The first was his 'Hymn to Camdeo', or Kāma, the Hindu god of love, a form of the Vedic fire-god Agni, born of the Primal Waters. Jones acknowledges a pagan god worshipped by 'blacks' (as the stubbornly unenlightened termed Indians) with profound intercultural respect. His ode counterpoints reassuring Graeco-Roman similitude and refreshing culture-specific difference in the subcontinental iconography: Kāma's sugar-cane bow with bowstring of entwined bees, and arrows tipped with passion-inducing sensuous flowers. Drawn to this 'potent God' by all kinds of love—of Anna, of India, of discovery—the poet who had voyaged across mighty seas in the 'sweet little *Crocodile*' was amused that Kāma's emblem was the *makara*. This crocodile-like creature was also the *vahana* (vehicle) of Gangā Mā (Mother Ganges), and of Varuna, the Vedic god of ocean. Confident he possesses no inordinate love of power, Jones hymns the universal 'soul-kindling, world-inflaming' power of love as he celebrates his own sexual fulfilment and the renewal of his own creativity:

> I feel, I feel thy genial flame divine,
> And hallow thee and kiss thy shrine.
>
> 'Knowst thou not me?' Celestial sounds I hear!
> 'Knowst thou not me?' Ah, spare a mortal ear!
> 'Behold'—My swimming eyes entranc'd I raise,
> But oh! they shrink before th' excessive blaze. (ll. 9–14)

Jones completed the 'Hymn to Camdeo' by 6 January 1784, and nine days later he read *A Discourse on the Institution of a Society* to the founder-members of the Asiatick Society in the courthouse Grand Jury Room. The audience included Wilkins; Jonathan Duncan, subsequently Governor of Bombay; David Anderson, close friend of Hastings, and later President of the Committee of Revenue; Charles Chapman, Hastings's emissary to Vietnam; Francis Gladwin, eminent Persianist, Brigadier-General John Carnac, former commander of the Company's army; experts on finance and revenue such as

Thomas Law and George Barlow; lawyers such as William Chambers and John Paterson; and Jones's fellow-judge, Hyde. Their investigations, Jones ambitiously announced, will be bounded 'only by the geographical limits of *Asia*', encompassing 'MAN and NATURE; whatever is performed by the one, or produced by the other.'

When the *Discourse*, together with his 'First Charge to the Grand Jury at Calcutta', and his 'Hymn to Camdeo', was speedily published in London in 1784, the critical world at once appreciated both the intensive nature of his activities in the few months of his residence in Calcutta, and the challenging horizons of his research programme.[15] Jones's 33-page pamphlet represents a tripartite agenda for imperial domination: research, embracing the power of knowledge and the knowledge of power; law, effective social control of disparate populations, both native and colonialist; and literary appropriation of the sources of power in Indian culture.

Edward Said's indictment of Jones's ambition to obtain a 'perfect knowledge of India' as complicit with imperial power states the blindingly obvious.[16] In 1784 how might it have been anything else? Neither Jones nor any of his Asiatick Society colleagues was in Bengal for the benefit of his health. Perhaps polemical postcolonialism might admit there can be no destruction of prejudice without the understanding that springs from knowledge. It would be equally unhistoric to view Jones's publication as an apolitical triumph of peace and love: a positive *trimurti* (trinity) of empathetic awareness, justice via respected indigenous law codes, and comparative religion. Metropolitan reviewers, apparently unaware of how Jones's pamphlet bolstered the cultural politics of Hastings's Orientalist regime, concentrated upon potential literary and historical gains. 'How grand and stupendous is the following plan!' enthused the *Critical Review*: 'We may reasonably expect to enlarge our stock of poetical imagery, as well as of history, from the labours of the Asiatic Society [...] to combine the useful and the pleasing', and the *Gentleman's Magazine*, praising Jones's ode, similarly expected 'a rich mine of Oriental literature, arts, and antiquities'.[17]

Indian knowledge was to adjust western thought, but in the East Hastings knew that it was information, rather than military superiority, that enabled a

---

15. *A Discourse on the Institution of a Society [...] Delivered at Calcutta, January 15th, 1784: a Charge to the Grand Jury at Calcutta, December 4th, 1783: and a Hymn to Camdeo* (London, 1784).
16. Edward Said, *Orientalism* (London, 1978), 36.
17. *Critical Review*, 59 (1785) 19–21; *Gentleman's Magazine*, 55 (Jan. 1785), 50–1.

comparative handful of Europeans to subdue and administer vast subcontinental territories. Hastings introduced rigorously Orientalist government policies to ensure that British sovereignty was exercised in Indian ways, and to facilitate these policies he tapped all available sources of information.

Hastings fostered the production of Orientalist knowledge to increase his comprehension of the complexities of the subcontinent; understanding of Hindu tradition and Mughal precedent seemed essential if he was to inherit the syncretic mantle of Emperor Jalaluddin Muhammad Akbar (r.1556–1605). A man of polymathic talents, Akbar was a fierce warrior and modernizing consolidator of Mughal power. This illiterate (possibly dyslexic) connoisseur and patron encouraged Hindu and Muslim artists and craftsmen to work side by side in his ateliers and on the construction of his sumptuous red sandstone capital Fatehpur Sikri, where an aura of Sūfi devotionalism was achieved by Bengali and Gujerati architects. This eclecticism and syncretism culminated in his initiation of religious debate between Muslim scholars and Hindus, Sikhs, Buddhists, Cārvāka sceptics, and Portuguese Jesuits. Akbar represented a potent symbol of enlightened Mughal government with which Hastings sought to identify his British Indian despotism.

Jones had helped to facilitate the governor-general's thinking. As early as 1771, he stressed the importance of the *Ā'īn-i Akbarī* (*c.*1590), containing 'a full account of every province and city in the dominions of the Mogul, of his revenues and expences, both in peace and war, and of all the customs and ceremonies in his palace; together with a description of the natural productions of his empire' (*Works*, 5: 320–21). Francis Gladwin communicated Jones's 'high encomiums' to Hastings who, intent upon restoring Indian government to its first principles in accordance with 'the original constitution of the Moghul Empire', commissioned Gladwin to produce a translation. With exquisite timing, the first volume of Gladwin's *Ayeen Akbery, or, The Institutes of the Emperor Akbar* (3 vols, Calcutta, 1783–6) was appearing as the *Crocodile* anchored.

The first two observations of Jones's 'The best practicable system of judicature', which he sent to Edmund Burke in April 1784, reflected the thinking of the Hastings administration:

> 1. A system of *liberty*, forced upon a people invincibly attached to opposite *habits*, would in truth be a system of cruel *tyranny*.
>
> 2. Any system of *judicature* affecting the natives in *Bengal*, and not having for its basis the old *Mogul* constitution, would be dangerous and impracticable.
>
> (*Letters*, 2: 643)

That a radical whig such as Jones should play a key role within an Indianized despotism was a situation fraught with ideological tensions. A humane despotism required a self-justifying dialectic. And, if the information that Jones gleaned from Orientalist researches was immediately relevant in the formation of government policies, both the governor-general and the new puisne judge realized that the prestige of such scholarship—published in Calcutta and London and translated throughout Europe—might reinforce the authority of Hastings's regime in both the East and the West. Although sympathetic to the governor-general's ideological objectives, Jones prudently maintained a judicial impartiality. On learning from England that Burke was threatening to recall him should he side with Hastings, Jones was furious with his friend, and this breach was never effectively healed.

Jones's wholehearted support for the policy that Indians should be governed by their own laws was in line with Hastings's realization that this also might achieve reconciliation as Indians appreciated their legal and religious traditions were being respected both in the colony and the metropolis. Jones recalled the enthusiastic reception of his Oxford friend, Nathaniel Brassey Halhed's *Code of Gentoo Laws* in 1776, the first example of a Sanskrit legal treatise compiled at the instance of the British. European fascination with Enlightenment comparativism and antiquarianism validated the governor-general's larger cultural agenda, comparing Indian polity with that of the Greeks. The *Critical Review* detected much wisdom and honesty in the Asiatic legislators and, with mordant irony, contrasted the colonial plunder enshrined 'in the more enlightened codes of European laws, in the sacred Shaster perhaps of European faith'.[18] It was an uphill task to cleanse 'India hands', whether in Company or Crown employ, of the stain of nabobery.

In 1785 both Hastings and Halhed were to leave India; it was to be the province of 'Oriental' Jones to adjust metropolitan perceptions of the Orientalist regime and revolutionize western conceptions of the subcontinent. He must convince Europe that India possessed an advanced civilization and a sophisticated culture when their British overlords were huddling in thatched huts. And this was not to be a narrative of sad decline, for Jones knew that India's syncretic traditions of religious and cultural pluralism still had much to teach its latest invaders.

What he was learning every day was more than satisfying his boundless intellectual curiosity: it was a genuine love affair, a profound delight in the

---

18. *Critical Review*, 44 (1777), 177–90; 180–1.

sheer multifariousness of India, her colours, scents, and vibrancy. By February 1784 he and Anna were settled in Chambers's garden house at Bhawanipur, conveniently close to Hastings at Alipore. Thanking Richard Johnson for an unusual gift, 'a basket of Minerva's favourites'—fledgling owls—he has sent Anna to care for, Justice Jones is on good form:

> [Y]ou have sent her a full bench of little judges, and she will prove her affection for one judge by her attention to the four new ones. Her own too is *animal bipes*, and not entirely *implume*, as he plumes himself much on your friendship.[19]

Their pastoral content is enhanced by their favourite pets: 'two large English sheep', which, 'having narrowly escaped the knife' on the voyage, are reprieved to grow old in India. In April the Joneses are 'literally lulled to sleep by Persian nightingales', after hearing Bengali musicians perform evening ragas mirroring the tranquil mood of the river at sunset. Jones has been reading Persian versions of Sanskrit musical treatises, and delight in Indian music's infinite variety of moods and modulations is convincing him that it is based 'upon truer principles than our own', for 'all the skill of the composer is directed to the great object of their art, the natural expression of strong passions' (*Works*, 3: 17).

Things were not always so serene. The lightning and violent wind of a mid-May storm terrified his horses and nearly overset his carriage as he returned from court, but he was saved by the courage of his servants who managed to unharness the horses. Though drenched to the skin, his enthusiasm for the wildness of India and its religion was nothing dampened. In the same letter to Hyde, he tells of his inexpressible pleasure in reading of Krishna in a Persian translation of the *Śrīmad Bhāgwatam*: '[I]t is by far the most entertaining book, on account of its novelty and wildness, that I ever read' (*Letters*, 2: 649). By June it sounds as if Jones has gone native. He is receiving the profoundly divine insights of *darśan*. In the impassioned erotic tones of a *bhakta* (Hindu devotee), he announces to Richard Johnson: 'I am in love with the *Gopia*, charmed with *Crishen*, an enthusiastick admirer of *Rām*, and a devout adorer of *Brimha-bishen-mehais* [Brahma, Vishnu, Siva: the *trimurti*]' (*Letters*, 2: 652).

---

19. *The Collected Works of Sir William Jones*, ed. Garland Cannon, 13 vols (Richmond, Surrey, 1993), 1: lxv.

Despite Jones's devotion, Sūrya, 'the Phœbus of *European* heathens', mounted in his seven-horsed chariot, was merciless. They were first hit by intense pre-monsoon heat and then William fell victim to the moisture-laden monsoon winds. Hyde, alone on the bench, notes that Chambers had been ill with rheumatism since the 19 June and that Sir William became 'dangerously ill' on the 26th 'and went for his Health as far as Banaras'. Heading upriver in their pinnace budgerow, Jones was confined to his couch by recurrent fever, followed by 'an obstinate flux'.

Though weakened by dehydration, his mind remained obstinately focused. On a stop near Plassey, the site of Clive's 1757 victory over Nawab Siraj ud-Daula (replaced by Mir Jafar Ali Khan), Anna decided to take an evening walk. When Jones realized the dangers to which she had exposed herself, he 'almost immediately wrote' the 14 stanzas of 'Plassey-Plain (Aug. 3, 1784)'

> 'Tis not of Jâfer, nor of Clive,
> On Plassey's glorious field I sing;
> 'Tis of the best good girl alive,
> Which most will deem a prettier thing.
>
> The Sun, in gaudy palanqueen,
> Curtain'd with purple, fring'd with gold,
> Firing no more heav'n's vault serene,
> Retir'd to sup with Ganges old.
>
> When Anna, to her bard long dear,
> (Who lov'd not Anna on the banks
> Of Elwy swift, or Testa clear?)
> Tripp'd thro' the palm grove's verdant ranks.   (ll. 1–12)

Where Clive had tamed the 'blood-thirsty *Subahdar*' (governor) on his own hunting grounds with 'Britain's vengeful hounds of war', Anna domesticates the wilderness through the powerful influence of her goodness. She is oblivious to the dangers of savage tigers, fierce boars, maddened buffaloes, deadly snakes; deaf to the friendly warnings of Hindustani-squawking rose-ringed parakeets thronging the trees (for 'she began her moors [Hindustani] of late'), Arabic-speaking dromedaries, or the trumpeting of elephants in Bengali. Language is the key to survival in a dangerous subcontinent, but Anna has other resources; she continues her botanical evening stroll secure in her inviolable virtue and impregnable innocence:

> To worth, and innocence approv'd,
> E'en monsters of the brake are friends:

> Thus o'er the plain at ease she mov'd:—
> Who fears offence that ne'er offends?   (ll. 21–4)

Despite the lightness of tone, and Jones's comparison of his wife to Spenser's lion-guarded Una, the final quatrain betrays the depth of his emotional reliance upon Anna:

> Yet oh! had One her perils known,
> (Tho' all the lions in all space
> Made her security their own)
> He ne'er had found a resting place.   (ll. 53–6)

Ultimately the greatest danger they faced was not the Bengal tiger but the Bengal climate. They proceeded slowly upriver; both unwell, and his violent fever returned. On 14 August from Afzal bagh, near the former Mughal capital of Murshidabad, he completed a letter to Richard Johnson begun in June: 'I must continue here until my emaciated body can bear the heat on the water.' In the earlier section Jones responded to descriptions of the scorching heat Johnson experienced at the rock temples outside Bezoara, near Masulipatam, with joking suggestions for the canonization of saltpetre: '[W]hy should *Salt Petre* remain a mere mortal in this deifying country? [. . .] If Saint Peter bequeathed the keys of heaven to the Roman pontiffs, those keys, which unlock stores of Salt Petre, certainly lead to heaven in India' (*Letters*, 2: 651). One of Bengal's key exports, saltpetre was as useful in the production of ice as the manufacture of gunpowder; Jones was thinking of the paper, 'The Process of Making Ice in the East Indies' in *Philosophical Transactions* (65 [1775], 252–7) by Sir Robert Barker who—by a fiery coincidence—had also commanded the artillery at Plassey.

Longing for ice, and panting for cooling streams, they sailed past mustard fields and mango groves, to visit Jones's Asiatick Society friend Peter Speke, Resident at Jangipur, and thence to Bhagalpur. On the veranda of Charles and Mary Chapman's bungalow, set in luxuriantly wooded countryside, the two couples relaxed. They talked of the recent tragic death—at 29—of Augustus Clevland, Chapman's predecessor as Collector, revered for pacifying the tribesmen of the nearby Rajmahal hills and establishing a *thana*, a settlement for invalided Bengal army sepoys. Sadly Jones himself was again reduced to an invalid by fever. He encouraged his physicians to apply native medicines, and Anna brought him crimson *bandhūcas* and golden champac—not for his sickroom vase but for meticulous botanical examination on the silken coverlet.

On hearing that Arthur Pritchard and his wife had arrived in Calcutta, Jones, though he could barely sit up, thoughtfully wrote on 1 October to offer them his study and dressing room at the courthouse as temporary accommodation, advising Pritchard to seek 'by respectful attentions, the good-will and protection of Mr Justice Hyde: he is one of the best men living'. Subsequently Hyde recorded Pritchard's admittance as an attorney of the court, subject to a period of being articled.[20] Amazingly, only four days later, at sunset on 5 October, Jones was surveying from his sickroom the snow-capped peak of Chomolhari in Bhutan. By triangulation he calculated the elevation of the Himalayas, convinced they surpassed the Andes (then considered the world's highest peaks): 'we saw from *Bhagilpoor*, the highest mountains in the world, without excepting the ANDES' (*Works*, 2: 46–8).

In early November Hastings met Jones at Bhagalpur, describing him as 'a perfect skeleton', but Jones always remembered the room in Chapman's bungalow where Hastings gave him his first invigorating 'taste' of Wilkins's *Bhagvadgītā* (*Letters*, 2: 660). By mid-month he was sufficiently recovered to continue their journey, via the ancient sites of Gaya, where Vishnu trod and his avatar Buddha preached the Fire Sermon. Finally they reached the holy bustle of Banaras, where Śiva dances the liberation of pure mind. They marvelled at the temples and the pilgrims, the bathing ghats and the burning ghats. Jones was surrounded by pandits, *maulavis* (Muslim teachers of law), and rajas, but he particularly valued the company of the historian and accomplished poet of Persian and Urdu, Ali Ibrahim Khan, whom Hastings had appointed chief judge at Banaras.

At Hastings's suggestion, they stayed a few miles outside Banaras at the Sicrole bungalow of the Resident, Francis Fowke and his devoted sister Margaret, who described the surrounding countryside as 'a perfect garden [...] wooded with such beauty, & variety that it altogether presents a most delightful scene'.[21] The air here was invigorating and they felt once more fully alive in the engaging company of the Fowkes.

Francis was a scholar of classical, French, and Oriental literature with a pronounced 'talent of raillery'. He informed them their friend Hastings had not always been so cordial. Fowke had been appointed Resident at Banaras by Philip Francis and Hastings's other Supreme Council opponents; he had

---

20. Victoria Memorial Hall, Kolkata; Judicial Notebooks of John Hyde and Sir Robert Chambers, vol. 5; Reel 3: 16 Nov. 1784.
21. NLW, MS Ormathwaite, FE 5/1 'Memoir of Margaret Walsh' (née Fowke).

2. View of the Ghats at Benares, 1787, by William Hodges. (Royal Academy of Arts, London)

been twice recalled by Hastings and twice reinstated by the Court of Directors: the Bandelure (yo-yo) of Banaras, Fowke quipped. The charming intercession of Margaret achieved a total reconciliation. Subsequently Hastings paid them a visit with the eldest son of Emperor Shāh 'Ālam, and the Mughal prince had thanked the Fowkes for 'giving him an Idea of social felicity, which he had not before entertained'. Anna and William endorsed this princely accolade for they had never been happier; there was 'riding of a morning and airings, chess, & music of an evening'. The Fowkes delighted in music and drama, setting up a Residency band, and building 'an elegant little theatre' for their amateur dramaticals.

Amongst the Ormathwaite papers in the National Library of Wales are manuscripts that capture a flavour of this social and intellectual milieu enjoyed by the Joneses. They reveal a brief period of stimulating relaxation for Jones, feeling lucky to be alive and far from the courtroom cares of Calcutta. Francis Fowke gently joshes Jones in a poem entitled 'Heliophobia', dedicated 'To Sir

William Jones, on his apprehensions from exposure to the sun during his recovery':

> Oft' at Apollo's eastern fane
> The bard vowed admiration, praise,
> Phoebus cajol'd in humble strain,
> Circled his brow with Persian bays.
>
> Th' ungrateful poet flies the ray
> Whence all his orient laurels bloom
> Avoids the illumined face of Day,
> And hides his guilt in mid-day gloom.
>
> Indignant Sol each effort tries
> To blast the wit He gave in vain.
> Sickness at least shall seize, He cries,
> The wretch who spurns a Doctor's reign.[22]

Ingratitude is Fowke's theme on behalf of Phœbus Apollo. As god of music and poetry, Apollo rewarded Jones with the soubriquet 'Persian', now as sun god he feels resentful to be shunned by his shade-seeking favourite. With his medical hat on, Dr Phœbus recalls his power to cause, as well as cure, ill-health. Fowke attempts a further description of Apollo's campaign 'Against th'ungrateful Cambrian bard', but runs out of steam. Jones immediately writes: 'In Answer to ——'s Heliophobia':

> Well has your ready Muse display'd
>   The cause of all the Poet's Pain:
> But, still devoted to the Shade,
>   He now, in *Health*, exalts the Strain.
> Phoebus, who strove to blast his Wit,
>   By Sickness little Triumph won,
> He now a surer Means has hit,
>   And animates a Rival *Son*.
> Yet, heed the Bard's Excuse,'Tis Fear—
>   View those who serve the God of Day*   * The Hindoos
> Then turn to —— & raptured hear,
>   What Powers she owns, who shuns the Ray.[23]

Jones is happy to avoid the blinding light, contemplating the sun god's son, Asclepius, god of medicine, whose potent art could restore the dead. He

---

22. NLW, MS Ormathwaite, FB 3/1.
23. NLW, MS Ormathwaite, FB 3/3.

neatly turns the conclusion into a compliment to the attractive powers of soprano Margaret's fair complexion. This playful extempore versifying leads him to display his classical laurels by translating a Horatian ode in complex Asclepiad metres more closely than Milton[24]—'simplex munditiis' (elegantly simple) if you're Jones!

Muslim and Hindu intellectuals continued to call and Jones was punctilious concerning Mughal courtesies to honour Ali Ibrahim Khan, the first Indian to publish a paper in *Asiatick Researches*:

> Should not I present *Aly Ibr. Khan* with *betel* and *otr* [*attar* of roses] at parting? If so (and I always do it at Calcutta) shall I beg, that you will order me three or four *paungs* [chunam and betel-nut wrapped in an aromatic leaf] to be made up, and to supply me with some *otr* to drop on his hand? I was dressing yesterday when Simbhoo Loll called, but shall be happy in seeing him to-day, when A. I. Khan is gone.[25]

Chess was an appropriately multicultural pastime, and a manuscript in Fowke's best copperplate is entitled: 'Curious move at chess which was first shown to me by Sir William Jones at Benares'. This 'Oriental' poem dramatizes a means of saving one's endangered queen by sacrificing a castle, a move that achieves the death of the shah or checkmate. Set in al-Andalus, where the game was introduced in the tenth century, the poem begins:

> Where the stream of Solofrena
> Winds along the silent vale
> Where the palm Trees softly murmur
> Waving to the gentle gale.
>
> By the myrtle woven windows
> Of an old romantic seat,
> Sat at Chess two noble Persians
> Shelter'd from the scorching heat.
>
> Here with beating breast Alcanzor
> View'd the deep eventful play
> There with black o'erarching eye-brow
> Sat the caliph Mehmed Bey.   (ll. 1–12)

As play progresses Alcanzor's anxiety reveals more is at stake than a noble contest of skill—they are gambling on the result. As his treasure and lands

---

24. NLW, MS Ormathwaite, FB 3/2. Cf. *Letters*, 2: 506–7.
25. BL, APAC, Fowke MS Eur E9, 121 [f. 259]; W. Jones to F. Fowke, n. d. 'Sunday Morn[g]'.

fall victim to the 'crafty caliph', a desperate Alcanzor 'pledges/Zaida's beauties, Zaida's love', but from the pierced stone *jaalis* of the haram above, a plaintive voice is heard:

> 'Tis the beauteous Zaida crying
> Half distracted—'Oh my life
> To thy foe concede thy Castle
> And from death preserve thy wife.' (ll. 33–6)[26]

This is another previously unattributed poem by Jones, fascinated by this Oriental power game since Harrow. One of the earliest texts in *Poems* (1772) was the mock-heroic 'Caissa, or; The Game at Chess', composed in 1763 when he was only 16, and singled out for praise by contemporary reviews. 'The Indian Game of Chess', Jones's account of its subcontinental origins, subsequently appeared in the second volume of *Asiatick Researches* (1790). The Banaras poem owes its married couple to the 'Moorish Tale' of forbidden love entitled 'Alcanzor and Zayda' by Jones's antiquarian friend Thomas Percy, in the same metre.[27] Its championing of female resourcefulness and intellect might well have been a tribute to Margaret Fowke from whom Jones learned a great deal. The enthusiasm of this self-confidently single 26-year-old for 'Hindostannie airs', which she transcribed from, and performed with, Indian musicians, was more than instrumental—indeed, charmingly vocal— in determining the course of Jones's own research into Indian music.

Jones helps compose a prologue for their latest dramatical performance in which an evening at Covent Garden is imaginatively recreated as 'England's gay scenes in brightest colours rise/And native charms before my dazzl'd eyes!' Other native charms, however, are the subject of a poem that Fowke had received from an army friend at Khanpur: those of the beautiful Kashmiri singer and dancer Khanum Jaan. She had dazzled officers, both young and old, and they lamented her departure:

> Let others of Tippoo hard-hearted complain,
> Of our losses by land, our defeats on the main;
> Another, but much greater loss I deplore,
> I mean the great loss we've sustain'd at Cawnpore.
> How sweetly of late did our time pass along

---

26. NLW, MS Ormathwaite, FB 3/16. This poem subsequently appeared in the *Monthly Magazine*, 9: 1 (May 1800), 365; and the *Sporting Magazine*, 16 (1800), 55–6, above the ascription: '*Middle Temple* M. E. Y', a piratical barrister, perhaps?
27. Thomas Percy, *Reliques of Ancient English Poetry*, 3 vols (London, 1765), 1: 324–9.

With a Nautch from the Connum, from Connum a song;
And who to lament will deny we have cause?[28]

Female camp followers were as numerous in the Company army as they were amongst Mughal troops, but the dynamic attractions of Khanum were of a different order. She created her own star-struck following throughout Bengal and was shortly to illuminate the pages of what some critics have claimed to be the first novel in an Indian language: Hasan Shah's *Qissa Rangeen*, originally written in Persian *c.*1790.[29] A fascinating autobiographical study of intercultural intimacy, it tells of how Khanum refuses the advances of 'Ming Sahib' (possibly Colonel Sir John Cumming, commanding Cawnpore) to marry his *munshi* (Persian translator), Hasan Shah. On her tragically early death, a devastated Hasan Shah, himself a poet and prose writer, entered the service of the famous Urdu poet, Qalandar Bakhsh Jurrat, at Lucknow.

The beauty of Hindu song was sensitizing 'Oriental' Jones to the Indian power of the feminine principle. It was intimately relating the concepts of *prakriti* (nature seen as female) and *śakti* (the female embodying active power), which he had previously viewed in a theoretical light, to his own feminine side. Margaret Fowke's compelling magnetism was swirling him into further creativity. Her extensive collaboration with Indian musicians and with Jones is illustrated in a letter she sent, together with transcriptions of 'some Indostaun Airs', to her father on the 11 January 1785. It was subsequently forwarded to Lady Clive:

> I have often made the Musicians tune their instruments to the harpsichord that I might join their little band. They always seemed delighted with the accompaniment of the harpsichord and sung with uncommon animation, and a pleasure to themselves, which was expressed in their faces. There is a great deal of vivacity in the second and fourth of these Songs [. . .] The subject of them is the Hindoo holidays, called the Hooley, and they are an invitation to join in the general rejoicing. The 3ᵈ Song is an address from one of the Gopia (nine ladies whom Sir William Jones supposes to be Grecian Muses) to Krishen or Crishna. Krishen [. . .] is passionately fond of dancing, and is always represented with a flute. He is so completely accomplished that Sir William is convinced he is Apollo himself. He takes notice of him in his hymn to the Hindoo God of Love:

---

28. NLW, MS Ormathwaite, FB 3/6; 'Song on the Departure of Connum from Cawnpore (By G—g)'.
29. The original is now lost, but it had been translated into Urdu in 1893, and this has received an English translation: Hasan Shah, *The Nautch Girl*, trans. Qurratulain Hyder (Delhi, 1992).

> Can men resist thy pow'r, when *Krishen* yields,
> *Krishen*, who still in *Matra*'s holy fields
> Tunes harps immortal, and to strains divine
> Dances by moonlight with the *Gopia* nine?

The 3^d Song which you will observe is in the minor key is original, wild, tender, and passionate in a very great degree [. . .] The fifth and sixth are two plaintive little airs, in which there is great delicacy and expression. They are both sung by women. [. . .] I am promised a poetical translation of these lines by Sir William Jones. They are in the Birgi [Braj Basha, a Hindi dialect] language, in which there is in my opinion great softness. It is spoken near Agra. Sir William's Moonshy understands it and will give the sense to him in Persian.[30]

If her understanding of Hindu culture and sensitive appreciation of the wildness and delicacy of the *bhakti* song tradition are remarkable, her enthusiastic interaction with native musicians is little short of astounding for an Englishwoman in India at this period. It mirrored Jones's close collaboration with Indian informants, inspiring him to the intercultural experimentation that illuminated the Sanskrit music treatises, such as Somanātha's *Rāgavibodha* (1609), which he was studying in Persian translations. In 'On the Musical Modes of the Hindus' (1792), the first western study of Indian music, Jones writes: '[K]nowing my ear to be very insufficiently exercised, I requested a *German* professor of musick to accompany with his violin a *Hindu* lutanist, who sung *by note* some popular airs on the loves of Crishna and Rádhá; he assured me, that the scales were the same' (*Works*, 4: 189).

Margaret did not have to wait long for her translations. Returning downriver, at Malda the Joneses met John Herbert Harington, a keen young Persian scholar and secretary of the Asiatick Society, and on the 17 January, Jones writes:

> I take the liberty to send you a double version of the three songs, the musick of which gave me so much pleasure at Sicrole; It was fortunate, that Mr Harington's munshy understood the dialect of *Birj*, and turned the songs literally into Persian; from which I have translated them in European measures as well as in an irregular sort of metre adapted syllable for syllable to the *Indian* tunes. If you should happen to receive more compositions from the holy land of *Matura* [Krishna's birthplace], I shall be much pleased with translating them in the same way; and by exchanging my brass for your gold, shall gain

---

30. NLW, Powis 1990 Deposit, 'Clive of India', packet 30.

considerably by the traffick, though not with near so much as if I could have the pleasure and advantage of hearing my words graced by your voice and improved by your taste and skill.[31]

Amongst the Hastings papers are two translations of Hindi songs in Jones's hand, which appear to be two of the three sent to Margaret. Their intensely loving content is typical of the devotional verse of many Krishna-*bhakti* poets, including celebrated singer-saints such as Sūrdās (*c*.1483–1563), or the Rajput princess, Mirabai (*c*.1498–*c*.1547). While the girls throw brightly coloured powders over each other to celebrate the spring festival of Holi, this lover longs only for the divine hue of Krishna's cheek:

> Still smiles the mirthful season bright
> But yields my bosom no delight:
> See the girls! how at Húly, sweet Húly, they play!
> I alone, when my charmer appears, can be gay.
> Since these fix'd eyes my darling bless'd,
> Nor eve nor morning brings them rest.
> ('The Gopy's [cowgirl's] Complaint' ['Jeb tayn lág'], ll. 13–18)

The other song, also in 18 lines of couplets, Jones entitles 'The Gopy's Confession' ('Her her leíney'), and it must be confessed that the *gopis* significantly outnumber the Muses. Jones read in the *Nārāyana Purāna* that in the days of Krishna, 'there *were sixteen thousand* modes [*ragas*], each of the *Gopis* at *Mathura* chusing to sing in one of them, in order to captivate the heart of their pastoral God'; other sources speak of 900,000 and how Krishna miraculously multiplied himself, making love to them all. The *gopis* flout convention with rapturous devotion, yet each enviously adores Krishna's favourite Rādhā, who symbolizes the soul and *prakriti*; each identifies with Rādhā as his *hlādinī-śakti* ('infinite energy of bliss') in a contemplation at once divine and erotic. This second song reflects the teasing nature of youthful Krishna, who steals not only the *gopis*' water pots but their saris while they are bathing in the fragrant Yamuna (Jumna):

> When on Jemna's banks thy daughter
> Fill'd her vase with hallow'd water,
> Seizing my flaggon he stood nigh reviling;
> Whilst other damsels in safety sat smiling.

---

31. BL, APAC, Fowke MS Eur E5, 65; Jones to Margaret Fowke, Maldah, 17 January 1785.

> That bright youth, who joy dispenses,
> Robs me, robs me, of my senses. (ll. 7–12)[32]

Though by no means robbed of his senses, the fact that William was extremely taken with the scholarly Margaret is reinforced by Anna's affectionate letters to her. The Joneses now find their pinnace rather chilly on the river, and Anna writes: 'Do you think you could send me one of the Benaras Fur Caps like Sir William's by the Dawk [post] bearers to overtake me at Patna or sooner if you can I shall be very glad of it for I feel the cold to my head very much & am afraid of it bringing on headaches.'[33] From Bhagalpur on 6 January 1785 Anna, writing 'in said cap', thanked her for 'the musick which will be a great amusement to me, as translating will be to Sir William, who says you ought to *command* and not to *beg* to have copies as fast as he finishes them and that he will make it his business, since you wish for them to send them as soon as they exist'. Anna promises to find Margaret 'a Pedal Harp' in Calcutta, and sends her compliments to Francis, adding: 'I can beat every body at Chess but him & I hope to have that pleasure when I visit Sicrole again.'[34]

Back in Calcutta in February, William writes to Margaret to thank her for sending more 'Hindustany songs, which I will not fail to translate and transmit to Benares'. Anna finds him describing herself as 'a little indisposed'. She seizes the pen from her husband and, on a separate sheet of her own, scrawls in mock anger: 'Very pretty truly! So I am to be quite neglected, & you *transfer your favours to my Husband*, I think you are so much in the right that I cannot find in my heart to scold.'[35] Anna knew she had no rival; she had met John Benn, assistant Resident at Banaras, intuiting his affection for Margaret. The following February when Francis resigned his post to return to England with Margaret, so did his assistant; they had each milked India sufficiently, amassing fabulous fortunes through private trading in opium and diamonds. Margaret married Benn in London in 1787. Eight years later, in a freezing English

---

32. BL, Add. MSS. 29,235, ff. 48–9. From the three-word indications of the originals, Ken Bryant of the University of British Columbia thinks it likely that they were in Braj Bhasha: '[I]n the context provided by the translation, the first, "jeb tayn lag", would be "Since they (i.e. my eyes) have set"; the second, "her her leiney", would be "To rob, rob"'; (Private communication).
33. BL, APAC, Fowke MS, Eur E5, 70; [Lady Jones] to Margaret Fowke, n.d., incomplete.
34. BL, APAC, Fowke MS, Eur E5, 63; Lady Jones to Margaret Fowke, 6 January 1785.
35. BL, APAC, Fowke MS, Eur E5, 72, 73; Jones and Lady Jones to [Miss Fowke], 27 February 1785.

January, Margaret presented a grieving Anna with a flawless Golconda diamond once given her by Hastings.

On St David's Day 1785 Jones was delighted to receive a Sanskrit book from Banaras. A present from a Muslim, Ali Ibrahim Khan, this Hindu volume was to shape the rest of Jones's life, and his immediate decision to access its contents by learning Sanskrit was to change Europe's self-understanding. It was the *Mānavadharmaśāstra* (Law-code of the school of Manu), an authoritative system of jurisprudence possessing great prestige amongst all Hindus and the respect of Muslim rulers.

It was as a judge, rather than as a lover of Indian literature, that Jones was thus inspired to learn Sanskrit. He had felt too busy to undertake yet another language, but it was inevitable that Jones should follow Wilkins, 'without whose aid I should never have learned [Sanskrit]'. His reasons were pragmatic and twofold. Firstly, it would facilitate his assembling, with the help of a team of Indian scholars, a digest of Hindu law, the capstone of the policy of legitimizing British rule through the recovery of native traditions. Secondly, it would help him on the bench, where he was loath to be reliant upon court pandits in interpreting law. It remains an abiding irony that Jones, soon to regard his Indian instructors with such warm affection, was initially led to learn Sanskrit through suspicion of Bengali pandits.[36]

Jones seems to have suspected the competence and/or probity of a court pandit named Ramachandra. For the appointment of Govardhana Kaula as second court pandit, Jones sought recommendations from the Hindu universities, and the 'real opinion' of Wilkins's pandit, Kasinath. 'It is of the utmost importance', Jones explains, 'that the stream of Hindu law should be pure; for we are entirely at the devotion of the native lawyers, through our ignorance of Shanscrit' (*Letters*, 2: 666). But problems attended learning Sanskrit, especially as Brahman pandits were reluctant to abandon their 'sacred' monopoly. Jones's solution was to spend the autumn vacation of 1785 at Krishnagar, near the university of Nadiya, the most distinguished centre of Sanskrit learning in Bengal, and 'my third university'.

Jones acquired a *bangla*, 'a thatched cottage with an upper story and a covered veranda' on the banks of the crystal-clear Jalangi, 'where *many a garden flower grows wild*'. He and Anna fell in love with the place, deciding

---

36. See Rosane Rocher, 'Weaving Knowledge: Sir William Jones and Indian Pandits', in *Objects of Enquiry: The Life, Contributions, and Influences of Sir William Jones (1746–1794)*, ed. Garland Cannon and Kevin R. Brine (New York, 1995), 51–91.

regularly to spend late summer in the 'pure air of Krishnagar'. They were soon introduced to the maharaja, Śiva Chandra, a great Sanskrit scholar, whose parents, Krishna Chandra and Rani Bhabani, were enlightened patrons. With the maharaja's help, Jones eventually found a pandit, a *Vaidya* (medical caste) scholar Rāmalocana who, though not a Brahman, was still reluctant to teach the 'language of the gods' to an 'unclean' meat-eating foreigner, even for 100 rupees a month. A persistent tradition suggests Rāmalocana imposed strict purification rules of *varna dharma*, ensuring their lessons were held in a separate room, especially floored with white marble and ritually cleansed with Ganges water. According to Abdul Haque Vidyarthi: 'Sir William was to receive instruction on an empty stomach; but occasionally, when he humbly implored the pandit, he was allowed to take a cup of tea.'[37]

Whether this submission to a Hindu 'of an irritable temper' is fact or embroidery, it reflects his determination to master Sanskrit. Jones actually refers to his pandit as 'a pleasant old man', and Krishnagar as 'my Indian *Arcadia*'. They would relieve routine with schoolboy jokes. Jones records Rāmalocana's irreverent parody of a Sanskrit prayer: 'In Snuff I place my zealous devotion; O Snuff, the universal preceptor, raise my spirits!'[38] Pupil and teacher hit it off so well that Jones persuaded Rāmalocana to accompany him back to Calcutta where Jones daily applied himself to detailed study of the *Mānavadharmaśāstra*.

Within less than a year, Jones's knowledge of the Laws of Manu was sufficient for him to arbitrate in cases where court pandits disagreed. One important cause, decided on 15 August 1786, had far-reaching implications. It concerned the disputed right of Gunga Bissen, a Hindu of the *Kshatriya* (military or ruling) caste, to will his land to Munnoo Loll, a low caste *Śūdra* whom Bissen had bought as a slave but lovingly brought up from childhood and treated as his son. The two court pandits, Śri Ramchurn Sermono and Śri Govardhana Kaula, had divergent opinions and, in the absence of Jones, the court requested William Chambers, as court interpreter, to consult other pandits. On Jones's return from Chittagong, he questioned all the pandits involved, 'look'd into the Shanscrit Books on the subject in the parts referr'd to by the Pundits, and now in Court read his own translation of a passage from one of the Hindoo Writers who is esteemed as a Saint or

37. Abdul Haque Vidyarthi, *Mohammad in World Scriptures* (Lahore, 1940), 11.
38. Bodleian MS Sansk: C.34 Vópadéva, *Mugdhabodha*, f. xiii.

Demi-God, and which Book all the Pundits acknowledge is of the highest authority'.[39] Creating an important precedent regarding caste inheritance, Jones ruled that Gunga Bissen's will was valid.

On 2 February 1786, only six months after he had begun to study Sanskrit, Jones read to the Asiatick Society his 'Third Anniversary Discourse', which contains this famous world-modifying statement:

> The *Sanscrit* language, whatever be its antiquity, is of a wonderful structure; more perfect than the *Greek*, more copious than the *Latin*, and more exquisitely refined than either, yet bearing to both of them a stronger affinity, both in the roots of verbs and in the forms of grammar, than could possibly have been produced by accident; so strong indeed that no philologer could examine them all three, without believing them to have sprung from some common source, which perhaps no longer exists: there is a similar reason, though not quite so forcible, for supposing that both the *Gothick* and the *Celtick*, though blended with a very different idiom, had the same origin with the *Sanscrit*; and the old *Persian* might be added to the same family. (*Works*, 3: 34)

Jones was making an imaginative scientific leap, which marks the beginning of Indo-European comparative grammar and modern comparative linguistics. His familiarity with 28 languages enabled him to compile word lists such as the following:

Sanskrit	matar
Greek	meter
Latin	mater
Persian	madar
German	mutter
Spanish	madre
Russian	mat'
Welsh	modryb; mam
Breton	mamm
Albanian	mëmë
French	mere; maman
Pashto	mor
Arabic	umm
English	mother; mum
Gaelic	mathair

---

39. Hyde Papers, book 9, reel 4; W. A. Montriou, *Cases of Hindu Law, Before H. M. Supreme Court* (Calcutta, 1853), 290–5; T. A. Venkasawmy Row, *Indian Decisions* (Old Series), vol 1, *Supreme Court Reports, Bengal* (Madras, 1911), 177.

But Jones did not simply base his thesis upon obvious word-list resemblance, he made detailed comparisons of grammatical roots to establish conclusively their identity as cognates. This emphasis upon roots and linguistic structure, rather than speculative etymology, rejects the philosophical a priori method of the eighteenth century for a new historical and comparative a posteriori method. Jones suggests the revolutionary idea of language evolution and, if languages can change over time, they may also become extinct—Jones's putative lost source is what we now term Proto-Indo-European. His paradigm-shifting researches in Calcutta reveal the most extensive language family in the world. Today linguists calculate that the Indo-European family includes languages and dialects spoken by about three billion people, including most of the major language families of Europe as well as many spoken in the Indian subcontinent, south and central Asia.

But if the linguistic thinking is radical, the racial ramifications are truly revolutionary. At a time when few Europeans expected—or desired—to find either refinement or family in India, this passage radically adjusted preconceptions of western cultural superiority, introducing disconcerting notions of familial relationship between the rulers and their 'black' subjects. Jones, who had felt at home in India since stepping off the *Crocodile*, speaks in terms of a family of languages as he links East and West in linguistic and racial terms. Even more importantly, within that family Sanskrit is seen as a more beautiful sister than her revered western siblings. The linguistic heritage of the Hindus is 'more exquisitely refined' than that of their imperial masters. Jones described this genetic affinity to Viscount Althorp, now Earl Spencer: 'I find Sanscrit to be a sister of the Latin.' To the new governor-general, Sir John Macpherson, he writes: 'By rising before the sun, I allot an hour every day to Sanscrit, and am charmed with knowing so beautiful a sister of Latin and Greek' (*Letters* 2: 711, 727).

This epoch-making formulation of the Indo-European thesis simultaneously founded the modern discipline of comparative linguistics and ensured the prominence of the inflected beauty of Sanskrit in future linguistic researches. Almost a century before Darwin's *Descent of Man* (1871), Jones initiates a theory of evolution by suggesting that languages such as Sanskrit and Greek descended from a language now extinct. He is the Darwin of linguistics; 'a far-seeing man', as Goethe described him, 'who seeks to connect the unknown to the known', nowhere more than in his application of genealogy to languages.

As we shall see, many other scholars of East and West had noted the similarities between Sanskrit and Persian, praising the refinement of the former; Amīr Khusrau, for example, had done so in late thirteenth-century Delhi. Successful science depends not only upon research and discovery but upon effective communication. Aristarchus of Samos argued a heliocentric model for the solar system 1,800 years before a Polish polymath established the Copernican revolution. Jones's international reputation and that of the *Asiatick Researches*, distributed and pirated throughout Europe, ensured the impact of his 'Third Anniversary Discourse'. Well-circulated, authoritative, and lucid, Jones's formulation was pioneering in its application of modern science to philology. The analysis was historical, comparative, and structural, involving morphology, phonology, the study of syntactic similarities, and the interdisciplinary use of the Linnaean taxonomy of the family, which Jones imported from his botanical investigations.

Although this scientific bent was precociously modern, Jones was also using linguistic evidence to develop an extremely venerable theory: the monogenesis of mankind descending from Noah's sons Shem, Ham, and Japhet in their diffusion across the globe. Thomas Trautmann has shown how Jones's proposal of the Indo-European language family was part of this project to substantiate 'Mosaic ethnology', to find Indian proof of the Mosaic narrative and thus to enlist Sanskrit literature as compatible with biblical chronology.[40] Jones allowed India to get its feet under the Mosaic ethnological table of the human family, achieving a memorable family reunion as Sanskrit re-enters the company of her sisters, Greek and Latin.

Jones's speculation about mankind's monogenesis and the primeval source of his civilization became the centre of scholarly enquiry throughout Europe. In some respects both his creative and scholarly endeavours presented something of a Romantic threat to existing systems of belief. His Sanskrit studies were tending towards the separation of language from religion and mythology, leading the new science of linguistics away from Genesis, the concept that all languages derived from Hebrew, God's gift to Adam, and the mutual unintelligibility attendant upon the destruction of the Tower of Babel.[41]

---

40. Thomas Trautmann, *Aryans and British India* (Berkeley, 1997), 165–89; 190–228.
41. Garland Cannon argues that 'Jones's theory presented a thorny challenge to biblical authority'; Garland Cannon and Michael J. Franklin, 'A Cymmrodor Claims Kin in Calcutta: An Assessment of Sir William Jones as Philologer, Polymath, and Pluralist', *THSC*, N.S. 11 (2005), 50–69. See also Michael J. Franklin, 'The Building of Empire and the Building of Babel: Sir William Jones, Lord Byron, and their Productions of the Orient', in *Byron East and West*, ed. Martin Prochazka (Prague, 2000), 63–78; 68.

Jones was incorporating ancient India into world history, anticipating his crucial identification of the 'Palibothra' of the Greeks with Pataliputra, the birthplace of Emperor Aśoka in the third century BCE, at that time the world's largest city, and 'Sandracottus' with the fourth-century BCE Maurya emperor, Chandragupta. This facilitated accurate correlation of eastern and western history. It was certainly no part of the Asiatick Society's project to essentialize Asia's timelessness and fixity, a practice which Edward Said has seen as a key element of the agenda of official academic Orientalism. Jones's Orientalist research, through its construction of India's past, helped to shape the way Indians perceived themselves.[42]

Libertarian Jones had set the Indian tiger of Aryanism amongst the colonialist pouter pigeons as subsequent British Orientalists worried away at the ethnological and political implications of the Indo-European language family and moved towards the modern concept of race as a social construction as opposed to a natural or biological division. Almost exactly a century later, in 1875, Sir Henry Maine, legal adviser to the colonial administration in India at the zenith of the Raj, was still taking in the ethnological and political impact of Jones's thesis: 'That peoples not necessarily understanding one another's tongue should be grouped together politically on the ground of linguistic affinities assumed to prove community of descent is quite a new idea.'[43] If the category of race was crucial to the maintenance of socially polite distance between the British and Indians, too much similarity was more than embarrassing; differences must be discovered, especially when such a dangerous idea as common descent was available to Indians in reinterpreting their own identity. To a Victorian British social elite the idea was certainly common and hardly decent; they had little desire to claim kin in Calcutta.

Jones bequeathed to an imperial world the enormous problem of a dark-skinned people possessed of an ancient and 'exquisitely refined' civilization. Racialism became central to nineteenth-century imperial thinking. This operated not merely at a simplistic level within the colony—if the glories of their sophisticated society had been foolishly lost by the noble lighter-complexioned Aryans intermarrying with the darker-skinned original Dravidian population here was a lesson to the Raj on the importance of

---

42. See O. P. Kejariwal, *The Asiatic Society of Bengal and the Discovery of India's Past, 1784–1838* (Delhi, 1988).
43. Sir Henry Maine, *Village Communities in the East and West* (London, 1876), 210.

avoiding 'miscegenation'—but in the wider context of national and transnational history. The next sentence of Maine's Cambridge lecture, *The Effects of Observation of India on Modern European Thought*, following the one quoted above, states that: '[W]e owe to it, [Jones's 'new idea'] at all events in part, the vast development of German nationality; and we certainly owe to it the pretensions of the Russian Empire at least to a presidency over all Sclavonic communities.' The deep and dark waters of an Aryanism perversely made Eurocentric, of institutionalized racial superiority and Nazi world hegemony lay in a twentieth-century future of unparalleled barbarism.

The resonance of this 1786 passage thus extended far beyond philology. It marked a turning point in the history of intercultural understanding and the awareness of multicultural interrelatedness. The politics of this new knowledge is revolutionary. Always fascinated by the vibrant and exotic, Jones had sought to locate similitude rather than difference in Asiatic literature. Now, in south Asia, his thesis of linked linguistic and racial affinities between pampered colonialist and palanquin bearer possessed a radical and liberating originality of world-changing dimensions. It was a gift from British despot to Bengali native of infinitely greater political consequence than the scholar's gift of a musket to the peasant in *The Principles of Government*. The following year in London, the Society for Effecting the Abolition of the Slave Trade designed a seal 'expressive of an African in Chains in a Supplicating Posture', bearing the motto: 'Am I Not A Man and A Brother?'. Jones in Calcutta had already displayed the subjugated 'Hindoo' not only as a sister, but a more sophisticated sister, in the Indo-European language family. In this way, early in the expansion of Britain's second empire, metropolitan rulers had to come to terms with the disconcerting conception of classical India as the *fons et origo* of world understanding.

Empire had facilitated Jones's famous discovery in that it had sent him to be a judge in Calcutta. Though a Crown appointee, he served a regime controlled by the world's first global corporation—the EIC, resplendent in its unconstitutional power and private army. The Honourable Company, as it was called, was the corporate creator of empire, Britain, and modernity. As globalizing commerce was shrinking the world, Jones's 'Third Anniversary Discourse' stressed global interconnectedness. Distance had not died nor was the world yet flat, but this new concept of Indo-European *Ursprache* inevitably drew East closer to West. Romanticizing Europe would be led on to speculate on the Aryan *Urvolk* and the Indian garden *Urheimat*.

3. Statue of Jones by John Bacon, in St Paul's Cathedral, 1799.

The impact of Jones's discovery was that in India we had found not only fortune but family—relatives worthy of respect, who had achieved a sophisticated culture when Britons were daubing themselves with woad. Such realizations were chastening at home and influenced the development of British imperialism by encouraging a tolerant if sometimes grudging respect for its Indian subjects at least until the 1830s. The success of Jones's cultural translation introduced a period of Indomania, which could relish a domesticated Hinduism 'safe for Anglicans'. This was more than reverse acculturation, it was a conquest of the metropole by alien wisdom and exotic poetry; the *dharmaśāstra* of Manu and Vishnu's Kūrma Avatāra (Tortoise Incarnation) invaded St Paul's through John Bacon's colossal statue of Jones.[44]

The work of Jones and his colleagues in the Asiatick Society involved appropriating Sanskrit culture just as efficiently as Robert Clive and his generation had appropriated Indian wealth. It is claimed that Clive gained £232 million for the EIC and up to £22 million for himself. The imperial aggression was so strident and the catalogue of pillage and corruption so complete, we even looted the Hindustani word 'loot'.

Jones would pillage Indian knowledge, he would rifle Sanskrit culture, but he realized that knowledge, although colonially produced and temporarily useful in bolstering colonial authority, is unchained, uncontainable, and universally available. Apart from destroying linguistic, cultural, and conceptual barriers, eradicating racial stereotypes, the power of such knowledge was free to serve a diverse range of political, cultural, and ideological purposes. Ultimately Orientalist knowledge might be used to challenge European dominance; in the following century it was deployed by Indian nationalists against British hegemony.

---

44. See Trautmann, *Aryans and British India*, 77–80.

2

'Persian' Jones, London Welshman, Surveys his Roots

On 23 August 1775, William Jones is relaxing with two lawyer friends on Sir Roger Mostyn's landscaped lawns. A month before his 29th birthday, he is enjoying his north Wales tour. The luncheon sewin, wrapped in bacon, had been delicious, and he was sampling nectarines and peaches from the greenhouses of his host, the MP for Flintshire. Looking out towards 'the isle of Anglesey, the ancient Mona, where my ancestors presided over a free but uncivilized people', Jones's feelings are conflicted. With the spacious mansion at his back, his gaze moves across ornamental gardens and deer park; the contrast with father's birthplace was all too stark. A rough-hewn stone cottage, it was known as Y Merddyn. As a romanticizing child, that name embraced Myrddin, the magical 'man of the sea' Merlin. The young poet imagined his father's parish, Llanfihangel Tre'r-Beirdd (the Parish of St Michael, Town of the Bards), as Druidically mysterious. He now realizes the cottage name was a variant of the word 'murddyn', ruin.

Our infant polymath was deprived of the opportunity of growing up under his father's loving influence. Jones senior died on 1 July 1749 before his son was three, but the paternal role model was ever present. Intellect and determination had enabled the father to escape rural poverty to pursue a career as a celebrated mathematician, culminating in election to the vice-presidency of the Royal Society, and the friendship of Isaac Newton, Edmund Halley, Lord Hardwicke, and Samuel Johnson. In later life he chose to live south of the Strand, first, shortly after his marriage to Mary Nix in 1731, at 13 Buckingham Street, and from 1739 at 11 Beaufort Buildings, close to the sights and sounds of the river. Young William always recalled sitting with his father on the smooth steps under the rusticated columns of

Inigo Jones's Italianate York Water Gate as they watched the sailing barges and wherries ply the Thames. As the child grew, he explored the nearby grounds of the Savoy, once John of Gaunt's magnificent palace—where Chaucer was thought to have been married—which was destroyed in 1381 by Wat Tyler and radically questioning peasants: 'When Adam delved and Eve span,/Who was then the gentleman?' It always struck him that his Beaufort Buildings birthplace was situated between Fountain Court and Dirty Lane; no. 11 backed onto the latter.

His father's mathematical skill at Llanfechell charity school came to the attention of Viscount Bulkeley of Baron Hill, who recommended him to a London merchant. The Welsh work ethic of Jones senior was employed in the service of capitalism and colonialism. He was sent on a commercial voyage to the West Indies but, though inured to the grinding poverty and low life expectancy of Anglesey, he was appalled by plantation slavery. Loving the sea, he entered the navy as a teacher of mathematics and navigation—the twin facilitators of empire—aboard a man-of-war. At the battle of Vigo Bay in 1702, 'Longitude' Jones joined shipmates in pillaging the town. According to Teignmouth's biography: 'he eagerly fixed upon a bookseller's shop as the object of his depredations; but finding in it no literary treasures, which were the sole plunder that he coveted, he contented himself with a pair of scissors, which he frequently exhibited to his friends as a trophy of his military success' (*Works*, 1: 6).

After leaving the navy, he lodged with scientific writer John Harris in Amen Corner, St Paul's, teaching mathematics; lecturing in the 'Penny University' sessions at Child's coffee-house; and finessing his own self-education at Royal Society public lectures in Crane Court. In 1702, Jones published his influential *New Compendium of the Whole Art of Navigation*. His *Synopsis Palmariorum Matheseos*, in which he was the first to use the symbol π with its modern signification, followed in 1706. Books and manuscripts remained his favourite plunder, and Jones published a key Newton manuscript on the origins of infinitesimal calculus as *Analysis per Quantitatum Series, Fluxiones, ac Differentias* (1711), demonstrating Newton's priority over Leibniz in the discovery of the calculus. With Jones's elegant Latin preface, engraved vignettes, and woodcut diagrams, this book showcased its editor's importance as both a bibliophile and a disseminator of Newton's work. Jones was elected Fellow of the Royal Society on 30 November 1711, the year of his prudent marriage to the wealthy widow of his merchant patron.

To move from a remote sheep farm to a position of intimacy with the movers and shakers of British science was a remarkable intellectual, cultural, and social achievement for William ap Siôn Siors (son of John George).[1] All that drive and determination he bequeathed to his son. The Anglesey heritage was even more powerful. The fiercely independent oppositional anti-Roman ideology described by Tacitus, a Druidic culture of law-giving, natural philosophy, and science associated with *Môn Mam Cymru* (Anglesey Mother of Wales) was cherished as a pre-Norman foundation of Welsh and British nationhood. There was a cultural continuity here, for London Welsh society was, in effect, Wales's only public sphere. The London Welshman wrote home in Welsh, but regularly corresponded in English, French, or Latin with a wide range of European savants, mathematicians, and astronomers. He belonged to an international circle of communicating scientists, 'Voyaging through strange seas of [Newtonian] Thought' together.

Jones's closest friend was Abraham de Moivre, a French Huguenot refugee. They gravitated to that centre of French émigrés, the Rainbow coffee-house in Fleet Street, where they talked with Halley and Newton and taught advanced mathematics to Lord Charles, and his uncle Lord James, Cavendish. Jones proposed these scientific scions of the whig Devonshires for Royal Society membership in 1719. De Moivre's circle exercised enormous influence upon the scientific interests of the whig political establishment. De Moivre produced the first study of probability theory, *The Doctrine of Chances: or, a Method of Calculating the Probability of Events in Play* (1718), and the two friends shared a fascination with the mathematics of capitalism: interest, insurance, mortgages, and annuities. Jones became the foremost expert on compound interest, and his much-circulated manuscript, 'The Practice of Interest', included a formula for the rate of interest in an annuity.[2] Apart from anticipating the work of the Welsh radical Richard Price on how to address the needs of the disadvantaged within a more equitable society, the influence of such ideas is seen in his son's lifelong commitment to rendering the faces of commerce, capitalism, and the law more acceptable to the weak and oppressed.

Some amusing insights into the character of Jones senior can be gleaned from the journals of mathematician Reuben Burrow, befriended by 'Orientalist'

---

1. Following Welsh practice he had taken his father's Christian name (Siôn, in English: John) as his surname.
2. Staple Inn Hall, High Holborn, Library of the Institute of Actuaries, Jones MS.

Jones in Bengal. Straight-speaking Will Jones was reluctant to suffer fools; his manner and his mathematics were exacting, acerbic, and precise. Satirical at the expense of intellectual opponents, he was passionately committed to the defence of the truth and the defence of his friends:

> He was a little shortfaced Welshman, and used to treat his mathematical friends with a great deal of roughness and freedom. He rated Mr. Thomas Simpson in such a manner about his paper against De Moivre, that Simpson said he would never go to see him more, but he did see him again however.[3]

Jones held no grudges, suggesting Simpson for the post of mathematics master at the Royal Military Academy. Jones also recommended Nathaniel Bliss, astronomer and rector of St Ebbe's, for the Oxford chair in geometry, despite having earlier refused him a copy of his unpublished 'Abstract of Conic Sections'. The canny north Walian farmer in his background is clear from his actual words as cited by Burrow:

> 'In the first place, if I gave them to him he does not understand them, and in the next it is in the way of the parsons to make everything they can get their own; besides, he would probably give them out at the University, and then some of them would publish the properties as their own, and I do not know but that I may some time or other wish to publish them myself.'

'Orientalist' Jones eagerly devoured such reminiscences of his father, relishing the proud independence and the strong vein of anti-clericalism, which he undoubtedly shared. As an old man, Samuel Johnson, in conversation with pious intellectual, Elizabeth Carter, was anxious to eradicate any suspicions of his own youthful infidelity by slating atheists he had known. He mentions 'one of ye most harden'd Infidels he ever met with, one Jones, a great Mathematician & a very Clever Man'.[4]

This self-conscious Anglesey Druid imbibed the pagan mysteries of freemasonry and the revolutionary celestial dynamics of Newton. 'Longitude' Jones frequented John Byrom's Cabala Club with Royal Society vice-president and fellow 'infidel', Martin Folkes, natural philosopher, antiquary, and pet-monkey owner. The Revd William Stukeley, leading authority on

---

3. T. T. Wilkinson, 'Mathematics and Mathematicians, the Journals of the late Reuben Burrow [pt 2]', *London, Edinburgh, and Dublin Philosophical Magazine*, 4th ser., 5 (1853), 514–22; 518.
4. *Mary Hamilton, Afterwards Mrs John Dickenson*, ed. Elizabeth and Florence Anson (London, 1925), 181.

the Druids, was profoundly shocked that Folkes 'professes himself a godfather to all monkeys':

> He thinks there is no difference between us & animals; but what is owing to the different structure of our brain, as between man & man. When I lived at Ormond Street in 1720, he set up an infidel Club at his house on Sunday evenings, where Will Jones, the mathematician, & others of the heathen stamp, assembled. [...] From that time he has been propagating the Infidel system with great assiduity, & made it even fashionable in the Royal Society, so that when any mention is made of Moses, of the deluge, of religion, Scriptures, &c., it is generally received with a loud laugh.[5]

This dynamic sceptical strain of Enlightenment radicalism was viewed very differently by Jones's son, although his own youthful desire to shock emerged in more explicitly political ways. 'Oriental' Jones might not have advertised the fact that he had a 'heathen' father, but his religious views were similarly deist, and two generations of William Joneses endorsed Martin Folkes's sentiments as expressed to a Jewish friend: 'We are all citizens of the world, and see different customs and tastes without dislike or prejudice, as we do different names and colours.'[6]

There are ironies, however, instinct in the fact that his comparative religious studies in Bengal made Jones keen not to laugh at Moses but to emphasize the authenticity of Mosaic history, allowing India enter the biblical ethnology of the human family. Yet Jones's language-family theory ultimately became the definitive rejection of the idea that God-given Hebrew was the language from which all others derived following the destruction of the Tower of Babel. 'Oriental' Jones's whole career was to be built on comparative systematizing, along Newtonian and Linnæan lines, and—like his father's—was to have much to do with 'heathens', their 'baboon jargon', and their 'Infidel systems'. If Jones senior, like Folkes, or his son's friend and correspondent, James Burnett, Lord Monboddo in *Of the Origin and Progress of Language* (1773–92), appreciated similitude between species and the humanity of the 'orang-outang' or chimpanzee, we may perhaps detect here an Enlightenment movement towards the mathematics of evolution in terms of man and his invention of language. It was a process that would culminate in the publication of *The Origin of Species* (1859) and *The Descent of Man* (1871). Indeed Garland Cannon

---

5. *The Family Memoirs of the Rev William Stukeley*, Surtees Society, 73, 3 vols (Durham, 1882), 1: 100.
6. John Nichols, *Literary Anecdotes of the Eighteenth Century*, 6 vols (London, 1812), 4: 637.

has seen Jones as 'a Darwin who meshed many isolated evolutionary facts known by predecessors into a grand theory of evolutionary change documented by his own field research'.[7] In 1792 Jones explicitly referred to 'the primitive language from which all others were derived, or to which at least they were subsequent' (*Works*, 3: 199). In separating language from religion Jones enabled linguistics to move towards science, and Jones's scholarly stature prevented his being attacked in the way that Darwin was ruthlessly monkified in the 1870s.

A fascinating sidelight is thrown on the question of Will Jones's 'infidel' nature—at least in his later life—by a letter surviving in the Llanstephan MSS of his friend, the eminent translator and bibliographer Moses Williams. Dated the 14 May 1745, it is from Jones's kinsman Richard Morris, who left Llanfihangel Tre'r-Beirdd for London in 1726. Richard refers to 'the progress I have already made in collating and correcting of orthography of the Welsh Bible, which I submit to your consideration, and beg the favour of your sentiments thereon'.[8] The Bibles, subsequently printed in 1746 and 1752 in editions of 15,000 copies, were subsidized by the Society for Promoting Christian Knowledge at a cost of £6,000 for the use of the Revd Griffith Jones, vicar of Llanddowror, Carmarthenshire, in his circulating free schools. Anxious to counter accusations that the Welsh translation was not 'from the original Hebrew and Greek but from the English', Morris writes: 'I believe the prefaces to these ancient editions you have by you, confute this reflection upon the ability of our countrymen.' So 'Longitude' Jones, 'of the heathen stamp', turns out to be charting the course of Welsh biblical scholarship.

It would be good to know more concerning the relations between these two kinsmen in London, especially as Morris became the first president of the Honourable Society of Cymmrodorion, the foremost intellectual and philanthropic London–Welsh society, in September 1751. Richard refers to Will's 'kind communicative temper and former favours to me', and it is likely that Jones helped him in the teaching of navigation, which he practised for some time before joining the Navy Office.

As a scholar and communicator, Jones senior was his son's father; education and intellect were stamped through the structural chemistry of the Jones genome like a stick of Ynys Môn rock. Both men were helping science

---

7. Cannon and Franklin, 'A Cymmrodor Claims Kin in Calcutta', 69.
8. Cited in John Ballinger, *The Bible in Wales: A Study in the History of the Welsh People* (London, 1906), 21.

emerge from natural philosophy. But the father endured the harder struggle of self-advancement, pointing the way for the son to achieve the treasured goal of absolute independence. Law figured largely in the family's advancement.

As mathematics master at the Dissenting academy of classical scholar Samuel Morland FRS in Bethnal Green, Jones senior in 1704 tutored Philip Yorke, future Lord Chancellor Hardwicke. He became Yorke's lifelong friend, often accompanying him, when chief justice, on the western circuit. The experience fascinated Jones who became a Westminster magistrate. Jones subsequently joined the household of Lord Chief Justice Thomas Parker of the King's Bench, later first earl of Macclesfield, as scientific advisor to Parker and mathematics and astronomy tutor to his son George. When Jones's banker failed, these valuable connections led to a series of sinecure offices and the posts of deputy teller of the exchequer and secretary to the Commissions of the Peace.

Jones lived for lengthy periods at Shirburn Castle, near Oxford, a moated manor house that Parker had splendidly modernized. By 1740 two superb portraits, which George Parker commissioned from William Hogarth, hung side by side in the library. Having painted Martin Folkes two years earlier, Hogarth's curved 'line of beauty' certainly embraced the Newtonian circle. Both the artist and his two sitters were connected by freemasonry and charitable work at Thomas Coram's Foundling Hospital. The portrait of Parker displays the second earl's sumptuously brocaded silk waistcoat: Jones, in an elegant but unostentatious brown velvet coat, displays only the quietly confident pose of a man who has arrived. The juxtaposition of the paintings set the seal on their close relationship.

Jones's talents extended beyond the coolly rational world of science. He resolved the 'difficulties' attendant upon an imprudent 'Italian wedding', which George Parker contracted on his Grand Tour. The epigram: 'Macclesfield was the making of Jones, and Jones the making of Macclesfield' might, however, refer to the possibility of his having fathered the third earl on George Parker's young bride one clear night when her husband was observing the zenith distance of the pole star. Will Jones certainly had an eye for young ladies. By this time a widower, he met his second wife, Mary, the attractive and intelligent daughter of George Nix, an eminent cabinet maker and friend of Thomas Parker, at Shirburn Castle. When they married, on 17 April 1731, Mary (1705–80) was 25; Jones was 56.

Too little is known about 'Orientalist' Jones's mother, who embarked upon a marriage to this exacting, rather crusty, partner. Mary's nature was described by her patriarchal husband with characteristically balanced preci-

4. William Jones (1675–1749), mathematician and father of Jones, by William Hogarth, oil on canvas, 1740. (National Portrait Gallery, London)

sion: 'She was virtuous, without blemish; generous, without extravagance; frugal, but not a niggard; cheerful, but not giddy; close, but not sullen; ingenious, but not conceited; of spirit, but not passionate; of her company, cautious; in her friendship, trusty; to her parents dutiful, and to her husband, ever faithful, loving, and obedient' (*Works*, 1: 14–18).

This angel of Beaufort Buildings was a model of conscientious adaptability and strong understanding. Their first child George died as a baby in 1732, but they were delighted when their daughter Mary was born in 1736. When not attending to the literary and scientific education of her intelligent daughter, she was learning the Jonesian specialisms of algebra, trigonometry, and navigation to help her nephew who was entering the navy. The transmission of intellect was her nostrum also, and when their son William was born on Michaelmas Eve 1746, he had—for a brief time—two loving and practised teachers at his behest.

Among the papers of the Macclesfield Collection is evidence that—as an earnest young man—Jones père extended Newtonian analysis into the realms of morality, education, and government, producing 'A System of Ethicks', 'A System of Politicks', and 'A System of Economics', illustrated with apophthegmatic verse couplets.[9] Sadly, there was no time for the father to expound his systematizing to his son, but the posthumous lessons recorded in the minute handwriting of this bound manuscript would absorb the growing child's attention. Loosely inserted in Jones's 'Notes on Newton's Principia', I discovered an unpublished letter revealing that in May 1749 magistrate Jones was instrumental in Henry Fielding's election as Chairman of the Westminster Sessions, as literary London toasted the phenomenal success of *Tom Jones*.[10]

Mary handled the tragedy of her husband's death less than two months later with stoicism (their friend, Newtonian physiologist Richard Mead, had previously informed her of the condition—an incurable polyp in the heart—but she never revealed it to her husband) and determination to hold the family closely together. The role of educator squarely settled upon her shoulders and she expertly rose to the challenge. Refusing a kind offer from Mary, Countess of Macclesfield, to reside at Shirburn, she applied in her Westminster home advanced educational ideas, already tested upon her daughter, to the stimulation of young William's mind. Despite the fact her husband had bequeathed,

---

9. Cambridge University Library, MS Add 9597/12/11, March 1700.
10. 'I have thought of the Affair you mentioned to me concerning the Chair at Westmr Sessions and have determined not to decline it if the Gentlemen think proper to do me the Honour of their Choice. To morrow I am told is the adjournment Day. If you please to go to Westmr I will wait on you and attend you thither.' Cambridge University Library, MS Add 9597/18/15, Letter of Henry Fielding to William Jones, 16 May 1749.

5. Sir William Jones as a boy, by Sir Joshua Reynolds, oil on canvas, *c*.1753. (Asiatic Society, Kolkata)

together with his gold watch, his 'study of Books' and manuscripts—reputed to be the best mathematical library in England—to George, Earl of Macclesfield, in 'acknowledgement of the many marks of his favour', a wide range of books remained at home.[11] These facilitated Mary's guiding maxim: 'read, and you will know'. When not examining his father's cabinets of 'shells, fossils, minerals, stones, and mathematical instruments', young William did just that.

As Jones's will provided a legacy of £1,000 to each of the two children on their reaching the age of 21, reserving funds for 'their respective maintenance, tuition and education'; the family was comfortably situated. His most important legacy, however, was a wealth of powerful, influential, and intellectual whig connections in parliament, at court, the inns of Temple, and the Royal Society. These were to prove immensely supportive to Mary, providing

11. NA PROB 11/772, sig. 252, Will of William Jones of Saint Clement Danes, Middlesex, London, proved 10 August 1749. Unwisely Jones willed to George Parker an immensely important library of Welsh books and manuscripts, which he had purchased from Moses Williams's widow in 1742; they long remained at Shirburn inaccessible to Welsh scholars.

significant introductions for her children. But the help was not entirely one way, and Mary's co-operation in a comparative experiment reveals that—even as an infant—William Jones was advancing the cause of science.

An old friend, Henry Baker, natural philosopher and teacher of the deaf, approached her in July 1750, for permission to take detailed measurements of young William to compare with those of a 22-year-old dwarf, John Coan, from Twitshall, Norfolk. The Royal Society was preoccupied with anatomical 'curiosities' and prodigies of nature, and Henry's son, David Erskine Baker, measured both the dwarf and William, who proved an admirable scientific 'control':

> [A] Child of 3 Years and not quite 9 Months old, Son of the late very worthy *William Jones* Esq. F.R.S. was measured and weighed. This Boy, tho' very lively and handsome, is no way remarkable for his Size; and therefore his Dimensions and Weight, compared with the Dwarf's, may give a tolerable Idea of the real Smallness of the Dwarf.[12]

[468]

" found his Height, with his Hat, Shoes, and Wig
" on, to be 38 Inches. His Limbs are no bigger
" than a Child of 3 or 4 Years old: His Body is per-
" fectly ftrait: The Lineaments of his Face anfwer-
" able to his Age; and his Brow has fome Wrinkles
" in it, when he looks attentively at any thing.
" He has a good Complexion, is of a fprightly Tem-
" per, difcourfes readily and pertinently confidering
" his Education, and reads and writes *Englifh* well.
" His Speech is a little hollow, tho' not difagreeable;
" he can fing tolerably, and amufes the Company
" that come to fee him, with mimicking a Cock's
" Crowing, which he imitates very exactly. In
" 1744 he was 36 Inches high, and weigh'd 27
" Pounds and an half. His Father fays, when about
" a Year old he was as large as Children of that Age
" ufually are, but grew very little and flowly after-
" wards."

On receiving the Account of this little Man, a Child of 3 Years and not quite nine Months old, Son of the late very worthy *William Jones* Efq; F. R. S. was meafured and weighed. This Boy, tho' very lively and handfome, is no way remarkable for his Size; and therefore his Dimenfions and Weight, compared with the Dwarf's, may give a tolerable Idea of the real Smallnefs of the Dwarf.

The Weight of the Dwarf, with all his Cloaths on, was no more than 34 Pounds.

The Child's Weight, with its Cloaths likewife on, was 36 Pounds (*a*).

The

(*a*) The Cloaths, being weigh'd afterwards by themfelves, were two

[469]

	Inches.
The Height of the Dwarf, with his Shoes, Hat and Wig on	$38\frac{1}{10}$
The Height of the Child, without any thing on his Head	$37\frac{7}{10}$

	Dwarf. Inches	Child. Inches
Round the Waift	21	$20\frac{1}{10}$
Round the Neck	9	$9\frac{1}{10}$
Round the Calf of the Leg	8	9
Round the Ancle	6	6
Round the Wrift	4	$4\frac{1}{10}$
Round the Thumb	2	$2\frac{1}{10}$
Length of the Arm, *viz.* from the Shoulder to the Wrift	15	13
From the Elbow to the End of the middle Finger	$10\frac{4}{10}$	10
From the Wrift to the End of the middle Finger	4	4
From the Knee to the Bottom of the Heel	$10\frac{4}{10}$	$10\frac{7}{10}$
Length of the Foot with the Shoe on	6	$6\frac{4}{10}$
Length of the Face	6	$6\frac{5}{10}$
Breadth of the Face	5	$4\frac{8}{10}$
Length of the Nofe	$1\frac{7}{10}$	$1\frac{3}{10}$
Width of the Mouth	$1\frac{8}{10}$	$1\frac{8}{10}$
Breadth of the Hand	$2\frac{1}{10}$	$2\frac{5}{10}$

It two Pounds fourteen Ounces; confequently the real Weight of the Child is thirty-three Pounds two Ounces; which is but fourteen Ounces lefs than the Dwarf's Weight with all his Cloaths.

6. *Philosophical Transactions of the Royal Society*, 46 (London, 1752), 468–9.

12. *Philosophical Transactions for the Years 1749 and 1750* (London, 1752), 46: 467–70; 468.

The biographer's task is to take the measure of the man, and it is no small help to find the measurements of the child so accurately recorded in the pages of *Philosophical Transactions*. Yet there is something crude about this juxtaposition of dwarf and infant, which smacks of the freak show—Coan was subsequently displayed at the Royal Society alongside a double-jointed African—rather than humane physiological research. Baker's table (see above) compares an unfortunate prodigy of arrested physical development with a prodigy of precocious intellect, making us ponder the perplexing semantic range of the word 'prodigy'. Remarkably Jones's early scientific 'debut' only documents his unremarkable normality. Yet when the 7-year-old won a scholarship to Harrow, he was frequently referred to as a prodigy, and the label stuck. Young Jones was the product of a loving, secure, woman-centred, intellectually rigorous environment. Admired, intelligent, and good-looking, he was the delight of mother and of his sister Mary. Indulged rather than spoiled, his female upbringing developed his sensibility and throughout his life he relished female company.

At Harrow, which he entered in Michaelmas term 1753, Jones enjoyed the novelty of a male environment, diligently keeping pace with older pupils. He loved gardening, but 'cissy' taunts evaporated when his schoolmates received some of the produce. In his second year a scramble for pears—which, allegedly, had fallen from the tree—resulted in a fractured thigh and a year's convalescence. With the devoted attentions he received at home, this was no real setback. His mother, a talented artist, improved his drawing and chose entertaining books but, against the advice of both Marys, he neglected his Latin. On his return, he was flogged and humiliated by a despicable master, William Prior, whose cruelty confirmed Jones's lifelong abhorrence of tyrannical authority and injustice.

Spurred to regain his place, he worked long hours on classical prosody and rapidly displayed his linguistic prowess, translating and imitating Pindar and Sophocles, Ovid, Virgil, Horace, and Cicero, not neglecting Dryden, Pope, or his beloved Milton. But unlike the author of *Paradise Regained* who confessed: 'When I was yet a child, no childish play/To me was pleasing', Jones's mindset was not exclusively serious. While Etonians were sweatily perfecting their Wall Game, Jones invented the classical war game. The surrounding fields were transformed into Aegina,

Sparta and the Cyclades, their peace disturbed by Persian invasions and heroic battles as Harrovian hoplites, led by Jones, practised citizen-soldiery.

His headmaster, the Revd Dr Thomas Thackeray, an avuncular and intelligent family man whose latitudinarian whig principles proved too advanced for Eton, remarked that Jones was 'a boy of so active a mind that if he were left naked and friendless on Salisbury Plain he would soon find his way to fame and riches'. Comfortable in the hand-sewn shirts sent from home by his beloved 'Mamma' and secure in the friendship of Joseph Banks, Samuel Parr (scholar and reformer, the 'whig Dr Johnson'), William Bennet (bishop of Cloyne), and Richard Brinsley Sheridan, Jones would arrive even sooner.

His rich diet of classical reading produced visionary moments and, like Thomas Gray, 'oft before his infant eyes would run/Such forms as glitter in the Muse's ray/With orient hues'. The earliest extant example of Jones's poetry is from a tragedy he wrote for a school production entitled 'Meleager' (in which he took the lead), describing the horrors of the hero's death, consumed by internal fire:

> Wildly he stares; his glittering eye-balls sink
> Beneath their sockets, and omit their light.
> His shiver'd hair hangs dangling o'er his face;
> He rends his silken vest, and wrings his hands,
> And groans, possess'd with agonizing pain. (*Works*, 1: 31)

These lines powerfully recall the trauma of two serious childhood accidents. Ten years earlier the 4-year-old Jones, briefly alone in the Beaufort Buildings sitting room, had been scraping soot from the chimney-back when he fell into the fire. Horrified servants extinguished the flames and calmed the screaming child, but he suffered serious burns to his face, neck, and arms. Shortly after, impatiently struggling while being dressed by the maid, a clothes hook wounded him in his right eye. Despite Mead's best efforts, the sight of that eye was always imperfect.

When not honing his histrionic skills, 'the Great Scholar' was teaching himself Hebrew and the Arabic script. He idolized his new headmaster, classicist Robert Sumner and, as they practised Ciceronian rhetoric, Sumner realized his pupil's use of idiom was superior to his own. So while William was composing, in tribute to Aristophanes, a Greek verse comedy entitled

'Mormo', a hideous female hobgoblin invoked to frighten children, what was dear sister Mary doing?

There had been no public school for her, but she had received a rigorous educational programme supervised by both parents. Genes conspired to make Mary also a genius, if an unsung one. Striding through London, a Greek folio under her arm, library-bound to learn languages, and little concerned about mud bedraggling her skirt hems, visiting Lady Hannah Prime at Kneller Hall, or playing cards with General 'Cupid' Martin, Mary appears to us only through the distorting prism of the arch comments of the class-conscious conservative intellectual Laetitia-Matilda Hawkins:

> Miss Jones was of no very sightly appearance; and her negligence of dress could hardly be carried lower; she was said to have pursued a track of learning similar to that which distinguished her brother. [...] she was one of a small number of persons, whose conversation seems to be made purposely trifling, as if to veil their own superiority.[13]

We judge people by their friends and one of her closest was Anne Welch, 'Miss Nancy' as Johnson patronizingly called her, or Mistress Welch as she pointedly called herself. Having taught herself music, mathematics, and seven languages, Welch's circle embraced artists Angelica Kauffman and Sir Joshua Reynolds; novelist and scholar Charlotte Lennox; socialite Lucy Ludwell and her husband, pro-American linguist John Paradise; and the sculptors Joseph Nollekens, who married her sister; and Joseph Wilton, whose daughter Frances married Sir Robert Chambers, later Jones's colleague in Calcutta. Anne and Mary Jones were *avant la lettre* feminists, rejecting the dubious delights of domesticity for the more vibrantly 'masculine' public sphere. At Beaufort Buildings these bluestockings enjoyed teaching young William, teasing him unmercifully for his precocious pomposity. Laetitia-Matilda's father, Sir John Hawkins, lawyer, musicologist, and biographer of Johnson, 'used to consider these two lady geniuses as excellently coupled'. Johnson himself respected Anne's 'powers and knowledge', but regretted to Hester Thrale that she 'has no art of making them agreeable'. Both Anne Welch and

---

13. Laetitia-Matilda Hawkins, *Memoirs, Anecdotes, Facts, and Opinions*, 2 vols (London, 1824), I: 247–53; 249.

Mary Jones turned their scholarly backs upon conventional powers of pleasing.[14]

Not so her brother who early mastered the complaisant arts. William's first extant letter, written to Mary in November 1762, reveals a 16-year-old Harrovian moralist offering the consolations of philosophy to his 26-year-old sister mourning a dear friend:

> The common strain is: ''Tis pity so virtuous a man should die:'—but I assert the contrary; and when I hear the death of a person of merit, I cannot help reflecting, how happy he must be who now takes the reward of his excellencies, without the possibility of falling away from them and losing the virtue which he professed, on whose character death has fixed a kind of seal, and placed him out of the reach of vice and infamy! (*Letters*, 1: 1)

This and much more from the earnest Jones; but as we smile with Teignmouth, 'at the gravity of the young moralist', there is a self-reflexive poignancy about his words when seen in the light of his own lonely death in his Ariśnagar bungalow at the age of 47 in April of 1794.

★ ★ ★

Lost time is inevitably a theme of a life cut tragically short; in our search for a man who employed 'each shining hour' we must investigate not the Proustian episode of the madeleine but the Jonesian episode of the nectarine. We should return to the Tudor pile of Mostyn Hall at Holywell and stand with Jones in the August of 1775 amidst the venerable oaks and limes of the ancient parkland overlooking the Dee estuary. The letter to Althorp, describing the prospect of his ancestral homeland as 'the most magnificent view my eyes ever beheld, and almost the finest my imagination, warm as it is, could conceive', is revealing. Intended as a colourful travelogue, it is instinct with national pride, documenting the revelation that Wales was for him. He describes the 'enchanting prospect' of Penmaenmawr, the 'noble ruin' of Caernarvon castle, 'venerable Snowdon', and 'the most romantick scenes in the world' of roaring torrents and stupendous cascades; he gathers 'excellent

---

14. Hester Lynch Piozzi, *Letters to and from the Late Samuel Johnson, LL.D.*, 2 vols (London, 1788), 2: 281. Mary Moser, R.A., who at 24 was a founding member of the Royal Academy, claims that Anne Welch, 'after her father's death [Saunders Welch; like Jones senior, a compassionate Westminster magistrate, a close friend of Henry Fielding at Beaufort Buildings and of Samuel Johnson at Bolt Court] whilst she was abroad, frequently travelled as a man, with sword and bag, attended by a man-servant only'; see J. T. Smith, *Nollekens and His Times*, 2 vols (London, 1828), 1: 322.

mushrooms' on Harlech marsh to accompany the fine herrings on which they dined at Barmouth, before cantering over the sands to Aberdovey.

Under the rigorous work ethic of the young barrister-poet runs a fierce and irrepressible vein of sensuous Celticism. It bursts out in his evocation of St Winifred's Well: 'The fountain is really wonderful; it bubbles up among a number of smooth pebbles and throws up an hundred ton of water in a minute, and the stream which it forms, turns six or seven mills at a small distance from the source' (*Letters*, 1: 198). Dining at Holywell to Welsh melodies played by a blind harpist, before riding into the fertile vale of Clwyd with its river running 'broad and rapid like the Durance in the south of France', almost prepares him for the Edenic beauties of Mostyn's 'charming hill'. The associations are Miltonic and erotic—all that was missing from his Welsh idyll was his beloved Anna. He had visualized her strolling by the sparkling Elwy, that romantic tributary of the Clwyd: 'Who lov'd not Anna on the banks/Of Elwy swift or Testa clear?' (*Works*, 2: 503). Jonathan Shipley had not only introduced Jones to the Spencers but to his own family, and Jones had taken a decided shine to his eldest daughter. He had met Anna Maria in 1766; she was to prove a devoted and extremely patient fiancée. Her brother disappointed Jones with the news that she was at Chilbolton on the banks of the Test.

Characteristically Jones feels a twinge of guilt in luxuriating in the abandonment of disciplined rationality: 'After all this visual luxury you will think me very sensual for even remembering the taste of the peaches and nectarines which we gathered in Sir R. Mostyn's fruit garden, and which were equal to the finest I ever tasted in England.'

But Jones had dared to eat a peach, even a nectarine, and experienced his romanticizing epiphany at the prospect of 'ancient Mona' and his princely ancestors. It was a crystallizing moment of conceptualization on the border between sensory perception and thought, a liberating awareness of the centrality of his own liminal roots. Here in the distant west otherness and selfhood were mingling in a nectareous solution.

As he surveys Ynys Môn, he marvels that on the very next farm in his father's village had been born the eminent polymath Lewis Morris (1701–65) who presided over a resourceful group of amateur scholars uncovering the wealth of the Welsh cultural heritage. Jones recalled a treasured family document, a letter from Morris to his father, claiming kin. It contained a detailed genealogy, showing that their families shared an ancestry deriving from Hwfa ap Cynddelw, Lord of Llyslifon, and the princes of Gwynedd:

> It was a custom among the Ancient Britons (and still retained in Anglesey) for the most knowing among them in the descent of families, to send their friends of the same stock or family, *a dydd calan Ionawr* [on New Year's day] a *calennig*, [New Year's gift] a present of their pedigree [...] The very thought of those brave people, who struggled so long with a superior power for their liberty, inspires me with such an idea of them, that I almost adore their memories. (*Works*, 1: 2–3)

This was a rich intellectual inheritance, a tradition of empirical research and radical autonomy. Inscribed in the genetic material of his Welsh patrimony were the skills of the communicator, and the polymath. The careers of his father and Lewis Morris reveal elements that nourished the Orientalist: a heady mixture of the pragmatic and the speculative, the practical and the antiquarian, the poetic and the scientific, all reinforced by the precision of the mathematician, or the composer in the strict metres of *cynghanedd*. As West Indian voyaging inspired his father's fascination with navigation, mapping of the waters absorbed Lewis as Admiralty surveyor of the Welsh coastline. Lewis's travels were geographically limited, but his boundless intellectual versatility, commitment to ancient Celtic literature, and personal magnetism united a circle of scholars who pioneered Welsh cultural renaissance.

'Orientalist' Jones would prove just such an intellectual navigator, redrawing the map of European thought. Welsh preoccupation with genealogy was extended far beyond the descent of individuals in his dedication to researching families of nations, and families of languages. Secure in his own origins, his capacity for original thought allows him to stress the interconnections between the familial and the familiar. As cultural mediator, Jones locates similitude rather than difference, reinforcing the homologizing tendencies of the Enlightenment even while inspiring Romanticism's yearning for Oriental otherness.

In the library Jones talked with Sir Roger of the poets of Wales, and the researches of the Morris circle. He handled a copy of the first Welsh periodical, entitled *Tlysau yr Hen Oesoedd* (1735) ('Jewels of Ancient Times'), which Lewis had printed on his own press at Caer-Gybi (Holyhead). This early step in the textual production of Celtic revival featured anonymous *cywyddau* and *englynion*, and poems by the famed Taliesin and by 'our Welch Ovid', Dafydd ap Gwilym. An English preface stressed the centrality of access for both a Welsh and an English readership. Poetry and genealogy were more than a matter of literary pride; they represented a cultural statement of organic nationality, anticipating Herder's organicist theorizing.

They discussed Morrisiaid member, Evan Evans (Ieuan Brydydd Hir [Tall Bard]), talented trilingual poet, and tireless rescuer of manuscripts from the ignorant depredations of mice, bookworms, and an Anglophone squirearchy. A correspondent of Thomas Gray and the antiquary Thomas Percy, Evans had discovered precious texts such as 'Y Gododdin' and the writings of Taliesin. *Some Specimens of the Poetry of the Antient Welsh Bards* (1764), his manifesto of bardic nationalism, was dedicated to Mostyn, who embodied the best traditions of Welsh poetic patronage. Evans unearthed early manuscripts of the 'Trioedd Ynys Prydain' (Triads of the Isle of Britain), mnemonic sets of three interlinked sentences, but as a scholar he harped on a new triad: access, research, and publication.

This crucial triad was key to Jones's investigation of diverse cultures, and Wales had much to teach him concerning his own cultural identity. Hiring a boat, the barristers were rowed across to Beaumaris to visit its 'finely preserved' concentric castle. Jones admired 'a beautiful white goat who sate brouzing the ivy on the summit of the highest wall, and seemed to hold us little folks below him in supreme contempt'. Jones was only a few miles from his father's birthplace and the parish of Llanbabo where his uncle farmed Tyddyn-bach (smallholding).

Could Jones not bear the thought of introducing his friends to his hard-handed Uncle Harri? Llanbabo, its very name comically reminiscent of Welsh 'babble', was perhaps an insupportable destination for those ignorant of its being the shrine of a sainted sixth-century Celtic king and monk, Pabo Post Prydain, (Pillar of Britain), or that 'Pabo' was the Morrises' nickname for Jones's father. Must William, like the Beaumaris billy goat, hold the 'little folks below him in supreme contempt'? As a rising circuit-barrister, perhaps it was socially safer to view his Anglesey origins at a certain poetical distance.

'We could not leave Beaumaris', he writes, 'without visiting Baron Hill, the elevated seat of Lord Bulkeley, who was so polite as to show us his house and grounds and to insist on our taking a cold collation with him.' But Jones was irritated by the remark of Thomas James, Viscount Bulkeley, that 'persons of rank were already treated with too little respect' (*Letters*, 1: 200). Egalitarian Jones uses the comment of one young viscount to advise another to avoid decadent aristocrats at Cambridge: '[D]istinguish yourself from the mob of noblemen, and consider birth, fortune, and so forth, as nothing more than steps by which you may climb more rapidly into the temple of virtue, which is far above them all' (*Letters*, 1: 205).

Jones fails to mention that it was Bulkeley's great-grandfather Richard who aided his father's 'climb' from charity school to Royal Society, facilitating his own entry, if not into 'the temple of virtue', at least into the Middle Temple. Admission to the Bar has erected a social barrier; his Anglesey relations remained unvisited.

Jones's new experience of Wales offers an empowering sense of self-identity, bolstered by a tradition of radical oppositional independence; acquired class prejudice, however, reduces him to something of a cultural tourist. The questing Jones requires a wider intellectual scope than a small island endeared by patrimonial, princely, and Druidic resonances. Ultimately it was all about prospects, whether viewed as commanding vistas or ambitious expectations of advancement.

More was to be surveyed than a picturesque prospect of Mona. 'What a boundless scene opens to my view!' he writes to a fellow-Orientalist: 'If I had two lives, I should scarcely find time for the due execution of all the public and private projects which I have in mind' (*Works*, 1: 167). It was high summer and high time to take stock; at his back he could hear 'Time's winged Chariot hurrying near' with the ominous ticking of his own 'Andrometer'.

He had sketched out this scale of achievements prescribing the career of the accomplished man of merit for Althorp's amusement. Though Jones insists it is a joke, the 'Andrometer' dictated for his late twenties concentration upon 'Publick Life; Law and Eloquence; [. . .] State Affairs; Speeches at the bar or in Parliament' (*Letters*, 1: 175). It was clearly not enough that he was 'Persian' Jones.

Perhaps it is best not to measure Jones by his own exacting impatience; his father would have said: 'Yn araf deg yr â gŵr ymhell' ('By going slowly a man goes far'); role model Cicero declared: 'Festina lente' ('Make haste slowly'). The 'Great Scholar' matriculated at University College on 15 March 1764, being elected Bennet scholar on 31 October of the same year. How—in little more than a decade—had he become the greatest Oriental scholar in Europe?

Jones owed the secret of his success to a Frenchman, born exactly a century before him, who travelled in Syria and the Levant; was employed in the French embassy at Constantinople and by the French East India Company; and whose mastery of Arabic, Turkish, and Persian enabled him to complete the groundbreaking *Bibliothèque orientale* (1697) of Barthélemy d'Herbelot de Molainville. He was Antoine Galland (1646–1715), whose *Les mille et une nuits* (Paris, 1704–17) achieved a publishing sensation, intensifying an enduring vogue for Oriental splendour and mystery that affected almost every aspect of European culture. Shahrazâd's subtle techniques of deferring sexual desire via textual curiosity encouraged a delighted audience to follow her life-sustaining narratives through the imagination's exotic bazaars. The moment young William pulled the first of Galland's twelve leather-bound duodecimo volumes from his father's library shelf the die of his life was cast.

Galland's example epitomizes the symbiosis between popular and academic Orientalism that was also to distinguish Jones's career. The respected Oxford tradition of Oriental scholarship stemmed from Edward Pococke (1604–91) and Thomas Hyde (1636–1703), successive occupants of the Laudian Chair of Arabic, but although they acknowledged the study of Arabic as a conduit of scientific learning, its centrality for biblical scholarship remained its *raison d'être*. Thomas Hunt (1696–1774), who held chairs in both Arabic and Hebrew, and Robert Lowth, bishop of Oxford, and author of *De sacra poesi Hebraeorum* (1753), encouraged Jones to read the Old Testament as figurative, rhythmic, and inspired Oriental literature. His youthful exuberance undiluted by his intellectual rigour, Jones saw that conspicuous consumption of Eastern luxury goods might be diverted into a genuine appreciation of Asiatic literatures. A more 'sexy' Orientalism could combine the sensational and the scholarly, the erotic and the erudite.

With this in view, and in the absence of sufficiently demanding lectures, Jones emulated Galland in a move initiating his lifelong reliance upon native informants. Galland had gathered Oriental narratives from Hanna, a Maronite Syrian from Aleppo. Jones improved his Arabic by similarly employing a native of Aleppo, a Syrian named Mirza, whom he lodged in his rooms, to help him translate *Les mille et une nuits* back into Arabic.

Exploring the manuscript treasures of the Pococke collection in the Bodleian, Jones became fascinated by the close linguistic relationship between Arabic and Persian. Unexpectedly, his research was aided by Company politics and the dismal failure of a Mughal mission.

By the treaty of Allahabad, signed by Clive on 12 August 1765, Emperor Shāh 'Ālam II granted Diwani rights, allowing the Company to collect the land revenues of Bengal, Bihar, and Orissa. In return, the emperor was promised annual tribute of 26 lakhs (a lakh = 100,000) of rupees together with military support, but Clive subsequently proved reluctant to commit Company soldiers to restore the emperor to his Delhi throne.

Shāh 'Ālam, anxious to establish personal diplomatic relations with George III, insisted on an embassy to entreat his majesty to 'send 5 or 6,000 young men practised in war [to] carry me to Shahjehanabad [Delhi], my capital'.[15] Clive conceded to his request that the embassy should be led by Captain Archibald Swinton, and Shaikh I'tisam ud-Din, a *munshi* from the *qasbah* elite of Nadia in Bengal, was chosen to translate the Persian letter at court. It was only at sea early in January 1766 that Swinton revealed to I'tisam ud-Din that neither the emperor's letter nor his *nuzr* (tribute) of a lakh of rupees was on board.[16] I'tisam—and possibly Swinton also—had been duped by Clive, but Shāh 'Ālam's loss was Jones's gain; the *munshi*, although never introduced at St James, was brought to Oxford by Swinton.

I'tisam ud-Din's travelogue, *Shigurf Namah-i-Velaët, or Excellent Intelligence concerning Europe*, makes a fascinating contrast with fictional texts such Montesquieu's *Persian Letters*, which placed an Oriental in Europe (a device also used by Voltaire, and by Jones's friend Goldsmith) to defamiliarize and satirize western society. One of the first members of the educated Indian elite to visit Britain, I'tisam helped adjust conceptions of south Asians created by lascars who had jumped ship from docked East Indiamen. For Jones it was an opportunity to enlist the assistance of an Indian intellectual.

During the voyage I'tisam had been reading with Swinton (former Persian interpreter to General John Carnac) the *Farhang-i Jahangiri* (1608) of Mir Jamāl ud-Din Husain Injū, an emigrant scholar from Shiraz who had impressed Emperor Akbar and was made governor of Bihar by his son Jehāngir.[17] I'tisam introduced Jones to the *Farhang-i Jahangiri*, an excellent dictionary and introduction to Persian grammar; I'tisam's copy of the dictionary section remains among Jones's manuscripts in the Oriental and India Office Collections. Jones and Professor Hunt showed the Persian and Turkish manuscripts of the Bodleian to I'tisam, who realized that Persian studies lagged well behind Hebrew, Arabic, and Aramaic at Oxford. Jones's ambition was to remedy this.

Researching at University College, and passing the vacations in London—reading European classics in Italian, Spanish, and Portuguese,

---

15. BL, APAC, Sutton Court Collection, MSS Eur F.128/111, ff.100–2, Shāh 'Ālam to the King of Britain.
16. See *Shigurf Namah-i-Velaët, Or, Excellent Intelligence Concerning Europe, Being the Travels of Mirza Itesa Modeen*, trans. James Edward Alexander (London, 1827), 9, 229–30. See also Gulfishan Khan, *Indian Muslim Perceptions of the West* (Oxford, 1998), 72–8.
17. *Shigurf Namah-i-Velaët*, 82–3.

learning fencing from Domenico Angelo and the Welsh harp from a musician called Evans, he was, in his own words, 'with the fortune of a peasant, giving himself the education of a prince' (*Works*, 1.59). In 1765 he hit upon the idea of funding his studies at Oxford by accepting the post of tutor to the 7-year-old George John Spencer, Viscount Althorp, an ancestor of 'the people's princess' Diana. He was recommended to the Spencers by Bishop Jonathan Shipley who, as visitor, had admired Jones's Greek oration on Harrow's founder, John Lyon. Shipley had been tutor to the family of Charles Mordaunt, Earl of Peterborough, whose niece, the beautiful Anna Maria Mordaunt, maid of honour to Queen Caroline, he had subsequently married. Shipley's rise from bourgeois origins was an instructive model. By this smart Shipley-inspired and Shipley-facilitated career move, Jones gained a lifelong friend and correspondent, access to a superb library, and entrée into the society of influential whig magnates. Moving between the Palladian grandeur of Althorp House and his book-lined rooms in Oxford he was making prestigious contacts and establishing himself as a linguist. 'Persian' Jones was on his way.

The summer of 1766 saw him elected fellow of University College, and offered the post of interpreter for Eastern languages at the Treasury by its new First Lord, Augustus Fitzroy, Duke of Grafton. His ambitions were larger, but he suggested with characteristic generosity and naive unworldliness that the post be given to Mirza. As Teignmouth observed, Jones might easily have accepted the post and appointed Mirza his deputy on full salary.[18]

Even before the beginning of Michaelmas term 1768, in which he was to graduate BA from University College, Jones attempted to gain a professorial post: the Regius Chair of Modern History and Languages, worth £400 a year. Lord Spencer was again enlisted to mention Jones to Grafton in whose gift this post also lay, but nothing came of it. While consoling himself that the university was not the universe, Jones received—possibly via Grafton—a prestigious commission from King Christian VII of Denmark: to translate the *Tarīkh-i Nādirī* of Mahdī Khān Astarābādī (fl. 1733–59) into French. This was a life of the Persian monarch Nadir Shah who invaded India in 1739,

18. It has been suggested that Jones's Arabic teacher Mirza, supposedly a Syrian of Aleppo, was in fact the Bengali I'tisam ud-Din, who was granted the honorific title of Mirza by Shāh 'Ālam; see Mohamad Tavakoli-Targhi, 'Orientalism's Genesis Amnesia', *Comparative Studies of South Asia, Africa and the Middle East*, 16: 1 (Spring 1996), 1–14, and Gulfishan Khan, 'Indo-Persian Scholarship and the Formation of Orientalism' (forthcoming).I feel the jury is still out on this issue.

sacked Agra and Delhi, slaughtered many non-combatants, especially Hindus, and carried off the Peacock Throne, together with the Koh-i-noor, to Persia.

The politics of Orientalism were again operating in Jones's favour, but multiple ironies surround his first publication: the *Histoire de Nader Chah* (1770). That the translation of a biography sympathetic to a Persian despot, commissioned by an absolutist king whose arbitrary power was being wielded in an increasingly pathological manner against his own queen, Caroline Matilda, George III's sister, should be the first publication of a scholar who advocated universal manhood suffrage remains a central irony.

Jones was deeply suspicious of unconstitutional authority. 'Power is always odious', he writes in the preface, 'always to be suspected, especially when it resides in the hands of an individual; and a free people will never suffer any single man to be more powerful than the Laws, which themselves have enacted or confirmed: but no kind of power is more licentiously insolent than that, which is supported by force of arms.' We may juxtapose this denunciation of imperial power with the dedication of Alexander Dow's *The History of Hindustan* (1768–72) to George III: 'The success of your Majesty's arms has laid open the East to the researches of the curious.' The resonance is increased by the fact that Lieutenant-Colonel Dow had refused King Christian's commission.

There was an integral relationship between conquest and Orientalism, between hegemony and historiography, as a private trading company reorganized itself into a colonial power. Evidently, 'insolent' power was not a Persian preserve. Interconnected power shifts and regime changes in the Middle East and India—in which Khorasan warlord Nadir Shah was a key player—proved most beneficial to western despotism. The decline of the cultured Iranian Safavid dynasty (descended from a long line of Sūfī sheikhs), aided Nadir Shah's rise to power, and his Indian adventure weakened both the Mughal empire and Hindu rulers in northern India to the Company's advantage. Christopher Bayly sees this series of events as perhaps the first 'truly global crisis'.[19] Nadir was part of a global historical process that would help facilitate Jones's own Indian adventure, his world-modifying ideas, and his central role in the development of world literature.

Jones derides our continuing infatuation with the lives of warriors and conquerors, whose claim to historical or biographical celebrity is drenched in blood:

19. Christopher Bayly, *The Birth of the Modern World 1780–1914* (Oxford, 2004), 90–1.

> This infatuation arises, partly from the deplorable servility of our minds, and our eagerness to kiss the foot which tramples on us; [...] and partly from our mistaking the nature of true Virtue, which consists, not in destroying our fellow-creatures, but in protecting them, not in seizing their property, but in defending their rights and liberties, even at the hazard of our own safety.
>
> (Preface to *Histoire de Nader Shah*; *Works*, 12: 313–14)

Never eager to kiss even the hand of unconstitutional power, Jones wrote to Hendrik Schultens, the Dutch Orientalist: 'My temperament cannot stomach the arrogance of princes and nobles, which has to be swallowed by poets and lovers of literature' (*Letters*, 1: 167). But power and patronage lay in connections; and here again the despot Nadir aided Jones's ascent, for Christian VII rewarded him with nomination to the Royal Society of Copenhagen and a recommendation to George III.

The biography of Nadir was 'the last manuscript in the world, I should have thought of translating', but with a shrewd opportunism Jones appended to *Histoire de Nader Chah*, 'Un traité sur la poësie orientale', supplying prose and verse translations of odes by his beloved Hāfiz. While reluctantly bolstering the fame of a recent Persian despot, he celebrates a fourteenth-century Persian poet. In accessing alternative classical traditions he could destroy despotic western power: the absolute sway that Graeco-Roman classicism held over European literature. The struggle against Eurocentric prejudices and stereotypes had begun in earnest.

Jones had two other Persian projects, a revision of Meninski's *Thesaurus Linguarum Orientalium* (1680–87), and a Persian grammar. Conversations with I'tisam, Swinton, and General Carnac convinced him that, as Persian was the language of Mughal diplomacy, he should seek EIC patronage for these works. Jones's letter of 19 November 1770 to Sir George Colebrooke, Chairman of the Court of Directors, dramatically illustrates that a grammar might prove valuable intellectual property to canny London publishers:

> In order to make my grammar as correct as possible, I entrusted it to a native of India now residing in London, requesting him to examine attentively the Persian part, as the book was to be printed in about a fortnight. While it was with him, a friend of mine received intelligence that a conspiracy was formed to procure a copy of my publication before it was made public, and consequently to deprive me not only of my property, but, by a more malicious cruelty, of my reputation as a man of letters and honour. He went immediately to the Indian's lodgings, where he found a person employed in transcribing my grammar, and so far advanced that he wanted but a few lines of the

conclusion. [. . .] [T]he person detected in it was George Nicol, the very man, who in concert with [Archibald] Hamilton, had advertised a Persian grammar, and dictionary *under the patronage of the East India Company*. On the sudden appearance of my friend, Nicol behaved like a man conscious of guilt; he turned pale, and strove to conceal my grammar and his copy; but they were both seized, and are now happily in my possession.[20]

If Jones was amazed at this attempted piracy on the part of two respected publishers, he was saddened that his Indian *munshi*—presumably I'tisam ud-Din—had proved so untrustworthy. The whole affair revealed the truth of what Jones had appreciated: that commercial and self-'interest was the charm which gave the languages of the East a real and solid importance'. Finding the directors insufficiently generous concerning the revision of Meninski, Jones left that project to Orientalist John Richardson. He concentrated on the market potential of his Persian grammar, pleased to let empire sponsor Orientalism.

The autumn of 1770 proved a time of crucial career decisions. Jones had grown discontent with the tutorly role model provided by his father. Jones refused to become a pedagogic adjunct to the Spencer entourage. The Reynolds portrait, which cost his mother £36.15s, reveals the ambitious self-awareness of the sitter in his elegant maroon velvet coat, set off by frilled lace cuffs and stock; this is a young man who knows his own worth. If Hogarth's portrait of his father reflected self-confidence, here is second-generation autonomy. Reynolds captures his sensitivity and charm, a hint of humour playing about the generous mouth and full sensual lips; determination is stamped in the set of his jaw and the searching intensity of his gaze. The book in his right hand emblematizes the means of his self-advancement.

Recently Jones had felt insecure about the relationship between his own self-image and the impression he created. He was disturbed to hear that a friend, having praised his intellectual abilities, had gone on to describe him as 'the most silent and unsocial of all beings, as a nonconformist in society, as a mere hermit, as one who locked himself up all day, and took no part in the amusements that usually employ young men' (*Letters*, 1: 14). He is obviously stung by this unflattering portrait, especially when he learns Countess Spencer thought that such 'apparent reserve' might be the product of 'some hidden discontent'. She proved remarkably perceptive, but perhaps did not fully appreciate how desperately Jones lusted after fame. To Hungarian Orientalist Count Reviczki he reveals his obsession:

---

20. Abu Taher Mojumder, 'Three New Letters by Sir William Jones', *India Office Library and Records* (1981), 24–35; 30.

7. Sir William Jones, by Sir Joshua Reynolds, oil on canvas, 1769. (Althorp Park)

I am as delighted as anyone with singing, dancing, wine-drinking in moderation, and the divine prettiness of the girls who are delightfully plentiful in London. But it is easy for me to put all these pleasures of life in second place to that one thing which I desire to distraction, glory. Glory I shall pursue through fire and water, by night and by day. (*Letters*, 1: 86–7)

The pleasures of life, even the pleasure of teaching intelligent children in the delightful ambience of Althorp Park or Wimbledon House, must be relegated to a single-minded pursuit of independence and reputation. Fame is undoubtedly the spur for the bourgeois genius; in this Jones was certainly not alone. During the 1770s two of Jones's most talented and politically committed friends, Joseph Priestley and the London Welshman Richard Price, were closely associated with that patron of bourgeois radicalism, Lord Shelburne, both viewing aristocratic life with a certain republican disdain. Jones concurred.

Yet he had certainly enjoyed teaching Althorp, a thoughtful boy who soon appreciated that Jones was training him, along Ciceronian and Miltonic classical republican lines, for civic duty. Teaching was in his blood, and he frequently discussed education with Richard Shepherd, a fellow of Corpus Christi, who acknowledged 'how much I have availed myself of those conversations' in *An Essay on Education in a Letter to William Jones, Esq.* (1782), urging a more progressive school syllabus. Jones also taught George's elder sister Georgiana, future duchess of Devonshire, Latin, French, and composition. She frequently sat in on her brother's lessons, imbibing many of Jones's advanced whig ideas, which leant gravitas to her charismatic blue and buff campaigning for Fox in the early 1780s.

There was a special bond between George and William and they became firm friends: 'The difference of twelve years in our ages will soon disappear', wrote Jones, 'and we shall be *young men* together' (*Letters*, 1: 143). His role as a species of '*domestick* tutour', however, emphasized their difference in rank. When Lady Spencer placed her son in his charge, she said, 'Make him, if you can, like yourself and I shall be satisfied.' Jones obeyed this instruction to the letter, but now he felt compelled to attend to his own self-fashioning.

The 24-year-old dogmatically stated to Lady Spencer her son should attend Harrow without interruption; failing that, Jones would continue to instruct him, but in a private house free from familial distraction. In establishing this specific contrast between private and domestic education, Jones draws upon Rousseau, 'whose pen, formed to elucidate all the arts, had the property of spreading light before it on the darkest subject, as if he had written with phosphorus on the sides of a cavern' (*Works*, 4: 176). *Émile, ou de l'éducation*, published eight years earlier in 1762, had stressed the usurping centrality of the tutor:

> No matter whether he has father or mother, having undertaken their duties I am invested with their rights. He must honour his parents, but he must obey me. That is my first and only condition.[21]

In response to the suggestion of the grandmother, Anna Maria Poyntz, that the boy could take his hours of instruction wherever the family was staying, 'Jean-Jacques' Jones insists in a letter to Althorp's mother: 'I do not want his hours only, but his months and years; I wish to be with him at meals, at our amusements, in our hours of rest as well as of study that I may give his thoughts a right turn upon every subject, and strengthen his mind while I seem to relax it.' Lady Spencer might have retorted that Rousseau had 'orphaned' Émile to eradicate parental influence, and that she didn't take kindly to being expunged, but Jones had announced his educational manifesto. If that were not sufficiently clear, he adds: 'I will only say that it is my firm resolution never to take orders, surely my birth and sentiments, and even my talents (if I may venture to mention them) raise me far above dependence' (*Letters*, 1: 67-8).

Celtic pride, intellectual arrogance, unbending principle, the egalitarianism of the meritocrat, and a callow lack of understanding of maternal protectiveness or parental rights: this all makes for a disconcerting mixture. It is hard to imagine Jones's father reacting like this. Even ten years later, Horace Walpole could barely conceal his irritation at a young man's arrogance: '[he] quarrelled with Lord Spencer, who he insisted should not interfere at all in the education of his own son'.[22]

That the breach was sharp but short-lasting is very much to the Spencers' credit. Anna Maria Poyntz praised the ethical education George had received from Jones, feeling sure its influence would be lasting. Perhaps they all realized that, as a young man with pretensions to gentility but without inherited fortune, Jones was condemned to a position of dependence and marginality if he remained a cultured appendage to an aristocratic household. Tutoring the aristocracy had given him a great start, but the road to liberty lay in a profession where intellect was the key to success. On 19 November 1770

---

21. Jean-Jacques Rousseau, *Émile*, trans. Barbara Foxley (London, 1938), 20.
22. *The Correspondence of Horace Walpole, Earl of Orford, and William Mason*, ed. Revd J. Mitford, 2 vols (London, 1851), 2: 87.

he entered the Middle Temple to begin studying for the bar. Significantly, the very first letter to benefit from his Middle Temple address was that to Sir George Colebrooke concerning the attempted Persian piracy.

With the publication of his *Grammar of the Persian Language* in April 1771 'Selim' Jones had arrived. Yunus Uksfurdi (Oxford Jones) produced not only a *Shakaristān* (a chest of sugar), as the grammar was titled in Persian, but a *gulistān* (bower of roses), replete with the beauties of 'the Persian Anacreon' Hāfiz, a *rubā'ī* (quatrain) and a half by Omar Khayyām, and the love-songs of Firdausi: 'If I could sleep one night on thy bosom, I should seem to touch the sky with my exalted head.'[23] A book proffering Oriental breasts and chests of rupees was likely to succeed. It perfectly balanced the aesthetic and the utilitarian; a text designed to train Company writers in the language of Mughal governance simultaneously inspired them to love mystical Persian poetry. In formally arranging the coming-out of the 'Turkish maid of Shiraz' in western drawing rooms, Jones was introducing not only the first English translation of a Hāfiz *ghazal* (ode), but the very first English verse translation of a Persian poem:

> Sweet maid, if thou wouldst charm my sight;
> And, bid these arms thy neck infold;
> That rosy cheek, that lily hand,
> Would give thy poet more delight
> Than all Bocara's vaunted gold,
> Than all the gems of Samarcand.
>
> Boy! let yon liquid ruby flow,
> And bid thy pensive heart be glad,
> Whate'er the frowning zealots say:—
> Tell them their Eden cannot show
> A stream so clear as Rocnabad,
> A bow'r so sweet as Mosellay.
>
> O! when these fair perfidious maids,
> Whose eyes our secret haunts infest,
> Their dear destructive charms display,
> Each glance my tender breast invades,
> And robs my wounded soul of rest,
> As Tartars seize their destined prey.
>
> ('A Persian Song of Háfiz', ll. 1–18)

---

23. *Kitab-i Shakaristan Dar Nahvi-i Zaban-i Parsi, Tasnif-i Yunus Uksfurdi, A Grammar of the Persian Language* (London, 1771), 43.

Jones has reimagined the Orientalist's role as cultural translator. If we consider these three stanzas we can begin to appreciate Jones's subtle mastery of mediating techniques. Hāfiz describes his beloved as a 'Shirazi Turk', but Jones realizes this traditional trope would mean little to metropolitan readers. At first sight it might seem that he is simply domesticating Hāfiz and that, in his youthful, proto-Romantic desire to locate inspired 'wildness and simplicity', he misses much of the poet's artful sophistication such as the geographical and cultural resonances of the Turk (light-skinned)/Hindu (black) juxtaposition. But Jones misses nothing, ensuring that his imagery enables his readers to view the fair-skinned and ravishingly beautiful beloved as a cruel plunderer and destructive invader like the Turkic Tartar.

In its careful construction Jones's creative paraphrase of Hāfiz reveals his techniques of affirmative Orientalism. His poetic version excises a mole or Indian beauty spot, perhaps thinking that the application of strategically placed beauty spots had become rather passé, but this is present in the literal translation also provided: 'I would give for the black mole on her cheek the cities of Samarcand and Bokhara.' More significantly, he firmly heterosexualizes the relationship where the grammar of Hāfiz's Persian makes no gender differentiation. Balancing familiarity of poetic diction with the 'singularity of the measure' (abcabc), Jones navigates artfully between Persian and English cultural traditions, between comforting similitude and exciting difference, and between poem and translation, to produce a triumph of acculturation. As the expert on translation theory, Ahmad Karimi-Hakkak has appreciated: 'Rather than giving an impression of chasms separating Hāfiz from his eighteenth-century English readers, Jones's creative and transformative strategies have resulted in a text that links new readers to the Persian poet.'[24]

Thus Romantic Orientalism is born, not in scented seraglio sheets or amidst the petals of a Turkish rose bed, but within the pages of a London Welshman's Persian grammar. It would delight young Company writers as they dreamed of the pagoda tree on their long passage to India; the

---

24. Ahmad Karimi-Hakkak, 'Beyond Translation: Interactions between English and Persian Poetry', in *Iran and the Surrounding World*, ed. Nikki R. Keddie and Rudolph P. Matthee (Seattle and London, 2002), 36–60; p. 48. Karimi-Hakkak compares Jones's strategies with those adopted by early twentieth-century Iranian poets in appropriating European poetry.

Romantic writers—Coleridge, Southey, Landor, Byron, Moore, Percy Shelley, Felicia Hemans, Charlotte Dacre, Sydney Owenson, to name but a few—who were to reap the literary rewards of 'sticking to the East' were as yet unborn.

In his preface Jones combats Eurocentric prejudice, insisting that the true savagery—then as now—is western philistinism:

> We all love to excuse, or to conceal, our ignorance, and are seldom willing to allow any excellence beyond the limits of our own attainments: like the savages, who thought the sun rose and set for them alone, and could not imagine that the waves, which surrounded their island, left coral and pearls upon any other shore. (p. ii)

As he laboured away among dusty legal tomes at the Temple, the romance of the East continued to exert its perfumed attractions. Yet he threw himself into case law and precedent with the same enthusiasm he devoted to Asiatic poetry. 'A singular, and astonishing proof of the vigour of his capacity', it was said of Jones at the time, 'is that he can dictate to two amanuenses, at the same time, on different subjects.'[25]

The student barrister observed causes in Westminster Hall: the renowned Orientalist continued to look eastwards. The spring of 1771 saw a second important publication, his *Dissertation sur la littérature orientale*, condemning the mutual suspicions and reciprocal prejudices of East and West as the product of ignorance and self-love. He recalls Voltaire's comment on those who judge foreign poetry on the basis of inadequate translation: 'They are like blind men who assure you that the rose can have no lively colours, because they feel the thorns with their hands' (*Works*, 12: 282). His solution, anticipating the scientific comparativist emphasis of his whole career, is to experiment:

> Take two odes, the one Arabic or Persian, the other Greek or Latin. Translate them literally into a common language without embellishment or variation. Make due allowance for idioms, topical circumstances, and manners, on both sides, then decide without prejudice between the works of the Eastern writers and those we commonly admire.[26]

He compares the tenth ode of Hāfiz and the thirty-second ode of Horace in French prose translations to demonstrate the ways in which respective

---

25. *European Magazine*, 4 (December 1783), 445–6.
26. See *Works*, 12: 283. This translation is by the poet and reviewer, John Langhorne; *Monthly Review*, 44 (June 1771), 425–32; 427.

traditions, contexts, connotations, and idiom may prove formidable mutual culture-specific barriers. All this was admirably empirical. But the barriers Jones erected with his third publication of 1771 demonstrate the very prejudice, ignorance, and self-love he had been anxious to dispel.

His *Lettre à Monsieur A*** du P**** blotted Jones's scholarly integrity as surely as it blighted the academic career of its addressee, Abraham-Hyacinthe Anquetil-Duperron (1731–1805). No one believed more firmly than Jones that international scholarly co-operation should rise above dynastic disputes. It seems almost inconceivable that he should entirely extinguish the possibility of co-operative research with a passionate Orientalist every bit as committed as himself to comparative historicism, egalitarian relativism, and the inalienable rights of humanity.

Anquetil-Duperron had written disrespectfully about Hyde's scholarship, wrongly accused Hunt of claiming a knowledge of Avestan, and complained about the lack of heating in the Bodleian. On the other hand, such was the insatiable curiosity of this young man on discovering some copied fragments of the Zoroastrian Avesta, he had immediately enlisted as a private soldier on a French East Indiaman bound for Pondicherry. By contrast, Jones waited years for the security of a knighthood and a fat-cat salary before venturing to India. With his keen sense of the romance of knowledge, Jones might surely have empathized with this intrepid intellectual explorer. Instead, commonplace anti-Gallic anger and Orientalist jealousy combined in the exquisitely elegant but deeply satirical French of Jones's demolition of the Frenchman's three-volume edition, *Zend-Avesta* (Paris, 1771).

Jones's misguided assertion that Anquetil-Duperron had been duped by the Parsis with modern forgeries is the result of his failure to conceive that such grotesque gods, primitive liturgy, and 'absurd rhapsodies' should be associated with prophetic law-giver Zoroaster. He ridicules the idea that ox urine was used in ritual purification, suggesting Anquetil-Duperron should take a dose '*d'urine de bœuf*' for his ingratitude to Oxford. The real bull at the gate is 'wrong-headed' Jones who retarded studies of the Zend-Avesta for half a century. Where Jones led, French and German *philosophes* Voltaire, Diderot, Grimm, Volney, and Christoph Meiners all followed. Jones applied the weight of his reputation to destroy that of his French counterpart; in the long term this would seriously besmirch his own.

Although this was the Voltairean letter of the *arriviste*, anti-Gallican sentiments did him little harm at the time. 'I think the whole nation', opined Thomas Hunt from Christ Church, 'as well as the University and its members, are much obliged to you for this able and spirited defence' (*Works*, 1: 92–3). To Charles Reviczki, Jones boasted that with his attack upon 'some smart Nobody [...] I have flabbergasted the whole nation of *Gaul*' (*Letters*, 1: 107).

Jones was ever the patriot, in the best classical republican sense, but such pre-Chauvin chauvinism sits ill with his admiration of the *philosophes*, the fact that three of his four publications had been written in French, or his family's tradition of befriending French émigrés. An émigré his mother and sister had welcomed to Beaufort Buildings was the fascinating novelist Madame Anne Marie La Cépèdes de Fauques de Vaucluse. This was the lady to whom Jones owed his superb French.

An even more colourful character than Anquetil-Duperron, she escaped from a nunnery to embark upon a Parisian career writing three-decker Orientalizing sentimental novels such as *Abbasaï, histoire orientale* (1753) and *Contes du sérail, traduits du turc* (1753). Moving into the more edgy territory of the *libelliste*, her political fable, *La Dernière guerre des bêtes* (1758), satirized Madame de Pompadour as a rapaciously luxurious leopard. To avoid the Bastille she fled to London, where she delivered the *coup de grâce* to Jeanne-Antoinette Poisson with her scathing *History of the Marchioness de Pompadour* (1758), indicting the regime of Louis XV as a sink of political and sexual intrigue.

On the recommendation of the queen blue of Hill Street, Elizabeth Montagu, Madame de Vaucluse undertook the education of the four daughters of Elizabeth, Lady Craven, travel writer and literary hostess. The two Elizabeths were as delighted as both Marys with her conversation, her intellect, and her eccentricities, and when not teaching the Craven girls, she gave French lessons to young William. Her popular Orientalism—continuing with *Oriental Anecdotes: or, The History of Haroun Alrachid* (1764)—inspired Jones with the romance of Asia, and as the years passed the linguistic relationship was reciprocal:

> This illustrious Scholar disdained not to receive improvement in the French language from this Veteran Lady; and, in return, condescended to polish the style of her English publications. Should this assertion be doubted, it may be sufficient to refer to 'The Vizirs; or, the Enchanted Labyrinth, an Oriental Tale, in Two Volumes: by Madame Fauques de Vaucluse;' in which the introductory Remarks from D'Herbelot and the History of Nader Shah sufficiently bespeak the learned Communicator.[27]

27. Nichols, *Literary Anecdotes*, 3: 246.

Lady Craven said of her respected governess: 'Madame de Vaucluse had one fault common to great geniuses,—she had every sense but common sense.'[28] While this observation might occasionally apply to the impetuous Jones, the piquant relationship between young scholar and erudite old lady was bolstered by many common interests. She provided him with an early entrée to Elizabeth Montagu's assemblies, frequented both by formidable bluestockings such as Elizabeth Carter and Elizabeth Vesey and many members of Johnson's Turk's Head Club. Jones was also introduced to Lady Craven's circle in London and at Benham Park, including influential Indian contacts, Lord Macartney and General Richard Smith. Jones also was making introductions. He encouraged the relationship between Madame de Vaucluse and her future husband, Prussian officer Henry Savile de Starck, many years her junior, to whom Jones wrote:

> You do right to cultivate the acquaintance of Madame de Vaucluse; and you cannot too frequently visit her. She possesses, what is rarely found joined with transcendent abilities, much affability, and a most engaging complacency of manner. The more you know her, the more you will perceive, by the depth and variety of her erudition, how superior she is to any idea we can form, by their works of the Maintenons, the Sevignés, &c—[29]

When not demolishing or lauding French genius, Jones was gratified to see his own 'transcendent abilities' celebrated by a discerning public. By 1771 'the ingenious Mr Jones' was as common an appellation in adulatory reviews as the soubriquets 'Selim' or 'Persian' Jones. The 1772 volume of *Monthly Review* contained a detailed two-part article on his *Persian Grammar*, 'obviously, a work of the greatest importance to the East India Company', by Leiden-trained professor of Hebrew at Edinburgh, James Robertson, and a glowing review of Jones's most important book to date: *Poems, Consisting Chiefly of Translations from the Asiatick Languages* (Oxford, 1772).

Taking its experimental cue from his *Dissertation*, this book displays an innovatory approach to comparative literature. The fact that most of its contents are certainly not 'regular translations' is made clear in the preface and fully understood by readers who praised the 'invention' of the poet, and

---

28. *Memoirs of the Margravine of Anspach*, 2 vols (London, 1826), 2: 107.
29. Memoir of Madame de Starck written by Henry Savile de Starck in 1780; Bodleian MS Beckford d. 28, cited in Fatma Moussa Mahmoud, 'Sir William Jones and Mme Vaucluse', *Revue de Littérature Comparée*, 54 (1980), 5–16; 14. In the 1780s Mme de Starck was employed as an amanuensis by William Beckford.

the 'charms of a flowing and harmonious versification'.[30] These poems are judiciously aimed at a readership that required to be taken gently and with propriety by the hand through the unknown delights of Arabia Felix and beyond.

Thirty years earlier William Collins published his *Persian Eclogues* (1742), which were so mildly orientalized that their candid author later admitted they might just as well have been called 'Irish Eclogues'. Jones's poems, instinct with sensuality are a far cry from such bloodless neoclassicism. Providing much more than local colour, they are exquisitely worked examples of how the transfusion of Oriental vigour might revive tired Augustanism with 'new expressions, new images, and new inventions'.

At the same time there is much that is old about Europe's desire to locate, appropriate, and inhabit an Eastern bower of bliss, and it is with a calculating hand that he introduces Spenserian and Miltonic elements, anxious to avoid 'the shock of the new' that the genuinely Oriental might produce. In 'The Palace of Fortune' the beauteous youth (Pleasure) implores the goddess to fulfil all his sensual desires:

> Let me on beds of dewy flowers recline,
> And quaff, with glowing lips, the sparkling wine;
> Grant me to feed on beauty's rifled charms,
> And clasp a willing damsel in my arms;
> Her bosom, fairer than a hill of snow,
> And gently bounding like a playful roe:
> Her lips, more fragrant than the summer air;
> And sweet as Scythian musk, her hyacinthine hair;   (ll. 183–90)[31]

The heroine, aptly named Maia—simultaneously suggesting the European 'May', the Sanskrit *māyā* (the power of illusion), and an Arabic name for the beloved—is shown in an enchanted mirror the youth's bower of libidinous bliss:

> The wanton stripling lies beneath the shade,
> And by his side reclined a blooming maid;
> O'er her fair limbs a silken mantle flows,
> Through which her youthful beauty glows,
> And part conceal'd, and part disclos'd to sight,   (ll. 199–203)

---

30. *Monthly Review*, 46 (1772), 508–17; 509.
31. *Sir William Jones: Selected Poetical and Prose Works*, ed. Michael J. Franklin (Cardiff, 1995), 42; hereafter *SWJ*.

Blushing to observe their love-making, she averts her eyes but, when she looks again, she sees 'how vain pleasures sting the lips they kiss,/How asps are hid beneath the bowers of bliss!' (ll. 241–2). This blend of the sensual and the didactic would appeal to young Percy Shelley, who was indebted to Jones's poem for the whole framework of *Queen Mab* (1813). Jones's pioneering introduction of moral allegory into the dramatic verse tale developed the genre of the Oriental verse tale.

'The Seven Fountains, An Eastern Allegory', in which a youth bathes in six fountains of sensuous delight with six ravishingly beautiful nymphs, proved more than a luxurious excursus into the pleasure principle to inspire Beckford's *Vathek* (1786). It uses Eastern sensuality to explore the aesthetic implications of Locke's theories of sense perception and Newtonian ideas of colour and light. Jones was providing fascinating materials and formative models for the orientalizing of Landor, Coleridge, Southey, Byron, Shelley, and Moore, their Romantic subjectivity underpinned by footnoted Orientalist objectivity. His proto-Romantic genre experimentation presented these poets with all the requisite apparatus of a textualized Orient culled from a variety of authentic sources. Jones's early poems are replete with spicy odours and musky scents, crystal fountains, caves of ice, damsels in diaphanous robes, and all the sensuous paraphernalia of the sumptuous pleasure dome. They create a paradisal pleasance out of Kashmir or Arabia Felix, ready to tempt any Romantic to inhabit the Oriental tale.

His success may be measured in the rapturous response of Elizabeth Montagu, a discriminating arbiter of literary taste, as confessed to the proto-Romantic Scottish poet and philosopher James Beattie:

> Pray have you met with Mr. Jones's imitations of Asiatic poetry? He possesses the oriental languages in a very extraordinary manner, and he seems to me a great master of versification. I wish he had given us translations, rather than imitations, as one is curious to see the manner of thinking of a people born under so different a climate, educated in such a different manner, and subjects of so different a government. There is a gayety & splendor in the poems which is naturally derived from the happy soil & climate, of the Poets & they breathe Asiatick luxury, or else Mr Jones is himself a man of most splendid imagination. The descriptions are so fine, & all the objects so brilliant, *that the sense aches at them*, & I wish'd that Ossians poems had been laying by me, that I might sometimes have turn'd my eyes from ye dazzling splendor of the Eastern noon day to the moonlight picture of a bleak mountain. Every object in these

pieces is blooming & beautiful; every plant is odouriferous; the passions too are of the sort which belong to Paradise.[32]

Jones has whetted her intellectual curiosity to read authentic Oriental texts by means of a direct sensuous assault upon this bluestocking reader. His poetic talent for imaginative Orientalizing re-creates his own impassioned response to Asiatic literature. The poems operate simultaneously at the level of cultural conduit and as colourful illustrations of what Romanticism might achieve by looking East. The 'silken mantle' of Jones's popular Orientalism 'part conceal'd, and part disclos'd to sight' his Asiatic source texts. Montagu's longing for the hyperborean plunge bath of Ossian after the superheated sensual delights of Asia testifies to the success with which both Macpherson and Jones finely judged metropolitan tastes. Novelty and difference were marketable features, but restraint had to be exercised in the transmission of 'alien' cultures. Montagu had spread Ossian's fame amidst bluestocking circles, subsidizing Macpherson's research trip to the Gaelic Highlands; now she was being dazzled by Jones. Her enthusiasm was reflected by whole sections of the reading public unconcerned about authenticity, reacting to the fashionable craze for things Oriental and the cultural relics of their own ethnic and political margins. Montagu's letter significantly juxtaposes two writers whose 'translations' were to exert such a profound influence upon European Romanticism.

Beattie's response—he had not yet read *Poems*—reveals exactly what Jones was up against. This catalogue of unreconstructed prejudice is from the pen of the sensitive and intelligent author of *The Minstrel*, later to have such a formative influence on Wordsworth:

> What is the reason, madam, that the poetry, and indeed the whole phraseology, of the eastern nations (and I believe the same thing holds of all uncultivated nations) is so full of glaring images, exaggerated metaphors, and gigantic descriptions? Is it, because that, in those countries, where art has made little

---

32. Elizabeth Montagu to James Beattie, 5 September 1772; Sir William Forbes, *An Account of the Life and Writings of James Beattie LL.D*, 2 vols (Edinburgh, 1806), 1: 298–9. An unpublished letter kindly sent me by Elizabeth Eger reveals that Montagu had earlier attempted to send *Poems* to Beattie: 'I will endeavour to convey to you by Mr Dilly some Asiatick poetry translated by a very ingenious Man & most extraordinary Linguist, a Mr Jones. I shd rather call these pieces imitations than translations. I wish they had been more of the latter for tho our Poet may have improved the poems, my greatest pleasure would have arisen from observing the turn of mind in the Oriental Poet. An Asiatick Bards address to a Sultan is more interesting to me than an English Poets birthday ode'; University Library, King's College, Aberdeen, Beattie Collection, MS 30/C.80, Montagu to Beattie, 8 June 1772.

progress, nature shoots forth into wilder magnificence, and every thing appears to be constructed on a larger scale? Is it that the language, through defect of copiousness, is obliged to adopt metaphor and similitude, even for expressing the most obvious sentiments? Is it, that the ignorance and indolence of such people, unfriendly to liberty, disposes them to regard their governors as of supernatural dignity, and to decorate them with the most pompous and high-sounding titles, the frequent use of which comes at last to infect their whole conversation with bombast? Or is it, that the passions of those people are really stronger, and their climate more luxuriant? Perhaps all these causes may conspire in producing this effect.[33]

The enlightened Montagu has certainly made him think, but Beattie's series of questions reveals a tissue of ignorant Occidental stereotypes as he complacently retreats to the classical reassurance of Greece 'by whose example and authority [...] simple and natural diction was happily established'. Jones must show Beattie and benighted western scholarship the light in the East.

To demonstrate that 'most of the figures, sentiments, and descriptions' in the first of the 1772 *Poems*, 'Solima, An Arabian Eclogue', are drawn from Arabian poets, Jones prints a transliterated extract from a pre-Islamic *qasīda* (ode), together with this accurate prose translation:

> The stranger and the pilgrim well know, when the sky is dark, and the north-wind rages, when the mothers leave their sucking infants, when no moisture can be seen in the clouds, that thou art bountiful to them as the spring, that thou art their chief support, that thou art a sun to them by day, and a moon in the cloudy night. (Preface, pp. ii–iii)

The corresponding lines of Jones's poem introduce a frisson of European gothic, and excise authentically Arabian elements, including the image of dereliction, the mothers abandoning their suckling babies, or the absence of life-giving rain. In a superficial and ahistorical view, it might appear that his poetic talents were not keeping pace with his critical theory. Jones's couplets might seem to reflect the tiredness not of the weary pilgrim, but of a certain Popean artificiality:

> When, chill'd with fear, the trembling pilgrim roves
> Through pathless deserts, and through tangled groves,
> Where mantling darkness spreads her dragon wing,
> And birds of death their fatal dirges sing,
> While vapours pale a dreadful glimmering cast,

---

33. Forbes, *An Account of the Life and Writings of James Beattie*, 1: 234–5.

> And thrilling horrour howls in every blast;
> She cheers his gloom with streams of bursting light,
> By day a sun, a beaming moon by night;
> Darts through the quivering shades her heavenly ray,
> And spreads with rising flowers his solitary way.
>
> ('Solima', ll. 69–78; *SWJ*, p. 34)

Interestingly in this context, some fifty-five years earlier Lady Mary Wortley Montagu (Elizabeth Montagu's cousin-in-law), who confessed to Pope, 'I am pretty far gone in oriental learning', was also experimenting with cross-cultural translation and thinking about reader response. From Adrianople she sent Pope a Turkish poem by Ibrahim Pasha, which she had translated, the opening of which reads:

> The nightingale now wanders in the vines;
> Her passion is to seek roses.[34]

Turning 'the whole into the style of English poetry' for a singularly Popean readership, her versification produces the following:

> Now Philomel renews her tender strain,
> Indulging all the night her pleasing pain;

The *gul u bulbul* (rose and nightingale) legend emerges with greater clarity in the simplicity of her literal translation, without the aid of western classical allusion. In the same way, modern readers would probably prefer Jones's prose translation of the Arabic text to his poem 'Solima', and those who know the original might wish that Jones had translated it in its entirety. It is the sixth-century female poet Janūb bint al-'Ajlan al-Hudhaliyya's passionate tribute to her warrior brother 'Amr Dhû'l-Kalb, ironically killed not in an epic battle, but by two leopards while sleeping:

> 'Amr Dhû'l-Kalb, best of them in esteem, lies in Sharyān valley, the wolves howling around him.
> Thrusting a thrust so wide that gush upon gush of his blood follows it like a mighty stream.
> Playfully up walk the eagles to him, [confident], strutting like maidens in their gowns.
> He it was who would bring out the lovely round-breasted girl, submissive among the captive women, perfume diffusing from her sleeves.

---

34. Letter of Lady Mary Wortley Montagu to Pope of 1 April 1717; *Turkish Embassy Letters*, ed. Malcolm Jack (London, 1993), 78–9.

> The like of 'Amr you will never see as long as foot treads earth and camels moan in yearning for their homelands.[35]

Jones admired Janūb's powerful mixture of eulogy and elegy achieved in the heroic resonances of the *qasīda* long line. Discovering it in a Pococke manuscript, he was transported from the dusty Bodleian to the wild beauty of Bedouin pastoral. Why did Jones not present to his readers this authentic product of desert pain? Simply because he judged the time was not yet ripe; too pure a vein of the exotic might repel rather than attract a sensitive audience. Jones intuited the truth of what Coleridge was later to assert: a great writer 'must himself create the taste by which he is to be relished'. This applied equally to the cultural translator; first Jones must create a public taste for the genuine ethnic commodity.

Poems aimed to achieve this by a three-fold strategy: firstly the acculturating influence of his own Orientalist poems; and secondly by his inclusion of translations of two carefully selected Asiatic poems: 'A Persian Song of Hafiz', which had already appeared to acclaim in his *Grammar*, and 'A Turkish Ode of Mesihi'. This 'Ode to Spring' by the Albanian-born Mesīhī (d. 1512), who in Constantinople seems to have preferred the tavern to the madrasa, has an appeal that is universal rather than culture-specific. For each stanza Jones supplies a refined metrical translation, a transliteration in Roman letters, and a precise prose translation, where one can locate the images absent from his more Augustan version: the vibrancy of sunbeams on scarlet tulips, which 'like sharp lancets, tinge the banks with the colour of blood', or the geographic specificity of 'the breath of the gale is full of Tartarian musk'. Jones thus enables his readers to access a product of Turkish civilization at a range of levels.

The third element in Jones's educative approach was arguably the most significant: the two essays appended to *Poems*. Seminal documents in the history of criticism, they install the lyric at the centre of poetry. 'On the Poetry of the Eastern Nations' establishes Jones as a major precursor of the Romantics. Here his desire to revive the pastoral involves not Arcadian shepherds, or even the pallid Arabism of 'Solima', but full-blooded Bedouin, and in his attempt to inject energy and reality into the genre he anticipates Wordsworth's 1800 preface to *Lyrical Ballads*.

---

35. *Arabic Literature to the End of the Umayyad Period*, ed. A. F. L. Beeston et al. (Cambridge, 1983), 85–6. My thanks are to Geert Jan van Gelder and Adam Talib for identifying this qasida.

In a path-breaking demonstration of poetry as the nuanced product of culture and environment, he focuses first on Arabia, specifically upon the Yemen, the Arabia Felix of the ancients, at the crossroads of Africa, the Middle East, and Asia on the fragrant south Arabian spice route. Anticipating the Wordsworthian concept that 'the passions of men are incorporated with the beautiful and permanent forms of nature', and developing some of Burke's ideas, Jones argues that Arab familiarity with 'natural objects' both '*sublime* and *beautiful*' is reflected in the graceful and delicate imagery of their language:

> they compare *the foreheads of their mistresses to the morning, their locks to the night, their faces to the sun, to the moon, or the blossoms of jasmine, their cheeks to roses or ripe fruit, their teeth to pearls, hail-stones, and snow-drops, their eyes to the flowers of the narcissus, their curled hair to black scorpions, and to hyacinths, their lips to rubies or wine, the form of their breasts to pomegranates and the colour of them to snow,*
>
> (*SWJ*, p. 323)

Warming to his theme, he celebrates the pre-Islamic *Mu'allaqāt*, especially the *qasīda* of Lebīd, 'purely pastoral, and extremely like the *Alexis* of Virgil, but far more beautiful, because it is more agreeable to nature'. Jones was the first to appreciate that these Bedouin descriptions of abandoned encampments, of passionate love-making; atmospheric evocations of desert journeys on swift she-camels; and vaunting praise of the poets' prowess in hunting, drinking, and fighting, constitute a species of invigorating heroic pastoral. These sixth-century 'Suspended' odes, once transcribed in gold upon fine Egyptian paper and hung from the walls of the holy Ka'ba in Mecca, were another Bodleian revelation. Jones paid an Oxford boy ten pounds to painstakingly trace the whole of Pococke's manuscript of the *al-Hamāsah*, a superb anthology of Bedouin poetry; the flimsy paper was carefully copied for him by Hājī Abdullah in Bengal.

For Jones the *Mu'allaqāt* recalled the Welsh heroic pastoral of the 'Gorhoffedd' (Exulting Boast) by Gwalchmai ap Meilyr, twelfth-century bard of Owain, Prince of Gwynedd, and comrade of Jones's ancestor, Hwfa ap Cynddelw. East and West, otherness and selfhood merged in a similar 'romantic' mixture: keen apprehension of natural beauty, reminiscences of the beloved, and pride in military resistance as the poet guarded the ancient stronghold of Môn:

> Sun up early, summer speeding near,
> Birds' sweet sound, delightful bright weather.

> Gold-mettled am I, dauntless in strife,
> Lion facing legions, lightning my charge.
> I kept night watch, guarding the border,
> Streams' murmur at Dygen Freiddyn's fords,
> Bright green the wild grass, water lovely,
> Nightingale loud, familiar lyric,
> Gulls play on the couch of the ocean
> Gleaming their feathers, querulous factions.
> Far-roving my mind as summer comes
> For love of a young girl of Caerwys.[36]

The Arab nomad, like the Celtic mountaineer or Ossianic rebel, offered a potent political symbol of resistance to tyrannical power. The Bedouin, as Jones points out, 'have never been wholly subdued by any nation'. If, as Abdulla el Tayib maintains, 'An ideally conceived Bedouin, imaginary though he be, exists forever in the Arab soul', it is clear see that wild bardic genius was alive and well and living in Jones's imagination.[37] This was oppositional pastoral for advanced whigs.

'On the Poetry of the Eastern Nations' provides a verse 'imitation' of lines from Lebīd's *mu'allaqa*; ten years later Jones judged the time right to publish a critical edition with accurate prose translations of all seven *Mu'allaqāt*. The 1772 'Essay' introduces the Arab maxim that 'the three most charming objects in nature are *a green meadow, a clear rivulet, and a beautiful woman*, and that the view of these objects at the same time affords the greatest delight imaginable'. In 1782 *The Moallakát* would treat the public to Tarafa's three youthful enjoyments:

> First, to rise before the censurers awake, and to drink tawny wine, which sparkles and froths when the clear stream is poured into it.
> Next, when a warrior, encircled by foes, implores my aid, to bend towards him my prancing charger, fierce as a wolf among the Gadha-trees, whom the sound of human steps has awakened, and who runs to quench his thirst at the brook.
> Thirdly, to shorten a cloudy day, a day astonishingly dark, by toying with a lovely delicate girl under a tent supported by pillars.
>
> ('The Poem of Tarafa', verses 58–60; *SWJ*, p. 208)

---

36. Evan Evans, *Some Specimens of the Poetry of the Antient Welsh Bards* (London, 1764), 83–4. As Evans provides only a Latin translation, the quotation is from Joseph P. Clancy, *The Earliest Welsh Poetry* (London, 1970), 119–20.
37. *Arabic Literature*, ed. Beeston et al., 35.

Moving his gaze to Persia, he compares Hāfiz's Ghazal 663, 'O sweet gale, thou bearest the fragrant scent of my beloved' with Shakespeare's Sonnet 99, 'The forward violet thus I did chide', demonstrating that 'Eastern imagery is not so different from the *Europeans* as we are apt to imagine.' Keen to dispel racial and political stereotypes, he includes a translation from Sa'dī's *Bostan* of the advice of King Nushirvan to his son Hormuz:

> *Be a guardian, my son, to the poor and helpless; and be not confined in the chains of thy own indolence. [. . .] Go, my son, protect thy weak and indigent people; since through them is a king raised to the diadem. The people are the root, and the king is the tree that grows from it; and the tree, O my son, derives its strength from the root.*

Jones defies any westerner—such as Beattie denouncing Asian peoples as 'unfriendly to liberty', using 'exaggerated metaphors, and gigantic descriptions'—to ignore evidence of Iranian enlightenment: 'Are these mean sentiments, delivered in pompous language?' Refuting notions of Asiatic tyranny and Oriental unreason, he encourages his readers to relocate 'Oriental' despotism in the Occident; such poems: 'a century or two ago [. . .] would have been suppressed in *Europe*, for spreading with too strong a glare the light of liberty and reason' (*SWJ*, pp. 332–3).

Jones understood that tastes must be educated incrementally and with subtlety. Translation of the Asian 'Other' involved delicate politico-cultural negotiations with the European 'Self'. On a personal level there was little doubt that he had seen the Middle Eastern light. Jones was a convert, despite his undying regard for western classicism, as he confessed in 1768 to his fellow-Orientalist Charles Reviczki:

> From my earliest years, I was charmed with the poetry of the Greeks; nothing, I then thought, could be more sublime than the Odes of Pindar, nothing sweeter than Anacreon, nothing more polished or elegant than the golden remains of Sappho, Archilochus, Alcæus, and Simonides: but when I had tasted the poetry of the Arabs and Persians . . .   (*Works*, 1: 78)

In public, however, he must not appear to have gone native. Consequently in his preface to *Poems*, Jones disingenuously claims not to be doing what he undeniably is: displaying the competing charms of Eastern classics:

> It must not be supposed, from my zeal for the literature of *Asia* that I mean to place it in competition with the beautiful productions of the *Greeks* and *Romans*; for I am convinced, that whatever changes we make in our opinions,

we always return to the writings of the ancients, as to the standard of true taste. (Preface, p. vi)

The conclusion of 'On the Poetry of the Eastern Nations' marks a subtle departure from the Occidental gold standard, a modification indicated by a significant 'yet', introducing the idea of a western diet tedious in its repetition:

> I must request, that, in bestowing these praises on the writings of *Asia*, I may not be thought to derogate from the merit of the *Greek* and *Latin* poems, which have justly been admired in every age; yet I cannot but think that our *European* poetry has subsisted too long on the perpetual repetition of the same images, and incessant allusions to the same fables. (*SWJ*, 336)

Presuming that his readers are with him, Jones indicates a way forward for the refreshment of European literature: annotated critical editions of Asian classics, and more departments of ancient and modern Oriental languages. This would achieve 'a more extensive insight into the history of the human mind; we should be furnished with a new set of images and similitudes; and a number of excellent compositions would be brought to light, which future scholars might explain, and future poets might imitate' (*SWJ*, 336).

This final word of his first essay might appear to lead seamlessly into his second: 'On the Arts, Commonly Called Imitative', except that the whole burden of the latter is to affirm that lyric poetry has little to do with imitation.

> In the preceding collection of poems, there are some *Eastern* fables, some *odes*, a *panegyrick*, and an *elegy*, yet it does not appear to me, that there is the least *imitation* in [any] of them: *Petrarch* was, certainly, too deeply affected with real *grief*, and the *Persian* poet was too sincere a lover, to *imitate* the passions of others. (*SWJ*, 344)

Here Jones again demonstrates that while reinventing Orientalism he is facilitating Romantic revolution. Both Eastern and European poetry are used to establish a groundbreaking expressive and emotionalist concept of art, which anticipates the subjectivity of Romanticism. He rejects Aristotelian mimetic concepts, establishing the lyric impulse as the primary and universal prototype for poetry and music. An ode of Sappho or the Song of Solomon is 'not an imitation of nature, but the voice of nature herself'. Nearly thirty years before Wordsworth's famous formulation, 'poetry is the spontaneous overflow of powerful feelings', Jones defines poetry as 'originally no more than a strong and animated expression of the human passions'.

A fascinating and influential *locus* for Romantic aesthetic theory, M. H. Abrams acknowledges its importance:

> [W]e find a conjunction of all the tendencies we have been tracing: the ideas drawn from Longinus, the old doctrine of poetic inspiration, recent theories of the emotional and imaginative origin of poetry, and a major emphasis on the lyric form and on the supposedly primitive and spontaneous poetry of Oriental nations. It was Jones's distinction, I think, to be the first writer in England to weave these threads into an explicit and orderly reformulation of the nature and criteria of poetry and of the poetic genres.[38]

Abrams places an unnecessary emphasis upon primitivism; Jones considered Firdausi and even the Bedouin authors of the *Muʻallaqāt* as products of sophisticated cultural traditions, illustrating a 'rich and creative invention, which is the very soul of poetry'. But Abrams sees Jones as a crucial synthesizer, weaving the very threads of Romanticism. With his youth, talent, and ardent enthusiasm, Jones was ideally suited to the role of popularizer. Accomplished, handsome, and highly spirited, he had not neglected the social graces; he was a great success with the ladies, whether bluestockings or bishops' daughters. 'Asiatic' Jones, frequently seen at fashionable Ranelagh in Persian dress, used the reflected glamour of the Oriental vogue to transform the public conception of the Orientalist. He was no dry bespectacled scholar but an intellectual celebrity.

Hester Thrale, the Caernarvonshire-born writer who presided with Johnson over her Streatham salon, uses Jones as a mental and moral exemplar. Society was weary of conspicuous display, she wrote in a frequently published letter 'To a Newly-Married Man' (John Rice, who had eloped with her husband's niece):

> The age we live in, pays, I think, peculiar attention to the higher distinctions of wit, knowledge, and virtue, to which we may more safely, more cheaply, and more honourably aspire. The giddy flirt of quality frets at the respect she sees paid to Lady Edgecumbe [a talented harpsichordist], and the gay dunce sits pining for a partner, while Jones the orientalist leads up the ball.[39]

A decade later the Calcutta judge reflected on the vanity of such gay dunces of the London beau monde in 'An Ethick Epistle' of his own:

---

38. M. H. Abrams, *The Mirror and the Lamp: Romantic Theory and the Critical Tradition* (New York, 1953), 87–8.
39. Hester Lynch Piozzi, *Letters To and From the Late Samuel Johnson, LL.D.*, 2 vols (London, 1788), 1: 99–100.

> E'en males (O shame to manhood!) have appear'd
> With cheeks high-crimson'd and blue-powder'd beard;
> Or kid-skin spiders [corsets], to contract their shapes,
> Have stiffen'd into poles the travell'd apes.   (ll. 61–4)[40]

Contemptuous of long pedigrees, inherited honour, rank, and wealth, Jones introduces the tale of a Yemeni Bedouin warrior, Amr ibn Madī Karib al Zubaydī. When the effete king of 'fertile IRAK' borrows the legendary sword 'al-Samsamah', with which Madī had vanquished all his enemies, he finds it as useless as his own, and the scimitar wins him no glory. Madī's comment to the king's servants underscores Jones egalitarianism:

> Oh would your mighty master learn to prize
> Worth prov'd his own, and lifeless aids despise,
> That yon keen blade high vantage might impart,
> This arm he should have borrow'd, and this heart.   (ll. 115–18)

The reviews certainly prized Jones's worth as an author of 'luxuriant imagination' and 'poetical genius'.[41] By the time he was called to the bar on 28 January 1774, 'Persian' Jones had gained election to the Royal Societies of London and Copenhagen, and to Johnson's exclusive Turk's Head Club, where he encountered the glitterati of the day—Edmund Burke, Oliver Goldsmith, David Garrick, Joshua Reynolds, and Edward Gibbon—on terms of friendly equality and mutual respect. Five years later in 1778 Jones found it supremely sweet to patronize his patron's son by nominating Althorp for admittance to the Club; in 1780 he similarly secured the election of a delighted Bishop Shipley. The seductive power of patronage enabled him to turn the tables of dependency.

On St David's Day 1774 Jones published his *Poeseos Asiaticæ Commentariorum*, a work of immense scholarship he had been perfecting since 1767. *Poeseos* was acclaimed throughout Europe. Michaelis, Herder, and Goethe were reading it, even before the Jena Orientalist, Johann Gottfried Eichhorn, reprinted it at Leipzig in 1777. Jones's detailed commentary on Asiatic imagery, diction, and metrics was lavishly illustrated with texts printed in Hebrew, Arabic, Persian, and Turkish, complete with Latin translations. A groundbreaking book in the history of comparative literature, it brilliantly

---

40. Rosane Rocher, 'Sir William Jones as a Satirist: An Ethic Epistle to the Second Earl Spencer', *Transactions of the Honourable Society of Cymmrodorion*, N.S. 11 (2005), 70–104.
41. See, for example, *Critical Review*, 33 (April, 1772), 314–8.

reflected his proselytizing zeal for Asian literature and its potential to reinvigorate the West. Jones had now championed and translated Oriental poetry in English, French, and Latin, which was still, to a large extent, the language of international European scholarship. In just over a decade Jones was conversing with Indian pandits in the superior language of subcontinental scholarship —Sanskrit.

For now, as Jones attempted to prevent peach juice staining his elegant muslin stock, he could reflect that his latest publication had set the seal upon his reputation as the foremost linguist in Britain and the most eminent Orientalist of his generation. But he had to get out of the greenhouse, and not just Sir Roger Mostyn's. He must quit the forcing house of the Orientalist's study, exchanging Persian dress for lawyer's gown.

Poeseos Asiaticæ concluded with his elegant 'Ad Musam', a much-admired eight-line farewell to Camena, the muse of poetry. The author of a two-part review in the *Gentleman's Magazine* offered his own translation of Jones's iambics as tribute to 'this truly classical writer':

> Parent of eloquence, of virtue nurse,
> Farewell, thou soft inspirer of my verse!
> Thy lute and laurel I must leave;
> But pleas'd thy vot'ry's homage to receive,
> O sweetest of the heav'nly throng,
> As Suada or as Pitho hear my song:
> Ne'er be my hand, or tongue, or gown,
> Sordid, ineloquent, or useless, known!
>
> (*GM*, 44 [Dec. 1774], 579–83, 622–4; 624)

His muse must now be the Greek Pitho, or the Roman Suada, goddess of persuasion, eminently useful at the bar. The muddy lanes of the Carmarthen circuit called.

3
'Druid' Jones on the Carmarthen Circuit: Radicalization and Recreation on the Celtic Fringe

In Jones's life plaudits and superlatives can become somewhat tedious. Let's begin by stripping this son of 'a shortfaced Welshman' down to size. The acerbic Laetitia-Matilda Hawkins did as much for his sister Mary. Thanks to her *Memoirs* we have an account of Jones's Westminster Hall debut, as witnessed by 'Classic Harry', her scholarly brother Henry:

> I remember to have heard him speak as a Counsel in the Court of King's Bench: the question before the Court, arose from private disagreements in a family, which made a separation between husband and wife necessary; and there being a child whose interests were to be taken care of, the interference of the Court was required. A perfect silence prevailed—the attention of all present being attracted to hear what 'Linguist Jones', as he was even then called, would say. Though he could not have been accustomed to hear his own voice in a court of law, for I believe this was his forensic debut, he, nevertheless, spoke with the utmost distinctness and clearness, not at all disconcerted by the novelty of his situation. His tone was highly declamatory, accompanied with what Pope has called 'balancing his hands', and he seemed to consider himself as much a public orator as Cicero or Hortensius could have done. His oration, for such it must be called, lasted, I recollect, near an hour. But the orator, however he might wish to give a grand idea of the office of a pleader, did not, in the course of the business, entirely avoid the ridiculous; for having occasion to mention a case decided by the Court, he stated in the same high declamatory tone in which he had delivered the whole of his speech, that he found 'that it had been argued *by one Mr. Baldwin*' Not being very conversant with the state of the bar, he did not know that this *one*

Mr. [William] *Baldwin* was, at the time of which I am speaking, a barrister in great business, and was then sitting not half a yard from the orator's elbow. It occasioned a smile, or perhaps more than a smile, on every countenance in Court; but the orator proceeded as steadily as before. In the course of his speech, he had had occasion to mention the governess of the child; and he had done it in such terms as conveyed, and must have conveyed to any one possessed of ordinary powers of comprehension, an idea that she was an extremely improper person to remain with a young lady: on the next day, therefore, Mr. Jones appeared again in the seat which he had occupied the preceding day; and when the judges had taken their seats, he began with the same high declamatory tone, to inform the Court, that 'it was with *the deepest regret* he had learned that, in what he had had the honour to state to their Lordships the preceding day, he was understood to mean to say that Mrs.— was a harlot!!' The gravity of every countenance in Court yielded to the attack thus made upon it, and a general laugh was produced by it.[1]

The studied theorist, the conscious Cicero, for all his self-possession, was totally deflated as the smiling judges hastened to assure him that no impression unfavourable to the governess's morals had been made upon the court. What a contrast with the triumphant debut of his friend Francis Hargrave in the Somerset case! Blushing at the gauche impression he had made, Jones vowed this would never happen again. Painstaking legal research and detailed preparation of his argument now became the hallmarks of his forensic career. Emulating the penetrating intellect that John Dunning, distinguished expert in common law, brought to the bar, Jones had by 1777 carved out a substantial London practice. As he wrote to Dutch Orientalist Hendrik Albert Schultens: 'My law employments, attendance in the courts, incessant studies, the arrangement of pleadings, trials of causes, and opinions to clients, scarcely allow me a few moments for eating and sleeping' (*Works*, 1: 267).

The nature of Jones's practice was shaped by the culture of the circuits. Defending tenant farmers and agricultural workers from powerful adversaries polished his courtroom skills as it honed a radical edge to his politics. The road to the West proved an educative one for Jones.

Lawyers have always sought fees, prestige, and social status, but the increasing professionalism of barristers in the second half of the eighteenth century was marred by their energetic pursuit of an aristocratic clientele. On the King's Bench, Lord Mansfield was something of an exception, and Jones

1. Hawkins, *Memoirs, Anecdotes, Facts, and Opinions*, 1: 244–6.

was influenced by the interest of its industrious chief justice in mercantile law and marine insurance. With his belief in commerce and the potential of professionals to encourage social change, Jones refused to serve the narrow interests of a privileged elite.

Legal scholar David Lemmings asserts that: '[D]espite a limited efflorescence of radical barristers at the time of the Wilkite agitation during the 1760s and 1770s, there is not much evidence that *lawyers* were normally expected to deliver the Englishman's birthrights, especially when it came to broad constitutional issues.'[2] Jones's career ran counter to 'normal' expectations. As jurist, in the Court of the King's Bench, on the circuits, and as a Commissioner for Bankrupts, Jones was attempting to secure those very birthrights: protection of the individual, his liberty, property, and constitutional representation.

The 'patriotic' barristers Jones admired, men like John Dunning, John Glynn, and Thomas Erskine, embraced popular and radical causes, but this was largely within the metropolis. Determined also to safeguard the Welshman's birthrights, he was soon made very aware of the geographical remoteness of Wales. First he must travel the 400 miles of the Oxford circuit.

On Monday, 6 March 1775, he set out for Berkshire and the Oxford circuit to ride its nine English counties and then to traverse five Welsh ones, on the Carmarthen circuit, timetabled at the conclusion of the Oxford. At Reading he met leading counsel Edward Bearcroft and Henry Howorth, and assisted his friends Thomas Milles and Serjeant-at-Law James Adair in 'three or four causes'. He valued the company of these reforming lawyers, who strongly opposed the American war. The circuit proceeded to the Oxford Assizes where Jones was well received. Stabling his 'little Grey', he hired two powerful hacks for himself and his manservant to travel the long journey to the next assize town of Worcester. There was a moonlit ride to a fine hostelry at Enville where the carp was excellent and the claret flowed, courtesy of Adair, who had just been elected to the parliamentary seat of Cockermouth. Jones's friend proved a staunch opponent to North's administration, advocating reform and Catholic relief.

From Stafford, where John Dunning arrived to lead a cause, Jones and Adair made an excursion to Buildwas, which had suffered a terrifying

---

2. David Lemmings, *Professors of the Law: Barristers and English Legal Culture in the Eighteenth Century* (Oxford, 2000), 326.

earthquake in the spring of 1773. They spoke to a farmer who had witnessed his house and fields move across the crumpled earth as the Severn ran backwards to its source. The circuiteers passed through the dramatic hills and hanging woods of Coalbrookdale, its erupting smelting furnaces recalling to Jones, as they subsequently would to Philippe de Loutherbourg and Turner, 'Vulcan's forges in the caverns of Ætna' (*Letters*, 1: 187).

The circuit moved southwards to Shrewsbury, 'an ugly town but delightfully situated. Here we had a tolerable ball.' The next day those without hangovers visited the 'venerable ruin' of Ludlow castle, a superb setting for the masque of *Comus* by his beloved 'Milton and Henry Lawes, the best poet and musician of their age'. At Hereford they 'were entertained with a concert, a poor one, indeed! but a ball, which followed it, in which I danced with a very pretty partner, made ample amends'. Jones and two friends left the Oxford circuit here, to follow the winding Wye upstream, skirting the snow-covered Black Mountains and heading for the delights of the 'Old Carmarthen'.

Entering Wales on the 30 March, they dined at Hay, and were at Brecon Priory in time for tea with Lady Camden, where they congratulated her on her husband's 'manly eloquence' in opposing a parliamentary bill to cripple the trade of New England. Jones had stood in the Commons the preceding month to hear Lord Camden quote John Locke on justifiable resistance to tyranny. The following day they rode on to Llandovery where they dined with the judges, first Justice John Pollen and second Justice Edward Poore, 'with whom we live in perfect familiarity'.

The circuit thus far, at least in Jones's correspondence with Althorp, seemed more fashionable tour than 'forensick campaign'. Crossing the border proved both geographically and culturally seamless. At Newton he visits George Rice, whig MP for Carmarthenshire, in his double-pile gentry house. Jones, like 'Capability' Brown later that spring, is delighted with 'perhaps, the finest situation in the whole island'. Like the Cambro-Norman Giraldus Cambrensis six centuries earlier, he is impressed by Dinefwr Castle, 'the summer palace of the old kings of South Wales', but Jones's own hybridity seems somewhat occluded.

The pen of Gerald of Wales quivered in his hand 'to think of the terrible vengeance exacted in our own times by the King's troops on the subject people of the commote of Caeo'.[3] By contrast, the fate of Jones's female

---

3. Giraldus Cambrensis, *The Journey through Wales and The Description of Wales*, trans. Lewis Thorpe (Harmondsworth, 1978), 139.

ancestor, Gwenllian, the Anglesey-born defender of Dinefwr, is far from our circuiteer's mind. Jones is high on the fashionable picturesque—and it's time for lunch: 'fresh oysters as fine as any I have tasted [...] trouts fresh from the river *Towy* (which is much more beautiful than its name is melodious) [...] the best tarts I ever tasted, they are made of *bogberries*' (*Letters*, 1: 189). He assures Althorp: 'I am not πολυφάγος' (a greedy eater) but, Welsh fare was certainly to his taste.

His description of 'Market-day at Llandilo' reveals a double exteriority of race and class:

> I could not help fancying myself in a Flemish town; it was at least wholly unlike an English one, as the language, manners, dress, and countenances of the people are entirely different from ours; I speak of the lower sort, for the gentry are not in any respect distinguishable from us. (*Letters*, 1: 189)

The Anglo-Norman conquerors had indeed introduced Flemish colonists to dilute indigenous culture, but Jones is here reacting to authentic Welshness, the 'otherness' of the internal colony that is the land of his fathers. Falling into tutorial mode, he reinforces some elementary Welsh: '[M]any Welch names begin with *Llan*, which signifies an *inclosure*; the double *l*, you know is pronounced in a very singular manner.' In fact Jones himself was at the foot of a very steep learning curve; but learning was what he excelled in.

Patrician condescension was rapidly abandoned as his professional experience caught up with his social expertise. Ancient Celtic liberties had been eroded by the arbitrary power of an Anglicized squirearchy, and Jones's egalitarian principles were confirmed in his legal representation of the colonized Welsh. Increasingly his letters to the Spencers describe the oppression of the 'yeomanry and peasantry of Wales' at the hands of rack-renting squires, monoglot-English magistrates and judges. It is fitting his education should begin here for Dinefwr was the ancient capital of the principality of Deheubarth, founded by Hywel Dda *c*.920, and embracing the three counties of the Carmarthen circuit. Jones would prove a codifier of law like Hywel; across the centuries they share a dedication to equity and compassion rather than retributive punishment. Having read at Trinity College, Cambridge, a thirteenth-century Latin manuscript of Hywel's code (in which it was no crime for the starving to steal food, and married women possessed property rights, and could initiate divorce proceedings), Jones lamented working within a far less humane legal system. Nevertheless, he would defend the Deheubarth disadvantaged in the courthouses of Carmarthen, Haverfordwest, and Cardigan.

Reaching Carmarthen at the beginning of April, Jones writes: 'Here began my legal campaign; [...] a Welsh court exhibits in miniature all the practice of Westminster-hall; we have a court of chancery as well as of common law, we make motions, we draw bills and special pleadings, and we try causes both civil and criminal.' Whereas the English circuits fell within the jurisdiction of the four courts sitting at Westminster, whence all proceedings, whether from Northumberland or Middlesex, originated, the Welsh courts were in many respects practically independent of London. These itinerant twice-yearly Courts of Great Sessions, instituted under the Tudor Act of Union to acculturate the 'wild' Welsh, fascinated the common lawyer and jurist in Jones. The Carmarthen circuit offered him as junior counsel a comprehensive range of experience in criminal, civil, and equity causes. Such wide experience prepared him for his future role on the Calcutta bench.

From his clients' point of view, fees were substantially cheaper, and justice remarkably rapid, causes being commenced, conducted, tried, and determined, within the assize week. This real benefit, as compared with the 'circumlocution' of the Court of Chancery, for example, could hardly be denied even by the patronizing author of a *Quarterly Review* account of the Select Committee reports, which led to the abolition of these courts in 1830:

> [T]he plaintiff, for instance, big with litigious choler against his neighbour, whose sheep have browsed the heather of his mountain, instructs his attorney on the spot, a fortnight before the assizes, to avenge his proprietary rights by a *capias quare clausum fregit,* [a writ of trespass for breaking the plaintiff's close] which is duly served on the defendant before the Great Session. On Monday, the first day of the session, Counsellor Griffiths is retained, and kept up till two in the morning drawing the plaintiff's declaration; while Counsellor Jones, just arrived from London, is roused from bed at four to prepare the plea for the defendant—a replication follows with equal deliberation. On Wednesday at two o'clock the pleadings are ripe, the parties are what is called 'at issue', and notice of trial is given. Wednesday night is spent by the attornies in drawing their briefs, under inspiring libations of *cwrw* [beer]. Being copied with extra expedition by the law-stationers, on Thursday evening they are duly delivered to the doughty leaders on each side, and to their comatose juniors—consultation marked for 'Friday morning, at six o'clock, before the sitting of the court'; while, in the meantime, the attorneys' clerks have been

scouring the country to collect the witnesses. On Friday, after convicting a prisoner of burglary, passing three fines, hearing a motion for a new trial, making ten rules absolute on affidavit of service, and deciding an equity suit that has been pending above a fortnight, the court of Great Session tries the important and only cause respecting the common of pasture. The witnesses being many, and Welsh, and prejudiced, the interpretation of their testimony occupies great part of the day. The senior judge, after committing a Welshman for prevaricating in Welsh, charges the Welsh jury in an eloquent English summing up, with all the law and the elegance of Mansfield. The jury, under the influence of this address, transmitted through an interpreter, return a verdict for the plaintiff, damages five shillings, which damages are expended in *cwrw dha*, and the costs are taxed, if not paid, and the victorious plaintiff returned to his mountain side by the end of the twentieth day from his first visit to his attorney. This is hardly an exaggerated representation of that celerity which marks the proceedings of the local judicature of Wales, which the Welsh appear to deem an advantage, and which, though it would be intolerable (if possible) where business is on a large and difficult scale, appears, from the evidence of most persons practically acquainted with the Welsh courts, to be attended with no evil in Wales beyond a little stimulus and excitement to the counsel and attornies engaged.[4]

Despite the sarcastic trivialization, this illustrates the frenzied forensic activity that 'Counsellor Jones' experienced—when might he find time for assize balls? It also demonstrates his familiarity with procedures involving court interpreters and complex questions of jurisdiction long before he arrived in multilingual Bengal. In west Wales the vast majority of the population were monoglot Welsh speakers and most witness testimony was translated for the benefit of judges and counsel. Much depended upon the proficiency of court translators, and Jones was appalled at the prospect of prisoners failing to comprehend arcane procedures conducted in an alien language. In the courtroom his own increasing proficiency in Welsh, gained with the assistance of David Jones, Clerk of Ingrossments at the House of Commons, assured his popularity with clients and jurors. For Jones undoubtedly attained what was lamentably rare on the Welsh circuits, a working knowledge of Welsh, despite joking to Louis XVI that he knew almost every language but his own.[5]

---

4. *Quarterly Review*, 42: 83 (1830), 182–226; 204.
5. The earliest version of this canard I have discovered reads as follows: 'In 1782, Sir William Jones made the tour of France, after which he resided for a few months in Paris, where he was introduced at Court. The French Monarch was much pleased with his conversation and made many inquires respecting some of the provinces he had travelled through, to all of which he

This sharply contrasted with the bigoted prejudice that regarded Welsh speaking as a virtual indicator of cultural and moral inferiority. Half a century later an infamous Commission of Inquiry provided its own Macaulay Minute, asserting: 'there is no Welsh literature worthy of the name'.[6] The commissioners claimed the courtroom reveals the 'evil of the Welsh language'; facilitating fraud, it 'abets perjury, which is frequently practised in courts, and escapes detection through the loop-holes of interpretation'. The report concluded: 'The mockery of an English trial of a Welsh criminal by a Welsh jury, addressed by counsel and judge in English, is too gross and shocking to need comment.'

Any trial where language proves a barrier to understanding is indeed a mockery, but Jones makes no mention of perjury amongst Welsh witnesses. This is made more significant by the contrasting frequency of his subsequent comments on the high incidence of perjury in Calcutta, and the need for adequate Hindu and Muslim oaths. What Jones found 'gross and shocking' were the attempts of wealthy landlords to use distraining actions in the courts to bolster their tyrannical power base.

Workaholic Jones enjoyed the intellectual buzz of the eight-day stints at each of the county towns, and he took in the balls, at least three generally, hosted by the foreman of the grand jury, the sheriff, and the county MP. The arrival of the circuiteers on the first day of 'size' week was a matter of immense excitement as the local populace followed the sheriff's carriage, preceded by liveried trumpeters and 'javelin men' to welcome judges, barristers, attorney general, prothonotary, and officials, at the outskirts of the town. At Haverfordwest, 'the handsomest, the largest, and genteelest town in south Wales', the Great Sessions were a biannual highlight of the social calendar.

The county gentry flocked in and, their carriages finding difficulty in negotiating the steep streets, they decanted into sedan chairs, giving rise to the town's nickname of 'little Bath'. A festive atmosphere enveloped the

---

answered him in the particular dialect of each province. After Sir William withdrew, the king turned about to one of his courtiers, saying, "He is a most extraordinary man! He understands the language of my people better than I do myself!" "Yes, please your Majesty," replied the courtier, "he is, indeed a more extraordinary man than you are aware of, for he understands almost every language in the world, but his own." "Mon dieu!" exclaimed the King, "then of what country is he?" "He is, please your Majesty, a Welchman!"' *The Asiatic Annual Register for 1799* (1800), 60.

6. *Reports of the Commissioners of Inquiry into the State of Education in Wales* (London, 1848), 309–10. On Macaulay's Minute, see Chapter 9.

town as justice boosted commerce to the benefit of attornies, innkeepers, tradesmen, drapers, and tailors. White gloves were especially in demand for the ladies to wear at the dances and for presentation to judges and barristers if it proved a 'maiden' assize, free from capital convictions. Courtroom drama was available, which the inhabitants generally preferred unaccompanied by the gruesome theatre of public execution in this 'gwlad y menyg gwynion' ('land of the white gloves'). Those who relished gallows confessions might enjoy the repentant George Barnwell's dire warning to youth in Lillo's *The London Merchant* presented by itinerant acting companies who synchronized their schedules with the circuits. Gentry, in town 'to rub off the rust a little' appreciated the appropriate social humour of the Covent Garden success, *She Stoops to Conquer* by Jones's friend, Goldsmith.

If monoglot Welsh jurors welcomed Jones as 'hanner Cymro' (half-Welshman), the arrival in the Assembly Rooms of a celebrity—and still single—barrister was certainly of interest to daughters of notable local families, the Philipps of Picton Castle, the Owens of Orielton, and the Edwardes of Johnston, who controlled Pembrokeshire's three parliamentary constituencies. London was the Mecca of the Anglicized gentry, but for Mahomet—in the handsome and fashionable shape of 'Oriental' Jones—to come to the Welsh mountain, was most convenient.

Jones never detailed the social milieu at these west Welsh balls, but a telling account is provided by Mary Morgan, wife of theologian Revd Dr Caesar Morgan. Although still basking in the afterglow of a meeting with Elizabeth Montagu and James Beattie at Sandleford Priory, she was not disappointed by the Haverfordwest assize ball given by the MP, Richard Philipps, Baron Milford. Some of the Welsh ladies lacked style but, apart from Lord and Lady Milford, and Lady Moriarty, the company was enhanced by the 'remarkably handsome' Granville Leveson-Gower, Lord Granville observing the proceedings with a Darcy-like reserve.[7] Such were the connections and attractions of this future diplomat that, after a long-term affair with Althorp's sister, Henrietta Frances, Countess Bessborough, he married her niece Lady Henrietta Elizabeth Cavendish, the daughter of Georgiana, Duchess of Devonshire.

Jones cut quite a figure in the allemandes and cotillions, but he had not chosen the Carmarthen circuit for its country dancing. The Orientalist scholar, fascinated by eastern alterity, was discovering in the West what

---

7. *A Tour to Milford Haven, in the Year 1791* (London, 1795), 221–2.

8. Sir William Jones, attributed to James Northcote, oil on canvas, c.1772. (National Museum of Wales, Cardiff)

made him different—his Celtic blood. And the harsh reality of impoverished agricultural life he witnessed fired that blood. It shocked him out of his complacently bookish appreciation of Wales as a bastion of ancient British liberty. He enjoyed viewing the superb Welsh landscapes of Merioneth-born Richard Wilson at the Royal Academy, at Mostyn Hall and Brecon Priory (Wilson was related to the Mostyns and Lord Camden was his cousin), tacitly endorsing these patrician representations of the Principality as an innocent haven of pastoral quietude and quietism. Even the bourgeois shrewdness of our Haverfordwest observer, Mary Morgan, deserts her as she offers a rose-tinted picture of Carmarthenshire:

> Men of fortune have a number of tenants, whom they can always command, as they have still a kind of lordship over the peasantry. But I believe they never exercise the least degree of tyranny. They rather consider them as under their protection, than as their vassals. It seems to be a land of perfect liberty. (p. 270)

In reality, as David Solkin observes, 'a landscape of liberty actually functioned, when we examine it closely, as a landscape of reaction'.[8] This was the reality Jones quickly came to understand. The Celtic Revival was spearheaded by Jones's kinsmen, but it was a far cry from hymning ancient liberties to protecting the rights of hard-pressed agricultural labourers. The social constraints preventing Jones from visiting family in Anglesey were removed by his professional Carmarthen-circuit commitment. He preferred empathizing with the rural poor as clients rather than relatives.

As poet he rejected the Arcadian shepherds of neoclassicism, as barrister he certainly found none in the boggy fields and exhausted upland grazing of west Wales. Yet a *Quarterly Review*er, writing fifty years after Jones rode the circuit, stubbornly romanticizes Welsh shepherds as akin to 'Bedouin Arabs'.[9] Cambria Felix indeed, but Jones's imagination was more firmly grounded. Welsh pastoral conditions starkly ironized the high-society 'shepherdesses' of Vauxhall Gardens. The county assizes provided an education to counterbalance the beau monde. His letters portray a vivid picture of crime, punishment, and widely divergent social conditions within the Principality.

On 7 April 1775 at Haverfordwest, Jones 'had the unpleasant task of defending four men accused of murder: they were all acquitted; but I suspect one of them to be guilty' (*Letters*, 1: 190). John Morris, of the parish of Begelly, had been indicted as principal for the murder of Mary Griffiths by 'striking her head with a hatchet'.[10] Her body had been dumped in one of the shallow bell coalpits on the outskirts of the village. Two brothers of the accused, George and William Morris, were charged, together with Thomas Morse, with aiding and abetting the murder. 'The story is long and very horrid', he writes to Althorp, 'you shall hear it, among my other Welch stories, when we meet.'

Less dramatic but more universally oppressive was his repeated story of 'the abject state of vassalage to which the peasantry and lower yeomanry of the counties through which I pass twice a year, are reduced, or the cruel insults and injuries, which they are forced to bear' (*Letters*, 2: 529). Jones relished applying his increasing legal skills to defend small tenant farmers and workmen against the virtually feudal oppression of unscrupulous

---

8. David Solkin, *Richard Wilson: The Landscape of Reaction* (London, 1982), 102–3.
9. *Quarterly Review*, 57: 113 (1836), 164.
10. NLW, MS 4 Wales 820/1; Gaol Files.

adversaries: 'while I wear the gown, no helpless or injured person of any nation shall want an advocate, without a fee, in any of our courts' (*Letters*, 1: 142).

> At Carmarthen last autumn I obtained a just verdict in favour of a poor farmer cruelly attacked by a powerful adversary, who commenced a fresh action, but durst not bring it on this circuit, because he knew full well, that I should lash him for his cruelty with redoubled asperity. I have made this man my bitter foe; but I have preserved a better, though a weaker man, from ruin; and, in truth, I desire nothing so much as the enmity and bad word of all scoundrels, since, if it be true that *similis simili gaudet*, the *approbation* of *such* men must be the greatest disgrace.   (*Letters*, 2: 468–9)

His determination to operate without fear or favour was illustrated by a striking case that came on at Haverfordwest in 1780. The combined maritime forces of France, Spain, and Holland were shaking the superiority of the British navy, and fears of French invasion were rife. Against this fraught political background, Isaac Phillips, a yeoman of St Martin, had been charged with 'alarming a village on the coast of Pembrokeshire that a hostile ship of war was approaching'. Phillips had made a simple mistake, but seventeen years later in Fishguard a genuine French invasion force was routed by pitchfork-wielding heroines from Llanwnda who, in their traditional scarlet flannel whittles (cloaks) and tall black felt hats, appeared more formidable than any English redcoats.

The indictment, however, was a serious affair: Phillips was languishing in the Castle gaol, having been charged that he:

> [D]id falsely, knowingly, wilfully and maliciously with Intention to excite great fear and Terror among his majesties liege subjects spread a false and malicious report and alarm [. . .] that an enemies privateer meaning a privateering ship belonging to certain sovereign persons then and now at open war with our said sovereign arrived within the Harbour of Milford Haven to the great Terror and alarm of his said majesties liege subjects [. . .].[11]

One of the prosecuting magistrates was Barrett Bowen Jordan of Waterston House, a wealthy landowner, later to distinguish himself as prime mover in an absurd witch-hunt to find Fishguard Welshmen supposed to have aided the French invasion forces, and in the resultant Haverfordwest high-treason trial of September 1797, which collapsed for lack of evidence. The second JP was a more significant figure. He was a former governor of Bengal, John

---

11. NLW, MS 4 Wales 821/5: Gaol Files.

Zephaniah Holwell, author of *Interesting Historical Events, Relative to the Provinces of Bengal and the Empire of Indostan* (1765), a survivor of the infamous Black Hole of Calcutta, and one of Voltaire's chief informants on India. Rupee-rich Holwell, having sold Chilton Lodge to General Richard 'Nabob' Smith, had built elegant Castle Hall in extensive grounds near Hakin. He was an influential figure with whom it might have been in the best interests of Jones (whose application for an Indian judgeship was pending) to curry favour. The sardonic account of his courtroom harangue that Jones provides for Althorp clearly reveals that no such thought occurred to him:

> The prosecutors were two magistrates, one of them *governor Holwell*, who were angry at having *been made fools of*; a point, however, which they could not easily have proved, inasmuch as they were fools *ready made*. I defended the prosecuted man with success, and mingled in my speech many bitter reflections on the state of the country at the time of the alarm, and on the attempt, because the English laws were not relished in India, to import the Indian laws into England, by imprisoning and indicting an honest man, who had done no more than his duty, and, whose only fault was fear, of which both his prosecutors were equally guilty. (*Letters*, 1: 431)

It is a piquant coincidence that Jones is opposing a governor of Bengal in legal combat eight years before his friend Burke opens the protracted impeachment of Governor-General Warren Hastings. They were hugely different trials, and Holwell was certainly not in the dock, but abuse of power was at the heart of both Haverfordwest and Westminster Hall proceedings. Jones was appalled at Holwell's high-handed disregard for Phillips' rights and liberties; caprice and discretionary power had no place in the judicial system. Scandalized that Pembrokeshire magistrates should behave like the popular perception of Eastern potentates, Jones vigorously obtained Phillips' release.

Causes like these—where his Welsh 'forensick rambles' could make a difference—brought him into conflict with Burke at the Turk's Head. Burke mocked the Welsh circuits, nicknaming Welsh judges 'the yellow admirals of the law' (superannuated naval captains unattached to active squadrons), and failing to understand the social consequences of their abolition. Jones deplored Burke's proposal as a petty economy, when government might save 'millions of guineas and myriads of lives by a speedy union with America'. His concern was for 'the poor suitors of this country':

Ought a few thousands to be saved to the revenue, by a plan which will either distress the yeomanry and peasantry of Wales or deter them from applying at all for justice? How many industrious tenants will then be greater slaves than they are now to the tyrannical agents and stewards of indolent gentlemen? (*Letters*, 1: 354)

His own convenience would be better served if he could conduct all his business in London, but Jones appreciated the financial implications for the underprivileged Welsh: 'I know so well the expense of instituting suits in Westminster Hall for the principality, and the convenience of watering the borders of my countrymen with the fountain of justice brought to their own doors, that I hope the Welch men will petition against the bill, and, if they please, they may employ me to support their petition at the bar of the House' (*Letters*, 1: 346).

If he was watering the floral borders of Wales from the fountain of justice, Wales and its borders were reciprocally refreshing him. On the Oxford summer circuit Jones joined the regular boat trip from Ross to Monmouth, drifting down the Wye, 'the loveliest river in England, [*sic*] if not in the world'. Pioneering picturesque tourism before Gilpin's *Observations on the River Wye* (1782), the barristers relished every bounteous meander: 'It winds in a most wonderful manner and its banks present a new beauty every five minutes; here we see a fine ruin of a castle, there the most romantick rocks, in another part the noblest and thickest woods, in another the sweetest meadows and prettiest farms' (*Letters*, 1: 204). In 1771 Thomas Gray rapturously described the Wye's banks as a 'succession of nameless beauties', but he lacked local knowledge. Some of these 'romantic rocks', as labouring-class poet Robert Bloomfield reveals in The Banks of the Wye (1811), were dignified not with Arthurian titles, but with the names of eminent circuiteers:

> A group of wranglers from the bar,
> Suspending *here* their *mimic* war—
> Mark'd towering BEARCROFT'S ivy crown,
> And grey VANSITTART'S waving gown
> And who's that giant by his side?
> 'SERGEANT ADAIR,' the boatman cried.[12]

Such appropriation of the Welsh landscape by leaders of the English bar, including Robert Vansittart, whose baboon terrified Sandwich, was not

---

12. Robert Bloomfield, *The Banks of Wye*, 2nd edn (London, 1813), 27.

resented by Jones, especially as a 'giant' rock memorialized his close friend, Bill of Rights Society member, James Adair. Had Vansittart been present, his licentious tastes would have equipped the 'sociable', as these pleasure boats of shallow draught were termed, with his own 'succession of nameless [female] beauties'. Immorality would have embarrassed Jones, for all his lyrical outpourings to the damsels of the Principality. His luxuriousness was limited to the prandial, and here the circuiteers were punctilious:

> We passed the day most luxuriously, having sent from London a store of excellent champaign and burgundy, and provided cold turkey pies and cold meat, lobsters, crabs and so forth for our dinner: we dined in the boat which was moored on the bank, and kept our wines perfectly cool, by putting the bottles into a natural well of the coldest water I ever tasted. (*Letters*, 1: 204)

Further west, few lanes would accommodate a chaise, but the rugged hills, dense woodland, and hidden valleys would more than compensate as they rode and talked. From Haverfordwest to Cardigan the first stop was the Nant-y-ddwylan Arms, a comfortable hostelry where horses were rested and thirsts slaked. Then they enjoyed panoramic views on the atmospheric track over the Preseli Mountains, dotted with Neolithic cromlechs and instinct with druidical and Arthurian mystery, crossing the fast-flowing river Nevern at Pont Cynon, to arrive at Eglwyswrw, a picturesque village on the slopes of Foel Drygan. Here they would repair to the Serjeants' Inn—conveniently close to the Sessions House of the Cemaes Assizes—to dine on turbot, and deplete the circuit wine cellar. A later traveller informs us: 'A *fête champêtre* at this place furnished Sir William Jones's muse with a subject', perhaps in the 'dingle prettily wooded' just outside the village.[13]

In his scarce leisure time, inspired by the researches into the *Cynfeirdd* (early poets) and *Gogynfeirdd* (fairly early poets [of the princes]) undertaken by his Anglesey relations, Jones indulged in re-creational Celticism. His brother-barristers knew all about the Romantic relationship between Jones's Celtic genealogy and his bardic identity; in his friend Thomas Warton's dissertation 'Of the Origin of Romantic Fiction in Europe' (1774), they had read of his patriarchal parish:

> The bards of Britain were originally a constitutional appendage of the druidical hierarchy. In the parish of Llanidan in the isle of Anglesey, there are still to

---

13. George Nicholson, *The Cambrian Traveller's Guide, and Pocket Companion*, 3rd edn (London, 1840), 207.

be seen the ruins of an arch-druid's mansion, which they call TRER DREW, that is the DRUID'S MANSION. Near it are marks of the habitations of the separate conventual societies, which were under his immediate orders and inspection. Among these is TRER BEIRDD, or, as they call it to this day, the HAMLET OF THE BARDS.[14]

Despite these impeccable credentials, Jones's decision to found the society of the 'Druids of Cardigan', was prompted by 'clubbability' and a taste for Teifi-side lobster and champagne fêtes champêtre rather than a desire to revive the bardic tradition. Though no shape-shifter like the medievalized Taliesin, Jones knew all about self-fashioning and his renegotiation of Cymric selfhood involved a certain ironic distancing. Against the dramatic backdrop of Cilgerran Castle, recently painted in oils by Richard Wilson and

9. Kilgarren Castle, South Wales, print by William Elliott after Richard Wilson, 1775. (British Museum)

14. Thomas Warton, *The History of English Poetry*, 4 vols (London, 1774–81), 1: xlvii.

later captured by Turner in a hazy watercolour sunrise, Jones's *awen* (genius) for extempore composition perfected him for the role of *pencerdd*, or chief bard. The barristers' profession allied them to learned, legislating Druids.

The refreshing hedonism of 'Damsels of Cardigan' (1779), sung to the popular tune of 'Rural Felicity', reveals Jones at his most relaxed, its lines flowing gently as the waves of Tivy. Its music and its message link Celtic past and Romantic future, reflecting Lewis Morris's celebration of the natural in Welsh poetry: 'Llywarch Hen, Aneurin, and the followers of the Druids, are our men and Nature our Rule', and anticipating the Rousseauistic themes of Wordsworth's 'Expostulation and Reply' and 'The Tables Turned'.[15] The lyric has a universality of appeal and was much reprinted, but it excels in appropriateness for its immediate audience, the hallmark of good occasional verse. The circuiteers emerge, like so many moles, from the legal black-letter of Statham and Brooke's *Les Reports del Cases en Ley*, into the bright light of their riverside picnic:

> How vainly we pore over dark Gothic pages,
>   To cull a rude gibberish from Statham or Brooke!
> Leave Year-books and parchments to grey-bearded sages,
>   Be Nature our law, and fair woman our book.
>   But weak is our vaunt,
>   While something we want.
> More sweet than the pleasure which Learning can give.
>   Come, smile, damsels of Cardigan,
> Love can alone make it blissful to live.
>
> (ll. 48–9; *SWJ*, pp.54–5)

The law-Latinists appreciated the Horatian epigraph: 'Curtæ nescio quid semper abest rei' (something is always missing from our imperfect fortune). They might wryly recognize the relevance of the preceding line: 'Riches, dishonestly acquired, increase, and yet' contentment proves elusive. What might these lawyers lack more sweet than the pleasures each stanza describes? The final two reveal much about Jones, relishing the prospect of riches and an elegant Welsh mansion: 'That India supplied us with long-hoarded treasure,/That Dinevor, Slebeck or Coedmore were ours' (ll. 57–8); or a long-awaited judgeship: 'Or say, that preferring fair Thames to fair

---

15. *Additional Letters of the Morrises of Anglesey (1735–86)*, ed. Hugh Owen, 2 vols (London, 1947–9), 1: 291.

Tivy,/We gain'd with bright ermine robes purple or red' (ll. 64–5). And yet still something would be missing. Was it the unknown equestrienne he playfully addressed in another Cardigan lyric, 'On Seeing Miss ★★★ Ride by Him, without Knowing Her':

> Her shape was like the slender pine,
>   With vernal buds array'd,
> O heav'n! what rapture would be mine,
>   To slumber in its shade.   (ll. 17–20; *SWJ*, p. 63)

On being invited to dine at the elegant mansion of Bronwydd, Jones subsequently discovered the beautiful rider was Ann Lloyd, whose glorious 'hyacinthine hair' flowed down her shoulders. Perhaps the missing element was in fact his own Anna, passing her 'long love's day' beside the gin-clear Test?

Jones's 'Kneel to the goddess whom all men adore' (1780) was written in response to the fires of religious sectarianism he had seen illuminating the London skyline. Even as Old Bailey colleagues were trying the Gordon rioters, Jones's poetic corrective invokes a deistic syncretism associated with the Druids. These priest-poets were hailed as civil and ecclesiastical law-givers, they must now 'Teach the world to be wise', kneeling under their oak to the universal goddess. The manuscript, found among the papers of Mary Granville, Mrs Delany, a bluestocking whose friends included Swift, Handel, and Frances Burney, illustrates how Jones's occasional verse had an impressively wide circulation. Reflecting the tolerant approach to world religions that distinguishes his cultural research, gentle humour aids its universalist message. Inevitably 'Persian' Jones touches on Iran in a central stanza, its only flaw being a reductive reference to Anquetil-Duperron:

> When sallow Parsees, in vain Anquetil's rant,
>   Repeat the strange lessons of false Zoroaster,
> Or hymn ruddy Mithra's in rapturous cant
>   As their surest preserver from every disaster,
>   They worship but one,
>   Warm and round as the sun,
> Which Persia's rich kings on their diadem wore:
>   The circle they prize
>   Had long left the skies,
> And they kneel to the Goddess whom all men adore.
>   (ll. 21–30; *SWJ*, p. 59)

Later in Calcutta, Jones got things right about Zoroaster through his friend Bahman, who 'lived with me as a *Persian* reader for three years', and frequently cited Firdausi's verses on Zoroastrianism: 'Think not, that they were adorers of fire; for that element was only an exalted object, on the lustre of which they fixed their eyes; they humbled themselves a whole week before God.'[16]

The next verse turns to Jones's goal—India—and here it is useful to compare the ideas of a very different poet, but equally revolutionary thinker, William Blake. Blake's illuminated book *All Religions are One* (1788) refers to religions as reflecting culture-specific 'reception of the Poetic Genius', and this, together with recent discoveries concerning Blake's access to Moravian traditions, has special relevance to Jones's fourth stanza:[17]

> When dark visag'd Bramins obsequiously bow
>   To the rock whence old Ganges redundantly gushes,
> They feign that they bend to the form of a cow,
>   And save by this fiction the fair maiden's blushes;
>   But from Sanscritan Vedes
>   The discov'ry proceeds
> That her aid, whom we honor, e'en Bramin implores;
>   Like us wildly they dance,
>   Like us lightly advance,
> And kneel to the Goddess whom all men adore.   (ll. 31–40)

Aware of traditions associating Druids and Brahmans, Jones stresses the identity of Oriental and Occidental enthusiasm in the repeated 'Like us'. As Zoroastrians are not fire-worshipping idolators, the Hindus do not worship the cow as a sacred end in itself. But Jones, in implying a censoring fiction to save maidenly blushes, ascribes to Brahmans something akin to his own delicate processes of cultural translation in 'Hymns to Hindu Deities' (1784–88). Sensitive as to what might offend European readers, Jones chooses in 'A Hymn to Gangá' (1785) to depict the purifying Ganges flowing from the beautiful brow of Śiva, but this 1780 verse reveals that his Hindu researches have already revealed that Vedic references to Śiva's head could refer to the *Śivalinga*. It is the 'Druid', not the Brahman, who feels the need to conceal the genuine object of Śaivite devotion: the Hindus

---

16. 'The Sixth Anniversary Discourse: On the Persians', *Works*, 3: 103–36; 128–9.
17. Marsha Keith Schuchard, *Why Mrs Blake Cried: William Blake and the Sexual Basis of Spiritual Vision* (London, 2006).

are not bowing to Nandin, Śiva's bull *vāhana* (vehicle), but to *Bīja*, or semen, worshipped as 'the Ganges flowing from the head of the *Śivalinga*'.

Blake's Moravians, characterized by advanced attitudes towards sexuality in marriage, similarly meditated upon the supreme phallic symbol of creative energy. A Moravian hymn celebrates that 'Member full of Mystery! Which holily gives, and chastely receives, the conjugal Ointments for Jesus's Sake, during the Embraces, invented by the Most Merciful himself, there being then Seeds of the Church sowed.'[18] Sacramental celebration of sexuality might be found in Europe as well as India. Moravian Christianity was becoming increasingly popular in England, and the practices of the sect were meeting with the kind of denunciation levelled at Hinduism.

Jones continues his poem with a display of Celtic arrogance as he jokes of his superiority to Taliesin, sixth-century founding father of Welsh bardism:

> See, Teifi, with joy see our mystical rite
>   On steep woody marge after ages renewed;
> Here once Taliesin thou heard'st with delight,
>   But what was his voice to the voice of our Druid? (ll. 61–4)

Jones loved the heroic immediacy of Taliesin's 'Battle of Argoed Llwyfain', a hard-fought victory against the Bernician Angles, when ravens crimsoned their feathers in gore. He knew Evan Evans's Latin version and subsequently compared the original with the poet laureate William Whitehead's English translation, in Edward Jones's *Musical and Poetical Relicks of the Welsh Bards* (1784). He admired Taliesin's 'prophetic rage', and the fatalistic acceptance of vatic lines he read in *Gorchestion Beirdd Cymru* ('Feats of the Welsh Bards', 1773), compiled by Rhys Jones with Evans's assistance:

> Eu Ner a folant
> Eu hiaith a gadwant
> Eu tir a gollant
>   ond gwyllt Walia.

[Their Lord they will praise, their language they will keep, their lands they will lose—except wild Wales.]

As long as its language survives, Wales will thrive as a nation. But while Evan Evans in the depths of Denbighshire tries to define an authentic Taliesin canon, Jones will soon be grappling with subcontinental insights

---

18. Henry Rimius, *A Candid Narrative of the Rise and Progress of the Herrnhuters, commonly call'd Moravians, or, Unitas Fratrum*, 2nd edn (London, 1753), 54.

into the origins and families of nations. Within six years, on the banks of the Hugli rather than the Teifi, Jones was celebrating the 'language of the gods'. In Bengal he repaired the damage done to linguistic scholarship by the eccentric theories of Inner Temple attorney, Rowland Jones, whose *The Origin of Language and Nations* (1764) declared in an excess of patriotic *hwyl* (fervour) that Welsh was the primeval Adamic language that had evaded Babel. His notion was rejected by Lewis Morris as 'an empty froth', and by the *Critical Review* (18 [1764], 306) as the words of 'a druid rising out of the grave after eighteen hundred years sleep'. 'Linguist' Jones discovered a far more disconcerting *Ursprache* in Indo-European.

Sometimes the 'Druids' deserted the Teifi river god for another secluded spot by the brink of a veritable fountain of justice and Jones was persuaded to hymn the erotic delights of its nymph:

> We dine, you must know on the circuit by the side of a beautiful spring, which, as I discovered it in one of my walks, I was bound to celebrate. I therefore wrote the song in a wild grotesque style to the tune of a very lively country-dance, and it was admirably sung by one of our party (*Letters*, 2: 498).
>
> > Why should old *Tivy*, boys, claim all our duty paid,
> > And no just homage freely be to charming youth and beauty paid?
> > See, where the Nymph of the Spring sits inviting us,
> > With sparkling waters crystalline refreshing and delighting us!
> > What tho' his margin proud be rocky steep and willowy,
> > Or what tho' his azure couch be spacious deep and billowy!
> > She from her sweet paps lilied and roseal
> > Lies feeding all the laughing birds with dew drops ambrosial.
> >   ('The Fountain Nymph', ll.1–8; *SWJ*, p. 67)

The Welsh landscape is sexualized in this extempore paean to the 'untamed bosoms' and the somatic sensuality of one of Jones's favourite poems: Michael Drayton's topographical epic *Poly-Olbion* (1612), with its sixth song's choreography of Cardigan's chorography. This Celtic Revival was very much about refreshing other than intellectual parts; the boozy barristers recline on the naiad's 'arched grot' and 'that green hillock's breast, around its rosy nipple, boys', while the mischievous triple rhymes of his *chanson à boire* inevitably produces 'tipple, boys'. Jones is seen here in unbuttoned mood but, in sending this poem to his impressionable young friend, he feels compelled to add this prosaically heavy-footed but morally upright coda:

Do not imagine, my dear lord, from these light pieces or from any light expression, that I am or ever was, in principle or practice, a libertine; [...] but let philosophers say what they will, *either a man must not live in society, or he must conform in a certain degree to the society in which he lives*: now it must be allowed, that the manners of my brother lawyers are most licentiously profligate, (worse, I verily believe than those of the *regular* officers) and, if I had seemed to censure them, and had not in any degree given in to them, I should have been disliked by them, instead of being popular. The fruit, therefore of one day's excess in wine has been perpetual temperance for the rest of my life; for as I convince them that I did not abstain from sullenness or reserve, they now let me drink as little as I please, and very little I please to drink. Even on the day when my song was produced, I confined myself to three or four glasses, with a copious mixture from the fountain. (*Letters*, 2: 498–9)

Such were the accommodations of clubbability. So for 'Oriental' Jones it was watered-down wine, women, and song. Like a good Muslim, or a Welsh Methodist, he was most inspired to sing by the combination of '*a green meadow, a clear rivulet, and a beautiful woman*'. The final couplet of the poem: 'And if any rebel youth shall miss the cup or mutiny,/Amerc'd shall be the miscreant without appeal or scrutiny', reveals—in appropriately legalistic terminology—his fears of discretionary penalties for social non-conformity.

The society Jones Celticized with the title of 'Druids of the Tivy' was in fact a variant of what was known to hard-riding and hard-drinking circuit lawyers as the Horseshoe Club, the rules of which demanded Saturnalian self-indulgence, outlawing any display of white feather. The Horseshoe or bar mess, for all its hilarity and public-school prankishness, actually marked a key stage in the professional self-regulation of the bar. The rising lawyer Henry Brougham was disciplined by a 'Grand Court' mock-assize at Durham, for abusing 'the etiquette of the circuit' by absenting himself without leave from club celebrations to dine with the judge. The 'prisoner' was sentenced to stand before the company in a white sheet—a tablecloth sufficed—for penitential confession.

In the late 1770s and early 1780s, Thomas Plumer, the 'roaring bull' of the Oxford circuit and subsequently one of Hastings's defence team, rode the Carmarthen circuit, 'at the end of which he joined in the revelry of the Horseshoe Club, instituted by the members for their relaxation and indulgence in all sorts of fun and nonsense'. Plumer's journal for 1778 records that, unlike Brougham's Northern circuit, the Carmarthen sanctioned bench and bar to dine and indulge in club drollery together. It also provides some tantalizing references to Jones's part in some of these antics:

Saturday, April 11,—Dined with the judge; had a special Horse Shoe for electing of officers; Price knighted; Dr. Benjamin, Recorder; Cuthbert and Achmuty, two Precentors, the former also Præcursor, and the latter Expositor; Mil[l]es, Remembrancer, and Deputy-Master of Ceremonies. Douglas, Historiographer; Poore, Primate, Bishop of the Carmarthen Circuit; Jones the Grand Vicar preached the Ordination Sermon on the text out of Isaiah—'And there were 29 knives', and the Proverbs of Solomon—'As iron sharpeneth iron, so doth a friend the face of his friend', in verse; his grace was also given a copy of verses composed on the Oxford Circuit; Sir Wm. Lewis, Representative and Plenipotentiary; Self (Plumer) Ld. Gore; Lorimer, unbeliever, candle-snuffer, &c.; Williams, Accountant, got drunk, and behaved so ill that Jones proposed his expulsion; but in consequence of his being drunk, and making an apology the next day, he was forgiven. Bragge, Inspector; Pemberton, Master of the Ceremonies.[19]

Circuiteers were appointed to club offices according to their characters, avocations, or talents: 'Historiographer' Sylvester Douglas (later to marry Catherine, eldest daughter of Lord North, and oppose Plumer as one of the prosecuting counsel in Hastings's impeachment) made his name publishing election reports; 'Precentors' Richard Cuthbert of the Middle Temple and John Ahmuty (who followed Jones to Bengal, becoming magistrate of Gorakhpur and an Asiatick Society member) had good voices to lead the singing of Jones's lyrics; Plumer himself had acquired the nickname of an affable Irish chief justice, Baron Gore, appropriate for a 'roaring bull'.

But it is 'Grand Vicar' Jones who is given the fullest mention, his listing immediately following that of second judge Edward Poore, a friend of Bentham in his Oxford days, whose profligacy earned the nickname of 'Bishop'. The soubriquet 'Grand Vicar', the deputy of a Catholic bishop, added to the mention of sermonizing, might imply that a certain pomposity or self-righteousness was being satirized; it is hard to believe Jones deputized for Poore in debauchery.

Unfortunately none of Jones's verse sermons are extant, so we may only speculate on how he might have pierced the hearts of his Carmarthen 'congregation' with his 'nine and twenty knives'. The text, from the first chapter of Ezra and not Isaiah as Plumer has it, concerns Cyrus, King of Persia, allowing the Jews to return from their Babylonian captivity, restoring to them the Temple's looted treasures, among which are numbered 'thirty chargers of gold, a thousand chargers of silver, nine and twenty

---

19. Cited in 'The Horse-Shoe Club' (signed 'Queen's Gardens'), *Notes and Queries*, second series, 12 (14 September 1861), 214–5.

knives'. The knives' significance was traditionally a test of sermon writers' allegorical ingenuity and 'Persian' Jones, fascinated by the prophecies of Jeremiah and Isaiah, and with his love of Metastasio's lyrical drama, *Cyrus*, and Handel's oratorio, *Belshazzar*, would have risen to this challenge. Jones had identified Cyrus with Kaikhrosru of the *Shahnama*, insisting that Firdausi's epic could prove as fascinating to western readers as the *Iliad*.

Evan Evans's 'Paraphrase of Psalm CXXXVII, Alluding to the Captivity and Treatment of the Welsh Bards by King Edward I', presented the exiled bards in Babylonian captivity hanging up their harps by 'the willowy Thames', silently disobeying with Druidic defiance the order to entertain their captors.[20] Jones could have followed this patriotic biblical precedent by aligning himself with Jehovah's anointed, Cyrus, as the deliverer of the chosen people, the Welsh, from their captivity; a Middle Templar sanctioning the reconstruction of the temple of Celtic justice.

It would be easy for 'Grand Vicar' Jones to link the Temple knives with his second text, 'Iron sharpeneth iron; so a man sharpeneth the countenance of his friend' (Proverbs 27: 17). Barristers hone their skills in courtroom conflict, employing the sharpened knives of reason and rhetoric as they cut to the quick of a forensic issue. Jones relished the play of keen and penetrating wit in company sharpened by the intelligent conversation of close friends. Though he found the politics of some fellow lawyers uncongenial, Jones enjoyed the camaraderie of the circuit. 'How sweet is the circle of friends round our table', he wrote in 'The Damsels of Cardigan': 'Where none are unwilling and few are unable,/To sing a wild song, or relate a wild tale!' Years later, recovering at his Chittagong bungalow from a fever that brought him close to death, he recalled circuit days with great affection. Writing in February 1786 to his friend, 'Remembrancer, and Deputy-Master of Ceremonies' Thomas Milles, he promised 'a General Epistle to the Druids of the Tivy', together with such 'occasional pieces' as he might write.

The 'copy of verses composed on the Oxford Circuit' presented by Jones to Judge Poore reminds us that his inveterate habit of versifying was potentially dangerous. It is likely these were the verses I discovered written on the endpaper of an edition of Jones's poems, bearing the ascription: 'Written by Sir W[m]. Jones on the Oxford Circuit on seeing Bearcroft intoxicated led by Mr Henry Howorth':

20. *Gwaith y Parchedig Evan Evans*, ed. D. Silvan Evans (Caernarfon, 1876), 128.

> Immortal Gods! Can this be he
> Who did the fiery Kenyon crush,
> Confounded Harding, soften'd Lee,
> And made the face of Cooper blush.
>
> Conduct him Howorth o'er the lea,
> Do thou his tottering footsteps guide,
> Young Hal of Monmouth shalt thou be,
> And he be Falstaff by thy side.[21]

This testament to the blunting powers of alcohol upon Edward Bearcroft KC, FRS, one of the sharpest barristers of the day, was no doubt widely circulated at the time. Bearcroft bided his time in extracting his revenge, but the opportunity would arrive, as we shall see, for him to insert his forensic knives, supported not by Henry Howorth, but by 'crush'd' Lloyd Kenyon, at Wrexham in 1783 and by 'blushing' Cowper at Shrewsbury the following year.

Jones's poem should be juxtaposed not only with his *chansons à boire* and his self-exculpating comments on drinking, but with the fascinating detail, provided by Plumer's diary, that handsome young John 'Bloom' Williams 'got drunk, and behaved so ill that Jones proposed his expulsion' from the Druids. Williams's infringement of professional etiquette was forgiven by an apology, but such incidents reveal the problems inherent in being a temperate composer of drinking songs. Jones's guarded socializing with roaring barristers can be viewed within the wider context of his balancing of self-interest, and moral and political principle in his relationships with the dissolute Medmenham 'monks' Sandwich and Wilkes.

He was gaining both a reputation and an education from the circuits, learning as much about human nature from his colleagues as his clients. As he wrote from Worcester on the Oxford circuit to Samuel Parr in the summer of 1779: 'Whether the ἀριστεία [prize for arguing most causes] has been assigned to me in Wales I know not; but the knowledge of men which I have acquired in my short forensic career, has made me satisfied with my present station, and all my φιλοτιμία [ambition] is at end' (*Letters*, 1: 303). If this sounds not a little disingenuous, by the spring of 1782, having been awarded the ἀριστεία on several circuits, he was boasting to his Atticus in a letter from Cardigan of 'so much money I can hardly count it' (*Letters*, 2: 525). Only a few lines later, Jones attacks his colleagues as mercenary: 'I am delighted with my profession but disgusted with the professors, very few have any

---

21. NLW, *The Poetical Works of Sir William Jones*, 2 vols (London, 1810).

publick principle or any view but that of exposing to sale in the best markets their faculties and their voices' (*Letters*, 2: 525).

Though there was ambivalence, there was little hypocrisy in Jones's position. His growing reputation as counsel allowed him to salt wealthy farmers in their mundane land-based equity causes, while picking up some of the more dramatic or complex briefs where his skills were more fully tested in defence of the oppressed. On the circuits he saw how the Waltham Black Act, originally an emergency measure to deal with the poaching of game from royal parks, had made more than fifty former misdemeanours punishable by death, making a total of over 200 offences capital within the 'Bloody Code' of retributive justice. From Shrewsbury in the spring of 1780 he wrote of the 'very sanguinary' nature of many of the criminal laws, recommending Althorp to attempt some 'mitigation of their severity' when he took his seat in parliament. At Worcester on the Oxford circuit he had been powerless to intervene in a case of infanticide:

> [A] girl was hanged for strangling her bastard: she had been seduced on a solemn promise of marriage. How much more deserving of death was her seducer! how powerful must the sense of shame be, that can so far prevail over the strong affections of a mother! and how unnatural (for the truth must not be concealed) are our manners which annex the idea of shame to the increase of the human species! (*Letters*, 1: 350)

Unrolling the tightly bound parchment of the Indictment Files of the Oxford circuit, one can discover only the cold official details of the sad story of Susannah Grigg from Dudley who, on St Valentine's day 1780, gave birth to a female bastard in a privy: 'not having the fear of God before her Eyes but being moved and seduced by the Instigation of the Devil [...] she did choake and strangle it'.[22] There is a profound and telling distance between the humanity of Jones's reflections upon the unnatural weight of the psychosocial pressures upon this girl and the stark legal record of her unnatural deed—as great as that between her real and imagined seducers.

The following spring at Haverfordwest a similar dread of social disgrace was a key feature in one of Jones's causes. Sexual shame was exacerbated here by the imputation of poisoning, widely regarded as the most odious homicide in its premeditation. On 12 April 1781, he defended George Williams of St Issells parish in east Pembrokeshire, a married man and collier

---

22. National Archives, ASSI 5/100/18, Worcestershire Lent Assizes, 1780.

by trade, charged with the murder of Sarah Powell from the same parish. The prosecution had been brought by her father, John Powell, also a St Issells collier. Jones provides an account of the legal arguments he had employed to Althorp:

> I was counsel for a man indicted for *poisoning* a woman: the evidence was 'that she was pregnant by him, and that he gave her a potion, *intended to procure an abortion*, which operated so strongly that it killed her.' This would clearly have been murder; but there was great reason to believe, that she took the medicine voluntarily and knowingly, *intending to procure an abortion*: this, I contended, was self-murder in the unhappy girl, and that the prisoner, who furnished her with the drug, was only an *accessory before* the fact, and must therefore be acquitted on an indictment as *principal*. (*Letters*, 2: 467)

Jones omits the gruesome scientific results of a post-mortem upon the body of Sarah Powell, exhumed from St Issells churchyard, and conducted upon a table in the church in the presence of several family members. Examination of stomach contents revealed that the unfortunate girl had swallowed a quantity of powdered glass and iron rust mixed with treacle; it is recorded that she took several days to die.[23]

Jones's successful defence of Williams was made in the immediate wake of one of the most notorious poisoning trials of the century, that of Captain John 'Diamond' Donellan (his ring displayed an enormous Golconda gem acquired as an EIC officer), master of ceremonies at the fashionable Pantheon assembly rooms in Oxford Street. Donellan was charged with the murder of his brother-in-law, twenty-year-old Sir Theodosius Boughton, to gain control of the estate. Leading prosecuting counsel at Warwick Assizes was Jones's Oxford-circuit colleague Henry Howorth, while another friend, surgeon John Hunter, expert witness for the defence, suggested that evidence of poisoning from a post-mortem ten days after death was unreliable. Unfortunately neither the eminent Hunter nor anyone else noted that the indictment specified arsenic, although Donellan was accused of distilling laurel leaves, which would have produced cyanide. Jones thought the conviction safe, hoping Donellan's 'only motive for denying his guilt to the last [he was hanged at Warwick on 2 April] was a tender regard to his children, whom the idea of his crime must always make very unhappy' (*Letters*, 2: 465).

---

23. NLW, MS 4 Wales 821/5; Gaol Files.

This 'society' murder attracted enormous public interest with exhaustive press coverage and at least six detailed accounts of the trial published within weeks. It was a long way, geographically and socially, from Jones's Pembrokeshire poisoning and the issue of a collier's guilt or innocence. In Warwick, Jones tells Althorp, 'three shorthand writers were in court': in Wales there were no newspapers in English or Welsh. For us this is frustrating, for Jones the legal plaudits were inevitably local and unrecorded, but it would appear that the Haverfordwest proceedings were conducted with as much rigour as the Midland circuit trial of Donellan, under the full glare of public gaze. If anything, the post-mortem seems to have been handled with a greater efficiency in St Issells church.

These modern forensic procedures give the lie to Henry Brougham's indictment of the Welsh judicature as 'the worst that was ever established'. Brougham's 'Recollections of a Deceased Welsh Judge' reveals the patronizing attitudes towards Welsh justice and Welsh intelligence enlisted in the cause of the abolition of the circuits of Wales. He refers to an absurd attempt to identify the infanticide mother following the discovery of the body of a newborn child 'in a certain parish in Cardiganshire'. The magistrates ordered every woman between the ages of fourteen and fifty living within a ten-mile radius to be medically examined. Over a hundred attended and when one woman protested, the surgeon 'attempted a forcible examination'. She successfully brought an action for assault, 'and the mother of the child remained undiscovered'.[24]

This apocryphal account substantiates nothing more than an age-old attempt to extract humour at the expense of the Welsh, its staleness underlined by the fact that Brougham's targets: 'the excessive stupidity of the people, both witnesses and jurors', their trifling disputes and litigiousness, were commonplaces of anti-Welsh (and indeed anti-Hindu) satire. Brougham even trots out an ancient anecdote of a 'jury which, after hearing a trial for sheep-stealing, [. . .] brought in [. . .] a safe verdict *of manslaughter!*', citing it as absurd example of linguistic misunderstanding rather than socio-cultural solidarity in the face of sanguinary laws that made sheep-stealing a capital offence.[25] Chancellor Brougham pretends to have ridden the Welsh circuits to contrast the 'clear air and fine scenery' with the benighted ignorance of its inhabitants for his own ethnocentric, political, and juridical purposes.

24. *The Law Review and Quarterly Journal of British and Foreign Jurisprudence*, 4 (May 1846), 46–51; 47.
25. Cf. E. B. [?Elias Bockett], A *Trip to North-Wales: Being a Description of that Country and People* (London, 1701), 5.

A reforming humanitarian liberal, his narrative nevertheless reveals pervasive prejudice.

Undermining ethnocentricities and the binary oppositions that structure racism was what Jones was about as an Orientalist. As a practising lawyer and comparative jurist, riding the Carmarthen circuit facilitated his acculturation, enabling him to come to terms with his own ethnic hybridity. He opened himself to the otherness of Wales only to discover it was part of himself. With one foot firmly planted in the dominant metropolitan culture, he empathized with his subaltern and marginalized Welsh countrymen. In 'my three counties' Jones experienced local and contingent aspects in the production of cultural and national identity, with the example of the sociolinguistic contrast between south and north Pembrokeshire mirroring the north/south divide in the Principality as a whole.

Jones admired the social cohesion of agricultural labourer and artisan in the face of endemic rural poverty, and found in their fierce independence a reflection of his own. This finding was a chastening one when he contemplated how very much greater was their struggle to achieve it. He appreciated their warmth: their vulnerability he might try to protect. Many of his country clients had little idea they were being represented by a metropolitan celebrity, but they shrewdly noted his skill as an advocate and valued his lack of condescension. Jones's mastery of jurisprudence, which he regarded as 'reducible to a few plain *elements*', allowed this born communicator to speak with simple authority: 'I found a retainer for a man of this town, who is to be tried for murder: if his account of the affair be true, I shall save his life' (*Letters*, 2: 499). The firmness of his belief that law is a science and not a self-generating mystery inspired confidence.

If Wales proved a 'contact zone' for his radical acculturation, opportunities for a reciprocal transculturation were offered both by his professional dedication to the defence of individual liberty and his widely circulated political ideas. In this way Jones, together with figures such as Richard Price, and the deist, educator, and universalist, David Williams, were linking Wales with metropolitan and international spheres of oppositional radicalism. Rational Dissent might accomplish more for Wales than the fatalistic acceptance taught by the profoundly conservative leaders of the Methodist Revival with all their moralizing and evangelizing vigour.

In his movement between centre and periphery and familiarity with London–Welsh societies Jones found that many of the staunchest Welsh patriots were in fact expatriates. Religious revivalism was encouraging circulating schools in Wales, but when might come the great cultural awakening of sleeping bards and national identity? With some notable exceptions, few of the resident gentry families, however polished or accomplished, took even a polite interest in the language or culture of the tenants who farmed their lands, paid their rents, and sat in their pews. In 1781, Evan Evans, attending a service in St David's Cathedral, was surprised and saddened to find it performed in English in so remote a corner: 'I suppose our clergy think that the vulgar have no souls, just as we are taught by travellers that the Turks suppose of the ladies. No great inducement to either to behave well.'[26] As St David's was a stronghold of staunch High Church Anglicanism this was unsurprising. More disturbing was Evans's lament to Lewis Morris that the Celtic Revival was being frustrated by the Celtophobe hostility of Anglophone Welsh bishops who 'look upon me with an evil eye, because I dare have affection for my country, language, and antiquities, which, in their opinion, had better been lost and forgotten, and which some of them have had the front to maintain in their sermons'.[27]

Amongst the mountains of Trecastle in the spring of 1781 Jones penned his 'Ode to Alcæus', defining the state as: 'Men, high-minded men,/With pow'rs as far above dull brutes endued/In forest, brake, or den/As beasts excel cold rocks and brambles rude.' Despite the defiant radicalism, Jones recognized that men, even the highest-minded men, like the most talented poets, need patrons. Two years earlier Evan Evans stood with Druid-democrat Iolo Morganwg at Gwernyclepa, near Basaleg, amidst the brambled ruins of the court of Ifor ap Llewelyn (Ifor Hael), the celebrated patron of Dafydd ap Gwilym. In powerfully wrought *englynion*, the oldest Welsh metres, in the consonantal chiming of *cynghanedd*, Evans mourned the decline of Welsh bardism and the ancient patronage system that maintained it:

> Llys Ifor Hael! gwael yw'r gwedd,—yn garnau
> Mewn gwerni mae'n gorwedd;
> Drain ac ysgall mall a'i medd,
> Mieri, lle bu mawredd.

---

26. NLW, MS 5497, Letter of Evans to Benjamin Davies, 18 June 1781.
27. *Gwaith y Parchedig Evan Evans*, p.182. Morris replied: 'What can you expect from Bis–ps or any officers ignorant of a Language which they get their living by, and which they ought to Cultivate instead of proudly despising. If an Indian acted thus, we would be apt to Call him Barbarous. But a Sc–t or Sax–n is above Correction', *Additional Letters of the Morrises*, 2: 623.

Yno nid oes awenydd—na beirddion
Na byrddau llawenydd,
Nac aur yn ei magwyrydd,
Na mael, na gwr hael a'i rhydd.[28]

[Ifor Hael's court, wretched sight,
A ruined pile amidst the alders.
Thorns and thistles inhabit there,
And bramble where once was majesty.

No Bard is there, no poets,
No feasting tables,
Nor gold inside these walls,
No bounty, no free-handed generosity.]

The single recorded meeting of Jones and Evans was at Carmarthen in the spring of 1779; the barrister was on circuit and the curate was learning Hebrew and Arabic at the Presbyterian Academy. When Evans's patron, Sir Watkin Williams Wynn, of Wynnstay and St James's Square, heard of this apparent neglect of Welsh studies, he withdrew Evans's pension of twenty pounds a year, proving that he was no Ifor Hael.[29] Yet Wynn was vice-president of the Society of Antient Britons, second president of the Cymmrodorion (the first, by contrast having been Lewis Morris's brother Richard, an £80 per annum Navy Office clerk), and co-founder with Lord Sandwich of the Concert of Ancient Music; could his patronage be impugned? Had he not appeared in a Ranelagh masquerade dressed as a Druid in 1770? In fact that year marked his coming of age and the Wynnstay celebrations cost over £1,600. The self-indulgent extravagance of this patron ran up enormous debts; consequently his land agents gained a tyrannical reputation as they racked the poor tenantry.

Evans describes Jones as 'gwr mwyn a rhadlon' (a gentle and gracious man), and Jones gave him an address to correspond. Evans's seminal *Antient Welsh Bards* had been encouraged by the interest of Thomas Gray, a long and mutually beneficial dialogue with Thomas Percy, and the negotiations of the antiquarian, Daines Barrington, with Dodsley, its publisher. It brought him scholarly prestige, the approbation of Samuel Johnson, but only twenty pounds. Ieuan Fardd spent his whole life in the service of Welsh culture, a perpetual thirty-pound-a-year curate, unable to obtain a living. Bishop Percy

---

28. *Gwaith y Parchedig Evan Evans*, 51–2.
29. *Gwaith y Parchedig Evan Evans*, 247.

and Johnson attempted to recommend Evans but had no acquaintance with the bishop of St Davids.

Jones's extensive connections might have provided invaluable help: the pluralist bishop of St Asaph was almost his father-in-law; Percy was his Turk's Head companion; Justice Daines Barrington, a Welsh-circuit colleague; Sir Roger Mostyn invited Jones to dinner whereas Evans only aspired to the library. The circuiteer in his chaise and the footsore indigent curate moved in different worlds, but a correspondence between a prime mover of the Celtic Revival and a facilitator of Oriental Renaissance would doubtless have proved mutually enlightening. Jones could have perfected Evans's Semitic studies while investigating the poets of the Welsh princes. What might the Druid have achieved in Celtic researches had the riches of Indian employment and culture not beckoned?

As it was, the opportunities presented by a chance Carmarthen meeting were lost. Evans returned to a damp room at Aberystwyth which imperilled both his precious manuscripts and his fragile health; Jones repaired to his 'very good lodgings' to study briefs and finalize plans for a Whitsun trip to see Benjamin Franklin in Paris. Though Jones's self-imposed regime was a punishing one, his 'lines and life' knew a freedom of which Evans, self-condemned to trudge the byways of Wales rescuing parchment from oblivion, could only dream.

Liberty is a relative term and there was damper accommodation in west Wales. In the same year that Mary Morgan was mixing with the *haut monde* in the Assembly Rooms, Edward Daniel Clarke, a fresh-faced Cambridge graduate who had distinguished himself at Jesus College by constructing and launching a balloon, was also visiting Haverfordwest with his pupil, the Hon. Henry Tufton. Having ordered their supper, they discovered a few steps from their inn: 'a place of confinement; but so barricadoed, and so miserable in its aspect, that I conceived it to be a receptacle for wild beasts'.[30] Within they discerned a man in a dishevelled naval uniform, attempting to read by the dim light that penetrated a tiny double grated window: 'Gentlemen, (said he) you see here an unfortunate officer of the navy, who, for a trifling debt, has suffered five months imprisonment in this abominable dungeon; without any support but from the benevolence of strangers and the uncertain charity of a few among the inhabitants, denied

---

30. *Edward Daniel Clarke, A Tour through the South of England, Wales, and Part of Ireland, made During the Summer of 1791* (London, 1793), 235.

even water to gratify his thirst, unless he can raise a halfpenny to pay for it, and condemned to linger here without a prospect of release.'

His name was Lieutenant G[riffi]th of HMS *Trimmer* who had been ashore when it sailed in pursuit of some smugglers, and the brig-sloop having failed to return, he had been forced to take lodgings in the town. The financial failure of his agent in Liverpool resulted in his inability to pay a 'paltry tavern-bill' and his prosecution by a pitiless landlady. Young Clarke, who was shortly to be appointed tutor to the son of Jones's friend, Sir Roger Mostyn, was so appalled by the fate of Lieutenant Griffith, who claimed to have 'accompanied Captain Cook in his navigations', that he called down shame upon the Aldermen of Haverfordwest who 'could not spare the price of one dinner, to relieve a fellow-creature in distress'.[31]

Imprisoned in a castle dungeon, Griffith was a victim of a Tudor statute (34–5 Henry VIII, cap. 26), which by oversight had not been repealed in Wales by the General Insolvent Act; consequently, as Richard Foley, the Secondary of the Carmarthen circuit, pointed out, 'an unfortunate debtor in Wales may be imprisoned for life for ever so small a debt, as the law now stands'. The *Analytical Review* insisted upon urgent action: 'This ruinous practice, by which the body of a debtor in Wales may be kept in perpetual bondage by a litigious and inhuman creditor, for a fractional part of a pound sterling, demands the immediate interposition of the legislature.'[32]

Although this was a matter for the inferior county court, it seems strange that Jones, with his extensive experience of working with debtors as both a Commissioner of Bankrupts and in his collaboration with Lady Spencer in the Society for Charitable Purposes, appears to have made no mention of this appalling legal injustice. It was exactly the kind of ancient infringement upon basic human liberty that he had been determined to eradicate. Jones's *Speeches of Isaeus Concerning the Law of Succession to Property in Athens* (1779), *Essay on the Law of Bailments* (1781), and *The Mahomedan Law of Succession to the Property of Intestates* (1782) had established him as a pioneering comparative lawyer, but here was a substantial and inequitable difference between the proceedings of the county courts of Wales and those of England that had apparently escaped his notice. It is also puzzling that on his regular visits to Haverfordwest Jones had not commented on gaol conditions that had appalled the philanthropist and

---

31. A 'J. Griffith' appears in the complement of the *Endeavour*; BL Add. MSS 27,885: logbook of Lieut. James Cook; 12 Feb.–23 Sept. 1770.
32. *Analytical Review*, 12 (March 1792), 279–82; 282.

prisoner reformer John Howard in an August 1774 visit: 'The two lowest are very Damp dungeons: in one of these, as I was informed, a prisoner lost, first the use of his limbs, then his life.'[33]

In India, Jones would continue to espouse the cause of insolvent debtors, frequently dedicating the profits from his publications to their use. As judge he also advocated improvement in prison design, making frequent unannounced or incognito visits to the gaols of Calcutta. From the Sundarbans in February 1785 Jones wrote to his friend, Prime Minister William Pitt, requesting him to insert a special clause in his next India bill for the relief of insolvent debtors, condemned by the high cost of solicitors' fees to languish for indeterminate years in unhealthy incarceration: 'A prison in Europe has enough of horror; but a place of close confinement in this climate must be worse than the worst dungeon in our western world' (*Letters*, 2: 661).

For now he was, both at Westminster and on circuit, studying ancient Ricardian statutes and the courts' complacency at their modern misuse for political ends. He was engrossed in a battle to prove the illegality of press-warrants, and the disturbing aftermath of a case at Haverfordwest confirmed his need to fight for 'the laws and liberties of our country'.

---

33. John Howard, *The State of the Prisons in England and Wales* (Warrington, 1777), 465.

4

Impressive Patrons and Impressing Mariners

In the evening of 12 April 1781 Jones writes to Althorp from his inn hard by Haverfordwest Castle, its dungeons recently converted into the new county gaol. Though exhausted after a long day in the Guildhall, he is still fuming about the illegality of impressment:

> [A] verdict being found for a client of mine against a military man, the unsuccessful party stood ready with a press-gang, and pressed the victor coming out of court, tho' he was no more a seaman than I am, nor so much: now had this man been unable to write, or had he found no one to convey his letter to me, he would have been sent on board the tender, and might have been in the Cove of Corke or in the straight course to America in a short time. I procured his enlargement, and an attachment against all persons concerned in this outrage. Be assured my dear lord (I speak coolly and deliberately) that, while the *illegal* power of pressing subsists, the peasantry of Britain are no more free than the people of Constantinople or Morocco. It is only a base mode of exercising cruel tyranny and of saving a large sum of money (which a *register of mariners* would certainly cost) in order to make the legislative part of government as bad as the executive. Pardon me, I cannot bear this oppression; nor can I reconcile it to my conscience to suppress much longer my argument proving to demonstration the illegality of press-warrants. Lord Sandwich may complain, and his fair nieces may rally me as much as they please; but a citizen must do his duty and what higher duty is there to than to preserve the laws and liberties of our country? (*Letters*, 2: 467–8)

This letter from the most westerly county of Wales, with its references to the fraught situation further west across the Atlantic and the incipient dangers of eastern despotism, situates 'Asiatic' Jones as defender of British liberty threatened by royal navy impressment. He saved his client from being shackled in the hold of a naval tender, but there are more subtle species of enslavement. Jones displays a proud Celtic aversion to the chains of his own dependence in negotiating the intricate network of interconnected patronage systems.

Jones's mention of John Montagu, fourth earl of Sandwich, and 'his fair nieces', the daughters of Kelland Courtenay of Powderham Castle: Anne, Lady Cork, and her sister Isabella, who had married Jones's friend, William Poyntz, reminds us of how 'the Great World' of 'the twice two thousand', as Byron described it, seems considerably smaller in the eighteenth century. These Courtenay nieces were cousins to William ('Kitty'), 3rd Viscount Courtenay with whom William Beckford was to have a scandalous affair. The hedonistic Orientalist *manqué* Beckford was introduced to Jones by Lady Craven. His coming-of-age celebrations at Fonthill Splendens that Christmas—courtesy of slave-plantation sugar—cost £40,000, more than might have facilitated Jones's Indian dream of independence. The Poyntz family was interlinked with the Spencers—Countess Spencer was a Poyntz. The Shipleys were related to the Spencers. Bluestocking Elizabeth Montagu, who loved Jones's poetry, was related by marriage to Lord Sandwich. Jones moved skilfully within intricate high society circles, but the strain was sometimes apparent.

Why should Lord Sandwich complain about Jones's attempts to prove the illegality of press-warrants? He was First Lord of the Admiralty and naval reliance upon impressment to man its ships had dramatically increased during the American War of Independence. Sandwich's irritation mattered because of his extremely powerful voting interests at India House. Three years earlier Jones had written of his 'Indian scheme': 'My success will depend wholly on lord North and lord Sandwich' (*Letters*, 1: 268). Jones learned that Sandwich told Lady Cork and Mrs Poyntz 'that he had heard I was a *violent patriot*' (*Letters*, 1: 301). Sandwich was a key player in EIC politics, in tune with North's thinking concerning Indian affairs; his patronage might prove decisive if Jones was ever to obtain the Calcutta judgeship.

This simple clash of prospects versus principles was complicated by the fact that the issue of naval impressment had brought Jones closer to Sandwich's former friend and fellow Medmenham Hell Fire Club member—now bitter enemy—the radical John Wilkes. Politics and ambition trapped libertarian Jones between these two dynamic libertines: Admiralty Sandwich and Liberty Wilkes.

Everyone knew the celebrated story of how these two friends had quarrelled. During a drunken Medmenham orgy, Sandwich was persuaded to invoke the devil; with immaculate timing Wilkes released from a box an Indian baboon, which jumped on Sandwich's back, reducing him to a paroxysm of terror.[1] Should Jones cultivate the devil-raiser of the East India Company or the monkey-handler's Phrygian cap?

Sandwich displayed ruthless political skill in exploiting sexual scandal to bring down his fellow libertine, the popular demagogue, John Wilkes. On 15 November 1763, while Wilkes's notorious 45th issue of the *North Briton* was being censured as seditious libel in the Commons, Sandwich read choice extracts from Wilkes's privately printed, obscene, and blasphemous *Essay on Woman* to an unusually receptive House of Lords. The following evening Sandwich attended Gay's *The Beggar's Opera* at Covent Garden and at Macheath's words: 'That Jemmy Twitcher should peach me I own surprised me', the audience erupted. In a spontaneous reapplication of political satire Sandwich gained the ineradicable nickname of 'Twitcher' for his hypocritical betrayal.

The mysterious moral scourge 'Junius', whose elegant oppositional letters were widely thought to have been written by Jones himself, labelled Sandwich 'the most profligate character in the kingdom'. Warming to his excoriation, Junius continues: 'To talk of morals or devotion in such company is a scandalous insult to common sense, and a still more scandalous mockery of religion.'[2] Yet Jones found Sandwich fascinating company. Augmenting the conventional Grand Tour, he had travelled in Turkey and the Near East. In 1741, with antiquarian William Stukeley (who labelled Jones's father a heathen), Sandwich was founding 'Grand Sheik' of the Egyptian Society for the preservation of antiquities, which boasted the scholarly traveller Richard Pococke as secretary. But the Orientalist Sandwich was always lavishly filled with libertinism. He was 'Vizier' of the Divan Club where Ottoman-travellers, including the rakish privy councillor, Sir Francis Dashwood, adorned in Turkish finery and jewelled turbans, cavorted with their harem. Their red morocco minute book, blasphemously inscribed 'Al Koran', records that Fanny Murray, dedicatee of Wilkes's *Essay on Woman*, was painted for the society in Oriental costume revealing her left breast.

---

1. Sent from Calcutta by Henry Vansittart, Governor of Bengal, the baboon was a gift for his brother Robert, who presented it to the society.
2. Letter of 17 January 1771; *Junius*, ed. John Wade, 2 vols (London, 1865), 2: 334–5.

Understandably, morally upright Jones had mixed feelings concerning 'Jemmy Twitcher':

> Lord Sandwich appears to me a wonderfully pleasant man in society; he is quite what the French call *aimable*, and possesses in a high degree the art of putting all around him at their ease. I never saw so much of him before: I like his conversation and his musick, but I fear that his politicks and ours would not make good harmony. Next Sunday I shall probably dine with him; but you know me too well, my dear lord, to imagine that my principles and sentiments can be altered by the company and conversation of ministers, on whom I never obtrude my own opinions, but always give them openly, when I am called upon.   (*Letters* 1: 338)

We know that at this particular Admiralty dinner, Jones had enthusiastically joined Sandwich and all his guests' 'triumphing in the favourable intelligence brought from Russia concerning our great navigator'. By the following week the copious toasts seemed sadly ironic as news reached London that James Cook, together with four of his marines, had been killed by Hawaiians in Kealakekua Bay the previous February. It was Sandwich who had appointed Cook to lead the Royal Society expedition of 1768–71, and the grateful commander named islands in the southern Atlantic and in paradisical Hawaii after his patron. Extending astronomical research and discovery, the *Endeavour* voyage established the international reputation of Jones's friend, Linnaean naturalist Joseph Banks, who was obliged to Sandwich for permission to join the expedition. The close bonds between naturalist and Admiralty lord were forged in London clubs and high-class brothels, but Sandwich, committed to scientific discovery as enhancing the royal navy's standing, knew the intellectual worth of his fellow carouser.

Sandwich represents a remarkable symbiosis of connoisseur, profligate, musician, and scientist. This 'Medmenham Monk', who lent his name to a speedy gaming-table snack, was a key facilitator of the Enlightenment union of research science and naval exploration. So, when dining at the Admiralty, Jones occasionally forgot that sections of the second edition of a book written at the instigation of Prime Minister Lord North—Charles Butler's *The Legality of Impressing Seamen* (1777)—were authored by Sandwich. Impressment was controlled by the Admiralty whose First Lord endorsed Butler's opinion: a sailor should be grateful for a press-warrant, which 'snatches him from disease, from misery, or perhaps an ignominious death; the inseparable attendants of idleness, intemperance and bad company' (p. 54).

Jones was not the first scholar to deplore the illegality of press-warrants. In 1752 David Hume had condemned this 'illegal power [...] tacitly permitted in the crown'. Like Jones, Hume recommends a register of seamen, possessing a much higher opinion of British 'hearts of oak' than Butler or Sandwich:

> Liberty, in a country of the highest liberty, is left entirely to its own defence, without any countenance or protection: The wild state of nature is renew'd, in one of the most civiliz'd societies of mankind: And great violences and disorders, amongst the people, the most humane and the best natur'd, are committed with impunity.[3]

A quarter of a century later, the situation was manifestly worse; violences against the people increased with Recruiting Acts of 1778 and 1779, which extended impressment to the British army. In November 1779 Jones witnessed the results at the Society for Charitable Purposes:

> A poor old woman, whose case I have known these three or four years and whom I have from time to time relieved, called here this morning with a fresh recital of her sorrows. Her son was pressed into land service (illegally, I believe, as he could have given a good account of himself) and he is now at Plymouth with his wife and an infant lately born and, by her account, must be dying. I have sent him a trifle, and will, if possible, procure his discharge; but his mother in the mean time is wholly destitute. (*Letters*, 1: 331)

With Lady Spencer's help, he procures temporary relief for this 'poor Welch woman'. By the new year Jones, through an application to the Duke of Rutland, a friend of Pitt and believer in reconciliation with America, obtained the discharge of her son, 'who will, if he recovers, be able to maintain his aged parent as well as his own little family'.

Individual intervention, backed by influential aristocratic connections, might achieve much, but the source of the injustice remained unassailed. Such was the dread of impressment that cases were reported of agricultural and industrial labourers mutilating themselves, usually by cutting off their right thumb and forefinger. Ironically these Recruiting Acts were designed to encourage volunteer enlistment; their success was limited and they were repealed in 1780. By contrast, naval press gangs were operating ever more blatantly.

---

3. David Hume, *Political Discourses* (Edinburgh, 1752), 153–4.

Despite Admiralty commitments, Sandwich found time for leisure pursuits. As news arrived of the British army's evacuation of Boston, and empire seemed to be unravelling, he was fly-fishing on the Kennet. In early May 1776 at an inn near Newbury, Hume encountered the fervently anti-American lord of the bedchamber, Lord Denbigh, who declared: 'that he, Lord Sandwich, Lord Mulgrave, Mr Banks, and two or three Ladies of Pleasure, had pass'd five or six Days there, and intended to pass all this Week and the next in the same Place; [...] Lord Sandwich in particular had caught Trouts near twenty inches long, which gave him incredible Satisfaction'.

As Hume reflected to his close friend, the publisher and MP for Malmesbury, William Strahan:

> That the First Lord of the Admiralty, who is absolute and uncontrouled Master in his Department, shou'd at a time when the Fate of the British Empire is in dependence, and in dependence on him, find so much Leizure, Tranquillity, Presence of Mind and Magnanimity, as to have Amusement in trouting during three Weeks near sixty Miles from the scene of Business, and during the most critical Season of the Year. There needs but this single Fact to decide the Fate of the Nation. What an Ornament would it be in a future History to open the glorious Events of the ensuing Year with the Narrative of so singular an incident.[4]

Indeed; and three of these philandering fishermen were good friends of the irreproachable Jones! Captain Constantine Phipps, Lord Mulgrave, was appointed by the Admiralty in 1773 to discover a northern route to the Pacific. His report, *A Voyage towards the North Pole* (1774), revealed that—like Banks, his schoolfellow—he was a serious research scientist as well as a man of action, exactly the kind of figure to win Jones's admiration.

Jones frequently dined with Mulgrave and they kept in touch even when Jones left for Bengal. Conveniently, Mulgrave became Commissioner for Indian Affairs in 1784, and on 6 January 1788, from Calcutta, Jones wrote to Banks of his plan to send Mulgrave 'a beautiful royal Tiger, as gentle as a Spaniel, who was nursed by a She-Goat in my house' (*Letters*, 2: 786).

Jones was moving amongst statesmen and heroes of science and empire; although he shared Hume's disgust, the 'clubbable' celebrity barrister accepted that many of his friends were more enamoured with libertinism than libertarianism. These were impressive men whose company might—

---

4. Hume to William Strahan, 10 May 1776; *The Letters of David Hume*, ed. J. Y. T. Greig, 2 vols (Oxford, 1932), 2: 318–19.

temporarily—divert his mind from naval impressment. Jones's personal reluctance to angle in the depths of the *demi-monde* did not prevent his secretly relishing any such piscatorial dilution of the war effort against the rebel colonists he so admired.

Music parties were more to Jones's taste and here again Sandwich was in the cultural vanguard *and* mired in scandal. In the year of America's Declaration of Independence he founded—together with Sir Watkin Williams Wynn, President of the Honourable Society of Cymmrodorion—the Concert of Ancient Music. Sandwich's private secretary was Joah Bates, organist, conductor, and outstanding Handelian.

Sandwich earlier inaugurated The Catch Club at his grand Tudor pile, Hinchingbrooke House, near Huntingdon, but Jones learned from Banks that Sandwich's most egregious catch was the beautiful 17-year-old Martha Ray, whom he first saw working in a shop in Tavistock Street. His purchases that day amounted to more than the silk cravats he had been examining. The debauched Sandwich paid £400, with an annuity of £30, to Martha's parents to purchase their 'daughter's honour' and body.[5] Such was Jones's '*aimable*' Sandwich and, if naval impressment rendered 'the peasantry of Britain [...] no more free than the people of Constantinople or Morocco', this commercial pressing of a young girl by 'Sheik' Montagu mirrored the worst excesses of Asiatic sexual despotism.

Discovering that Martha also had an exquisite voice, it received the best training from Joah Bates and the celebrated Italian composer Felice Giardini. Soon regarded as one of the finest singers of her generation, she transformed Sandwich's elaborate Christmas concerts at Hinchingbrooke, which Banks and Mulgrave urged Jones to attend.

Writing to Althorp on New Year's Day 1774 from Emmanuel College Cambridge, where he was immersed in legal manuscripts, Jones mentions that many mutual friends have 'gone to Hinchinbrook, where lord Sandwich is entertaining the county and the University with Musick for a whole week; he has Giardini with him, and Leone, the Jew [Myer Leoni, German operatic tenor], who is said to have a wonderfully fine voice; I have been pressed to go to these Oratorios, but have my hands, as usual, so full of work, that Orpheus himself could hardly tempt me to leave college' (*Letters*, 1: 139).

But others were tempted, not least by Ray's bravura performances of delightful airs such as 'Brighter scenes I seek above', from Handel's *Jephtha*.

---

5. *Westminster Magazine*, 7 (April 1779), 171.

The following year a young ensign, James Hackman, engaged on recruitment business, was invited to dinner at Hinchingbrooke. He became erotically obsessed by Ray, but when his regiment was sent to Ireland, her reluctance to leave a life of luxury to take up a knapsack led to his resigning his commission. Exchanging his red coat for a black one, Hackman became ordained as an Anglican deacon to facilitate his pursuit of her. The Tahitian Omai, being fêted by Banks and Sandwich, discovered the lovers together at Hinchingbrooke.

On the evening of 7 April 1779, Ray, together with mezzo-soprano Caterina Galli, attended a production of Isaac Bickerstaff's *Love in a Village* at Covent Garden. The jealous Hackman, who had been downing brandy at the Bedford Coffee House opposite, seeing her being handed into her coach after the performance, rushed up to her, and without saying a word, put a bullet in her head. The frenzied Hackman turned his other pistol on himself but at an insufficient angle, managing only to inflict a head wound. Falling beside his murdered love, he had to be restrained from beating his skull with the butts of both pistols.

At the Old Bailey Jones witnessed his sentencing by Mr Justice Blackstone; James Boswell, who had a taste for such things, saw Hackman 'turned off' at Tyburn on 19 April. Sandwich was distracted. Martha Ray had borne him nine children, one of whom was Basil Montagu, later the friend of Samuel Parr, William Godwin, Mary Wollstonecraft, Wordsworth, Coleridge, Southey, and Lamb.

Shortly after Jones dined with Sandwich early in 1780, everyone was reading Sir Herbert Croft's anonymously published *Love and Madness: A Story too True in a Series of Letters* (1780), which went into seven editions. The Ray–Hackman letters were fiction, but Croft's scandalously opportunistic epistolary novel contained the genuine letters of Thomas Chatterton. Written shortly before the 17-year-old poet's death in London on 24 August 1770 from an overdose of laudanum, Croft duplicitously obtained them from the poet's mother in Bristol in 1778. Chatterton's 'medieval' Rowley poems went into posthumous editions in 1778 and 1779 and, while the controversy concerning their authenticity was raging in literary London, Croft's novel presents Martha Ray encouraging Hackman to investigate Chatterton's works. If Croft's tasteless publication embarrassed the grieving Sandwich, its smoke and mirrors technique of simultaneously revealing and disguising forgery intensely irritated the scholarly Jones.

Following intense discussions at the Turk's Head, Jones, together with Thomas Percy and Oliver Goldsmith, visited Chatterton's lodging house in Brooke Street, Holborn, to conduct his own investigations. Jones revealed his opinion to Walter Pollard and Thomas Maurice: Chatterton invented 'a jargon of every species of dialect, ancient and modern, of every age and date'.[6] Maurice communicated Jones's findings to Croft who plagiarized them in *Love and Madness*.

Turning from the scandalous Sandwich to the 'scandalous father of civil liberty', in 1768 Jones described Wilkes as a man 'of energy and intelligence, but a trouble-maker and a sort of fire-brand to light the flames of sedition' (*Letters*, 1: 10). By the following February, as Wilkes's political career became united with the concept of liberty in the popular imagination, Middlesex freeholder Jones signed a pro-Wilkes petition. If this seems a curious volte face, Jones was not alone. In the Commons on 17 February, the day after Wilkes had again been returned for Middlesex, the strongest opposition to a motion: 'That John Wilkes, esq., having been expelled this House, was, and is, incapable of being elected a member to serve in this present parliament', came from two of Jones's friends: Sir George Savile and Earl Mulgrave. They, like Jones, were angered at parliament's flagrant disregard for the electorate, citing the Bill of Rights as enshrining the people's prerogative to petition the throne should Wilkes again face expulsion.

The fact that Wilkes was once more expelled led directly to the inauguration on 25 February 1769 of the Society of Gentlemen Supporters of the Bill of Rights to support the cause of Wilkes and the rights of freeholders to elect whom they chose. Although Jones was not a member, the Bill of Rights Society included men he respected: John Horne (Tooke), the radical philologist; reforming lawyers, such as Jones's mentor, John Dunning, and Wilkes's counsel, John Glynn; and radical politicians, James Townsend, Brass Crosby, and John Sawbridge, brother of republican historian Catharine Macaulay. Many of these men of vast legal and political expertise joined Major John Cartwright's Society for Constitutional Information, to which Jones was subsequently elected.

Throughout the early 1770s, Wilkes, his power base firmly in London, but pioneering nationwide popular politics, came to represent the very things Jones held dearest: the protection of the individual, his rights, and

---

6. Thomas Maurice, *Memoirs of the Author of Indian Antiquities*, 3 vols (London, 1819), 2: 156–7.

his property. Wilkes's fight against the arbitrary power of press-warrants brought Londoner and London Welshman into close political association. And in the Falkland Islands crisis the contrast between Jones's unlikely friends, Wilkes and Sandwich, was at its clearest.

The Spanish seizure in June 1770 of Britain's base at Port Egmont in the Falklands led directly to Sandwich's return to office as First Lord of the Admiralty (1771–82). The crisis dramatically increased the issue of press-warrants. Wilkes maintained that a press-warrant had no more validity than the general warrant used against him because it failed to specify the name of the individual upon whom it was served. This opinion received strong support from Judge Charles Pratt, first Earl Camden, and was fundamental to William Jones's thinking on the matter.

Both slavery and press-warrants were obnoxious to those who cherished traditions of liberty and these two evils intertwined their malicious tentacles in a trial that proved to be a fascinating forerunner to the landmark case of James Somerset, and encouraged the tireless abolitionist Granville Sharp to become a major force in the campaign against impressment.

In July 1770, Mrs Sarah Banks, mother of Joseph Banks, heard screams coming from the river at the foot of her garden at 22 Paradise Row, Chelsea. They were the cries of Thomas Lewis, an escaped black slave; his 'owner', Robert Stapylton, with the help of two burly watermen, was violently bundling him into a skiff. Sarah Banks contacted Sharp; a writ of habeas corpus was served upon the captain of the Jamaica-bound *Snow*, and Lewis was discovered 'chained to the mainmast, bathed in tears, and casting a last mournful look on the land of freedom'.[7]

On the morning of 19 February 1771 and the following day, while awaiting the trial of Stapylton, attempts were made to seize Lewis by a press gang 'employ'd by the opposite party'.[8] These attempts were foiled by representations 'to Mr Dunning, & to Lord Mansfield', but they emphasized the point that both Sharp and Jones were keen to stress: impressment was tantamount to enslavement.[9]

---

7. New York Historical Society, Sharp Papers, copies of letters received, 1763–73, MS Notebook on the Thomas Lewis case.
8. Diary entry of Elizabeth Prowse (Sharp's sister) for 20 February 1771, cited in E. C. P. Lascelles, *Granville Sharp and the Freedom of Slaves in England* (Oxford, 1928), 28.
9. See Granville Sharp, *An Address to the People of England: Being the Protest of a Private Person against every Suspension of Law* (London, 1778), 57.

At Stapylton's trial John Dunning held up Sharp's anti-slavery tract before Lord Mansfield and the King's Bench jury as he maintained that 'that no man can be legally detained as a slave in this country [...] our laws admit of no such property'.[10] The jury concurred, several of them crying out 'No property, no property!' Mansfield, aware of the enormous potential colonial repercussions, was reluctant to resolve this question.[11] Liberty was the predominant issue; the fundamental Lockean liberty that 'every Man has a property in his own Person'.

Within six months, on 3 December 1771, the trial of *Sommerset* v. *Steuart* came on at Westminster Hall. James Somerset was a black slave who, having been brought to England by his 'owner', Virginian planter Charles Steuart, had escaped only to be recaptured and shackled on board the Jamaica-bound *Ann and Mary* lying in the Thames. Sharp applied for a writ of habeas corpus, and Jones's friend, Francis Hargrave, volunteered his services as part of the legal team to represent Somerset. Hargrave, only recently called to the bar, provided a powerful, carefully researched argument, outshining serjeants John Glynn and William Davy, and amazing John Alleyne, his fellow junior, to convince the jury that no man could ever be a slave in England.[12] This was a splendid debut and one that Jones would have given his eye teeth to have made, but he would have to bide his time.

Jones realized that Mansfield's decision of 22 June 1772 had not in fact made slavery illegal in Britain for he had only ruled that common law recognized no power of a master to transport his slave out of Britain. Nevertheless there was cause for celebration that evening with Hargrave at Lincoln's Inn and at the party given by Francis Barber, Johnson's black manservant, in Johnson's Court. Yet even while they toasted the words of Somerset's counsel that English air is 'too pure for a slave to breathe in', the downwind stench of a slaver remained an indictment of British humanity.

Jones heard from Johnson the story of how, in 1759, believing that his dear servant Francis Barber, had been pressed, he had urged his friend Tobias Smollett (whose *Roderick Random* had vividly depicted the horrors of the press gang) to write to Wilkes in order to secure Barber's liberty from

---

10. *Memoirs of Granville Sharp, Esq*, 2 vols (London, 1828), 1: 81–2.
11. Mansfield actually remarked in open court: 'I don't know what the consequence may be, if the masters were to lose their property by accidentally bringing their slaves to England. I hope it never will be finally discussed; for I would have all masters think them free, and all Negroes think they were not, because then they would both behave better', *Memoirs of Granville Sharp*, 1: 91.
12. *An Argument in the Case of James Sommerset a Negro* (London, 1772).

the naval frigate *Stag*. Jones, whose father had served as a teacher of navigation on a man-of-war, did not share Johnson's view that a sailor's lot was inferior to that of a prisoner who has 'more room, better food, and commonly better company'. Johnson has acquired the reputation of being an opponent of press gangs, but Granville Sharp records an interview in which he was depressed to hear the great Cham describe impressment as 'a condition necessarily attending that way of life; and when they entered into it, they must take it with all its circumstances'.[13] Jones passionately believed that neither slave master nor press-gang officer should have power to transport men out of Britain against their will.

One dramatic case that highlighted the dreadful social consequences of impressment was that of Mary Jones, whose husband, William, fell yet another victim to a press gang at the time of the Falklands crisis. It is not recorded whether the tragic story of Mary's trial and execution in the autumn of 1771 impinged upon the young Middle Temple student who shared her husband's name and whose sister, like their mother, was another Mary Jones. We do know that our William Jones, refreshed after his sea-bathing at Weymouth, was preparing to attend the new term at the Court of the King's Bench at Westminster Hall, as the case of Mary Jones came on at the Old Bailey. Here, on the 11 September 1771, she was indicted for shoplifting, together with her friend Ann Styles, with whom she lived in Angel Alley off the Strand, a few minutes' walk from Jones's birthplace in Beaufort Buildings.

Her trial received little press attention at the time. Six years later on 13 May 1777, however, during a Commons debate upon the security of dockyards, Sir William Meredith, a fierce opponent of sanguinary laws, made a powerful speech in which he forced the honourable members to face their own responsibility for Mary's fate. Deploring how many crimes had been made capital 'that scarce deserve whipping', he referred to the Shoplifting Act of 1699:

> Under this act, one Mary Jones was executed; it was at the time when press warrants were issued on the alarm about Falkland's Islands. The woman's husband was pressed, their goods seized for some debts of his, and she, with two small children, turned into the streets a-begging. 'Tis a circumstance not to be forgotten, that she was very young, (under nineteen) and most remarkably handsome. She went to a linen-draper's shop, took some coarse linen off

13. *Memoirs of Granville Sharp*, 1: 251.

the counter, and slipped it under her cloak; the shopman saw her, and she laid it down: for this she was hanged. Her defence was, (I have the trial in my pocket) 'That she had lived in credit, and wanted for nothing, till a press-gang came and stole her husband from her; but, since then, she had no bed to lie on; nothing to give her children to eat, and they were almost naked; and perhaps she might have done something wrong, for she hardly knew what she did.' The parish-officers testified the truth of this story; but, it seems, there had been a good deal of shop-lifting about Ludgate; an example was thought necessary, and this woman was hanged for the comfort and satisfaction of some shopkeepers in Ludgate-street. When brought to receive sentence, she behaved in such a frantic manner, as proved her mind to be in a distracted and desponding state; and the child was sucking at her breast when she set out for Tyburn. [...] Compare this [her crime] with what the State did, and with what the Law did. The State bereaved the woman of her husband, and the children of a father, who was all their support; the Law deprived the woman of her life, and the children of their remaining parent, exposing them to every danger, insult, and merciless treatment, that destitute and helpless orphans suffer. Take all the circumstances together, I do not believe that a fouler murder was ever committed against Law, than the murder of this woman by Law. Some who hear me, are perhaps blaming the judges, the jury, and the hangman; but neither judge, jury, nor hangman are to blame: they are but ministerial agents; the true hangman is the member of Parliament; he who frames the bloody law is answerable for all the blood that is shed under it.[14]

It matters little that Meredith had minimized her crime to one of stealing 'some coarse linen'; Ann Styles testified that Mary 'wanted to buy a child's jam'(a child's dress, from *Jammah*, the long muslin dress worn in India) and she was actually indicted, 'for stealing 4 pieces of worked muslin, containing 52 yards, value £5: 10s'.[15] Whether this single parent had stolen inexpensive linen or costly Indian piece-goods, the more heinous state crime of husband-stealing was beginning to be acknowledged at the time as it was later by Charles Dickens. He reprinted Meredith's speech in his preface to the 1849 edition of *Barnaby Rudge: A Tale of the Riots of Eighty*, putting into the mouth of Edward Dennis, the public hangman who placed the noose around Mary's neck, the wry comment: 'That being the law and the practice of England, is the glory of England, an't it Muster Gashford.'

14. *The Parliamentary Register; or, History of the Proceedings and Debates of the House of Commons* (London, 1778), 7: 178–9; *Gentleman's Magazine*, 41 (1771), 471.
15. *Old Bailey Proceedings Online* (www.oldbaileyonline.org, 17 June 2008), 11 September 1771, Trial of Mary, wife of William Jones, and Ann Styles for Theft: Shoplifting (t17710911-32).

One may speculate upon whether it was the beauty of Mary Jones, on which Meredith lingered, the iniquity of impressment, or the sickening ritual of execution that was uppermost in the mind of the black-robed Sheriff of London, John Wilkes, as his coach followed the open cart from which she was launched into eternity at Tyburn on 16 October 1771.

The drapers of Ludgate Street no doubt slept safer in their beds that night, but a case such as this stresses that experience, whether at Westminster Hall or the Old Bailey, might encourage an appreciation of the interconnections between the need for political and judicial reform. Jones, like Wilkes, saw that commerce and the free market were intrinsically linked with defence of private property and the rights and sovereignty of the individual, but any system that denied equality before the law and common humanity was ultimately indefensible.

By the time Sir William Meredith, who had also opposed general warrants, and championed the rights of Middlesex electors and American colonists, gave his impassioned speech about the legal murder of Mary Jones in 1777, Jones was inevitably moving closer, both politically and socially, to 'Wilkes and Liberty'. In the winter of 1776, Jones was dining with Wilkes at the house of publishers Edward and Charles Dilly who specialized in books of Dissenting and American interest. At their excellent dinners in 22 the Poultry even 'Johnson and Wilkes forgot the animosities of Tory and Whig'. Nathaniel Wraxall, judge-advocate in Bombay, later recalled:

> I found myself seated very unworthily among several distinguished individuals. Wilkes, Jones, afterwards so well known as Sir William Jones, De Lolme, Dr. Dodd, with three or four others, composed the company. We were gay, animated, and convivial. Before we parted, Dodd invited us to a dinner at his residence in Argyle-street.[16]

Jones, Wilkes, and Messrs Dilly questioned the ingenious Swiss lawyer John Louis de Lolme concerning his opinions of the infant transatlantic republic. His *English Constitution* (1775) was acclaimed by readers keen to bask in foreign praise of Britain's tolerance, its free press, and trial by jury. Jones found it a rosy-tinted, if not Panglossian, picture ignoring imbalance in the

---

16. Like the rest of the company, Jones found 'the Macaroni parson' Revd Dr Dodd engaging, but the following February Dodd obtained £4,200 on a forged bill of exchange in the name of the earl of Chesterfield, and in June this 'plausible, agreeable man' was hanged at Tyburn; Nathaniel William Wraxall, *Posthumous Memoirs of His Own Time*, 3 vols (London, 1836), 2: 24.

mixed Constitution created by growing royal power, or deplorable facts such as rotten boroughs returning MPs, but not Birmingham or Manchester.

These were dark days for believers in liberty and the Constitution. A closing of the ranks was taking place on both radical and reactionary sides. Through the bleak February of 1777 Jones followed the progress of a bill penned by Attorney General Edward Thurlow to suspend habeas corpus, allowing the king to detain at his pleasure persons suspected of treason in North America or on the high seas. The strongest opposition came from Fox, who detected 'strides not only to destroy the liberty of America, but this country likewise'. Wilkes, opposing its third reading, refused to 'arm ministers with an unconstitutional power', contrasting American and British politics in language Jones radically endorsed: 'Would to God, Sir, our Parliament equalled that congress of heroes in wisdom, in love of their country, in uncorruptedness, in public virtue!'[17]

Wilkes informed the House of the case of Ebenezer Smith Platt, a Georgia 'liberty man' lying in chains in Newgate, charged with high treason for diverting a cargo of muskets and gunpowder, intended for pro-British Native Americans, to the grateful use of General Washington at the siege of Boston. Labelled by the press as 'the first American that Government has meddled with', Platt had been in custody for fourteen months, without trial and without bail.[18]

Jones was familiar with the case via Platt's barristers, John Alleyne (a friend of Franklin and of America), and the celebrated criminal barrister, Henry Howorth. From Wilkes he learned of the efforts of Long Island-born Patience Wright, wax-modeller to high society, to obtain justice for the handsome 24-year-old Platt with whom her daughter Elizabeth had fallen in love. Her petitioning enlisted the London help of the painter Benjamin West and the Paris assistance of Benjamin Franklin.

Involvement in a cause espoused by Wilkes would scarcely endear Jones to ministers. Nevertheless Jones joined Platt's defence team researching legal precedents, and consulting Dunning in this unprecedented situation. Any lawyer worth his salt was keen to defend habeas corpus, and here injustice

---

17. *The Parliamentary Register; or History of the Proceedings [...] During the Third Session of the Fourteenth Parliament* (London, 1777), 230–66; 246. Sheldon S. Cohen, 'The Odyssey of Ebenezer Smith Platt', *Journal of American Studies*, 18: 2 (1984), 255–74.
18. *The Universal Magazine*, 60 (February 1777).

was compounded by a prisoner of war being treated as a traitor. Jones endorsed connections Granville Sharp was making between suspension of habeas corpus and impressment: 'that other most notorious and *iniquitous* mode of *suspending*, or rather *annulling*, all *the laws* of British freedom, in the case of *seamen*; I mean the IMPRESSING them into service'.[19] These two inflammatory issues were intertwined in Jones's career; he was shortly offered the valued opportunity of aiding Westminster Hall's leading common law barrister, John Dunning, both in the Platt cause and in a high-profile case of impressment.

A huge increase in legalized 'man-stealing' was occasioned by the American war in 1776 and 1777. Within the City of London press-warrants required an alderman's countersignature, which was generally unforthcoming, and the pressing of Thames watermen was frequently obstructed. Admiralty solicitors became more determined. It was time for Jones to consolidate his growing reputation as a constitutional lawyer and advocate of human rights. There could be no better means of accomplishing this than by assisting John Dunning in representing the City in the infamous case of lighterman John Millachip, freeman of the Needlemaker's Company, and liveryman of London.

Jones was enjoying a brief respite amongst Oxford's 'philosophick bowers' when Millachip was impressed early in March 1777. The aldermen's Court of Common Council obtained a writ of habeas corpus and on 3 April Millachip was liberated from the *Monarch*, a 74-gun ship of the line, in the Thames estuary.

Jones rode to London to confer with Dunning: 'If the question concerning the legality of pressing mariners should be argued (which it will not be, if the governing powers can prevent it) I shall have the pleasure, and a great pleasure I shall think it, of speaking on the subject, and of being able to say hereafter "prima causa *publica* pro Libertate dicta" ' (*Letters*, 1: 232).

Jones had only been back at Lamb's Buildings a week when, on 23 April, John Millachip was again impressed on board his Thames lighter. Jones primed Dunning with his trenchant arguments on the illegality of press-warrants. Meanwhile the indefatigable Granville Sharp met Sandwich's secretary, the Handelian Joah Bates, and Colonel Windus of the Shipping Committee, to impart the discordant information that Admiralty opposition

---

19. Sharp, *An Address to the People of England against the Suspension of Laws*, 57.

'made to the Habeas Corpus was improper and would endanger Lord Sandwich as well as Lord Mansfield if he remanded' Millachip.[20]

Impatient for the Millachip trial to come on, Jones was kept confoundedly busy. He had hoped to ride to Cambridge to see Althorp at Whitsun, having bought a fine 40-guinea chestnut stallion 'with a long light coloured tail' for the purpose. He was prevented by the pressure of work. While his powerful horse lacked exercise, its owner 'vibrate[d] from day to day between Guildhall and Westminster hall'. With only a few days' notice, he learned that the Platt cause was finally to be heard.

On 12 May 1777, Ebenezer Platt, looking drawn and drained, was brought from Newgate to Westminster Hall: 'The Arguments against bailing him were advanced by the Attorney-General [Thurlow], Mr [Thomas] *Wallace* [future attorney general], Mr [James] *Mansfield* [future solicitor general] and Mr [Edward] *Bearcroft* [KC]; for bailing him, by Mr *Dunning* and Mr *Jones*.'[21] Debate centred on the words of the Act: 'no judge or justice of peace shall bail or try any such person or persons' (suspected of treason in North America or on the high seas), without an order signed by at least six privy councillors.

Dunning insisted: 'the Words *no Judge* cannot sure be extended to a *Court*'; the power of the Court of the King's Bench 'is of so high and transcendent a Nature that it cannot be destroyed or abridged without *express words*' (pp. 3–4). Thurlow claimed the meaning and intention of the statute was clear. Jones sarcastically agreed; it was clearly 'intended to answer the pious End of detaining any Person whatsoever, that the Minister thinks proper, in Prison, without a Chance of Trial or Enlargement'.

Jones believed the humanity of British laws lay in their stringent interpretation: 'if any Law is to be construed strictly, surely that is which affects an unfortunate Man denied the Privilege of evincing his Innocence to the World, and that boasted Birth-Right of every *Englishman*, a Trial by his Peers, one torn from his country, from every social and domestic Connection, and upon the pretended suspicion, perhaps, of a capital Offence,

---

20. Granville Sharp's Diary, 2 May 1777; cited in John A. Woods, 'The City of London and Impressment 1776–1777', *Proceedings of the Leeds Philosophical and Literary Society*, 8: 2 (1956), 111–27; 118. Bates, like Sandwich and a host of music lovers, including Lord North, Goldsmith, Garrick, and Mrs Sheridan, frequently attended Sharp's Handelian soirées on the Thames or at his house in Old Jewry.
21. *An Argument in the Case of Ebenezer Smith Platt, now under Confinement for High Treason* (London, 1777), 1.

consign'd to a gloomy Cavern, there, without a Friend, without a Hope, to await the further Persecutions of his Oppressors' (p. 6). *The Morning Chronicle* praised the 'minute and critical examination' to which Dunning subjected the wording of the act: 'He was followed by Mr Jones, a very able, learned, and ingenious young Counsel, who apologized very modestly for his taking the brief from Mr Alleyne, without a transfer of his abilities.'[22]

Dunning's practised harangue and Jones's modest ingenuity were all to no avail. This was a deeply politicized hearing, a crucial test case for the repressive statute, as Attorney General Thurlow's presence attested. Westminster Hall and St James's were intimately hand-in-glove. Mansfield's ruling that the prohibition to bail or try applied to the King's Bench was supported by his brother judges, and Platt was returned to his Newgate dungeon.[23]

Such failure was doubly depressing; Jones feared for the liberty of Britain as well as for that of a luckless American patriot. He was physically exhausted as he lamented to his friend on 16 May:

> Why alas! do I boast of liberty? Why am I proud of being an Englishman? I spend days and nights in endeavouring to free others, and yet I am not free myself [...] A cause at Guildhall, which may be brought on suddenly! Bankrupts on *Tuesday*! And a consultation on Monday evening, [...] and the labour of searching old records to prepare for the battle with the attorney and solicitor general on the question of pressing!   (*Letters*, 1: 236)

The Millachip cause was finally brought before Mansfield the following day. Dunning declared counsel's intention of arguing upon two grounds: first, the general question of the legality of impressing; and secondly, the particular circumstances constituting Millachip's exemption.[24] Dunning intended to leave the first ground to his junior, for Jones was prepared to speak 'at least three hours' in 'the great cause of Millachip'. But Jones was denied his Francis Hargrave star appearance by contrived adjournments. Jones had abandoned a research trip to Rome to be ready for the hearing: 'Had I been absent, I should not have forgiven myself, as the City honoured me with its confidence, and as I am a master of the subject' (*Letters*, 1: 241).

22. *Morning Chronicle and London Advertiser*, Tuesday, 13 May, 177. The *Morning Post and Daily Advertiser* reported Jones's citing of many cases, adding that 'Mr Brass Crosby, Mr Wilkes, Sir Watkin Lewes, and several other *patriots* attended.'
23. Following a Lords' debate in which the Duke of Richmond attacked and Lord Sandwich defended Platt's treatment, Platt was released by royal warrant on 15 March 1778.
24. *The Annual Register for the Year 1777* (London, 1778), 186–7.

The Court of the King's Bench, under its hammer-beam roof, had as little desire to debate the legality of pressing mariners as it had to debate that of the slave trade. Although Millachip was discharged 'as being of the Livery', this 'prima causa *publica*' was postponed and, like the Somerset case, never satisfactorily brought to issue by the disingenuous Mansfield. But Jones's detailed briefing of John Dunning had moved his mentor far beyond his earlier position as signatory of a legal response to the Lord Mayor's queries on the legality of press-warrants. In that 1770 document, Dunning, John Glynn, and Alexander Wedderburn, largely endorsed Sir Michael Foster's 1743 judgement upholding their legality:

> [Impressment] appears to us to be well established by ancient and long continued usage, [...] we see no objection to this power's being executed by the Lords of the Admiralty under the authority of his Majesty's orders in Council.[25]

Jones vehemently opposed this opinion on two grounds: his researches had convinced him that the 'ancient usage' argument was fundamentally flawed; his second legal and political objection was to any such arbitrary power being vested in *the Crown* rather than parliament. He wanted these key issues thrashed out in open court. Proactive steps to establish the illegality of impressment were required, not reactive concentration upon exemptions or abuses of process. It was an uphill struggle. The American war precipitated a determined increase in repressive governmental power: 'the right of pressing seemed to grow in strength, and all idea of local or personal exemptions to lose ground very considerably'.[26]

Jones found this all profoundly discouraging but his continued success on the Carmarthen circuit, where he was gaining a real reputation, his legal work in London and at the Oxford quarter sessions, the intellectual and social rewards of both cities, and the enthusiastically reviewed appearance of a second enlarged edition of his *Poems*, dedicated to Lady Spencer, all filled his life with a sense of purpose, service, and achievement that his teeming— if not hyperactive—brain demanded.

He relished the forensic drama of the courtroom and the interplay of finely tuned minds, but circuit experience made him regret 'the custom of retaining advocates before the merits of the cause are disclosed'; he envied

---

25. *The Annual Register for the Year 1770* (London, 1771), 232.
26. *The Annual Register for the Year 1777*, 28.

Roman republican lawyers who had the ability 'to chuse their side' (*Letters*, 1: 232). In terms of his career, the question of which side he should choose was encapsulated and dramatized in his relationship with those two dissolute Medmenham monks: Sandwich and Wilkes.

Jones had planned, should the legality question be evaded, to publish the speech he had intended to give at Westminster Hall, despite his keen awareness that this would do little for his career. As he acknowledged to Althorp:

> This opposition to *prerogative* is not, you will say, the road to preferment. I know it, my dear friend, and am wholly unconcerned about it. We all seek happiness; now I am so framed that I must act conscientiously, or I cannot be happy: is it not better then to live as I do, moderately yet independently, like a philosopher yet like a gentleman, than to hanker after silk gowns, or all the trumpery of a courtly bar? I am sure you think so; but you must not therefore expect to see your friend decorated with honours and titles, which being conferred by the breath of an individual (for what else is a King?) are at least as empty as the breath that confers them. No: I seek and expect more solid glory, the applause of my countrymen for having laboured in their service with the best intentions; and if not with the best success, yet they may give me the praise, which was given to Varro after his defeat, *non desperavit de republicâ*. (*Letters*, 1: 241–2)

In confessional mode the 31-year-old reveals to the 19-year-old Trinity student Spencer that a happy Jones is a 'Conscientious' Jones. Yet we wonder why his argument on the illegality of press-warrants—which he declared he would 'infallibly print and publish'—never appeared? Was it that the high road to preferment appeared more attractive to the proudly pacing stallion of his ambition than the hock-clogging mud of the Cardiganshire lanes? Perhaps he simply never found time—as with the promised notes for *The Moallakát*, the planned printing of his father's mathematical works, or the 'many tracts on jurisprudence', which he mentions having written. Or perhaps Jones *did* in fact publish his argument against impressment.

Early in 1778 *A Discourse on the Impressing of Mariners; wherein Judge Foster's Argument is Considered and Answered* appeared anonymously from the prestigious firm of Thomas Cadell, who had published two of Jones's Orientalist works. But was Jones the author?

Here the frustrations of historical research intrude. A single double-sided page of Jones's account with Cadell survives in Dunedin, listing the sales of *Poeseos Asiaticæ Commentariorum* (1774), and books purchased during

1773–7.[27] We learn that Jones bought Butler's *The Legality of Impressing Seamen* on 12 November 1777, three days before its publication. Jones's account with Cadell for 1778, which might have proved Jones's authorship of *A Discourse on the Impressing of Mariners*, a rebuttal of Butler, does not appear to have survived. Without recourse to the dubious arts of computer stylistic analysis, we must turn to internal evidence.

The *Discourse* has some critical things to say of lawyers, and this might not simply be a ruse to obscure authorship. It could well be the product of intense frustration with the King's Bench, under judges such as Mansfield, which 'has always waived coming to any formal decision; left the matter [of impressment] nearly as it found it; and seems to have been satisfied with getting rid of it, as one would do with a troublesome acquaintance'.[28] However that might be, the *Discourse* is a profoundly scholarly and closely argued work.

Its 139 pages proceed from a research discovery of a mistranslation of the Anglo-Norman in a late fourteenth-century statute of Richard II. Examining the manuscript of this earliest authority cited to justify impressment (2 Richard II cap. 4), the author maintains this statute has absolutely nothing to do with any such practice. It was enacted to impose penalties on mariners who, having contracted in the king's navy and received pay in advance, absconded with the money. On seeing the Anglo-Norman word 'arestuz', the lawyers had inevitably translated it as 'arrested', ignoring its alternative meaning of 'to hire' (as in 'arrêter un domestique') which 'the context and whole tenor of the statute plainly evinced' (p. 23).

The impassioned description of the civic horrors associated with press gangs provides the flavour of a breathless courtroom harangue:

> [L]awless and desperate fellows, hardened in iniquity and inured to violence, armed with bludgeons, staves, and clubs, and sometimes even with hangers [short swords], and fire-arms, insolently parading through the streets in lawless triumph, knocking down one person, hacking the limbs of another, and dragging along, with brutal cruelty, an innocent victim, who has offended against no law; and breaking and forcing their way into houses, without any legal authority, and all this even in the face of open day, to the terror and

---

27. Dunedin Public Library, Reed Collection, Cadell's statement of Jones's account for 1773–7.
28. *A Discourse on the Impressing of Mariners; wherein Judge Foster's Argument is Considered and Answered* (London: Cadell [1778]), p. 111. In the same way, the only other element in this work which seems incompatible with a thesis of Jones's authorship, the remark: 'I must not confess I have not that sacred veneration for common law which lawyers entertain for it' (p. 66) might simply reveal irritation at the circularity of Foster's argument that common law had invested the Crown with the right of issuing press warrants (pp. 57–9).

consternation of the peaceable members of the community; rioting along, and insulting with blasphemous oaths and daring language, whomsoever they please with impunity, and accompanying every action with curses and imprecations. I would seriously ask any one, if these are not the frequent practices of these desperadoes; and whether the like is to be countenanced or even tolerated under a civilized Government, not in a land of freedom, but even under the severest despotism? (pp. 35–6)

This mixture of stylistic elegance, practised rhetoric, vehement argument, legal *nous*, and linguistic assurance testifies to the strong likelihood of Jones's authorship, as do the Ciceronian epigraph; repeated exhortations to a vigilant defence of 'the property and liberty of the public'; reminders of the dangers of court government and the power of the crown; the reference to Hessian troops plundering and murdering in America; and perhaps, above all, a pronounced egalitarian response to those who had parroted Judge Foster's point that 'all private interest must give way to the public safety'. It was cant to say 'all'; what they meant was that it was the *poor man*'s private interest and his safety that must be sacrificed:

Why not openly and at once declare all the inferior ranks of the People our slaves; as much so as the negroes in America? Why not, in pity to them, stop short at labour; was not that enough, without claiming their unwilling service in war? in the army? in the navy? I entertain not the same idea of these people: I consider them as the firm rock on which every Government is founded; from them it derives its stability, permanency, wealth and prosperity (p. 124)[29]

The author declares: 'I have no desire to survive Public Liberty', determined, like Jones, who regularly practised firelock drill, to don a red coat in time of emergency:

When an enemy appears, I will not quit this post: I think it my duty to defend it. My ancestors left me in possession of Liberty, and I will deliver it in the best condition I am able down to posterity (p. 17)

If Jones did not write these words, he would endorse them with every fibre of his being.[30] So much so in fact that the very absence of any comment

---

29. Cf. 'I am convinced that on the *popular* part of every government depends its real force, the obligation of its laws, its welfare, its security, its permanence'; Jones to Althorp, 4 February 1780; *Letters*, 1: 344.
30. Cf. 'Do not imagine, that, in case of an actual invasion, your friend would be idle [...] in the heat of action, every man who can load and fire may be serviceable [...] I will be your pupil in war and die or conquer by your side'; Jones to Althorp, 18 July 1779; *Letters*, 1: 300.

from Jones on the appearance of a discourse so relevant to his preoccupation with impressment must be weighed against the absence of any documentary evidence of his authorship. The *Monthly Review* lauded its persuasive argument and humanitarian bias:

> If ever there was an act of disinterested patriotism, it is that of defending the cause of poor enslaved mariners: because those who undertake this benevolent office, are above the danger, and are only interested by their humanity in the sufferings of men who can neither plead their own cause, nor resist the oppression.[31]

That this reviewer was no radical Wilkite is apparent in his linking a sardonic comment on the Bill of Rights Society with a quotation from the latest Samuel Foote comedy at the Theatre Royal to stress the real importance of the assault upon human rights posed by impressment:

> When we consider the noise and bustle made some few years since by an association who on a particular occasion assumed the high-sounding title of SUPPORTERS of the BILL OF RIGHTS! a man might be tempted to exclaim with Prig in *The Cozeners*, 'D—n me, Jack Wilkes's affair is but a flea-bite to this!'

The graphic nature of this *Discourse* was a revelation to a wider public sphere of periodical writers and readers unfamiliar with Wapping, Portsmouth Point, or the grim and grimy dockyard areas of any seaport. This must have proved encouraging to its author, whoever he was; but it was not enough for Jones. Consciousness-raising among the middling chattering classes was a step in the right direction, but Jones wanted the matter brought once and for all to judicial issue.

By the end of November 1777, which had perhaps seen Jones writing this *Discourse*, he learned 'the great cause [of Millachip] concerning impresses of seamen' was scheduled to come on in the new year. The opposition plea stated: 'that, when the press-warrants issued, there was *an open & unnatural rebellion* in America; but as there was full time for parliament to have authorized such warrants, there could be no *necessity* for the King alone to issue them *without parliament*' (*Letters*, 1: 250). He had no doubt that increasing royal power and court influence were pushing the country dangerously close to absolute government. Jones shared his doctor—Sir George Baker—with the king, but little else.

---

31. *Monthly Review*, 58 (May 1778), 341–2; 341. See also *Gentleman's Magazine*, 81 (October 1811), 309–10, reprinted in *The Monthly Magazine*, 38: 2 (1814), 401–2.

On the advice of that royal physician, Jones spent a Christmas vacation in Bath to take the waters and ride on the downs. Exhausted by his punishing regime of legal work and research, he had already self-diagnosed his lassitude as the *morbus literatorum*, poor digestion, caused by 'stooping to read & write'. His remedy was simple: 'abstinence from too much food, literary and culinary'.

On the morning of 29 December 1777 Jones visited Wilkes, also at Bath for his health. Wilkes proudly showed Jones a letter from Denis Diderot, philosopher and author of the monumental *Encyclopédie*. Jones's virtually photographic memory enabled him to relay 'a translation almost literal' to Althorp. Jones endorses Diderot's praise of Wilkes's eloquent speeches denouncing the American war; not so the man-to-man sexual advice that follows:

> 'As to yourself, he adds, be cheerful and drink the best wines, keep the gayest company; and should you be inclined to a tender passion: address yourself to such women as make the least resistance: they are as amusing and as interesting as others; one lives with them without anxiety, and quits them without regret.'[32]—I want words, Diderot, to express the baseness, the folly, the brutality of this sentiment: I am no cynick, but as fond as any man at Paris of cheerful company and of such pleasures as a man of virtue need not blush to enjoy; but if the philosophy of the French Academicians be comprised in your advice to your friend Wilkes, keep it to yourself and to such as you: I am of a different sect. (*Letters*, 1: 252–3)

This is the Diderot who preferred Tahitian sexual mores, famously—if honestly—announcing: 'There is no moral precept that does not have something inconvenient about it.' By contrast the Jonesian role model was Cicero rather than Catullus. If his principles were not to be altered by the conversation of ministers, neither were they to be corrupted by the communications of Enlightenment savants. Jones was a 'water-drinker' not only at Bath; he was all for 'Wilkes and Liberty' but never for Wilkes and licence.

Yet, apart from oppositional politics, the lawyer and the former outlaw had much in common. Elected to the Royal Society even before his election to the Beefsteak Club, Wilkes was no mean scholar, having acquired Greek and Latin at the age of fourteen and attended the prestigious university of Leiden. In 1765 he had even applied to be Ambassador to Constantinople.

---

32. Diderot's French vindicates Jonesian accuracy: 'Au milieu du tumulte public, portez-vous bien; soyez gai; buvez de bons vins; et lorsqu'il vous prendra fantaisie d'etrê tendre, adressez-vous à des femmes qui ne fassent pas soupirer longtems. Elles amusent autant que les autres; elles occupent moins; on les possède sans inquiétude, et on les quitte sans regret', *Denis Diderot: Correspondance*, ed. Georges Roth and Jean Varloot, 16 vols (Paris, 1968), 14: 199.

They shared many mutual friends such as the eminent poet and critic, Joseph Warton, a member of Johnson's Club.

What loomed large in their minds was General John Burgoyne's letter from Albany, detailing a series of bloody defeats culminating in the surrender of his entire army to American militia forces at Saratoga. Deploring the huge losses on both sides, Jones was especially anxious for his friend Captain Watson: 'If he is killed among the many officers, who are said to have fallen at Mud Island, I shall grieve that, though he perished bravely, he did not perish in a better cause' (*Letters*, 1: 254).

The Revolutionary War was turning in favour of the Americans and Jones anticipated ever more desperate governmental measures to increase taxation and recruitment. The Christmas recess saw unprecedented ministerial and Loyalist activity in raising city subscriptions for the formation of new regiments.

Burke, seeking oppositional ammunition, urgently consulted Jones on the constitutional implications of raising troops by such extra-parliamentary means. Concerned that 'the Crown should continue the Progress it has made towards absolute Government', Jones saw private subscriptions establishing a dangerous precedent in which donations might grow 'by usage into arbitrary Exactions' (*Letters*, 1: 258). Jones's constitutional arguments also fed into a powerful parliamentary speech of Dunning, the opposition's ablest lawyer, deploring the illegality 'of using *private* subscriptions to raise men and money to defend Government'. That was on the 4 February and on subsequent days key speeches by Burke (opposing the use of Native Americans) and by Charles James Fox (lamenting the war had cost the lives of 25,000 soldiers and £25,000,000) led to Lord North's announcement of a new Conciliation Commission to treat with the Americans.

The spring of 1778 proved a crucial one for Jones. Mid-April found him relaxing at Midgham House, the sumptuous Berkshire seat of his friend—and Althorp's uncle—William Poyntz. Jones described it as 'a sweet place [...] the seat of perfect Liberty'. The company was lively, attractive, and talented, including Sandwich's niece Lady Cork, the 'very pretty and extremely clever' Lady Granard, and her intellectual 'beau', the agronomist Alexandre-Henri Tessier. Visits were made to General Smith's magnificent Chilton Lodge, and to Lord and Lady Craven at their Palladian Benham Park, newly designed by 'Capability' Brown.

Elizabeth Craven and Jones spoke of mutual friends, the ingenious Madame de Vaucluse, and the dynamic Polish patriot, Orientalist couple

Prince Adam Czartoryski and Princess Izabela Czartoryska. They also talked Turkey; it was Jones's enthusiasm that inspired Elizabeth's visit to Constantinople, finding the Turks an example to the West in their treatment of women. Charitable amateur dramatics were the order of the day with a performance of Lady Craven's elegant translation of Pont de Vile's *La Somnambule* for the benefit of Newbury infirmary. Jones modestly understudied George Berkeley, son of the immaterialist philosopher, in the title role. General Smith played a major role—not in the French comedy, but in Jones's 'Indian scheme'.

Richard Smith had succeeded Clive as Commander-in-Chief of the Bengal army, supporting Shāh 'Ālam's return to his Delhi throne. No immaterialist he; this prominent EIC stockholder was reputedly worth between £200,000 and £300,000 (multiply by a hundred for today's value). He was the model for Sir Matthew Mite (Smith's father was a cheesemonger) in Samuel Foote's successful satire on the Company, *The Nabob*, currently being printed at Cadell's. This close friend of Philip Francis and Burke was a notorious gambler—he allegedly lost £180,000 to Fox—and prominent racehorse owner; he purchased a Harley Street house and a Berkshire mansion. Smith also bought votes, attempting to become MP for the rotten borough of Hindon, Wiltshire, for which 'General Gold', as the voters called him, was fined a thousand marks and gaoled for six months.[33] This intimate of the fashionable Cravens, discussing Company affairs with Jones, was both committed rake and convicted criminal.

But nothing is simple, as Jones had long discovered, in personal relationships, or indeed in the strange world of eighteenth-century politics. Convicted alongside Richard Smith at the Salisbury Assizes, as 'Guilty of notorious Bribery', was none other than Thomas Brand Hollis, principled radical and friend of religious and political reformers such as John Jebb, Theophilus Lindsey, Christopher Wyvill, and respected republican Thomas Hollis, whose surname Brand adopted in honour of his benefactor. Purchasing a rotten borough seems a bizarre method of advancing parliamentary reform, but Brand Hollis subsequently became a founder-member of the Society for Constitutional Information in 1780, to which Jones was elected two years later.

The Nabob's portrayal of 'the borough of Bribe'em' might have been immeasurably improved had Foote introduced this corrupt combination of

---

33. T. B. Howell, *A Complete Collection of State Trials*, 21 vols (London, 1816), 20: 1225–84.

nabob and radical; it would have proved far more hilarious than any Pont de Vile comedy. The Hindon farce dramatized the enormous difficulties involved in reconciling opposites: was it possible for Jones to become a radical nabob?

In conversation with Smith at Midgham, Jones learned of the vacancy caused by the sudden death of Stephen Charles Lemaistre, puisne judge of the Supreme Court of Bengal, on 22 October 1777. Jones's brain raced at the thought. General Smith, a well-connected member of the Company's court of proprietors, might prove a valuable ally.

Jones had commitments at Oxford, and now a grand new Indian project, but he was determined not to miss a performance of *Othello*, which Lady Cork had arranged for the evening of Monday, 27 April. Having enjoyed the play, he rode through the night to rejoin the sessions: 'I set out for Oxford at midnight and reached it at five in the morning: at eight my chambers was beset with clients, my floor spread with maps and plans, my table covered with briefs' (*Letters*, 1: 266–7).

At ten o'clock on Wednesday night he received a note from William Poyntz, inviting him to the royal naval review at Portsmouth. He left Oxford at four in the morning, riding hard for Midgham, only to miss Poyntz by half an hour. Failing to find his friend, Jones hired a cutter at Southampton and sailed—helped by 'a brisk gale and a strong tide'— through the serried ranks of warships at Spithead to arrive in Portsmouth on May Day morning. The reason for his haste was his impatience to canvass Sandwich concerning his 'Indian scheme'. He met his friend Mulgrave, but Sandwich was too much in demand:

> Lord Mulgrave invited me to see the naval review on board his ship the *Courageux*, which he has taken in exchange for the *Ardent*: the names of both his men of war suit the disposition of their commander, who is both courageous and ardent in a high degree. I shall go on board to-morrow at eight.— Lord Sandwich is attending the King, and is so much engaged that I think it improper to wait upon him.   (*Letters*, 1: 267)

A minor setback, but Jones's imagination was fired. With 'Nabob' Smith's conspicuous wealth fresh in mind, Jones realized a five- or six-year stint in Calcutta might see him return with a fortune of £30,000, a passport to economic and political independence. Typically, Jones reveals these plans in the context of his inability to stomach aristocratic arrogance, and this in a letter to a viscount! He extols meritocracy in terms high-minded, 'manly' (a favourite epithet), and philosophic: 'I acknowledge no man as my superior, who is not so in virtue or knowledge, and if this be pride, I am not free from it; but I call it only a sense of that manly ἰσονομία [political equality], which ought to be the basis of every good government, and which is certainly founded on reason' (*Letters*, 1: 269). But reason dictated that he required court patronage; Jones determines 'to spend the next three months in strengthening my interest, ministerial, professional, and [EIC] *directorial*'.

Receiving sanction to 'shake the Pagoda tree' with a Supreme Court judge's £6,000 salary was to take slightly longer than three months. But then Jones wasn't always intent upon strengthening his interest. He seems to have created a strangely ambivalent impression upon that powerful Company 'Mogul', Laurence Sulivan: 'I hold Mr Jones (who is the first in this country of the Persian class) to be a mere superficial smatterer, with this merit, however, that he knows more of the language than any other man and perhaps with such lights and materials as are here within reach he may not be equalled.'[34] Certainly, moving closer to Wilkes than to Sandwich was a serious mistake for anyone with an eye to the main East India chance.

From Lamb's Buildings on 24 May Jones writes to Lady Spencer of the 'great probability' of being appointed, and how 'my predilection for the East and my desire to unite Persian and Law' increased his eagerness for the post (*Letters*, 1: 271). He had been doing the court rounds: at Lord North's levee; with Lord Mansfield, who was always interested in Jones's career; and with Lord Chancellor Bathurst at his imposing Adam-designed red-brick Apsley House. His optimism is unbounded: 'with such a triumvirate I can hardly fail'.

Jones had a loyal friend in good-natured Bathurst to whom he would shortly dedicate his pioneering work of historical comparative law: *The Speeches of Isæus in Causes concerning the Law of Succession to Property at Athens* (1779). Bathurst had appointed Jones a Commissioner of Bankrupts and now, having declared: 'he means to recommend me to the King as Mr LeMaistre's successor', it seemed Bathurst might make his fortune. Unluckily imperial politics were working against both men. One of the things that had drawn them together—the desire for a negotiated peace with America—was unpalatable to the king, who personally intervened to replace Bathurst with his own man.

---

34. Bodleian Library, MS Eng. Hist. c. 269, f. 29; cited in George McGilvary, *Guardian of the East India Company: The Life of Laurence Sulivan* (London, 2006), 243.

The passing of the Great Seal to Edward Thurlow on 3 June 1778 sealed Jones's fate. The strength of Thurlow's desire to bring North American colonists and domestic radicals to heel would heighten his suspicion of Jones's politics. Thurlow enthusiastically supported impressment, detesting metropolitan radicals who obstructed Admiralty warrants: no friend of Wilkes could be tolerated by Thurlow. In the light of this development, Jones's fear that 'they may keep me in suspense for the whole summer', and enquiries concerning late autumn sailings for Bengal, seem dismally optimistic.

Thus the summer of 1778 passed with Jones doing all the right things, such as waiting on Sir Grey Cooper at the Treasury, and the wrong ones, such as communicating with American diplomats in Paris. Simultaneously qualifying and disqualifying himself for the Calcutta judgeship, he was not impressing ministers by opposing the impressing of mariners. On 29 June he responded to a lengthy letter—with a Parisian postmark—from Arthur Lee on that very topic.

Lee was a Middle Temple friend, called to the bar a year after Jones in 1775; and acting as Congress's agent in London. This Virginia diplomat, brother of the Wilkite alderman William Lee, was now a Commissioner to France alongside Franklin. The Americans in Paris had been busy and the February of 1778 had seen Franco-American Treaties of Amity, Commerce, and Alliance signed and ratified by the Continental Congress.

Lee is confident Jones will exert his 'utmost strength upon the great question of impressment'. As students they had shared their opinions on the subject; Lee's description of the illegality and constitutional dangers of this practice might almost have been written by Jones:

> For what can more abase the dignity of the constitution, or endanger the security of the subject, than that the least enlightened and most abandoned of the community, for of such press-gangs are usually composed, should be supposed to have a legal power of judging and executing in what concerns the dearest object of legal protection, personal liberty?[35]

Lee requests the details of Jones's arguments on this question, lest any one might be 'inclined to introduce it into the United States'. Royal navy ships crewed by pressed mariners were actively impressing American sailors from

---

35. Letter of 18 October 1777; Richard Henry Lee, *Life of Arthur Lee, LL.D., Joint Commissioner of the United States to the Court of France*, 2 vols (Boston, 1829), 1: 119–22.

neutral merchantmen. Jones excuses his delayed response to Lee on the ground that he 'had been expecting from term to term, that the case of John—would be argued in Westminster Hall'. This obviously refers to the case of John Millachip, about which Lee was well aware, but Lee's biographer finds 'the word illegible'. As Cannon speculates, Jones might have scrawled the surname to frustrate prying eyes, for a letter to Lee might well be opened.[36] Certainly, Jones, apart from expressing his pleasure that 'our opinions so exactly coincide', does not elaborate on his arguments concerning impressment, as he turns to sad news of John Alleyne's early death. After another editorial hiatus in the letter, Jones refers to his needing to spend a week or two in Paris to interview witnesses concerning a property cause in chancery.

The political sensitivity of impressment was increasingly daily, especially as Britain was now at war with France, but for Jones to 'encrypt' a reference to Millachip, while openly mentioning a planned French visit, seems oddly inconsistent. What we can be sure of is that Jones was completely unaware—because at this stage so was Lee himself—that Lee's private secretary, Mr John Thornton, was in fact Major John Thornton in secret British government employ. That May, Thornton, under Lee's instructions, was at Portsmouth to obtain information on naval strength and troop movements.[37] While patriot Jones was watching the naval review, so was double agent Major Thornton. He was there to receive secret instructions from his Admiralty masters, communicate intelligence concerning the French fleets at Brest and Toulon, and send Lee false reports of British naval unreadiness. Suspicions were rife; there was a need for caution whereas Jones's ardent enthusiasm often led to impetuous decisions. His continental trips attracted both press speculation and governmental mistrust.

Jones had followed the trial, in March 1777, of James Aitken, known as John the Painter, for setting fire to the rope-house of Portsmouth dockyard in the cause of the American Revolution. The names of Franklin, Silas Deane, another American diplomat in Paris, together with their friend Dr Edward Bancroft FRS, research chemist, and novelist, were mentioned in the trial. In Paris Aitken visited Deane who, with the celebrated Pierre de Beaumarchais, directed a French government-funded company supplying

---

36. Lee, *A Life of Arthur Lee*, 2: 342. *Letters*, 1: 274n.
37. See *The Revolutionary Diplomatic Correspondence of the United States*, ed. Francis Wharton, 6 vols (Washington, 1889), 1: 545.

Congress with guns and uniforms. Aitken confessed that, after setting the rope-yard alight, he travelled 'to Doctor Bancroft, No. 4, Downing-street, Westminster, to whom he had a verbal recommendation from Mr Deane'.[38] What the arsonist didn't know, and what Franklin and Deane never discovered, was that Dr Bancroft was another double agent.

Serjeant-at-Law William Davy, opening the prosecution case, considered who might be behind this atrocious attempt to make Britain 'bow its neck, not only to the yoke of America, but to the most petty sovereign in Europe'. Davy's conclusion, tinged with ominous meaning: 'I wish Mr Silas Deane were here; a time may come, perhaps, when he and Dr Franklin may be here', elicited from the prisoner an impassioned response: 'He is the honestest man in the world.' In this opinion of Franklin, barrister Jones and arsonist John the Painter were of a mind; in that irony lay the whole danger to the London Welshman's prospects.

Concerning those prospects, Jones learned in late June of a talented rival for the Calcutta post. It was none other than Francis Hargrave! Jones still envied his brilliant King's Bench debut; would he now eclipse him in the East? Hargrave had no celebrity soubriquet or Oriental expertise but, more to the political point, he was 'devil' (research assistant) to 'the beast', as Jones nicknamed Thurlow. Immediately, Jones wrote to Hargrave asking 'if the situation of a Master in Chancery would not prove equally agreeable?' almost as if such a position were in his gift.

The reply from Hargrave's chambers on 5 July 1778 is more than friendly, it verges upon the self-abnegating. He acknowledges Jones's 'rare and extraordinary endowments', courteously bowing out before the Orientalist's superior claims to the Bengal bench.[39] Hargrave's brief postscript: 'One line, assuring me that the explanation I now send is satisfactory, will relieve me from a great deal of pain', underscores how very fortunate Jones was to have such a sensitive and scrupulous friend. Jones was certainly relieved, remaining confident that: 'It is still the opinion and wish of the bar, that I shall be the man' (*Letters*, 1: 276).

Jones wants the Calcutta post with a passion, it was the key to independence 'in parliament as well as at the bar, without selling my liberty to a patron' (*Letters*, 1: 276–7). In order to be free of patronage he required it—

---

38. Howell, *State Trials*, 20: 1,317–68; 1,365.
39. 'Sir William Jones', *The Annual Obituary and Biography for the Year 1817* (London, 1817), 1: 444–76; 458–9.

that was the double bind. Yet he is determined to make no compromises: 'if the minister be offended at the style in which I have spoken, do speak, and will speak, of publick affairs, and on that account should refuse to give me the judgeship, I shall not be mortified'. To this stubborn if principled inflexibility was added the perverse delight he took in mystifying the government with his cross-Channel business trips.

The American war was becoming global; Britain now faced the combined powers of France, Spain, and the Dutch Republic. The theatres of war extended beyond Europe and the Mediterranean to the West Indies and India. Sending a copy of his *Speeches of Isæus* to Edmund Burke on 28 February 1779, the state of the nation reminds Jones, as that of Rome reminded Cicero, of some lines of Ennius: '"*Pellitur è medio sapientia, vi geritur res; Spernitur orator bonus, horridus miles amatur*"' ['wisdom is exiled, violence rules; the honourable speaker is disdained, the fearsome soldier is loved'] (*Letters*, 1: 287). Perhaps 'orator bonus' Jones was exiling some of his own wisdom in making this French trip. The advertisement to *The Moallakát* stated his hope: 'that the war will raise no obstacle to this intercourse with the scholars of Leyden, Paris, and Madrid; for men of letters, as such, ought, in all places and at all times, to carry flags of truce'. But this was something of a pious academic hope.

The Moallakát was dedicated to the generous linguist John Paradise, who gave Jones a beautiful Arabic manuscript of these poems; Jones's legal business was to secure Paradise's American estate, threatened by Virginia legislation disinheriting non-residents. The friends arrived in Calais in time for dinner on 16 May 1779. To ease their travel within France, Jones obtained from Lady Spencer an introduction to the respected duc de Nivernois who, as Ambassador Plenipotentiary to Britain, helped negotiate the Peace of Paris (1763), ending the Seven Years' War.

Inspired by this, the ambitious Jones, desirous to *act* as self-appointed intermediary between Britain and her rebellious colonists, presented Franklin with 'A Fragment of Polybius'.[40] This pretended Hellenistic fragment formulates terms for a treaty reconciling Athens (England) and the Greek Islands (the United States). Franklin figures as Eleutherion (protector of freedom) whom Jones praises for 'the deepest knowledge of nature, the most solid judgement, most approved virtue, and most ardent zeal in the cause of general Liberty'. Jones's self-description is most revealing:

---

40. Polybius (*c*.203–120 BCE) originated the concept of the mixed republic.

> An Athenian, who had been a pupil of Isæus together with Demosthenes and begun to be known in his country as a pleader of causes, was led by some affairs of his clients to the capital of Caria [France]. He was a man unauthorized, unemployed, unconnected; independent in his circumstances as much as in his principles; admitting no governor under providence, but the laws, [...] he sometimes took occasion [...] to lament the increasing calamities of war, and to express his eager desire of making a general peace on such terms as *would produce the greatest good from the greatest evil.* (*Letters*, 1: 292)

There are mordant ironies here. Jones was at Passy to ensure Paradise continued to receive remittances from his wife's slave-worked tobacco plantations. Jones recalled intense discussions with Congressman Henry Laurens, and with Thomas Day, his roommate at the Middle Temple, about how slavery discredited the American cause. Day, together with their lawyer friend John Laurens Bicknell, had written *The Dying Negro* (1773), a widely influential poem inspired by a newspaper account of a runaway slave, who had married a white woman, and shot himself in despair when recaptured. Henry Laurens, a former slave dealer, had promised to free all his Carolina slaves shortly after 1776. Would Jones as a vehement opponent of the slave trade be capable—at the bar of his own conscience—of convincing himself that his errand to safeguard Paradise's Virginia plantations would produce 'the greatest good from the greatest evil'?

In compensation, perhaps, he envisages a grander mission: 'peace in our time', the treaty drafted by jurist, philosopher, and 'international negotiator' Jones. He was in truth an ardent lover of liberty but this love came shackled to his equally burning desire to impress. This same mixture of ambition and naiveté inspired 'Persian' Jones's youthful attempt to gain the post of ambassador to Turkey. Franklin would not have resented such presumption; the opening of his *Autobiography*, written at Shipley's Twyford house, announces that vanity 'is often productive of good in the possessor'.[41]

It was sheer hypocrisy for Jones to claim he was 'unconnected'. The forging of powerful connections had been uppermost in his mind since being introduced as an apple-cheeked schoolboy to Shipley. Franklin was one such impressive friend. Jones may have been 'unauthorized' as peace negotiator, but the groundwork of his 'treaty' dealt intelligently with the major sticking-point: independence. In March Shelburne told the Lords that should America become independent, 'the sun of England's glory was set for

---

41. Jared Sparks, *The Life of Benjamin Franklin, containing The Autobiography* (Boston, 1856), 3.

ever'. Jones realizes that inevitably government must recognize American independence as surely as one day ministers would facilitate his own.

This visit to France, together with successive ones in 1780 and 1782 created intense speculation, on both sides of the Channel and the Atlantic, that he was involved in international diplomacy. Although the 'Fragment' reveals more of the scholar than the politician, Jones's self-aggrandizing made a lasting impression. As late as 1827 a reviewer of *The Secret Journals of the Acts and Proceedings of Congress* categorically states: 'there can be little doubt, it was, that lord Shelburne sent the celebrated Sir William Jones, as a secret agent to Paris, to sound the American minister on the subject; and probably, with directions, ultimately to proceed to America'. The 'Fragment' was seen as a 'diplomatic paper' creating political repercussions: 'The count de Vergennes, along with the American ministers, was apprehensive that Mr Jones was, in reality, on his way to America, to attempt a separate peace; and these apprehensions were, by them, communicated to congress.'[42]

Rumours concerning 'Plenipotentiary' Jones infuriated ministers as much as his advanced whig principles. Meanwhile he was relishing the company of Franklin. Exactly forty years older than Jones, he was much more of a role model than a father figure: 'No man ever derived so much advantage as he has, from a literary and philosophical reputation', wrote the aspirant of the established polymath. They shared unbounded intelligence and stubborn idealism.

Jones and Franklin talked together at Passy like the two Honest Whig Club members they were. Franklin might have been privileged with the secret of Jones's authorship of *A Discourse on Impressing Mariners*, for the revolutionary politician shared his anger. 'If impressing seamen is of right by common law in Britain', Franklin furiously scribbled in his copy of Judge Foster's *Reports*, 'slavery is then of right by common law; there being no slavery worse than that sailors are subjected to.'[43] Franklin would serve his own press-warrants:

> The first person I would press should be Mr Justice Foster, because I have need of his edifying example, to show how impressing ought to be borne with; [...] Then I would press the rest of the judges; and, opening the Red Book, I would press every civil officer from £50 a year up to £50,000, [...] Lastly, I think I would impress the King [...] for, to say the truth, I am not

---

42. *The American Quarterly*, 1 (March and June 1827), 129–52; 148–9.
43. Jones had read these comments: 'a copy of it [Foster] exists in England (though few know of it) with manuscript notes by Dr Franklin', *Letters*, 333.

quite satisfied of the necessity or utility of that office in Great Britain, as I see many flourishing states in the world governed well and happy without it.[44]

When not recalling mutual friends such as Richard Price and Joseph Priestley with Franklin, Jones was impressing and being impressed. Dining with the 'romantick politician', free-trade economist Turgot, they toasted Franklin who 'snatched the lightning from the skies and the sceptre from the tyrants'. Jones met the entertaining Encyclopediste Jean-François Marmontel; applauded the meritocratic sentiments of Beaumarchais's *Le Barbier de Séville*; and attended one of the first performances of *Iphigénie en Tauride*, conducted by its composer Gluck. At Auteil, Paradise and Jones visited the renowned salonnière, Anne-Catherine de Ligniville Helvétius, to whom Franklin had proposed marriage. Pleasure was mingled with duty in a 'very polite' meeting with the duc de Nivernois; Monsieur le duc required to be warmly remembered to Lady Spencer and the Duchess of Devonshire, and they successfully arranged an exchange of naval prisoners.

This transaction reminds Jones it is time to return; an important case was coming up at Westminster Hall in which Jones was the leading counsel. Jones and Paradise embarked for England at two o'clock on Saturday, 5 June. Arriving shortly after six, Jones raced back to his chambers. The diplomat *manqué* must dust down his black gown. The trial, scheduled for the following Wednesday, involved a brutal case of impressment. Jones spent long hours studying his brief; here was an opportunity to prove the illegality of press-warrants.

The King against John Borthwick and sixteen Others illustrates the domestic impact of mobilization and the commonplace horrors of impressment. The original indictment tried at Bury Assizes concerned the actions of Midshipman Richard Hatton and a party of sixteen press-men in an Ipswich tavern late in the evening of the 7 December 1778. They belonged to the *Charlotte* tender, lying off Harwich, a vessel specifically assigned to the pressing of seamen, whose commander, Lieutenant William Palmer, held an Admiralty press-warrant. Entering a room where the seamen were drinking, the naval personnel wielded 'large sticks in their hands such as are usually carried by press-gangs'. They ignored the information that some of the drinkers belonged to the *Brilliant* storeship and were already on his Majesty's service.

---

44. *The Posthumous and Other Writings of Benjamin Franklin*, ed. William Temple Franklin, 2 vols (London, 1819), 2: 109–18; 118.

A confrontation seemed inevitable and the only man who escaped the room relied upon his own threat of violence: 'Sharpe then drew a knife out of his pocket, and brandishing it, said: "The first man that hinders me from going home to my wife and family, I'll stick him!" ' The others had no weapons, but 'Bennet drew a poker from the fire for his defence, and said he would not be taken alive.' In the ensuing affray, furniture was overthrown, candles extinguished, and the publican, Thomas Nichols, who was encouraging resistance, received a fatal blow on the head from the cudgel of one of the press gang.

The Suffolk jurors had failed to determine who dealt the blow and Sir William Ashurst brought in a special verdict, requesting the judgement of the King's Bench. Ashurst saw 'several points of law arising thereon, among which is that most important and long-contested question respecting the right of impressing seamen for his Majesty's service [...] as the acquittal or condemnation of the prisoners must depend in a great measure upon the legality or illegality of that practice'.[45] The case came on at Westminster Hall on 9 June 1779, with Jones for the prosecution.

Jones trenchantly argues that the men had assembled for an unlawful purpose and with malicious intent: 'they are all equally, and in the same degree, criminal', and guilty of murder.[46] Counsel for the prisoners, Robert Graham, agreed that 'it should first be argued upon a supposition that the assembling was unlawful, provided that if it should on this ground be given against him, he might then be allowed to prove the legality of their purpose'. In reply, 'Mr Jones proceeded to say, that the laws of this country allowed not of executing any process, however legal, in the manner in which the present was attempted, men armed with bludgeons, without assigning any cause, forcibly and with threats endeavour to arrest and imprison others, who naturally resist.' Graham's counterargument insisted that the prisoners acted without malice and under orders.

In the report of the Borthwick case, subsequently published by Jones's Carmarthen-circuit colleague, Sylvester Douglas, we read:

> The counsel for the prosecution came prepared to argue the general question of the legality of pressing; but the court intimated an opinion, that it was unnecessary

---

45. *Morning Chronicle and Public Advertiser*, 20 March 1779. The next article reports: 'Yesterday morning a Lieutenant and ten sailors impressed several young men on the parade in St James's Park, who unwarily stopped to see the guards relieved, they were secured in the guard house, where they were hand-cuffed and sent on board the Nightingale tender.'
46. *Lloyd's Evening Post*, 9 June 1779.

to agitate that point in this case, as the warrant stated could not authorize a parol delegation of the power vested in the lieutenant, and, indeed, it was admitted by the counsel for the prisoners, that they were trespassers.[47]

Lieutenant Palmer's press-warrant failed to authorize a merely oral delegation of the power vested in him; the prisoners were not justified in the execution of the warrant, had no deputed power, and were therefore trespassers. Whereas Jones wanted to establish the illegality of impressment as a practice, the court was concerned with this case representing an illegal act of pressing, an abuse of properly warranted procedure.

Judge Edward Willes's summing-up made it crystal clear:

> In this case, the counsel for the prosecution offered to argue the general question, whether the warrant was legal or not. But, unless the prisoners had a power to execute it, and conducted themselves legally in the execution, there is no occasion for the court to consider that question.

As with the Millachip case, the King's Bench was determined to avoid the political hot-potato of the legality of press-warrants. Again Jones is denied the opportunity of displaying his thoroughly researched mastery of the subject. Deprived of his Westminster Hall 'Hargrave moment' and with no news of the post concerning which Hargrave had deferred to him, Jones threw himself into the summer circuits.

Early September 1779 finds Jones bathing at Weymouth; scouring rock pools to augment his collection of beadlet sea-anemones ('called *Actiniæ* by the naturalists'); and counting the ships of Sir Charles Hardy's Channel fleet sailing westward past Portland Bill to attack a Franco-Spanish force—rumoured to be an invasion fleet—off Plymouth. In an excess of self-sacrificial Celtic-inspired enthusiasm, he contemplates a dramatically glorious death:

> [I]f my death could procure the total loss of the combined fleets followed by an *union* with America on terms of general Liberty, I should not hesitate to throw myself from that rock, like Gray's bard, into the gulph below. (*Letters*, 1: 315)

The same letter contains some mysteriously self-dramatizing hints of future revelations—not to be trusted to the post—concerning: 'an *attempt* of mine to procure peace and liberty, which no man living but yourself [Althorp] shall know'.

---

47. *Reports of Cases Argued and Determined in the Court of King's Bench, in the Nineteenth, Twentieth, and Twenty First Years of George III*, ed. Sylvester Douglas, 3rd edn, 2 vols (London, 1790), 1: 210.

Jones is darkly cynical about the self-seeking rock pool of British life: its cities full of the effete pursuit of pleasure and patronage, its country gentlemen ignorant, prejudiced, and corrupt: '[B]oth houses of parliament are so totally depraved, and the legislative part of our constitution so perfectly dependent on the executive.' He despairs of 'manly, rational, intelligible Liberty'. Where are 'virtuous men and real patriots' to be found? Jones's only hope lies 'in our rising countrymen of rank, property, virtue, and talents; the *two first* of which qualities are necessary to give them opportunity of exerting the *two last* early enough'. This hardly sounds egalitarian, but it gives us an insight into Jones's thinking, not least concerning property. The privileged Althorp possesses all four of these 'qualities', but Jones self-referential slip is showing here.

Over many years the 33-year-old Jones had been using his intellectual gifts to play the patronage system while accruing social, academic, legal, and linguistic capital. All this had been bankable, but he lacked the economic capital essential for effective independence. If he was a realist, he was also profoundly conventional. Money crystallizes relationships. Intimate association with aristocrats and gentry had reinforced his belief in landed property as the ultimate guarantee of civic autonomy. Conversations with Adam Smith at the Turk's Head had convinced him that *homo economicus* might come equipped with enlightened self-interest and a substantial moral mission. The example of Franklin convinced Jones that he could not wait until he was 70 to make his mark. The 'nabob wealth' of a Bengal salary would enable him to short-circuit, and attempt to reform, the system.

Jones's '*trembling Hope*' rests upon the youth of Britain. '[T]he *old* and *middle-aged* are so corrupt (I speak with some exceptions, no doubt) that, if England can be saved at all, it must be saved by the *young*' (*Letters*, 1: 319). Jones's holiday is over and, having liberated his Actiniæ, he must return to his own struggle in the specialized microhabitat that is London. He is getting no younger and must continue to interact with 'corrupt' ageing men such as Sandwich and Wilkes.

Jones longs for the time when 'I can be of more service to my country by acting rather than speculating' (*Letters*, 1: 327). The merely theoretical never provides sufficient stimulation: this is a predominating theme of Jones's life. Capacious intellect and burning ambition fuel his frustration: '[A] good citizen ought to *act*.' Serving one's country is not the binary of self-serving; for Jones it is the only road to self-fulfilment. It is not enough to put forth delicately beautiful feelers twice a day like the rock pool sea-anemone, if one stubbornly remains a beadlet of jelly: 'I consider myself as related to society, and not as a mere insulated animal, like an Actinia on a rock, solicitous only for *my* subsistence and *my* pleasure.'

Heartily sick of waiting upon ministers and courtiers and impassively reacting to an adverse current of political events, a new and determined conviction has taken hold—it is time for Jones to act.

5

Republican Jones and the 'Poetry of Politics': Fragments of Liberty

The spring and summer of 1780 saw things come to a head in a confusing concatenation of events. That January Jones was convinced: 'The present session of parliament will entirely put an end to my suspense in regard to the India judgeship' (*Letters*, 1: 341). Some hope!

Jones had done quite enough on his own account to hamper his Indian prospects. Now political developments beyond his control were threatening the Calcutta appointment. The EIC charter was coming up for renewal in March and North's desire for greater governmental control brought him into conflict with both its chairman and the opposition forces of Burke, and of Fox who asked the minister if, not content with having lost America, 'he wished to ruin the company's possessions in India'.[1] This was against the background of Company complaints concerning the Supreme Court's jurisdiction, which they saw as obstructing the Supreme Council in Calcutta. Petitions had been sent to parliament from both Hastings and British inhabitants, detailing native complaints about the unsympathetic introduction of English law into Bengal. It remains deeply ironic that the appointment of Jones, who was to play such a key role in Hastings's project to govern Indians by Indian laws, should be jeopardized by a political situation in which there were even parliamentary calls to abolish the Supreme Court.

On 10 February, Jones and Philip Yorke (great nephew of Lord Chancellor Hardwicke, Jones senior's pupil) attended 'the new spouting society' in Soho Square: 'More than six hundred persons were assembled; men and

1. *The New Annual Register for the Year 1780* (London, 1781), 145–6.

women of fashion, lawyers, parsons, officers, tradesmen, people of all sorts: the question was "whether parties were beneficial in a free state".' Sickened by a vehemently vociferous schoolfellow whose eloquence issued from a wine bottle, Jones took no part in the debate, but it made him think all the more. In this parody of parliament the drunken Harrovian represented the worst aspects of corrupt privilege in an increasingly servile House. Though he 'will not enlist under the banners of a party', Jones wants to step forth— but on a more significant stage than a Soho soapbox.

The following day Jones, moving from the ridiculous to the sublime, heard Burke brilliantly 'spouting' in the Commons, attacking extravagance and corruption in his advocacy of economical reform. Jones regarded his friend as an overzealous defender of the concept of party, but whenever he heard him in parliament he envied that access to political power.

Power repelled and attracted him. In the hands of an individual he found it odious, but the republican in Jones longed for the means to place power in the hands of a free people. Enlightenment belief in the power of association drew him towards the Association Movement, modelled upon political reformer Christopher Wyvill's Yorkshire Association, which petitioned parliament for the abolition of sinecures, rotten boroughs, governmental waste, and the abuse of executive power. But these electors were men of property and Jones found their calls for reform too cautious. Jones had limited patience with this gradualist extra-parliamentary approach. With the election approaching, a more decisive remedy might be achieved through the ballot box.

At this critical moment, theory and practice were symbiotically associating in Jones's thinking. His constitutional research was reinforced by professional experience of arrant injustice. The bourgeois radical was increasingly acknowledging his own roots and his belief in universal manhood suffrage.

If impressment was enslavement so also was disenfranchisement. Jones was moving closer to the distinguished parliamentary reformer, Major John Cartwright, who, in the momentous year of 1776, declared: 'I can conceive no clearer idea of slavery, than for one man to be obliged against his will to be the soldier of another.'[2] Cartwright's *Declaration of the Rights of Englishmen* (1780) argued that the unfranchised '*do not enjoy* liberty, but are absolutely *enslaved* to those who have votes, and to their *Representative*'. Of this Jones was heard to say, 'it ought to be written in letters of gold'.

---

2. *Take your Choice! Representation and Respect: Imposition and Contempt. Annual Parliaments and Liberty: Long Parliaments and Slavery* (London, 1776), 27.

A letter from Shrewsbury of 12 March expresses his frustration; his need to act decisively could not be clearer:

> [T]he general election approaches, a time when every lawyer wishes to step forward to the scene of action: I can ill brook the necessity of remaining so long at my age without taking a part in the affairs of my country. [...] renounce all idea of the judgeship, and to enter boldly on my political career. (*Letters*, 1: 352)

The next few weeks proved exciting, but friends urged caution. Accordingly, when he learned of the death of Dr Richard Browne at Oxford, Jones applied for the lord almoner's professorship of Arabic. This prestigious chair hardly involved 'taking a part in the affairs of my country', but politics worked against him. The university appreciated the reflected glory of Jones's international reputation, but they had long memories in Oxford. High tories and ministerial supporters recalled how Jones's *Oration intended to have been spoken in the Theatre* (1773) lacked the requisite 'slavish compliment' to North as chancellor. With its panegyrics of Milton, Selden, and Locke, it was a paean to political as well as academic liberty and had to be withdrawn. Many academics were chary of Jones's growing reputation as a radical whig. In the event nepotism and politics triumphed; the Arabic chair went to a comparative nonentity, Henry Ford, the husband of Bishop Lowth's niece.

Destined not to become *homo academicus*, Jones had yet more interviews with North. Indirectly, one of his firmest friends was not helping matters. On 6 April 1780 Dunning triumphed in the Commons; his motion 'that the influence of the crown has increased, is increasing, and ought to be diminished' was carried by eighteen votes. As a political animal Jones was delighted, but this weakening of North's government brought uncertainty for the aspirant puisne judge:

> Lord North is fearful of offending him [Lord Chancellor Thurlow] and waits for his recommendation, which he will never give in favour of me or anyone else. Thus I am kept *between hawk and buzzard*, approved by both and advanced by neither. (*Letters*, 1: 357)

Late April brought news of another Oxford vacancy, but this was no academic post. It was caused by the surprise resignation of the High Church tory and Gothic revival architect, Sir Roger Newdigate, as MP for Oxford University. The story of Jones's decision to stand as a whig candidate for the university is a complex but fascinating one. It would submerge him even deeper into a welter of patronage and enlistment in party politics.

On 29 April, Jones wrote to Johnson's former tutor, the Revd Dr William Adams, Master of Pembroke College, enquiring what his chances might be if nominated as a candidate. What he did not realize as he wrote this letter was that his Oxford friend Dr William Scott, for whose admission to the Turk's Head Jones had voted, was at that moment being selected as college candidate for University College. Scott, the brother of John, future Lord Chancellor Eldon, had been canvassing hard behind the scenes. On learning of Jones's interest in the seat, Scott had secured Jones's promise of secrecy while he insidiously solicited the support of Jones's friends, including Burke, Reynolds, and Dunning. Jones had been completely outmanoeuvred by Scott's duplicitous behaviour. Jones wrote to Adams, pointedly stressing his Celtic candour to this archdeacon of Llandaff: 'I should grieve, if this matter should end in a breach between Scott and me: but I am a plain Briton, as my father was, and must speak out.' Jones felt Scott had 'invaded my most heartfelt friendships'.[3]

An inauspicious start to Jones's campaign, but friends assured him he might rely upon 'all the literary and Whig interest in the nation'. Announcing his candidature on 2 May, Jones realized the election of a whig member for Oxford would represent a major political step. The third candidate was an experienced parliamentarian, Christ Church's Sir William Dolben, whom Jones respected for anti-slavery convictions, but who generally voted for the tory interest. Jones pinned his hope on Scott and Dolben splitting the tory vote, but here too Scott was devious. Though Scott had always opposed 'every proposition favourable to popular government', he disguised his political sentiments to pick up whig votes: 'Now he is a perfect Janus, with a Tory face at Oxford and a Whig Face in London' (*Letters*, 1: 384).

Despite these setbacks, Jones threw himself into action. Eminently practised in canvassing and cementing key contacts in high places, he merely switched the focus from ministerial and EIC to Oxford voting interests. Again he must play the patronage system: 'Patronage, I fear, will carry votes against me: it must therefore be exerted for me.' His campaign involved strategic complexities:

---

3. Letter of 15 May 1780 to William Adams; Garland Cannon, *The Life and Mind of Oriental Jones* (Cambridge, 1990), 364.

> Lord Onslow influences *Turner* of Merton who is a Whig and much inclined to oppose Sir W. Dolben. Duke of Portland might easily carry *Dyer* of Queens. Sir George Savile (my friend) will carry the 2 Hartleys, and they, Booth of Merton. *Hewson* of Queens [is] swayed by Sir R. Worsley. (*Letters*, 1: 365)

Jones despatched his 'zealous friend' John Paradise to Oxford to obtain lists of electors from college butlers. This enabled Jones to compile a list of 847 voters, which he sent to powerful whig contacts, including the celebrity canvasser Georgiana Cavendish, Duchess of Devonshire, and the Spencers. But the rules of the patronage game required a deftness and subtlety that fell victim to Jones's impetuous enthusiasm. An ill-judged circular letter, written by the unworldly Paradise, irritated many recipients; its praise of Jones sounding too much like 'being one's own Trumpeter' (*Letters*, 1: 367).

Some Oxford MAs were puzzled at Jones's not being an official college candidate; others were justifiably confused at exactly what 'Persian' Jones wanted: was it to be Indian judge, Arabic professor, or Oxford MP? Worse than this, Jones proved too energetic in peppering his patronage targets. Introduced to the waspish Horace Walpole, Jones lost no time in canvassing this Cambridge man. Walpole describes his contemptuous reaction to poet William Mason:

> Mrs. Vesey presented him to me. The next day he sent me an absurd and pedantic letter, desiring I would make interest for him. I answered it directly, and told him I had no more connection with Oxford than with the Antipodes, nor desired to have. [. . .] the man it seems is a staunch Whig, but very wrong-headed.[4]

Walpole had a point; if the circular was Paradise's fault, Jones made little effort to prevent its distribution. Even more 'wrong-headed' was Jones's decision to include copies of his pro-American 'Carmen ad Libertatem' in his mailshots. Jones depicts Liberty as practically a-wing, drawn westwards by the republican devotions of thirteen states:

> Altaribus te jam tredecim vocat,
> Te thure templisque urget America:
> Audis; Atlanteumque pennis
>   Ire paras levibus per æquor.
> Ah! ne roseta et flumina deseras
> Dilecta nuper: nam piget,—heu piget

4. *Correspondence of Horace Walpole*, 2: 86–7.

>   Martis nefasti fratricidæ,
>   Imperiique malè arrogate.   (*Works*, 10: 399)

[America is already hailing you at thirteen altars, and on your light wings you are preparing to cross the Atlantic. O do not desert the rose gardens and rivers you have recently loved: for we repent,—O we repent of the fratricide of a wicked war and of a wrongly-arrogated authority.]

This ode hardly impressed staid Oxford voters, earning him the damaging sobriquets of 'American' or 'Republican' Jones.

Offering her active support, Georgiana, Duchess of Devonshire quizzed him for deserting the Muses, but Elizabeth Montagu, canvassing Sir William Weller Pepys, declared: 'If the Muses were the Electors he would carry the election from every candidate that could offer. He possesses the keys of all their treasures and can deal them forth for the world.'[5] Unfortunately it lay in the power of neither the Muses nor his eminent female champions to matriculate in, let alone graduate MA from, Oxford. Although not electors, such women were prime movers in the public sphere and proved 'powerful engines of support' in his energetic campaign.

In the midst of all this frenzied activity, on Wednesday 17 May, Jones was devastated by the sudden loss of his much-loved mother, the woman who had taught him 'to love the rights and liberties of my countrymen', and 'to detest the abettors of unconstitutional power' (*Letters*, 1: 374). It was too late now to buy her a carriage and a house in the country. In the knowledge that she had always urged him on to public service, he sadly declared: 'I have no parent left but my Country', and threw himself into campaigning to assuage his grief.

His letters at this time are filled with the names of the great and the good, even the not so good, as long as they possessed, controlled, or might canvass, an Oxford vote: Joseph Banks (despite his intimacy with Sandwich), along with most members of the Turk's Head Club, John Dunning, Colonel Isaac Barré, a prominent champion of the colonists, Lord Craven, Lord Abingdon, 'General Smith canvasses Berkshire and the India connexions', Admiral Keppel, Charles James Fox. An election meeting on 25 May chaired by circuit colleague Thomas Milles was encouraging, but news from Oxford less so. There was resentment of Jones's reliance upon non-resident MAs, and the London support of radical whigs such as John Wilkes, Richard

---

5. *Mrs Montagu 'Queen of the Blues': Her Letters and Friendships from 1762–1800*, ed. Reginald Blunt, 2 vols (London, 1923), 2: 84–5.

Price, and Edmund Cartwright, poet and inventor of the power loom. The fatal blow to Jones's political hopes was delivered in early June as London and the whole nation were appalled by the anti-Catholic Gordon riots.

On the evening of Tuesday 6 June 1780 a future 'prophet against empire' and a would-be legislator of colonial governance were both caught up in the events of riot-torn London. The 22-year-old William Blake, according to his biographer, Gilchrist, was entangled in the surging mob, which plundered and burnt the newly erected Newgate prison. The extent to which Blake was celebrating the 'fierce rushing' of the 'Glad Day' of Albion rising midst the flames engulfing the London Bastille has been the subject of well-worn critical debate. We know, however, that the 33-year-old Jones, was lamenting this anti-Catholic 'phrenzy' as 'a poniard in the heart of Liberty' (*Letters*, 1: 401). The legacy of this divisive turmoil would help frustrate Jones's own attempts to argue the constitutional basis for extending the suffrage, contributing to almost a decade of dormancy for the parliamentary reform movement.

Jones saw that radicalism itself was being fragmented, and this piquant juxtaposition of celebrity lawyer and journeyman copy-engraver, of documented and alleged (perhaps mythic) presences, reveals the intricate relationship between political and poetical liberty. It is simplistic to imagine enlightened demystifier Jones and Romantic seer Blake as situated on opposing sides of any putative barricade. Both were to prove mythographers, energizing Enlightenment projects with a Romantic vision of radical realignment. The divide between them was purely social. Blake's 'entanglement' in the 'mobility' ('The mob, the rabble; the common people; the working classes', *OED*) symbolizes the contrast with Jones's 'vertical' mobility and his wealth of powerful connections that constituted effective liberty.

The rioters, having heard that the Templars were assembling in their college, raised the cry of 'The Temple—Kill the lawyers!' in Whitefriars and Essex Street. John Scott (later Lord Chancellor Eldon) was barely able to protect his beautiful young wife Elizabeth from the harrying of the mob on leaving their house in Carey Street. Her bonnet was ripped off and her dress torn by the time they reached the safety of the Temple's massive gate.

Armed with a 'light horseman's carbine', Jones commanded a volunteer company of barristers and students in defence of the Middle Temple. The very 'stones of Law' of which, as Blake later claimed, 'prisons are built', were being protected by a zealous advocate of liberty and universal manhood suffrage, a close friend of Edmund Burke and Sir George Savile who had respectively designed and introduced the 1778 Catholic Relief Bill. The supreme irony was that on 2 June, while a crowd estimated at between 20,000 and 60,000 invaded parliament to demand the repeal of Savile's Act, roughing up lords and bishops in the process, the radical Duke of Richmond was attempting to introduce a bill in the Lords advocating manhood suffrage and annual parliaments.

Huge crowds destroyed Catholic property throughout London, torching the Bavarian embassy chapel in Golden Square, and wrecking the Sardinian embassy chapel of St Anselm and St Cecilia in Lincoln's Inn Fields. Savile's Leicester Square house was set ablaze and gutted, valuables looted, his coach and furniture smashed. Targeted for his enlightened position on religious toleration, Lord Mansfield and his wife narrowly escaped, but their Bloomsbury Square house, including his precious library, was pillaged and burnt to the ground.

Rumours spread as rapidly as the fires. Jones heard 'a well-dressed man' claim Mansfield had been murdered, whereas Jones had only just left him 'very cool and composed' at a friend's house. Jones was furious that the Commons had adjourned and martial law declared unconstitutionally by the king. On the night of the 8 June he was 'playing at soldiers from eight to four in the morning', and had only had a few hours' rest before arguing a cause in the Court of Exchequer: '[T]he courts of *common* law and *equity* are sitting: how then can we be under *martial* law?'

In the confusion Jones and Wilkes, equalled enraged at the inaction, were thinking along the same legal lines: voluntary association and the common-law authority of the *posse comitatus* or sheriff's posse. At the Temple, although 'every lawyer wishe[d] to step forward to the scene of action', Jones was frustrated by the difficulty of teaching colleagues how to reload a musket: 'We have five hundred gentlemen, who are divided into companies and supplied with muskets which they will only fire once, and with bayonets which they know not how to push' (*Letters*: 1: 405). Meanwhile Henry, the son of Domenico Angelo, Jones's teacher of sabre and *épée*, was watching Wilkes at the head of a party of soldiers defeat a mob attempting to torch London Bridge. As City chamberlain this former colonel in the militia put Farringdon ward under military control, and defended the Bank of England; Johnson wrote to Hester Thrale; 'Jack Wilkes headed the party that drove them away.'[6] No one knew better than Wilkes how crowds

---

6. *Reminiscences of Henry Angelo*, 2 vols (London, 1830), 2: 150; *Letters to and from Johnson*, 2: 154.

might be mobilized in the cause of liberty, but he saw as clearly as Jones how the rioters were making political reform anathema to men of property.

The Blakean contraries are further complicated if the rioters believed, as David Erdman claimed, that freeing Newgate prisoners represented 'a step towards freeing Albion from its oppressive war with America'.[7] No object was closer to the heart of Jones, the defender of the 'law-built heaven' of the Temple and vilifier of the counterproductive horrors of the volatile mob, 'the *bourreaux* [executioners] of our Liberty'. For Jones this was sectarian strife not extra-parliamentary politics. If Blake heard in the rioters' cries 'the voice of the people, arising from valley and hill,/O'erclouded with power', the mordant irony was that this association was simultaneously being made by the forces of retrenchment, much to Jones's disgust:

> A very great magistrate said to me yesterday, 'This is the voice of the people!' Good god! No sober man ever used that expression without meaning the voice of the *nation*, of the *whole community*; such as was heard to call so loudly at the Revolution. (*Letters*, 1: 404)[8]

Later, in his 1793 prophecy, Blake envisaged the intertwined energies of freedom and tyranny spreading eastward from the American Revolution. In the midst of the 1780 confusions Jones saw exactly what was happening. The mob had made the king 'the happiest prince in Europe' by handing him an all too plausible 'pretext for strengthening the prerogative (already too strong for the freedom of the parliament)'.[9] Glorious, American, and future French revolutions are brought into ironic counterpoise by the voices Jones hears in the metropolis:

> Many of our best-intentioned men, well inclined till now to our mixed constitution, are continually saying, 'How much more secure we should have been in France'! [...] An officer of some rank said to me an hour ago: 'This is the fault of our constitution!' Those were his very words; and, if I hear them often repeated, my alarms will encrease. I sincerely think that our constitution is in the greatest danger. (*Letters*, 1: 409)

---

7. David Erdman, *William Blake: Prophet against Empire*, 3rd edn (Princeton, 1977), 9.
8. *The French Revolution*, 1: 206–7; *The Complete Poetry and Prose of William Blake*, ed. David V. Erdman (New York, 1982), 295. Vicesimus Knox wrote: 'The Tory and Jacobite party exulted over the ruins, and would have rejoiced in building a Bastille with the dilapidations. "See," said they, as they triumphed over the scene, "the effects of power in the hands of the PEOPLE!"' *The Spirit of Despotism* (London, 1795), 62–3.
9. Jones was enraged by rumours that the riots were '"a most diabolical plot of the French and Americans" [...] the Americans had no more to do with the riot than the Chinese', *Letters*, 1: 414–15.

The orchestrated bigotry of the Protestant Association had, according to Jones, 'ruined the cause of Liberty beyond hope of recovery'. His immediate reaction is a strong desire 'that every man in the City and in the country will carry his firelock and know how to use it', now for the defence of the Constitution rather than the Temple. Jones also saw the Gordon Riots had effectively extinguished his political hopes, making 'the resident Oxonians more adverse than ever to the advocates for Liberty, which they absurdly confound with Licentiousness' (*Letters*, 1: 417).

Raising a volunteer company of barristers and students reinforced Jones's opposition to a standing army. In July he published his first political tract: *An Inquiry into the Legal Mode of Suppressing Riots, with a Constitutional Plan of Future Defence* (1780), advocating a civilian militia and the citizen's constitutional duty to bear arms. Jones avoided a contemporary instance of the effectiveness of civilian force, which would have been impolitic to mention. Conversations with British officers and American friends inspired his admiration for the Massachusetts minutemen, trained to respond 'at a minute's warning', whose conspicuous bravery had met with considerable success in urban and irregular warfare. The first two heads of his six-point plan read as follows:

> I
> Let all such persons in every county in ENGLAND as are included in the power of that county, and *are of ability to provide themselves with arms*, and pay for learning the use of them, be furnished each with his *musket* and *bayonet*, and their necessary appendages.
> II
> Let several *companies* be formed, in every such county, of sixty men or more, voluntarily associated for the sole purpose of joining the power, when legally summoned, and, with view, of learning the proper use of their weapons, street-firing, and the various evolutions necessary in action.

Although the first edition did not bear his name, 'street-firing' Jones circulated his ideas so widely there was no doubt of its authorship. The *Gentleman's Magazine* stressed its timely importance, its 'candour and learning', even echoing Jones's privately declared determination 'to step forward':

> At a crisis of distress, when the despondence of some and the servility of others seem disposed to surrender the constitutional rights of the people to the crown [...] the present author has stept forward, and discussed with learning, temper, and decency, a question, of all others, most interesting to an English-

man, viz. 'Whether the still subsisting laws and genuine constitution had not armed *the civil state* with a power sufficient [...] to have suppressed ever so formidable a riot, without the intervention of the *military*.'[10]

Major Cartwright praised the tract's clarity and eminent practicality: 'It bespeaks the hand of a master, deep in legal knowledge, and the heart of a citizen truly virtuous.'[11]

Jones's plan to arm the civil state was nearly adopted in London. As he wrote on 21 July to Samuel Parr: '[James] Townsend moved for it in the Court of Aldermen, and lost it by two votes.' That disappointed Jones but, 'what vexes me most is, that I shall be in Wales on the 3d of next month, when I had resolved to give the County of Middlesex a little speech, and propose a general measure in support of the civil power' (*Letters*, 1: 423).

Jones's first political speech would have to wait but, as he left London for the delayed Carmarthen circuit, he recalled the compensations of Wales. The topicality of his August poem for the 'Druids of the Tivy' was dictated by his experiences of early June. Written 'in one hour', 'Kneel to the Goddess whom all men adore' supplies a tolerant corrective to the violence of narrow sectarianism:

> What means all this frensy, what mad men are they
>   Who broil and are broil'd for a shade in religion?
> Since all sage inspirers one doctrine convey
>   From Numa's wild nymph to sly Mohamed's pigeon.
>   Then Druids arise
>   Teach the world to be wise,
> And the grape's rosy blood for your sacrifice pour,
>   Th'immortals invoke,
>   And under this oak
> Kneel, kneel to the Goddess whom all men adore. (ll: 1–10; *SWJ*, p. 58)

The poem's playful emphasis upon the universality of the divine female (Astarte, Diana, Venus, or Mary) and the ubiquity of inspired revelation, whether Egerian or avian, anticipate the comparative mythology and imaginative syncretism of Jones's path-breaking essay 'On the Gods of Greece, Italy, and India' (1784). It was appropriate to place such teaching in the mouth of a half-Welsh 'Druid' and Cymmrodor, for Druidic lore anciently

---

10. *Gentleman's Magazine*, 50 (1780), 335.
11. *Monthly Review*, 63 (August 1780), 142–3.

taught the Blakean lessons that 'All Religions are One', and that 'There is no Natural Religion'.

Returning to metropolitan politics at the end of August, Jones realized the hopelessness of his Oxford candidacy. Declining the poll on 2 September, he devoted all his energies to canvassing for Fox in Westminster and supporting Wilkes on the hustings. It felt liberating not having to watch his back for adverse university reaction, but in thanking Wilkes for his 'kind exertions' in the Oxford campaign, Jones asked him to return the list of voters. Clearly Jones had not abandoned parliamentary ambition, and his planned address to Middlesex freeholders at the Mermaid Tavern, Hackney, on 9 September, *A Speech on the Nomination of Candidates to Represent the County of Middlesex* (1780), contains some of his most radical political writing.

An ambitious state of the nation address, it condemns the American war prolonged by an 'angry, vengeful, and implacable parliament'. Government had shown how a 'colonising and commercial' people might 'alienate their colonies and destroy their commerce'. 'Oriental' Jones asks the electors to 'turn their eyes to the East' where sources of infinite public and private wealth, of 'every precious, every valuable commodity; gold and gems, spices and elegant apparel' are threatened by the prospect of native revolution and governmental obstruction of 'our India company'. His desire 'to pass with haste by the coast of Africa' does not prevent Jones from providing an impassioned denunciation of the slave trade, subsequently much cited by abolitionists on both sides of the Atlantic:

> Sugar, it has been said, would be dear, if it were not worked by Blacks in the Western Islands; as if the most laborious, the most dangerous works, were not carried on in every country, but chiefly in *England*, by freemen, in fact, they are so carried on with infinitely more advantage, for there is an alacrity in the consciousness of freedom, and a gloomy, sullen indolence in a consciousness of slavery; but let sugar be as dear as it may, it is better to eat none, to eat honey, if sweetness only be palatable; better to eat aloes or coloquintida, than violate a primary law of nature, impressed on every heart not imbruted by avarice, than rob one human creature of those eternal rights of which no law upon earth can justly deprive him. (pp. 5–6)

Commitment to inalienable rights and universal liberty reinforces his enthusiasm for the infant republic. He attacks British blindness to 'how their own liberties are blended and interwoven with those of the Americans', their insanity in assailing what is geographically impregnable:

> I was last summer at Paris, in company every day with sensible and experienced men of different nations; who knew *America* perfectly, and as perfectly knew the strength of the *British* navy. 'Your countrymen,' said they, 'must be *mad* in the extreme [...] The virtuous republicans can subsist [...] by *agriculture* alone, and your armies will never penetrate, to our positive knowledge, into the *heart* of their provinces.' (p. 8)

This argument, as insuperable as the American continent itself, Jones frequently expressed in private letters:

> Did you know that Americans had flourishing settlements *seven hundred* miles from the coast? Every man among them is a soldier, a *patriot*—Subdue such a people! The king may as easily conquer the moon or wear it on his sleeve. (*Letters*, 2: 517)

Jones recommends 'a double remedy for all our evils': to return a parliament eager to reach an honourable reconciliation with America, and to restore the balance of 'our mixed system', threatened by the unconstitutional growth of monarchical power: 'I have heard undue prerogative compared to a giant, who bestrides our narrow island, and may at his discretion suspend his massy club over our heads or reduce us to powder with its weight.' In supporting Wilkes's candidature, Jones recalls the *North Briton* warning that: 'the giant *prerogative* is to be let loose, and stalk about, to create unusual terrors'. It also recalls a sardonically conclusive remark made by Jones in an interchange that Boswell recorded at the Turk's Head:

> Goldsmith in high spirits: spoke of equality. Said Burke, 'Here's our monarchy man growing Republican. Oliver Cromwell, not Oliver Goldsmith.' Said Goldsmith, 'I'm for Monarchy to keep us all equal.' 'Ay,' said I, 'a King like a great rolling stone to make all smooth.' JONES, 'To grind to powder.'[12]

Jones's Hackney speech—ironically never delivered as Wilkes and George Byng were nominated (and subsequently returned) without opposition—was praised by prominent publisher John Nichols: 'He expresses his opinion, without reserve, in the strong language of the County Petitions and Parliamentary Debates of 1780', and was judged by distinguished antiquarian, Richard Gough, as 'to the full as BOLD as the BOLDEST of Mr Wilkes's'.[13]

---

12. *Private Papers of James Boswell*, ed. Geoffrey Scott and Frederick A. Pottle, 18 vols (New York, 1928–34), 6: 130.
13. John Nichols, *Literary Anecdotes of the Eighteenth Century*, 9 vols (London, 1812–15), 8: 78. *Gentleman's Magazine*, 74: 2 (1804), 1,214.

More than a demonstration of how effective he might have proved as an MP, it marks a new confidence in Jones. The next two years saw a series of publications that convinced many government ministers he was a card-carrying republican.

Jones was preparing for another Paris trip with Paradise who intended to become 'a complete member of an American republic', one of the first naturalized American citizens.[14] On his way to Dover, Jones dined with Turk's Head friend, Bennet Langton, who, adding military engineering to his skills in ancient Greek, had helped design new fortifications for Chatham docks. As Jones toured 'the redoubts, merlins, and embrasures' with Langton's bright 8-year-old son George, he was innocently thinking that such knowledge would be useful in writing an 'impartial history of the American war' (*Letters*, 1: 440). Such activities—shortly followed by a voyage to France—might have appeared much more suspicious to any lurking government spy.

Apart from meeting Franklin and 'as many of the American leaders as I could', Jones observed French legal processes at the Palais de Justice and consulted royal library manuscripts on Arabic literature. Jones realized that, 'In my profession the reputation of a scholar is a dead weight' (*Letters*, 1: 450), but such was his fascination with Bedouin culture he found it impossible to quit the republic of letters.

Orientalism had much to do with the poetics of politics. Jones wanted to see exquisite Sūfi poetry translated into English as the writings of Hāfiz and Sa'di stressed the path of physical and spiritual reconciliation. In poetry as in politics, reconciliation and synthesis between Asia and Europe, between America and Britain, would be mutually enriching. Not for nothing was he called 'Harmonious' Jones. At Hackney he had urged the need for a conciliating government to heal the breach with America and to restore 'the broken harmony of our limited republick'. Relieved from the stresses of seeking votes and patronage from all and sundry, he had a brief window of leisure to review both his own position and that of his country. Through the spring of 1781 two important fragments were running in his head.

The first embodied an opinion of Cicero 'that no man can justly be called a speaker, unless he unite in the highest degree the powers of instructing, delighting, and moving, every audience on every subject' (*Works*, 9: 29).

---

14. Letter of Paradise to Franklin, 2 October 1780; cited in A. B. Shepperson, *John Paradise and Lucy Ludwell* (Richmond, VA, 1942), 150.

Jones early recognized the power of sensibility in educating young Althorp. Jones's tutoring was crowned by his pupil's entering parliament at the same election in which the master withdrew the contest. As Orientalist and as barrister Jones was moving audiences of readers and of jurors, earning substantial and growing reputations in both fields. His failure to address the nation's representatives was no real setback. There were powerful extra-parliamentary ways to enlist instruction and delight to mobilize the emotions of a wider audience. The poetry of politics was very much on Jones's agenda.

In many respects he anticipates, and would have endorsed, Friedrich Schlegel's *Lyceums-fragment* 65: 'Poetry is republican speech: a speech which is its own law and end unto itself, and in which all the parts are free citizens and have the right to vote.'[15] For the second important fragment upon which Jones's imagination was working embraced—like that of Schlegel—both poetical form and political structures. It was Fragment 29 of the Greek lyric poet Alcæus (late 7th–mid 6th century BCE), as cited by James Thomson in his preface to Milton's *Areopagitica*: 'What is it that makes a city [. . .] it is not walls and buildings: no, it is being inhabited by men; by men who know themselves to be men, and have suitable notions of the duty of human nature: by men, who know what it is alone that exalts them above the brutes.'[16]

The remarkable publication history of the resultant poem, *An Ode in Imitation of Alcæus* (1781), which Jones described as '*the last sigh of my departed hope* for a renovation of our free Constitution', charts his incremental success in achieving political ends by aesthetic means. Fittingly for a poem 'composed in my chaise between Abergavenny and Brecon' and written down 'in the mountains of Trecastle', this text has a *mobilité* reflecting that of its author. Initially a private 'conversation poem' sent to the viscount addressed in the first line: '*Althorp*, what forms a state?', it was 'set to *Attic* notes' by musicologist Charles Burney, for after dinner recitals. Subsequently privately printed, its opening adjusted to omit the addressee, it was distributed to fellow members of the Club of Honest Whigs such as Richard Price, Joseph Priestley, Charles Dilly, Ralph Griffiths, Thomas Day, William Hodgson, and Benjamin Franklin.

---

15. *German Aesthetic and Literary Criticism*, ed. Kathleen M. Wheeler (Cambridge, 1984), 42.
16. Francis Blackburne, *Remarks on Johnson's Life of Milton* (London, 1780), 208.

Reprinted anonymously by the *Annual Register* and the *European Magazine*, it was given a huge popular audience through being distributed gratis in broadsheet by Cartwright's Society for Constitutional Information (SCI), to which Jones was elected in March 1782. Established as an inherently public and democratic document, the 1790s saw Jones's ode quoted at length in the Commons by Charles Grey (later Prime Minister Earl Grey, architect of the 1832 Great Reform Act) and published in full by Thomas Spence in the radical journal *Pigs' Meat; or, Lessons for the Swinish Multitude*, and by *The Chartist Circular* of 28 December 1839.[17]

A closer look at the poem demonstrates exactly how all the parts are 'free citizens' of a political and literary *res publica*, embracing not only Alcæus, Milton, and Thomson, but also including the French Huguenot poet Guillaume du Bartas (1544–90), who provided the divine model for *Paradise Lost*, his translator, Josuah Sylvester (1562/3–1618), and Jones's friend William Hawkins, Oxford professor of poetry. Jones's ode was frequently republished in America, and it is fascinating to consider the possibility of its 'republican speech' helping to inspire the American national anthem.

Francis Scott Key, the Maryland attorney who in the dawn of 14 September 1814 penned on the back of a letter 'The Star-Spangled Banner' after seeing the American flag proudly flying over Fort McHenry despite intensive British shelling of Baltimore, might well have recalled Jones's reference to 'starr'd and spangled courts' (l. 60). It is, of course, impossible to establish whether Jones (or indeed Key) was influenced by Milton's reference, in his version of Psalm 136, to the stars as 'spangled sisters bright', or by the phrases 'star-spangled canopy' or 'bright star-spangled regions' from Sylvester's translations of du Bartas to which Milton's indebtedness was pointed out in an important work of literary criticism by Charles Dunster.[18]

What is to be charted here is not the interrelationship of glittering fragments or the processes of influence, but the mingling of the individual and the collaborative. Disparate voices and genres are being brought into play across history. This is poetry as process. Jones's ode, inspired by an antityrannical fragment, accords with Schlegel's *Athenaeum-Fragment* designa-

---

17. *Authentic Report of the Debate in the House of Commons, on the 6th and 7th of May, 1793, on Mr Grey's Motion for a Reform in Parliament* (London, 1793), 12. *Pigs' Meat; or, Lessons for the Swinish Multitude*, 3rd edn (London, [1795?]), 59.
18. Charles Dunster, *Considerations on Milton's Early Reading and the Prima Stamina of his Paradise Lost* ([London], 1800), 27.

tion of Romantic poetry as 'progressive, universal poetry', forever 'in the state of becoming'. Jones's poem becomes part of the emergent republican state.[19]

In response to the ode's opening question, 'What constitutes a state?' the answer is supplied:

> Men, who their duties know,
> But know their rights, and knowing dare maintain,   (ll: 13–14)

Jones forges a line borrowed from a young Prince Henry in William Hawkins's play, *Henry and Rosamond* (1749): 'I know my Right, and knowing, dare maintain it', into an enduring political aphorism, which played a key role in the British political reform movement and entered the universal currency of American republican rhetoric.[20] Jones's clipped coinage, 'Who Know Their Rights And Knowing Dare Maintain', was stamped by the radical bookseller, coin minter, and member of the London Corresponding Society, Thomas Spence, on a variety of political tokens. The aphorism was cited by presidents such as Thomas Jefferson, Andrew Jackson, and countless United States senators throughout the nineteenth century. It appeared on the Great Seal of Maryland; became the motto of the Pennsylvania Volunteers in the American Civil War; entered the rhetoric of abolitionism; and was chosen as the state motto of Alabama as late as 1939.

Without prejudice to questions of plagiarism or intellectual property, Jones is concerned with the property that inheres in a man's trade and should qualify him for suffrage. The poetic 'parts', in Schlegelian terms, 'are free citizens and have the right to vote'. As princely rights are transmuted into civil rights, encouragement of their recognition and of the daring to maintain them is balanced by concomitant civic duties.

In tracing this polyglossal and progressive proceeding from an Alcæus fragment towards the Schlegelian aesthetic of the aphorism, it can be seen that Jones's political thinking is not bounded by the select republic of letters to which he belongs. Unlike the Jena Romantics, who theorized the politics

---

19. 'Romantic poetry is a progressive, universal poetry. Its goal is not merely to reunite all the separate forms of poetry and to put poetry in contact with philosophy and rhetoric [...] Other kinds of poetry are finished and can be completely analysed. Romantic poetry is still in a process of becoming; indeed that is its true essence: that it can only eternally become and never be perfected'; *The Early Political Writings of the German Romantics,* ed. Frederick C. Beiser (Cambridge, 1999), 116–17.
20. William Hawkins, *Henry and Rosamond. A Tragedy* (London, 1749), 24.

of an exclusively literary world and would soon be dazzled by the textualized idea of India he helped to create, Jones moved within a variety of groupings—professional, private, public, and counter-public spheres. His republican aesthetic was grounded in a versatile adaptability.

What is particularly striking is his ability to diminish the perceived aesthetic gap between artist and middle or working-class reformers. Another oppositional poem, Jones's tyrannicidal *Ode in Imitation of Callistratus* (1782), was regularly sung at anniversary dinners of the SCI.[21] Jones's effortless mobility was energized by the tensions underlying the English class system to reverse the patron–client nexus. Whether successfully recommending Viscount Althorp, or his future father-in-law, the America-supporting Bishop Shipley, for admission to Johnson's Club; attending the Grecian Club with Richard Paul Jodrell, Thomas Day, and Sir Robert Chambers; at the SCI, the Club of Honest Whigs at the London Coffee House, or addressing the mercantile and artisan supporters of Wilkes he acquired in the metropolis the political, social, and cultural capital to augment his celebrity status as Orientalist and barrister-jurist.

Horace Walpole, with his usual acerbic wit, locates Jones for us, on Sunday, 4 February 1781, amidst cerulean celebrities in Berkeley Square:

> at Lady [Margaret] Lucan's [miniaturist], who had assembled a *blue stocking* meeting in imitation of Mrs Vesey's Babels [every table discussed a different topic]. It was so blue, it was quite Mazarine-blue. Mrs. Montagu kept aloof from Johnson, like the West from the East. There were Soame Jenyns [wit, essayist, and whig placeman], *Persian* Jones, Mr. [Martin] Sherlocke [continental traveller], the new court wit Mr [John] Courtenay [reforming MP and author], besides the out-pensioners of Parnassus. Mr. Wraxall was not, I wonder why, and so will he, for he is popping into every spot where he can make himself talked of, by talking of himself; but I hear he will come to an untimely beginning in the House of Commons.[22]

In the absence of Nathaniel Wraxall, former EIC judge advocate, the talk was of the forthcoming marriage between Althorp and Lavinia Bingham: *the high-society event of 1781*. Walpole had already presented some 'immortal'

---

21. *An Ode, in Imitation of Callistratus, sung by Mr Webb, at the Shakespeare Tavern, on Tuesday the 14th day of May, 1782*. A regicidal version was sung at a joint meeting of SCI and the London Corresponding Society (LCS) on 2 May 1794; see John Barrell, *Imagining the King's Death: Figurative Treason, Fantasies of Regicide 1793–6* (Oxford, 2000), 214.
22. *The Correspondence of Horace Walpole*, 2: 148.

doggerel to Lady Lucan.[23] By contrast, Jones's epithalamium is a masterpiece of outright political audacity.

The Muse Recalled; an Ode on the Nuptials of Lord Viscount Althorp and Miss Lavinia Bingham, written at the insistence of Georgiana, Duchess of Devonshire, confidently turns ceremonial convention into pro-revolutionary public harangue. The ode as requested occasional commodity is hijacked in the republican cause of oppositional ideology; celebration of aristocratic union is replaced by dismay at colonial rupture and metropolitan decadence. The 'crimes [...] and recreant baseness' of 'Albion's sons', characterized as 'slaves of vice, and slaves of gold!' have resulted in the westering flight of Freedom and Concord. Borne aloft 'on starry pinions', together with 'Truth, Justice, Reason, Valour', they have sought 'a purer soil, a more congenial sky':

> Beyond the vast Atlantick deep
> A dome by viewless genii shall be raised,
> The walls of adamant compact and steep,
> The portals with sky-tinctur'd gems emblaz'd:
> There on a lofty throne shall Virtue stand;
> To her the youth of Delaware shall kneel;
> And, when her smiles rain plenty o'er the land,
> Bow, tyrants, bow beneath th'avenging steel! (ll: 129–36; *SWJ*, p. 74)

At Baron Lucan's direction and despite the scant praise of his daughter, the ode was published by Walpole at Strawberry Hill. The publisher, having forgiven Jones's 'wrong-headed' ingratitude, was delighted with both its aesthetics and its politics. Where Wraxall regards *The Muse Recalled* as evidence that Jones 'lent his powerful Assistance to the Cause of Rebellion',[24] Walpole's whig republicanism, opposing the American war and reviling contemporary decadence, celebrates Jones's ode:

> [T]he eighth, ninth, and tenth stanzas have merit enough to shock Dr. Johnson and such sycophant old nurses, and that is enough for me. How precious is any line of Demosthenes that offended King Philip and the whole Court of Macedon![25]

---

23. This is the final stanza of Walpole's 'Nuptial Ode': 'Your best wishes bring'em,/Your best roses fling'em/O'er the hammock, where Bingham/And Althorpe shall swing'em,/With ding, ding, a dong'; *Letters Addressed to the Countess of Ossory by Horace Walpole*, ed. Vernon Smith, 2 vols (London, 1848), 2: 23.
24. Nathaniel Wraxall, *Historical Memoirs of My Own Time*, 2 vols (London, 1815), 2: 80.
25. *Letters Addressed to the Countess of Ossory*, 2: 49.

Jones radicalizes the genre of the epithalamium, exploring and exploding its potential in line with the noble genre of history painting. The history is inherently contemporary, the theory is the civic and public role of poetry and painting, and the model is James Barry's etching and aquatint, *The Phoenix or the Resurrection of Freedom* (1776). This print depicts a group of mourners, Sydney, Milton, Marvell, Locke, and Barry himself, around the tomb of Britannia who died when Liberty departed for America.[26] Their gestures direct our attention across the water to the phoenix-like rebirth of Liberty atop a domed classical temple, set in an untainted Utopia of agriculture, commerce, the arts, and Graces dancing on the shore.[27] The westerly progress of Thomson's Liberty and Gray's Poesy is extended in both print and poem, and this at a time when Jones himself was also contemplating becoming a Virginia legislator.

Barry, like Jones, was a close friend of Edmund Burke, and their circles overlapped in the Venn diagram of London society. His mourning heroes were those of Jones also. Amongst the 'friends of America', Barry was also a hero to Blake, who admired his muscular, defiantly heroic depictions of Satan, and shared Samuel Johnson's enthusiasm for the painter's 'grasp of mind'. He became the second Royal Academy professor of painting, succeeding Sir Joshua Reynolds. But he was to die in poverty and Blake, following Barry's expulsion from the Royal Academy for inflammatory remarks against his colleagues, could only protest in furious annotations to his copy of Reynolds's *Works*:

> Who will Dare to Say that Polite Art is Encouraged or Either Wished or Tolerated in a Nation where The Society for the Encouragement of Art Suffer'd Barry to Give them his Labour for Nothing. A Society Composed of the Flower of the English Nobility & Gentry? [...] Barry told me that while he Did that Work, he Lived on Bread & Apples.[28]

Blake's marginal tirade reflects his own marginalization. Ultimately freedom was all about connections and the right sorts of associations: Jones was a genius and self-made man like Barry and like Blake, but the liberties he

---

26. Cf. the observation of the republican Thomas Hollis that 'Liberty seems to be flying from this country & making a desirable progress' in America; *The Diary of Sylas Neville, 1767–1788*, ed. Basil Cozens-Hardy (Oxford, 1950), 49.
27. Cf. 'Commerce with fleets shall mock the waves,/And Arts, that flourish not with slaves,/ Dancing with ev'ry Grace and ev'ry Muse', *The Muse Recalled* (Strawberry Hill, 1781), ll. 137–9.
28. BL C.45.e.18: *The Works of Sir Joshua Reynolds*, ed. Edmund Malone, 2nd edn, 3 vols (London, 1798), 1: blank verso between Contents and dedication.

enjoyed—even to publish radical tracts—were predicated upon his social, intellectual, and professional celebrity. Operating reluctantly, but efficiently, within the ubiquitous patronage system, Jones amplified the power of influential private connections with the new associational tendencies and bourgeois radical thinking of the public sphere. Though Jones believed as strongly as Blake in the concept of meritocracy, Reynolds and 'the Flower of the English Nobility & Gentry' were his friends. Jones's claims to moral authority based upon ideals of republican virtue would have been anathema to Blake whose ethical priorities were truly revolutionary.

There were different ways of avoiding slavish dependence, but 'Illuminated' prophecies prove expensive and Blake's millennial vision of artistic and intellectual liberation was often impeded by the demands of rich patrons. Inky-fingered 'Blake the Engraver', as Jon Mee argues, possibly lacked even the liberty to be recognized as a radical intellectual within the Joseph Johnson circle.[29] As a tradesman Jones would have given him the vote (see p. 191), but where exactly was Blake to stand within the fragmented constituencies of radicalism? Upwardly mobile Jones dined with Sir Joshua Reynolds, despised by Blake; he discussed Milton with William Hayley, Blake's patron and employer, rather than with the journeyman poet-engraver. Enthusiastic mysticism and prophetic inspiration, as Blake realized, would be rewarded only by a meritocracy of the mind, but Jones had the liberty to argue the virtues of merit in aristocratic circles. While Reynolds painted Jones, Blake, in marginalized obscurity, lamented an art world obsessed by the massaging of societal self-image in the expensive mirrors of commissioned portraits.

> While Sir Joshua was rolling in Riches, Barry was Poor & Unemploy'd except by his own Energy; [...] & only Portrait Painting applauded & rewarded by the Rich & Great. Reynolds & Gainsborough Blotted & Blurred one against the other & Divided all the English World between them. Fuseli, Indignant, almost hid himself. I am hid.[30]

The helpless passivity of 'I am hid' underlines Blake's subordinated social position and the political and artistic frustrations of his autotelic labours ally him with 'the stern bard' who sings the Preludium to *America* (1793). The

---

29. See Jon Mee, '"The Doom of Tyrants": William Blake, Richard "Citizen" Lee and the Millenarian Public Sphere', in *Blake, Politics, and History*, ed. Jackie DiSilvo et al. (New York and London, 1998), 97–114, 103.
30. BL C.45.e.18. See n. 28 above.

lines he engraved on plate 2 underneath the emergent figure of revolutionary Orc were subsequently masked/suppressed/hid:

> The stern Bard ceas'd, asham'd of his own song; enrag'd he swung
> His harp aloft sounding, then dash'd its shining frame against
> A ruin'd pillar in glittring fragments; silent he turn'd away,
> And wander'd down the vales of Kent in sick & drear lamentings.   (2:18–21)[31]

Erased (in all but three copies), these lines chart Blake's relationship with visionary self-doubt and his disillusion with the failure of revolutionary art and politics. They displace his psychological insecurity and self-doubt onto the figure of the bardic author, auditor, and 'auto-destructive' critic of his own inspired song as he dashes his harp into glittering fragments.

By contrast, a decade earlier Jones's recalled Muse reveals not disillusion with revolutionary realities but ravishing American visions: 'What floods of glory drown my sight!/What scenes I view! What sounds I hear!' (ll. 143–4).

> Then, fatal harp, thy transient rapture o'er,
>   Calm I replace thee on the sacred wall.
>   Ah! see how lifeless hangs the lyre,
>   Not lightning now, but glitt'ring wire!
>   Me to the brawling bar and wrangles high
>   Bright-hair'd Sabrina calls and rosy-bosom'd Wye.   (ll. 147–52)[32]

The calm replacement of the London Welshman's harp on the wall of 'Astræa's fane' emphasizes his dedication to the virgin goddess of Justice and the professional enfranchisement that she represents as he returns invigorated from aristocratic nuptials to the Carmarthen circuit. Abandoning the 'glitt'ring wire' for forensic wrangles in the West was no hardship. The glittering prize of a Bengal judgeship seemed far off as ever, but at least Jones had no need to search for spiritual 'Bread & Apples' down the Old Kent Road.

Throughout 1781 Jones was working at a blistering pace—even for a hyperactive polymath. In addition to his legal work, he was increasing his interest with major EIC proprietors by compiling, at the direction of Admiral Hugh Pigot, the *Report of the Committee of Correspondence* into the involvement of Paul Benfield, the nabob banker to the Raja of Tanjore,

---

31. *Complete Poetry and Prose of William Blake*, ed. Erdman, 52.
32. Cf. 'Me wrangling courts and stubborn law,/To smoke, and crowds, and cities draw', Sir William Blackstone, 'The Lawyer's Farewell to His Muse' (written 1744); *The Biographical History of Sir William Blackstone* (London, 1782), 3–4.

in the coup that deposed Baron George Pigot, the admiral's brother, as governor of Madras.[33]

He was also preparing for the press *An Essay on the Law of Bailments* (1781), employing comparative historical method to examine this neglected but increasingly relevant area of contract law. Jones felt that the legal profession was not adequately serving Britain's 'polite and commercial people'. A major contribution to jurisprudence, his *Essay* was 'one of the most remarkable books of this period'.[34] Bailment, the entrusting of goods to a temporary custodian, was as central to the development of commercial shipping, warehousing, and carriage as his friend Richard Price's work on insurance.

Commerce was the engine to drive reform in a society peopled by industrious men of moveable property. Pro-American Jones would be amused that a clinching extract from his 1781 book was read to a 1988 Tennessee court in *Shepherd Fleets, Inc.* v. *Opryland USA, Inc.*, concerning a hotel's liability for damage to a guest's parked car. Indeed James Oldham credits Jones with the earliest formulation of the legal concept of 'the reasonable man' and the standard of care he might be expected to demonstrate.[35]

In June Jones sent his *Essay* to upholder of republican virtue and fellow Club member, Edward Gibbon, promising a copy of *The Moallakát* on its publication. His happiness, he claims, does not depend upon the Calcutta appointment. If there is no positive news by the end of autumn, he will, like a postcolonial Prospero, 'entirely drop all thoughts of *Asia*, and, "deep as plummet sounded, drown my *Persian* books"' (*Letters*, 2: 481). On the other hand, if he *were* to be appointed, he would not be found spreading republicanism in Bengal: 'I should hardly think of instructing the Gentoos [Hindus] in the maxims of the Athenians.' He would travel overland to India, procuring eastern law tracts on the way, so as to 'become a good *Mahomedan* lawyer before I reached Calcutta'. In this he had already made a good start, being actively consulted by both the promoters and opponents of the Bengal Judiciary Bill. Burke writes in mid-June:

> I beg, if you have leisure for it, that you would be so kind as to breakfast with me, and assist me with your opinion and advice on the conduct of the Bengal

---

33. *Report of the Committee of Correspondence, Confirmed by the Court of Directors [...] Relative to* Mr Benfield ([London], 1781); see *Letters*, 2: 524.
34. W. S. Holdsworth, *A History of English Law*, 17 vols (London, 1938), 12: 393–4.
35. See James Oldham, 'The Survival of Sir William Jones in American Jurisprudence', in *Objects of Enquiry: The Life, Contributions, and Influences of Sir William Jones*, ed. Garland Cannon and Kevin R. Brine (New York, 1995), 92–101; 96–8.

Bill. The natives of the East, to whose literature you have done so much justice, are particularly under your protection for their rights. (*Works* 1: 360)

The bill was steered by a commons select committee, chaired by Jones's Midgham friend, General Smith, in which Burke was very influential. The resultant Act confirmed the principles of Warren Hastings's 1772 plan to govern Indians by their own laws. Jones immediately set to work on translating Ibn al-Mutaqqina's *Bughyat al-bahith*, from Pococke's Aleppo manuscript in the Bodleian. Here Jones was not so much concerned with the poetry of politics but the poetry of law, for the tract was written in verse to help Arabic students learn it by heart. The fundamental object of Jones's *The Mahomedan Law of Succession to the Property of Intestates* (1782) was to aid British lawyers implement the East India Judicature Act, which stated that all causes involving '*inheritance and succession to lands, rents, and goods*, and all matters of contract and dealing between party and party, shall be determined, *in the case of* Mahomedans [...] *by the laws and usages of* MAHOMEDANS' [and in the case of Gentoos by the laws and usages of Gentoos] (*Works*, 8: 161). At a time when many intellectuals still claimed Asiatic despotism denied the very existence of private property in land, Jones's book marked real progress in the struggle against prejudiced representations of the East.

Jones was also compiling—at the behest of Chancellor Thurlow—a detailed report on the '*Bengal judicature* from its first establishment', while continuing to speak out against the American war and 'the rolling tide of prerogative and influence' (*Letters*, 2: 487). At Oxford he was still labelled a republican, 'very unjustly, if they mean one, who wishes to see a republick in *England*; but very justly, if they mean one, who thinks a republick *in the abstract* the only rational, manly, intelligible form of government' (*Letters*, 2: 499).

Meanwhile Jones's protégé was making his Westminster mark. On the 27 February 1782 Viscount Althorp seconded the motion of seasoned parliamentarian General Henry Seymour Conway against the further prosecution of offensive war in America. Althorp rejects the argument that we should force the Americans to sue for peace; it was high time to end 'the calamities of war [...] the burning of towns and spreading destruction wherever we went'.[36] It was carried by 234 votes to 215 and within a month North's government was to fall. Jones was lavish in his praise of his friend's noble speech, but a twinge of jealous pique made him carp at Althorp's use of the

---

36. *The Parliamentary History of England* (London, 1814), 22: 1071–2.

word '*sovereign* as applied to the king', providing the pedantic—if republican—correction that 'the legislature only is our *sovereign*' (*Letters*, 2: 519).

Jones would have to get used to being congratulated on his pupil's success. Though the Rockingham–Shelburne coalition ministry was unstable from its beginnings, it represented, in Jones-speak, 'the glorious Victory which the constitution, almost at its last gasp, has obtained over a monstrous government compounded of tyranny and folly'. Jones's problems were complicated by the fact that quarrels between Shelburne and Rockingham were centred in rival claims to the power of patronage, a ministerial conflict set within the larger issue of how to limit Crown patronage.

A friend told Jones that Chancellor Thurlow's rule was 'sole patronage or none'. Would an approach to Lord Rockingham make Thurlow take umbrage? Did North still have the king's ear? Who, in fact, was the 'judge-maker'? So Jones rang the changes on images of uncertainty, comparing his position between bar and bench with 'Homer's "Man in a Dream", *pursuing without approaching*', or even with Mahomet's coffin suspended midway between ceiling and floor. It was an intolerable situation, especially as Anna and William had mutually, if unromantically, agreed their marriage should be predicated upon the Calcutta post.

Jones writes to Lady Spencer on 12 April 1782 from Charles Powell's fine Tudor house, Castle Madoc, near Brecon, built on the bailey site of his ancestors' eleventh-century castle. Powell was widely respected as a magistrate and former major in the militia, an intelligent, unaffected, public-spirited, and improving landlord. While praising this 'good Whig', and other Welsh gentlemen like him, Jones expounds his '*democratical*' principles:

> I know many such in these counties, and some in other parts of the island; and this knowledge cannot but add to the strong tincture of republican principles (consistent with the kingly office properly understood) of which I cannot divest myself; for I cannot find that virtue, honour, or good sense, are conferred by patent or descend like heirlooms in great families, nor can I discover any substantial difference between man and man but a difference in those qualities, which are attainable equally by the prince and the peasant. These principles are as remote from lawless licentiousness as they are from lawless tyranny; and, however *democratical* they may be thought, I am not likely to part with them.
>
> (*Letters*, 2: 529)

Is it significant that such thoughts should be addressed from a Welsh castle to an English countess? The ironies are deepened by the fact that the Powells—like Jones's Anglesey ancestors—were princes when the Spencers were sheep-tending peasants, as hard-handed, sun-burned and, unsophisticated as Jones's unmentioned (unmentionable?) Llanbabo relations.

The eighteenth-century class system was as rigid and as impenetrably mysterious as Hindu caste, which involved complex interrelationships of social, religious, and economic determinants: *varna* (colour), *jāti* (birth), *ārya* (nobility), *dasa* (servility). The Laws of Manu, which within a few years Jones was translating, stated that the lowest class, the *śūdra*, was born from the foot of the Supreme Creator. Johnson would scarcely have known this, but the 'great Cham' of Bolt Court had decided views on 'maintaining subordination of rank'. Johnson's anecdote of Catharine Macaulay's footman reveals the universalism of class prejudice; in terms of belief in hierarchy and subordination even the most enlightened Tory might be compared with the least enlightened Brahman:

> Sir, there is one Mrs. Macaulay in this town, a great republican. One day when I was at her house, I put on a very grave countenance, and said to her, 'Madam, I am now become a convert to your way of thinking. I am convinced that all mankind are upon an equal footing; and to give you an unquestionable proof, Madam, that I am in earnest, here is a very sensible, civil, well-behaved fellow-citizen, your footman; I desire that he may be allowed to sit down and dine with us.' I thus, Sir, shewed her the absurdity of the levelling doctrine. She has never liked me since. Sir, your levellers wish to level *down* as far as themselves; but they cannot bear levelling *up* to themselves.[37]

Where Jones met intellect he certainly did believe in 'levelling *up*'. A vivid illustration is found in his close relationship with a young Welshman, Arthur Pritchard, his part-time legal secretary. Jones candidly acknowledges to Pritchard: 'You were for a long time wholly indifferent to me, until I discovered your mental qualities, which pleased me because they are in many respects similar to my own, and you are in possession of my regard, that, if you were my brother, I could not esteem you more affectionately.' He invites Arthur to write frequently and 'with *frankness*'; discusses his poems with him, revealing he 'was an early lover' and alluding to his relationship with Anna; takes a genuine interest in his family; and repeatedly expresses his concern for the health, happiness, and working situation of his clerk. Anxious for Arthur to make wise career choices, Jones is reluctant to see him in service, 'because I know the sentiments and conduct of masters'.

---

37. James Boswell, *The Life of Samuel Johnson, LL.D.*, 3 vols (London, 1793), 1: 412.

Encouraging his secretary to emulate his own proud independence, Jones assures him: 'You are so much superior to most masters in the *fine world*, that you would soon despise them; and I earnestly hope you will not hastily enter into so precarious and humiliating a station' (*Letters*, 2: 496–7).

A prestigious station was lost to Jones through his absence from London and Oxford. His post-circuit sojourn at Castle Madoc was followed by a visit to Pritchard in Oldbury-on-Severn; it was not until six o'clock on the 15 April that he collected his letters at University College. As he breathlessly explains to Pritchard:

> [O]ne of them was from Lord Shelburne dated the 9th desiring to see me *instantly*: I put four horses to my chaise; travelled all night, and saw his Lordship early the next morning: the same day I was presented to *all* the new ministers. A great place had been kept open for me above a fortnight: not hearing from me, nor knowing where I was, they desponded and disposed of it. Particulars you shall know when we meet: had parliament been dissolved I should have had a seat in it immediately.   (*Letters*, 2: 542)

The post of undersecretary of state at the Home Office was not destined for Jones. It was his own secretary's loss also, for Jones continues: 'I thought of you and resolved, if possible, to procure you some genteel place in an office of state: this resolution I will never abandon.' Jones explains his planned Virginia trip with John Paradise. One can imagine Pritchard's excitement on reading this dramatically revealing letter, especially when Jones invites him to accompany them across the Atlantic. More than this, Jones generously announces that Pritchard 'will stand first in my *will*, (after my female friend)' and, in the case of Jones's death during the voyage, he will leave him a thousand pounds. Arthur will be no republican's footman, but 'wholly on the footing of a gentleman' and, repeating this 'levelling *up*' phrase, Jones urges him to 'put yourself wholly on a footing with me', for 'You know my opinion that all honest men are equal, and the prince and the peasant are on a level.'

Democratic adjustment of levels is very much on 'Leveller' Jones's mind in writing to Thomas Yeates, the young SCI secretary (and future Orientalist):

> Care must now be taken, lest, by reducing the *regal* power to its just level, we raise the *aristocratical* to a dangerous height; since it is from the *people* alone that we can deduce the obligation of our laws and the authority of magistrates. On the *people* depend the welfare, the security, and the permanence of every legal government; in the *people* must reside all substantial power.

This letter was published by the SCI in the *General Advertiser and Morning Intelligencer* of 6 May, and in a reprinting of his *Inquiry into the Legal Mode of Suppressing Riots*, which Jones hurriedly produced in reacting to political events at Westminster.[38] On 10 May the Commons debated a Plan of National Defence—drawing on Jones's 1780 plan—which Shelburne had circulated to chief magistrates of principal towns and cities. Four days later Jones anonymously published—in an open letter signed by 'A Volunteer'— a detailed response to Shelburne's twenty-point plan. It removed 'unconstitutional' references to the king and to the Lords Lieutenant who should 'have no more to do with this great business than the bench of Bishops'. Officers should be commissioned by high sheriffs and chief magistrates rather than by the king, and their rank determined by the size of contribution to the defence fund as opposed to their monetary or real estate.[39] Foremost in Jones's mind was the example of Lord Charlemont's volunteers in Ireland whose responsible conduct not only ensured national defence, but advanced the cause of constitutional reform and legislative independence.

Privately Jones maintained: 'I wish to God, that every elector of Britain had as bright a bayonet as mine' with the resolution to use it in opposing arbitrary aristocratic and royal power (*Letters*, 2: 527). 'The great business', he emphasized to Wilkes, is that 'of arming the nation *legally* and *constitutionally*. The people of England have it now in their power to be really, not nominally a people; a people of highth and mightiness, and capacity for action; not a people of *words* and *quills*, like a nation of parrots and porcupines' (*Letters*, 2: 540).

Congratulating Major Cartwright on his 'excellent paper', *Give us our Rights!* (1782), Jones adds an unguarded postscript: 'It is my deliberate (though private) opinion, that the people of England will never be a people, in the majestic sense of the word, unless two hundred thousand of the *civil state* be ready, before the first of next November, to take the field, without rashness or disorder, at twenty-four hours' notice' (*Letters*, 2: 547). Urging readers to consult the Virginian 'Declaration of Rights', Cartwright vindicated

---

38. *An Inquiry into the Legal Mode of Suppressing Riots. With a Constitutional Plan of Future Defence* (London, 1782).
39. *A Plan of National Defence* [London, 1782]. Jones's printed open letter of 14 May 1782, signed 'A Volunteer', is catalogued by the British Library by means of its opening sentence: '*Sir, I take the liberty of submitting to your serious attention the plan of national defence lately suggested by government, compared with a different plan now approved, though subject to revision, by a company of loyal Englishmen, of which I have the honour to be one.*

'the natural rights of the people' (p. 39). Jones advances the discussion beyond natural rights to legal and constitutional rights. The brain of this 'lawyer, soldier, and citizen' was working at its highest pitch. Careful research into English jurisprudence led him to conclude the Constitution did more than justify a democratic militia: it demanded a vast extension of the franchise.

On the evening of 28 May, Jones addressed the 'Quintuple Alliance', the radical reformers of London, Westminster, Southwark, Middlesex, and Surrey, at the London Tavern in Bishopsgate Street. The 'judicious and spirited oration' he delivers in its capacious third-floor room embodies his conviction that the people must be armed with votes as well as muskets.[40] He urges his audience to take home with them a proposition of the utmost importance: 'the spirit of our constitution requires a representation of the people nearly equal and nearly universal'.[41] Jones anchors radical Dissenting thought in constitutional history. Despising 'the gabble of the feudal lawyers' and trusting in trade and the market, Jones rejects 'the evil principle of feudalism' for 'the good principle of commerce':

> What caused the absurd yet fatal, distinction between property, personal and real? The feudal principle [...] What raised the silly notion that the property, not the person, of the subject, was to be represented? The feudal principle. (p. 12)

Jones's political thinking remains dependent upon the Lockean theory of possessive individualism; if there must be a property qualification, individuals have property in their own labour.

> I consider a *fair trade* or *profession* as *valuable property*, and an Englishman, who can support himself by honest industry, though in a low station, has often a more independent mind than the prodigal owner of a large encumbered estate. (p. 15)

At the time when less than 3 per cent of adult males could vote, this was effectively universal manhood suffrage, excluding only those 'unable or unwilling to gain anything by art or labour'. Economic productivity united self-interest and the public good in a Lockean contract, offering equality of opportunity and independence of mind; the self-reliant working man

---

40. *Monthly Review*, 67 (August 1782), 148–9.
41. *A Speech of William Jones, Esq. to the Assembled Inhabitants of the Counties of Middlesex and Surry, the Cities of London and Westminster, and the Borough of Southwark. XXVIII May, MDCCLXXXII* (London, 1782), 10.

deserved a vote. Here Jones reveals his political position as more rigorously egalitarian than many contemporary English radicals.

As one of the two stewards for Middlesex, Jones is playing an energetic part in the Quintuple Alliance, together with influential political reformers such as Dr John Jebb, Charles Lennox, Duke of Richmond, Aldermen James Townsend, Brass Crosby, and James Sawbridge. His political schedule is now as hectic as his legal one. At noon the following day, the 29 May, Jones attended a packed meeting of Middlesex electors at the Mermaid Tavern in Hackney. He applauds an impassioned speech by philologist radical John Horne Tooke (who in the darkly paranoid days of 1794 found himself in the Tower charged with high treason) urging the electors to petition the Commons on 'the Right of the People to an equal Representation'. Following an unanimous vote to petition parliament, Jones rose to present a motion concerning an armed civil militia: 'That it be a Recommendation to the Committee to consider of and prepare a proper Plan of Defence against Tumult or Invasion, to be reported the next General Meeting for their Opinion and Adoption.'[42] His motion, seconded by Horne Tooke, was also passed unanimously.

In his London tavern speech Jones had alluded somewhat cryptically to 'a very particular and urgent occasion, which calls me for some months from *England*'. Whereas this might seem simply to refer to his projected legal trip to Virginia, it is clear from his letter to Pritchard of the preceding week that Jones thought he might be 'named a commissioner for peace' (*Letters*, 2: 544). Intense press speculation surrounded Jones; the *Public Advertiser* of 26 June announced:

> The destination of Mr Jones is not Asia, as from his skill in Asiatic Languages might have been inferred, but *America*; and not having any private Concerns in any Part of America, it is supposed that the Object of his Departure is Business of a Public Kind.
>
> When we call to Mind some other Circumstances connected with the above mentioned Mr Jones, such as his very confidential Intimacy with all the Spencer Family, his peculiar Enthusiasm for Liberty of every Kind and in every Place, and above all, his Fame not only for Literature, but the Business of Politics, it seems to the highest Degree probable that Mr Jones is now appointed, and surely with the best possible Reason appointed, to assist in the Pacific Negociation with America.

---

42. *Public Advertiser*, Friday, 31 May 1782.

By the time London readers were devouring this information, Jones and Paradise had been in France a week, and at Passy on the 27 June they were introduced to John Jay, a shrewd New York politician, whose help Franklin requested in negotiating a peace treaty. Jay records that Jones spoke warmly of the republic: 'Mr Jones said he despaired of seeing constitutional liberty re-established in England, that he had determined to visit America, and in that happy and glorious country to seek and enjoy that freedom, which was not to be found in Britain.' But hard-nosed Jay read this as empty rhetoric. By an enormous irony, while British public opinion had virtually convinced itself that Jones was a peace commissioner, Jay suspected that Shelburne was employing him in a very different role: as a spy!

Writing to Robert R. Livingston, secretary of foreign affairs to the continental congress, Jay outlines his suspicions: 'It appeared to me a little extraordinary that a gentleman of Mr Jones's rising reputation and expectations should be so smitten with the charms of American liberty, as "to leave all, and follow her".' On reading Jones's printed speeches, he 'became persuaded that Mr Paradise and American liberty were mere pretences to cover a more important errand to America, and I was surprised that Mr Jones's vanity should so far get the better of his prudence, as to put such pamphlets into my hands at such a time'.[43] Jay avoided providing Jones and Paradise with introductory letters, mentioning his suspicions to Franklin and the Marquis de Lafayette. Franklin, of course, had no doubts of his friend's integrity and provided glowing letters of recommendation to Jefferson and to James Bowdoin, describing Jones as 'a particular friend of mine, and a zealous one of our Cause and Country'.[44]

That summer saw a sad end to the close friendship of Jones and Paradise. From rural Passy they travelled to Nantes, 'la ville des négriers' (slave ships). The slave-trade capital of France proved a culture shock for the sensitive and scholarly plantation owner Paradise. Jones was enthusiastic about the transatlantic voyage, boarding all the ships 'bound *for the land of virtue and liberty*' and choosing the *Annette*, Captain Jean Audubon, to sail within five weeks.[45] A letter from Shelburne (now prime minister, Rockingham having died on

---

43. *The Diplomatic Correspondence of the American Revolution*, ed. Jared Sparks, 12 vols (Boston, 1829–30), 8: 130–3.
44. Cited in Edward E. Hale, *Franklin in France*, 2 vols (Boston, 1888), 2: 328; 214.
45. He became the father of the naturalist, J. J. Audubon.

1 July), announcing that 'he had nothing more at heart than to procure a desirable station for me in Bengal', changed everything (*Letters*, 2: 579).

Despite Jones's fine words concerning a republic of liberty, freedom to fulfil his Indian ambitions lay in Britain. He exhorted Paradise to sail with Henry Laurens, former president of the continental congress, whom Jones had helped during his two-year imprisonment in the Tower. Paradise could face neither the rigours of the journey nor the complicated legal transactions without Jones; they quarrelled bitterly and parted in Nantes.[46] It is hard not to see this as a desertion of his friend and, to some extent, of the republic. Yet, even while he self-justifyingly described Paradise's weakness to Franklin, Jones was keeping his American options open by requesting 'information concerning the profession of a *lawyer* in the state of Pennsylvania' (*Letters*, 2: 564).

As Jones explained to Burke: 'I soon waked from my dream of being able to assist my unfortunate friend in Virginia, and to be again in England, according to my engagements, before the end of the year' (*Letters*, 2: 579). His timetable had been vastly over-optimistic. Rapid transatlantic business trips were far in the future; as it was the American dream turned into a nightmare. Jones would never be able to recall Nantes without a feeling of residual guilt. The long-cherished dream of India, union with Anna, and an independent fortune, totally eclipsed the western expedition. When Anna's cousin, Georgiana, Duchess of Devonshire, wrote that autumn, she innocently mentions being presented with a copy of Jones's *Ode in Imitation of Callistratus*:

> I wish I understood Greek, that I might read something Mr Paradise has written at the top of it. I will attempt to copy it; and after the various characters I have, *in days of yore*, seen you decipher, I will not despair of your making out Greek, though written by me.   (*Works*, 1: 399–400)

Jones had no difficulty with her transcription but its sentiment stuck in his throat: 'The Graces, seeking a shrine that would never decay, found the soul of Jones.'

Jones returned to London via the Dutch Republic (with whom Britain was still at war), spending a few days with Hendrik Schultens at Leiden, where patriot civil militiamen were attempting to assert the sovereignty of the people. It was an apt moment to present Schultens with his *Ode in Imitation of Callistratus*, which opens with a vision of citizens armed against tyrannical power with swords and muskets:

---

46. See Shepperson, *John Paradise and Lucy Ludwell*, 173–8.

> Verdant myrtle's branchy pride
> Shall my biting falchion wreathe:
>   Soon shall grace each manly side
> Tubes that speak, and points that breathe.   (ll. 1–4; *Works*, 10: 391)

Jones 'received infinite civilities' from the modernizing Dutch as a libertarian Orientalist and friend of Adam Smith. In Holland, as in Britain against a similar background of increasing urbanization, a vast variety of provincial learned societies, literary and debating clubs enriched the public sphere. Here also the power of association was transforming bourgeois radicalism, and linguist Jones soon discovered the Dutch word *burgerij* denoted both 'citizens' and 'civil militia'. Their 'Patriots' cherished the right to bear arms as a public duty, ready to handle them effectively in resistance to invasion or in advancing constitutional reformation and the rights of the populace.

Dutch republicanism was promoting the ideal of the sovereignty of the people more energetically than many of the bourgeois radicals in Britain. Jones realized education must be enlisted in the cause of liberty; constitutional rights must be made intelligible to the whole populace. Jones showed Schultens a Socratic *jeu d'esprit* he had written in French to convince Franklin and the comte de Vergennes that the first principles of the state might be understood by the working man.

On his return he was delighted to find Anna at Chilbolton rectory and to relax in the warm, feminized Shipley ambience. He brought Parisian *cadeaux* for all five beautiful daughters, and letters from Franklin to their father and to Franklin's favourite, the wayward Georgiana. Having studied with Reynolds, she had exhibited at the Royal Academy and was a talented harpsichordist, poet, and Latin scholar, added to which she was getting irritatingly good at chess! Georgiana confessed she had written to Franklin that Shelburne would do better to strengthen his administration by appointing Jones to a ministerial position than send him to Calcutta. Pretending to be furious, Jones enjoyed quizzing her, but neither of them realized his *jeu d'esprit* might threaten both prospects.

At Oxford Jones translated the dialogue into English, and Cartwright quickly published it as a free pamphlet under the auspices of the SCI. *The Principles of Government, in a Dialogue between a Scholar and a Peasant* (1782), a seminal document in the history of the reform movement, is also a remarkable example of adult extra-mural education. It begins with a question:

> Why should humble men, like me, sign or set marks to petitions of this nature?
> It is better for us peasants to mind our husbandry, and leave what we cannot
> comprehend to the King and Parliament.   (*SWJ*, p. 396)

The scholar, determined to extract a signature for his electoral reform petition, insists: 'You can comprehend more than you imagine; and, as a *free member of a free state*, have higher things to mind than you may conceive.' The negative definition of freedom in the peasant's response identifies him as a tenant farmer and symbolizes the conceptual prison from which he must be liberated: 'If by *free* you mean *out of prison*, I hope to continue so, as long as I can pay rent to the squire's bailiff; but what is meant by a *free state*?' Release into an imaginative realization of his own rights will be more complete if facilitated by his own discovery. Accordingly, the scholar uses a heuristic method of teaching, answering the farmer's question with another, encouraging the farmer to think laterally or centrifugally from his own experience: 'Tell me first what is meant by a club in the village, of which I know you to be a member.' Through a series of skilfully leading questions, an analogy between the state and the mutual benevolent box-club is elucidated and the tenant farmer is guided towards understanding that 'a free state is only a more numerous and more powerful club'.

Club life did not necessarily entail Medmenham debauchery, Turk's Head exclusivity, bizarre wagers at White's, venison and turtle at the Beef Steak Society, or even the articulate debate of metropolitan and provincial learned societies beloved of middle-class professionals. The exponential growth of artisanal or village box-clubs at this period was a testimony to working-class self-help. Tom Paine declared: 'Benefit clubs, though of humble invention, merit to be ranked among the best of modern institutions.'[47] Their members were free, independent, and equal, bound only to each other by a network of reciprocal obligations, co-operating and pooling resources to avoid economic reliance on local magnates and social superiors. Enfranchised in the election of club officials, the members were learning the emancipation of collectivity. Jürgen Habermas documents club membership as a 'training ground for what was to become a future society's norms of political equality'.[48] But whereas Habermas views the Enlightenment associational tendency as 'an exclusively bourgeois affair', 'clubbable'

---

47. Thomas Paine, *Rights of Man. Part the Second* (London, 1792), 125.
48. 'Further Reflections on the Public Sphere', in *Habermas and the Public Sphere*, ed. Craig Calhoun (Cambridge, MA, 1992), 423–4.

Jones did not. More lay in the box than sickness benefit: it contained the seeds of trade unionism.

As for the ballot box, when informed that six men in seven have no votes, the farmer is eager to sign the scholar's petition for 'the restoration of you all to the right of chusing those law-makers, by whom your money or your lives may be taken from you' (p. 400). On being asked 'what ought to be the consequence, if the King alone were to insist on making laws, or altering them at his will and pleasure', the answer of this representative of the labouring poor is simple and momentous: 'He too must be expelled.' The farmer has also realized that, in the defence of the state against arbitrary power, a quarterstaff is no match for a firearm: 'We ought always, therefore, to be ready: and keep each of us a strong firelock in the corner of his bedroom.' In a daring enactment of what he described to Wilkes as 'The great business of arming the nation *legally* and *constitutionally*', Jones's scholar makes a gift to the peasant of a musket 'with complete accoutrements'.

This present of a musket was shortly to prove a gift to those opponents of reform anxious to charge 'Republican' Jones with sedition. Jones was a genuine trendsetter in 'poisoning' the minds of box-club members. A decade later in the years following the French Revolution, reactionary bourgeois forces were also associating, and the Association for Preserving Liberty and Property against Republicans and Levellers, founded in 1792 by Middle Temple barrister, John Reeves, published a satiric tract specifically warning against the infiltration of box-clubs by democratic reformers. *Address to the Members of the Various Box-clubs and Benefit Societies in Great Britain* was authored by Joseph Moser, a Westminster magistrate, under the pointedly anti-Paineite pseudonym 'Strap Bodkin, staymaker'. The infiltrators, who persuade members to purchase *The Rights of Man* and divert funds to the relief of striking workers, are given legal and SCI connections, the chief culprit being: 'Mr Dott, who wrote for Mr Brief, who was clerk to Mr Capias, who was agent to Serjeant Magpie, who belonged to the Constitutional Society.'[49] One thing of which Mr Dott was not accused was supplying members with muskets!

'Incendiary' Jones was busily working on what was to prove his last political pamphlet, *A Letter to a Patriot Senator, including the Heads of a Bill for a Constitutional Representation of the People* (1783). The senator is Althorp,

---

49. *Liberty and Property Preserved against Republicans and Levellers. A Collection of Tracts* (London, 1793), 10–13.

who requested further elucidation of Jones's ideas on extending the suffrage. The resultant open letter educates the people in their constitutional heritage of political liberty. The people's rights are enshrined in 'the common and publick law of England which neither the craftiness of the TUDORS nor the tyranny of the STUARTS, could wholly supersede or abrogate' (p. 6). Archival research is used to substantiate the 'nearly equal and nearly universal' representation advanced in his London Tavern speech. Jones is angered to hear the rich speak of *boroughs on their estate* with as much composure, as if they were speaking of *burrows* in a warren' (p. 20). He supports more equal electoral districts, advocating annual parliaments to eliminate corruption and concentrate the minds of MPs.

Anticipating entrenched opposition to his appended bill, Jones shows political *nous* in avoiding the Duke of Richmond's radical proposal that all tax payers should be enfranchised. The bill Richmond attempted to introduce in the Lords—frustrated by the Gordon rioters—argued that even the poorest consumer paid taxes in his purchase of food and clothing. More wisely, Jones sets his sights on enfranchising the self-sufficient worker by incorporating annual income qualifications of £25 for voters (roughly the average labourer's wage) and of £300 for candidates. Despite this sop, Jones was realistic enough to admit: 'The whole system, it will be said, is *democratical*, big with danger to public peace, and evidently tending towards revolution, by giving to the people a greater share of power than is consistent with general tranquillity' (p. 33). He directly addresses this fear of the working classes:

> For my own part, I have so far habituated myself to consider all men as from nature equal, that I never give alms to a beggar without reflecting, that nothing perhaps has prevented my accepting them from him, but the accidental difference between us in birth, connexions, and the culture of our minds. (p. 38)

Ingrained class prejudice was the overwhelming obstacle to increasing the suffrage. At fashionable dining tables Jones had been sickened by an all-pervasive contempt for the labouring classes. Jones's focus displays a passionate, if condescending, commitment to the aspirant working classes:

> But when I view the yeomen and traders of England, firm, intrepid, liberal, industrious, benevolent and bearing on their very countenances a consciousness of dignity and freedom, I cannot help revering as much as I love, a people superior to the rest of mortals. Their ignorance of their rights I lament; and

their failings I deplore; but, were I not fully convinced, that the proposed reformation would soon enlighten and improve them, and, by restoring their liberty, restore their virtue, and promote their happiness, I would never have opposed many friends, and possibly raised many enemies (to my ruin, perhaps, as far as a man of small independent fortune but a great independent spirit can be ruined) by writing thus so freely on such a delicate and momentous subject. (p. 38)

Neither his assumed position of exteriority, nor his rose-tinted reliance upon the clichéd idealism of the yeomanry of old England, fully disguises the sources of his partiality. The linking of their cause with his own fortunes, as we have seen, was no mere rhetoric; arguably it betrays an awareness of his own roots. Restoration of the people's liberty was indeed a 'momentous subject', but his use of the epithet 'delicate' reminds us of the incipient dangers of being seen as beyond the politely acceptable political pale. Admiring the yeomanry was one thing: to advocate the presentation of muskets to 'peasants' was something rather different. Reference to the threat of 'ruin' might seem hyperbolic, but very shortly 'Republican' Jones's *Principles of Government* was the subject of a seditious libel prosecution.

For many tories, Jones was transforming the Druidic oak into the liberty tree, with a little help from his whiggish future brother-in-law, Dean William Shipley. Marriage to Penelope Yonge, the heir of Sir John Conway, had brought Shipley enormous wealth from land-holdings including Rhuddlan Castle and sugar plantations at St Kitt's and Nevis. This pluralist and slave-driver by proxy was also chairman of the Flintshire Association for parliamentary reform to whose members he read *The Principles of Government*, carrying a resolution that it be translated into Welsh. Although this project was abandoned, Shipley, determined to give Jones's agitational tract a wider north-Welsh audience, reprinted it in English, replacing the words 'scholar' and 'peasant' with 'gentleman' and 'farmer'.

The high sheriff of Flintshire, Thomas Fitzmaurice, promptly indicted Shipley at Wrexham Great Sessions in April 1783 for publishing a paper designed 'to raise seditions and tumults within the kingdom;—and to excite His Majesty's subjects to attempt, by armed rebellion and violence, to subvert the state and constitution of the nation'. Jones missed this momentous treason trial. When the case came on that September, before two former circuit colleagues: judges Lloyd Kenyon and Daines Barrington, he was nearing Madras. Jones learned of the indictment before embarking, but it failed to constitute even a small cloud on his expanded horizon.

He writes to Dunning, now Baron Ashburton, with absolute assurance: 'as an indictment for a theoretical essay on government was I believe never before known, I have no apprehension for the consequences' (*Letters*, 2: 615–6).

The SCI retained the flamboyant Thomas Erskine as Shipley's counsel, but the dispersal in Wrexham of a SCI paper on the rights of juries in libel cases played into the hands of the prosecution and the case was removed by a writ of *certiorari* to the Shrewsbury Assizes where it was heard before Mr Justice Francis Buller and a special jury of Shropshire gentlemen on 6 August 1784.

Opening the indictment, Edward Bearcroft, whom Jones's verses had mocked as an inebriate Falstaff, cuts straight to the quick: the gentleman's gift of a musket and bayonet. He stresses the disastrous consequences if all adult males were not only enfranchised but drilled in the 'Prussian exercise': 'taught to load and prime quick, and to make use of a bayonet—picture to yourselves all the men of this populous kingdom that can write twenty-one, attending at elections, with a musket upon their shoulder, and a bayonet at their side'.[50] Bearcroft portrays this as an incitement to armed rebellion especially in the light of the farmer's words: 'He [the king] too must be expelled', conveniently ignoring that this response was to the speculative idea of the Crown governing contrary to law. With eloquent and painstaking logic, Erskine in reply comprehensively demolishes Bearcroft's argument:

> Then follows a *third* speculation of a government dissolved by an aristocracy, the king remaining faithful to his trust; for the Gentleman proceeds thus: 'But what if a few great lords or wealthy men were to keep the king himself in subjection, yet exert his force, lavish his treasure, and misuse his name, so as to domineer over the people, and manage the parliament?' Says the Farmer, 'We must fight for the king and ourselves.' What? for the fugitive king; whom the dean of St. Asaph had before expelled from the crown of these kingdoms! Here again the ridicule of Mr. Bearcroft's constructions stares you in the face; but using it as an abstract speculation of the ruin of a state by aristocracy, it is perfectly plain.[51]

Erskine's task in revealing Bearcroft's palpable misconstructions of Jones's 'theoretical essay' was comparatively easy. He knew the crucial historical importance of this cause was the issue of the jury's powers in cases of

---

50. Howell, *State Trials*, 21: 887.
51. Howell, *State Trials*, 21: 912.

seditious libel, and here he was matched against his former master in chambers, the commanding Buller. Erskine, at his best in appealing to jurymen, cautioned them against being bullied into deciding merely the fact of publication, reserving issues of law to the judges. The jury, contrary to Buller's direction, wanted to return a verdict of 'guilty of publishing *only*', and Erskine strongly argued that this implied that they found no libel. This led to a dramatic courtroom clash between peremptory judge and defiant pupil:

> Mr. Justice *Buller*. Sit down, Sir; remember your duty, or I shall be obliged to proceed in another manner.
> Mr. *Erskine*. Your lordship may proceed in what manner you think fit; I know my duty as well as your lordship knows yours. I shall not alter my conduct.[52]

Buller recorded the verdict as 'guilty of publishing, but whether a libel or not the jury do not find'. Erskine moved for a new trial before the King's Bench, on the ground of misdirection by the judge, and at Westminster Hall in November he argued persuasively for the rights of juries, especially in cases such as Shipley's involving a nice but absolute distinction between the politics of speculation and the politics of incitement. He failed to convince Lord Mansfield, however, who was preoccupied with the incendiary potential of a free press: 'The licentiousness of the press is Pandora's Box, the source of every evil' (21: 1040). In words significantly absent from the 'official' *State Trials*, but recorded by the reporter of the *London Chronicle* (20 November 1784), Mansfield judged the indictment defective, but considered Jones's pamphlet seditious:

> [Y]et it was seditious, perhaps treasonable, as it excited the people to dissention. It incited them to petition for a reform in parliament, under pretence of rights taken from them. It excited to resistance in case such petition was rejected. What did it excite them to do? It said you are to arm, not when danger comes but now.

Despite Mansfield's *opinion*, Erskine was ultimately successful in his motion for arrest of judgement and the whole proceedings against Shipley were set aside.

The Wrexham reprinting of Jones's *jeu d'esprit* established Erskine as a champion of civil liberties, constituting a major legal milestone in the

---

52. Howell, *State Trials*, 21: 951.

history of the freedom of the press and the rights of jurors. Erskine's arguments led to Charles Fox's Libel Act (1792), granting juries the right to decide on the libellous tendency of any publication, passed in the very year in which Paine was prosecuted for publishing *The Rights of Man*.

Shipley was celebrated by crowds of villagers and bonfires burning effigies of Fitzmaurice as he neared his father's house in Twyford, Hampshire. His triumphal return to north Wales was met with similar public 'paroxysm'; the Flintshire zoologist Thomas Pennant was not amused at the yahoo antics:

> The Dean was met some distance from Wrexham and brought in with all patriotic honours, his carriage divested of the horses and drawn by much more irrational animals. [...] the two-legged brutes seized his carriage and drew it to Llanerch, where they were received with bonfires, &c.[53]

A reactionary cartoon depicted Shipley's carriage drawn by prancing billy goats, the caption proclaiming:

> I've escap'd with my Ears & from Newgate you find
> And as for my honour, that's left far behind;
> Which all the World knows, but Welch Goats whom I blind.[54]

But the 'Welch Goats' of Gwynedd were clear-sighted enough to hit upon a masterstroke. The local radicals boosted the audience of Jones's pamphlet way beyond the ten thousand copies distributed by the SCI, by incorporating the text, together with a history of the trial, into an *anterliwt* (interlude), performed at fairs and markets to the literate and illiterate alike. The robust language of *Barn ar Egwyddorion y Llywodraeth, mewn Ymddiddan rhwng Pendefig a Hwsmon*, 'Gan Fardd anadnabyddus o Wynedd' (*A Judgement on The Principles of Government, in a Dialogue between a Gentleman and a Farmer*, 'By an obscure Poet of Gwynedd', 1784), argues the authorship of Thomas Edwards (1738–1810), Twm o'r Nant, or TE Nant, as this castigator of landlords styled himself.[55] The stock *anterliwt* characters Llawenddyn y Ffŵl (Merriman the Fool) and Siôn Gybydd (John Miser) enact Gentleman and

---

53. Letter of 29 December 1784 to Lloyd Kenyon; George Thomas Kenyon, *The Life of Lloyd, First Lord Kenyon* (London, 1873), 124.
54. 'The Triumph of Turbulence or, Mother Cambria Possessed', Pennant Collection, NLW 2598C.
55. See Emyr Wyn Jones, *Yr Anterliwt Goll: Barn ar Egwyddorion y Llywodraeth... Gan Fardd Anadnabyddus o Wynedd* (Aberystwyth, 1984); id., *Diocesan Discord: A Family Affair, St Asaph 1779–1786* (Aberystwyth, 1988).

Farmer respectively, and Jones's pamphlet is given a faithful and forceful colloquial translation:

> Ff. Pe mynnei'r Brenhin wneud deddfe ei hun
> Au troi wrth ei wyn pan fynne.
> Cyb. Ei droi ynteu allan fydde raid'n hollol. (p. 21)
>
> [Fool. If the King should wish to make his own laws
> And alter them as he pleases.
> Miser. He too must be turned out.]

The dialogue is rehearsed in a context rich in local colour and folk satire. The Hon. Thomas Fitzmaurice, owner of a bleach works for imported Irish linen at Lleweni, is disrespectfully termed 'y cannwr' ('the bleacher') for his attempt to blacken Shipley's name. (Another) William Jones, a Rhuthun solicitor, who handled the prosecution for the 'Gwyddel tingam' ('crooked-arsed Irishman') Fitzmaurice, is portrayed as a fiercely conniving swindler, 'Ai wyneb fel maen y Felin' ('His face like a millstone').

There is extravagant praise of Shipley, and of the consummate eloquence of 'Counsler' Erskine in wrong-footing Bearcroft. Repeated toasts are drunk, at the Miser's expense, to the dean and his supporters: Sir Roger Mostyn, Sir Watkin Williams Wynn, Colonel Richard Middleton. In an alcoholic glow, the Ffŵl sings 'Advice to the girls' to the tune of 'Haste to the wedding', with much salacious description of moist lasciviousness and its inevitable consequences. This might annoy the Methodists but, with its lively mixture of satire, politics, beer, and sex, Twm's interlude was first-class tavern entertainment. The end, as we have it, of this powerfully idiomatic publication is suitably joyous and radically republican as the prime minister's brother is shot in effigy:

> Y cleucheu tryw'r wlad yn canu
> A *Phontffires* mhob man'n cynnu,
> A Ff—z yn eu canol bydd'n rhyfeddol fyth,
> Wedi osod yn syth iw saethu.
>
> [The bells through the land ringing out
> And Bonfires everywhere being lit,
> And Ff—z in their midst will be wondrous ever,
> Set up straight to be shot.]

Apart from its importance in the establishment of a free press, and the rights of juries in libel trials, *The Principles of Government* became a key text at the heart of the movement for parliamentary reform and extension of the franchise. A new English edition appeared in the wake of the infamous Peterloo massacre (1819), and another Welsh translation at the height of the Chartist movement of the 1840s. Its international dimensions illustrate Jones's uncanny ability to situate himself at the hub of events in pre-revolutionary Europe. The dramatization of the pamphlet and its trial in the *anterliwt* further exemplifies how Jones could link the metropolis and the margins, his sympathies centred in the colonized and the oppressed, whether of Wales or of India. With the help of Twm o'r Nant, 'Oriental' Jones, 'bardd adnabyddus' (well-known poet) whose father was 'o Wynedd' (of Gwynedd), had become the author of the first Welsh political tract.

In a letter of 27 January 1783, a few months before the eruption of the seditious libel trial, Jones had asked Attorney General Lloyd Kenyon 'to place me in a favourable light with the Chancellor' (Thurlow). Concerned that his politics, founded on 'the true spirit of our constitution', were being misrepresented, he adds: '[H]is Lordship may be assured that I am no more a republican than a *Mahometan* or a *Gentoo*' (*Letters*, 2: 601). In the April of the following year, from the Calcutta courthouse, he employs an interesting simile: 'As to raising sedition, I as much thought of raising a church' (*Letters*, 2: 642).

In 1804 Teignmouth's biography sought to portray Jones as substantially orthodox in both politics and religion; Cambridge philosopher and theologian William Paley protested at what he saw as a distortion of the truth:

> He was a great republican when I knew him. The principles which he then avowed so decidedly, he certainly never afterwards disclaimed: and his sentiments on questions of great publick importance ought neither to be extenuated nor withheld. He might be justly deemed a republican, in the literal acceptation of that term; for, uninfluenced by any selfish motives, he seems, through life, to have devoted his labours to advance the essential interests of the community. Such men are the benefactors of their species, and the appointment of Sir William Jones, to a high judicial situation in India, was probably the greatest blessing ever conferred, by the British government, on the inhabitants of the East.[56]

Such was Paley's opinion but, without prejudice to the old canard of Jones being a radical at home and a despot abroad, or to the newer Saidean insight that all representations are inevitably misrepresentations, we must judge the judge at the bar of India.

---

56. George Wilson Meadley, *Memoirs of William Paley, D.D.* (London, 1809), 154.

6

Knowing India: Asiatic Researches/Recreations

> It gave me inexpressible pleasure to find myself in the midst of so noble an amphitheatre, almost encircled by the vast regions of *Asia*, which has ever been esteemed the nurse of sciences, the inventress of delightful and useful arts, the scene of glorious actions, fertile in the productions of human genius, abounding in natural wonders, and infinitely diversified in the forms of religion and government, in the laws, manners, customs, and languages, as well as in the features and complexions, of men. I could not help remarking how important and extensive a field was yet unexplored, and how many solid advantages unimproved; [...] such inquiries and improvements could only be made by the united efforts of many, who are not easily brought, without some pressing inducement or strong impulse, to converge in a common point, I consoled myself with a hope, [...] that, if in any country or community, such an union could be effected, it was among my countrymen in *Bengal*.
>
> <div align="right">(<i>Works</i>, 3: 1–2)</div>

Sir William Jones's meditation on the deck of the *Crocodile* in August 1783 has become an icon of Orientalism. Determined to prove a leading actor in the amphitheatre of Asia, he reveals his visionary plan in 'A Preliminary Discourse on the Institution of a Society', to its founder-members on 15 January 1784. Jones stresses unparalleled opportunities for intellectual exploration presented by their geographic convergence. Their society inaugurated scientific Indology; its research programme encompassed Indian languages, literature, science, philosophy, and civil and natural history. Their studies are limited 'only by the geographical limits of *Asia*'. In distinct opposition to Eurocentrism, Jones encourages a re-centring of perspective from the hub that is India. He invites his colleagues to join him in 'considering *Hindustan* as a centre, and turning your eyes in idea to the North' to contemplate 'the ancient and wonderful empire of *China*', '*Japan*, with the cluster of precious islands', and beyond the Himalayas to Tibet and Tartary. The organ of their Indocentric society, *Asiatick Researches*, would transform western conceptions of a marginalized subcontinent, placing a vibrant India at the centre of European Romanticism.

Jones cites the Royal Society model, at first 'a few literary friends at *Oxford*', rising 'to that splendid zenith, at which a *Halley* was their secretary, and a *Newton* their president'. He modestly omits to add that a *Jones* was vice-president at that celebrated time. His own presidency of the Asiatick Society would focus world scholarly attention upon Bengal.

Thirty founder-members converged that Thursday night at the Calcutta courthouse in response to the reputation of Europe's foremost Orientalist. They had been drawn to Bengal 'by the most powerful incentive': pecuniary self-interest. This, as Jones pointed out thirteen years earlier in his *Persian Grammar*, 'was the magick wand which brought them all within one circle'. Jones's only wand was the abracadabra aura of celebrity status: it worked its magic on the Hastings circle. Communicator par excellence, it was only someone of his polymathic propensities who could envisage such a grandiose research programme, let alone inspire the diverse interests of the members. He sees that empire might become the vehicle of Orientalism; self-enrichment was not limited to sicca rupees.

As a young tutor, inspired by *Confucius Sinarum Philosophus* (1687) in Père Couplet's translation, he sketched out his 'Plan of an Essay on Education', opening with the words of the 'sublime' Confucius: 'The perfect education of a great man, consists in three points: in cultivating and improving his understanding; in assisting and reforming his countrymen; and in procuring to himself the chief good, or a fixed and unalterable habit of virtue' (*Works*, 1: 154). Knowledge acquisition must entail its distribution; research must 'benefit mankind and ourselves'. The wisdom of China, imported to Europe by a Belgian Jesuit, is reapplied in Calcutta by a half-Welsh Orientalist for the benefit of 'Company hands'; it is within their hands to enrich the West, and indeed India, by their researches.

Of course, not all the British in Bengal were sufficiently interested or intellectually capable of becoming Indologists. They devoted themselves—according to their social or financial circumstances—to private trading or money-making scams; to Indian *bibis* or Portuguese prostitutes; to arrack (fermented coconut palm sap), lal shrub (claret), or Mango shrub; to opium, betel leaf, hookah, or cheroot. Anything which might allay the tedium of long hot hours between breakfast and dinner was welcomed, and most especially gambling. Two months after the Asiatick Society's first meeting, its president was sitting, on 16 March, together with Sir Robert Chambers and John Hyde, to try a cause between two young Company writers:

> *John Taylor v Philip Younge*. An action on a bet that the Plaintiff could make a million of distinct dots with one point within the space of twenty four hours. [...] No machine was to be used and he was to use only One Point, Pen or Pencil. [...] the bet with Mr Younge was two thousand rupees [...] the court sate till half an hour after seven in the evening.[1]

The cause was argued over more long hot hours with judgement finally given for the defendant, Mr Younge. There was little opportunity for Jones's expertise in comparative law, although the pages of Hyde's notebook attest his mathematical interest in this feat. Gambling had much in common with commerce. While some made millions of dots, a fortunate few made millions of rupees. The universal desire to gain a fortune or a competence united bored gamblers and their Asiatick Society judges: what separated them, apart from the huge salaries of the latter, was the deployment of precious leisure time.

The adolescents arriving as Company servants were denominated 'Writers', but only a tiny minority of these minors ever saw their writing in print; their clerkly, bureaucratic duties accorded with the scribal culture of the Mughal empire. Hastings himself began his career as a five-pound-per-annum writer in 1750 at a comparatively mature eighteen. Not until 1793 was a minimum age of fifteen established for writers and cadets, a situation targeted by Burke's colourful parliamentary rhetoric. In 1783 he fulminated: 'Young men (boys almost) govern there, without society, and without sympathy with the natives [...] birds of prey and passage.'[2] On this issue as on many others, the two implacable opponents thought alike. Hastings had written a decade earlier: '[T]he boys of the service are the sovereigns of the country under the unmeaning title of supervisors, collectors of the revenue, administrators of justice, and rulers, heavy rulers of the people.'[3]

---

1. Kolkata, Victoria Memorial Hall, Hyde Papers vol. no. 5: '1784 Jan. 31 to Dec. 29'.
2. 'Speech on Fox's India Bill', 1 December 1783, *The Writings and Speeches of Edmund Burke*: V *India: Madras and Bengal*, ed. P. J. Marshall (Oxford, 1981), 402.
3. Hastings to Josias DuPre, 26 March 1772, *Memoirs of the Life of the Right Hon. Warren Hastings*, ed. G. R. Gleig, 3 vols (London, 1841), 1: 234.

Intrepid traveller Eliza Fay discovered, 'It is not uncommon to see *writers* within a few months after their arrival dashing away on the course *four in hand*: allowing for the inconsiderateness of youth, is it surprising if many become deeply embarrassed.'[4]

Nathaniel Brassey Halhed, an impecunious 23-year-old writer, had acquired no phaeton and four during a fifteen-month sojourn in Bengal. Writing on 5 November 1773 to Samuel Parr, he lamented that the pagoda tree (so-called from a southern Indian coin) had been shaken to its roots:

> India (the wealthy, the luxurious, and the lucrative,) is so exceedingly ruined and exhausted, that I am not able by any means, not with the assistance of my education in England, and the exertion of all my abilities here, to procure even a decent subsistence. I have studied the Persian language with the utmost application in vain; I have courted employment without effect.[5]

In England this writer was a published author, having completed with Sheridan a verse translation of the erotic *Love Epistles of Aristaenetus* (1771). Love letters also featured in Halhed's rivalry with Sheridan for the hand of the talented singer-composer Elizabeth Linley. Unlucky in love at home, in Calcutta his writing talents were similarly employed in poetic compliments to the most attractive women—married or single—of Fort William.[6] This rapidly brought him to the attention of the husband of the beautiful Marian Hastings. The governor-general redirected Halhed's talents, transforming a dissipated prodigal into a disciplined Orientalist.

Hastings was blamed by Henry Thomas Colebrooke, who arrived in April 1783, six months before Jones, as a 17-year-old writer, for failing to secure him a rewarding post. As son of Sir George Colebrooke, former Company chairman, Henry came with great expectations. He also criticized Hastings for the lax morality of a Calcutta inhabited by 'harpies' with 'one pursuit—a fortune'. That this was also Henry's pursuit resonates in the subtext of a disillusioned letter to his father: 'The truth is, India is no longer a mine of gold; every one is disgusted, and all whose affairs permit, abandon it as rapidly as possible.'[7]

But Colebrooke did not abandon India; the twenty papers he contributed to *Asiatick Researches* made him, on Jones's death, its foremost Orientalist.

---

4. Eliza Fay, *Original Letters from India, 1779–1815*, ed. E. M. Forster (London, 1925), 182.
5. Samuel Parr, *Works*, ed. John Johnstone, 8 vols (London, 1828), 1: 469–71.
6. Rosane Rocher, *Orientalism, Poetry, and the Millennium: The Checkered Life of Nathaniel Brassey Halhed, 1751–1830* (Delhi, 1983), 40–3.
7. 'A Memoir of the Late Henry Thomas Colebrooke', *Journal of the Royal Asiatic Society*, 5 (1839), 1–60; 4.

Completing Jones's 'Digest of Indian Law', he was elected the society's president in 1807.

Henry's cousin, Robert Hyde Colebrooke, arrived in 1778 as a cadet in the Bengal Infantry. Promoted to lieutenant, he completed, under the botanist Captain Robert Kyd, pioneering surveys of the Andaman and Nicobar Islands in the Bay of Bengal. Appointed Surveyor-General of India, Colebrooke produced, in the Jonesian linguistic tradition, an Andamanese vocabulary, publishing in the fourth volume of *Asiatick Researches* five articles on geographical, anthropological, and astronomical topics. A talented artist, his *Twelve Views of Places in the Kingdom of Mysore* (1793–4) precisely record military details of Cornwallis's 1790–2 campaign against Tīpū Sultān, overshadowed by the monumentally dramatic backdrop of the Eastern Ghats.

Clearly, the Colebrookes were not your average writers or cadets, but their differing careers exemplify how the Asiatick Society nurtured researchers' individual specialisms, providing for their publications an international platform, underwritten by the president's incomparable reputation. The Society developed the exploratory scientific and literary culture encouraged by Hastings, communicating and underscoring the political and cultural resonance of British Indian research. For those whose mental ambition ranged beyond wagering on millions of dots, Jones outlines a vast sphere of intellectual and imaginative space unavailable within the class-bound confines of the metropolis. 'If our countrymen here', Jones writes to the poet Edward Jerningham, 'will learn that wealth is not the only pursuit fit for rational beings, my object in proposing and supporting the Society will be attained' (*Letters*, 2: 868). India offered the bourgeois ambitious, such as himself, alternative routes of social mobility and intellectual aspiration.

With, in Marilyn Butler's phrase, 'the grandeur of one of the great moghuls of the Enlightenment',[8] Jones charts the challenging horizons of their research programme in 'A Discourse on the Institution of a Society':

> [Y]ou will investigate whatever is rare in the stupendous fabrick of nature; will correct the geography of *Asia* by new observations and discoveries; will trace the annals, and even traditions, of those nations, who from time to time have peopled or desolated it; and will bring to light their various forms of government, with their institutions civil and religious; you will examine their improvements

---

8. See Marilyn Butler, 'Culture's Medium: The Role of the Review', in *The Cambridge Companion to British Romanticism*, ed. Stuart Curran (Cambridge, 1993), 120–47; 128.

and method in arithmetick and geometry, in trigonometry, mensuration, mechanicks, opticks, astronomy and general physics; their systems of morality, grammar, rhetorick and dialectick; their skill in chirurgery and medicine, and their advancement, whatever it may be, in anatomy and chemistry. To this you will add researches into their agriculture, manufactures, trade; and, whilst you inquire with pleasure into their musick, architecture, painting, and poetry, will not neglect those inferior arts by which the comforts and even elegancies of social life are supplied or improved.   (*Works*, 3: 6)

Did he miss anything out? The *nawab* of knowledge requires his colleagues to be sultans of all they survey. If this sounds imperious, well so it was; if it sounds imperialistic, it was that also; he was building an empire of science. Within four short months Jones has identified areas where Indian science and civilization excelled. His predominant emphases are upon Indian scientific 'improvements and method', 'their skill [...] their advancement', and the sophistication of India's artistic heritage. Revealing this to the West will enhance European research and advance European science, while demonstrating the originality of Indian rationality, science, and culture.

As for what he missed out, 'Linguist' Jones had left out the languages: 'I have ever considered languages as the mere instruments of real learning, and think them improperly confounded with learning itself; the attainment of them is, however, indispensably necessary; and if to the *Persian, Armenian, Turkish* and *Arabick*, could be added not only the *Sanscrit*, the treasures of which we may now hope to see unlocked, but even the *Chinese, Tartarian, Japanese*, and the various insular dialects, an immense mine would then be open, in which we might labour with equal delight and advantage' (*Works*, 3: 7). This reductively instrumental conception of languages reveals a typical perversity as if Jones were a mere locksmith. The poet and translator knows full well that languages are an integral part of the treasure, not merely the keys to cultural riches.

His audience of Crown and Company servants included Sanskritist Wilkins, pioneer of printing in Bengali and Persian, Charles Hamilton, translator of the *Hedaya*, a guide to Muslim law, and Persianist Gladwin, founder-editor of *Calcutta Gazette*, and most published author in late eighteenth-century Calcutta.[9] They realized their power to create new

---

9. See Michael J. Franklin, '"The Hastings Circle": Writers and Writing in Calcutta in the Last Quarter of the Eighteenth Century', in *Authorship, Commerce and the Public: Scenes of Writing, 1750–1850*, ed. Peter Garside, Caroline Franklin and Emma Clery (Basingstoke, 2002), 186–202.

audiences for substantially new discourses and often proved more successful in earning European reputations than in achieving mercantile profit.

Towards the end of his 'Preliminary Discourse', Jones turns to publication: 'let us present our *Asiatick* miscellany to the literary world'. His model was German physician Engelbert Kaempfer, whose sympathetic account of Japan's closed society had fascinated Europe. Jones's society must open western eyes to the reality of India, its illustrious past and exciting present. He promises the 'fruits or flowers' of his own research: 'I shall offer my humble *Nezr* [ceremonial gift] to your society with as much respectful zeal as to the greatest potentate on earth.' Respect for the potential authority of this infant meritocracy, couched in a polite image of Mughal gifting, reveals Jones's shrewd understanding of the ways in which power is mediated by knowledge and knowledge mediated by power.

Muslim politesse is reciprocated in Wilkins's gift of a Hāfiz *ghazal* to Jones as popularizer of the Shirazi poet. It symbolizes the Sūfi concept of *suhl-i kul* (peace with all), suggesting universal toleration as the Society's keystone as it had been of Akbar's Fatehpur Sikri. Gladwin reported in his *Calcutta Gazette* of 3 June:

> The contents of the Ode did credit to Mr Wilkins's choice [...] Indeed the President possesses claims upon the gratitude of this settlement which no compliments can ever repay.

Gladwin offers a 'free translation' of Hāfiz's ode, printed in parallel with the Persian original set in *nasta'liq* font, to the newspaper-purchasing public:

> The crown of the king of flowers has
>   Appeared from the border of the garden;
> O God! May its approach be auspicious
>   To the Cypress, and Jasmine.
>
> Fortunate was this acceptance of a seat of
>   Pre-eminence in this assembly:
> As every associate may now occupy his
>   Respective place with honour.
>
> Impart to the ring of Solomon the joyful
>   News of a successful conclusion;
> As the most powerful name of God has
>   Restrained from it the hands of Demons.
>
> May this house be for ever inhabited,
>   From the earth of whose threshold

>   Is continually wafted the breeze of prosperity,
>   Fraught with the fragrance of the sweet basil.
>
> [...]
>
>   If afterwards thy bud shall expand, disclosing
>   The fragrance of thy amiable disposition,
>   The odour of the musk of Tartary shall
>   Arise from the plain of thy cheek. (ll. 1–16; 28–32)[10]

'[A]s the expressions of Hafiz are supposed to have a prophetick virtue', Gladwin trusts, '*the house may ever be inhabited*, or that the Society may ever flourish.' Wilkins's choice of *Ghazal* 390, with its perfumed floral compliments to 'planting the tree of Justice', is apposite. If Jones's signet-ring, inscribed with a bust of Cicero, reflects the virtue of 'Jamshid's [Solomon's] seal-ring' it will reveal everything he wants to know, and perhaps provide the power to subdue Eurocentric demons.

This *ghazal*, tribute to enlightened despot Jones, was originally dedicated to an arbitrary Muzaffarid patron. Hāfiz's delicate negotiations with religious and secular structures of authority remind us that the politics of religion and art were as intricately interconnected in fourteenth-century Iran as they are in today's Kashmir. For Hastings's Orientalist regime the mystical aspects of Sūfism, quietist and potentially syncretist, were inherently useful to the state in bringing Muslim and Hindu closer together within the intercultural tradition of Dāra Shikūh's *Majma'al-bahrayn* or 'The Mingling of the Two Oceans' of Hinduism and Islam.

Jones would link the politics of Islamic mysticism to the politics of Advaita Vedānta (the non-dual end of the Vedas), the most intensely mystical aspect of Hinduism. It has long been argued that the concentration of these early Indologists upon the *Upaniṣads*, constituting the religious and philosophic tradition of Advaita Vedānta, had a pronounced political dimension. Niranjan Dhar claims that this reflected the Orientalists' desire to foster what they saw as its spiritualized, conservative, and quietist tendencies to encourage the stability of British India. Such concerns obviously increased in the years following the French Revolution with the dangers of French expansionism in India, and Governor-General Marquis Richard Wellesley's fears that the young minds of writers at the College of Fort William might be polluted by Jacobin ideas.

Dhar contrasts the political motivation underlying the 1800 establishment of Fort William College with that of Jones's Asiatick Society, which 'owed

---

10. *Calcutta Gazette*, 1: 14 (3 June 1784), 5.

its origins to a disinterested love for the hoary culture of India'.[11] But the members of the Hastings circle were not politically naive and love is rarely disinterested. Jones's deep love for Sūfistic writers such as Hāfiz and Saʿdī long predated his appointment as acknowledged legislator in Bengal. It was in accord with his deistic emphasis upon reason and his own fascination with the traditions of Cambridge Platonism and Protestant mysticism. Jones sought similitude between West and East, and part of this overarching project was to stress the compatibility of Hindu and Islamic mysticism. There was an imperialist ideological dimension here; it was a means of aligning the regime's need to appear both neo-Brahmanical and neo-Mughal. The establishment of authoritative texts of the *Bhagavadgītā* and Hāfiz bolstered the authority of the colonial regime, encouraging socio-political stability. Nor was this political instrumentality reductive; the Hastings circle revered these Hindu and Muslim texts, admiring their potential to transcend differences of birth, of culture, and of religion.

Hastings spells out the political rationale of Orientalism in his letter to EIC director Nathaniel Smith, prefixed to Wilkins's *The Bhăgvăt-Gēētā* (1785). He respects this devotional section of the vast Sanskrit epic, *Mahābhārata*, as 'almost unequalled in its sublimity of conception, reasoning, and diction; a work of wonderful fancy', but devotion could serve governance.

His letter should be read in the context of the enormous difficulties facing the governor-general. Hastings had to deal with more than Mysore and the Marathas; in Calcutta there was opposition on the Supreme Council, at home there was the Court of Directors, more concerned with trade figures than colonial administration or Sanskrit literature; the suspicions of Parliament and the Crown, reacting to a confusing spectrum of public opinion: condemnation of colonial rapacity; concern for investments in Company Bonds; sympathy for the victims of Bengal famine; fears of luxury and desire for luxury goods; irritation at the social pretensions of returned nabobs; disgust with the demon gods of Hindu polytheism; contempt for childlike/feminized/luxurious Hindus and for devious/despotic/cruel Muslims.

The publication of *Bhăgvăt-Gēētā* highlighted EIC employees as cultivated scholars rather than dissolute fortune hunters, for 'it is on the virtue, not the ability, of their servants, that the Company must rely for the permanency of their dominions':

---

11. Niranjan Dhar, *Vedanta and the Bengal Renaissance* (Calcutta, 1977), 31.

Nor is the cultivation of language and science [...] useful only in forming the moral character and habits of the service. Every accumulation of knowledge, and especially such as is obtained by social communication with a people over whom we exercise a dominion founded on the right of conquest, is useful to the state: it is the gain of humanity: [...] it attracts and conciliates distant affections; it lessens the weight of the chain by which the natives are held in subjection; and it imprints on the hearts of our own countrymen the sense and obligation of benevolence. Even in England, this effect of it is greatly wanting. It is not very long since the inhabitants of India were considered by many, as creatures scarce elevated above the degree of savage life; nor, I fear, is that prejudice wholly eradicated, though surely abated. Every instance which brings their real character home to observation will impress us with a more generous sense of feeling for their natural rights, and teach us to estimate them by the measure of our own. But such instances can only be obtained in their writings: and these will survive when the British dominion in India shall have long ceased to exist, and when the sources which it once yielded both of wealth and power are lost to remembrance.[12]

With disarming confidence and candour, Hastings expounds Orientalist governance in terms of cultural empathy and Enlightenment relativity; 'rights of conquest' are balanced by 'natural rights', short-term strategic utility by long-term cultural enrichment. Hastings, the empire builder, has the vision to conceive of a postcolonial reality with Indian empire forgotten and Indian literature celebrated.

Jones underscored every word of Hastings's letter. It makes us realize why the Society sought to elect Hastings as president; they knew his achievement in the promotion of Oriental learning and the patronage of Indian poets, artists, and musicians.[13] His refusal, on the grounds of insufficient leisure, led to the election of founder Jones as president, who similarly acknowledged Hastings's learning: 'As to myself, I could never have been satisfied, if, in traversing the sea of knowledge, I had fallen in with a ship of your rate and station, without striking my flag' (*Letters*: 2; 629).

Jones shared Hastings's awareness of the power of public opinion, both in Bengal and in London. Though Jones requests Robert Orme to 'give my affectionate remembrance to General Smith' (*Letters*, 2: 717), he had no desire to be tarred with the nabob brush by metropolitan factions anxious to

---

12. Charles Wilkins, *The Bhăgvăt-Gēētā* (London, 1785), 12–13.
13. See P. J. Marshall, 'Warren Hastings as Scholar and Patron', in *Statesmen, Scholars and Merchants: Essays Presented to Dame Lucy Sutherland*, ed. Anne Whiteman et al. (Oxford, 1973), 242–62.

taint the Orientalist administration with pursuit of plunder. Jones need not have worried; he was being celebrated in Britain for bringing an end to colonial rapacity. The London press was singing his praises:

> By the last accounts from India we learnt, that in the great question between the Company and the army, on the plunder of Cheyt Sing, Sir William Jones has given an ultimate decision, by which it is declared, that the plunder belongs to the Company, and not to the army. This is one of the most memorable decisions in the Supreme Court of Judicature of Bengal; for by this decree a stop will be put to that system of rapacity and plunder which has degraded us in the East. (*London Chronicle*, 2 September 1784)

Jones was battening upon new plunder: India knowledge. East Indiamen would ship this precious cargo to Europe, amidst the silks, spices, and muslins. This could achieve the culmination of the political and cultural 'System' Hastings described in a letter to John Scott of 9 December 1784:

> My letter to Mr Smith introducing Mr. Wilkins's Translation of the Gheeta is also Business, though began in Play. It is the effect of part of a System which I long since laid down, and supported, for reconciling the People of England to the Natives of Hindostan.[14]

The Asiatick Society was, in effect, Jones's institutionalizing of Hastings's 'System'. The production of India knowledge might accomplish Hastings's important goals: to reconcile Indians with their imperial masters; 'free the inhabitants of this country from the reproach of ignorance and barbarism'; and free Company servants from accusations of 'moral turpitude'. Their research programme would initiate a new scheme of scholarly, ethical, and cultural values to compensate for the colonial theft of the Clive generation. The textual dimensions of Indian research might underpin notions of legitimacy and continuity in the subcontinent and in the metropolis. The task of representing Indians to European prejudice was intrinsically connected to that of (re)presenting Company employees. Jones's long-awaited arrival galvanized research within the colony. Throughout Europe it advertised the meritocratic aspects of British Orientalist government.

Papers read to the Society in its first two months established predominating areas of research in ancient Indian history, chronology, epigraphy, and linguistics. Thomas Law, Collector of Bihar, (whose trials of the '*mukarari* system', treating the *zamindars* as landowners rather than tax collectors,

---

14. BL, Add. MSS. 29,129, f. 275.

anticipated the 1793 permanent settlement), provided 'A short account and drawing of two pillars situated to the north of Patna' on the 29 January. A fortnight later, it was the turn of Francis Balfour, whose *The Forms of Herkern* (1781), supplied Persian models of business and personal correspondence, using Wilkins's excellent *nasta'liq* types. Balfour's 'Treatise on the introduction of the Arabic into Persian and the languages of Hindostan', reflected the linguistic versatility of this eminent physician who attended Anna.

On 19 February two papers were read, the first by John David Paterson, a Dacca judge, who sent 'A letter shewing the agreement between the Hindoo and Greek chronology, accompanying tables composed by the Moonshy [*munshi*, secretary] of Dara Shikuh'. The second was Jones's 'Dissertation on the Orthography of Asiatick Words in Roman Letters', pioneering 'the Jonesian System' of phonetic transliteration for Sanskrit, Persian, and Arabic characters. These contributions reveal the incremental and collaborative nature of the society's research. Jones's observation that ancient Greeks converted 'foreign names to a *Grecian* form', together with what he gleaned from Dārā Shikūh's comparative chronological tables in Paterson's paper, broke the ground for establishing historical synchronicity.

William Chambers, brother of Sir Robert, describes the Pancha Rathas, monolithic temples carved whole from outcrops of pink granite at Mahabalipuram, south of Madras. Admiration for these splendid sculptures was clouded by his evangelical contempt for the 'wretched superstitions' they celebrated, but Chambers, a talented linguist, communicates frustration with his inability to date architecture in a land where 'poets seem to have been their only historians'.[15] Chambers's solution of 'comparing names and grand events, recorded by them, with those interspersed in the histories of other nations, and by calling in the assistance of ancient monuments, coins, and inscriptions' aided Jones's 1793 breakthrough in tracing India's history.

Such intellectual activity reveals the competence and confidence of professionals working outside the comfort zones of their own discrete disciplines. They were not ivory-towered academics lingering in a remotely textualized India, but eminently practical men for whom the subcontinent was very much a dynamic reality. As Jones explains:

---

15. William Chambers, 'Account of the Ruins and Sculptures at Mavalipuram', *Asiatick Researches*, 1 (1788), 145–70; 157.

> It is not here, as in Europe, where many are scholars and Philosophers professedly, without any other pursuit: here every member of our Society is a man of business, occupied in his respective line of revenue, commerce, law, medicine, military affairs and so forth: his leisure must be allotted, in great part, to the care of his health, even if pleasure engage no share of it. What part of it remains then for literature? Instead, therefore, of being surprised, that we have done so little, the world, if they are candid, will wonder that we have done so much.   (*Letters*, 2: 747)

His inspirational presence motivated the members; when a seriously ill Jones left Calcutta to travel upriver in late June 1784, there was precious little societal activity. But even in his weakened state, he was encouraging friends to contribute papers. We gain some insight into his formidable intellectual energies from Charles Grant, the intensely driven evangelical who was commercial Resident at Malda.

Returning from the reinvigorating company of the Fowkes at Banaras, Jones realized that the shrewd administrator Grant would prove a valuable friend. The first Grant knew of their intended stay was the 'appearance of letters here for Sir W. Jones'. Although this must have appeared highhanded, the Grants welcomed the convalescent couple on 17 January 1785. William and Charles were exact contemporaries, and Anna enjoyed the company of Grant's intelligent wife Jane. Grant found Jones 'polite and entertaining in a high degree', but his 'depth of learning, facility and variety of genius' was intimidating: 'The shame of being unlearned and the desire for some acquisition in that way took again possession of my mind.'[16]

Jones's personal magnetism and polymathic intellect daunted and inspired. Grant took Anna and William to Gaur, the medieval capital of Bengal, where they viewed the impressive Adina Masjid, one of the largest mosques in India. Built in 1369 by Sultan Sikandar Shah, it was formerly a Hindu temple rich in carved basalt statuary, over which the authority of Islam had been asserted in massive brick domes. Jones was excited by images of Vishnu and the elephant-headed Ganeśa, which had escaped the iconoclastic hammer; it was a fascination the scrupulous Grant, to whom both temple and *masjid* were anathema, was unable to share.

Grant's missionary zeal had deep roots. As a newly married man, obsessed with making an Indian fortune, he became addicted to gambling.

---

16. Journal entry for 6 February 1785, cited in Henry Morris, *The Life of Charles Grant* (London, 1904), 82.

10. Sir William Jones, by Robert Home, oil on canvas, c.1785. (Asiatic Society, Kolkata)

The numbing tragedy of his two baby daughters dying of smallpox within days of each other in April 1776 he saw as a punishment revealing 'the just displeasure of God' at his immorality. Grant's repentant evangelicalism and determination to support Anglican and Methodist missions in Bengal was blessed by the arrival of four more children, Jane being pregnant with their fifth when the Joneses arrived.

While Jones consults Bernard Picart on 'the ceremonies of idolatrous nations' in the library, Grant receives an enquiry concerning a Bengal mission from Welshman Thomas Coke, Wesley's man in America. Jones composes a paper establishing comparative mythology while Grant rehearses gross ethnocentric stereotypes in replying to Coke: 'The leading features in the character of the Mahometans are pride and cruelty, treachery and love of power; those of the Hindoos are abject servility, cunning, lying, dishonesty, and excessive love of money.' Shackled to his own conception of a justly vengeful Creator, Grant finds it 'hardly possible to conceive any people more completely enchained than they [Hindus] are in their superstition'.[17]

Grant represented everything that might have made Jones more cautious in his enthusiastic advocacy of Hindu culture. A man of ability and integrity, he was extremely well connected and would return to England to become a close friend of Wilberforce, and EIC director. Though humane and concerned about Bengal weavers and his own workers pioneering indigo cultivation, he lacked artistic or imaginative vision. His journal records: 'Sir W. was curious at Gour only about the remains of art'; Grant viewed the polished marble in a much more practical light: how well it would look paving the new Calcutta church. On 10 July he writes to the commission secretary for the building of St John's: 'I have now the pleasure to dispatch to you a boat laden with Gour Stones.'[18] Appalled at such vandalism, Jones refused to contribute to the building fund.

Jones became expert in negotiating tensions in his relationships with mutual friends: the equally earnest evangelicals, John Shore, future governor-general, and William Chambers, who married Jane Grant's sister Charity. Jones is as accommodating in his domestic arrangements as in appearing orthodox: 'Sir W., who slept in his budgerow [to enjoy cooling river breezes] came ashore early Sunday morning, and joined us at family prayer, afterwards at Church, and read to us one of Secker's discourses on

---

17. Letter of Grant to Thomas Coke of 19 February 1785, cited in Jonathan Crowther, *The Life of the Rev. Thomas Coke, LL.D* (Leeds, 1815), 200–1.
18. Letter of Grant, dated 10 July; St John's Church Minute Book.

"Whatsoever things are pure".' Jones had chosen carefully, for the polymath Thomas Secker, archbishop of Canterbury, excellent Hebraist, and patron of Jones's friend, Hungarian Orientalist Joannes Uri, encouraged missions to Native Americans. Jones informed the Grants that centuries before Christ, Hindus taught that evil should be repaid by good, 'as the Sandal-tree in the instant of its overthrow, sheds perfume on the axe, which fells it' (*Works*, 3: 243). Charles was impervious to praise of Indian ethics; its people walked in darkness and the stern voice of evangelical duty dictated that they must be shown the great light. Jones failed to convince Grant there was anything whatsoever pure in Hinduism, but persuaded him to join the Asiatick Society nevertheless.

On the 27 January, the Joneses sailed down the Mahananda and the Padma-Ganges to the Sundarbans, freshwater swamp forest and brackish-water mangrove jungle intersected by a maze of tidal creeks. To Charles Chapman he describes their delightful expedition: 'The Mahananda was beautiful, and the banks of some rivers in the Sunderbunds were magnificent; we passed within two yards of a fine tiger' (*Letters*, 2: 667). But in a 'new' letter to Grant I recently unearthed at the India Office, the content is more Society-focused and the tiger reduced to a leopard:

> We found the passage through the Sunderbunds by no means disagreeable, except that our rest was disturbed at night by the loquacity of the rowers and their continual invocations of Gházy, who preserves them, they suppose from tigers: we had no serious alarm of any kind, and saw only one leopard, who seemed to stare at us, as we passed within two yards of him, with careless contempt. [...] the term begins on Tuesday, and I must plunge again into the ocean of law. I found on my table a most polite letter from Mr Cox of Canton with a present of Chinese drawings [...] He ought to be a member of our society, and would be a valuable correspondent. I [...] request you to present my compliments to Mr Baillie, whom I should also be happy to propose as a member of our Asiatick body.[19]

Significantly Jones offers Grant this sleep-disturbing reminder of Indian devotion. He learned from his *dandies* (boatmen) that Bada Khan Ghazi was a popular Muslim warrior-saint invoked by Muslims and Hindus alike for protection against tigers. He subsequently read the *Rāy-Mangala*, by Bengali poet Krishnaram Das, portraying symbolic conflict between Ghazi and the Hindu tiger-god Dakshin Ray, reconciled by a divinity appearing as half-Krishna and half-Muhammad. Such bodily syncretism, eroding the

---

19. BL, APAC, Eur. MSS C864; W. Jones to [Charles Grant], Calcutta, 27 February 1785. This is Jones's only extant letter to Grant.

boundaries between religious communities in lower Bengal, complemented the syncretic mysticism Jones celebrated in Sūfī poetry.

This letter reveals Jones's untiring efforts to strengthen his infant society. John Henry Cox was the son of James Cox, whose Spring Gardens museum, featuring spectacular automata, was a fashionable London attraction. He came to India to develop trade with China in watches, clocks, and intricate toys, becoming a substantial private merchant whose Bengal-built ships supplied Canton with opium, cotton, and—in a daring trans-Pacific venture—American furs. Jones desperately wanted to visit China, having translated one of the odes of the *Shi-Ching* (*c*.800 BCE) from a Royal Library manuscript in Paris in 1770, and having met a fascinating Cantonese, Whang Atong, at dinner with Sir Joshua Reynolds. From Calcutta Jones urged Whang to translate the *Shi-Ching*, and encourage Chinese artists to visit Bengal. Via 'Canton' Cox, Jones received the *Lun Yu* (Analects of Confucius), the *Ta Hsüeh* (Great Learning), together with a *Shi-Ching* manuscript, but Whang demurred at the huge task of translating its 300 odes.

A translation became one of his 'great objects in Asia', but Jones failed to introduce Europe to the beauties of ancient Chinese poetry. He imagined printing literal and poetic versions after the model provided in his 'On the Second Classical Book of the Chinese' for this sublime censure of a tyrannical minister:

> O how horridly impends yon southern mountain!
> Its rocks in how vast, how rude a heap!
> Thus loftily thou sittest, O minister of YN;
> All the people look up to thee with dread.
>
> Which may be thus paraphrased:
>
> See, where yon crag's imperious height
>   The sunny highland crowns,
> And, hideous as the brow of night,
>   Above the torrent frowns!
>
> So scowls the Chief, whose will is law,
>   Regardless of our state;
> While millions gaze with painful awe,
>   With fear allied to hate.   (*Works*, 4: 122)

William Baillie also became a valued 'member of our Asiatick body'. An officer in the Bengal Engineers until 1785, Baillie was a talented artist, map and printmaker, a friend of landscape painter Thomas Daniell and portrait painter Ozias Humphrey. Jones found Baillie's *Views of Calcutta* strangely unpopulated, much as his map excises the non-English 'Black town'. Jones preferred the livelier topographical prints of Daniell. He hoped artists might delineate the 'many noble remains in *Bihar*, and some in the vicinity of *Malda*'. This was not exclusively for the historical record, before they were ravaged by builders of churches or mansions; even the ruins of Indian splendour might 'furnish our own architects with new ideas of beauty and sublimity' (*Works*, 3: 19).

Jones's 'Second Anniversary Discourse' indicates the enormous amount he still has to learn about the subcontinent. Written early in 1785, it bristles with Eurocentric preconceptions, rapidly shed during subsequent years.

A key locus of prejudice concerns the Indian status of the mathematical sciences. He claims that in these disciplines 'the *Asiaticks*, if compared with our Western nations, are mere children'. Jones regales his audience with Johnson's remark that in ancient Athens, Newton would have been worshipped as a divinity, adding with uncharacteristically ethnocentric relish: 'how zealously then would he be adored in *Hindustan*, if his incomparable writings could be read and comprehended by the *Pandits* of *Cashmir* or *Benares!*' Though aware of Arabic algebraic expertise, he expects nothing in the way of 'new *methods*, or the analysis of new *curves*, from the geometricians of *Iran, Turkistan*, or *India*'.

It was the work of two of Jones's closest friends in India that proved him wrong. The convivial Reuben Burrow was a first-rate mathematician. Expert in classical geometry and modern artillery, he assisted Nevil Maskelyne, Astronomer Royal and brother of Lady Clive. Hastings recognized his talent, and he obtained a Calcutta post as mathematics master to the corps of engineers. Burrow set about learning Arabic, Persian, and, subsequently, Sanskrit. Appointed chief surveyor, this model Society member discovered that the Hindus possessed a more accurate method of calculating the parallaxes of the moon than that provided in the *Nautical Almanack*, published by Maskelyne and the Board of Longitude.[20]

Burrow revealed that the 'mere children' of Indian science had priority over the West in several branches of algebra, and complete knowledge of the binomial theorem.[21] Together with his account of Brahman astronomical tables, he sends Hastings suggestions 'for discovering, collecting, and translating whatever is extant of the ancient works of the Hindoos'.[22]

20. Reuben Burrow, 'A Method of Calculating the Moon's Parallaxes in Longitude and Latitude', *Asiatick Researches*, 1 (1788), 320–5.
21. Reuben Burrow, 'A Proof that the Hindoos Had the Binomial Theorem', *Asiatick Researches*, 2 (1790), 487–95.
22. BL, Add. MSS 29,233, f. 237, account of Brahman astronomical tables.

Muzaffar Alam and Seema Alavi note Burrow's observation, 'that the Brahmins of Benares used algebraic formulae which derived from a familiarity with the Newtonian doctrine of "series" to compute eclipses'.[23] Burrow exemplifies the best traditions of intercultural enquiry. Relaying his compliments to Major William Palmer, Jones informs him that 'his friend Tafazzul Husain Khān is reading Newton with Burrow, & means to translate the *Principia* into Arabick' (*Letters*, 2: 839–40).

The other man who convinced Jones of the accuracy of Hindu astronomy was the brilliant young half-Welsh Orientalist, Samuel Davis. In Banaras, Davis showed Jones one of Raja Jai Singh II's observatories on the roof of Mana Mahala, overlooking the Ganges. Using the sublime architecture of these massive, but high-precision, instruments of masonry and stone, Davis was making detailed astronomical calculations by contemporary Hindu formulae. They talked of Buddhism and Bhutan, where Davis had travelled with Samuel Turner's diplomatic mission to Tibet, but the beauty of mathematics drew them together. Becoming firm friends, Jones's poems were exchanged for Davis's detailed watercolours. In a fashion exemplifying society co-operation, Davis obtained a manuscript of the astronomical *Sūrya-siddhānta* from Robert Chambers, but, as many technical terms were obscure even to Davis's diligent pandit, 'the *Tita*, or Commentary' was supplied by another founder-member, Jonathan Duncan, Resident at Banaras.

Davis and Burrow were astounded by the accuracy of astronomical tables that the pioneering Guillaume Le Gentil, French Resident at the Faizabad court of Nawab Shuja ud-Daula, obtained from Tiruvallur Brahmans on the Coromandel Coast, two decades earlier. They revealed scientific Indian astronomy dating back to the third century BCE. Encouraged by Jones, Davis was learning Sanskrit and studying Hindu texts in the light of his own empirical research. With the help of Indian experts, unavailable to other scholars of Indian astronomy, such as Jean-Sylvain Bailly in Paris or John Playfair in Edinburgh, he amplified and corrected Le Gentil's work. Jones chauvinistically anticipated Anglophone victory: '[You] will have the honour of a triumph over Le Gentil, Bailly, and all the oriental Astronomers of France' (*Letters*, 2: 909).

---

23. *A European Experience of the Mughal Orient: The I'jāz-i Arsalānī (Persian Letters, 1773–1779) of Antoine-Louis Henri Polier*, ed. Muzaffar Alam and Seema Alavi (New Delhi, 2001), 45–6; BL, Add. MSS 29,233, f. 268.

Le Gentil was elected an honorary member of the Asiatick Society, but he was a close friend of Anquetil-Duperron, and Jones was evidently still touchy about his own errors concerning the *Zend-Avesta*'s authenticity. Le Gentil had given Anquetil-Duperron a manuscript of Dārā Shikūh's the *Sirr-i Akbar* ('The Great Secret'), a Persian translation of the *Upaniṣads* completed with the help of Banaras pandits. When Jones learned that Anquetil-Duperron had translated four of the *Upaniṣads* from the *Sirr-i Akbar* into French in 1787, he seized the Sanskritic priority. Jones's *Isa-Upaniṣad* was the first translation of an *Upaniṣad* direct from Sanskrit into a western language; translations from Persian intermediaries were now obsolete.

And there was that other Frenchman, who had been using Hinduism as a stick with which to beat Christianity. Determined to answer Voltaire, Jones took his cue from Davis's paper, 'On the astronomical computations of the Hindus' (1790), and attempted to align the four Yugas (aeons) of Indian time with their truncated Mosaic counterpart. Jones was working at the crucial interfaces between astronomy and astrology, between chronology and religion: 'in our conversations with the *Pandits* we must never confound the system of the *Jyautishicas*, or mathematical astronomers, with that of the *Paurānicas*, or poetical fabulists'. But he failed to 'reck his own rede' regarding the poetic fables of Genesis. If Indian astronomy and chronology were 'bedecked in the fantastick robes of mythology and metaphor', perhaps Jones should look to his own Mosaic garb.

Despite this idée fixe, the expertise of Davis, the scientific rigour of the 80-year-old mathematician Rāmachandra, and the precision of astronomer Vināyaca, made Jones appreciate the originality of Indian astronomy. Thomas Trautmann claims Jones's 'On the Antiquity of the Indian Zodiack': 'showed (rightly) that the Greek and Indian zodiacs were the same and argued (wrongly) that the Greek was derived from the Indian'.[24] But Jones actually wrote: 'the *Indian* Zodiack was not borrowed mediately or directly from the *Arabs* or *Greeks*; [...] both *Greeks* and *Hindus* received it from an older nation, who first gave names to the luminaries of heaven, and from whom both *Greeks* and *Hindus*, as their similarity in language and religion fully evinces, had a common descent' (*Works*, 4: 72).

This re-employs the 'common source' argument used concerning the ancestry of Sanskrit, Greek, and Latin. Greeks and Hindus derived their zodiac—like their language—from an 'older nation'. In observing that

---

24. Trautmann, *Aryans and British India*, 88.

astronomy did not begin, as Newton claimed, with the Egyptians, but with the Chaldeans, Jones provides evidence of what Trautmann himself considers a major strength of the Sanskrit scientific tradition: 'the astronomy-astrology-mathematics area, with which Indians were major participants in an extended dialogue involving Chaldeans, Greeks and Arabs'.[25]

Collaboration with Davis was familiarizing Jones with the work of brilliant mathematical astronomers such as Aryabhata (475–550 CE) of Banaras, who explored concepts of gravitational pull and celestial attraction over a millennium before Newton. By the time he gave his 'Eleventh Anniversary Discourse: On the Philosophy of the Asiaticks' on 20 February 1794, Jones had dramatically revised his 1785 opinions: 'I can venture to affirm, without meaning to pluck a leaf from the neverfading laurels of our immortal Newton,—that the whole of his theology and part of his philosophy may be found in the *Vedas* and even in the works of the *Sufis*: that *most subtil spirit*, which he suspected to pervade natural bodies, and, lying concealed in them, to cause attraction and repulsion, the emission, reflection, and refraction of light, electricity, calefaction, sensation, and muscular motion, is described by the *Hindus* as a *fifth element*' (*Works*, 3: 246).

Going back nine years, from the Eleventh to the Second discourse, we exchange this celebratory tone for the polite note of earnest encouragement. In 1785 his emphasis is upon the mundane utility of Asian scholarship. Indian civil history will interest the British public, and aid the Orientalist regime: 'we have a still nearer interest in knowing all former modes of ruling *these inestimable provinces*, on the prosperity of which so much of our national welfare, and individual benefit, seems to depend'. A detailed knowledge of Indian geography and its vegetable and mineral productions 'are momentous objects of research to an *imperial*, but, which is a character of equal dignity, a *commercial*, people'. In this colonialist adaptation of Blackstone's description of the British as 'a polite and commercial people' lurks a substantial irony. Blackstone was contrasting 'a nation of freemen' with arbitrary despotic governments; the British in India *were* the despots.

Jones was determined to prove a polite despot. Eager that the society should not neglect contemporary indigenous scholarship, he had raised the question of Indian membership at the inaugural meeting. His collaboration with pandits and maulavis (Muslim legal experts) on the law digest encour-

---

25. Thomas Trautmann, 'Indian Time: European Time', in *Time: Histories and Ethnologies*, ed. Diane Owen Hughes and Thomas Trautmann (Ann Arbor, MI, 1995), 167–97; 189.

aged very different attitudes from those of more Eurocentric colleagues, such as Charles Grant or Charles Hamilton. Rosane Rocher has carefully explored Jones's work with Indian pandits; it is this co-operative process and the rich opportunities it presented for transculturation that Edward Said ignores when, in his totalizing theoretical discourse, he writes of the West as producing the knowledge and the East as the passive object of knowledge.[26]

Expecting much from '*learned natives*, whether lawyers, physicians, or private scholars', eager to submit research, Jones suggests the annual award of a medal inscribed in Persian and Sanskrit to the author of the best paper. The first Indian contribution was his friend Ali Ibrahim Khan's 'On the Trial by Ordeal among the Hindus', translated from Persian by Jones, and communicated to the society by Hastings on 10 June 1784.

Although the Society was displaying every sign 'of a healthy and robust constitution', that of its president required frequent recourse to physicians and Jones's mind inevitably turns to Indian medicine. In exhorting his colleagues to consult Sanskrit books, he was not simply advocating emergency rescue of palm-leaf manuscripts, but envisaging the possibility of Sanskrit's becoming unintelligible 'through a want of powerful invitation to study it'. When he describes the personal physician of Emperor Aurangzeb, François Bernier, as being 'himself of the Faculty', Jones is referring to membership of a linguistic as well as a medical faculty. Bernier learned Sanskrit from the pandit who taught Dārā Shikūh, and Jones was convincing himself of the necessity of doing likewise.

Having benefited from indigenous digestive and febrifugal herbal remedies, Jones is convinced 'the works of *Hindu* or *Muselman* physicians' will reveal invaluable cures. He enthuses like an aficionado of Ayurvedic medicine: 'The noble deobstruent oil, extracted from the *Eranda* nut [castor oil], the whole family of *Balsams*, the incomparable stomachick root from *Columbo*, the fine astringent ridiculously called *Japan* earth, but in truth produced by the decoction of an *Indian* plant [*Acacia catechu*], have long been used in *Asia*; and who can foretel what glorious discoveries of other oils, roots, and salutary juices, may be made by your society?' (*Works*, 3: 15).

Yet despite the eminent rationality of Indian medicine, Jones infamously declares: '[R]eason and taste are the grand prerogatives of *European* minds, while the *Asiaticks* have soared to loftier heights in the sphere of imagination.' Jones's studies in both the Hindu and Islamic *materia medica* soon led him to abandon

---

26. Rocher, 'Weaving Knowledge: Sir William Jones and Indian Pandits', 51–91.

this simplistic binarism. Further reading of favourite twelfth-century Persian poets such as Khāqāni and Nizāmī confirmed his earlier error; their startlingly original imagery reflected advanced scientific medicine. In a Khāqāni poem Jones discovers flowers adopting the roles of physician and patient: 'You have jaundice (*yarqān*) like the narcissus, and tachycardia (*khafaqān*) like the tulip.'[27]

Exactly a month after the second discourse, on 24 March 1785, Jones himself soared to Olympic imaginative heights in his 'On the Gods of Greece, Italy, and India'. It might have seemed to his audience that he was hardly following his own advice concerning the utility of their researches. Their president's essay established parallels between Occidental and Oriental deities—how useful is that?

The more discerning realized this paper was for export, and that its transcultural ramifications were profoundly revolutionary. Adapting the psychological use the West was making of the Orient, Jones inaugurates comparative mythology, exploiting cultural relativism to familiarize Europe with the 'alien' beliefs of the subcontinent. Keen to illustrate the 'general union or affinity' between eastern and western mythologies, he investigates parallels between Indian and Graeco-Roman deities to reveal Hinduism as 'the living cousin' of western antiquity. If his comparisons were speculative, Trautmann maintains that Jones's concept of 'a genetic relation between the sets of divinities has proved a useful and durable one'.[28] Jones's essay was foundational in the development of syncretic mythology; such divine affinities anticipate the familial relationship he later discovers between the languages 'of Indian and European heathens'.

But Jones could not let Hinduism be seen as running counter to biblical history—that would prove counterproductive in the West. Thus he commits himself to Mosaic history: 'Either the first eleven chapters of *Genesis*, all due allowances being made for a figurative Eastern style, are true, or the whole fabrick of our national religion is false; a conclusion, which none of us, I trust, would wish to be drawn.' There is a real failure of nerve here. It is signalled in the words 'none of us', as he retreats behind the superior claims of the Oriental book on which 'our national religion' is founded. To draw potentially 'irreligious' conclusions would be a step too far for 'Harmonious' Jones.

---

27. See Anna Livia Beelaert, 'Medical Imagery in the Description of the Seasons in Classical Persian Poetry', *Persica*, 14 (1990–92), 21–35; 31.
28. Trautmann, *Aryans and British India*, 59.

Considering the difficulties facing Jones, P. J. Marshall shrewdly comments: 'Perhaps not surprisingly, his researches ended in the vindication of Moses.' Elinor Shaffer implies intellectual cowardice: 'He is aware of the revolutionary implications of his work on the antiquity of Hindu civilization and on the parallelism of mythologies, but rejects them.' Alun David detects ambivalence, if not Jonesian equivocation: '[T]o declare faith in biblical history, even if not necessarily in good faith, is to give oneself space, within the broadest bounds of orthodoxy, for speculative activities which might yet prove corrosive of traditional authority.'[29] Jones was not shaking 'the adamantine pillars of our Christian faith', but he was undermining any Christian monopoly on truth.

Attracted by the colourful and bewildering diversity of the Indian pantheon, Jones ultimately reflected the deistic or Unitarian bias amongst the Hastings circle, which sought to identify an essential monotheism in pristine Hinduism: '[L]earned *Indians*, as they are instructed by their own books, in truth acknowledge only One Supreme Being, whom they call BRAHME, or The Great One in the neuter gender: they believe his Essence to be infinitely removed from the comprehension of any mind but his own; and they suppose him to manifest his power by the operation of his divine spirit, whom they name VISHNU, the *Pervader,* and NÁRÁYAN, or *Moving on the waters* ('On the Gods of Greece, Italy, and India', *Works*, 3: 350).

Opening the book of Genesis, he prefaces his quotation with the ultimate praise: 'a sublimer passage, from the first word to the last, never flowed or will flow from any human pen':

> *In the beginning* God created the heavens and the earth.—And the earth was void and waste, and darkness was on the face of the deep, and the spirit of God moved upon the face of the waters; and God said: *Let Light be*—and *Light was.* (*Works*, 3: 352)

Where Oriental creation myths compete, the Middle Eastern sublime must outshine its south Asian counterpart. Though Genesis lacks the Hiranyānda, the golden cosmic egg of Brahma, its version has been ratified by the West. In measuring the immeasurable, religious prejudices come into play: 'The sublimity of this passage is considerably diminished by the *Indian* paraphrase

---

29. P. J. Marshall, *The British Discovery of Hinduism in the Eighteenth Century* (Cambridge, 1970), 35; E. S. Shaffer, *'Kubla Khan' and 'The Fall of Jerusalem'* (Cambridge, 1975), 117; Alun David, 'Sir William Jones, Biblical Orientalism and Indian Scholarship', *Modern Asian Studies*, 30: 1 (1996), 173–84; 175–6.

of it, with which Menu, the son of Brahma, begins his address to the sages, who consulted him on the formation of the universe':

> This world, says he, was all darkness undiscernible, undistinguishable, altogether as in a profound sleep; till the self-existent invisible God, making it manifest with five elements and other glorious forms, perfectly dispelled the gloom. He, desiring to raise up various creatures by an emanation from his own glory, first created the *waters*, and impressed them with a power of motion: by that power was produced a golden Egg, blazing like a thousand suns, in which was born BRAHMA, self-existing, the great parent of all rational beings. The waters are called *nárà*, since they are the offspring of NERA (or ÍSWARA); and thence was NÁRÁYANA named, because his first *ayana*, or *moving*, was on them. (*Works*, 3: 352–3)

To this *Mānavadharmaśāstra* passage Jones adds the words of 'the Supreme Being to Brahma' in the *Bhagvadgītā*: 'I AM THAT WHICH IS; and he, who must remain, am I.' His audience would immediately recognize the parallel with Yahweh's self-defining tautology in Exodus 3: 14: 'And God said unto Moses, I AM THAT I AM.' Jones follows this with a sentence perfectly illustrating his perceived difficulties in terms of parallelism and priority, in a situation where orthodoxy problematizes comparative mythology and comparative literature: 'Wild and obscure as these ancient verses must appear in a naked verbal translation, it will perhaps be thought by many, that the poetry or mythology of *Greece* or *Italy* afford no conceptions more awfully magnificent: yet the brevity and simplicity of the *Mosaick* diction are unequalled.'

In communicating the profound effect such 'wild' Hindu obscurity had upon him, Jones realizes he could be both more relaxed and more deeply reverential as a poet rather than as a polymath. In hymning the Hindu deities he discovers his own personal *moksha* (self-release), without Moses sitting on his shoulder. In Bengal Jones appreciates how essential to his psychological integration is his creative imagination. 'A Hymn to Náráyena', which Jones was composing concurrently with 'On the Gods', is the most powerful poem he ever wrote.

> Spirit of Spirits, who, through ev'ry part
>   Of space expanded and of endless time,
>   Beyond the stretch of lab'ring thought sublime,
>   Badst uproar into beauteous order start,
>   Before Heav'n was, Thou art: 5
>   Ere spheres beneath us roll'd or spheres above,

> Ere earth in firmamental ether hung,
> Thou satst alone; till, through thy mystick Love,
> Things unexisting to existence sprung,
>   And grateful descant sung.   10
> What first impell'd thee to exert thy might?
> Goodness unlimited. What glorious light
> Thy pow'r directed? Wisdom without bound.
> What prov'd it first? Oh! guide my fancy right;
>   Oh! raise from cumbrous ground   15
>   My soul in rapture drown'd,
> That fearless it may soar on wings of fire;
> For Thou, who only knowst, Thou only canst inspire.
>
>   ('A Hymn to Náráyena', ll.1–18; *SWJ*, p. 108)

Jones produces hybrid Pindaric *bhakti* at once inherently classical and disturbingly postcolonial. For the western reader, the Hindu sublime is 'dignified' by Miltonic resonances and the long Pindaric stanza, here significantly of 18 lines, the number of *Purāṇas* (texts conveying Vedic learning), and the number of Hindu deities Jones planned to hymn. Faced with the problems of representing the infinite, the eternal, and the ineffable, while focusing upon human adoration of the divine, Jones enlists the dialectics of the ode. Thus the spatial and temporal flow of the first ten run-on lines follows the expansive sweep of the lengthy verse sentence, interrupted only by juxtaposition of perfect ('was') and present continuous ('art') tenses in the median fifth line ('Before Heav'n was, Thou art:'), itself a revisioning of the opening of the Lord's Prayer.

The second sentence (ll.11–18) serves as terrestrial antistrophe to the supernal strophe, its breathless effusion created by the caesurae of three questions and two answers, the third ('What prov'd it first?') requiring divine enlightenment and inspiration. In this way Jones establishes the dialectics of the cyclical and the diurnal, of the self-existent and the devotee, and of the creator Spirit and the creative singer, mediated and resolved only by 'mystick Love', which binds them together. Jones appreciated that strophe and antistrophe—the turning of the choric ode as the chorus moved across the stage from east to west and back—possessed an appropriate symbolism for his Oriental/Occidental synthesis.

The hymn's prefatory Argument claims Vedic doctrine is compatible with Platonic thought in conceiving 'that the whole Creation was rather an *energy* than a *work*, by which the Infinite Being, who is present at all times in all places, exhibits to the minds of his creatures a set of perceptions, like a wonderful picture or piece of musick, always varied, yet always uniform; so that all bodies and their qualities exist, indeed, to every wise and useful purpose, but exist only as far they are *perceived*; a theory no less pious than sublime, and as different from any principle of Atheism, as the brightest sunshine differs from the blackest midnight'. His thinking here again is synthetic and transcultural, linking Plato, the immaterialism of Berkeley, and the *Upaniṣadic* doctrine that this world is not the ultimate reality but *māyā* (illusion). In distant Lambeth, Blake listened as 'India rose up from his golden bed.'[30]

'A Hymn to Nárávena' is more than a proto-Romantic bridge between 'We know this only, that we nothing know' of Pope's *Essay on Man* and the mystical pantheism of Percy Shelley's 'Hymn to Intellectual Beauty'. Jones's originality lies in his exploration of analogies between poetic and divine acts of creation and perception, foreshadowing and facilitating Romantic fascination with beauty, power, and knowledge. 'Nárávena', like other Jones hymns, traces the metaphysical relationship between the variegated veil of nature and the Supreme Mind that continuously creates it, and, as John Drew valuably points out, these poems 'implicitly deal with their own nature even while they deal with the nature of existence'.[31]

From a bustling courthouse during a brief break in proceedings, Jones sends a draft of 'A Hymn to Nárávena' to Wilkins, requesting more of Vishnu's names for a fifth stanza. Its subject is 'the sublimest that the human mind can conceive; but my feeble Muse cannot do justice to it'; he laments his 'inability to read the two Purāns of the *Egg* and the *Lotos*' (*Letters*, 2: 669). It is Thursday, 14 April 1785, and the Society was meeting that night. Jones is also attempting to complete his introductory paper for Ataher Ali Khan's dissertation 'On the Cure of the Elephantiasis', and enquiring whether Wilkins might be able that evening to give his paper on the Sanskrit inscriptions found in a cave near Bodh Gaya—he couldn't, so Jones read Khan's paper. Such a mind-numbing whirl of activity encompassing the sublime and the mundane, the mystical and the medical, the legal and the linguistic, illustrates a day in the life of a polymath. The publication and reception

---

30. 'Sir William Jones might have written expressly for Blake his remarks upon the *Hymn to Narayena*'; Kathleen Raine, *Golgonooza, City of Imagination: Last Studies in William Blake* (New York, 1991), 45.
31. John Drew, *India and the Romantic Imagination* (Delhi, 1987), 73–4.

history of 'Náráyena' highlight both the intellectual diversity of Calcutta and potential areas of tension between pioneering amateur Indologists.

It was all about publication, and the problem was a poached periodical title. A week earlier Jones reiterated that the Society should present its *'Asiatick* miscellany to the literary world'. In Europe, the appetites of scholars, poets, and theorists of early Romanticism had been whetted by Wilkins's *Bhăgvăt-Gēētā*. They were looking to Bengal for authentic texts, eagerly awaiting the authoritative research Jones had promised. The self-made scholars of Calcutta were correspondingly anxious to show the West what they had achieved, and the entrepreneurial Francis Gladwin seized the moment. Appropriating Jones's title, he brought out the first number of *The Asiatick Miscellany* in Calcutta in 1785.

This was not attempted piracy, such as that of Jones's *Persian Grammar*, it was a really professional job, priced 10s 6d in large quarto. What Gladwin really hijacked was the research impetus. Stealing the initiative from overburdened Jones, Gladwin edited his own prestigious collection, aided and abetted by authors who, inspired by the example of Jones and Wilkins, sought an international audience. Its contributors were, almost without exception, active members of Jones's Society. But the first volume of Society proceedings was only to appear four years later in 1789, under the title of *Asiatick Researches*.

Gladwin was a prime mover in the Calcutta print market. His periodical presented a rapid publishing opportunity to Orientalists impatient to place their work before receptive publics in Calcutta and London. Gladwin's scholarly bias was literary, linguistic, and historical, rather than scientific; he did not intend to poach Asiatick Society papers. One notable exception was Henry Vansittart's 'A Description of Assam, translated from Mohammed Cazim's *Alemgirnamah*', read on 12 May 1785. This was published first in *The Asiatick Miscellany* and in the second volume of *Asiatick Researches* five years later. The fact that Vansittart, son of Henry, former governor of Bengal, and an enthusiastic Persian scholar who died tragically early on 12 October 1786, never saw his work in *Asiatick Researches* illustrates how Gladwin offered prompter publication.

The translations of classical poets such as Sa'dī, Jāmī, Hāfiz, and Amir Khosrau within *Asiatick Miscellany* were printed in parallel with the originals set in *nasta'līq* or *naskhī* characters for Persianists. They represented the work of skilled linguists such as Captain William Kirkpatrick, Persian interpreter to the commander-in-chief, later Resident of Poona, and John Gilchrist, later principal of Fort William College, and Asiatick Society secretary. These men, according to Christopher Bayly, were 'associated with the vanguard of the imperial information collectors'; their cultural interests extended to the vernaculars of India, and the writings of the Indian intelligentsia.[32] Gladwin included Gilchrist's translation of an ode by the renowned contemporary Hindustani poet Sauda (1713–80), accompanied—in Jonesian fashion—by both original and transliteration.

Gladwin reacted to market demand in India and the West for a periodical with a wide appeal publishing original poetry, Oriental tales, and translations from Asian verse already circulating in manuscript form. Aimed at the enquiring metropolitan and colonial bourgeoisie, *Asiatick Miscellany* was, as Gladwin's preface announced, 'designed to interest lovers of poetry' as well as 'the learned and the curious'. In this it was a triumphal coup. The first number includes the first publication of no fewer than four of Jones's 'Hymns to Hindu Deities', and a reprinting of *The Enchanted Fruit, or the Hindu Wife*.

In 1993 Jerome McGann underscored his conviction that Jones's Argument might serve as fitting epigraph for a Romantic anthology by placing 'A Hymn to Náráyena' as the opening text of his *New Oxford Book of Romantic Period Verse*.[33] Two centuries earlier Gladwin gave this seminal text in the emergent poetics of Romanticism similar prominence. *Asiatick Miscellany* revealed to the West the beauties of Jones's hymns, and 'A Hymn to Náráyena' was reprinted throughout the capitals of Europe, with Beethoven copying lengthy extracts into his *tagebuch* (diary).

Within the colony, even before its first publication in *Asiatick Miscellany*, Gladwin brought Jones's ode to the attention of a wider audience. Jones had had some handsome copies run off by the government printers to circulate 'Náráyena' to friends. In Gladwin's *Calcutta Gazette* of 26 May 1785 we have the first published reader response in an anonymous contributor's poem addressed 'To the Author of the Hymn to Narayena':

> Proceed! Reclaim us—for our guilt atone;
> Bid India's nations pardon all our wrongs;
> A British Brahma they already own!
> We worship GOD in NARAYENA's songs.   (ll. 41–44)

---

32. Christopher Bayly, *Empire and Information: Intelligence Gathering and Social Communication in India, 1780–1870* (Cambridge, 1997), 291 and passim.
33. McGann unfortunately describes Jones's hymns as 'celebrated translations from the Sanskrit'; *New Oxford Book of Romantic Period Verse*, ed. Jerome McGann (Oxford, 1993), xxi–xxii; 783.

Imperial guilt, moral reclamation, proprietary deism, and the syncretic empathy of 'A British Brahma' all make for a heady (post)colonial brew. In hailing Jones as the 'Pundit' who 'from the Shanscrit leaf' read 'the mystic origin of Plato's page' (ll. 25–8), the poem redefines 'the riches of the East' in response to metropolitan accusations of extravagance, frivolity, and materialism. It might legitimize their economic and social behaviour if Company servants could demonstrate that even the seeking of financial independence was an activity that need not be divorced from cultural responsibility. The acquisition in Bengal of 'social self-knowledge' involved an attempt to understand the operations of the imperial order they were instrumental in establishing. At the sharp end of empire, the Calcutta intelligentsia was anxious not only to read about itself, but to (re)write itself; print was revealing colonial society to itself.

We have no record of Jones's reaction to being hailed as Calcutta's moral reclaimer, but he was rather sniffy about Gladwin's *Miscellany*. The poet was pleased with a wider readership, but the president did not want the Society associated with what he saw as a populist production. He testily corrects the misapprehension of Irish antiquarian, Joseph Cooper Walker:

> The *Asiatic Miscellany*, to which you allude, is not the publication of our society, who mean to print no scraps, nor any *mere* translations. It was the undertaking of a private gentleman, and will certainly be of use in diffusing Oriental literature, though it has not been so correctly printed as I could wish. (*Letters*, 2: 770)

Walker was not alone in his confusion. Arriving in Europe with its title page bearing no editor's name, Gladwin's periodical was taken to be Asiatick Society proceedings, edited by Jones. John Parsons, fellow of Balliol, and future Oxford vice-chancellor, clearly thought he was reviewing Jones's promised 'Asiatick miscellany'. After two pages of paean, culminating in: '[N]ow only in the bloom of manhood; possessed of integrity unimpeached, and of manners the most attracting; in his judicial capacity, the glory of the British name in India; and, as a scholar, still indefatigable in those pursuits, which render him at once the patron and example of the poet, the philosopher, and the critic', Parsons describes the periodical as marking 'a new epoch in the annals of eastern literature'.[34] Jones's poetry is seen as its 'highest ornament', but Parsons cannot help but wonder why 'no provision is here made for researches into the antiquities, or natural history, of India'.

It is surprising that the productive Gladwin never seems to have presented a paper to the Society.[35] He was, however, a regular attender and Jones bore no grudge, for his notebook records Gladwin's name among an inner circle of friends whose dining club convened after Society meetings. No publication of Orientalist activity in Bengal could be bad publicity, and a little intellectual drama in Calcutta complemented what was available at the Chowringhee Theatre. *Asiatick Researches* was the groundbreaking journal that Europe awaited, but its unofficial precursor proved a worthwhile curtain-raiser.

On Saturday, 6 August 1785, Jones was dining at home and thinking of London friends with the romantic EIC army ensign and Armenian nationalist, Emin Joseph Emin. We know this as Emin wrote on Sunday to bluestocking Elizabeth Montagu: 'Yesterday I dined with my boy at Sr Williams, he told me he was going to write both to Mrs Montague and to Mr Burke and promised to remember me to your Ladyship, to him, and to all his and my Noble Friends, which makes me still happier.' He was a remarkable guest and Jones was as impressed as Elizabeth Montagu who wrote of him: 'I wish his patriot spirit was communicated to a dozen or two of our great men.'[36] Emin's mother and younger brother died during Nadir Shah's siege of Baghdad, and his father, like many of his countrymen, had emigrated to India where entrepreneurial Armenians had been welcomed since the days of Akbar.

Driven by a fierce love of political freedom, he was determined to study British military and artillery tactics, and enlist the aid of Erekle II of Georgia in uniting Armenians against Ottoman and Persian oppression. In 1751 Emin worked his passage to England on the East Indiaman *Walpole*. After labouring as a bricklayer in Drury Lane, a chance meeting with Edmund Burke in St James's Park gained him not only employment as a copyist, but the patronage of a prestigious swath of high society, including Mrs Montagu's friends George, Lord Lyttelton, and Dr Messenger Monsey, the

---

34. *Monthly Review*, 77 (May 1787), 414–23; 414. Parsons's epithet 'unimpeached' would have resonance in this month when the Articles of Impeachment against Hastings were presented to the Lords.
35. *Proceedings of the Asiatic Society*, vol. 1: *1784–1800*, ed. Sibadas Chaudhuri (Calcutta, 1980), 351–67.
36. *The Letters of Mrs Elizabeth Montagu*, ed. Matthew Montagu, 4 vols (London, 1813), 2: 51.

royal mistress Amalie, Countess of Yarmouth, the dukes of Northumberland and Cumberland, and William Pitt the elder.

Sponsored as a cadet officer in the Royal Military Academy at Woolwich, Emin cut his military teeth in the Seven Years' War as a gentleman officer attached to British and Prussian armies in turn. This charismatic cavalry officer then spent a decade awakening the youth of Armenia, sometimes at the head of 12,000 wild Caucasian mountaineers, often in bloody internecine guerrilla action. His impassioned attempt to realize his vision of a free Armenia, allied with Georgia and under Russian protection, was sadly doomed to failure, and in 1770 Emin voyaged to Calcutta where he joined the Bengal army irregular cavalry.

By the time Jones met him in 1784 Emin was recently back from Persia and yet another venture to reignite his Armenia dream. Jones helped obtain a posting to the 3rd European Invalid Regiment, describing the 60-year-old soldier of fortune to Governor-General Macpherson as 'a fine fellow; and if active service should be required, he would seek nothing so much, as to be placed in the most perilous edge of the battle' (*Letters*, 2: 700). As Emin writes to Elizabeth Montagu, Sir William is his 'guardian Angel':

> I am gratefully under Obligation to Sr William, who has honored me with the inexpressible Indulgence to be with him, to enjoy almost every day in the Week at his house his learned improving Company, in a word I am in Love with his benevolent Heart and greatness of Soul. His mind is exactly like my dear uncle Mr Edmund Burke's, and my Lady Jones's affable Cordiality Care and Indulgence towards me and my Son, much resembling my Princess Patroness the aimable Mrs Montague.[37]

Jones might not have approved the Burkean comparison, but the reason for Emin's frequent visits to Garden Reach was that Jones was encouraging him to compose his memoirs (published in London in 1792). Jones corrected 'errors in language and orthography', advising his 'dear Emin' to abandon 'the Asiatick style of panegyrick': 'Swift has misled you by inculcating that men of wit love praise, be assured that every man of wit (unless wit and sense be at variance) must prefer plain food to sugarplumbs, and would rather be rubbed with a coarse towel than Dacca Muslin with all its flowers' (*Letters*, 2: 808).

---

37. *The Life and Adventures of Emin Joseph Emin 1726–1809; Written by Himself*, 2nd edn, ed. Amy Apcar (Calcutta, 1918), 486, 491.

The same letter makes clear that Jones, like many diasporic Armenians in India, opposed monarchical government. He reflects on Emin's Armenian project: 'I know mankind too well to be surprized at the failure of your enterprize; nor am I fully persuaded, that it was just, since Heraclius [Erekle] had a claim on Armenia; unless you intended to establish a republican government, and could have been satisfied with the station of a private citizen.' Jones lectures this heroic precursor of the nineteenth-century Armenian liberation movement: 'A pure democracy is the only natural form of government', but a mixed government—like that of Britain—is more likely to be lasting.

Persian-born Emin, who had voyaged to England to learn what liberty is, resented application of the term 'Oriental', even by the elder Pitt: 'But give me Leave to say Sr that your hint with the Word Oriantal, as if I was telling one of the Arabian Tails, I own, it choacks in the Throat me nor can I swallow it with any Comfort. I am hurt to the Soul, I see that success is necessary to make a man seem honest as well as wise.'[38] As functionary of a British Asiatic despotism, 'Oriental' Jones's own position—both politically and theoretically—might be seen as just a little 'flaky'. But Jones's chief crusade was scholarly.

In a serial letter of 4–30 August 1787 to Spencer, Jones describes his privileged position as cultural translator:

> To what shall I compare my literary pursuits in India? Suppose Greek literature to be known in modern Greece only, and there to be in the hands of priests and philosophers; and suppose them to be still worshippers of Jupiter and Apollo: suppose Greece to have been conquered successively by Goths, Huns, Vandals, Tartars, and lastly by the English; then suppose a court of judicature to be established by the British parliament, at Athens, and an inquisitive Englishman to be one of the judges; suppose him to learn Greek there, which none of his countrymen knew, and to read Homer, Pindar, Plato, which no other Europeans had even heard of. Such am I in this country; substituting Sanscrit for Greek, the *Brahmans*, for the priests of *Jupiter*, and *Vālmic*, *Vyāsa*, *Cālīdāsa*, for Homer, Plato, Pindar. Need I say what exquisite pleasure I receive from conversing easily with that class of men, who conversed with Pythagoras, Thales, and Solon, but with this advantage over the Grecian travellers, that I have no need of an interpreter. (*Letters*, 2: 755–6)

---

38. Letter of Emin to William Pitt, 1758; *Life and Adventures*, ed. Apcar, 485.

The classical Romanticism of his rhetoric stresses his singularity and his delight in collaboration with Indian informants. By this time, his proficiency in Sanskrit—'my last language; & I will know it perfectly or die in the attempt'—was sufficient to write poetry in it. At Krishnagar he composed, 'a *Sanscrit* stanza, signifying that "as the thirsty antelope runs to a pool of sweet water, so I *thirsted* for all kinds of knowledge which was sweet as nectar"'. The scholarly Raja Śiva Chandra copied it, his son learnt it by heart, and the Brahmans declared him worthy of the Kshatriya caste, 'a Hindu of the *Military* tribe, which is next in rank to the Brahmanical' (*Letters*, 2: 748).

Jones was honoured to be accorded 'a place among the Hindu poets', but initially the Brahmans objected to 'thirsty' as metaphor, thinking it 'applicable to *water literally*, but not *literally* to *learning*'. Rāmalocana, Jones's pandit: 'urged that I, as a poet & consequently inspired, could not err, & he produced an authority to prove that my word *trishnà* means not only thirst, but any *ardent desire*'. Jones is illustrating Hindu literary criticism, but this incident not only establishes inspired Jonesian infallibility, it symbolizes his deepest motivations. As scientist and Sanskritist, as jurist and poet, his insatiable thirst holds him in a double bind of Augustinian desire, caught between *libido sciendi* (desire of knowledge) and *libido dominandi* (desire of power). These cravings, individually or in concert, can prove more powerful than the sexual *libido sentiendi* (desire of sensations), but there is no need to venture into post-Freudian realms of Foucauldian sexuality. We can psychoanalyse Jones tangentially with the sixth-century help of one of his favourite Bedouin. The hedonistic Tarafa, who knew all about thirst, implores:

> Suffer me, whilst I live, to drench my head *with wine*, lest, having drunk too little in my life-time, *I should be thirsty in another state*.
> I see no difference between the tomb of the anxious miser, gasping over his hoard, and the tomb of the libertine lost in the maze of voluptuousness.
> Death, I observe, selects the noblest heroes for her victims, and reserves as her property the choicest possessions of the sordid hoarder.
> I consider time as a treasure decreasing every night; and that which every day diminishes soon perishes for ever.
> ('The Poem of Tarafa', verses 62; 64; 66–7; *SWJ*, p. 208)

Jones was a man of unquenchable thirst, sharing with Tarafa the urgent sense that one's drinking time is severely limited. In the same letter Jones admits: 'I hold every day lost, in which I acquire no new knowledge of man or nature.' But Jones was no 'anxious miser'—his hoard of Sanskrit treasure was donated to world literature. Yet his 'exquisite pleasure' in knowing what 'none of his countrymen knew', and reading 'what no other Europeans had even heard of' is a species of intellectual gloating. The *libido dominandi* was also known to theologians as *libido excellendi*, and Jones's voluptuous desire for pre-eminence flourished in the burgeoning climate of Bengal.

His vaunted European singularity in Sanskrit within the Athens of Calcutta was exaggerated, despite Wilkins's return to England in 1786. It implies isolation, but Jones never complains of being removed from metropolitan intellectual circles by vast oceanic miles. Corresponding with a huge range of scholars, including Johann David Michaelis, the leading Hebraist, and Orientalist friends such as Hendrik Albert Schultens at Leyden, and Adam Czartoryski in Poland, Jones avoids the loneliness of the long-distance polymath. Cutting-edge collaboration with indigenous experts bolsters his sense of being *the* man on this crucial Asiatic spot. This was not Saidian intellectual domination, inevitably linked to political hegemony: it was straightforward egocentricity, a consciousness of being the conduit. Arguably it was not even egotism, but simple fact, ratified in Europe by the appearance of *Asiatick Researches*.

Following meticulous proof-reading, the first sheets came off the Company's press as early as September 1786, and Jones was confident 'that the learned in Europe will not be disappointed by our first volume' (*Letters*, 2: 699, 708). Progress was frustratingly slow as government business took priority, and Jones finally contracted Calcutta printer Manuel Cantopher. Although the title page bears the date 1788, the appendix, listing society members, was not printed until late February 1789.[39] On 27 February Jones writes to Wilkins: 'The ships of this season will carry home seven hundred copies of our first volume of Transactions; and the second will be ready, I hope, next year' (*Letters*, 2: 827–8).

Jones's reputation sold *Asiatick Researches* in the West, and society members in Calcutta deferred to his enormous erudition and enthusiasm to communicate the Indian revelation. His contributions span a vast subject-spectrum: Indian anthropology, archaeology, astronomy, botany, ethnology, geography, music, literature, physiology, languages and inscriptions, mythology and religion. This represents a phenomenally polymathic

---

39. Graham Shaw, *Printing in Calcutta* (London, 1981), 121–2.

output achieved despite long hours in court, and his major task of codifying Indian laws. He authored over a third of the papers read to the society, and the six he included amongst the twenty-eight in the first volume of *Asiatick Researches*, were of such length as to constitute a similar proportion of its pages.

Jones includes four important articles by Indian scholars. Ali Ibrahim Khan's balanced rationalist observations 'On the Trial by Ordeal'; Govardhana Kaula's valuable survey, 'On the Literature of the Hindus'; Pandit Rāmalocana's expert translation of 'An Indian Grant of Land', engraved on copper plates discovered on Salsette Island, north of Bombay, and sent by Jones's friend, General John Carnac; and Rādhākānta Sarman's skilful deciphering of (most of) the 'Inscriptions on the Staff of Firuz Shah', which had been copied by Lieutenant-Colonel Antoine Polier, avid collector of manuscripts and constructional engineer of Calcutta's new fort. The oldest inscriptions on this Aśokan pillar—which the fourteenth-century Delhi sultan, Firuz Shah, the son of a Hindu Rajput princess, re-erected to display his Indic credentials—baffled both Rādhākānta and Jones. Recognizing elements of an abjad (alphabet of consonants only), Jones thought them Ethiopian, but the language was Brāhmī, finally deciphered by James Prinsep in 1837. None of the four papers had been read by its author, for Jones's suggestions regarding Indian membership were ignored. *Asiatick Researches* was the first 'European' journal to publish research by indigenous intellectuals, but it was only in 1829, during Horace Hayman Wilson's presidency, that Indians were allowed membership.[40]

For Jones the 'greatest, if not the only, obstacle' is lack of research time: '*Give us time for our investigations, and we will transfer to* Europe *all the Sciences, arts, and literature of* Asia' (*Works*, 5: 1). But his example integrated 'Business' and 'Play', his vacations were never vacant: 'It rarely happens that favourite studies are closely connected with the strict discharge of our duty, as mine happily are; even in this cottage I am assisting the court by studying Arabic and Sanskrit' (*Letters*, 2: 762). Such eradication of the distinction between work and leisure became characteristic of the society's research culture, which married the enthusiasm of the amateur with the discipline of the professional.

But what of Anna, what part did she play in all this happy porousness of leisure and employment? She was the pivot of his emotional life, the focus of his domestic happiness, but also the source of his deepest concern. His

---

40. On the subsequent Indianization of the Asiatic Society, see Tapan Raychaudhuri, *Europe Reconsidered: Perceptions of the West in Nineteenth-Century Bengal* (Oxford, 1988).

love for India was as boundless as his curiosity concerning the peoples of the East. The contact zone was for him a comfort zone, but its climate threatened Anna, whose sensitive digestion could not even cope with 'half of a small Patna onion'. As he explains to his Oxford and Oxford circuit colleague, Thomas Caldecott:

> I never was unhappy in England; it was not in my nature to be so; but I was never happy till I was settled in India. My constitution has overcome the climate; and if I could say the same of my beloved wife; but she has perpetual complaints, and of course I am in perpetual anxiety on her account. (*Letters*, 2: 778)

That letter was from Krishnagar in late September 1787, and by the following St David's Day, back in their 'pastoral retreat' on the banks of the Hugli, they have decided upon her early return, yet this is repeatedly delayed because: 'When she is well, or rather when she is not ill, we pass our time as happily as if we lived in the golden age.' Their having no children made them even more reliant upon each other. Writing to Georgiana, Duchess of Devonshire, Anna adopts a humorous tone: 'You will have just one dozen & a half to make amends for setting about it so late.—I shall never set about it at all'; but it must have been a constant regret.[41]

Jones's baby was his Society and, though it sometimes seemed a 'puny, rickety child', it was to grow strong. It was one they could not fully share. The public sphere of Calcutta was gendered more rigidly than that of London. Jones advocated Indian membership, but his concepts of equality, although embraced as universal, in practice applied only to male citizens. Jones's wife, like his sister Mary, was an accomplished scholar, but the Asiatick Society's doors remained closed to her. The Royal Society would not admit women until 1945; the Bengal Club, established in 1827 as a bastion of British male exclusiveness, banned women, Indians, and dogs until well after the end of colonial rule. The relatively small number of British women in Calcutta made the situation worse. Whereas Anna and William had joint access to the philosophical bluestocking salons of Elizabeth Vesey and Elizabeth Montagu, the separate spheres of Calcutta were more severely demarcated.

At the pinnacle of colonial society, Anna had intelligent and lively friends, including the mixed musical circles of sisters-in-law Sophia and Elizabeth Plowden. Lady Jones took a leading part in major social events

---

41. Chatsworth, Devonshire Collection, Letter of 9 December 1785.

such as governor's balls, where she would open proceedings by dancing with Governor-General Lord Charles Cornwallis. She devoted herself to charitable work at the Calcutta orphanage, and was elected Honorary Governess of the Free School Society, along with Lady Frances Chambers and that venerable Calcutta institution, Mrs Frances 'Begum' Johnson. Mrs Johnson was a survivor: of the climate, the 1756 sack of Calcutta, and four marriages, her last being to Revd William 'Tally-Ho' Johnson, dissolute hunting chaplain of St John's, whom she eventually paid to leave India!

The Joneses, by contrast, were celebrated for their mutual fondness, but by no means regarded as dull. A letter from John Wade, a surgeon at Chunar, to Francis Fowke, decisively emphasizes that they were much in demand:

> Lady Jones, I think, is still more agreeable than she appeared at Benares, and Sir Billy has grown much less professorial in his Conversation. They are incomparably the best Company to which I had access in Calcutta; there may possibly be better, but I do not believe there is.[42]

It is good to learn that modest, pompous, clubbable Jones, 'Grand Vicar' of the Carmarthen circuit, has lost some of his pedagogic intensity, but Wade's compliment is to wife and husband equally. When a typical day is described for Spencer, Anna appears as something of a passive adjunct—being read to by one man, or carried by four—and again we lament the destruction of *her* journal:

> Would you like to know how I pass the day? I will give you a sketch of my employments during the term and sittings, and during the vacation. In term time I rise an hour before the sun, and walk from my garden to the fort, about 3 miles: thence I go in a palanquin to the Court-house, where cold-bathing, dressing and breakfast take up an hour; so that by seven I am ready for my Pandit, with whom I read Sanscrit; at eight come a Persian and Arab alternately with whom I read till nine except on a Saturday, when I give instructions to my Mogul secretary on the correspondence with the Mussulman scholars. At nine come the attornies with affidavits: I am then robed and ready for court, where I sit on the bench, one day with another, five hours. At three I dress and dine; and, till near sunset, am at the service of my friends, who chuse to dine with me. When the sun is sunk in the Ganges, we drive to the Gardens either in our postchaise, or Anna's phaeton drawn by a pair of beautiful Nepal horses. After teatime we read; and never sit up, if we can avoid it, after ten. But for four months in the year I must sit three evenings in

---

42. BL, OIOC, Fowke MSS, Eur E8, 72, J. P. Wade to F. Fowke [n.d.].

11. Drawing of Anna Maria Jones from Sir William Jones's notebook. (Yale, Beinecke Library, Osborn Collection)

the week as a justice of the peace. In the vacation, when we are at our villa in summer, and at our cottage in autumn, I rise when I happen to wake, and, after bathing and coffee, read *Sanscrit* only, till about eleven, when I read English or Italian to A.M. for an hour, (and on Sundays, books of Theology) after which I finish the rest of my day's task till dinner-time. At sunset I walk two or three miles, while she is carried by four men in a chair, called a *Tānjān*, pronounced *Tonjong*, and used in the Eastern peninsula, from which she brought it. On our return, we pass our evenings as we generally do in term-time. You will judge, therefore, whether I wish to change this calm course of life for the house of commons, from which I should return three or four nights in seven with *despair* & the head-ach. Farewell! (*Letters*, 2: 757–8)

Inevitably for her his long term-time hours brought tropical longueurs at their 'charming villa, the eye of the Ganges', despite her superintendence of 'flocks and herds & an excellent dairy, which produces the best butter in India'. But the milkmaid of Ariśnagar had her own creative outlets, foremost amongst which was that Anna Maria was publishing poems in *The Asiatic Mirror*, and *Calcutta Morning Post*. These were highly accomplished pieces reflecting the mannered sensuality and self-conscious sensibility of the Della Cruscan school. This fashionable trend was initiated by British expatriates in Italy, where Hester Piozzi, Bertie Greatheed, William Parsons, and Robert Merry (Della Crusca) had published *The Florence Miscellany* (1785), inspiring Jones's friend, Edward Jerningham, 'Laura Maria' (Mary 'Perdita' Robinson), and 'Anna Matilda' (Hannah Cowley) in Britain, and 'Anna Maria' in Bengal.

While William was measuring the potential of the Pindaric ode to encompass the Indian sublime, Anna's experiments in the poetry of sensibility also anticipated the interiority of Romanticism. He was fascinated by the devotion of *bhakti* and the sensibility of *rasa*: she was the devotee of a European cult of sentiment. He wrote hymns to Krishna: she wrote odes to Della Crusca. At the heart of British India, they acknowledged in differing ways the hegemony of what William Godwin termed 'the empire of feeling'. Calcutta musical tastes, reflected in Jones's appreciation of the latest Haydn trios, were as advanced as those of London. Anna Maria's poems, well received in the colonial capital, reveal a similar openness to the latest metropolitan literary vogue.

She published her elegant slim octavo, handsomely printed and expensively priced at one gold mohur (a guinea and a half), under the title *The Poems of Anna Maria*, her Christian names serving as Della Cruscan soubriquet. Her dedication to the 'Polished People' of Calcutta records her pride in their encomiums, but regrets 'her ill State of Health' prevented a more extensive volume. In London, where Della Cruscanism was being excoriated by Tory satirist William Gifford, her reviews were most favourable, but surprisingly no critics connected 'Anna Maria' with Lady Jones. *The New Annual Register* saw her work as 'distinguished by great tenderness of sentiment, harmony of numbers, and pleasing poetic imagery'.

Unitarian minister William Enfield, in the *Monthly Review*, praised this 'ingenious young Poetess', noting that her 'decorations and imagery, however, have been but little influenced by the local habitation of the author; who, on the banks of the Hougly, still talks as she would have done in Europe, of *green-hair'd Tritons and their Nymphs*, of *Elves*, and of the *Muse*'.[43] But though it is the female Cynthia, rather than the male Chandra, who illuminates her evening walks by Hugli's 'sapphire stream', Enfield fails to notice that her 'Ode, inscribed to Della Crusca' enlists the aid of Krishna and Brahma to deck with praise the brows of Robert Merry:

> Where INDIA's GOD in secret roves,
> Through the rich consecrated Groves;
> Where BRAHMA pours his pious Pray'r
> To the religious list'ning Air;
> And from the Fervour of his lays,
> I'll weave a Wreath of magic praise;
> Shall circle round thy crescent brows . . .[44]

The poetry of sensibility was appreciated by husband and wife. Jones sends Shore their thanks for Charlotte Smith's *Elegiac Sonnets*: 'the tender strains of the unfortunate Charlotte [. . .] have given us pleasure and pain' (*Letters*, 2: 761). This makes it even more remarkable that in the extant correspondence Jones makes no mention of his wife's poetic talent. It is inconceivable that he might have been jealous of a wife he so dearly loved, but she achieved what he had not, for he never published a separate volume of his Indian hymns.

Above all, it was botany that allowed them to collaborate in an engrossing interest where sensual delight and classificatory rigour, the aesthetic and the academic, mingled in precise observation of similarity and difference. Acutely conscious that he was 'no Lynx like Linnaeus', he could rely upon Anna's skills in the examination of minute blossoms. The burgeoning flower borders of their Garden Reach villa testified to her artistry as an ornamental Oriental gardener, and her botanical sketchbooks reveal her

---

43. *The New Annual Register for 1794*, (1795), 251; *English Review*, 24 (1795), 144–6; *Monthly Review*, 15 (November, 1794), 352.
44. *The Poems of Anna Maria* (Calcutta, 1793), 47.

growing skills as an illustrator. Though far inferior to the work of the superb artist Zayn al-Din from whom the Joneses commissioned many paintings, her ability to produce an accurate record was invaluable. Her sketches, annotated by Jones, demonstrate that everywhere they went—in the profusion of the Sundarbans, the fertile plain of Krishnagar, the dramatic hill country above Chittagong, or at home, along the fragrant lanes of Ariśnagar—William dissected and described while Anna, 'whose progress in drawing and colouring is wonderful', delineated. A loose sheet in which Jones gives Anna advice, gleaned from Reynolds, on the mixing of naturalistic greens, illustrates the scholarly dimensions of their 'principal amusement'.[45]

What began as a convalescent pastime expanded into a scientific enterprise linking Sanskrit learning and modern medical research. One day when deeply involved in taxonomical study of the lotus, consulting Sanskrit books concerning the use of its seeds and rhizomes as food and medicine, while Anna attempted to capture its beauty in a watercolour, they received a unexpected visit from 'a native of Nepal [who] made prostrations before it on entering my study, where the fine plant and beautiful flowers lay for examination'. The incident set a sacred seal upon the cultural importance of their investigative and recuperative labours.

Jones's collaboration with botanist Johann Gerhard Koenig, former pupil of Linnaeus; Dr John Fleming, who first lent Jones Linnaeus's *Philosophia Botanica* at Bhagalpur; Dr Patrick Russell, FRS, Koenig's successor as Madras presidency naturalist; Dr William Roxburgh, author of *Plants of the Coast of Coromandel* (1795–1820); and Colonel Robert Kyd, founder of the Botanic Garden in Calcutta, confirmed the medicinal and commercial imperatives of this British Indian botanical research programme. His letters to Sir George Yonge, secretary at war, detailing valuable medicinal, food, and spice plants suitable for transportation to the newly established botanic garden at St Vincent in the West Indies, stressed intercolonial co-operation. This emphasis received scholarly amplification in his extensive correspondence with Sir Joseph Banks, President of the Royal Society, concerning the identification of Linnaean genera, trialling of plant species, and dispatch of seeds and specimens to England.

All this was eminently practical, but Jonesian curiosity was also aroused by the magical word 'spikenard', the precious plant of 'The Song of Songs':

45. Royal Asiatic Society, Jones Collection, 025.037.

'Spikenard and saffron; calamus and cinnamon, with all trees of frankincense; myrrh and aloes' (4: 14), the finest of which grew, according to Ptolemy, near Rangamati in Bengal. The opening of Jones's 'On the Spikenard of the Ancients' also opens a window into the mind of the polymath:

> It is painful to meet perpetually with words, that convey no distinct ideas; and a natural desire of avoiding that pain excites us often to make inquiries, the result of which can have no other use than to give us clear conceptions. Ignorance is to the mind what extreme darkness is to the nerves: both cause an uneasy sensation; and we naturally love knowledge, as we love light, even when we have no design of applying either to a purpose essentially useful. This is intended as an apology for the pains which have been taken to procure a determinate answer to a question of no apparent utility, but which ought to be readily answered in *India*, 'What is *Indian* Spikenard?'   (*Works*, 5: 13)

For Jones the sublime of ignorance represents profound sensory deprivation, the painful darkness of 'a spring shut up, a fountain sealed'. His search for illumination involved the help of friends Indian and European, not forgetting their gardeners; communications with botanist and surgeon Robert Saunders, a member of Samuel Turner's Bhutan mission; and a scholarly dispute with eminent naval physician Sir Gilbert Blane. Having received samples of a perfumed grass of the Andropogon genus, known as *Terankus* ('fever-restrainer') from his brother William, physician to Nawab Asaf-ud-daula at Lucknow, Gilbert Blane declared in a 1790 Royal Society paper that this was the elusive *Nardus Indica*. Convinced that Blane was wrong, Jones consulted ancient texts and modern scientists, Indian and European, to prove conclusively that Indian Spikenard or *Sumbul* (spike/ear) was *Jatamansi*, of the Valerian family, today classified as *Nardostachys jatamansi*.

As Mary Pratt has shown, the largely Eurocentric natural historians of the eighteenth century, in the application of their totalizing taxonomic vision, had no interest in indigenous knowledge about landscape, flora, and fauna.[46] Jones's research, by contrast, was deeply sensitive to both the Sanskrit names of species and their place in Hindu culture, literature, and medicine. In his 'Botanical Observations on Select Indian Plants', Sanskrit and Bengali or Hindi names precede the Linnaean (where it exists) and, following a precise botanical description, indigenous cultural detail illuminates the entries for specialist or general readers. In describing *Sép'hálicá*,

---

46. Mary Louise Pratt, *Imperial Eyes: Travel Writing and Transculturation* (London, 1992), 36–53.

Jones rejects its Linnaean name, 'Sorrowful Nyctanthes': 'This *gay* tree (for nothing *sorrowful* appears in its nature) spreads its rich odour to a considerable distance every evening; but at sunrise it sheds most of its *night-flowers*, which are collected with care for the use of perfumers and dyers.' He stresses his reliance upon pandits; Rādhākānta, his younger brother Ramākānta, and Servōru Sarman all assure him: 'that the plant before us is their *Sép'hálicá*, thus named because *bees* are supposed *to sleep* on its blossoms'.

The *Nágacésara* tree is 'one of the most beautiful on earth, and the delicious odour of its blossoms justly gives them a place in the quiver of Cámadéva'. Jones refers to a couplet by twelfth-century poet Sri Harsha comparing 'the white of the *Nágacésara* from which the bees were scattering the pollen of the numerous gold-coloured anthers, to an alabaster wheel, on which Cáma was whetting his arrows, while sparks of fire were dispersed in every direction'. He dismisses the Linnaean name 'Iron Mesua': 'Surely, the genuine appellation of an *Indian* plant should be substituted for the corrupted name of a *Syrian* physician who could never have seen it; and, if any trivial name were necessary to distinguish a single species, a more absurd one than *iron* could not possibly have been selected for a flower with petals like silver and anthers like gold' (*Works*, 5: 140).

Pioneering ecological anthropology, he urges his botanist friends to learn Sanskrit, convincing them Linnaeus himself would have employed 'their true Indian appellations' had he known the language of the gods. In 'The Design of a Treatise on the Plants of India', read to the Society on 1 April 1790, his excitement is apparent: 'Some hundreds of plants, which are yet imperfectly known to European botanists, and with the virtues of which they are wholly unacquainted, grow wild on the plains and forests of India' (*Works*, 5: 2). With the aid of Indian doctors, the intensive study of ancient Sanskrit dictionaries such as the *Amarcòsh*, the *Médìni*, and the *Dravyábhidhána, or Dictionary of Natural Productions* would access the medicinal properties of these plants and vegetables to modern science.

Enlightenment was occasionally accompanied by a little heat. Jones prefers sexual symbolism applied to the poetics, rather than the classification, of plants. Despite having 'twice read with rapture the *Philosophia Botanica*', Jones was not so happy about the anthropomorphic aspects of Linnaeus's sexual system; botanists 'have no business to inflame their imaginations'. Inadvertently revealing his own reading as occasionally inflammatory, he declares: '[F]ew passages in *Aloisia* [*Aloysia Sigea* (1665), by French attorney, Nicholas Chorier], the most impudent book ever composed by man, are more wantonly indecent than the hundred-forty-sixth number of the *Botanical Philosophy*.' He is referring to this Linnaeus passage: '[T]he ANTHERS are the testicles, the POLLEN is the sperm, the STIGMA is the vulva, the STYLE is the vagina.'[47] It was a hot night in the Old Court House, and Jones appeared something of an April fool in asserting to colleagues, who knew the couple's favourite recreation: 'Hence it is, that no well-born and well-educated woman can be advised to amuse herself with botany' (*Works*, 5: 6).

Anna Seward, the accomplished poet and critic, agreed. An admirer of Jones's poetry, the 'Swan of Lichfield' was a friend of botanist Erasmus Darwin but, when he suggested she compose a Linnaean poem for which he would provide scientific notes, she judged the plan 'not strictly proper for a female pen'.[48] He set about it himself and *The Loves of the Plants* appeared anonymously in 1789. Darwin thought the Linnaean system 'undiscovered poetic ground', but Jones ventured into this virgin territory five years earlier. *The Enchanted Fruit; or, The Hindu Wife* (1784), based upon an incident in some *Mahābhārata* recensions concerning the polyandrous princess Draupadī, married to the five heroic Pāndava brothers, demonstrates Linnaean concepts of the familial and the generic running in his mind:

> For *India* once, as now cold *Tibet*,
> A groupe unusual might exhibit,
> Of sev'ral husbands, free from strife,
> Link'd fairly to a single wife!
> Thus Botanists, with eyes acute
> To see prolific dust minute,
> Taught by their learned northern *Brahmen*
> To class by *pistil* and by *stamen*,
> Produce from nature's rich dominion
> Flow'rs *Polyandrian Monogynian*,
> Where embryon blossoms, fruits, and leaves
> *Twenty* prepare, and ONE receives.   (ll. 61–72; *SWJ*, pp. 82–3)

Draupadī is '*Polyandrian Monogynian*', and Linnaeus orientalized as a 'learned northern *Brahmen*'. This mock-epic narrates the Draupadī sextet's trespass in a Brahman's garden and Arjuna's (one of her husbands) unintentional sin in

---

47. 'The calyx could also be regarded as the *lips of the cunt* or the *foreskin*'; see *Linnaeus' Philosophia Botanica*, trans. Stephen Freer (Oxford, 2005), 105.
48. Anna Seward, *Memoirs of the Life of Dr Darwin* (London, 1804), 131.

separating with his arrow an ambrosial fruit from its 'parent stalk'. Jones's playful comparativism reveals the contrasting significance of Hindu fruit and Judaic apple. This is no irrevocable original sin, for 'Crishna' himself advises that the holy fruit may be restored to its branch if each of the Pāndavas and their wife Draupadī confesses his/her innermost sins. Such shrift will avoid the dire prospect of a Brahman's curse. The poem's climax highlights Draupadī's confession of a youthful crush on her handsome pandit as he relates the divine eroticism of Krishnā's dance with the milkmaids:

> 'While this gay tale my spirits cheer'd,
> So keen the *Pendit*'s eyes appeared,
> So sweet his voice—a blameless fire
> This bosom could not but inspire.
> Bright as a God he seem'd to stand:
> The reverend volume left his hand,
> With mine he press'd'—'   (ll. 473–9)

Although the culmination of Draupadī's confession—'The *Brahmen* ONLY KISS'D MY CHEEK' seems innocent enough for this feisty heroine, it is sufficient to return the enchanted fruit to its native bough. This representation of Hindu reparation contrasts with the Mosaic linkage of disobedience, knowledge, and loss of Eden. The Hindu 'Golden Age' is epitomized in the accommodating morality of the capitalized rule, 'WHAT PLEASETH, HATH NO LAW FORBIDDEN' (l. 21). When not actively shaking the pagoda tree, what pleased Jones and his colleagues was the prospect of acquiring 'a complete knowledge of India'. The tree of knowledge was not forbidden in the Indian garden; here was no bitter apple of the fall.

7
Europe Falls in Love with Śakuntalā

Willst du die Blüthen des frühen, die Früchte des späteren Jahres,
Willst du, was reizt und entzückt, willst du was sättigt und nährt,
Willst du den Himmel, die Erde mit Einem Namen begreifen,
Nenn ich, Sakontala, dich, und so ist Alles gesagt.

[If you want the spring's blossoms and the fruits of the maturer year,
What is seductive and creates joy, or what is satisfying and nourishing,
If you want to encompass Heaven and Earth in one single name,
Then I name you, Sacontala, and everything is said.]

This celebrated Goethe quatrain published in the *Deutsche Monatschrift* of 1791 captures the essence of the *Śakuntalā* fever that gripped Europe in the early 1790s.[1] The tradition of popular Orientalism stemming from texts such as the *Arabian Nights* intimately linked the exotic and the erotic. The blending of these elements in a play reflecting an enchanted world of pastoral romance where mortals and gods interacted ensured that the sensational reception of *Śakuntalā* outstripped even that which had greeted Galland's *Les Mille et une nuits*. European longing for the East is simultaneously sacred and profane and there is a specifically sexual charge to the enraptured enthusiasm for this Indian play. The monstrous gods and demonic devotees that thronged so many western representations of Hinduism are thrust to the wings of the European imaginary as Śakuntalā appears centre stage. Goethe saw the purity of Kālidāsa's play and its eponymous heroine as devouring the 'Bestien in dem Götter-Saal' (beasts

---
1. Johan Wolfgang von Goethe, *Werke*, Weimar edn,.143 vols in 4 parts (Weimar, 1887–1912), 1: 4, p. 122; (my translation).

in the hall of gods), occluding his horror of Hindu statuary. Here was an Orientalism at once intensely seductive and profoundly classical; the lips of Śakuntalā changed everything:

> Kalidas und andere sind durchgedrungen;
> Sie haben mit Dichter-Zierlichkeit
> Von Pfaffen und Fratzen uns befreit.
> In Indien möcht ich selber leben,
> Hätt es nur keine Steinhauer gegeben.
> Was will man denn vergnüglicher wissen!
> Sakontala, Nala, die muss man küssen,
>
> [Kalidas and others have got our attention;
> They have with their poetic elegance
> Freed us from caricatures and stupid priests.
> I should like to live in India myself,
> If only there had not been any sculptors.
> And this is what one should know of the more pleasant aspects!
> Sakontala, Nala, they have to be kissed,][2]

That Goethe should, on encountering this daughter of a Brahman *rishi*, lose his head so completely remains an enduring tribute to Jones's skill as cultural mediator.

Jones published his translation as *Sacontalá, or the Fatal Ring* on 8 October 1789; printed by Joseph Cooper, it cost 12 sicca rupees (30 shillings). Its first notice announced: 'A work so perfectly novel, curious, and interesting, and the purchase of which amounts only to the price of a play ticket, will no doubt have a large sale; more particularly as the liberal and humane translator has appropriated the amount, free from all expence, to the relief of insolvent debtors.' This *Calcutta Chronicle* journalist wrote truer than he knew; this play not only provided a ticket to a golden-age pastoral, it utterly changed Europe's conception of India. A revolutionary contribution to Orientalism, Śakuntalā received, in the century following its publication, no fewer than forty-six translations in twelve different languages.

Jones announces his 'discovery' of the Śakuntalā in a serial letter to Althorp, now Lord Spencer, of 1–11 September 1787 and the context is highly significant. On vacation at their charming rural *aśram* (hermitage) at Krishnagar near the gently flowing Jalangi, the couple were perfectly

---

2. 'Zahme Xenien', Goethe, *Werke*, 1: 3, p. 251. Jones was also working on the *Mahābhārata* narrative, 'Nala and Damayanti'; New York, Fales Library, Jones MSS, 2/44.

content. On the verandah the air felt fresh after sultry Calcutta, and Jones was contemplating things worldly and unworldly. His letter opens with his *'embarras des richesses'*, remittances to England to the tune of '£4,130.14.7 which, with what I sent last year, are above ten thousand pounds'. On 2 September, he and Anna have been reading 'an excellent discourse by that excellent man' Richard Price: 'On the subject of future punishment he expresses himself inclined to think that it will be *temporary*, that is for *a length of time proportioned to the offence*, but he leaves it doubtful, whether this opinion [. . .] can be justified by the *language* of Scripture' (*Letters*, 2: 765).[3] Jones, the dispenser of temporal justice, categorically states he would 'give up Scripture rather than embrace' the idea of an eternity of pain, which he conceives as divine injustice. He outlines Hindu belief in reincarnation where the soul, according to its good or evil deeds, rises more closely towards, or falls away from, assumption into the divine nature. Jones confidently asserts: 'I am no Hindu, but I hold the doctrine of the Hindus concerning a future state to be incomparably more rational, pious, and more likely to deter men from vice, than the horrid opinions inculcated by Christians on punishments *without end*.'

Jones's deistical openness to central tenets of Hindu eschatology separated him from evangelical friends within Bengal. These remarks were intended for private consumption; by contrast his celebration of the *'embarras des richesses'* of Hindu literature was something he wished to communicate to the whole of Europe:

> I must tell you the subject of a Drama in Sanscrit by Calidāsa (pronounce always as in Italian) the Indian Shakespeare, or Metastasio, who was the chief poet at the court of Vicramāditya near two thousand years ago.[4] The dramatick piece, which is neither Tragedy nor Comedy, but like many of Shakespeare's fairy-pieces, is called *Sacontalá*, and the story is this.
>
> A pious man, whose name was Viswamitra, or Universal Friend, had by his devotion attained such power over all nature, that Indra, the God of the Firmament, began to fear, lest his own dominion might be in danger, and to check the ambition of the Saint, commanded an *Apsara*, or Celestial Nymph, to descend from heaven and seduce the hermit from his vows of Chastity. She—What she did, you shall hear to-morrow morning, *si je ne dors pas*. Adieu!   (*Letters*, 2: 766)

---

3. Probably his *Sermons on the Christian Doctrine as Received by the Different Denominations of Christians* (London, 1787).
4. Jones places Kālidāsa too early. Despite his pre-eminent status, critical uncertainty continues concerning his dates. A persistent tradition names him chief of the *Navaratna* (Nine Jewels) at the court of Chandragupta Vikramaditya (CE 375–414).

4 Sept. I am no Hindu; but I hold the doctrine of the Hindus concerning a future state to be incomparably more rational, more pious, and more likely to deter men from vice than the horrid opinion inculcated by Christians on punishments without end. — Since I have lately said so much of the Hindus, I must tell you the subject of a Drama in Sanscrit by Calidása (pronounce always as in Italian) the Indian Shakespeare, or Metastasio, who was the chief poet at the court of Vicramaditya near two thousand years ago. The dramatick piece, which is neither Tragedy nor Comedy, but like many of Shakespear's fairy-pieces, is called Sacontalá; & the story is this.

A pious man, whose name was Viswamitra, or Universal Friend, had by his devotion attained such power over all nature that Indra the God of the Firmament began to fear lest his own dominion might be in danger, and to check the ambition of the Saint commanded Sacontala the daughter of an Apsara, or celestial nymph, to descend from heaven and seduce the hermit from his vow of chastity. What she did you shall hear to-morrow morning since he does pass. — adieu

12. Letter from Jones to 2nd Earl Spencer, Crishna-nagar, 1-11 September 1787. The folios illustrated are of 4 and 5 September. (British Library, Althorp Papers)

5 Sept. — (for the Saint had the weakness
She — of other mortals) overpowered his austerity,
and was delivered of a lovely daughter,
who was named Sacontalá. The
child, being born on earth, was necessarily
to go through life before she could be
admitted into Swerga, or the heaven of
Indra; to which her mother ascended,
having intrusted her to the care of
another holy man whose name was
Canna. After she had received a
divine education, she was seen in a
forest by Raja Dushmanta, when he
was hunting, and her beauty inflamed
him with such passion that he
married her. Soon after the nuptials
a Brahman, named Durbása visited
the king, who being in a very thoughtful
mood, on account of some publick
business, took no notice of him; which
disrespect so provoked the Brahman
that he pronounced this imprecation
against Dushmanta. "May she
whom thou lovest best forget
thee, and not recollect thee till
she has seen the ring on thy finger!"
Dushmanta, not attending to him, or
disregarding the curse, went, as it
was his custom every morning, to bathe
in a sacred pool called Sasitertha
or the Moon's Pilgrimage, and sprinkling
his head with the water — but
as it is noon, you shall know what
he did to-morrow, if the Sultan allow me to live
another day!" Farewell!

In teasing Shahrazâd style Jones narrates the heroine's conception, revealing his understanding of *tapas* (spiritual power accumulated through asceticism). Within three years, or a thousand and one nights, Śakuntalā eclipsed Shahrazâd as a focus of wide-eyed European attention. Mary Wollstonecraft, reviewing the 1790 London edition, discovered delicacy, refinement, and a pure morality in *Śakuntalā*, the very qualities Jones desired to highlight when representing Hindu culture. She emphasizes its novelty and breadth of appeal:

> This Indian drama, translated by Sir William Jones, if we may credit common fame, will undoubtedly be thought not only by the man of taste, but by the philosopher, a precious *morçeau*; for whilst the latter has the opportunity of tracing human passions clothed in a new modification of manners, the former will be immediately gratified by the perusal of some pathetic scenes, and beautiful poetic similes.[5]

Wollstonecraft maintains the play must be a work of 'great intrinsic excellence' to surmount the difficulties of being read 'in a different climate' where it is necessary 'to refer to our memory, or to illustrative notes, to account for expressions, which allude to foreign customs'. Sensitively aware of such problems as face the translator where the limited experience and innate prejudice of the reader tend to make 'every thing strange appear absurd', she praises Jones's skill in 'the poetic delineation of Indian manners which come home to the human bosom in every climate'.

This is a substantial tribute to the success of Jones's 'elegant translation' in presenting Indian culture as both sophisticated and accessible to metropolitan audiences. Though fascinated by the dramatic Otherness of India, Jones has found similitude everywhere. He revolutionized European language theory by recognizing Sanskrit as a more refined sister of Latin and Greek. Now the beauteous Śakuntalā embodies that Indian refinement in all her seductive elegance. His very linguistic method in translating Kālidāsa—using an intermediate interlinear Latin translation—symbolizes this East–West rapprochement, but it is his skill as a poet that enables him to draw in his contemporary readers.

In the *Monthly Review*, Thomas Ogle, Surgeon Extraordinary to the Prince of Wales, reveals a similar universalist Enlightenment response; he finds in the play:

> much which irresistibly calls forth the tender feelings. 'The great passions of the mind,' as has been remarked, 'do not partially prevail: they are the same in

---

5. *Analytical Review*, 7 (August 1790), 361–73; 361.

every country: in the breast of the European, as in that of the inhabitant of Asia:' the affecting parts here are the natural parts: every one has felt similar sensations; and every one must be pleased with having them recalled to his imagination.[6]

The play's full title is *Abhijñānaśākuntala*, 'The Recognition of Śakuntalā', and in the sensitive reaction of this authoritative critic we appreciate Jones has simultaneously effected both its literary recognition and a world-shrinking acknowledgement of an Indian's power to move an Englishman. The following month, James Anderson, political economist and friend of Bentham, praises Jones as a reuniter of kin, beatifying him as global peacemaker:

> 'Blessed are the peace-makers, saith a high authority.'—Blessed then are those who by painful researches, tend to remove those destructive veils which have so long concealed mankind from each other, and occasioned this destructive estrangement; who, by discovering the human heart, without disguise, naked as it came out of the hands of the creator, enable all nations, languages, and people, to recognise each other as relations, and induce them to embrace each other as kindred.[7]

Citing extracts describing Raja Duṣyanta's saddened realization of his cruel behaviour towards Śakuntalā, Anderson invokes Wedgwood's powerful abolitionist motto to assert the brotherhood of man:

> 'O my darling, whom I treated with disrespect, and forsook without reason, when will this traitor, whose heart is deeply stung with repentant sorrow, be once more blessed with a sight of thee.'
>
> Dost thou, O reader, recognize the savage in these features? Is he not a man? Is he not thy brother?

This is the revolutionary politics of sensibility. Jones could not have been more delighted with the warmth of this impassioned and affective reception. Its universalist, fraternalist, and familial empathy was precisely the response he wanted to encourage. Yet in his preface, such was his confidence in the literary excellence of Kālidāsa's play, that Jones avoided anticipating such intercultural enthusiasm, coolly retiring behind the subjectivity of *quot homines, tot sententiae*:

> On the characters and conduct of the play I shall offer no criticism; because I am convinced that the tastes of men differ as much as their sentiments and

---

6. *Monthly Review*, 4 (February 1791), 121–37; 124.
7. *The Bee, or Literary Weekly Intelligencer*, 2 (March 1791), 111–20; 149–51; 111–12.

passions, and that, in feeling the beauties of art, as in smelling flowers, tasting fruits, viewing prospects, and hearing melody, every individual must be guided by his own sensations and the incommunicable associations of his own ideas. (SWJ, p. 218)

Despite Jones's emphasis upon individual tastes, 'incommunicable associations' recalls David Hartley, whose application of Newtonian scientific method to the regions of the human mind implied that its associative powers were chemical, neurological, and, above all, universal. The natural taste of pleasure—whether in eating a delicious fruit or watching a sophisticated drama—may transcend the culture-specific. Jones's desire to find likeness in the East, amplified by his exposure to the Vedantic philosophy of Hinduism, was moving him towards a syncretic theological position that was annihilating the distance between Occidental and Oriental mysticisms. His linguistic and legal researches, his ethnological and literary discoveries, were convincing Jones of the truth of what François Fénelon (1651–1715), whose ideas were currently resonating in French Revolutionary idealism, had asserted as the grand principle of moral and political reform:

> [T]hat all the world is but one republic, of which God is the common Father, and every nation as it were one great family. From this beauteous and luminous idea arise what politicians call *the laws of nature and nations*, equitable, generous, full of humanity. Each country is no longer considered as independent on others, but the human race as an indivisible whole. We are no longer limited to the love of our own country; the heart enlarges itself, grows immense, and by an universal friendship embraces all mankind.[8]

'Universal Friend' is the name of Śakuntalā's father, the *rishi* (poet-seer) Viśvāmitra, and her drama is universally embraced. The accomplished poet Anna Lætitia Barbauld, writing to Mrs Beecroft in September 1790, agrees that 'the language of nature and the passions is of all countries', and this private female correspondence also focuses upon Duṣyanta. Here is the ultimate accolade to Jones's success as cultural translator: a Hindu raja is favourably judged by the measure of a popular novel of sensibility:

> The hero of the piece is as delicate and tender a lover as any that can be met with in the pages of a modern romance; for I hope you can pardon him a little

---

8. Sir Andrew Michael Ramsay, 'A Discourse on Epic Poetry', in *The Adventures of Telemachus, the Son of Ulysses*, 2 vols (London, 1742), 1: xix.

circumstance relative to the *costume* of the country, which is just hinted at in the poem: I mean the having a hundred wives besides the mistress of his heart.[9]

Barbauld's playful emphasis upon sexual 'costume' anticipates the continental reception of the following year, subsequent to the appearance of Georg Forster's German translation of Jones's *Sacontalá*. British enthusiasm appears tepid in comparison with the rapturous German response. With no empire, German Romantics might feel genuinely cosmopolitan, free from imperial anxiety, more in tune with the *Weltgeist*. Yet their reaction to the heroine may be seen as a perfect example of imperial rhetoric whereby a colonized land is allegorized as a female body. India **was** Śakuntalā, without italics, but with bold sensual emphasis, in an elaborate fantasy of seduction. Forster sent Johann Gottfried von Herder his translation on 17 May 1791; it was a revelation to him. Herder had found 'the mistress of his heart', the ideal for which he was seeking:

> *Sakontala* is a drama which can equal any drama [...] a delicate fable of destiny [...] The language is ornate, floral and yet never overdone, the behaviour of characters or classes towards each other, be they gods or mortals, is so decent and good that it would be difficult to find a play which equals it, in all the languages, among all the nations. Also the intertwined voices of music, the elements of painting, of decor, of humour are as original as they are delicate, finally, the concepts of religion, especially in the dwellings of Paradise, are (who is to deny it) themselves paradisiacal.[10]

Goethe later explained to Orientalist Antoine-Léonard de Chézy, who produced the first French translation from the Sanskrit, *La Reconnaissance de Sacountala* (1830), his profoundly personal response to the blissful dawning of 'the *Sacontalá* era':

> The first time I became aware of this unfathomable work it aroused such enthusiasm in me, attracted me so much, that I did not cease studying [...] this highly treasured work, it determined such an epoch in the course of my life [...] Here the poet appears to us in his highest role, as a representative of the natural state, of the finest way of life, of the purest moral striving, of the most dignified majesty and the most earnest contemplation of God.[11]

---

9. *The Works of Anna Lætitia Barbauld*, 2 vols (London, 1825; repr. London, 1996), 2: 83.
10. *Sämtliche Werke*, ed. Bernard Suphan, 33 vols (Leipzig, 1877–1913), 24: 580.
11. Goethe to de Chézy, 9 October 1830; cited in A Leslie Willson, *A Mythical Image: The Ideal of India in German Romanticism* (Durham, NC, 1964), 69.

Kālidāsa's play became a vibrant source of archetypal values linking ancient and modern, East and West, making Goethe rethink his preconceptions concerning Indian art, Vedic thought, and Aristotelian dramatic theory. Although he never produced *Śakuntalā* at Weimar, he used its introductory prologue with its conversation between stage manager and actress as a model for the 'Vorspiel auf dem Theater' of his *Faust*, written in 1797. Kālidāsa's introduction of the leading actress who was to perform the role of Śakuntalā, emphasizing the artificiality of theatrical performance, might seem a fifth-century anticipation of Brecht's alienation effect. Far from disrupting emotional involvement in the play, however, the actress's delightful song is designed to encourage it:

> Mark how the soft blossoms of the Nágacésar are lightly kissed by the bees! Mark how the damsels delicately place behind their ears the flowers of Sirísha! (*SWJ*, p. 221)

Herder's reservations concerning Indian art are similarly swept away by the aesthetic and religious impact of reading *Śakuntalā*. He admires its artistic harmony, its mingling of the marvellous and the commonplace, its pastoral innocence, balancing poetry and nature, the devotional and the erotic. This cultural icon, reflecting the holy land of mankind's childhood, is more valuable than anything the Greeks, or any other nation, had produced. Herder speaks of the play with an enthusiasm and proprietary zeal, at once possessive and proselytizing. He passionately writes '*Sakontala* heisst mein Drama' ('*Śakuntalā* is the name of my drama'), it is his 'Indische Blume', its heroine likewise is a flower unfolding her innocent sexuality in a fragrant *āśrama*.

Eighteen years earlier, Jones's *Persian Grammar*, illuminated by Hāfiz, had initiated Romantic Orientalism; now the translator of Kālidāsa lit the blue lotus touchpaper of Romantic Indophilia. *Śakuntalā* was inspiring poets, philologists, ethnologists, and mythographers throughout Europe. Herder's enthusiasm infects the young Jena Orientalist Friedrich Majer, who became the chief German purveyor of Indic knowledge, introducing Schopenhauer to Sanskrit culture; the whole Romantic Jena circle falls under the *bhaktic* spell. In the *Athenäum* both Schlegels championed Sanskrit language and literature. August Wilhelm describes the perfection of Sanskrit as the language of heaven, its characters designed by God Himself.[12] Friedrich wants

---

12. *Athenäum, eine Zeitschrift*, ed. August Wilhelm Schlegel and Friedrich Schlegel, 3 vols (Berlin, 1798–1800), 1: 23.

the treasures of Oriental literature made as accessible as those of Graeco-Roman antiquity; the source of '*Universalpoesie*' will be found in India: 'Im Orient müssen wir das höchste Romantische suchen' ('In the Orient we must seek the most sublime Romanticism').[13] Convinced of the unity of poetry and mythology, and captivated by the idea that the source of religion might be revealed in the language of ancient India, Schlegel encourages his countrymen to study Sanskrit and reveal its mysteries.

Friedrich Schlegel's meeting in Paris early in 1803 with Alexander Hamilton (a cousin of his namesake, the Federalist founding father of America) marks an epoch in German Indology. The enormous continental influence of *Asiatick Researches* was now focused in the French capital by the presence of one of its contributors. In Calcutta Hamilton was influenced by Wilkins and Jones to learn Sanskrit and, on his return, he took advantage of the 1802 Peace of Amiens to study Europe's finest collection of Sanskrit manuscripts at the Bibliothèque Nationale. On the resumption of hostilities with Napoleonic France, the single man in continental Europe to hold the key to Sanskritic treasure was locked up as a prisoner of war. The Orientalist ironies of this situation were deepened by the intervention of the expert on the near East, philosopher and politician Constantin Volney, to allow Hamilton liberty to collaborate with Louis Mathieu Langlès in cataloguing Hindu manuscripts. Though opposed to imperial aggression, Volney's publications upon Egypt and Syria had, in the words of celebrated whig hostess Lady Elizabeth Holland, 'serve[d] as guides', or in those of Edward Said, 'justified in advance', Napoleon's Egyptian campaign of 1798–9.[14] German interest in the Orient was national in more subtly political ways. Here Jones's comparative linguistic research and Sanskrit translations served as a guide for an ethnological model embracing a sophisticated Asian cultural inheritance.

Friedrich Schlegel, in Paris to study Persian with de Chézy, could not believe his luck. Having found 'the only one in Europe apart from Wilkins who knows Sanskrit and knows it thoroughly', his Persian studies were eclipsed by his devoting three hours daily to lessons with Hamilton. Franz Bopp, the pioneering comparative linguist, was also taught Sanskrit by Hamilton, as were Volney and Langlès, On 15 May 1803 Friedrich wrote to August Wilhelm that soon he would be able to read *Śakuntalā* in the

---

13. *Athenäum, eine Zeitschrift*, 3: 320.
14. *Journal of Lady Elizabeth Holland* (London, 1908), 199; Said, *Orientalism*, 39.

original.[15] Orientalism was on the march and the 'language of the gods' was spreading across the continent.

Many European thinkers, having read Jones's 'On the Philosophy of the Asiaticks' (1793), began to see Hindu idealism as outshining its Greek counterpart. 'The incomparable Jones', as Goethe termed him, had directed Europe's attention to 'the incomparable SANCARA' (Śankara; late eighth century CE) who argued, 'that external appearances and sensations are illusory, and would vanish into nothing, if the divine energy, which alone sustains them, were suspended but for a moment' (*Works*, 3: 239). Friedrich Schlegel, desiring to find in India a unifying spiritual revolution that might synthesize religion, philosophy, and art, was encouraged to emphasize similarities between Vedantic philosophy and the German idealism of Spinoza.

Introducing *Śakuntalā* to the West, Jones indicates the 'spectacularly new' might possess reassuring familiarity. In comparing the play with mature Shakespearean romance he refuses the condescension of viewing Kālidāsa as a more naïve Bard. On the contrary, he announces that *Śakuntalā* is:

> so much like Shakespeare, that I should have thought our great dramatick poet had studied Cālidāsa. There are a hundred fine Tragedies, Comedies, & Operas in Sanscrit; & I am convinced, that the Indian Court was formerly one of the most brilliant in the world.   (*Letters*, 2: 806)

Kālidāsa's source for the *Śakuntalā* narrative is the first book of the *Mahābhārata*, 'the great (*mahā*) [tale] of the Bhārata dynasty'; Bhārata is the son of Śakuntalā and Raja Duṣyanta, or Dushmanta, in Jones's transliteration. In this epic original the hunting raja, for whom ten thousand slaughtered deer were insufficient, is driven by lust for the beautiful but ambitious Śakuntalā who agrees to a *gāndharva* (clandestine) marriage on condition that their firstborn son be heir to the throne. When the raja breaks his promise, a heavenly voice resounds:

> 'A wife splits her body to give birth to a child
> Therefore, Duṣyanta, treasure Śakuntalā's son,
> Or welcome disaster!'[16]

Kālidāsa transforms this spare narrative, adding psychological depth of characterization and a delicate range of subtle emotions in accordance

---

15. *Friedrich Schlegels Briefe an seinen Bruder August Wilhelm*, ed. O. Walzel (Berlin, 1890), 522–3.
16. W. J. Johnson includes a translation of the *Mahābhārata* source in his excellent edition: *Kālidāsa: The Recognition of Śakuntalā* (Oxford, 2001), 135.

with Sanskrit literary theory. Removing all traces of the *Mahābhārata* couple's cynical self-interest, he celebrates their mutual attraction in the closely observed detail of Duṣyanta's tentative courtship of the shy 16-year-old Śakuntalā. The raja has learned little of woman or love in his *zenana* (Indian haram); now he discovers the delicious pain of *fin' amor* (refined love) and the profound female power of *śakti*. Kālidāsa dramatizes the reciprocal links between *kāma* (love) and *dharma* (duty) in the lovers' emerging relationship and at the level of plot. Duṣyanta is recalled to his court but promises to return, giving Śakuntalā a ring as pledge of his eternal devotion. Abstracted and deeply in love, Śakuntalā fails to pay homage to Durvāsa, a visiting *rishi*. Her dereliction of *dharma* is punished by the irascible *rishi*'s curse that she will be forgotten by the one who loves her best. Priyamvadā implores Durvāsa to forgive her friend, and he allows that her lover's memory will be restored if she produces a token of recognition. With the curse Kālidāsa introduces potentially tragic elements. The mitigation Priyamvadā secures concentrates audience attention upon 'the Fatal Ring', Śakuntalā's accidental loss of which increases dramatic tension. Kālidāsa's sophistication appears in balancing the secular and the divine, the intuitive and the imaginative, the natural and the artistic. The fifth-century playwright has effectively 'romanticized' *Mahābhārata* materials and at the hands of an eighteenth-century poet-translator, the *Śakuntalā* is ready to play its dramatic role in European Romanticism.

The hunter Duṣyanta, invading the sacred ground of the *aśram*, is seen not only as the powerfully austere Śiva with his bow Pināka, resembling the rainbow, but, as a man of sensibility, empathizing with his antelope prey:

> Oh! there he runs, with his neck bent gracefully, looking back, from time to time, at the car which follows him. Now, through fear of a descending shaft, he contracts his forehead, and extends his flexible haunches; and now, through fatigue, he pauses to nibble the grass in his path with his mouth half opened. See how he springs and bounds with long steps, lightly skimming the ground, and rising high in the air! And now so rapid is his flight, that he is scarce discernible! (*SWJ*, p. 222)

At the level of religious symbolism, Duṣyanta, associated with the *linga* or procreative power of the phallus, intrudes within the holy garden, the wholly feminized space of *prakriti*. Here fawns are tame, 'tender female parrots feeding their unfledged young' recall the birds (*śakunta*) who protected Śakuntalā when abandoned as a baby, and sacred streams bathe the roots of trees bearing fragrant and exquisite blossoms. Appropriately in a play whose prologue announces water to be 'the first work of the Creator', Śakuntalā, muskily 'soft as the fresh-blown Mallicà', and her friends Anusúyá and Priyamvadá, are discovered watering delicate exotic plants.[17]

Duṣyanta is captivated at first sight, and his aesthetic and erotic entrancement is intensified by compassion for her labours and annoyance with her foster-father Káṇva who 'must have an unfeeling heart' to allot her such 'mean employment' and dress her soft loveliness in a 'coarse mantle of woven bark'. Unfeeling and its binary opposite are visually and deliciously counterpointed: 'He, who could wish that so beautiful a creature, who at first sight ravishes my soul, should endure the hardships of his austere devotion, would attempt, I suppose, to cleave the hard wood Sami with a leaf of the blue lotos' (*SWJ*, p. 225). The scented purple-brown heartwood of the *samī* tree is associated with weapons in the *Mahābhārata* but, as Jones reveals in his 'Botanical Observations', it was also 'used by the *Bráhmens* to kindle their sacred fire'. Kālidāsa is about his equally sacred task of kindling emotions. The contrast between the masculine hardness of sacred *samī* wood and the feminine delicacy of the blue lotus, which Jones was to make the fragrant emblem of Romantic India, reflects Duṣyanta's distress that she should endure such hardship, a compassion transculturally reminiscent of Miranda's sympathy for her 'patient log-man' in *The Tempest*.

The harmonies produced by this emotional antiphony refine the sensibilities of the audience who see the beauteous Śakuntalā watering the summer shrubs. Awareness of her sensual loveliness, the beauty of her *dharma* revealing her love for the thirsty flowers, the perfumed beauty of the blossoms themselves, and that of the handsome Duṣyanta, added to the rightness of his mingling passions, all encourage each individual in the audience to indulge in a synaesthetic banquet of the emotions. This is the 'romanticism' of *rasa*. Both transcendental and transcultural, it explains the remarkable level of western audience identification with an Indian raja's enthralment with Śakuntalā. Goethe's response is completely in accord with classical Indian aesthetics as Gupta *rasa* meets Romantic sensibility.

The concept of *rasa* is a triumph of Sanskrit aesthetics, refined through a continuous tradition of sophisticated drama lasting from several centuries before Christ to the twelfth century—an incredible one and a half millennia. Uniting the objective and the subjective, the quality in a literary work that

---

17. 'The *Brahméns* in the west of *India* distinguish this flower [Mallicà] by the name of *Castúri*, or *musk*, on account of its very rich odour', 'Botanical Observations', *Works*, 5: 73–4.

gives delight and the delight itself, the poetics of *rasa* link audience, author, and characters as emotions are cultivated in an enchanting pastoral of love and poetry. *Rasa* is an emotion or sentiment relished as an aesthetic distillation, a purified essence to be savoured. Whereas Aristotle's *Poetics* defined catharsis as a cleansing of emotion, a purging that results in feelings of peace and well-being, the *rasas* represent the aesthetic heightening of eight emotions which, being cleansed of any disagreeables, can delight the learning soul.[18] The *rasas* were achieved through the harmonious arrangement of eight corresponding *bhāvas* or moods. As the eleventh-century philosopher Abhinavagupta describes the experience of theatre-going: 'One's heart becomes like a spotless mirror, for all one's normal preoccupations have been completely forgotten, and one is lost in aesthetic rapture.'[19]

The audience identify with Duṣyanta as an embodiment of *rasika* sensibility, a connoisseur of the passions, the man of *rasa* if not the man of feeling. As Robert Goodwin has argued:

> The *rasika* approaches a work of art with [...] an indefinable longing that can only be expressed in the Indian context, as a dim remembrance of an ideal love in a former life. Art, then, seems to promise a recovery of the memory of who one really is and a primal sweetness that has been left behind in the process of living.[20]

When Duṣyanta from a position of concealment observes Śakuntalā in the privacy of her sacred grove, his sensual voyeurism is focused by her request to her friend to loosen her constricting bodice of bark fibres. The *rasa* of his captivation is the product of his savouring the nuances of his emotional responses: a mingling of *karuna* (compassion) for Śakuntalā's pain, 'her coarse mantle', her 'mean employment', and of *śṛngāra* (eroticism) of her beauty intensified by his invasion of female intimacy. The unseen observer endorses Priyamvadá's compliment to Śakuntalā's breasts as he lovingly attempts to capture their beauty in image and symbol:

> *Dushm.* [*Aside*] Admirably spoken, Priyamvadá! No; her charms cannot be hidden, even though a robe of twisted fibres be thrown over her shoulders and

---

18. The eight *rasas* are: the erotic (*śṛngāra*), the comic (*hāsya*), the compassionate (*karuna*), the furious (*raudra*), the heroic (*vīra*), the fearful (*bhayānaka*), the horrific (*bībhatsa*), the marvellous (*adbhuta*). A ninth, the peaceful (*śānta*), was an eighth-century addition.
19. See Raniero Gnoli, *The Aesthetic Experience according to Abhinavagupta* (Varanasi, 1968), 12ff. and 55ff.
20. Robert E. Goodwin, 'Aesthetic and Erotic Entrancement in the *Śakuntalā*', *Acta Orientalia Academiae Scientarium Hungaricae*, 43:1 (1989), 99–123, 111.

conceal part of her bosom, like a veil of yellow leaves enfolding a fragrant flower. The water lily, though dark moss may settle on its head, is nevertheless beautiful; and the moon with dewy beams is rendered yet brighter by its black spots. The bark itself acquires elegance from the features of a girl with antelope's eyes, and rather augments than diminishes my ardour. Many are the rough stalks which support the water lily; but many and exquisite are the blossoms which hang on them.   (SWJ, pp. 225–6)

The West shared Duṣyanta's entrancement. The cult of sensibility was much in vogue, but whereas it had been seen as a modern susceptibility, enshrining the idea of civilizational progress, Europe now discovered how remarkably late they had come to the banquet of the senses. The self-indulgence of sensibility was associated with capitalistic consumerism, itself facilitated by the importation of Oriental luxury goods. Now the literary riches imported by East Indiamen confirmed that the ethics of feeling and the morality of taste had been theorized eighteen hundred years earlier. 'The Shock of the Old', perhaps, for it was a shock to a metropolitan eighteenth century in which the feminization of taste was in its infancy.

India was a holy land for which mind, soul, and body yearned; it was here that German Romanticism might discover 'a strain of Earth's sweet being in the beginning'. Johann Joseph von Görres, the Heidelberg historian of mythology, recorded the intensity of this Indo-Germanic longing:

> Do you know the land where the youthful mankind lived its joyful childhood? [. . .] Our soul feels itself wonderfully drawn to the Orient, to the banks of the Ganges and the Indus.[21]

In arousing this profound desire, Jones had accomplished a spiritual and erotic revolution in the representation of India. There was, however, one lingering doubt harboured by some of the German intellectuals: that Jones might have bowdlerized Kālidāsa in conformance with drawing-room sensibilities. Having fallen in love with a Śakuntalā tightly constricted by woven bark, they longed for further revelation. They had read only Jones—in the English, or Forster's translation of Jones—and, with a certain prurient itch, wondered if the Sanskrit concealed more enchanting delights. In this they were encouraged by the sexually explicit content found in Jones's translation of the *Gītagovinda*, from which Jones omitted only those passages 'too luxuriant and too bold for an *European* taste'.

---

21. Quoted in Willson, *A Mythical Image*, 106.

On learning in 1804 that Friedrich Schlegel was contemplating his own translation of Śakuntalā, Goethe remarked to the friend of Wordsworth and Coleridge, Henry Crabb Robinson: 'That's Capital, I shall rejoice to read it free from the changes which the moral Englishman has made in it.' Robinson concurred: 'I take it for granted that Sir W. Jones has corrected certain pruriencies of oriental fiction—And this would not be allowed in a German translator', noting that the term 'Engländerei' (Englishism) had been coined for 'such Puritanism in language and excess of delicacy in matters of physical love'.[22] Robinson recalls that Goethe placed 'a sarcastic emphasis on the words "des moralischen Engländers"', revealing a certain ingratitude towards the half-Welshman who transformed his vision of India and whose popularizing of Hāfiz inspired his *West-östlicher Divan*. Schlegel's growing proficiency in Sanskrit confirmed that Jones had translated Śakuntalā 'with the utmost fidelity', and he abandoned his proposed translation; nevertheless suspicions of Jones's 'excess of delicacy' have proved tenacious.[23]

Jones acknowledged an enormous responsibility in being the first to transmit this pearl of Sanskrit high culture to the West, but the delicacy is not so much the production of 'the moral Englishman' as of the moral Kālidāsa. This, of course, is not to deny substantial cultural differences with regard to the representation of sexuality whether in Gupta literature or Ajanta temple sculpture. Jones was fully aware of such explicitness and never found it at all offensive. But he also understood the potential subtleties of *rasa* and how indulgence in such a complex palette/palate of 'tastes' was by no means incompatible with standards of taste—subcontinental or metropolitan.

When in the first act Śakuntalā is fatigued after her watering labours, emphases upon her dishevelled hair and her glowing body may be interpreted by the *rasika*, ancient or modern, Asian or European, as a suggestive anticipation of the exhaustion produced by energetic intercourse. A twenty-first-century critic remarks of Śakuntalā's fatigue that it resembles: 'a description of a beautiful and delicate girl tired during the act of lovemaking, or of the girl practising purushayita or inverse position in relation to

---

22. *Goethe: Begegnungen und Gespräche*, ed. Ernst Grumach and Renate Grumach (Berlin, 1985), 5: 475–6.
23. Garland Cannon writes of Jones's 'rather puritanical rendering of the sensual lines', while arguing that this feature was 'predictably unobserved by his European readers'; 'Sir William Jones's Introducing Śakuntalā to the West', *Style*, 9 (1975), 82–91; 89.

her lover'.[24] Goethe, with advanced ideas on sexuality, might have shared this reader-response on reading Jones's translation:

> Her arms, graced with palms like fresh blossoms, hang carelessly down; her bosom heaves with strong breathing; and now her dishevelled locks, from which the string has dropped, are held by one of her lovely hands. (*SWJ*, p. 231)

Jones omits one key descriptive element, captured in the translation Chandra Rajan completed exactly two centuries later: 'The Śirisa blossom adorning her ear,/caught in the sparkling web of beads of sweat,/ceases its delicate play against her cheek.'[25] Gentlemanly Jones presents a glowing—rather than a sweating—heroine, but Eurocentric elisions are infrequent. In Śakuntalā's third act portrayal where Rajan has: 'With Uśīra-balm spread thick over her breasts' (p. 201), Jones's version: 'medicine extracted from the balmy Uśīra has been applied, I see, to her bosom' (*SWJ*, p. 243), more clearly stresses the subtle *śṛṅgāra* eroticism of Śakuntalā, or her friends, applying aromatic lotion to her breasts. Jones's translation reads:

> Her forehead is parched; her neck droops; her waist is more slender than before; her shoulders languidly fall; her complexion is wan; she resembles a Mádhaví [jasmine] creeper, whose leaves are dried by a sultry gale: yet, even thus transformed, she is lovely, and charms my soul. (Ibid.)

And Rajan's:

> Wan face with sunken cheeks, breasts no longer firm,
> slender waist grown more slender, shoulders drooping despondent,
> complexion dulled by pallor—O how woebegone she looks,
> limp, struck by maddening love, yet how lovely
> —a Mādhavī, its leaves touched by a scorching wind. (pp. 202–3)

Jones modifies the hyperbolic element of the Indian tradition, wherein physical symptoms of a woman's love-sickness can seem tantamount to emaciation. His western audience is habituated to the code of *fin' amor*, which presents a lovelorn *male* in despair at the pretended indifference of an immaculate 'Belle Dame sans Merci'. For the moment Jones judges it sufficient that Europe should appreciate that there is no dissembling in the Indian female. Jones is reluctant to impugn the loveliness of Śakuntalā;

---

24. M. L. Varadpande, *History of Indian Theatre* (New Delhi, 2005), 117.
25. *Kālidāsa: The Loom of Time*, ed. and trans. Chandra Rajan (New Delhi, 1989), 183. Cf. William Johnson's superb version: 'On filmy sweat the mimosa's bloom/Slides from ear to cheek'; *The Recognition of Śakuntalā*, 18.

languor and pallor, even a drooping neck, are acceptable, but not drooping breasts. His chivalric 'protectiveness' towards 'his' heroine is an aspect of his powerful desire to nurture a radically different representation of Hindu culture of which she remains a perfect emblem.

Goethe is the beneficiary of this desire to destroy prejudice and adjust preconceptions. Having created the West's desire for Śakuntalā, it is deeply ironic that Jones should be suspected of occluding her seductive charms; 'the moral Englishman' hides little from Goethe. The representation of Hinduism and its feisty heroines was not always so straightforward; Kālī being a case in point.

Kālidāsa was a devoted follower of the Saivite strand of Hinduism; his name means 'servant of Kālī', consort and śakti of austere Śiva. When Jones composed his 'Hymn to Durgá' (another aspect of Kālī) he avoided portraying her as a four-armed emaciated naked black woman, adorned with necklaces of bloody skulls. He represents the goddess in her Pārvatī aspect, the pious and beautiful neophyte who was a divine model for the half-divine Śakuntalā. In this he was influenced by another celebrated Kālidāsa text, the *Kumārasambhava* ('Birth of Kumara'), but he draws a veil over the violent love-making of Śiva and Pārvatī graphically described in the eighth canto of Kālidāsa's epic poem:

> The rest, my song conceal:
> Unhallow'd ears the sacrilege might rue.
> Gods alone to Gods reveal
> In what stupendous notes th'immortals woo.
>   ('Hymn to Durgá', VI. 2. 1–4)

Jones understood that to represent the overt eroticism of any religion requires profound cultural tact. The union of Śiva and Pārvatī is no private moment of sexual adoration; it is one of the most central and crystallizing encounters of Hinduism. Europe was not ready for such revelation, but there was little for Jones to conceal in the *Śakuntalā*. Jones used the Bengali recension of Kālidāsa's play, which includes more erotic dialogue between Śakuntalā and Duṣyanta in Act Three than the Devanāgarī version. At the climax of this act Anusúyá and Priyamvadá persuade Śakuntalā to allow Duṣ yanta room on her 'flowery couch' and artfully withdraw on the pretext of comforting a distressed fawn:

> Why should not I, like them [Śakuntalā's friends], wave this fan of lotos leaves, to raise cool breezes and dissipate your uneasiness? Why should not I, like

them, lay softly in my lap those feet, red as water lilies, and press them, O my charmer, to relieve your pain? (*SWJ*, p. 247)

If we compare this with Rajan's translation of Duṣyanta's words we can see the extent of Jones's omission:

> Shall I raise cool breezes, waving over you
> these broad lotus-leaf fans, moist and refreshing
> to relieve your languid weariness?
> Shall I place your lotus-pink feet on my lap.
> O lady with beautiful tapering thighs!
> And press them tenderly to ease your pain? (pp. 207–8)

Though his simile, 'red as water lilies' more precisely realizes her delicately hennaed feet, Jones avoids celebrating Śakuntalā's thighs; 'O my charmer' hardly seems adequate! The Sanskrit word Jones encounters here is '*karabhoru*', glossed by Monier-Williams as 'the thick part of the hand, "the part between the wrist and the fingers"; it is also "a young elephant". [...] "having thighs gracefully tapering like the trunk of an elephant"'.[26] Cultural, rather than linguistic, translation is the issue here: what is suggestive in a Sanskritic tradition might prove less so in a European one.

Far from exemplifying a prudish 'Englanderei', Jones's avoidance of carpal or elephantine similitudes reflects a reluctance to introduce elements that might appear bizarre to a readership he is nurturing. His pandit friends appreciated these transcultural difficulties. Jones was assisted by Rāmalocana, and William Johnson considers the unanswerable question 'of exactly how the pandit he was working with mediated the sense to him in the absence of dictionaries—there may have been some indigenous censorship'.[27] Nevertheless, although *Mahābhārata* also describes Śakuntalā as: 'The woman with the lovely thighs', both Miller and Johnson, in translating the less explicit Devanāgarī recension, avoid this textual crux.

Thighs or no thighs, continental enthusiasm continued unabated. Friedrich Schiller, the innovative playwright and authority on aesthetics, rhapsodized about Śakuntalā as the ideal of beautiful femininity, for which he yearned as keenly as Duṣyanta. Novalis (Friedrich von Hardenberg) lovingly addressed Sophie von Kühn, his teenage fiancée, as 'Sakontala'. Chateaubriand fell under its spell; Heine composed *Śakuntalā*-inspired sonnets;

---

26. Monier Monier-Williams, *Śakuntalā, or Śakuntalā Recognised by the Ring* (Hertford, 1853), 126.
27. Private communication.

Lamartine declared *Śakuntalā* displayed 'the threefold genius of Homer, Theocritus and Tasso combined in a single poem'; Schubert, appreciating its blend of idealism, magic, and romantic love, began work on a three-act opera (Sacontala, D. 701); and Théophile Gautier was involved in a ballet version for the Opéra de Paris.[28]

In a remarkable appropriation of the Hindu heroine, Friedrich Adolph Krummacher, theology professor at Duisberg, composed dedicatory parables, addressing Queen Louisa of Prussia as Sacontala. The universally respected Louisa, seeing Prussia's imminent defeat, made an unsuccessful personal appeal for favourable terms to the emperor at Tilsit, but Napoleon's attempts to destroy her reputation only endeared her more deeply to her subjects. Krummacher portrays himself as a Brahman presenting his literary works to his beloved queen as a basket of flowers from her native *aśrama*:

> But the Bramin boldly drew nigh to the throne, and he placed the basket at the feet of Sacontala, and said: Behold, thou amiable sovereign and mother of thy people, these rushes of the basket, and the tender moss of the hills, and these simple flowers, are the produce of that distant valley on the extreme border of thy spacious dominions, where thy feet walked when the early spring of life did smile upon thee.[29]

That a Prussian queen should become Śakuntalā was a significant straw in an easterly wind. Jones's radical readjustment of *Weltanschauung* (world view) had decidedly political implications, especially for a fragmented Germany, where Indo-European was proprietorially termed Indo-German. Jones's research encouraged cultural and linguistic 'elective affinities' with the *Urheimat* of India in early nineteenth-century Orientalist conceptions of German nationhood.

Jones's translations have been seen by some cultural theorists as interpellating a colonial subject, constructing 'a Hindu character, a Hindu psyche, a Hindu way of life' in an authorized version of Indian civilization, imposed by western cultural hegemony upon a subject and subjectified people.[30] It is undeniable that *Śakuntalā*'s European reception established

---

28. Raymond Schwab, *The Oriental Renaissance: Europe's Rediscovery of India and the East, 1680–1880*, trans. Gene Patterson-Black and Victor Reinking (New York, 1984), 57–64.
29. 'The Bramin's Gift (1805)', in F. A. Krummacher, *Parables*, trans. Frederic Shoberl (London, 1824), 2.
30. Tejaswini Niranjana, *Siting Translation: History, Post-Structuralism, and the Colonial Context* (Berkeley, 1992), 33.

this text as not merely evidence, but as the representational icon, of Indian civilization. But this was no Eurocentric imposition: it reflected the judgement of the Indian poetic tradition. The Romantic image of India reflected India's own self-image. Kālidāsa's play, according to Edwin Gerow, is 'the validating aesthetic creation of a civilization': 'The Śakuntalā is not merely a document that provides evidence about culture, it is not just a cultural exemplar; it defines an integral part of an outlook and internal relationship of a civilization.'[31] In consulting Rādhākānta Sarman as to which of the Indian plays was 'most universally esteemed', Jones was enlisting Brahmanical authority, a cultural hegemony that can scarcely be seen as 'western'. Alternatively, in translating Śakuntalā with the help of a non-Brahman scholar Jones was arguably fostering an anti-Brahmanical stance.[32] Subsequently, this play would inspire national self-consciousness among the Indian intelligentsia. Orientalism, through its retrieval of Sanskrit texts and its reconstruction of India's past, shaped the way Indians perceived themselves, facilitating the Bengal Renaissance. As S. N. Mukherjee has stated; 'His Śakuntalā had a profound effect in India. By saving Kālidāsa from the medieval commentators he ushered in what has been called "an Indian Renaissance".'[33] Although a key member of the colonial administration, Jones's Enlightenment aspirations were ultimately to work in the service of Indian nationalism.

Jones combined his antiquarian researches with a modernizing and enlightened belief in progress. Although demonstrating India's distinguished past, in which Hindus had been 'splendid in arts and arms, happy in government, wise in legislation, and eminent in various knowledge', he proved reluctant to indulge in any intellectual nostalgia for an Indian golden age. Unlike many of his Asiatick Society colleagues, such as Wilkins or even Hastings himself, Jones refused to dismiss contemporary Hinduism as a degraded falling-away from a pristine monotheism. Whereas Halhed subscribed to a common prejudice against popular Hinduism, Jones appreciated that this theory of historical deterioration was somewhat simplistic. Nor did he support a caste-based dichotomy. Jones was reluctant to reinforce the

---

31. Edwin Gerow, 'Plot Structure and the Development of Rasa in the Śakuntalā', Journal of the American Oriental Society, Pt. 1, 99 (1979), 559–72; Pt. 2, 100 (1980), 267–82; 1: 564.
32. Rocher, 'Weaving Knowledge: Sir William Jones and the Pandits', 51–79; 58.
33. S. N. Mukherjee, Sir William Jones: A Study in Eighteenth-Century British Attitudes to India (Cambridge, 1968), 3. See also David Kopf, British Orientalism and the Bengal Renaissance: The Dynamics of Indian Modernization 1773–1835 (Berkeley, 1969).

distinction between a rational ethical Brahman élite and the 'repulsive superstitions' of the masses.

In general Jones remained sympathetic to the devoted fervour of popular ritual, applying a tolerant relativism to the overt eroticism of Hinduism. In 'On the Gods of Greece, Italy and India' (1784) Jones observed that 'it never seems to have entered the heads of the legislators or people that anything natural could be offensively obscene; a singularity, which pervades all their writing and conversation, but is no proof of the depravity of their morals' (*Works*, 3: 367).

Jones views Bengal as a crucial site in the evolution of Hinduism, reflecting a vigorous continuity between classical devotional texts and contemporary Hindu devotees. Daily discussion with learned pandits, and enjoyment of recitals of the Hindi and Bengali songs sent him by Margaret Fowke contribute to his appreciation that the dynamic tradition of *bhakti* linked popular religious enthusiasm and learned Vedantism. His fascination with Vaiṣnavism (devotion to Vishnu, especially in his eighth *avatār*, as Krishna) is apparent in 'A Hymn to Náráyena' (1785) and 'A Hymn to Lacshmí' (1788). Understanding the immense influence the *Gītagovinda* exerted upon popular Krishna devotion in Bengal, he decides to translate this devoutly erotic poem of the twelfth-century Bengali poet-saint Jayadeva ('victorious Lord'), whose name is also an epithet of Krishna.

On completing his translation of *Gítagóvinda* in the spring of 1789, Jones sent a copy to John Shore, future governor-general. It pleased Shore but, characteristically of the future founder of the evangelical Clapham Sect, he reciprocated by sending Jones a theological text by Richard Hooker. Jones appended *Gítagóvinda* to his paper, 'On the Mystical Poetry of the Persians and Hindus', read to the Asiatick Society on 8 December 1791.

Five years earlier, in his 'Third Anniversary Discourse' (1786), Jones had declared it impossible 'to read the Vedanta, or the many fine compositions in illustration of it, without believing that Pythagoras and Plato derived their sublime theories from the same fountain with the sages of India' (*SWJ*, pp. 362–3). Confining his 1791 brief to mystical poetry, Jones develops his ideas concerning the common identity of the Platonic, Vedantic, and Sūfistic traditions. Such similarities had been noted as early as the eleventh century by the Muslim historian al-Biruni, but it was during the period of liberal religious toleration ushered in by the reign of Akbar that such speculative syncretism had flourished. On the metaphysics and theology of the Sūfis, Jones recommends 'the pleasing essay, called *The Junction of two*

Seas' by Prince Dārā Shikūh, the eldest son of Shāh Jahān. Dārā Shikūh's interest in comparative mysticism had led him to Banaras, where Brahmans had helped him translate some of the *Upaniṣads*, but his cruel death at the hands of his strict Sunni younger brother Aurangzeb effectively ended such syncretic investigation. Jones also reveals his reliance upon the authority of the *Dabistan*, a work of comparative theology written by Mohsen Fani, 'a *sufi* who, like other Muslims of his persuasion, was particularly attracted to Kashmir as a home of religious mysticism'.[34]

Jones focuses such syncretic reflection for European readers by quoting at length from an essay 'Of the Love of God' by Isaac Barrow, the teacher of Newton and 'deepest theologian of his age'. He claims it 'differs only from the mystical theology of the *Súfis* and *Yógis*, as the flowers and fruit of *Europe* differ in scent and flavour from those of *Asia*, or as *European* differs from *Asiatick* eloquence; the same strain, in poetical measure, would rise up to the odes of SPENSER on *Divine Love* and *Beauty*, and, in a higher key with richer embellishments, to the songs of HAFIZ and JAYADÉVA, the raptures of the *Masnavì*, and the mysteries of the *Bhágavat*' (*Works*, 4: 216).

Jones's essay includes twenty-six couplets, which represent the first European translation of the mystical *Masnaví* by Jalāl ud-Din Rūmī (1207–73). He acknowledges the *Masnaví* as an 'astonishing work', and prefaces his translation with Rūmī's description of the Sūfi poets: 'they profess eager desire, but with no carnal affection, and circulate the cup, but no material goblet; since all things are spiritual in their sect, all is mystery within mystery'. Jones explores points of contact between 'figurative modes of expressing the fervour of devotion' in various Oriental cultures, such as the nuptial contract of the Song of Solomon, Nizāmī's *Laylī and Majnūn*, and the marriage of Krishna and Rādhā, all of which illustrate 'a singular species of poetry, which consists almost wholly of a mystical religious allegory, though it seems on a transient view to contain only the sentiments of a wild and voluptuous libertinism'.

Eager to prompt his readers to experience fascination—rather than alienation—in difference, Jones's philosophy as cultural mediator is simply stated: 'if we think it worth while to read their poems, we must think it worth while to understand them'. Throughout this essay Jones stresses the contemporary

---

34. John Drew, *India and the Romantic Imagination* (Delhi, 1987), 54. Cf. 'The Sixth Anniversary Discourse', in *Asiatick Researches* 2, repr. in *Representing India*, vol. 8.

relevance of the allegorical tradition within both Muslim and Hindu cultures, referring to modern Sūfis and 'Hindi poets of our own times'.

Introducing his translation of Gítagóvinda at the conclusion of the essay, Jones dates its author far too early, but what is more important is his keen awareness of a living tradition of religious performance of this twelfth-century work, enlivened by village pride and rivalry:

> Let us return to the *Hindus*, among whom we now find the same emblematical theology, which *Pythagoras* admired and adopted. The loves of CRISHNA and RADHA, or the reciprocal attraction between the divine goodness and the human soul, are told at large in the tenth book of the *Bhágavat*, and are the subject of a little *Pastoral Drama*, entitled *Gítagóvinda*: it was the work of JAYADÉVA, who flourished, it is said, before CALIDAS, and was born, as he tells us himself, in CENDULI, which many believe to be in *Calinga*: but, since there is a town of a similar name in *Berdwan*, the natives of it insist that the finest lyrick poet of *India* was their countryman, and celebrate in honour of him an annual jubilee, passing a whole night in representing his drama, and in singing his beautiful songs.

In modern Bengal this tradition is still vibrant; as Barbara Miller observed, 'the singing of *Gítagovinda* is especially prominent at an annual spring fair in the village of Kenduli in Birbhum district'.[35]

The *Gītagovinda*, or 'Song of Krishna as cowherd', is an elegant example of *kāvya* (literature informed by *rasa*) poetry and marks the flowering of the medieval Vaiṣṇava devotional tradition. It celebrates the pastoral god Krishna and his love for the daughter of his foster-father, the most radiant of the *gopīs*, Rādhā. The tradition of Krishna sporting with the *gopīs* is an ancient one, but it is only in *Gītagovinda* that Rādhā emerges as a fully developed figure allegorizing the god's union with *prakriti* and symbolizing the infinite love that is the essence of Krishna. Rādhā contrasts with her fellow *gopīs* in her proud, ambitious, and jealous desire for an exclusive relationship with Krishna. Though a mortal woman, Rādhā is made divine through her passion for her dark lord and in the ultimate *rasa* of their union.

In the Rādhā–Krishna cult, disciples of Krishna of both sexes identify with Rādhā as his *hlādinī-śakti* ('infinite energy of bliss') in a contemplation at once divine and erotic. *Gītagovinda* operates simultaneously on the corporeal and metaphysical planes. Such emotional erotic worship was at

---

35. See *Love Song of the Dark Lord: Jayadeva's Gītagovinda*, trans. Barbara Stoler Miller (New York, 1977), xi.

the heart of the *bhakti* movement in Bengal with which Jones demonstrated a profound empathy, announcing that he was 'in love with the *Gopia*, charmed with *Crishen*'.

Devotion to Krishna, however, must be balanced by his responsibility to his metropolitan audience. Despite the eroticism of the Hebrew songs, such as the Song of Songs, the schism between body and soul has been long-standing in the West, apart from the erotic spirituality associated with Christian mystics such as Hildegard of Bingen or Teresa of Avila. If there was little celebration of sexual desire even within marriage—the words of the mid-twelfth-century Sarum Missal wedding liturgy, 'with my body I thee worship' standing as an enlightened exception—Hindu veneration of the details of the courtship and intercourse of Rādhā and Krishna was likely to prove alien or abhorrent to western sensibilities. In the pagan Greek pantheon, the adulteries of Zeus are legion, but even his love-making with his wife Hera, when Mount Ida put forth fresh grass, dewy lotus, crocus, and hyacinth, is enfolded in a tasteful golden cloud (*Iliad*, 14); there is certainly no attention to the symbolism of their sexual positions. The overt eroticism of Jayadeva's text rendered the translation of *Gītagovinda* a much harder task than that of the *Śakuntalā*. What Jones accomplished is a triumph of intercultural empathy and genuine devotion.

The religious climax of the poem comes in Canto X where Lord Krishna requests Rādhā to place her delicate foot upon his head to symbolize her triumph over her god. Legend has it that Jayadeva, reluctant to write such potentially impious words, went to perform his ritual ablutions; on his return he found the couplet completed by an approving Krishna. Here is Jones's translation of this divinely inspired and ratified passage:

> Speak but one mild word, and the rays of thy sparkling teeth will dispel the gloom of my fears. My trembling lips, like thirsty *Chacóras*, long to drink the moon-beams of thy cheek. *O my darling, who art naturally so tender-hearted, abandon thy causeless indignation. At this moment the flame of desire consumes my heart: Oh! grant me a draught of honey from the lotos of thy mouth.* Or, if thou beest inexorable, grant me death from the arrows of thy keen eyes; make thy arms my chains; and punish me according to thy pleasure. Thou art my life; thou art my ornament; thou art a pearl in the ocean of my mortal birth: oh! be favourable now, and my heart shall eternally be grateful. Thine eyes, which nature formed like blue water-lilies, are become, through thy resentment, like petals of the crimson lotos: oh! tinge with their effulgence these my dark limbs, that they may glow like the shafts of Love tipped with flowers. Place on my head that foot like a fresh leaf, and shade me from the sun of my passion,

whose beams I am unable to bear. Spread a string of gems on those two soft globes; let the golden bells of thy zone tinkle, and proclaim the mild edict of love. Say, O damsel with delicate speech, shall I dye red with juice of *alactaca* those beautiful feet which will make the full-blown land-lotos blush with shame. (SWJ, p. 312)

The religion of courtly love, itself an Oriental importation via Mozarabic Spain, placed such language on the lips of troubadours and trouvères immortalizing mortal mistresses by means of their lyric devotions. The spiritual revolution of Hinduism allowed the West to witness a god deifying his beloved through his adoration. Demonstrating his deep understanding of sacred pastoral and of Indian flora and fauna dense with symbolic allusion, Jones portrays the homage of a suffering and supplicant god in a faithful rendering of *Gītagovinda*'s *bhaktirasa* (essence of devotion). If we compare his compact and effective line: 'My trembling lips, like thirsty *Chacóras*, long to drink the moon-beams of thy cheek' with Lee Siegel's literal translation: 'may the moon which is your face cause the *cakora* [bird] which is my eye to long for the intoxicating-nectar from your quavering lower-lip',[36] we can see that on occasions Jones allows himself a certain freedom, but only in the service of clarification. Jones's line spells out for a western audience what the indigenous reader already knows: the *cakora* drinks only moonbeams. The transference of this image from Krishna's eye to his lips is intensified by further transferring the 'quavering' of Rādhā's lower lip to the lips of her Lord. This heightens our sense of Krishna's submissive entreaties.

The single bowdlerization in this key passage is of Krishna's references to love bites and nail wounds, regarded in Hindu tradition, but less so in Europe, as socially acceptable means of exciting and recording passion. Where Siegel's translation has: 'give me a wound with the arrows that are your sharp nails, bind me with the fetters which are your arms or bite me'; Jones provides: 'grant me death from the arrows of thy keen eyes; make thy arms my chains; and punish me according to thy pleasure'. Thus only his juxtaposition of pleasure and punishment remains to hint at these mildly sado-masochistic aspects of love-making to which the *Kāmaśastra* devotes a whole chapter (2: 4).

Jones, however, does not expurgate all such references. And one he does include illustrates not only tact in cultural translation, but the way in which his understanding of Jayadeva's devotional text was deepened by a poet's

---

36. Lee Siegel, *Sacred and Profane Dimensions of Love in Indian Traditions as Exemplified in The Gītagovinda of Jayadeva* (Delhi, 1978), 274.

appreciation of the contrast of actual and symbolic colour. In the fourth verse (*sloka*) of the eighth canto (*sarga*), Rādhā is rebuking Krishna for making love to another beautiful *gopi*; his body announces the tell-tale signs in the language of colours. His teeth are as blue as his skin from kissing the blue mascaraed eyes of Rādhā's rival. His broad chest is reddened, 'stained by the bright lotos of her foot', decorated with lac, from her sitting astride him. And in her passionate orgasm her nails have been at work. Barbara Miller's translation reads as follows:

> Etched with scratches of sharp nails in the battle of love,
> Your body tells the triumph of passion in gold writing on sapphire.[37]

In Jones's version we have:

> [T]hy limbs marked with punctures in love's warfare exhibit a letter of conquest, written on polished sapphires with liquid gold.   (ll. 351–2)

Jones's version of 'marked with punctures' is arguably less explicit than 'Etched with scratches of sharp nails', in reflecting physical aspects of the battle of love with the dark god. Furthermore, 'exhibit a letter of conquest' possesses an Augustan formality, which is also evident in his use of 'limbs' (as opposed to 'body'), and the second person singular. On the other hand, Jones's translation, with its suggestion that the 'conquest' is not merely of passion, as Miller has it, but triumph over the god himself, is arguably closer to the original as given in Siegel's literal version, which reads: 'Your body, which has lines of wounds from hard curved-nails [inflicted] in the battle of love, resembles a record of [her] victory in love-pleasure' (p. 271). Jones's adaptation of Jayadeva's image also reinforces the traditional and symbolical colour of the god, 'liquid gold' effectively conveying Krishna's blood standing out against his cerulean skin.

Krishna's descent has re-established his Mount Meru (the Hindu Olympus) paradise of Goloka (the Cow-World) in Gokula, a pastoral area watered by the Yamunā, whose dark-blue waters reflect his ethereal colouring as he dances his erotic Rasa-Līlā with the milkmaids. Their love-play is so violent and sustained that the perfumed waters are churned like the primordial ocean of milk in the Hindu creation myth. From these engendering waves arose the beauteous goddess of fertility and fortune, Śrī

---

37. Miller, *Love Song of the Dark Lord*, 106.

Lakshmī, bounteously portrayed in Jones's 'A Hymn to Lacshmí' as an Oriental Botticelli's Venus:

> And those firm breasts, whence all our comforts well,
>   Rose with enchanting swell;
> Her loose hair with the bounding billows play'd,
> And caught in charming toils each pearly shell,
>   (ll. 41–4; *SWJ*, p. 156)

Jones reverentially describes Lakshmī's loving focus upon the dark lord Vishnu (the azure of ether symbolizes his nature as Pervader and Preserver), here addressed as Hari, Remover of ignorance and affliction:

> On azure HERI fix'd her prosp'ring eyes:
>   Love bade the bridegroom rise;
> Straight o'er the deep, then dimpling smooth, he rush'd;
> And tow'rd th'unmeasur'd snake, stupendous bed,
> The world's great mother, not reluctant, led:
> All nature glow'd, whene'er she smil'd or blush'd;
>   The king of serpents hush'd
> His thousand heads, where diamond mirrors blaz'd,
> That multiplied her image, as he gaz'd.   (ll. 64–72)

As the love-making of Lakshmī and Vishnu on the causal waters is infinitely reduplicated in the jewelled reflections of the serpent Ananta's hood, so in the Jumna Krishna multiplies both himself and the *gopīs* to enjoy simultaneous intercourse with nine lakhs of milkmaids.[38] And the intrinsic link between these two stupendous acts of divine sexuality is established in '*Vrindavan*'s od'rous grove', where Lakshmī and Vishnu are reborn to embody the mutuality of *bhakti-darśana* (vision of adoration):

> Blythe RÁDHÁ she, with speaking eyes, was nam'd,
> He CRISHNA, lov'd in youth, in manhood fam'd.   (ll. 89–90)

In the mystical springtime forest of Vrindavan where Rādhā seeks her beloved the air is heavy with the scent of musk and aromatic fragrances from a bewildering variety of flowering shrubs and blossoming trees. Their nectareous fragrances, their colours, their flower and leaf shapes, their manner of growth, and their pollens all possess sensual and symbolic significance. The Kadamba tree, from which Krishna watches the naked milkmaids as they come to retrieve their stolen clothes, bears spherical orange

---

38. Cf. Jayadeva's concluding prayer to Vishnu; *SWJ*, 316.

flowers covered in tiny white filaments, symbolizing the infinite worlds of Krishna's love and wisdom.

Jones's botanizing made him fully attuned to Jayadeva's descriptive luxuriance. In his 'Botanical Observations' he writes of the Kadamba: 'The flowers have an odour, very agreeable in the open air, which the ancient *Indians* compared to the scent of new *wine*; and hence they call the plant *Halipriya*, or *beloved by* HALIN, that is, by the third RÁMA, who was evidently the Bacchus of *India*' (*Works*, 5: 90). The third Rāma, another *avatar* of Vishnu, and Krishna's elder brother in Vrindavan, is more interested in the liquor which wine goddess Vāruni distils from Kadamba flowers; it is their intoxicating scent that drives Rādhā and Krishna to drink deep of each other's eyes.

Jones shares Rādhā's delight in the vibrant orange-scarlet 'clustering blossoms of the voluble *Asóca*' (l. 108): 'The vegetable world scarce exhibits a richer sight than an *Asóca-tree* in full bloom; [. . .] JAYADÉVA gives it the epithet *voluble*: the *Sanscrit* name will, I hope, be retained by botanists, as it perpetually occurs in the old *Indian* poems and in treatises on religious rites' (*Works*, 5: 113). Botany, fascination with mystical eroticism, love of Hindi and Bengali songs of *bhakti*, delight in the detailed naturalism of contemporary Kangra paintings of Vrindavan, all feed into his deep appreciation of Jayadeva's text. Jones understands the colour symbolism of the duality of Krishna and Rādhā recalling the cosmic coitus on the causal waters, as the blue (ether) and gold (sun) of Vishnu mingle with the water lily and lotus of Lakshmī:

> [H]is heart was agitated by her sight, as the waves of the deep are affected by the lunar orb. His azure breast glittered with pearls of unblemish'd lustre, like the full bed of cerulean *Yamunà*, interspersed with curls of white foam. From his graceful waist, flowed a pale yellow robe, which resembled the golden dust of the water-lily scattered over its blue petals. His passion was inflamed by the glances of her eyes which played like a pair of water-birds with azure plumage, that sport near a full-blown lotos on a pool in the season of dew. (ll. 482–9)

Love in separation (*viraha*) is the emotion which dominates the *Gītagovinda*, and the sexual climax in *sarga* twelve portrays their ecstatic reunion. Here Jones might have been expected to bowdlerize, but we have quite the reverse. In Krishna's address to Rādhā at the opening of the *sarga*, Jones has:

> 'Set the lotos of thy foot on this azure bosom; and let this couch be victorious over all, who rebel against love. *Give short rapture, sweet* RÁDHÁ *to* NÁRÁYÁN [Vishnu], *thy adorer.*' (ll. 505–7)

Ironically, Jones's translation of Krishna's invitation that Rādhā should set her foot on his 'azure bosom' is more explicitly erotic than the original. It indicates his desire that she should adopt an inverse coital position in which her feet are placed upon his chest (*viparīta-rata*, astride her lover), symbolizing sexual and religious dominance. This female-superior position is clearly indicated several times in *Gītagovinda*, but it is not actually being referred to here.[39] Krishna invites Rādhā to place her foot not on his chest, but on his forest couch of fragrant flower-buds and delicate shoots. Miller has: 'Leave lotus footprints on my bed of tender shoots, loving Rādhā!'

Jones's inadvertent error intensifies the eroticism of this climactic moment, establishing a Rādhā-superior *maithuna* (union) as his own tribute to the cult of Rādhākrishna. It celebrates Rādhā's victory as the triumph of female *śakti* and *prakriti* over male passivity, familiar in depictions of the goddess Kālī dominantly astride Śiva. Earlier in the poem Jayadeva had touched upon the ancient tradition of the lovers' exchange of clothes. In her longing for sexual union and for identity with the godhead, Rādhā 'dresses herself like her beloved, and looking at herself in sport, exclaims, "Behold the vanquisher of MADHU [Krishna]!"' (ll. 250–51). Jones realized that such playful cross-dressing and exchange of roles reflected spiritual indivisibility in a non-dualistic androgyny deeply mystical and deeply divine. But we should return to his version of their *sarga* twelve ecstasy:

> I do thee homage; I press with my blooming palms thy feet weary with so long a walk. O that I were the golden ring, which plays round thy ankle! Speak but one gentle word; bid nectar drop from the bright moon of thy mouth. Since the pain of absence is removed, let me thus remove the thin vest that enviously hides thy charms. Blest should I be, if those raised globes were fixed on my bosom, and the ardour of my passion allayed. O! suffer me to quaff the liquid bliss of those lips; restore with their water of life thy slave, who has been long lifeless, whom the fire of separation has consumed. Long have these ears been afflicted, in thy absence, by the notes of the *Cócila*: relieve them with the sound of thy tinkling waist-bells, which yield musick, almost equal to the melody of thy voice.' (ll. 507–17)

Bearing in mind that *kāvya* literature, with its concentrated intensity provided by patterns of assonance and alliteration, compounded units of words, rhythmic musicality, and the mirroring of sound and sense, has often

---

39. For examples of *viparīta-rata*; see ll. 225–8; 251; 351–2; 361; on its sexual and religious significance; see Siegel, *Sacred and Profane*, 167–9.

13. 'Radha and Krishna Exchange Clothes', opaque watercolour and gold on paper, Himachal Pradesh, Kangra. c.1800. (Los Angeles County Museum of Art)

been described as 'essentially untranslatable', Jones's version is both decorous and elegant.[40] The literal translation, 'Compose an obliging speech like nectar trickling from the nectar-storing moon which is your face', is rendered by Jones, 'Speak but one gentle word; bid nectar drop from the bright moon of thy mouth.' This is more delicately sensual than Miller's 'Consent to my love; let elixir pour from your face!'[41] An uncharacteristic reluctance to refer to 'breasts' is apparent in the periphrastic 'charms', but his clumsy reference to Krishna's longing that 'those raised globes were fixed on my bosom' is not improved upon by Miller's blunt: 'Rest these vessels on my chest!' Where Jones departs from scholarly accuracy, as in 'O that I were the golden ring, which plays round thy ankle!' it represents an attempt to nudge the reader, conversant with Occidental poetic traditions, into a sense of reassuring familiarity.

In fact, Jones's only bowdlerizing is his omission of *sloka* twenty-three of the final *sarga*, which Siegel translates thus: '"Put ornaments, clothes and the jewelled girdle, O good-hearted one, upon my passionate hips which are firm and beautiful, which are the cave-dwelling of the elephant who is Love!"' (p. 284). Here Siegel follows the sixteenth-century commentary of Śankara Miśra who explains that Rādhā's 'hips possess that cleft in which the powerful elephant of Love resides'. Differing conventions in the description of female beauty demand the exercise of a certain *délicatesse*. Barbara Miller exchanges the apparently incongruous elephant for the frankly explicit 'My beautiful loins are a deep cavern to take the thrusts of love.' Had Jones produced such a line he might have satisfied Goethe's prurience, but would have offended a readership he wished to delight. Such sexual explicitness from the lips of the divine Rādhā would prove unacceptable; Jones might almost imagine a mid-twentieth-century barrister intoning: 'Is this a Sanskrit devotional text you would even wish your wife or your servants to read?'

Jones's treatment of Jayadeva's devotional mysticism simultaneously reveals sensitivity to Hindu culture and European sensibilities. Such profound respect for Indian religion, communicated by an Orientalist of unparalleled repute, riveted western attention. The physician and friend of Erasmus Darwin, John Aikin observed: 'The president has not endeavoured to spiritualize the composition', and that 'this *sacred drama* is replete with all that is tender and amatory, in the appropriate imagery of the country; and

---

40. A. B. Keith, *A History of Sanskrit Literature* (Oxford, 1920), vii–viii.
41. *Love Song of the Dark Lord*, 122.

related in a style extremely sweet and delicate'.[42] In Germany Johann Friedrich von Dalberg's verse re-translation of Jones initially delighted Goethe who wrote to Schiller on 22 January 1802: '[T]he enclosed will be sure to give you pleasure. [...] What struck me as remarkable are the extremely varied motifs by which an extremely simple subject is made endless.'[43] Goethe soon realized that, contrary to his expectations of German precision, von Dalberg's version contained omissions and inept errors, but Friedrich Majer published a more accurate version of Jones's translation in the *Asiatisches Magazin* of the same year.

Friedrich Schlegel was intoxicated by the 'joy and ardent inspiration of love' of the *Gítagóvinda*, drawing from its 'high lyrical beauties' an 'idea of the beauty of Indian imagination'.[44] The power of Jayadeva's text, undiluted by Jones's translation, was sufficient to impart to German Idealism the colour and fragrance of the blue lotus. *Gítagóvinda* was received in a mood of European *bhakti* as a key to universal religion.

Jones's translations inspired the Romantic Orientalism that flooded across Britain in the 1790s and the early decades of the nineteenth century. His earlier experimentation in combining moral allegory and dramatic verse tale established the Oriental verse tale. Having developed the genre, the exotic translated materials he supplied, bolstered by his enormous erudition, exercised a profound influence upon the next generation of poets, enabling Walter Savage Landor, Thomas Campbell, Robert Southey, Byron, and Thomas Moore to root their Romantic subjectivity in scholarly, annotated objectivity.[45]

'Stick to the East;—the oracle, [Madame de] Staël told me it was the only poetical policy', wrote Byron to Moore in May 1813.[46] It proved sound advice; the public was indeed orientalizing, and Longman's advance for Moore's *Lalla Rookh* (1817) brought the poet three thousand guineas. Meanwhile Byron was instrumental in the publication of another celebrated poem of the Orient, Coleridge's 'Kubla Khan' (1816). Percy Shelley had already

---

42. *Monthly Review*, 13 (April, 1794), 561–74; 574.
43. Johann Friedrich von Dalberg, *Gita-Govinda* (Erfurt, 1802). *Correspondence between Schiller and Goethe*, trans. L. Dora Schmitz (London, 1909), 2: 395.
44. Friedrich Schlegel, *Lectures on the History of Literature, Ancient and Modern*, 2 vols (Edinburgh, 1818), 1: 213.
45. To take a single example, the notes to Robert Southey's *The Curse of Kehama* (1810) contain sixteen lengthy extracts from Jones's translations, essays, and poems, and nineteen from *Asiatick Researches*.
46. *Byron's Letters and Journals*, ed. Leslie Marchand, 12 vols (London, 1973–82), 3: 101.

discovered both the value of his friend Byron's advice and the worth of Jones's *Works*, which he ordered in December 1812. The power of Southey's *The Curse of Kehama* (1810) had impressed the young poet, but his enthusiasm for Sydney Owenson's (Lady Morgan's) novel *The Missionary: An Indian Tale* (1811), in which the relationship between the Catholic monk Hilarion and the Brahman priestess Luxima creates an infinitely more sympathetic picture of Hinduism, drew Shelley even closer to Jones's position.

Owenson can be seen to follow Jones in reading Hinduism as analogous to European deism; Luxima reveals herself as a Romantic mouthpiece for Jones's Orientalism. In her nature-worship, exquisite sensibility, and pet fawn, Luxima is also deeply indebted to the figure of Sacontalá. Shelley's immediate empathetic response was his 'Zeinab and Kathema' (1811–12), in which Zeinab, a Kashmiri maiden, is abducted from her idyllic home by 'Christian murderers' and shipped to England where she turns to prostitution and rebellion. Preoccupied with India throughout his poetic career, the influence of Jones is apparent in Shelley's subject matter, imagery, and poetic style. John Drew has produced a detailed critique of Shelley's image of India, reading *Prometheus Unbound* (1820) in terms of Kashmiri mythology, and demonstrating that Jones was the mediating factor.[47]

Jones's translations revolutionized European conceptions of India. *Sacontalá* and *Gítagóvinda* reveal him as a tactful mediator of Hindu culture, treating with skill and sensitivity those elements that continued to cause the westerner some difficulty. In 1965 the Sanskritist Daniel Ingalls declared that the treatment of female-superior copulatory positions 'depart[s] the farthest from Western standards of propriety' reflecting 'the heroine's desire to please her lover rather than herself'. His grasp of the Indian concept of *śakti* seems as limited as his understanding of female sexuality. With breathtaking Eurocentricity, he adds: 'The Westerner should be cautioned against taking such verses as evidence of the effeminacy of Indian lovers.'[48] The lingering longevity of one of the oldest of ethnocentric stereotypes, that of the effeminate Hindu, in the mind of a mid-twentieth-century translator can help us understand the difficulties Jones faced almost two centuries earlier. Jones admirably judged the extent to which *rasa* was culture-specific.

---

47. *India and the Romantic Imagination*, 229–82. See also Nigel Leask, *British Romantic Writers and the East: Anxieties of Empire* (Cambridge, 1992), 68–169.
48. Daniel H. H. Ingalls, *Sanskrit Poetry* (Cambridge, MA, 1965), 153.

Acutely aware of the historical and cultural significance of his role as interpreter of India and anxious to avoid creating any impression of grossness or vulgarity, he attempted to demonstrate to the West the ways in which Sanskrit texts integrated religious, aesthetic, and erotic meaning. His success may be gauged by the fact that even James Mill, to whom the idea of Hindu culture was effectively an oxymoron, and Jones, a profoundly uncritical reader, grudgingly conceded that Kālidāsa's play represented a perfect example of pastoral.[49] Jones's apparent failure was marked by the triumph of Anglicist forces in the subcontinent, a triumph so complete that in the Raj of 1853 Śakuntalā was condemned as a work of 'the greatest immorality and impurity', unfit for use as a text for study in Indian schools and colleges.[50]

According to the formula, *traduttore traditore,* all translations constitute textual betrayal, but such massive philistinism on the part of an Anglicizing Raj represented the real betrayal. This was, however, only a temporary setback. Even while western aesthetic principles were being inculcated, Bankim Chattopadhyay (1838–94), the first important Bengali novelist and composer of the patriotic anthem, *Bande Mataram,* maintained that Miranda and Śakuntalā could have been portrayed by the same pen.[51] The future lay with a pluralism for which William Jones had beaten the path.

---

49. James Mill, *History of British India* (1817), with notes by Horace Hayman Wilson, 6 vols (London, 1858), 2: 111. In his voluminous notes Wilson attempts to recuperate the Orientalist position from Mill's savaging Utilitarian attack.
50. Gauri Viswanathan, *Masks of Conquest: Literary Study and British Rule in India* (London, 1990), 5–6.
51. See Tapan Raychaudhuri, *Europe Reconsidered: Perceptions of the West in Nineteenth-Century Bengal* (Delhi, 1988), 172–3.

8

Life and Death in Calcutta: A Courtroom View of the Ethics of Empire

On Thursday, 24 April 1788, after five hours in court, Jones is working on his 'Ode to Durgá', in which he depicts the fierce goddess not in her bloodthirsty Kālī aspect, but as the gentle mountain-born Pārvatī. He is anxious to adjust the representation of this enormously popular *śakta* divinity, generally portrayed to the West as a hideous creature propitiated only by blood. This is how she is represented by Nathaniel Halhed, in Banaras with Hastings early in 1785, while the Joneses were with the Fowkes. Stained with red ochre and paved black with trodden blood of sacrificed goats, the Durgā temple, its gaudily horrific idol standing over an ithyphallic Śiva, its clamorously ecstatic devotees and chattering, jumping monkeys were all too much for the sensitive Halhed. His 'To Brăhm or Kreeshna: An Ode on Leaving Benares' contrasts the elevated 'monotheism' of pristine Hinduism, with 'primeval Reshees' worshipping, 'One great eternal, undivided Lord' and what he sees as debased and debauched cult ritual in the temples of Varanasi:

> What pious *Hindu* hails not *Doorgha*'s vault?
> Nich'd in an angle of the seven-foot space
> Stands a gaunt semblance of th' ill favour'd hag:
> Her grizzled carcase and unseemly base
> Veil'd in a squalid yard of scanty rag.
> A silver'd convex marks each garish eye,
> Her hideous visage shines imbrued with ink:

> And as the bramin waves his lamp on high
> The satisfied adorer sees her wink.   (ll. 40–8)[1]

Jones presents her, not in a tropical gothic vault, but against a serene Himalayan backdrop, weaving flower garlands for her beloved ascetic, the destroyer and creator of all, Śiva:

> A vale remote and silent pool she sought,
> Smooth-footed, lotos-handed,
> And braids of sacred blossoms wrought;
>   II. 2.
> Not for her neck, which, unadorn'd,
> Bade envying antelopes their beauties hide:
> Art she knew not, or she scorn'd;
> Nor had her language e'en a name for pride.
> To the God, who, fix'd in thought,
> Sat in a crystal cave new worlds designing,
> Softly sweet her gift she brought,   (*SWJ*, p. 170)

Having written these lines focusing upon the purity of Hindu devotion to the supreme power of intellect, we can only imagine his reaction on picking up the *Calcutta Gazette* and reading this editorial:

> We are credibly informed that on the night of Sunday, the 6th instant, which was the night of the new moon, a human sacrifice was actually offered to Kâly, the Hindoo Goddess of Destruction, at her temple at Chitpore. [...] the trunk of the man sacrificed was found before the threshold, and the head within the Pagoda, at the feet of the Idol, which had been invested, during the sacrifice, with new robes made of rich and costly manufactures, and several new necklaces, and bracelets of gold and silver.

The authorities suspected 'some opulent and well-read Hindoo', and the Brahman superintendent of the temple was taken in for questioning concerning the low '*Chandál caste*' victim. In a fascinating juxtaposition this lurid picture is immediately followed by a starkly contrasting representation of Hinduism. The editor, Francis Gladwin, affirms:

---

1. BM, Add. MSS 39,899, ff. 6–8. See Rosane Rocher, 'Alien and Empathic: The Indian Poems of N.B. Halhed', in *The Age of Partnership: Europeans in Asia before Dominion*, ed. Blair B. King and M. N. Pearson (Honolulu, 1979), 215–35. On the iconography of Durgā/Kālī, see my 'Cultural Possession, Imperial Control, and Comparative Religion: The Calcutta Perspectives of Sir William Jones and Nathaniel Brassey Halhed', *Yearbook of English Studies*, 32 (2002), 1–18.

It is a fact that the conduct of Mr. H[enckel] in the Sunderbunds has been so exemplary and mild towards the poor Molungees or Salt manufacturers, that to express their gratitude they have made a representation of his figure or image, which they worship amongst themselves. A strong proof that the natives of this country are sensible of kind treatment, and easily governed without coercive measures.   (*Calcutta Gazette*, 24 April 1788)

This representation of 'mild Hindoos' responding to colonial mildness with the touching devotion of superstitious idolaters, serves a dual purpose. On one level it reveals an attempt to provide a compensatory balance (even while implying Hindu statue-erection would inevitably be idolatrous), at another it suggests that worship of the 'exemplary' Henckel is more beneficial than that of the sanguinary Kālī.

Jones admired Tilman Henckel, an exact contemporary and fellow-Londoner, realizing that he not only protected the 'poor' *malangis* (middlemen) from the government salt agent, but also the forced labourers, *maihándárs* (salt boilers), from the oppression of the *malangis*.[2] As Judge and Collector of Jessore, Henckel leased plots of land to local farmers to reclaim and cultivate areas of mangrove forests. Hastings financed Henckel's plan for promoting 'the future security of the province, and the peace of the inhabitants, in a country so infested with dacoits [armed gangs of robbers]'.[3] Jones understood the direct relationship between dacoity and rural poverty and appreciated Henckel's achievement in ridding much of the Sundarbans of both.

An anonymous letter in the *Calcutta Gazette* of 18 May expresses concern that the Chitpore 'human sacrifice' editorial 'may have an effect very prejudicial to the Hindoos in general'. The writer allows that such sacrifice was considered meritorious by some Hindus 'in times of great antiquity', but that now it 'is expressly forbidden', adding that 'the Byeshnoos [Vaishnavites] never admitted the sacrifice even of animals'. He rejects the idea that 'respectable Hindoos' were involved: 'I have not a doubt myself that it has been committed by Dacoits: "The votive offering for a deadly deed".'

The goddess Durgā, whom Jones was hymning, was cherished by the people of Calcutta as Kālī of the Kalighat temple, and invoked not only in the hope of offspring or cure from disease, but for aid in committing

---

2. W. W. Hunter, *A Statistical Account of Bengal*, 20 vols (London, 1875–7), 2: 301.
3. Letter of 21 December 1783 from Tilman Henckel to Warren Hastings; cited in *The Calcutta Review*, 61 (December, 1858), 391–2.

desperate crimes. In their suffering and poverty they turned to Kālī Ma, the dark mother, to help them against the violent iniquities of colonialism. Did Jones, the defender of Welsh peasants, make transcultural connections here? He lamented the lack of improving landlords at home: in Bengal humane Collectors such as Thomas Law or Tilman Henckel were similarly rare. In their absence, dacoity shaded into political resistance in British India just as it does today in Indian India, where the dacoit Bandit Queen, Phoolan Devi (1961–2001), champion of caste resistance, is still revered by her followers as an avatar of Kālī. As Rajeshwari Sunder Rajan has explained:

> Dacoity is not identical with these [Marxist–Leninist, or Maoist, peasant groups] since its action is not directed at the state, for one thing, but at upper-caste men of property, and it is pursued as a way of life and a livelihood rather than followed as a political program. All the same it constitutes a challenge to the modern state as it invariably shades into, or is taken over by, political demands.[4]

Friends of upper-caste Hindus and 'opulent and well-read' Muslims, such as Hastings, Jones, and the anonymous letter-writer, would recognize this twenty-first-century description of the threat posed by dacoity to the greatest democracy in a globally warming world, where half of the rural populace do not own a light bulb. Appalling extremes of wealth and poverty inextricably link the Indias of past and present. In 1787 Jones learned of the success of Lieutenant Ambrose Brenan against an infamous dacoit named Bhavani Pathak in the Rangpur district. Brenan's report provides a tantalizing reference to one of Pathak's associates, Debi Chaudhrani, a woman dacoit, and embodiment of *śakti*. She 'lived in boats, had a large force of *barkandazs* [bandits] in her pay, and committed *dakaitis* on her own account'.[5] Perhaps she was another rural Kālī, the Phoolan Devi of her age, and her dacoits were 'social bandits', redistributing wealth to the starving poor. That is how Bankimchandra Chatterjee, a leading figure in the Bengal Renaissance, who was heartily sick of colonialist representations, would portray her in his novel *Devi Chaudhurani* (1884).

While insurgents such as Debi Chaudhrani and Bhavani Pathak are being subdued, Jones is celebrating divine aspects of *śakti* and *prakriti* in 'The Hymn to Bhavani' (1788), goddess of fecundity. Illustrating Hindu

---

4. Rajeshwari Sunder Rajan, *The Scandal of the State: Women, Law, and Citizenship in Postcolonial India* (Durham and London, 2003), 220.
5. Hunter, *A Statistical Account of Bengal*, 7: 159.

interrelationships between human sexuality, animal reproduction, and crop fertility, Jones presents 'rich nature's queen' worshipped in pastoral superabundance by dancing 'maids and youths on fruitful plains' (*SWJ*, p. 182).

In Bengal the prosaic reality—then as now—was often very different. Bankim Chatterjee himself acknowledged an honest representation of one of the cruellest famines in Indian history by a 19-year-old revenue assistant at Murshidabad:

> Still fresh in Memory's eye the scene I view,
> The shrivelled limbs, sunk eyes, and lifeless hue;
> Still hear the mother's shrieks and infant's moans,
> Cries of despair and agonizing moans.
> In wild confusion dead and dying lie;—
> Hark to the jackal's yell and vulture's cry,
> The dog's fell howl, as midst the glare of day
> They riot unmolested on their prey!
> Dire scenes of horror! which no pen can trace,
> Nor rolling years from Memory's page efface.[6]

The author was John Shore. Jones never witnessed the appalling 1769–70 famine that scarred the memory of his friend, but famine recurred with dreadful regularity and poverty was endemic in the countryside through which he sailed in the luxurious insulation of his pinnace-budgerow. Excessive rainfall produced severe famine in eastern Bengal in 1787 as swollen rivers destroyed mud, and even brick, houses. The town of Burdwan was wrecked, and a ferocious cyclone destroyed crops in districts as far apart as Midnapore, Sylhet, and Rangpur, where, despite distribution of rice, 'mortality was great indeed'. Widespread drought followed in 1788, the Collector of Dharmpur reporting that no rain had fallen after 12 September.

On 19 September Jones is 'composing an Ode to *Pedma* [Lakśmī], the Ceres of Hindustan', adding: 'The Goddess of Abundance, indeed has not been kind this year; for we are just escaped from a famine: thousands have perished in the late dearth, and thousands are now fed every day in Calcutta, where rice is distributed by English gentlemen, most of whom have subscribed 500 rupees to purchase it: I subscribed 1000, & will double my subscription, if the dearth be not removed by the approaching harvest' (*Letters*, 2: 813). Jones's letter turns to the pleasure that Anna and he have

---

6. Charles John Shore, Baron Teignmouth, *Memoir of the Life and Correspondence of John Lord Teignmouth*, 2 vols (London, 1843), 1: 25–6.

had in reading his friend Adam Smith's *Wealth of Nations*. Perhaps it was this text and his hopes for the coming harvest that inspired the following lines:

> And shouting hills proclaim th' abundant year,
> That food to herds, to herdsmen plenty brings,
>   And wealth to guardian kings.
> Shall man unthankful riot on thy stores?
> Ah, no! he bends, he blesses, he adores.
>
> ('A Hymn to Lacshmí', ll. 212–16; *SWJ*, p. 161)

Jones's unfortunate poetic timing is not helped by the connotations of 'riot' in both English and Urdu; his use of this verb meaning 'to indulge to excess'—ironic in itself—is distorted in the reader's mind by images of desperation at the food distribution. The impoverished *ryot* (tenant farmer) must be grateful for his dole of rice, blessing not only Lakṣmī, but the 'guardian kings' of the Company.

In examining the causes of inundation and famine, Jones's hymn incredibly singles out the vices of the natives, which arouse the displeasure of Lakṣmī:

> But, when his vices rank thy frown excite,
> Excessive show'rs the plains and valleys drench,
> Or warping insects heath and coppice blight,
> Or drought unceasing, which no streams can quench,
> The germin shrivels or contracts the shoot,
>   Or burns the wasted root:
> Then fade the groves with gather'd crust imbrown'd,
> The hills lie gasping, and the woods are mute,
> Low sink the riv'lets from the yawning ground;
> Till Famine gaunt her screaming pack lets slip,
>   [...]
> The mother clasps her babe, with livid eyes,
>   Then, faintly shrieking, dies:
> He drops expiring, or but lives to feel
> The vultures bick'ring for their horrid meal.
>
> (ll. 217–26; 231–4; *SWJ*, p. 162)

This is powerful writing, but the poet's sympathy at the plight of suffering humanity is tainted by the idea of divine retribution and our suspicions of political evasion. As Charles Grant viewed the deaths of his baby girls as God's punishment for his dissolute gaming, Jones here blames the *rangī* (blight), and the resultant famine upon the goddess's anger at Indian vice, conveniently exculpating the Company from all responsibility in failing to control the price of food grains. His employment of retributive religious dogma aligns enlightened Jones with the aboriginal hill tribesmen of Orissa who believed their goddesses created famine to punish their sins.

The next stanza appears to confirm that, unlike Shore, Jones had not witnessed such horrors: 'From ills, that, painted, harrow up the breast,/ (What agonies, if real, must they give!).' Self-obsessed with his own pain in merely contemplating such suffering, he compounds his insensitivity with the parenthetical 'if real', in the face of reports of widespread starvation. The appeal to Lakṣmī to 'Preserve thy vot'ries: be their labours blest!/Oh! bid the patient *Hindu* rise and live' is vitiated by Jones's description of the Hindu mind as benighted—is it by Hinduism, by Brahmanism, by Lakṣmī herself?

> His erring mind, that wizard lore beguiles
>   Clouded by priestly wiles,
> To senseless nature bows for nature's GOD.   (ll. 238–40)

Should the Hindu 'rise and live', or to whom should he bow? Jones's answer here is in uncharacteristic Serampore missionary mood. The Hindu should look westward:

> Now, stretch'd o'er ocean's vast from happier isles,
> He sees the wand of empire, not the rod;
> Ah, may those beams, that western skies illume,
>   Disperse th' unholy gloom!   (ll. 242–5)

Lakṣmī must have been spinning in her sea of milk, for this undoubtedly marks the lowest point in Jonesian Hindu hymnology. Such Eurocentric prejudice is all the more perplexing for its appearance in a hymn that reverently describes the churning of the ocean creation myth; the passionate union of Vishnu and Lakṣmī; and the loving narrative of Krishna's schoolfellow Sudāman, an exemplar of *bhakti*.

Human suffering was not always caused by natural disasters or goddesses in the 'garden of Bengal'. The 1783 Rangpur peasant revolt was aimed at the coercive tactics of revenue farmers such as Raja Devi Singh and his agent Hari Ram. A contemporary song recorded that 'under severe torture a wail of agony arose' from starving peasants who descended on the raja's palace:

> In the fusillade of stones,
> Some suffered broken bones,
> And the palace of Devi Singh
> Was reduced to a pile of bricks.[7]

---

7. Ratiram Das's 'Rangpurer Jager Gan', cited in Atis Dasgupta, 'Early Trends of Anti-Colonial Peasant Resistance in Bengal', *Social Scientist*, 14: 4 (1986), 20–32; 29–30.

This Rangpur poem came back to haunt Hastings in February 1788 at Westminster Hall on the opening of the impeachment. Elizabeth Sheridan fainted as Burke described unsubstantiated reports of the raja's reprisals: horrific brutality, daughters raped in front of their fathers, vaginal violation, nipples torn from breasts.[8] Though such hideous accounts provided powerful ammunition against the former head of the Company-state, the Rangpur uprising was targeted at the Company's intermediaries. By contrast, throughout the last three decades of the eighteenth century, outbreaks of the Fakir–Sannyāsī rebellions, in which ascetic Hindu *sadhus* and Muslim fakirs united to fight the British over control of revenue collection, were clearly regarded as politically motivated. Hastings, seeing such inter-religious co-operation as the unacceptable face of pluralism, labelled these peasant insurgents 'enemies of the state'. His detestation of dacoity as a 'hereditary profession' inspired the notorious Regulation 35 of his Judicial Plan, ordering that dacoits should be executed, their villages fined, and their families made 'slaves of the state'.[9]

While it is doubtful whether such official enslavement was ever enacted by the local courts, in 1772 the Supreme Council's mealy mouthed justification of Indian slavery as radically different from the American model: '[H]ere slaves are treated as the children of the families to which they belong, and often acquire a much happier state by their slavery', muddied the judicial waters of the regime.[10]

How was Jones to take to the polluted waters of despotic justice? In Britain he condemned the African slave trade with a passion that impressed Wilberforce. What of its Bengal counterpart? In his 'Charge to the Grand Jury' of 10 June 1785 Jones refers to how they 'would have seen large boats filled with such children coming down the river for open sale at *Calcutta*', the majority either 'stolen from their parents, or bought, perhaps, for a measure of rice in a time of scarcity' (*Works*, 7: 16). The trade defied a government order made 'after a consultation of the most reputable *Hindus*

---

8. See Michael J. Franklin, 'Accessing India: Orientalism, "Anti-Indianism" and the Rhetoric of Jones and Burke', in *Romanticism and Colonialism*, ed. Tim Fulford and Peter Kitson, (Cambridge, 1998), 48–66.
9. BL Add MSS 29, 079, fols 14v-15r, Hastings to Council at Fort William, Murshedabad, 3 August 1773.
10. General Regulations for the Administration of Justice, 15 August 1772, cited in J. W. Kaye, *The Administration of the East India Company* (London, 1853), 381.

in *Calcutta*, who condemned the traffic as repugnant to their Śastra'. This would seem to give the government an absolute right to dismantle the practice, but the circumstances to which Jones refers: 'the number of small houses in which these victims are pent', and that their complaints, 'may expose them to still harsher treatment; to be tortured, if remanded, or, if set at liberty, to starve', reflect police inadequacy and lack of political will.

Even more disconcerting is the slippage in Mr Justice Jones's moral absolutes. 'Eternal rights' disappear down the Hugli as his application of the modifier 'absolute' to slavery marks the sad dawning of a moral relativity. Jones now states his abhorrence of '*absolute unconditional*' slavery, betraying a colonialist accommodation with the 1772 'justifications' cited above: 'the continuance of it [domestic slavery], properly explained, can produce little mischief'. His position is indistinguishable from that of Alwi of Anjouan, which he had condemned two years earlier. It is hard to believe that Jones is speaking these words: 'I consider slaves *as servants under a contract*, express or implied, and made either by themselves, or by such persons, as are authorized by nature or law, to contract for them, until they attain a due age to cancel or confirm any compact that may be disadvantageous to them: I have *slaves*, whom I rescued from death or misery, but consider them as other *servants*, and shall certainly tell them so, when they are old enough to comprehend the difference of the terms' (*Works*, 7: 15).

By cynically redefining household slaves as 'contracted' domestic servants to exculpate Calcutta practice, Jones's attempts to make household slavery acceptable succeed only in lowering the status of domestic service. Insisting slaves should be treated as humanely as servants, Jones refers to an horrific case brought before him 'as a justice of the peace, concerning the death of a *slave girl*, whom her master had beaten', but there is no record of this trial. Six days later, on 16 June 1785, in a murder trial involving a runaway slave boy, Jones was faced with how little humanity might be accorded to a servant. In *Rex* v. *Humphrey Sturt Esq.*, a well-connected Company writer, the son of the MP for Dorset, was indicted: 'for the wilful murder of Munsa at Ranny Tullaub in the Province of Bahar'. We know, from a letter he wrote to Lord Macartney, that Sturt disliked India, finding 'the manners and ideas of the people very discordant with his own'; what he loved was hunting.[11]

---

11. Helena H. Robbins, *Our First Ambassador to China: An Account of the Life of George, Earl of Macartney* (London, 1908), 166.

In his defence, published by Sturt in an effort to exonerate himself, he relates how on his return from pig-sticking he learned his European cook's slave boy was missing; chowkeydar Munsa, assigned to guard the boy's tent, was suspected of connivance. Sturt commanded his interrogation. When Munsa refused inducements, 'I ordered one of my Toorcksewars [cavalrymen] to flog him.'[12] With slips of bamboo, borrowed from nearby basketmakers, he was tied to a tree and beaten. In his writhing he received some strokes on his belly, so Sturt positioned another guard 'to strike him when he should turn that Way'. While taking tea Sturt learned that Munsa was dead.

Summing up, Chambers explained the different species of homicide: 'I made considerable use of the annexed analysis of the case which my brother Jones took the trouble to draw up for me.' After a marathon sitting, not unusual at Calcutta—Sturt's trial lasted thirty-one hours—the jury found him: 'Not Guilty of Murder, but Guilty of Manslaughter, whereupon the Prisoner was burnt in the hand & discharged.'[13]

The verdict, according to *The Oriental Magazine; or, Calcutta Amusement* (June 1785, p. 169), was 'to the intire satisfaction of the Court and the wishes of a very numerous audience'. Sympathy for a recalcitrant servant, who had aided the escape of 'property', was at a premium. Yet in his 1785 'Charge' Jones asserts he has evidence: 'that the condition of slaves within our jurisdiction is beyond imagination deplorable; and that cruelties are daily practised on them, chiefly on those of the tenderest age and the weaker sex, which, if it would not give me pain to repeat, and you to hear, yet, for the honour of human nature, I should forbear to particularize'. Is Jones reverting to his pre-colonial unconditional condemnation of slavery? Unfortunately not; this is another exculpation of the 'English', for his information 'relates chiefly to people of other nations, who likewise call themselves *Christians*'.

It seems strange that a judge addressing jurymen, whose duties involve hearing painful details, 'should forbear to particularize'. Jones the slave owner must demonstrate he is also a man of sensibility, unlike those 'low caste Portuguese at Dacca [who] had taken advantage of the distress occasioned by a scarcity of grain, to purchase vast numbers of children from their parents'.[14] Perhaps we should particularize. A disturbing case heard on 12

---

12. *The Defence of Humphrey Sturt; Esquire, on a Charge Exhibited against him for Murder* (Calcutta, 1785), 13–14.
13. Kolkata, Victoria Memorial Hall, Hyde Reports, vol. 13, reel 6: June 1785.
14. BL, APAC, P/50/60, Matthew Day (Collector of Dacca) to William Cowper, 2 March 1785.

December 1793 illustrates many deplorable aspects in the lives of the Calcutta underclass, not the least of which was their difficulty in obtaining justice. The prosecution was brought against a Frenchman, Pierre Bouton, by John Drake for the rape of his former slave, 10-year-old Mary Serraun. It was recorded in Hyde's notebook as 'An assault *with intent* to ravish Mary Serraun' (emphasis mine).

Drake describes himself as 'a Christian and a Roman Catholic', a watchmaker, who had lived in Calcutta for sixteen years. On her mother's death, he had bought Mary 'from a Portuguese called Anthony for twenty rupees and a bottle of gin'; Drake christened her at the age of five. On the day of her alleged rape, she had asked if she might watch 'a festival of the Mahomedans'. 'I gave her leave, and two lesser girls who are my only servants, to go one at a time', and Mary left his house at eight in the morning. Later Drake was summoned to the police office: 'I saw there Mr [William Coates] Blaquière, the Prisoner, and the girl, the girl was bleeding, and was in a very bad condition.' Blaquière, Persian translator, chief interpreter to the Supreme Court, and JP, immediately enquired 'whether the girl was a maid or not. I said she was when she left my house'.

At a pre-trial hearing in chambers, Justice Hyde asked the prisoner 'if he was not ashamed to lie with such a young girl'; Bouton claimed 'she had been debauch'd before that time, and was not a maid'. Hyde questioned Drake as to 'whether Mary was a Child or a Woman', receiving assurances that she had been a virgin. This was corroborated in court by the sworn evidence of Seedoo Dai, police midwife, who testified she had known Mary for some years, and that she was not more than ten years old, had not begun menstruating, and that her genitals were those of a child. Seedoo added that Mary's 'bleeding continued ten days, and it was a month and an half before the sores were cured'.

What lay behind the questioning concerning Mary's virginity were interlinked assumptions on the part of these two august members of the Asiatick Society, Blaquière[15] and Hyde, that Indian or Eurasian girls

---

15. Blaquière was a cross-dressing freemason, who used female disguise in effecting surprise arrests. Zoffany used him as the model for St John the Divine, resplendent in long blond locks, in his Calcutta church altarpiece. John Clark Marshman described him as a 'Brahmanised European, notorious for his hostility to Christianity and his indifferent character.' He learned Sanskrit, but police experience had given him a taste for the gruesome; he published the *Kālika Purāna* section concerning human sacrifice: 'The Rudhirádhyáya, or Sanguinary Chapter', trans. W. C. Blaquière, *Asiatick Researches*, 5 (1799), 371–91.

reached sexual maturity much earlier than English girls; and that, in the Portuguese or mixed-race compounds of Calcutta's 'Black Town', standards of morality were deplorably lax. In this latter context, Drake's testimony is deeply revealing:

> I told Mr Justice Hyde the girl was now ruin'd and I did not wish to take her again into my family. I said people had heard all this and it would be a great shame for me to take her into my house. Mr Justice Hyde said I might sell her, I said she was not a slave, when I Christen'd her I tore her paper.[16]

Trapped between a court presupposing sexual precocity and immorality, and the 'moral' shame of a former owner and father figure, what hope is there for this child rape victim? The voice of justice—in this case, Mr Justice Hyde—suggests Drake might cut his losses, but the watchmaker's response shames the Supreme Court judge. Drake had torn 'her paper', her Jonesian contract; she is now free to be abandoned.

What of the Frenchman who had torn her flesh? According to the testimony of Kitty de Rozario, a Portuguese Eurasian, living in the same compound, Bouton crucially asked Mary: 'Are you a maid?' Thinking he meant was she a servant, she had answered no, perhaps proud that Drake treated her as a daughter, unlike the 'two lesser' servant girls. Bouton had the linguistic cunning to dupe his victim, providing himself with a potential exculpation, but the English of the artless Kitty was gravely limited. Despite her claim that the prison chowkeydar had heard Bouton boasting about deflowering the child, her testimony was disregarded. De Rozario made this inevitable as soon as she opened her mouth; her unsolicited denial that she was a prostitute implied the opposite:

> I am about sixteen years old. I do not know whether I am eighteen. I know that girl. I know that Prisoner about four months ago. He came to dine at a French Man's house, I do not know that French Man's name. I knew him two months. He never gave me any money.

The paedophile rapist Bouton was acquitted; we may only surmise what happened to Mary. Life was one of the few things that was cheap in Calcutta. In many respects this case typifies—even symbolizes—the tragic violence of colonialism.

---

16. Kolkata, Victoria Memorial Hall, Hyde Reports, vol. 13, reel 5: 12 December 1793.

A significant step was made towards ending the East Indian slave trade by a case heard on 27 July 1789: *The king against Peter Horrebow for Manstealing or Kidnapping*. The indictment states that Horrebow 'assaulted, carried away and transported four women named Dooly, Nooseinee, Newgee, and Mary in a certain ship called *The Friendship* lying in the Hoogly. And also of abducting male and female children.' The scale of the operation is revealed in the testimony of Jacob Hollanson, second mate. Horrebow sent him to Chandernagar to purchase slaves: 'I think there were 130 of them, of different ages from 8 years of age to upwards of 20', they were 'black with long hair [. . .] not like Negroes'.[17] They were brought downriver in a pinnace-budgerow, and transferred at Fultah to *The Friendship*, which set sail for Mauritius. Hollanson insisted the slaves 'slept between decks, not in the hold' and were given curry and clothes, but several grew sick so Captain Horrebow changed course for Ceylon: 'I cannot say exactly but I believe upwards of 20 died in the passage.'

Under cross-examination Hollanson was encouraged by defence counsel to stress Horrebow was born in Copenhagen, Chandernagar was a French settlement and Fultah, a Dutch settlement, in an unsuccessful attempt to place their client beyond the court's jurisdiction. Chambers's summing-up referred to Islamic prohibitions upon the sale of slaves; he stated: 'it was the first time such an offence had been committed under the British Flag', and his hope it should prove the last.

Horrebow was convicted and sentenced to three months' imprisonment, a Rs 500 fine, a bond of Rs 10,000, and two Rs 500 sureties of future good behaviour. Jones recommended a harsher exemplary sentence, but was overruled by Chambers and Hyde. As a result of Horrebow's petition to Governor-General Cornwallis, claiming: 'I had not an idea that it was illegal, being myself well acquainted with Merchants of the finest credit in England who openly and avowedly carry on a similar Traffick on the coast of Africa', Jones was contacted by his two brother-judges, desiring mitigation of the sentence. They saw that Horrebow had a point, for Cornwallis actually published his 'Proclamation against the Slave Trade' in the *Calcutta Gazette* on the very day the trial began. Jones's reply from Krishnagar reveals an ambivalent mixture of professional politeness and forensic rigour, a readiness to acquiesce, yet 'doubt[ing] whether it can legally be done':

---

17. Kolkata, Victoria Memorial Hall, Hyde Reports, vol. 26, reel 11.

'I confess I have no compassion for him; my compassion is for the enslaved children and their parents' (*Letters*, 2: 845).

Jones was wrongly informed that Horrebow's health was not likely to be affected by imprisonment; he died in gaol. But the settlement looked after its own celebrities. Sophia, Horrebow's wife, a much-fêted young actress on the Calcutta stage, of whom the *India Gazette*'s drama critic enthused: 'She looked as charming as she performed, and *that* is *saying much*' (22 March 1790), was the sister of a darling of Drury Lane, Anna Maria Crouch. According to John Wade, Jones's surgeon friend, 'Mrs Horrebow condescended to appear on the Stage & to accept a benefit of about £1,500 sterling', which allowed her to return home in 1791.[18]

Though the slaver's wife fared far better than the freed slave Mary, Jones had been instrumental in the abolition of the Bengal slave trade almost two decades before the 1807 act outlawed the trade throughout the British Empire. Yet Jones's friend, Hājī Mustafā, claims that British attempts to subdue the trade 'caused in the years 1787, 88, and 89, the death of three hundred thousand boys and girls that have died of famine in Bengal'.[19] The 1790 decision of the Court of Directors to commend Cornwallis and his council for Horrebow's conviction boosted the abolitionist movement in the metropolis. In some respects India was showing the way, but profits from the trafficking and labour of slaves remained a global blot upon British commerce and empire long after its ostensible abolition.

A murder trial that came on a few months later revealed the atrocious way in which servants might be treated, sullying the reputation of the Supreme Court. On 10 December 1789, the indictment was of 'William Townsend Jones, Gent. for Murder of Sheriut Ullah with a horsewhip'. This gentleman was a Supreme Court barrister. Sheriut was not actually employed by the prisoner, he had been staying with his brother, Wahadar, Townsend Jones's *durwān* (gate-porter). Suspecting Sheriut of stealing one of his dogs, an unlikely crime for a Muslim, the barrister called for a *chambuck* and flogged Sheriut, who was 'rolling about' in pain. When the terrified Wahadar returned with some water, he found Sheriut dead.

The *Calcutta Gazette* condemned: 'the custom of flogging servants under any provocation as highly dangerous and repugnant to the feelings of a

---

18. BL, APAC, Fowke MSS, Eur E8, 72, J. P. Wade to F. Fowke [n.d.].
19. *Some Idea of the Civil & Criminal Courts of Justice at Moorshoodabad, in a Letter to Capt. John Hawkshaw, at Behrampore, of the 30th May 1789* (Calcutta, 1789), 35.

gentleman', but referred to depositions read in court, 'which tended to prove the innocence of Mr Jones'. Key evidence was provided by defence witness Thomas Martin, a surgeon. Opening the body, he dropped the stomach contents into water, discovering 'a black substance at the bottom of the vessel, from its appearance & smell I was convinced it was opium'. Martin convinced the jury that Sheriut had committed suicide, referring to a similar case encountered when surgeon to the 28th Battalion of Sepahies at Chunar. Captain Lambert had given 'a trivial flogging' to his cook: 'The man being of a peculiar cast, felt himself so degraded that he ate opium in the presence of his wife.'[20]

'What happy wretches the natives are!' Frances Parks later exclaims in describing the enviable lot of a *durwān* on his five rupees a month.[21] And how peculiar to feel such shame at receiving a trivial flogging—administering a severe horsewhipping did not degrade Townsend Jones; he was acquitted and continued to practise in the Supreme Court.

Of course, a native might make a happier choice of employer, and a petty larceny case heard only two days after that grim murder trial provides some welcome relief. In *Rex* v. *Bakhtyar, and Saheb Ram*, indicted for theft of a chubdar stick (staff overlaid with silver), we have a fascinating glimpse into the lives of a judge's retinue. The first witness is Ragonaut Chubdar, who testifies:

> I am Sir William Jones's Chubdar (staff-bearer). I had in my custody the Chubdar stick and was responsible for the care of it. I went to the Phousdarry [criminal court for minor offences] in the Laul Bazar. I returned to this house and when Sir William Jones gave me leave to go home which was about eleven o'clock at night, I went home. After eating my supper, I went to sleep at my house which is nigh Tiretta's Bazar in Calcutta. I laid the stick by me. About four or five Bengal gurries, [*ghari*, an hour measured by water clock] before day light I waked and the stick was not there. I am sure I laid it there when I went to sleep. On missing the stick I made an outcry and the Chokydars came. I said my stick is stolen. I found the rope with which my door had been tied was cut.

Having failed to see Thomas Motte, Superintendent of Police, 'he was not well', and police commissioner Edward Maxwell, 'he was asleep', Ragonaut returned to tell Sir William Jones of the theft: 'He bid me inquire and find

---

20. Kolkata, Victoria Memorial Hall, Hyde Reports, vol. 27, reel 11.
21. *Wanderings of a Pilgrim in Search of the Picturesque*, 2 vols (London, 1850), 1: 142.

out who has stolen my stick that the thief might be punished.' Ragonaut followed these instructions to the letter. His suspicion fell upon Bakhtyar, 'a Peon (footman) in the House of Sir Wm. Jones', who had departed without receiving his wages. With the help of Cumloo, another of Jones's *peons*, he learned that Bakhtyar had gone to Murshidabad from where he returned 'finely dressed'.

The next witness was Ragonaut's friend, Sooroup Singh, Soontabardar (staff-bearer) of Sir Robert Chambers. Sooroup had spoken to witnesses who heard a drunken Bakhtyar admit to stealing 'three silver sticks from Sir William Jones' and delivering them to Saheb Ram, 'a Gold Smith belonging to the Mint, who had melted and sold them'. Ragonaut and Sooroup are no Dogberry and Verges; they are conscientious servants and their do-it-yourself investigations, relying upon local knowledge and a sophisticated web of contacts, led to the criminals' arrest.

Unfortunately, the evidence having literally melted away, both the accused were found not guilty. At this distance it is fascinating to hear, albeit via court interpreters, the subaltern voices of ordinary Indian men and women, Hindu and Muslim; the details of their interconnected lives emerge from their testimony to give a precious flavour of what is so rarely recorded in the pages of history. The time devoted to this cause might appear to reflect its importance as involving Justice Jones's property. But the same meticulous attention to detail, carefully recorded by the judges in turn, is reflected in trivial cases of petty larceny brought by Indian inhabitants of Calcutta, such as the theft of a chest with two brass hookahs, 'value ten pence', or of a pair of gold earrings.

The reports and notebooks of Jones, Hyde, and Chambers await the detailed attention of legal and social historians for the intriguing light they throw upon the complex melting pot that was the colonial capital. The enormous range of causes, in the court's performance of its civil, equity, criminal, admiralty, and ecclesiastical jurisdiction; the bewildering variety of nationalities and languages, reflecting the global nature of Company trade, and requiring accurate translation—a witness, Caesar de Rosario, states: 'I understand Bengally better than Portuguese'; of court procedures requiring the legal opinions of maulavis and pandits; oaths sworn upon Ganges water, the Koran, the Bible, or by Parsees 'oblating the Sun, the four Elements & the Supreme God'; all demanded an extraordinary level of legal expertise from court barristers as much as judges. Jones's years on the Carmarthen circuit, with its wide jurisdiction and bilingual procedures, made him an ideally versatile judge. And in complex cases concerning property and inheritance, his profound knowledge of both Islamic and Hindu law proved invaluable.

A link with another of Jones's metropolitan legal specialisms is his prominence in Calcutta cases of wrongful imprisonment. His judgement in *George Tyler* v. *Fred. Deatker and Henrik Deatker*, which David Ibbetson describes as 'probably his most celebrated constitutional case', was actually much embroidered in *The Memoirs of William Hickey*.[22] Hickey was a dissolute deputy sheriff of Calcutta, with an extensive practice as Supreme Court attorney; George Tyler, a wealthy rice merchant, was his friend. In Hickey's account, Tyler had been dining with Captain Daniel Fitzgerald Griffin of the Madras native cavalry, when constables Frederick and Hendrik Deatker, 'attended by at least a dozen dirty black fellows, burst violently into the room', to serve a writ upon a Mr Barnet, for whom they started to search the house. Griffin drew his sword, while Tyler sent a servant to summon his attorney Hickey, who on arrival abused the constables. Subsequently, the Deatkers obtained an arrest warrant for breach of the peace from Justice Hyde, and, according to the indictment, Tyler and Griffin were 'dragged through the streets under military guard to prison', where they were detained for four hours.

The trial opened on 13 April 1786, and Griffin's barrister James Dunkin attempted to woo the jury with high-octane zenophobia: '[I]t is a great and alarming grievance that a Constable who is not a British Subject [Deatker was a Dane] but an outcast of some foreign settlement should have Sepahies at his command to arrest British subjects & English gentlemen.' Dunkin further argued that the statute enabling judges to act as magistrates did not extend to Calcutta. Chambers and Hyde, aware of Jones's relevant experience, ordered an adjournment, so that key legal points 'might be argued a second time when Sir Wm Jones should be present'.

Jones gives his opinions in a letter to Chambers: 'First, I strongly incline to think that the Stat. 24 Geo. II. Ch. 44 extends to this country & that we *are Justices of the Peace* within the meaning of it.' Jones considers that Deatker failed to 'execute the warrant literally'; Griffin should have only been kept in custody if Deatker had obtained a detaining order from the justice. 'This was not done: the motive was bad; no law justifies the act', wrote Jones,

---

22. David Ibbetson, 'Sir William Jones as a Constitutional Lawyer', in *Sir William Jones, 1746–94, A Commemoration*, ed. Alexander Murray (Oxford, 1998), 19–42; 24.

convinced that the imprisonment was illegal, and consequently that judgement should be for the plaintiff, 'but the damages should not be large'.[23]

At the end of the trial, Jones gave his observations first, stressing the improper execution of the warrant, but he was overruled by the casting vote of Chief Justice Chambers, who pronounced judgement for the defendants, the Deatkers. So much is recorded in the judges' notes and the Calcutta press.

Hickey's *Memoirs* transform Jones's summing up into a two-hour harangue 'in the most pointed, elegant and nervous language' excoriating the 'magnitude and atrocity' of the defendants' offence. It was, according to Hickey's ventriloquism of Jones: 'a case of greater enormity, of more gross, wanton and outrageous oppression than had ever come to his knowledge as having occurred within the British Dominions'.[24] Thus and much more from Hickey's Jones, whose 'blood boiled' at such arbitrary tyranny. Rewriting judicial history and his client's defeat, Hickey awards himself an absurdly audacious role, announcing loudly to Chambers in open court: 'You are a contemptible animal!'

It is fascinating that Hickey should enlist this ostensibly credible representation of Jones, who is actually made to announce 'that throughout his public life he had been a strenuous advocate for the rights of Britons and the liberty of the subject', for his own self-serving ends. Had Hickey been a better lawyer, he would have noted what Thomas Curley shrewdly does, that both Jones and Chambers avoided reference to 'the illegality of the arrest warrant itself'.[25] In that Hyde named only Tyler, Griffin should not have been arrested; as Jones realized: 'Offender must be named; description will not do.' In effect Hyde's warrant had been used as a general warrant; the illegality of which Jones had frequently argued in impressment cases.

While Hickey and his cronies were drinking the health of Sir William Jones 'three times three', did the subject of their toasts entertain any scrupulous second thoughts about his complicity in repressing a material fact to protect his colleague, the steadfast John Hyde? Jones often refers to the 'dark and undefined' powers of police officers in Calcutta, and the evidence of his own legal notebooks reveals minute examination of this and similar causes.[26]

---

23. Kolkata, Victoria Memorial Hall, Hyde Reports, vol. 15, reel 7.
24. *Memoirs of William Hickey*, ed. A. Spencer, 4 vols (London, 1913–25), 3: 247–60; 253.
25. Thomas M. Curley, *Sir Robert Chambers: Law, Literature and Empire in the Age of Johnson* (Madison, 1998), 506.
26. NLW, MS 5467D, Notes on Legal Cases; BL Add MSS 8885, notes of legal cases argued in Bengal.

Jones was also concerned with illegal use of police powers against the Indian population. In *Kissenpersand Tagore* v. *Edward Maxwell & Thomas Motte*, the plaintiff, from a respected Calcutta family, sought damages for 'Assault, Battery & false imprisonment'. Attacked by a drunk named Imam Baksh in the Muchy Bazaar, Tagore was accused of causing the brawl and dragged to Motte's office, where he 'received 20 strokes with a rattan'. On 2 December 1785, judgement was given for Tagore, but there was disagreement concerning the level of damages, 'assessed at 2000 SR by the opinions of Chambers and Hyde, Justice Jones being of opinion that 5000 SR ought to have been given'. Jones was appalled that Police Commissioner Maxwell, on ordering the caning, remarked: 'no B—Shaster will do Justice'. Jones recorded his ruling:

> I said (inter alia), the justice of punishing a beating by a beating has been generally admitted in Bengal & I believe most men, whether Europeans or natives, who have resided long in Calcutta will admit the necessity of some power by which petty offences may be tried in a very summary way & punished by fine, or for inability to pay a fine by whipping. But I agree that no such power resides in the Defendants and I am further of opinion that if they had such power they would abuse it by inflicting such a punishment as leaves an indelible mark, perhaps in any case but certainly in such a case as this.[27]

Jones's approval of whipping, following due legal process, for trivial crimes, reflects the difficulty of devising effective secondary punishments in a climate where lengthy imprisonment, particularly for a European, often proved a capital sentence. At the Old Bailey, the punishment of whipping, either public or private, was frequently accompanied by a substantial prison term, but generally in Calcutta corporal punishment was followed by release, or a short gaol-term. The judges agreed 'the Legislature in England should make an Act declaring what offences should be capital and how other offences should be punished'. In the absence of legislation, punishment—for natives and colonists alike—tended to be more lenient than in the metropolis. Designed to be exemplary and shaming, there was a judicial scale of beatings, according to the gravity of the crime, administered by slipper, or rattan, up to a maximum of twenty strokes. For example, Aumen Mahomet, Tannadar (police station chief) convicted of 'debauching a slave girl who had run away from her mistress and was entrusted to his

---

27. Kolkata, Victoria Memorial Hall, Hyde Reports, vol. 12, reel 6: 2 December 1785.

care' was sentenced to be given '20 Rattans, be drumm'd round the town and his crimes published by beat of Tom Tom; then to be turned out of the Service'.

Jones detested sanguinary sentencing in Britain, and approved 'that Chambers scruples the conviction of any man capitally for any crime except murder'. Chambers was junior judge to Impey at the 1775 forgery trial of Hastings's political enemy, the Brahman Nandakumar, who was subsequently hanged, and he retained doubts about the wisdom 'of punishing Forgery with Death in this country'. Jones agreed, and also ruled that 'the death sentence for stealing out of a dwelling house (unaccompanied with actual violence) did not extend to this Country'. Jones further argued against the imprisonment of bankrupts in Bengal: 'The Law takes from the Bankrupt all his Property: it would be inhuman if the Law after that should permit the Creditor to confine his person.'[28] He was horrified at the 'old *Hindu*', and current Islamic, practice of amputation to punish the offending part but, such was Jones's detestation of perjury, he thought perjurers should have '*both ears nailed to the pillory*'. Happily, this Elizabethan punishment was never inflicted in the Calcutta pillory at the north end of the Cossitollah Bazaar.

Jones's suggestion was not the most enlightened idea of 'the most enlightened of the sons of men', as Johnson described him. Yet it was the frequency of this crime, in a city where poverty enabled affidavits to be purchased in its marketplaces, that determined Jones to improve his Bengali and Urdu, and learn Sanskrit in order to deal with unscrupulous pandits who make Hindu law 'at reasonable rates, when they cannot find it ready made' (*Letters*, 2: 684). So eradication of perjury led to enlightenment, and Jones's discovery of ancient Indian acknowledgment of the sovereignty of law. In a courtroom break, Jones copies out a sentence from the *Yajurvéda* (1500–1200 BCE): 'Then God produced Law, and Law is the king of kings, by whose help the weak are made strong', adding his own comparative reflection: 'Montesquieu was abused in Europe for a sentiment, which occurs in the oldest book of a country governed immemorially by despotism.'[29]

If ancient Indian enlightenment compared well with its modern European counterpart, the notion of continuity also reinforced Jones's sense that he was right to concentrate his legal codification upon the *Mānavadharmaśāstra*.

---

28. Kolkata, Victoria Memorial Hall, Hyde Papers, vol. 5, reel 3; no. 7, reel 3, 16 March 1785.
29. Kolkata, Victoria Memorial Hall, Hyde Reports, vol. 39, reel 15, 12 March 1793.

This indigenous system of jurisprudence possessed great prestige amongst all Hindus and was respected by Muslim rulers. Jones's focus upon such high culture law was at the expense of the diverse customary law of the villages, but, like Hastings, he was attempting to arrive at what was universal and authoritative. Crucially, on the bench, Jones's knowledge of the *Dharmaśāstra* helped him make the weak strong.

This was exemplified in *Kissnochurn Mullick against Ramnarain Mullick*, a cause involving a younger brother who, with his wife, had been driven from the family home by his elder brother in an attempt to engross their father's estate. On learning that their mother Tillukshuma was still alive, Jones, having quoted from his friend Halhed's *Code of Gentoo Laws*, read his own translation of the original text: 'After the civil or religious death of the father although the sons have an absolute right to his property, yet, while their mother lives, it is *illegal* for them to divide that property.'[30]

Many Calcutta causes enable us to compare the patriarchal nature of Oriental and Occidental cultures and law systems. A good example is provided by *Sree Ooday Cower against Mohun Lall Bussey*, heard on 1 December 1790. This action was taken by Ooday Cower against her husband to enforce a gift to her of land, following a marital quarrel occasioned by Bussey's taking a second wife, because Ooday had not brought him male issue. Leaving aside the question of bigamy, such an action was not possible in England where, as Blackstone makes clear, husband and wife 'are one person in law, so that the very being and existence of the woman is suspended during the coverture, or entirely merged or incorporated in that of the husband'. The case was submitted to the pandits who agreed that the *Dharmaśāstra* supported the wife's right to recover her property. This is the beginning of Govardhana Kaula's opinion:

> I adore the Supreme!
>
> Whatever property a man that has married two wives has given to the first wife by means of a Paper witnessed, in order to satisfy her in all respects, such Property, termed *Adhivedanikam*, i.e. given by one who marries another wife, is the Property of the Wife.
>
> In order to recover such property of Females as is called *Adhivedanikam*, the Wife may sue the Husband (according to what the *Dherem Shaster* directs) in like manner as when a debt is recovered.[31]

---

30. Kolkata, Victoria Memorial Hall, Hyde Reports, vol. 21, reel 9, 26 November 1788.
31. Kolkata, Victoria Memorial Hall, Hyde Reports, vol.. 30, reel 12.

Justice Jones having concurred with their reading of the relevant texts, the court was unanimous in giving judgement for the plaintiff. Ooday was no *feme covert*; though supplanted in her husband's affections, she had rights—anciently prescribed her—which no Englishwoman possessed.

Jones had been working on the rights of women according to both the Mitākṣarā and the Dāyabhāga schools of Hindu law and, with the help of his respected pundit Jagannātha Tarkapañcānana, was attempting to integrate them into his Digest. It is true that Jones imported English modes of thought and procedure, but such importations were necessary for the effective application of a universal Indian law, interpreted alike by native and English judges.

Many modern cultural historians are busily (re)discovering what was well known to Jones: Rosalind O'Hanlon and David Washbrook, for example, find that 'principles of individualism, notions of contract, private property rights and commercial rationalism' were concepts by no means alien to an India in transition to colonial rule.[32] A cursory consideration of Manu or the Muslim laws of inheritance translated by Jones would have confirmed this finding. Indeed, even the playwright Kālidāsa, in complimenting justice under Gupta rule, reveals, in *Sacontalá*, Raja Dushmanta considering the cause of the title to the property of a merchant 'Dhanavriddhi, who had an extensive commerce at sea', lost in a shipwreck:

> *Dushm.* Whether he had or had not offspring, the estate should not have been forfeited.—Let it be proclaimed, that whatever kinsman any one of my subjects lose, Dushmanta (excepting always the case of forfeiture for crimes) will supply, in tender affection, the place of that kinsman. (*SWJ*, p. 282)

The emphasis Jones placed upon inheritance, contracts, disputed accounts, and debts was at the centre of his vision of establishing property rights, 'both real and personal'. This not only reflected the Company's commercial concerns, but his everyday courtroom experience of contract and litigation, which were functions of the dynamic and sophisticated commercialism of the natives of Calcutta.

Jones deployed a discourse, drawing analogies between British and eastern Roman imperial codification of law, which cast him in the role of

---

32. See Rosalind O'Hanlon and David Washbrook, 'Histories in Transition: Approaches to the Study of Colonialism and Culture in India', *History Workshop Journal*, 32 (1991), 110–27; 116.

Tribonian to Cornwallis's Justinian. This was also the popular metropolitan view, the two men being seen as something of a dream duo:

> With such a Governor General as Lord Cornwallis, reinforced by the wholesome authority of the newly amended act of Parliament, and with such a law chief as Sir William Jones, what should there be in reason to check the most thriving expectations of our Asiatick concerns? (*Public Advertiser*, 27 March 1786)

In reality Cornwallis found Jones intimidating; military logistics were more to his taste than scholarly logic. Their relations were cordial but guarded. Years later at dinner with Pitt and Wilberforce, Cornwallis talked of 'the happiness we diffused [in India], and the equity of our government'; he 'gave great praise to [George] Barlow. Afraid of Sir William Jones; and always found him much to do, and took him into his council; where otherwise he might have thwarted.'[33] Cornwallis might well have been recalling the occasion when Barlow, founder-member of the Asiatick Society, and secretary to the Revenue Department, submitted to Jones the first draft of the permanent settlement of the land revenues of Bengal in 1793. Jones drew his pen through the first three words of Barlow's opening sentence, which had run: 'The two principal objects which the government ought to have in view, in all its arrangements, are, to insure its political safety, and to render the possession of the country as advantageous as possible to the East India Company and the British nation.' Jones added in the margin: 'Surely the *principal object* of every Government is the happiness of the governed.'[34]

It was a telling emendation. Jones favoured the permanent settlement's attempt to safeguard the rights of both *zemindars* (land-holders) and peasants, but Barlow's opening emphases upon political security and pecuniary advantage betrayed Cornwallis's chief imperatives. The need for Jones's correction was recalled following the 1857 Sepoy Revolt as revealing the self-interest of the Company's administration.[35] The contrast Francis Gladwin discerns between two governors-general: 'Under your [Hasting's] patronage, oriental learning was cultivated with success, but his Lordship, despising every branch of Science, there is not the smallest encouragement for publication so that my literary labours have also ceased to be of any

---

33. Robert and Samuel Wilberforce, *The Life of William Wilberforce*, 5 vols (London, 1839), 3: 49.
34. Kaye, *The Administration of the East India Company*, 1.
35. 'Some Moral Causes of the Indian Rebellion', *The Evangelical Repository*, 4 (June 1858), 277–86; 281.

value', similarly throws light upon the differences between Cornwallis and Jones.[36]

While Cornwallis remained contemptuous of Indians, unshakeable in his belief that every native was corrupt, Jones was busily salting away his salary, transmitting it to England by means of Company China bills. Jones preferred the moral high ground, but he was not exclusively concerned with the natives' pursuit of happiness: his own happiness involved working with indigenous scholars. As he continued to arrange Sanskrit texts 'in a scientific method' to establish the universality and impersonality of law on a western model, collaboration with his teams of pandits and maulavis was always a labour of love. His love of India enabled him to see that the river of Indian law was fed—like Gaṅgā Mā herself—by many tributaries.

With Jones's self-representation as a modern Tribonian in mind, it is fascinating to consider the picture of the 'celebrated Orientalist' by a young 'griffin', newly arrived with 'a very favourable introduction from Samuel Parr'. The 17-year-old Thomas Twining was invited—not to tea—but to dinner at no. 8, Garden Reach:

> Sir William was very cheerful and agreeable. He made some observations on certain mysterious words of the Hindoos and other Indian subjects. While sitting after dinner he suddenly called out with a loud voice 'Othello, Othello'. His particularly fine voice, his white Indian dress surmounted by a small black wig, his cheerfulness and great celebrity rendered the scene extremely interesting. I was surprised that no one—Mussulman or Hindoo—answered his call. At last I saw a black *turtle* of very large size, crawling slowly towards us from an adjoining room. It made its way to the side of Sir William's chair, where it remained, he giving it something which it seemed to like. Sir William observed that he was fond of birds, but had little pleasure in hearing or seeing them unless they were at liberty; and he, no doubt, would have liberated Othello, if he had not considered that he would be safer by the side of his table than in the Ganges.[37]

Jones's pet reminds us of how Reginald Heber, bishop of Calcutta and husband of Amelia Shipley, Anna Maria's niece, later earned a reputation for griffinism by feasting on the 'extremely sweet' turtles hauled from the Ganges where they had been feeding on floating corpses. If Othello was not dressed for dinner, its master was wearing comfortable Indian dress, the neat

---

36. BL Add MSS 29,172, f. 48, Gladwin to Hastings, 15 Feb. 1790.
37. *Selections from Papers of the Twining Family*, ed. Richard Twining (London, 1887), 305.

wig indicating he had not gone completely native, like Colonel Charles 'Hindoo' Stuart, who bathed in the Hugli every morning, performing *puja* to Śiva. Twining was influenced by meeting Jones; he later joined Colonel Stuart and Hastings's agent, Major John Scott-Waring, in asserting that India had no need of Christian missionaries. The Joneses' proselytism extended only to advocacy of a temperate Hindu regimen, to cold bathing, and the relaxing head-massage known as shampooing.

Twining was shown the Joneses' pastoral farm where 'our flocks and herds eat bread out of our hands' and Anna Maria outshone 'shepherdess' Marie Antoinette as the genteel *gopi* of Ariśnagar. Their friend and financial agent, Richard Johnson, deputy Resident at Lucknow, had sent them a consignment of goats.

> There never, I hope, was a *Gwilym ap Shôn* (Anglicè William Jones) who had not a love of goats, his brother-mountaineers, but I have an additional reason for valuing those now sent—They come from you. I will send them instantly to my farm. I would thank you this evening in person, but must go at sunset to the gardens where Lady Jones now is. My evenings are not at my disposal; and I dare not dine out. Have the charity when you can to eat blazing mince-pies & roast beef with Dear Sir, ever faithfully yours, W. Jones.[38]

Their consumption of beef and pork necessitated extra ritual ablutions for Hindu and Muslim servants, but their respect for life was encapsulated in a couplet of Firdausī, quoted by Sa'dī: 'Ah! spare yon emmet, rich in hoarded grain:/He lives with pleasure, and he dies with pain' (*Works*, 3: 221). Hastings took this to heart; back in England he assiduously attempted to avoid crushing ants in his Daylesford garden walks. Jones cites this couplet when surveying natural history in his 'Tenth Anniversary Discourse' (1793). Though insisting it was not 'a boast of peculiar sensibility', he would never allow 'the *Cocila*, whose *wild native woodnotes* announce the approach of spring, to be caught in my garden for the sake of comparing it with BUFFON's description'. When a young pangolin was brought to him from the mountains, 'I solicited his restoration to his beloved rocks, because I found it impossible to preserve him in comfort at a distance from them.'

Such imaginative sympathy, however ecological, was unlikely to advance comparative anatomy or zoology. Jones despaired that scientific examination of creatures involved their pain: 'I never could learn by what right, nor

---

38. NLW, MS 12857C.

conceive with what feelings, a naturalist can occasion the misery of an innocent bird and leave its young, perhaps, to perish in a cold nest, because it has gay plumage and has never been accurately delineated, or deprive even a butterfly of its natural enjoyments, because it has the misfortune to be rare or beautiful.' Ten years earlier he had captured the plight of such fledglings in a translation of an Arabic poem he dedicated to Anna:

> While sad suspense and chill delay
> Bereave my wounded soul of rest,
> New hopes, new fears, from day to day,
> By turns assail my lab'ring breast.
>
> My heart, which ardent love consumes,
> Throbs with each agonizing thought;
> So flutters with entangled plumes
> The lark in wily meshes caught.
>
> There she, with unavailing strain,
> Pours thro' the night her warbled grief:
> The gloom retires, but not her pain;
> The dawn appears, but not relief.
>
> Two younglings wait the parent bird
> Their thrilling sorrows to appease:
> She comes—ah! no: the sound they heard
> Was but a whisper of the breeze.   (*Works*, 1: 407–8)

In their childless marriage a positively parental love was lavished upon pets such as Jones's slender loris, 'my little favourite, who engaged my affection, while he lived, and whose memory I wish to perpetuate'. His 'On the Loris, or Slow-paced Lemur' did so, correcting the Comte de Buffon's inexact description, and providing accurate accounts of its habits and distribution. Yet its personal touches make more impact: '[T]o me, who not only constantly fed him, but bathed him twice a week in water accommodated to the seasons, and whom he clearly distinguished from others, he was at all times grateful.' What Twining witnessed was a new Jonesian dispensation of universal justice, out of the Orientalist's favourite Isaiah, where 'the leopard shall lie down with the kid': 'Lady J. is pretty well; a tiger about a month old, who is suckled by a goat, and has all the gentleness of his foster-mother, is now playing at her feet' (*Letters*, 2: 785).

Jones in his golden-age idyll, like the legendary raja, Chinna Govinda, had achieved the wondrous power of feeding tigers and sheep in the same fold. How different he appears from the young barrister of Lamb's Buildings who urged room-mate Thomas Day to kill a spider emerging from behind some books. Day famously responded:

> 'No, I will not kill that spider, Jones; I do not know that I have a right to kill that spider: suppose when you are going in your coach to Westminster Hall, a superior being, who, perhaps, may have as much power over you as you have over that insect, should say to his companion, "Kill that lawyer! kill that lawyer!" how should you like that, Jones? and I am sure, to most people, a lawyer is a much more noxious animal than this poor spider.'[39]

This lesson on relativity and his own lawyerly noxiousness from the Rousseauistic Day was only partially learned. It is certainly untrue to claim, with Arberry, that Jones 'abhorred blood sports of every kind'.[40] When Spencer communicates his passion for hunting, Jones makes nice distinctions. While he finds: 'Hunting *foxes* and shooting *noxious* birds are rational exercises', he abhors 'making *innocent* beasts miserable and mangling *harmless* birds'. Jones weighs in the element of comparative danger: 'After all, you English hunters must not imagine, that you rival us hunters of wild boars and tigers in India; nor is our exercise to be compared with the manly and military sport of lion-hunting in Africa' (*Letters*, 2: 750).

Despite his reference to 'us hunters', no evidence survives of his pig-sticking, or indulgence in the Mughal sport of tiger-hunting. The opening of a letter from Sir John Day, featuring a detailed account of a tiger-hunt: 'Although you could not partake of the pleasure, I am resolved that you shall not entirely escape the fatigue of our enterprize', might imply that such pleasure was not unknown to Jones. Day lightly dismisses the danger to his wife, Benedicta, when a tiger leapt on the flank of her elephant. With five tigers shot, Day's sympathies are aroused by the 'piteous spectacle' of a woman whose family had been carried off by the man-eaters: 'in a wild scream she demanded her husband and her children from the tigers'.[41] Such far from uncommon incidents would enable Jones, whose tiger cub was named Jupiter, to label tigers as 'noxious' creatures to be rationally controlled. It is, however, something of a surprise to discover the presence of our flower-collecting couple at a 'sport' reminiscent of imperial Roman decadence.

---

39. *The Leeds Mercury*, 6 October 1821.
40. A. J. Arberry, *Asiatic Jones* (London, 1946), 24. See also *Letters*, 1: 251–2.
41. BL, APAC, Eur E5, 77, [Sir] J[ohn] D[ay] to Sir W. J. Chinsura, 22 April 1784.

On the invitation of Charles Croftes, former accountant-general and business partner of Hastings, the Joneses travelled to Chittagong in early February 1786. Delighted with 'this Indian Montpelier, where the hillocks are covered with pepper vines, and sparkle with the blossoms of the coffee tree', they purchased a hilltop villa at Jafferabad, with a superb sea view, backed by a magnificent mountain range. Writing to Samuel Davis, Jones thought the scene 'sublime enough to be worthy of your pencil'. They had discovered another Arcadia to rival Krishnagar; their walks were scented with blossoms of the champac and the nágacésar and, on the 4 March, the smell of hot blood. Croftes invited them to a wooden circus compound, complete with viewing room, from which they watched a fight between a buffalo and a tiger.

Jones supplies no description of the amusement but, from contemporary accounts of this popular contest, the size and strength of the Indian buffalo makes more than a match for the royal tiger. Frequently reluctant to fight, the tiger was goaded with firebrands and boiling water, and the buffalo

14. Anna Maria Jones, Drawings: a) 'Fight between Buffalo and tiger', 4 March 1785

14. Continued b) 'Pandit Ramalochan', 15 Oct. 1785

14. **Continued** c) 'Ch'hātiyāna / Septaparna, or Seven-leaved', pen-and-ink and watercolour. (Royal Asiatic Society)

infuriated with powerful infusions of capsicums and nettles. The buffalo's violent onslaught often crushed the tiger against the walls of the compound, as here at Rungmaul. We know the result because Anna provided an annotated drawing, with sketches of victorious buffalo and dying tiger. These incongruously survive amongst her botanical drawings, recording one of the Joneses' more bizarre leisure pursuits.

It is easy to see why he never mentioned an entertainment that treated with such contempt the wild tiger *vahana* (mount) of Durgā, whom Jones in his hymn to the goddess, depicted defeating Mahisa, the buffalo demon of death. Shortly Cornwallis would be battling in southern India with the defiant 'Tiger of Mysore', Tīpū Sultān, who had appropriated both Hindu and Islamic symbolism of the tiger's implacable fierceness. The Rungmaul spectators knew all about Tīpū, but might have recalled the Bengal tradition that whoever kills a *vyaghra-raja* (royal tiger) without respect will fall victim to one; indeed Croftes was dead within the year, though of a cerebral and not feline stroke. It seems incongruous to see Jones as a potential contributor to *Oriental Field Sports*, but it is easier to understand a moral lapse as evidence of common (in)humanity, than to comprehend what separates him from us: the vast scope of his intellect.

We can counterpoise the 'sportsman' with the veterinary Jones attempting to alleviate suffering: 'I gave one of such pills night and morning for a fortnight to a she-goat of mine, whose body was covered with sores and botches: she was torn to pieces by a jhackal; so my experiment proved only that the four grains of arsenick which she had taken in the fortnight, did her no harm; I thought, indeed, that she grew better.'[42] He is writing from Krishnagar to Dr James Anderson, president of the Madras Medical Board, whose experiments with native medicines, included analysis of 'Tanjore pills' containing arsenic, and said to cure those bitten by venomous snakes and rabid dogs. Jones had translated a paper by Ataher Ali Khan, son of Nadir Shah's physician, on the use of arsenic in the cure of elephantiasis, syphilis, and other blood disorders. Initially he suppressed publication, but learning that arsenic had been successfully prescribed in England for intermittent fevers, he printed it in the second volume of *Asiatick Researches*. In an introductory note, Jones advises that the crucial balance between therapeutic benefits and harmful side effects requires trialling 'under the inspection of our European surgeons'. Ancient Hindu medicine, transmitted by a Muslim doctor, subjected to collaborative research between colonial presidencies, given local trials and metropolitan analysis, might vindicate Indian chemistry and enrich western science.

Jones appreciated that for both colonizer and colonized, the treatment of tropical disease required tropical medicine. In praising Sūrya, hymned in the *Ṛg Veda* as the source of health and immortality, Jones acknowledges the sun's blazing power and beseeches a cure:

> And now, on lowly knee,
> From him, who gave the wound, the balsam prays.
> Herbs, that assuage the fever's pain,
> Scatter from thy rolling car,   ('A Hymn to Súrya', ll. 175–8; *SWJ*, p. 151)

Though the Indian glare was insufferable for eyes weakened by study, Jones seeks the living light of science, liberating medical learning from the abysm

---

42. London, Natural History Museum, Botany Library, 'Correspondance', MSS. Rox, Jones to James Anderson, Letter of 14 September 1789. I am grateful for the transcription of Pratik Chakrabarti. See his '"Neither of meate nor drinke, but what the Doctor alloweth": Medicine amidst War and Commerce in Eighteenth-Century Madras', *Bulletin of the History of Medicine*, 80: 1 (2006), 1–38.

of the past. And if the sun nurtured febrifugal medicinal herbs, it could also produce the welcome inundation of the monsoon. When even 'Ocean, smit with melting pain,/Shrinks' from the suffocating heat:

> Less can mild earth and her green daughters bear
> The noon's wide-wasting glare;
> To rocks the panther creeps; to woody night
> The vulture steals his flight;
> E'en cold chameleons pant in thickets dun,
> And o'er the burning grit th'unwinged locusts run!' (ll. 149–54)

'Behind the glowing wheels' of Sūrya's chariot, drawn by seven bright green mares, 'six jocund seasons dance', and the 'cloud-riding' thunder-god Indra with his torrential restoration of colour, fertility, and sensuality. Jones's love of the cyclical drama of the Indian seasons drew him to Kālidāsa's youthful work, the *Ritusamhāra*, a lyrical evocation of natural phenomena, instinct with the female power of *śakti*. The *Calcutta Gazette* of 29 March 1792 announced as 'just published' *The Seasons: a Descriptive Poem by Cálidás, in the original Sanscrit*. Jones's Advertisement explains the significance of the royal octavo volume:

> THIS book is the first ever printed in *Sanscrit*; and it is by the press alone, that the ancient literature of *India* can long be preserved: a learner of that most interesting language [. . .] could hardly begin his course of study with an easier or more elegant work, than the *Rĭtusanhára*, or *Assemblage of Seasons*. Every line composed by CÁLIDÁS is exquisitely polished; and every couplet in the poem exhibits an *Indian* landscape, always beautiful, sometimes highly coloured, but never beyond nature: four copies of it have been diligently collated; and where they differed, the clearest and most natural reading has constantly had the preference.

Another milestone of Sanskrit philology, the entire text was in Sanskrit, printed in Bengali characters on high-quality woven Whatman paper, as befitted a work of recuperation and preservation. From the Company's press, it was another text liberated from exclusive Brahmanical control and the depredations of bookworms and white ants. Jones's enlightened educational ideas link this publication with his *Persian Grammar* two decades earlier. It was an admirable choice; learning would be encouraged by delight for readers discovering the sensuality of Kālidāsa's imagery, as erotic relationships are affected by the changing seasons. Early spring vies with the rainy season as the time for love-making in Sanskrit poetry, but Kālidāsa shows nature in all her moods encouraging passion in a mingling of the divine, the human, and the environmental. In the *varṣa ritu* (monsoon season) huge dark clouds, heavy with rain, gleam like the blue-black petals of the *utpala* lotus, like globules of mascara, or like the darkened nipples on breasts of pregnant women, also swollen with life-giving nourishment (*Ritusamhāra*, 2: 2).

Without a translation, the poem's audience was limited, but Jones was not here nurturing a drawing-room readership. His edition was aimed at the Indian intelligentsia and those colonial and European scholars he urged to join him in spreading the light of Sanskrit literature. He sent a copy to Wilkins in Bath, requesting his 'acceptance of a little Sanscrit poem [...] which you are the only man in Europe who can read and understand' (*Letters*, 2: 914). It was a gift to India and the world, exemplifying his own self-description in 'A Hymn to Súrya':

> He came; and lisping our celestial tongue,
> Though not from *Brahmà* sprung,
> Draws orient knowledge from its fountains pure,
> Through caves obstructed long, and paths too long obscure.
>
> (ll. 184–7; *SWJ*, p. 152)

Throughout the years Jones had been in India, his once-close friend Burke had also been labouring to create imaginative sympathy for an obscure subcontinent and bring justice to its natives. To make India comprehensible was the common endeavour of these two literary lawyers. Burke, as Peter Marshall has argued, 'envisaged an empire not of administration but of justice'.[43] These were never alternatives for Jones who saw justice in an Orientalist administration founded upon understanding of indigenous cultures, languages, and traditions. 'I am', Burke wrote, 'as all members ought to be just now, on Hindu', as if he were, like future Romantic opium-eaters, addicted to a compulsive drug.[44] While Burke's meticulous study of Indian information cost him sleepless nights, Jones, after long hours on the bench, worked late on Sanskrit texts.

The imperial theatre of the impeachment was largely erected on the gothic monstrosity of Hastings's criminality: the sublime refinement of Indian language and culture was symbolized in *Śakuntalā*, the product of a much earlier imperial theatre. At Westminster Burke knew the difficulties

---

43. *The Writings and Speeches of Edmund Burke*, vol. 6 India: *The Launching of the Hastings Impeachment, 1786–88*, ed. P. J. Marshall (Oxford, 1991), 35.
44. *The Correspondence of Edmund Burke*, ed. Holden Furber (Cambridge, 1978), 5: 124.

of creating empathy for India 'whilst we look at this very remote object through a false and cloudy medium'.[45] At Krishnagar, in imagery linking the biblical and the scientific, Jones agreed: 'In Europe you see India through a glass darkly: here, we are in a strong light; and a thousand little *nuances* are perceptible to us, which are not visible through your best telescopes, and which could not be explained without writing volumes' (*Letters*, 2: 749).

Burke considered peninsular politics as the imperial and ethical challenge of his time but, obsessed as he was with colonial guilt, he failed to produce any nuanced reading of India. By contrast Jones's own poetic representations of India, though richly nuanced, are, perhaps, too little troubled by colonial anxiety or imperial guilt for modern postcolonial tastes. The contemporary opinion was voiced by John Aikin, the brother of Anna Laetitia Barbauld: 'As a poet, he would probably have risen to the first class, had his ardour for transplanting foreign beauties allowed him leisure for the exercise of his own invention.'[46] Anna Seward, addressing the spirits of the Asian poets, acknowledges their debt to 'Persian' Jones:

> The veils that hid you thro' the rounds of time
> From European eyes, are torn away,
> And all the fire of oriental rhyme
> Glows in our isle with undiminish'd ray.
>
> Spirits of eastern bards, where'er shall rove
> Your British guardian, from your musky vales,
> Sun-hallow'd hills, and each odorous grove,
> Bring the rich incense that perfumes your gales!
>
> O'er his young head the spicy treasures blend,
> And from your brightest gems a crown obtain!
> On him may all the tribute stores descend
> Who hung with Persian wreaths the Albion Muses' fane!   (ll. 21–32)[47]

John Parsons praised Jones's linguistic ability 'to woo the Asiatic Muses from the spicy groves of Arabia to the more chilly climate of Britain', but Romantic Orientalism was not the only beneficiary of his transcultural ardour. In south Asian terms it was his role in enabling India to represent herself that marked his most substantial achievement in accessing Oriental knowledge.

---

45. *Writings and Speeches of Edmund Burke*, 6: 390.
46. John Aikin, *General Biography*, 10 vols (London, 1799–1815), 5: 561.
47. 'Invocation to the Shade of Petrarch, and to the Spirits of the Persian Poets, on their Compositions being Translated into English by Sir William Jones', *The Poetical Works of Anna Seward*, ed. Walter Scott, 3 vols (Edinburgh, 1810), 1: 113–14.

***

On the 24 November 1793, at home at Ariśnagar, Anna Maria completed her 'Adieu to India':

> Alas!—fond Mem'ry sweeps the Vision past,
> '*For ever fled, like yonder sweeping Blast;*'
> Those hours of Bliss, those Scenes of soft Delight,
> Vanish like Mists before the Rays of Light;
> But still Remembrance holds the Objects dear,
> And bathes their *Shadows* with Regret's pure Tear;
> Nor shall th'oblivious Pow'r of TIME subdue,
> The painful Feelings of the last—ADIEU!

The same day Jones wrote to Spencer of preparations for the voyage and of financial arrangements; he calculated that they should have at least £50,000 by March 1795, 'if it shall please the Giver of Life to prolong mine till that time'. Ominously he also mentions that he suffered a two-day rheumatic fever at Bandel, a vacation resort for Calcutta residents. Jones named the octagonal house he rented here: the 'Temple of the Winds', but he paid insufficient respect to Vayu, god of the wind, or to his wife's advice: 'having heated myself in the evening by walking on a botanical excursion, I dressed myself on my return but not in so warm a coat, as Anna advised me wear, the wind from the river being very strong; the consequence of neglecting her advice was that I had an acute rheumatism when I went to bed' (*Letters*, 2: 923).

Until then they had been enjoying themselves with an excursion to the Kumbh Mela pilgrimage site at Prayag, known as Triveni Sangam, the '*tīrtharaj*' (king of holy places) at the confluence of three sacred rivers. The Celt in Jones understood the Hindu reverence for rivers, springs, and sources as points of access to the pervasive powers of the Otherworld, and the couple were delighted to locate 'the rivulet of *Saraswatī*' joining the Ganga and Yamuna, and at 'blest *Prayāga*'s point' to 'behold three mingling tides,/Where pilgrims on the far-sought bank drink nectar, as it glides' ('Hymn to Gangá', ll. 77–8; *SWJ*, p. 129).

Anna and William also visited the Triveni home of Jones's friend and colleague, Jagannātha Tarkapañcānana, 'eighty nine years old, a prodigy of learning, virtue, memory, and health'. They were introduced to three generations of his family, including fourteen great-grandsons, 'the eldest of whom is married, and his wife is in a fair way of producing a descendant from the old man in the fourth degree'. Jones had secured for this 'venerable

15. Sir William Jones, aged 47, by Arthur William Devis, oil on canvas, 1793. (British Library, Oriental and India Office Collection)

sage' a pension to match his 300 rupee salary. To see Jagannātha surrounded by his family evoked poignant feelings in the childless couple.

Jones was not fated to see the publication of Jagannātha's compilation, the *Vivādabhaṅgārnava*, or 'Oceans of resolutions of disputes', the product of Jones's supervisory, editorial, and collaborative labours. This digest of Hindu law, to which Jones dedicated over six years of tireless effort, was translated by Henry Thomas Colebrooke, and published in 1798. According to J. Duncan Derrett, it was 'a success', eagerly cited by the court pandits.[48] It represented a profound contribution to the integration and organization of a vast body of belief, myth, ritual, custom, practice, and law into the Hinduism of modern India. Its compiler, Jagannātha, born in 1694, had obviously 'pleased the Giver of Life'; he lived until 1807.

The Joneses had been in India for just over a decade, 'and if it had not been for the incessant ill health of my beloved Anna, they would have been the ten happiest years of a life always happy because always independent' (*Letters*, 2: 920). Anna had been promising to return for over two of those years, but she simply could not bring herself to leave her dear Sir William. On her doctors' insistence, a passage had been booked on the *Princess Amelia*, her luggage was in the hold, and the East Indiaman was due to leave on 28 November. There was a short reprieve; the ship sailed on 7 December. Anna Maria would reach Portsmouth five days before her husband's death.

Alone and fearing for Anna's safety, Jones kept thinking of the fate of the *Crocodile* in which they had happily voyaged out together. On its return the beautiful frigate had hit the deadly rocks of Prawle Point, the southernmost headland of south Devon, in thick fog on the morning of 9 May 1784.[49]

Ever the workaholic—'his business is all day & every day', Anna had written to Georgiana, 'in a temperate climate it would be reckon'd hard duty[;] think what it is in this'—Jones now threw himself into in his labours with an energy he could not spare. Throughout the first three and a half months of 1794 he was working at a punishing rate. Hyde's notebooks confirm that Jones was on the bench until the third week of April. He was correcting the proofs of the *Institutes of Hindu Law*, working with Rādhākānta on the Digest, and completing his eleventh presidential address.

---

48. J. Duncan Derrett, *Religion, Law and the State in India* (London, 1968), 245–9.
49. Although Jones had read with relief that the passengers and its complement of 170 crew had been saved, the *Crocodile* was a total loss, and the hazards of the long passage now assailed his mind.

He was thinking with admiration of the Vedic *rishi* Kapila and Sankhya philosophy advocating renunciation of material desires; with astonishment of 'an entire *Upanishad* on the internal parts of the human body; with an enumeration of nerves, veins, and arteries, a description of the heart, spleen, and liver, and various disquisitions on the formation and growth of the fetus'; and with anxiety of Anna on the wide ocean. Jones had empathized with a distraught Hastings exactly ten years earlier when his beloved Marian left for England without him. Now Jones re-read a poem Hastings had written in his loneliness: 'Rooroo and Promodbara, a Hindu tale, borrowed from Mr Wilkins's translation of the Mahabhaurut'. Virgil and Ovid also borrowed it from the *Mahābhārata*, for it is the origin of the Orpheus and Eurydice myth.

The young sage Ruru, distraught at the death of his beloved bride, Pramadvarā, killed by snake-bite, implores the gods for her return. The god Dharma (judge of the dead) proves more gracious than Proserpine who stipulates the cruel mytheme of not looking back. Where Orpheus's tragic error kills Eurydice a second time, the bargain that Ruru gladly seals is that he should give half his remaining years to his bride. The dharmic wisdom and romantic rightness of such a gift reveal a Hindu emphasis upon restitution and renewal. Addressing Marian, Hastings stresses the relevance of the moral to his own sense of loss:

> 'Tis true, no Serpent of envenom'd Breath
> Hath stung my Love, ere yet a Bride, to Death,
> And O! may Heav'n, for many Years to come
> Preserve her Life from Nature's final Doom!
> Yet is she lost to me, in Substance dead,
> With half the travers'd Globe between us spread.
> [...]
> Ah Me! no Gods, nor Angels now descend,
> My sufferings else might some kind Spirit move
> To give me back on Terms the Wife I love.
> And more than Half my Life would I resign
> For Health, her Purchase, and herself for mine.[50]

In the same way, Jones, unbearably lonely without Anna, feels what he had never before felt in India—an irresistible pull homewards. He re-read the tale of Shirin and Farhād in the *Khosrow va Shirin* of the great Persian poet,

---

50. BL Add. MSS 39, 891, ff. 7–8.

Niẓāmī (1141–1209). In his Eleventh Anniversary Discourse 'On the Philosophy of the Asiaticks' on 20 February, he cites a 'most wonderful passage on the theory of attraction' from the *Farhād va Shirin* of Vahshi Bāfqi (d. 1583), which draws heavily upon a very similar description in Niẓāmī:

> 'There is a strong propensity, which dances through every atom, and attracts the minutest particle to some peculiar object; search this universe from its base to its summit, from fire to air, from water to earth, from all below the Moon to all above the celestial spheres, and thou wilt not find a corpuscle destitute of that natural attractability; [...] which taught hard steel to rush from its place and rivet itself on the magnet; it is the same disposition, which impels the light straw to attach itself firmly on amber; it is this quality, which gives every substance in nature a tendency toward another, and an inclination forcibly directed to a determinate point.' *(Works, 3: 247)*

His principal object in quoting this is to ask his audience, 'whether the last paragraph of NEWTON's incomparable work goes much farther'; in fact, John Dalton, who pioneered the idea of atomic weight, cites this very passage as 'striking' evidence that 'the Oriental sages recognised the fact of matter being ponderable and permanent'.[51] But in the 'poetical fire' of Farhād's love for Shīrīn Jones sees reflections of his own for Anna, intensifying the physical force of his desire to be reunited with her in a mingling of neoplatonic and atomic attraction. For both Hastings and Jones to measure their deepest emotions by an Oriental standard reveals the completeness of their engagement with Indian civilization.

On St David's Day Jones writes to Henry Dundas, president of the Board of Control, informing him that the *Institutes of Hindu Law: or, The Ordinances of Menu* had been published, and requesting royal permission to resign his office 'in the year 1795, or (if the Digest should not then be completed) in 1796'. Jones also writes to Samuel Davis in Burdwan, thanking him for his valuable book on the Indian constellations and offering to translate the Sanskrit verses of the illustrations. He seems in good spirits as usual when writing to his compatriot. Jones jokes that the Hindu representation of Ursa Major is 'as complete a Bear as that which attacked you at Pandua', tells him that at the last society meeting his health had been drunk 'in a full glass of liquid rubies from Shiraz', and hopes he will visit at Ariśnagar, coming 'like

---

51. John Dalton, 'A Sketch of the Atomic Theory', in Henry Lonsdale, *The Worthies of Cumberland* (London, 1874), 168.

Crishna, decked with holy Tamāla blossoms'; botanical Jones desires to examine 'their *private parts*' (*Letters*, 2: 931).

Jones wanted to include the medicinal properties and cultural symbolism of the Tamāla, whose dark blue-gray trunk was embraced by Radhā as she longed for Krishna, in his 'Botanical Observations', which he read on 3rd April. Some specimens arrived—a new species of bread-fruit with a similar leaf to the Tamāla—but Samuel did not. Shortly he was bitterly to reproach himself for this was the last paper Jones gave.

Davis also missed the other paper Jones read that Thursday night: 'On the Duties of a Faithful Hindu Widow', which Henry Thomas Colebrooke, now Collector of Natore, had sent from northern Bengal. With his first Society essay—on the abhorrent and aberrant gynophobic practice of *satī*, the ritual self-immolation of widows—its author is determined to make a real intellectual impact. In attempting to demonstrate that *satī* had ancient religious sanction, Colebrooke aligns himself with the Company's rigorous policy of non-interference in Hindu ritual and custom; however, their investigations of this practice had been seriously flawed.[52] Reports of *satī* had horrified the West since Alexander's expedition to India, and Strabo had claimed the practice was customary for widows of *kṣatriyas* (the warrior caste). It would seem, however, that in Vedic times *satī* was a purely mimetic ceremony in which the widow lay down beside her dead husband on the funeral mound, perhaps to mime a final act of copulation, and was then enjoined, as in the *Ṛg Veda* Burial Hymn, to 'Rise up, woman, into the world of the living', before the corpse was buried or cremated.[53] Subsequent confusion in Vedantic commentaries and transcriptions, resulting in a literal interpretation of a symbolic rite, may have been created by unscrupulous priests or families anxious to gain control of the widows' property, or by simple errors in the oral transmission of texts.

In his last extant letter, dated the 13 April, Jones extends the Society's thanks for this 'very interesting paper', but urges Colebrooke to forward his sources, especially 'the original of the *Rigvéda* Mantra, and of the verse from the *Bhágavat* in which I see the word *Sahótaja* [cabin of grasses erected on the pyre] which I have never met with'.[54] Jones needs to investigate these for

---

52. See Franklin, *European Discovery of India*, 6: x–xii. See also Ludo and Rosane Rocher, *The Making of Western Indology: Henry Thomas Colebrooke and the East India Company* (forthcoming), ch. 2.
53. *Ṛg Veda*, X.18.8, cf. *Atharva-Veda Samhitā*, XVIII.3.1.
54. Published from NLW, MS 16098E in *Collected Works*, ed. Cannon, 1: lxx.

the light they might throw on the consideration of *sahamarana* (dying together) in his 'new compilation of Hindu law', the *Vivādabhangārnava*. But it was left to the conscientious Horace Hayman Wilson—some sixty years later—to insist that 'the text of the *Rig Veda* cited as authority for the burning of widows enjoins the very contrary, and directs them to remain in the world'.[55]

On the evening of 20 April, Jones called on his neighbour—now governor-general—John Shore, 'complained of aguish symptoms, mentioned his intention to take some medicine, repeating jocularly an old proverb, that "an ague in the spring is medicine for a king"'. He 'had no suspicion at the time, of the real nature of his indisposition, which proved in fact to be a complaint common in Bengal, an inflammation in the liver' (*Works*, 2: 260). 'Oriental' Jones died a week later on Sunday, 27 April 1794.

A fuller picture emerges from the diary of Richard Blechynden, a building contractor, who greatly admired Jones. He was told by his friend Charles Rothman, magistrate and Asiatick Society member, that Jones had been complaining of being ill 'for about a week or ten days':

> Dr [James] Hare attended him and gave him some medicine for a pain in the stomach—which he said hurt his Bowels. Dr Hare on this beg'd to feel his Belly and passing his hand over to the right side found a tumour as big as his fist. Enquiring when this came he said it appeared about 4 or 5 months ago—but, that as it came of itself he imagined it would go away in the same manner—& had taken no notice of it.[56]

We can only echo the amazed reaction of the sensitive Blechynden: 'on hearing this one is tempted to call out, oh the *weakness* of a *Strong* mind!' The man of science who had been enthralled by John Hunter's anatomical lectures, admired Percival Pott for detecting the connection between cancer and the working environment, and who had consulted the best physicians in England and Bengal, thought his spring 'ague' would go away of its own accord. Though in pain so severe, 'that he would not go through such another period for all the Riches & Honours in the world', Jones confessed to Hare his only resort had been to exercise, 'walking every day before his Carriage to and from the Garden upwards of 4 miles'.

---

55. H. H. Wilson, 'On the Supposed Vaidic Authority for the Burning of Hindu Widows, and on the Funeral of the Hindus', *Journal of the Royal Asiatic Society*, 16 (1856), 201.
56. BL Add. MSS 45,589, Blechynden Diaries, 30 April 1794. On Blechynden, see Peter Robb, *Clash of Cultures? An Englishman in Calcutta in the 1790s* (London, 1998).

If there was folly, there was also pride: 'He said he thought it beneath him to let the mind bend to the pains of the Body.' During periods of delirium he would not allow anyone to come near, 'not even his favourite slave boy Otho', and had refused Shore's offers to sit up with him. On Saturday night there was some remission and his doctors suggested he might return to England 'on the *Boddington* or the *Sugar Cane*—Botany Bay ships, by which time they hoped to have him able to undertake the voyage—professing first to salivate him'. Such hopes were delusory: the *Sugar Cane* carried the news of his death to Britain.

> Early on Sunday morning the Consummah (house-keeper) ran over to Sir John Shore's & said his master was *Mad*—by which he understood he was delirious & accordingly went there accompanied by Sir Robert Abercromby, the General. Just as they came to the premises another servant came out and said that since the Consummah had left the house Sir Willm had called for a Dish of Tea—drank it and died! On their entrance they found him reclined on the couch his head against his right hand & the forefinger upwards towards his forehead—his usual attitude—his extremities were warm. Thus ended the mortal career of that truly great man Sir William Jones!

Blechynden's diary provides disturbing material that would never have seen publication at the time. Learning of Jones's death from Edward Tiretta, the Venetian political refugee and architect, Blechynden was grief-stricken: 'I almost cursed my own Existence to think that such really great and good men as he should be thus snatched away while the wicked and ignorant are permitted not only to walk this planet but to commit their depredations upon it!' Though little more than an acquaintance of Jones, he immediately drove down to the Ariśnagar house, 'and to my great astonishment found no one friend there'. The servants showed him where the body lay in a darkened room: 'I was obliged to open the Window that leads into the Verandah to get light—found him much reduced—but a fine placid smile upon his countenance—ordered a couple of candles to be lighted to keep away the Rats & desired a Musselman servant or two would wait in the Room.' Blechynden felt his forehead, 'it was scarcely cold—tho' he had died early in the morning—whether this was owing to the heat of the weather and the window shut up or to a Consuming fomentation of the Juices I know not'.

That it should be left to a comparative stranger to make these practical arrangements and human touches reinforces the sadness of a lonely death. That our last description of Jones should be overshadowed by thoughts of rats and rapid putrefaction adds to the burden. On his return Blechynden, 'met the Hearse on a full trot with Maudsley the undertaker sitting with the Driver on the box going thither'; it was more lucrative work for Thomas Maudsley in the city of palatial death.

At a quarter to seven on Monday morning, the hearse left from Hyde's Chowringhee house and the procession advanced towards the burial ground, 'accompanied by a very numerous attendance of the gentlemen of the Settlement in their carriages and palanquins and preceded by all the European Troops in garrison, with arms reversed and drums muffled, and the Artillery band playing sacred music, while minute guns were fired from the ramparts of Fort William' (*Calcutta Gazette*, 1 May 1794).

With his friend Lieutenant Wales, who assisted in the surveying of the Andaman Islands, Blechynden joined the crowds waiting over an hour to see the funeral procession. The contrast between Jones's empty house on the Sunday and the hastily organized, but immaculate and elaborate public ceremonial was all too stark. Blechynden insisted there should have been an autopsy: 'it was indisputably necessary to open him—& this neglect will undoubtedly astonish all Europe who will enquire into every particular of this uncommon Genius'. As the sun rose higher, the service was performed at the graveside by the Revd Blanchard with Mr Justice Hyde and Sir William Dunkin as chief mourners, and the pall borne by the barristers and attorneys of the Supreme Court: 'the body being laid in the earth, the solemn ceremony was concluded by the troops firing three vollies of musquetry over the grave'.

In 1760 the 13-year-old Jones had contemplated 'How quickly fades the vital flower', anticipating in his version of Horace's Ode 2:14 his long Park Street sleep:

> Our house, our land, our shadowy grove
> The very mistress of our love,
>   Ah me, we soon must leave!
> Of all our trees, the hated boughs
> Of Cypress shall alone diffuse
>   Their fragrance o'er our grave.   (*Works*, 1: 53)

A profound gloom was cast over Calcutta, despite it being inured to brief lives. Close friends, united by a sense of diminishment, were stunned by the suddenness of it all. Gladwin, in his *Gazette*, attempted to convey the sense of national loss at 'so great and good a man being snatched from the meridian of his glorious and useful career'. Prosaic in his sadness, John

Hyde calculated by adjusting the Julian and Gregorian calendars, 'that Sir WJ when he died was forty seven years, six months and seventeen days old'. Samuel Davis thought of the poignant quatrain Jones had translated from the Persian of the eleventh-century Sūfi poet Abu-Said Abil-Kheir:

> On parent knees, a naked, new-born child,
> Weeping thou sat'st, while all around thee smil'd:
> So live, that, sinking in thy last long sleep,
> Calm thou may'st smile, when all around thee weep.   (*Works*, 2: 70)

While many mourned a consummate scholar, a generous and unforgettable friend, Richard Johnson, indigo planter and attorney, (not to be confused with Jones's friend who returned to England in 1790) was calculating an opportunity for advancing the debt-ridden biographer and laird of Auchinleck. On the 2 May he sent overland a letter to James Boswell: 'The Sugar Cane, a Company's ship will sail in about five or six days, which will carry home the news of Sir William's death, and that you may have timely notice, I take the liberty of writing this, that you may instantly apply to the Minister to succeed him, before his death appears in the publick Prints.'[57]

Life goes on amidst the lamentations, but this reference to 'Oriental' Jones being succeeded underscores the impossibility of his being replaced. Realizing this, Brahman pandits wept openly with Muslim maulavis at the governor-general's *durbar* (public audience). The depth of their feeling may be gauged by the words of a respected pandit with whom Jones had worked on the compilation of the *Vivādā-sārārṇava*, 'the ocean of all disputes', the Mithila lawyer, Sarvoru Śarmā Trivedi:

> To you there are many like me; yet to me there is none like you, but yourself; there are numerous groves of night flowers; yet the night flower sees nothing like the moon, but the moon.   (*Works*, 2: 307)[58]

On the day of the funeral, Anna Maria was still unpacking in Bolton Street, relieved to be 'home' after the long voyage, especially as the *Princess Amelia* had run into some 'danger of being taken by the Sans Culottes' in the Atlantic. Reunited with her mother and her sisters (her father had died in 1788), she spent the whole year making plans and viewing suitable country properties. Now she was concerned for her husband's safety. He had long

---

57. Beinecke; Boswell Collection, Gen MSS 89, Ser. II. 24, 581, C1593, Letter to James Boswell from Richard Johnson, Calcutta, 2 May 1794.
58. Coleridge copied these lines into his Notebook in the summer of 1807.

planned to return via the Persian Gulf, to see the tomb of Hāfiz at Shiraz, to 'let my whiskers grow and wear a Persian dress' in the company of scholars and poets. She knew how difficult it would be for her husband to tear himself away from Persian delights, and then there were dangers—and delaying attractions—on the long overland journey. She wrote on 14 December 1794 to Lord Spencer: 'If you had had no letters by late Ships from Sir W. Jones you will not know that a continuance of the Civil War in Persia has made him abandon all thoughts of returning by that Route (The only good consequence I ever knew from War).' Poignantly unaware, Anna asks Spencer that if he knows of any 'over land Packet to India, perhaps you could contrive to send a little slip of letters for me as well as for yourself'.[59]

The cruel news was still on the ocean. Letters composed with infinite care lay amongst the official dispatches in the postal chest of the *Sugar Cane*; they did not reach India House in Leadenhall Street until Monday, 5 January 1795. Anna would never forget how bitterly cold it was that January; the Thames was frozen over below Westminster Bridge and all navigation entirely stopped by ice. Mercifully she was saved by her sister Elizabeth from reading the announcement in the papers of the following day. Elizabeth's letter to Sarah Ponsonby, one of the Ladies of Llangollen (Jones and Sarah's friend, Lady Eleanor Butler, had kept up a yearly exchange of letters detailing their reading) reveals the sanitized account of Jones's death that Anna Maria received. It bears all the hallmarks of John Shore:

> He suffered extreme pain without a murmur. The morning of his death he was taken up and carried into his Dressing Room. There some of his most intimate acquaintances visited him, but after a short time he beg'd to be left quite alone, saying—'I must not now be disturb'd, a few minutes will probably convey me into the presence of the Almighty.'[60]

Though she reproached herself severely for having left him, Anna Maria showed great courage in her loss. Even in the rawness of her grief, she was concerned to collect and preserve all his writings, applying—with her brother William's help—to all Jones's correspondents for autograph letters. Her thoughts returned to what she had often heard her husband remark: 'The best monument that can be erected to a man of literary talents, is a good edition of his works.' In mid-April 1795 she sought the advice of

---

59. BL Add. MSS 75,981, Lady Jones to Lord Spencer, 14 December 1794.
60. *The Hamwood Papers of The Ladies of Llangollen and Caroline Hamilton*, ed. Mrs G. H. Bell (London, 1930), 274–5.

Spencer at the Admiralty—he was now its First Lord—concerning who might be the best editor: '[I]f departed spirits know anything of what passes on Earth I can not but be persuaded that *his* would feel pleasure in knowing *you* were employed' in the choice.[61] The precious chests of books and manuscripts did not arrive until mid-December of the following year, 1796, and even then Spencer and Charles Grant had to intervene to prevent potentially damaging examination by India House officials.

By the time Anna took delivery on 15 February 1797 she had made up her mind: she would be the editor. She clearly saw this as the duty of a faithful widow. The literary world had produced its elegies, by Thomas Maurice, whose books were highly reliant upon Jones, and William Hayley, who had long admired him, but it was the Della Cruscan poet Anna Maria who showed them what scholarship was. Handling his autograph manuscripts she was beset with 'cento memorie e cento', as she put it in the words of their beloved Metastasio, but with the concentration of a *rishi* she converted the intensity of her feelings into fiery intellectual energy. Her superb six-volume quarto edition of his works was in the bookshops by June 1799, an incredible feat. As epigraph to her editorial preface she cited the first couplet of a Nizāmī quatrain she had watched him translate:

> He was a pearl too pure on earth to dwell,
> And waste his brightness in this mortal cell.

An edition worthy of Jones, it was a memorial to their intellect and a testament to her love. He had testified to his love for Anna in many poems; she broke down when she saw again one he had dedicated to her:

> Au Firmament
>
> 'Would I were yon blue field above,'
> (Said Plato, warbling am'rous lays,)
> 'That with ten thousand eyes of love,
> On thee for ever I might gaze.'
>
> My purer love the wish disclaims,
> For were I, like Tiresias, blind,
> Still should I glow with heavenly flames,
> And gaze with rapture on thy mind. (*Works*, 2: 507)

---

61. BL Add. MSS 75,981, Lady Jones to Lord Spencer, 13 April [1795].

9

'Indo-Persian' Jones and Indian Pluralism[1]

On the 9 February 2005, *The Hindu*, 'India's National Newspaper', headlined a story by Mandira Nayar entitled 'Lost in minutes: 800 years of history':

> NEW DELHI, FEB. 8. The tomb of Delhi's foremost poet, Amir Khusro, at the Nizamuddin dargah in South Delhi was vandalized early morning today, allegedly by a man from West Bengal. Wreaking havoc at the tomb, he single-handedly broke the intricately carved marble 'jaalis' adorning the poet's grave and vandalized more than three finials. While the police suspect he is mentally unstable, over 800 years of history have been lost forever. The accused, identified by police as Mohammad Bukhal Khan, has been arrested.

Almost exactly three years earlier, on 27 February 2002, a mob of angry Muslims set fire to the packed Sabarmati Express at Godhra in the western state of Gujarat, killing at least fifty-eight people. The train had been carrying Hindu activists or 'Ram sevaks' returning from the northern town of Ayodhya, where they had been campaigning for the building of a temple on the ruins of the Babri Masjid, a mosque the destruction of which ten years earlier by Hindu zealots provoked the worst rioting in India since partition, killing more than three thousand. This horror provoked an enormous wave of communal violence in which over two thousand people, mainly Muslims, were killed. The 'collateral' cultural damage was also appalling; in Ahmedabad, as Luke Harding reported for the *Guardian* on 29 June 2002:

> Two hundred and thirty unique Islamic monuments, including an exquisite 400-year-old mosque, were destroyed or vandalized [...] Experts say the

---

1. A version of this chapter was delivered to the Asiatic Society on 8 February 2006.

damage is so extensive that it rivals the better publicised destruction of the Bamiyan Buddhas in Afghanistan or the wrecking of Tibet's monasteries by the Red Guards. [...] Hindu gangs have smashed delicate mosque screens, thrown bricks at Persian inscriptions, and set fire to old Korans. [...] One of the monuments razed was the tomb of Vali Gujarati, the grandfather of Urdu poetry and inspiration of many later poets and singers, who died in, Ahmedabad, the state's main city, in 1707. [...] On the night of March 1 Hindu gangs with pickaxes smashed it and replaced it with a small brick temple dedicated to the Hindu monkey-god Hanuman. [...] Several of Vali's fans have pointed out his own verse almost anticipates his ending:

The city of whose songs I have always sung
Why can I not bear to live in that city now?

Thus Godhra, and what became known as the 'post-Godhra riots', imperilled a long and valued tradition of Gujarati religious tolerance for, as Harding points out:

[L]ike many of India's Muslim rulers, Ahmedabad's 15th-century sultan and founder, Ahmad Shah I, married a rajput (Hindu) princess. His mosques and civic buildings incorporated Islamic and rajput elements and he employed Hindus in the highest offices of state.

These disturbing twenty-first-century developments cast a long and deep shadow over both the past and future of the peaceful, plural, and often syncretic co-existence of the great religions of India. But one of the ironies that unites both the New Delhi and the Ahmedabad desecrations is that the lives and writings of the two poets whose tombs were targeted, Amīr Khusrau of Delhi (1253–1325), and Vali Mohammed Vali (1667–1707), aka Vali Aurangabadi, Wali Daccani, or Vali Gujarati, exemplify a sympathetic and productive mingling of Muslim and Hindu traditions. Perhaps this was the reason they were targeted. This final chapter illustrates the fascination of Jones and the Hastings circle with such Indian pluralism and multiculturalism. It also seeks to demolish the persistent idea that Jones and other Asiatick Society members were exclusively concerned with the glories of a Hindu past, whether it be classical Sanskrit Gupta culture as exemplified by Kālidāsa's *Śakuntalā*, or twelfth-century *bhakti* devotional literature such as Jayadeva's *Gītagovinda*.[2]

---

2. 'Even British "orientalist" scholars who are known for their admiration of Indian culture and traditions confined their interests to ancient India and specifically to the achievements of the Aryans', Kumkum Chatterjee, 'History as Self-Representation: The Recasting of a Political Tradition in Late Eighteenth-Century Eastern India', *Modern Asian Studies*, 32: 4.

To facilitate the transition from saddening postmodern times to the revolutionary 'Modern Times' of northern India in the last quarter of the eighteenth century we can do no better than to enlist the aid of Ghulam Husain Khan Tabatabai (1727–1806), whose fascinating history of India from the time of Aurangzeb down to 1781, the *Sëir Mutaqharin* (*View of Modern Times*), was published in Calcutta in 1789.[3] Jones had sent home a copy of the *Sëir Mutaqharin*, with warm recommendations, to C. W. Boughton Rouse, secretary to the Board of Control for India, in an attempt to secure financial security for the 'venerable old man', Ghulam Husain. He described it as 'an excellent impartial modern History of India [...] containing very just Remarks on the Administration of Government and Justice by our Nation, but *sine irâ aut odio*' [without anger or hatred] (*Letters*, 2: 723–4; 805–6). Addressing the Asiatick Society on the 28 February 1793, in his presidential 'Tenth Anniversary Discourse, On Asiatick History, Civil and Natural', Jones praises the accuracy of the *Sëir Mutaqharin*:

> GHULÁM HUSAIN, many of us personally know, and whose impartiality deserves the highest applause, though his unrewarded merit will give no encouragement to other contemporary historians, who, to use his own phrase in a letter to myself, may, like him, *consider plain truth as the beauty of historical composition*. From all these materials, and from these alone, a perfect history of *India* (if a mere compilation, however elegant, could deserve such a title) might be collected by any studious man, who had a competent knowledge of *Sanscrit*, *Persian*, and *Arabick*; but, even in the work of a writer so qualified, we could only give absolute credence to the general outline; for, while the abstract *sciences* are all truth, and the fine *arts* all fiction, we cannot but own, that in the *details of history*, truth and fiction are so blended as to be scarce distinguishable. (*Works*, 3: 214)

Before we consider Ghulam Husain's impartial history, it is intriguing to look at the strange narrative of its colourful translator. The *Sëir* was translated—with substantial help from 'Orientalist' Jones—by the pseudonymous 'Nota Manus' ('the hand is known'), but this writer, though well known in

---

(1998), 913–48; 945. Cf. Robert Travers, *Ideology and Empire in Eighteenth-Century India* (Cambridge, 2007), 245

3. Ghulam Husain Khan Tabatabai, *A Translation of the Sëir Mutaqharin; or, View of Modern Times, being an History of India, from the Year 1118 to the Year 1195 (this year answers to the Christian year 1781–82)*, 3 vols (Calcutta, 1789 [1790]). On Ghulam Husain, see Khan, *Indian Perceptions of the West*, 84–92.

Calcutta, was no 'India hand' in Company employ.[4] A remarkable exemplar of hybridity, Jones's friend was M. Raymond, a French Creole born in Constantinople, who assumed the Muslim name Hājī Mustafā upon his conversion to Islam. He was accused in print of being a spy by the influential EIC director Luke Scrafton, and probably was one. As well as being translator to Clive, it would seem that, during the duplicitous post-Plassey period, Hājī Mustafā was a double agent simultaneously working for both Coja Hadjee, general of the Nawab of Bengal, in his communications with the French, and for Henry Vansittart, Governor of Bengal (1760–64).[5]

Hājī Mustafā's translator's preface is a puzzling representation of British India in its mingling of political Orientalism and Oriental romance. He presents himself as an avid early Orientalist, like Hastings and Vansittart, but, when his 'Persian and Indian books, miniatures, and curiosities' were plundered on his pilgrimage to Mecca (the Hajj), he abandons book collecting and assembles 'a collection of Female Beauties'. Is the circumcised Mustafā metamorphosing into a stereotype of the despotic Oriental male, or is this an extraordinary example of 'colonial mimicry'?

Many of Jones's closest friends had fallen in love with Indian women: Major William Palmer was devoted to his Mughal wife Fyze Baksh, and their loving family portrait, painted by Zoffany, hangs at the entrance to the India Office Library; Colonel Antoine Polier maintained two Indian wives in Fyzabad; even the evangelical John Shore kept a mistress with whom he had three children. This was far from uncommon. William Dalrymple's important research has revealed that in a third of the Bengal wills proved between 1780 and 1785, bequests are made to 'Indian wives, companions, or their natural children'.[6]

As neither native nor Englishman, Mustafā's mimicry could work both ways, subversively imitating/mocking both genuine and 'White Mughals'; to adjust Homi Bhabha's terms, '*Almost the same but not white*', nor black.[7] Ownership of a haram would enable him to cut 'a capital figure' in Calcutta society and his use of this Anglicism emphasizes the disjunctions of East and

---

4. See Jones's manuscript of sections of the *Seïr Mutaqharin* in Persian *nasta'liq* with characteristic interlinear autograph translation; Yale, Beinecke MS Osborn fc 163.
5. Luke Scrafton, *Observations on Mr Vansittart's Narrative* ([London], 1766), 16–17; BL, APAC, Eur. MSS Orme OV 6, letter from Mustafā to Scrafton, 2 Jan. 1768, pp. 35–7.
6. William Dalrymple, *White Mughals: Love and Betrayal in Eighteenth-Century India* (London, 2002), 34.
7. Homi Bhabha, *The Location of Culture* (London, 1994), 89.

West in his self-divided self-representation. What is truly remarkable is that he should publish the details of his purchases in the preface to a history and in a pamphlet that contains an open letter to Cornwallis. He sends his servant to Lucknow 'to purchase four girls from Sixteen to twenty five, tall and slender', but the servant receives 'a box on the ear' for acquiring 'two black children, and two other women as small as children, very ugly'.[8] The cool and deliberate fashion in which Mustafā represents his new venture of enclosing carefully selected living 'objects', not within cabinets or bookcases but behind elaborately carved haram *jaalis*, is instinct with Asiatic otherness.

It is also very strange to find Justice Jones offering such assistance to a man who publishes his criticism of British and Mughal justice in Murshidabad, and explains with connoisseurial expertise the reasons why Abyssinian female slaves are so highly priced. They possess: 'a mobility and versatility of body that amazes a philosopher; and an animal warmth, and personal elasticity, that surpasses all belief; hence eight hundred Mohurs have been offered in India for an Habissinian virgin of sixteen, and refused'.[9] Though no libertine, Jones was also a slave owner, and Mustafā the philanderer was also something of a philologer, including in his translation of the *Sëir* a list of related Persian and English words. He had many influential friends, such as John Wombwell, Company Accountant at Lucknow, and the respected Captain Cuthbert Thornhill, Master Attendant of the Port of Calcutta, an 'eighteenth-century Sinbad', and friend of James Bruce, author of *Travels to Discover the Source of the Nile* (1790).

That the publication of *Sëir Mutaqharin* should be indebted to a series of events that seem to inhabit the world of the *Arabian Nights* is strange indeed. In this authentic 'Oriental tale', 'truth and fiction' (to recall Jones's definition of history) seem 'so blended as to be scarce distinguishable'. Mustafā himself agrees: 'Such a narrative, I acknowledge, would figure pretty well at the end of the one thousand and one nights, but it is nevertheless true, and to my sorrow, but too true' (*Sëir*, 1: 18).

When one of his seraglio, 'a beloved girl of mine', falls in love with one of his servants, Mustafā procures for his haram-slave a husband (a 'man of Mogul origin, a trooper') in Lucknow. Despite her protests, '"You want

---

8. *Some Idea of the Civil & Criminal Courts of Justice at Moorshoodabad, in a Letter to Capt. John Hawkshaw* (Calcutta, 1789), 25.
9. Ibid., 15–16.

then to turn me out of the house, and to chain me to that man?"—"Be it so," added the girl,—after a pause—"But you shall one day repent of it" ', she is carried off, with a dowry of 300 rupees, by her husband. Within two months she returns, bitterly complaining of her Mughal husband's cruelty and vehemently threatening to throw herself down a well. Mustafā arranges for her to be secretly transported—doubly contained within a hamper inside a covered coach—to Banaras where she might start a new life, and they 'parted with tears on both sides'.

> Seven days after, as I was getting out of my house at day-break to take an airing, I perceived a bag close to my door; and on my ordering one of my people to see what it could be, I went to look at it myself, and the first object that caught my sight, was an arm with a mole and an elegant hand, on a small finger of which I soon recollected a ring made of hair and gold wire. There was no standing such a spectacle. I returned into the house, and my troubled imagination made me see in the hall, right before me, the girl in tears, and saying: 'be it so—but you shall repent'. (*Seïr*, 1: 20–21)

Thus is the *object d'art* returned to the collector. Unanswerable questions are raised by this 'Oriental tale': is she killed by a cruel husband or by a family member according to an honour code incomprehensible to Western understanding? And what does it say of the self-division or indeed the culpability of Hājī Mustafā himself, as purchaser and sexual predator turned unsuccessful paternal protector? At one level, the story simply confirms Eurocentric stereotypes of the capricious and arbitrary power of the 'Asiatic' male and the corresponding victim-like powerlessness of woman. How completely is the female subaltern effaced—identified ultimately not by an arm with a mole, or an elegant hand, but by 'a ring made of hair and gold wire', entwining human with economic value, and symbolizing her former beauty and commercial worth.

In another way this disturbing narrative of containment and imprisonment hints darkly at collusion between the elite 'native' and the colonial project. For if colonial imagination gendered both territory and peoples as feminine spaces to be violated, controlled, and plundered, Mustafā's collection symbolizes incrimination in imperial subjugation, graduating from textual control (Orientalist library) to political control of woman/land (seraglio). The binary opposition of colonizing self/colonized other is undermined as Mustafā moves between the roles of Oriental actor and Orientalist commentator.

The news, a few weeks later, that Governor-General Hastings, 'the principal author of my well-being', was departing for Europe 'completed the unhinging of my mind, as if by some unexpected stroke'. The return of this seraglio-slave/silenced wife and the recall of Warren Hastings are arrestingly juxtaposed in the *poetic* construction of Mustafā's narrative and in the temporary dislocation of his senses. The 'Oriental' presents himself as talking to a portrait of Hastings, 'a picture of striking likeness, by the inimitable Zophani', and his distraction was only relieved by a fortunate accident, which restored him to his former avocation and his mimicry of the Calcutta Orientalists:

> On my going into one of the Nawab's seats, an old woman, among other articles of sale, offered me some broken leaves of a decayed book, in which the author talked with encomiums of the English Parliament in Europe, and with some asperity of the English Government in Bengal. A Persian discourse upon English Politics! strange indeed! I took the broken leaves, and perused some of them in the Garden. (*Sëir*, 1: 21)

Thus he discovered the *Sëir Mutaqharin*, resolving to translate his history with a mingling of Oriental and colonialist motives as a means of abating the sorrow of his seraglio tragedy, and provide funds to send two of his children to school in England.[10] Considering Ghulam Husain's criticism of Mubarak ud-Daula, Nawab Nazim of Bengal, Bihar, and Orissa as a sad example of Mughal government, it is easy to see why the *Sëir Mutaqharin* was thrown out from 'one of the Nawab's seats'. It is, however, Ghulam Husain's criticism of the imperial British rather than of modern Mughals that Mustafā desires to underline in his prefatory remarks. He feels he owes it to his 'adopted Countrymen (the English)' to provide some timely warning:

> The general turn of the English individuals in India, seems to be a thorough contempt for the Indians (as a national body). It is taken to be no better than a dead stock, that may be worked upon without much consideration, and at pleasure: But beware! that national body is only motionless, but neither insensible, nor dead.—There runs throughout our author's [i.e. Ghulam Husain's] narrative, a subterraneous vein of national resentment, which emits vapours now and then, and which his occasional encomiums of the English, can neither conceal nor even palliate; and yet he is himself but a voice that has spoken among a million of others that could speak, but are silent. (*Sëir*, 1: 22–3)

This is an important reminder that the enthusiasm for Indian and Indo-Persian culture that we have witnessed in Jones and his colleagues was far

---

10. *Sëir*, 1: 22. Mustafā reveals his mimicry of Jones in determining to direct any profit from the sale of his translation to 'British insolvent debtors in Bengal' (*Sëir*, 1: 5).

from universal. The contempt recognized by both the nawabi gentleman Ghulam Husain and the 'renegade' Mustafā would culminate in the zealous evangelizing and improving Anglicizing of the early decades of the next century, but it had never been absent. Jones had helped introduce a brief period of sympathetic and syncretic admiration for India, between the acquisitiveness of the Clive generation and the utter contempt for Indian culture later displayed by Mill and Macaulay. But one wonders how deeply it had penetrated the colonialist psyche. Inevitably even Asiatick Society members were most enthusiastic about the subcontinent when bagging up rupees. While Jones kept notebooks detailing the names of poets and intellectuals, pandits and maulavis, the names of respected professors and the numbers of students at 'his' university of Nadiya, he also made detailed accounts of the money he was remitting to Europe.[11] It was why they were there: but how long would they be tolerated?

Hājī Mustafā's admonitory representation of both the colonists and the colonized is rendered more powerful by his choice of trope and our recollection of a fair body in a bag. The elegant hand is no longer the signifier of wanton destruction, but is transformed into that contemporary printer's device, its finger extended to mark crucial content. For this body, though motionless, is neither insensible, nor dead, and will not be contained by representations out of *Les Mille et une nuits*. It is a national body, an 'imagined community' that looks forward, beyond even Bengali renaissance, to throwing off the shackles of imperialism.

In some respects this imagined community seems more fantastically imaginative than either Mustafā's or Shahrazâd's seraglio narratives. Historians of India have responded with utter disbelief that anyone at this time might refer to Indians as 'a national body', or speak of a 'vein of national resentment', but the words are there, Calcutta-printed in 1789.[12] It flies in the face of the historical facts of limited Company possessions and a vast congeries of princely states. In contemporary usage 'nation' as applied to India invariably meant a people or race, as in Colebrooke's 'the *Gurjaras* should be considered as the fifth northern nation of India',[13] rather than a putative nation-state. Yet Jones himself when enquiring if Cornwallis agrees

---

11. See Beinecke Library, Osborn Collection, c.400, Jones Notebook.
12. Despite 1789 being on the title page, the third volume was not printed until 20 January 1790; see Shaw, *Printing in Calcutta to 1800*, 129.
13. H. T. Colebrooke, 'On the Sanscrit and Prácrit Languages', *Asiatic Researches*, 7 (1803), 199–231; 229.

'that a digest, of Hindu and Mohammedan laws would be a work of national honour and utility—I so cherish both, that I offer the nation my humble labour', seems to elide the distinction between British and British Indian 'national honour and utility' (*Letters*, 2: 799).

Bearing in mind the publication date of *Seïr Mutaqharin*, one might suppose that it was the Gallic blood of its French Creole translator that suggested the idea of potential national revolution, but the translator's preface is dated 'Calcutta, 2d November, 1786' (*Seïr*, 1: 39).[14] Perhaps it was Mustafā's racial and religious liminality that enabled him to prise apart the adjective and noun in 'British India'. Whatever the reason for this apparent anachronism, we might compare the privately 'subversive' remarks of Anna Maria Jones in a letter to the Duchess of Devonshire: 'I believe this Country has been & is most wretchedly governed & so must every Country be that has a number of Chiefs all pulling different ways.'[15] It is impossible to resist misinterpreting her comment as 'too many chiefs and insufficient Indians', especially as Cornwallis replaced all senior Indian officials with Company servants.

Though describing himself as a 'Semi-Englishman', Mustafā, like Anna Maria, has few illusions about this brave new British empire. Not content simply to echo Ghulam Husain's gentlemanly complaints concerning the apathy and inaccessibility of colonial administrators, Mustafā represents the imperial credo in stark postcolonial terms: '*We are come in India to gather taxes, kill people, and make conquests,—and—and—and—care little about the rest*' (*Seïr*, 2: Appendix, p. 25).

He writes of Murshidabad reaction to the insurrection at Benares in 1781 where Hastings had faced significant personal danger as a result of which rumours of his death had abounded. Following a report that a *hircarrah* (messenger) had 'seen his head and right hand hanging at the gate of Bidjäigur':

> [N]umbers were deeply affected (and to be affected for *an* European governor, or indeed for any European at all, is a very novel matter in India) and they used to say: 'Pity! a great pity! the father of the Hindostanies is gone,—we shall never see such another man.' But others, and this was the majority, left the person out of the question; and minded only the crisis. 'What! are we not men as well as Chëyt-Sing's People? and what could prevent me from giving a slap to one or two of his chairmen? *(the Governor's)* they would have dropped his

---

14. Tīpū Sultān, ruler of Mysore, would shortly be in communication with the French Republic who addressed him as 'Citizen Sultaun Tippoo'; see *Copies and Extracts of Advices to and from India, relative to [. . .] the late Tippoo Sultaun* (London, 1800), 169.
15. Anna Maria to Georgiana, Duchess of Devonshire, 9 December 1785; cited in *Letters*, 2: 689.

palanquin, as by a signal, and any man could have killed him with ease. I saw him at Barwa: he had not an armed man by him; and his chairmen were but a dozen of people; and this would have at once produced a revolution [...] we are such multitudes here—with each a brick-bat in our hands, we could knock them down to a man.' (*Sëir*, 1: 23-4)

This is an intriguing representation of the Indian colonized, of many subaltern voices crying '*Afsoos, Afsoos*' ('Alas, Alas'), but even more inciting rebellion, speaking out of the silence imposed by colonialism and its 'official' discourses. Their thoughts of revolution are aided by the perceived vulnerability of the supreme colonial power in the area, whose team of palanquin-bearers (chairmen) number a mere dozen. According to Mustafā, the rank and file of Murshidabad had thought the unthinkable—of overturning the palanquin of state, and of the end of British colonial control.

Dedicated to Warren Hastings, sections of Mustafā's rough manuscript were hurried to London two years before its publication, 'through the channel of Colonel Allan Macpherson', Quartermaster General, Asiatic Society member, Persian translator to Governor-General Sir John Macpherson, and, like him, cousin to James 'Ossian' Macpherson. Mustafā wanted 'to afford some timely assistance to that great man [Hastings], by elucidating upon so competent and so unconcerned an evidence as our historian' (*Sëir*, 'Proposals', 1: 3).

Ghulam Hussein's *Sëir Mutaqharin* seeks to contextualize the earlier *inqilab* (reversal of fortune, revolution) effected by the East India Company as these 'alien' capitalists consolidated colonial hegemony in northern India. The Mughal empire was in terminal decline; in 1788 heated wires were drawn across the eyes of Emperor Shāh 'Ālam in Delhi. Ghulam Husain attempts in his history to come to terms with a world changed utterly, a world where Mughal nobility, customary authority, and good nawabi government had been displaced. As the prestigious Mughal poet of Urdu, Mīr Taqī 'Mīr' (1722–1810) observed:

This age is not like that which went before it.
The times have changed, the earth and sky have changed.[16]

Jones's praise of Ghulam Husain's 'impartiality' reflects his belief that the best traditions of Mughal government had indeed encouraged peaceful pros-

---

16. Khurshidul Islam and Ralph Russell, *Three Mughal Poets: Mir, Sauda, and Mir Hasan* (Delhi, 1991), 22.

perity and cultural synthesis. Jones admired the historian's celebration of Indian emperors who had 'cherish[ed] (their subjects) in the palm of the hand of benevolence' until mutual strangeness grew into familiar coalescence:

> And although the Gentoos seem to be a generation apart and distinct from the rest of mankind, and they are swayed by such differences in religion, tenets, and rites, as will necessarily render all Musulmen aliens and profane, in their eyes; and although they keep up a strangeness of ideas and practices, which beget a wide difference in customs and actions; yet in process of time, they drew nearer and nearer; and as soon as fear and aversion had worn away, we see that this dissimilarity and alienation have terminated in friendship and union, and that the two nations have come to coalesce together into one whole, like milk and sugar that have received a simmering. (*Seïr*, 2: 584)

This trope of the mingling of milk and sugar represents an image of reconciliation close to the heart of the Orientalist regime. Jones's attempts to reconfigure the binaries of imperialism place a similar emphasis upon cultural synthesis and syncretism. Admiration for the eldest son of Shah Jahān, the scholar prince Dārā Shikūh, was doubtless influenced by Jones's reading of the sympathetic portrait within the pages of Ghulam Husain's *Seïr Mutaqharin*. Dārā Shikūh's Persian text entitled *Majma 'al-bahrayn* or 'The Mingling of the Two Oceans' maintained that the fundamental tenets of Hinduism were essentially monotheistic and identical with those of Islam. According to Ghulam Husain, Dārā Shikūh 'seemed to inculcate the precepts of Quietisme and Mysticisme, and openly to give his approbation, and even preference, to some tenets of the Gentoo law' (*Seïr*, 3: 348). In describing his execution at the hands of his strictly orthodox Sunni brother, Aurangzeb, Ghulam Husain refers to Dārā Shikūh as 'the unfortunate prince [...] made an example of, to terrify the pretenders to the crown' (*Seïr*, 3: 349).

When Jones introduces Dārā Shikūh into his essay 'On the Mystical Poetry of the Persians and Hindus' (1792) he echoes Ghulam Husain's epithet, referring his readers for 'detail of their [Sūfī] metaphysicks and theology to the *Dabistan* of MOHSANI FANI, and to the pleasing essay, called the *Junction of two Seas*, by that amiable and unfortunate Prince, DÁRÁ SHECÚH' (*Works*, 4: 232; 13: 365). It is, however, important to contextualize this foregrounding and juxtaposition of Mohsanī Fani's *Dabistan* and Dārā Shikūh's *Majma 'al-bahrayn*.

It might seem that in learning Sanskrit Jones had moved on from the Middle East, but although this appeared an even greater revelation than his earlier discovery of Arabic and Persian poetry, it by no means displaced his first

16. Equestrian portrait of Dara Shikoh as a young man, by Chitarman, gouache, c.1640. (Royal Asiatic Society)

Oriental love. He was, after all 'Persian' Jones, and India was affording still more Persian delights. In delivering his 'Sixth Anniversary Discourse: On the Persians' to the Asiatic Society on the evening of the 19 February 1789, he acknowledges both his excitement and a debt of gratitude at being introduced to the *Dabistan*: 'A fortunate discovery, for which I was first indebted to *Mír* MUHAMMED HUSAIN, one of the most intelligent *Muselmàns* in *India*, has at once dissipated the cloud, and cast a gleam of light on the primeval history of *Iràn* and of the human race, of which I had long despaired, and which could hardly have dawned from any other quarter.'[17] This excitement was shared in Calcutta, and almost immediately the enterprising Francis Gladwin set about translating the *Dabistan*, selections from which he speedily published in his periodical, *The New Asiatic Miscellany*.[18]

In studying the remarkable parallels between Islamic and Hindu mysticism, Jones reveals his fascination with the mystical allegories of Sūfism. To the zealous admirers of Hāfiz Shirazi a glass of Shiraz might signify a toast to sublime devotion. To illustrate this Jones cites a literal translation of 'a most extraordinary ode' by the celebrated Ismat of Bokhara (d. 1436):

> Yesterday, half inebriated, I passed by the quarter, where the vintners dwell, to seek the daughter of an infidel who sells wine.
>
> At the end of the street, there advanced before me a damsel with a fairy's cheeks, who, in the manner of a pagan, wore her tresses dishevelled over her shoulder like the sacerdotal thread. I said: *O thou, to the arch of whose eye-brow the new moon is a slave, what quarter is this and where is thy mansion?*
>
> She answered: *Cast thy rosary on the ground; bind on thy shoulder the thread of paganism; throw stones at the glass of piety; and quaff wine from a full goblet;*
>
> *After that come before me, that I may whisper a word in thine ear: thou wilt accomplish thy journey, if thou listen to my discourse.*
>
> ('On the Mystical Poetry of the Persians and Hindus', *Works*, 4: 428-9)

This is intoxicating stuff, and insofar as the damsel wears her tresses in the style of the Brahman's sacred thread, which she advises the poet to bind on his shoulder, this Sūfi ode serves to some extent to prepare the metropolitan reader for the bold luxuriance and divine eroticism of that more explicit Hindu 'Song of Songs', Jayadeva's *Gītagovinda*.

---

17. *Works*, 3: 110. Jones had quoted an elegy of Mir Muhammad Hussain in his 'On the Orthography of Asiatic Words', ibid., 301–5.
18. *The New Asiatic Miscellany* (1789), 86–136.

In this way Jones makes his own important contribution to the 'Mingling of the Two Oceans' of Islam and Hinduism. As we have seen, Jones also followed Dārā Shikūh's lead in being drawn to the late Vedas, the Upaniṣads, but introducing his own translation of the Íśávásyam or Isa-Upaniṣad from the Sanskrit, Jones refers to Dārā's Persian version, the Sirr-i Akbar, with some reservation:

> [T]hough sublime, and majestick features of the original were discernible, in parts, through folds of the Persian drapery; yet the Sanscrit names were so barbarously written, and the additions of the translator has made the work so deformed, that I resolved to postpone a regular perusal of it till I could compare it with the Sanscrit original. (Works, 13: 366)

Such comments have been viewed as reflecting hostile condescension towards Persian and Indo-Persian scholarship, but this is not the case. They simply reveal the linguist's enthusiastic desire to study the original. Jones would have found a Sanskrit translation of Hāfiz equally irritating. In the same way, when pursuing his path-breaking ethnomusicological research into Hindu music via a study of Sanskrit, rather than Persian, texts, Jones's remark: 'that a man, who knows the Hindus only from Persian books, does not know the Hindus; and that an European, who follows the muddy rivulets of Muselman writers on India, instead of drinking from the pure fountain of Hindu learning, will be in perpetual danger of misleading himself and others' (Works, 4:181), underlines both his own priority in being a Sanskrit scholar and his determination to study original sources.

Only a very few of the Company servants who devoted some of their leisure time to Orientalist researches had learned Sanskrit. Persian, an essential political tool of diplomacy, was much more widely studied by the members of the Asiatick Society. Since 1780 Richard Johnson, a scholar of Arabic, Persian, and Urdu, had enjoyed the lucrative post of deputy to the Resident at the court of the wazir of Oudh, and his experience in Lucknow, effectively the foremost centre of artistic patronage since Mughal decline in Delhi, encouraged him to commission a lithographic edition of Hāfiz.[19] 'I hope some years hence', wrote Jones, 'to offer up a copy of it on the tomb of the divine poet near the crystal stream of Rucnabad' (Letters, 2: 702). In Calcutta, Johnson had helped Jones investigate Hindu mythology, but they also shared an immense respect

---

19. Dīvān-i Khvājah Hāfiz Shīrāzī madībāchah va qaṣāid. The Works of Hafez; with an account of his life and writings (Calcutta, 1791).

for Persian literature and the friendship of poets and scholars such as Abū Ṭalēb Khān Isfahānī, the editor of Hāfiz, Mir Muhammed Husain, and Mir Qamar ud-Din Minnat, whose diwan, dedicated to Johnson, and containing elegant miniatures of both Johnson and Hastings, earned for Minnat the governor-general's accolade of 'King of Poets'.

An interesting note to Colonel Allan Macpherson, which escaped Garland Cannon's masterly edition of the letters, reveals that even in snatched moments on the judicial bench Jones found time to seek patronage for a talented Persian poet fallen upon hard times:

In Court, 6th Jan. 1786.

Dear Sir,

Mirza Zainuddin Ishky is a man of genius and probity. I presented the Governor General last year with his works, and an Ode which I translated. He has been so poor that he has been forced to sell his darling books: but his son in law, who is in the service of the Vizier's Minister, has now invited him to settle at Lucknow. It would be very honourable to him if the Governor would favour him with a recommendatory letter to the Nabob Vizier. His literary merit I can answer for.[20]

Another brief letter reveals Jones's hitherto unknown friendship with William Augustus Brooke, Revenue Chief at Patna, who—throughout fifty-six years in India—gave patronage and practical help to many Indo-Persian writers, including Abū Ṭalēb Khān Isfahānī, and 'Abd al-Qādir Khān, the author of a history of Kashmir, dedicated to Hishmat al-Dawlah ('Splendour of the State'), Brooke's Persian honorific.[21] Both men were keen to assist Muslim and Hindu scholars:

Shall I trouble you to forward a letter to our friend Ghúlam Hussain Khan? *Dhuphnarayen* desires me to mention him to Genl. Sloper. Do you know what he particularly desires and in what capacity he served Mrs Wheler? When shall we have the pleasure of seeing you?[22]

---

20. *Soldiering in India 1764–1787*, ed. W. C. Macpherson (Edinburgh, 1928), 345. Jones presented Zainudeen's works, together with 'a hasty translation [...] of the best couplets', to Sir John Macpherson on 22 May 1785, and arranged for the poet to receive an interview with the acting governor-general; see *Letters*, 2: 673–5.
21. Mohammed Ahmed Simsar, *Oriental Manuscripts of the John Frederick Lewis collection in the Free Library of Philadelphia* (Philadelphia, 1937), 67.
22. See Ralph J. Crane, 'Letters of Sir William Jones in the Dunedin Public Library', *Notes & Queries*, 39: 1 (March 1992), 66–7; Crane fails to identify Jones's correspondent.

Brooke married a Muslim servant, whose literary talents he encouraged with the help of his *munshi* Khurran-mal. 'The *Lady* of Mr William Augustus Brooke' compiled the *Miftāhi Kulūbu-l-Mubtadln* ('The Key of the Hearts of Beginners'), a collection of moral tales and anecdotes from Persian authors, to assist their children's trilingual education.[23]

A verse 'Epistle to Sir William Jones' (1790), written by Captain John Horsford, one of Bengal's most battle-hardened artillery commanders during the Third Anglo-Mysore War, implored Jones not to let his mind be clouded by 'the cares of war', but 'to Persian lore devote the hour'. Jones's war effort must be exerted in the 'tender field' of Persian translation:

> KHAKANI's thoughts t' admiring ears express,
> Or your lov'd HAFIZ bring in English dress:
> With KHOOSRU sing how gentle pangs t' assuage,
> And trace pure SADI thro' his moral page;
> But if fatigu'd in this too tender field,
> Then seek the joys GILLALIDEN can yield,
> With ATTAR join in philosophic taste,
> Th' enlighten'd ROCHFOUCALT of half the East:[24]

Horsford, an expert in the deployment of cannon, mortar, and rocket to counter Tīpū's formidable artillery, though inured to blowing Muslims into little pieces, is also married to one. With his beloved Saheb Jaun, Horsford had six children, and the soldier longs for peace and the 'divine sublime' of Sūfi poetry as revealed by Jones: 'The spoils of war no real joys can give,/ 'Tis POESY's soothing voice that makes us live.'

In 1771 Jones's *Grammar of the Persian Language* had provided Europe with the very first English translations of one and a half quatrains (*rubā'īyat*) by Omar Khayyām (d. 1131).[25] In Bengal he transcribed, transliterated and

---

23. Bibi Brooke, *The Key of the Hearts of Beginners*, trans. Annette S. Beveridge (London, 1908).
24. *A Collection of Poems Written in the East Indies By J—H—* (Calcutta, 1797), 29–32. Jones describes the *Habsiyya* (Prison Poem) of Khāqānī (c.1127–87) as 'the wildest and strangest poem that was ever written [...] The fire of Khakani's genius blazes through the smoke of his erudition' (*Letters*, 2: 763).
25. 'At the time that the dawn appears, dost thou know for what reason the bird of the morning complains? He says, that it is shown in the mirror of the day, that a whole night of thy life is passed, while thou art lost in indolence'; 'By the approach of spring, and the return of December, the leaves of our life are continually folded'; *Works*, 5: 308; 185. This was first pointed out by L. P. Elwell-Sutton in a note to his introduction to Ali Dashti, *In Search of Omar Khayyam*, trans. L. P. Elwell-Sutton (London, 1971), 13, n. 4, but, despite the continuing popularity of Khayyām, the scholarly world seems to have taken little notice of this fact.

translated a hitherto unknown *rubā'ī* which he attributes to this philosopher, mathematician, and astronomer. Jones gave it the title 'Quatrain on the Vanity of Kingly Grandiosity By Khiyyám':

> I allow that thy throne, O *King*, may be formed of beryl & jasper: but he who has a discerning eye, esteems it a common stone: this royal seat of ermine & sable & precious fur appears in the sight of those who sit *contented* upon mats to be merely Vulgar Wool.[26]

Jones was drawn to this quatrain as it reflected his continuing suspicion of arbitrary monarchy. Influenced by imagery drawn from the thirteenth-century classic of Islamic mysticism, Rūmī's *Masnavi*, its author displays a scholarly Sūfi aloofness from the trappings of secular power.[27] Arguably, in the contrast drawn between ermine and wool there might be an allusion to the fact that Sūfi derives from the Arabic word *sūf* (wool), connoting the pious mystic wool-wearer, a dervish dress of radical renunciation.

Jones had listed others of his favourite Sūfi poets in 'On the Mystical Poetry of the Persians and Hindus', including 'Sáib, Orfí, Mír Khosrau, Jámi, Hazin, and Sábik, who are next in beauty of composition to Hafiz and Sadi', mentioning also 'Mesíhi, the most elegant of their *Turkish* imitators; [...] a few *Hindi* poets of our own times, and [...] Ibnul Fáred, who wrote mystical odes in *Arabick*' (*Works*, 4: 232). Such poets featured largely among the manuscripts and books that lined the shelves of his Ariśnagar study. They were also widely translated by many other Company and Crown employees in Calcutta and the other presidencies.

Abundant evidence of this is provided by a single number of Francis Gladwin's Calcutta periodical, *The New Asiatic Miscellany* (1789) mentioned above. Apart from Gladwin's own translations of sections of the *Dabistan*, the contents include Captain William Kirkpatrick's 'Introduction to the History of the Persian Poets'; translations of 'The Death of Mahomet' and 'The Death of Fatima' from one of the first Urdu prose works of North India, the *Deh Majlis* by Faz'li; a letter from Emperor Akbar to the Ruler of

---

26. New York, Fales Library, Jones MSS, 1: 19.
27. On the cover of his manuscript of Rūmī's *Masnavi*, Jones wrote: 'So extraordinary a book as the Mesnavi was never, perhaps, composed by man. It abounds with beauties, and blemishes, equally great; with gross obscenity, and pure ethicks; with exquisite strains of poetry, and flat puerilities of wit; with ridicule on established religions, and a vein of sublime piety: it is like a wild country in a fine climate overspread with rich flowers and with the odour of beasts. I know of no writer, to whom the Maulavi can justly be compared, except *Chaucer* or *Shakespeare*', *Works*, 13: 401–26; 417.

Turan, translated by John Stonehouse;[28] 'The Institutes of Ghâzân Khan, Emperor of the Moghuls', translated by Kirkpatrick; substantial extracts from Sa'dī's *Bostan*; and a fascinating example of enlightened Calcutta relativism entitled 'Doctor Franklin's Celebrated Parable against Persecution, Compared with a Passage in the Bostan of Sâdi'.

This comparativist article describes Sa'dī's *Bostan* as 'a work abounding in the purest morality, and in some of the highest strains of piety', and perfectly exemplifies the same open-minded syncretic acceptance of Oriental poetry and Oriental piety to be found in the writings of Jones. Furthermore, the whole periodical, its scholarly bias attested by many of the translations being accompanied by the originals set in Persian *nasta'līq* types, reflects a virtually exclusive focus upon Persian and Arabic texts concerned with ethics and good Mughal government. The only specifically 'Hindu' contents are the opening item, which was the first publication of Jones's own 'Hymn to Lacshmí', and 'The Stanzas called the Five Gems ('Pánca Retnáni'), composed by five Poets, who attended the Court of ADÍSÚRA, King of Bengal'.

One other significant item in *The New Asiatic Miscellany* is a poem entitled 'Raikhtah, or Ode from Wulli', which is printed in *devānagrī* (Skr. 'language [or 'town-script'] of the gods') characters with an interlineal transliteration and accompanying translation. This 'Wulli' is Vali Gujarati, the first poet to compose *ghazals* in an Indian language, Urdu, rather than in Persian, and whose Ahmedabad tomb, a site of pilgrimage for Indian poets of all languages, was desecrated in 2002. Vali, though not a Sūfi poet, was greatly inspired by Sūfi themes, and Urdu poetry has continued to reflect the profound influence of Sūfism. Vali was a revolutionary integrator and his celebrated visit to Delhi in 1700 encouraged poets to combine the dynamic vigour of Persian diction and imagery with the sensuous Indianized beauty of Urdu vocabulary.

'Rekhtah' was the old name for Hindi/Urdu,[29] and Vali's example encouraged a new wave of Indo-Muslim poets to use Rekhtah. 'By the

---

28. Akbar stresses how throughout 'the vast country of Hindustan [...] many and various descriptions of people, though differing widely in manners and in customs, now maintain the most friendly intercourse with each other', *New Asiatic Miscellany* (1789), 75.
29. Hindi–Urdu, the Indo-Aryan *lingua franca* of the Indo-Pakistani people, is one language with two names: Hindi when written in *devānagrī* script by Hindus, and Urdu when Arabo-Persic *nasta'līq* script is used by Muslims. Sharing the same grammatical, syntactical, and phonological systems, Hindi vocabulary is largely derived from Sanskrit whereas that of Urdu is

mid-eighteenth century', as Shamsur Rahman Faruqi points out, 'the Hindus, too, who had also been concentrating on Persian, began to adopt Rekhtah.'[30] The fact that this *ghazal* by Vali is printed by Gladwin in *devānagrī* rather than Perso-Arabic characters may be seen as important evidence of literary-cultural mingling. According to John Gilchrist's *Dictionary English and Hindoostanee* (1787–90), 'rekhtu' can mean a mixture as in plaster or mortar and, in the building of the new poetics of Urdu, Muslim and Hindu elements combined.

This new and syncretic poetic idiom excited young writers in Delhi at the beginning of the eighteenth century and reflected the cultural mingling of milk and sugar to which Ghulam Husain refers. Gopi Chand Nārang maintains that the 'indigenous base and syncretic qualities' of Urdu enables it to perform a 'syncretizing role in a pluralistic, secular and democratic India', and it would seem that Vali Gujarati, whose poetry the Calcutta Orientalists were reading and translating in the late 1780s, played a key role in this process of reconciliation.[31]

Gladwin's *New Asiatick Miscellany* reveals a marked emphasis upon the poetry and prose of politics, a politics of reconciliation that had been central to Hastings's Orientalist government, although Hastings himself in 1789 was being harangued by Sheridan for his 'monstrous behaviour' towards the Begums. In Bengal Hastings had appreciated that Mughal policies concerning the exchange of cultural and doctrinal information and of artistic and intellectual collaboration were valuable means of creating a measure of integration in the vast heterogeneity that was northern India.[32] He had set the tone and it was generally followed by Company servants. There was certainly no anti-Muslim bias among these periodical contributors, quite the reverse in fact, and they appeared to appreciate that in the building of empire the mortar of Rekhtah might prove useful.

---

    borrowed from Persian and Arabic. In the written language there are lexical differences, but as a means of oral communication in many ways there is an effective mingling and merging.

30. 'A Long History of Urdu Literary Culture, Part 1: Naming and Placing a Literary Culture', in *Literary Cultures in History: Reconstructions from South Asia*, ed. Sheldon Pollock (Berkeley, 2003), 805–63; 849, n. 100.
31. Gopi Chand Nārang, *Urdu Language and Literature* (New Delhi, 1991), vii.
32. 'Persian literary culture had a certain logical connection with the Mughal political ideology. It helped generate and legitimate the Mughal policy of creating out of heterogeneous social and religious groups a class of allies. Like the emperor and his nobility in general, this class also cherished universalist human values and visions', Muzaffar Alam, 'Persian in Precolonial Hindustan', in *Literary Cultures in History*, ed. Pollock, 131–98; 171.

The origins of Rekhtah and of *sabk-i Hindī* (Indian-style diction) are the subjects of heated dispute among linguistic and literary scholars of pre-colonial northern India.[33] But there is a general acceptance of the key role of Amīr Khusrau (1253–1325), the greatest of the pre-Mughal poets and the second victim of twenty-first-century tomb desecration, in the development of both *sabk-i Hindī* and Rekhtah. Amongst the Calcutta Orientalists there was significant interest in this Indo-Persian Sūfī poet, whose writings exemplify a profoundly multicultural or pluralistic position.

Amīr Khusrau was born in Patiali in Uttar Pradesh, of an Indian mother and a Turkish father; his life and his Arabic, Persian, and Hindi/Urdu writings anticipate the cultural synthesis between Hindu and Muslim civilization later to flourish at the court of Akbar. Jones was particularly attracted to the polymathic versatility of this 'Indian parrot' and Turco-Indic 'Renaissance man'. Historian, poet, literary critic, courtier, musician, and mystic, Khusrau, like Jones, was alive to the sensuality of India, its beautiful Hindu women, its flora, fauna, and languages.

Aziz Ahmad observes unreconciled tensions in Khusrau's *'Āshiqa*, which celebrates the love of the Muslim prince Khizar Khān for the Hindu princess Dewal Rānī. Whereas Wahīd Mirza described the poem as 'fragrant with the smell of *kewrā*, the *karnā*, the *champak*, and hundreds of sweet Indian flowers and spices, and is luminous with the bright Indian sun, and the pale cool moonlight', Ahmad claims the poem reveals 'that the India he loves is the land of the splendour of Islam, where the *sharī'a* is honoured and secure, and Hinduism has been conquered'.[34] Perhaps such orthodoxy was expected by his Sultan patron. On the other hand, Ahmad cites many contrasting examples of Khusrau's polemical defence of Hinduism, and his emphasis upon its essential similarities with Islam. What is important is that the lionizing of Amīr Khusrau is part of a revered tradition in India, especially amongst those who have wished to encourage cultural harmony within the subcontinent. This political motive was stressed in a review of a 1975 tribute volume:

> Several of the essays [...] do little more lionize the poet—stressing his religious tolerance towards Hindus and other religious groups and his raptur-

---

33. Conflicting accounts may be found in Amrit Rai, *A House Divided: The Origin and Development of Hindi-Urdu* (New Delhi, 1991) and Shamsur Rahman Faruqi's *Early Urdu Literary Culture and History* (New Delhi, 2001).
34. Aziz Ahmad, *Studies in Islamic Culture in the Indian Environment* (Oxford, 1964), 115.

ous pronouncements about all things Indian. It is not by chance that the publisher of this volume is the Government of India.[35]

It would seem that the poetry of politics was operating along remarkably similar lines for the world's largest democracy in the 1970s as it had within the 'enlightened' despotism of British India two centuries earlier. Much of the Hindi/Urdu poetry attributed to Khusrau, it is now clear, was not written by him and, although there is conclusive evidence of his interest in combining Persian and Hindu traditions of music, the tradition that he invented the sitar, developing it from the indigenous *vina*, which Jones and Francis Fowke had studied, is similarly apocryphal. Amīr Khusrau, in his freedom from ethnic, religious, or social prejudice, is a potent icon; had he not existed, it might have proved expedient to invent such a symbol of India's plural heritage. But invention is not necessary, and even the attributions to this inventive genius remain inherently interesting.

Imre Bangha cites and translates 'a popular poem attributed to Amīr Khusrau' in which the first half of each line is in Persian and the second in Brajbhasha, a dialect of Hindi:

> Do not be indifferent towards the condition of the poor one. You hide your eyes and invent excuses.
> I do not have the strength for separation, oh my love, why don't you embrace me?[36]

This mixing of languages symbolizes a cultural embrace, such as was not to be seen again until the time of Akbar. Furthermore, as Carla Petievich has shown, this may be compared with the *viraha bhakti* ('love-in-separation') theme of Sanskrit, for what was to develop in Rekhtah or Urdu was the fascinating 'gender-mingling' of the genre of *rēkhtī*, in which the female point of view is assumed by a male poet. This might well have much to do with the fact that the grammar of Urdu, unlike that of Persian, allows gender differentiation, which means that a poet such as Vali Gujarati can hymn the female beauties of Surat.[37]

These *rēkhtī* poets were, almost without exception, male, but, interestingly, one exception was Naubahār Zalīl, a maidservant of Prince Sulaimān

---

35. Carlo Coppola, review of *Amir Khusrau Memorial Volume* (1975), *Journal of Asian Studies*, 37: 4 (1978), 767.
36. See Imre Bangha, 'Early Rekhta Poetry in the Nāgarī script', (forthcoming).
37. Carla Petievich, 'The Feminine and Cultural Syncretism in Early Dakani Poetry', *Annual of Urdu Studies*, 8 (Winter 1993), 110–21; 112.

Shikūh.[38] British Romanticism encountered this brave and handsome son of Dārā Shikūh in a novel of sentiment written by the celebrated Sydney Owenson. Influenced by the theories of Jones's correspondent Colonel Charles Vallancey, her *Wild Irish Girl* (1807) suggested that Gaelic culture had Oriental origins, having been colonized by the enlightened Phoenicians. She was reversing received stereotypes of Irish barbarity, spelling out the civilizing effects of Eastern culture all too frequently destroyed by Western barbarism. In a spirit of Indo-European and Indo-Hibernian solidarity she turned her attention to India.

Her novel, *The Missionary: An Indian Tale* (1811), appeared amidst the heated debate preceding the renewal of the East India Company's Charter, and especially the 'Pious Clause' concerning the question of whether missionaries should be allowed to operate on Company territory. Opposed to missionary activity, Owenson introduced Sulaimān Shikūh into the novel to complete both a love triangle (of Kashmiri Hindu priestess, Islamic prince, and Franciscan monk) and a triad of three great Oriental religions, whose major tenets are not only seen in terms of a Jonesian syncretism, but expressed in Jones's words. This Romantic novel, which has been described 'as a perfectly extraordinary fictionalization of the psyche of William Jones', popularizes a cultural synthesis in which *bhakti*, *śakti*, Vedantic philosophy, Sūfism, and deism commingle like the waters of sacred Hindu *tirthas* (confluences/river shrines) within a paradisal Kashmiri setting.[39]

To return to Jones and Amīr Khusrau via Owenson and Dārā Shikūh's son has a certain syncretic inevitability. Certainly, Jones, like Khusrau, celebrated India in all its bewildering multifariousness. He was discovering interrelationship everywhere and the work of Persian intellectuals played a major role in the development of Jones's linguistic ideas. Jones knew the philological works of the eighteenth-century Mughal writer, Sirāj al-Din 'Alī Khān Ārzū (d. 1756), and had read in his *Sirāj al-Lughat* of the correspondence (*tavāfuq*) between Persian and Sanskrit.[40] But Ārzū's findings had been anticipated by more than four centuries by none other than Amīr

---

38. See C. M. Naim, 'Transvestic Words?: The Rekhti in Urdu', *Annual of Urdu Studies*, 16: 1 (2001), 3–26; 3.
39. Drew, *India and the Romantic Imagination*, 253; Michael J Franklin, 'Passion's Empire: Sydney Owenson's Indian Venture, Phoenicianism, Orientalism, and Binarism', *Studies in Romanticism*, 45 (Summer 2006), 181–97.
40. On Jones's study of 'Sirajaid'din Arzu'; see 'A Catalogue of Oriental Manuscripts', item 102n., *Works*, 13: 419.

Khusrau. In his *Nuh sipihr* (The Nine Heavens/Spheres), completed in the year 1318, Khusrau described Sanskrit in the following terms:

> But there is another language more select than the others, which all the Brahmans use. Its name from of old is Sahaskrit, and the common people know nothing of it. A Brahman knows it, but Brahmaní women do not understand a word of it. It bears a resemblance to Arabic in some respects, in its permutations of letters, its grammar, its conjugations, and polish.[41]

Khusrau's references to the 'select' and polished character of Sanskrit are echoed in Jones's emphasis upon its 'perfect', 'copious', and 'refined' nature in the 'philologer' passage of his 'Third Anniversary Discourse'. Crucially, Khusrau, like Jones, stresses key similarities in grammatical forms. While Jones the linguist is noting comparative philology centuries earlier than his own, Jones the poet is exhilarated by Khusrau's linguistic experimentation, and the intriguing humour of his wordplay. Aziz Ahmad informs us of Khusrau that: 'For the amusement of his friends he wrote mixed Persian and Hindi verses. These *dhu'l-lisanāyn* (bilingual) quatrains tail off in *jeux d'esprit* which could be read with *double entendre* as Persian or as Hindi.'[42] Jones had composed *jeux d'esprit* on the banks of the Teifi and the banks of the Ganges, but he had never produced anything so delightfully plural as the humorous occasional verse of Khusrau.

Included within a British Library collection of documents reflecting Jones's Persian studies in India is a contemporary Indian blind-stamped leather-bound book containing his transcriptions and translations of poems by Amīr Khusrau. One of Jones's favourites is the following translation of a Khusrau quatrain, perfectly exemplifying this playful linguistic pluralism:

> I went to recreate myself on the bank of a rivulet
> I saw on the brink of the stream a *Hindú* woman.
> I said: 'My idol, what is the price of your locks?'
> She cried out: 'Dur dur múy': that is, in *Hindy*,
> 'Keep your distance, sirrah!'
> In *Persian*, 'a pearl for each hair.'[43]

---

41. Khusrau, *The Third Sphere, Packard Humanities Institute; Persian Literature in Translation*: http://persian.packhum.org/persian/main
42. Ahmad, *Studies in Islamic Culture*, 116–17.
43. BL, APAC, MSS Eur. C 274.

Many aspects of intercultural relationship may be appreciated in this riverside meeting at bathing ghat or *tirtha*. Water is important in both religions for re-creation and for ritual purification or indeed both, if we think of Krishna sporting with the *gopis* in the Yamuna River. It highlights potentially divisive, but ultimately resolvable, issues of religion (idolatry) and love (*fin' amour*)—itself originally an Oriental discourse. In this interracial relationship, productive tensions play around the fact that the Hindu woman is both his worshipped 'idol' and an idol worshipper. The humour involved in her rejection of what on one level is an insolent question, is perfectly caught in Jones's translation of the Hindi by the words: 'Keep your distance, sirrah!', combining a mixture of contempt, reassertion of authority, reprimand, with a hint of playful rejection. The Persian meaning of the words adds a superbly haughty self-compliment encapsulating the treasure of her own beauty and, by association, the beauty of the subcontinent.

In his addition of a bilingual dimension to the rhetorical device of *īhām* (playing on multiple meanings of a word), Amīr Khusrau produces a highly sophisticated poetic that goes far beyond simple *double entendre* or punning. This is the semiotics of the syncretic. Its radical importance in terms of cultural interaction lies in its power to disconcert, and to re-create imaginative spaces (mirrored in Jones's choice of the Augustan-sounding term 'recreate myself') in the re-creation of reading/translating. Khusrau creates new interrelationships between words, seemingly identical but etymologically discrete, within the diverse linguistic family, which—as a result of Jones's researches—would be grouped as Indo-European.

William Jones, even more than the Indian-born Amīr Khusrau 500 years earlier, was an invading imperialist. Within the subcontinent, however, an indigenous tradition of religious pluralism stretches back a millennium before the Mamluk dynasty, which Khusrau and his father served. It is at least as old as the edicts of the Maurya emperor, Aśoka (r. 273–232 BCE), the four-lion capital from one of whose pillars provided the emblem of India's republic. The Maurya empire was founded in 322 BCE by Chandragupta whose identification by Jones had enabled Indian history to be aligned with that of the West. Aśoka, his grandson, proved a ferocious warrior in extending the boundaries of empire, but his victory over the fearless resistance encountered in Kalinga (Orissa) involved such horrific bloodshed that he converted to Buddhism. Adopting *ahimsa* or non-violence, his future conquests would be by *dharma* rather than the sword.

Aśoka's edicts, cut in rocks and in polished Chunar stone, record, according to Richard Gombrich: 'a personality and a concept of rule unique not merely in Indian but perhaps in world history'.[44] They order abolition of the death penalty, the protection of animal species, and embody respect for universal justice and for the intrinsic morality of all religions. Two edicts in Afghanistan bear Greek inscriptions, for the remnants of Alexander's colonists, one of which is also carved in Aramaic, the language of the Persian empire. Rādhākanta and Jones were unable to translate the oldest inscriptions on the Aśokan pillar, which Firuz Shah, Muslim son of a Hindu princess, had re-erected at Delhi. They would have been delighted to read Aśoka's words:

> How can the welfare and happiness of the people be secured? I give attention to my relatives, to those dwelling near and those dwelling far, so I can lead them to happiness and then I act accordingly. I do the same for all groups. I have honoured all religions with various honours. But I consider it best to meet with people personally. (Pillar Edict 6)[45]

Aśoka's twelfth edict states: 'There should be growth in the essentials of all religions [...] all of them have as their root restraint in speech, that is, not praising one's own religion, or condemning the religion of others without good cause.' This ancient encouragement of amicable inter-religious discourse underlines the central importance of what the distinguished Nobel Prize-winner, Amartya Sen, has termed the Indian 'argumentative' tradition of tolerance and pluralism over almost two and a half millennia.[46] Unlike his fellow Nobel laureate V. S. Naipaul, Sen refuses to view the entry of Islam into the subcontinent as destructive of Hindu civilization, seeing Mughal emperor Akbar as an integral part of this continuity of tolerant pluralism. To see Jones's role in Hastings's Orientalist regime as bringing Europe and a distant subcontinent much closer philosophically and linguistically is to honour the invading West's contribution to India.

The textual construction of India achieved by Jones's comparative philological, historical, and literary researches can be viewed against this back-

---

44. Richard Gombrich, *Theravada Buddhism: A Social History from Ancient Benares to Modern Colombo* (London, 1988), 95.
45. 'The Edicts of King Ashoka', trans. Ven. S. Dhammika (Kandy, Sri Lanka, 1994): http://www.cs.colostate.edu/~malaiya/ashoka.html
46. Amartya Sen, *Identity and Violence: The Illusion of Destiny* (London, 2006).

drop of a pre-existent Indian pluralism in which a multiplicity of beliefs coexisted and sometimes coalesced. But in the textualizing of India the Orientalists played into the hands of their Anglicist, Utilitarian, and evangelical adversaries. A textual subcontinent could be contained within the range of James Mill's bookshelves, and Mill, who viewed his failure to visit India as a positive benefit to his objectivity, could produce his hegemonic *History of British India* (1817) without stirring from his study.

In some respects the future seemed to rest with philistinism. Thomas Babington Macaulay also rejected the vast imaginative space that Jones had discerned in India. He too was obsessed with shelf-space, and in his infamous 'Minute on Education' of 1835 pronounced that: 'A single shelf of a good European library is worth the whole native literature of India and Arabia.' Ignorance and prejudice were compounded by the issue of new Enfield rifles to the Company sepoys in 1857. Where Ghulam Husain had written of Gentoo and Musulman coalescing like the mingling of sugar and milk in Indian tea, it was the mixture of beef fat and lard with which the cartridges were greased that brought Hindus and Muslims, alarmed at being polluted and Christianized, together into open revolt.

The violent suppression of the Sepoy Revolt brought the end of Company rule and introduced a virtual apartheid, with the rigorous policing of racial and religious boundaries. The incredible imbecility that had led to the cartridge contract symbolized the cultural ignorance of the Raj. As a leading Calcutta journalist, Girish Chandra Ghose, wrote in 1862:

> As regards Indian literature [...] history, antiquities, the present race of Anglo-Indians [the British in India] are lamentably ignorant. Jones, Colebrooke, Wilson [...] respected our fathers and looked upon us hopefully at least with melancholy interest, as you would look on the heir of a ruined noble. But to the great unwashed abroad today, we are simply niggers—without a past; perhaps without a future. They do not choose to know us.[47]

Ghose detects the same 'thorough contempt for the Indians (as a national body)' that Hājī Mustafā had lamented over seventy years earlier. But both men underestimated the revolutionary power of comparative philology. Jones had demolished Western claims to intellectual superiority. In the words of the German Orientalist, Friedrich Max Müller: 'These silent influences often escape the eye of the politician and the historian, but at

---

47. *Selections from the Writings of G.C. Ghose*, ed. M. M. Ghose (Calcutta, 1912), 434.

critical moments they decide the fate of whole nations and empires.' Müller cites an article by 'a native writer', published at Calcutta in the *Indian Mirror* of 20 September 1874:

> When the dominion passed from the Mogul to the hands of Englishmen, the latter regarded the natives as little better than niggers, having a civilisation perhaps a shade better than that of the barbarians. [...] The gulf was wide between the conquerors and the conquered. [...] There was no affection to lessen the distance between the two races. The discovery of Sanskrit entirely revolutionised the course of thought and speculations. It served as the 'open sesame' to many hidden treasures. It was then that the position of India in the scale of civilisation was distinctly apprehended. It was then that our relations with the advanced nations of the world were fully realised. We were niggers at one time. We now become brethren. [...] The advent of Scholars like Sir William Jones found us fully established in a rank above that of every nation, as that from which modern civilisation could be distinctly traced. It would be interesting to contemplate what would have been our position if the science of philology had not been discovered. [...] It was only when the labour of scholars brought to light the treasures of our antiquity that they perceived how near we were to their races in almost all things that they held dear in their life. It was then that our claims on their affection and regard were first established. As Hindus we ought never to forget the labour of scholars. We owe them our life as a nation, our freedom as a recognised society, and our position in the scale of races.[48]

William Jones's retrieval of Sanskrit texts and reconstruction of India's past did not simply inspire Oriental renaissance for Western Romanticism, it reshaped India's self-perception, encouraging cultural renaissance in Bengal. Sanskrit texts became defining political symbols of Hindu resistance to British rule; but for Jones, as for Pandit Nehru, India was more than *Hindutva* (Hindu-ness). His lifelong fascination with Indo-Persian linguistic and ethnological affinities entailed both his intellectual investment in pluralism, and his fervent belief in the syncretic co-existence of Hinduism and Islam. Both Nehru, in his *Discovery of India* (1946), and Mahatma Gandhi, the two architects of Indian nationalism, would represent the inherent difference of India as the dynamism of cultural synthesis, but ultimately subcontinental liberty was sadly yoked with the fragmentation of partition.

As the streets of its summer capital Śrinagar throng with armed Indian troops and paramilitaries rather than mystics and pilgrims, Arundhati Roy

---

48. Max Müller, *Chips from a German Workshop*, 4 vols (New York, 1876), 4: 372.

has stressed that Kashmir is 'the unfinished business in the partition of India and Pakistan', the 'gift of British colonialism'. The 'beautiful valley of *Cashmír*', as Jones described it, the 'perfect garden' of the blue lotus is polluted by a *Hindutva* increasingly associated with Hindu supremacists. Where is now the revered tradition of *Kashmiriyat*, encouraged by Akbar, influenced by Buddhism, Śaivism, Sikhism, and Sūfism, and characterized by religious harmony and cultural pluralism? The crisis continues with Indian media censorship, and the silence of the international community concerning human rights abuses in this cruelly divided territory.

In March 2003 I discovered a letter from Sir William Jones to Harford Jones, East India Company Joint Factor at Basra, expressing his passionate desire to see '*Persia*, the most delightful, the most compact, the most desirable country of them all', to view its cultural treasures and ancient monuments, and to talk to its respected poets.[49] While I read his words: 'I burn with a desire of seeing Shiraz', Baghdad was in flames. Jones's enduring fascination with Indo-Persian linguistic and ethnological affinities, his intellectual investment in pluralism, and his enlightened commitment to a syncretic East–West synthesis remain something of a beacon in a world where 'intelligence' is squandered upon missiles, and where the shrines of Sūfi saints are targets of Taleban explosives, intolerant Saudi-sponsored Wahhabism, and all those seeking to destroy the diversity and plurality of Islam.

As I write this concluding chapter, 'breaking news' of the latest outrage in the escalating crisis of the Punjab: 'Scores killed in suicide attack in Lahore', intrudes as a tragic coda. Late last night (Thursday, 1 July 2010) as thousands gathered at the beautiful green-domed Data Sahib shrine to worship, recite the Qur'an, and hear devotional music, two suicide bombers struck. Web photographs show the marble courtyard awash with blood. The puritanical jihadists chose the shrine of Afghanistan-born Hazrat Data Ganj Bakhsh Hujwīrī (d. CE 1071), Lahore's most revered Sūfi saint-protector, respected also by Hindus, Sikhs, and Parsees, by those who address their God as Rām or Rahim or a thousand other names.

A quarter of a century ago, Akbar S. Ahmed maintained that dominion over the Muslims of South Asia has always veered between the contrasting leadership styles of Dārā Shikūh's Sūfi-inspired syncretism and Aurangzeb's

---

49. See my 'I burn with a desire of seeing Shiraz': A New Letter from Sir William Jones to Harford Jones', *Review of English Studies*, N.S. 56: 227 (2005), 748–56.

fundamentalism, a polarity reflected in Zulfikar Ali Bhutto and General Zia respectively.[50] But perhaps that analysis is too simple. In Pakistan, as elsewhere, as long as the hopeless poverty of the people and the corruption of their military or 'feudal' landowning leaders continues to allow fundamentalists to represent themselves as fighting for social justice, the 'heretical' tolerance of Sūfīs will remain the softest of targets.

Lahore's patron saint, Hujwīrī composed the *Kashf-ul Mahjub* (The Unveiling of the Veiled), a founding icon of Indo-Persian culture. This most venerated early Persian Sūfī treatise emphasizes individual spiritual development and a deep humanitarianism, revealing an openness to Vedantic and Hellenistic thought and to Buddhist traditions. The veils that obscure one's knowledge of God, according to Hujwīrī, are the product of ignorance; for revelation and enlightenment to dawn, veils must vanish and the heart must expand. We recall James Anderson's words on peacemakers: 'Blessed are those who by painful researches, tend to remove those destructive veils which have so long concealed mankind from each other.'

Gautama the Buddha, the ninth avatar of Vishnu, though he received enlightenment under a Pipal or 'Bodhi tree', was born under an Aśoka tree. It was especially fitting that, in the year following Jones's death, this beautiful evergreen, with its fragrant orange-red flowers sacred to Hindus, Buddhists, and Jains, was named by botanist, William Roxburgh, as '*Jonesia Aśoca*'. Jones had declared: 'The vegetable world scarce exhibits a richer sight than an *Aśóca-tree* in full bloom' (*Works*, 5: 113). Aśoka means 'without sorrow' in Sanskrit and it is with joy that we celebrate the life of William Jones: 'the Celt [who] knew the Indian'.[51]

---

50. Akbar S. Ahmed, *Pakistan Society: Islam, Ethnicity and Leadership in South Asia* (Karachi, 1986).
51. See Percy Bysshe Shelley, *Prometheus Unbound: A Lyrical Drama in Four Acts* (London, 1820), II. iv. 94 (p. 86).

Select Bibliography

MANUSCRIPT SOURCES

Aberdeen University Library, King's College, Beattie Collection.
Library of the Institute of Actuaries at Staple Inn Hall, High Holborn, London, Jones MS
Asiatic Society, Kolkata, Manuscript Proceedings.
British Library, London (BL)
   Add. MSS 75735 Althorp Papers.
   Add. MSS. 29,235 Hastings Papers.
   Add. MSS 45589 Blechynden Diaries.
   Asia, Pacific and Africa Collections (APAC), formerly Oriental and India Office Collections (OIOC), Fowke MS Eur E9, 121 [f. 259].
   APAC, MSS Eur C 274: Jones's Persian Studies
   APAC, MSS Eur. A 172: Diary of Lady Frances Chambers, dated 1784.
   APAC, Sutton Court Collection, MSS Eur F.128/111, ff.100–102: Shāh 'Ālam to the King of Britain
Bodleian Library, Oxford
   MS. Beckford d. 28
   MS Sansk, C.34 Vópadéva, *Mugdhabodha*, f. xiii
Cambridge University Library MS Add 9597/12/11
Devonshire Collection, Chatsworth, Family Papers
Dunedin Public Library, New Zealand, Reed Collection
The Papers of Benjamin Franklin http://www.franklinpapers.org/franklin/
The National Archives, Kew
   ASSI 5/100/18: Worcestershire Lent Assizes, 1780.
   PROB 11/772, sig. 252.
Natural History Museum; Botany Library: 'Correspondence', MSS. Rox.
National Library of Wales (NLW)
   MS Ormathwaite, FE 5/1 'Memoir of Margaret Walsh'(née Fowke).
   Powis 1990 Deposit, 'Clive of India', packet 30
   MS 4 Wales 820/1
   2598C: Pennant Collection
New York, Fales Library: Jones MSS
New York Historical Society, Sharp Papers

Old Bailey Proceedings Online, www.oldbaileyonline.org
Packard Humanities Institute; Persian Literature in Translation, http://persian.packhum.org/persian/main
St John's Church, Kolkata, Minute Book
Victoria Memorial Hall, Kolkata, Hyde and Chambers Papers
Royal Asiatic Society, Jones Collection, 025.037
Yale University: Beinecke MSS Osborn Collection, FC. 163: c. 400, Jones Notebook
Beinecke, Boswell Collection GEN MSS 89, Ser., II. 24, 581, c 1593

PERIODICALS

The American Quarterly
Analytical Review
Asiatick Researches
The Annual Obituary and Biography for the year
The Annual Register
The Asiatic Annual Register
The Asiatick Miscellany
The Bee, or Literary Weekly Intelligencer
Calcutta Gazette
The Calcutta Review
Critical Review
English Review
European Magazine
The Evangelical Repository
Gentleman's Magazine
Journal of the Asiatic Society
Journal of the Royal Asiatic Society
The Monthly Magazine
Monthly Review
New Asiatick Miscellany
Pigs' Meat; or, Lessons for the Swinish Multitude
Quarterly Review
The Law Review and Quarterly Journal of British and Foreign Jurisprudence
New Annual Register
The Universal Magazine
Westminster Magazine

NEWSPAPERS

Calcutta Gazette
Indian Mirror
The Leeds Mercury

Lloyd's Evening Post
Morning Chronicle and London Advertiser
Morning Chronicle and Public Advertiser
Morning Post and Daily Advertiser
Public Advertiser

PRINTED PRIMARY SOURCES

Aikin, John, *General Biography*, 10 vols (London, 1799–1815).
Alam, Muzaffar and Seema Alavi (eds), *A European Experience of the Mughal Orient: The I'jāz-i Arsalānī (Persian Letters, 1773–1779) of Antoine-Louis Henri Polier* (New Delhi, 2001).
Alexander, James Edward (trans.), *Shigurf Namah-i-Velaët, Or, Excellent Intelligence Concerning Europe, Being the Travels of Mirza Itesa Modeen*, trans. (London, 1827).
Angelo, Henry, *Reminiscences of Henry Angelo*, 2 vols (London, 1830).
Apcar, Amy (ed.), *The Life and Adventures of Emin Joseph Emin 1726–1809; Written by Himself*, 2nd edn (Calcutta, 1918).
An Argument in the Case of Ebenezer Smith Platt, now under Confinement for High Treason (London, 1777).
Authentic report of the debate in the House of Commons, on the 6th and 7th of May, 1793, on Mr. Grey's motion for a reform in Parliament (London, 1793).
Bangha, Imre, 'Early Rekhta Poetry in the Nāgarī script' (forthcoming).
Barbauld, Anna Lætitia, *The Works*, 2 vols (London, 1825; repr. London, 1996).
Beiser, Frederick C. (ed.), *The Early Political Writings of the German Romantics* (Cambridge, 1999).
Bell, G. H., *The Hamwood Papers of The Ladies of Llangollen and Caroline Hamilton* (London, 1930).
Blackburne, Francis, *Remarks on Johnson's Life of Milton* (London, 1780).
Bloomfield, Robert, *The Banks of Wye*, 2nd edn (London, 1813).
B. E. [?Elias Bockett], *A Trip to North-Wales: Being a Description of that Country and People* (London, 1701).
Boswell, James, *The Life of Samuel Johnson, LL.D.*, 3 vols (London, 1793).
Brooke, Bibi, *The Key of the Hearts of Beginners*, trans. Annette S. Beveridge (London, 1908).
Cannon, Garland (ed.), *The Letters of Sir William Jones*, 2 vols (Oxford, 1970).
——, *The Collected Works of Sir William Jones*, 13 vols (Richmond, Surrey, 1993).
Cartwright, John, *Take your Choice! Representation and Respect: Imposition and Contempt. Annual Parliaments and Liberty: Long Parliaments and Slavery* (London, 1776).
Clarke, Edward Daniel, *A Tour through the South of England, Wales, and Part of Ireland, made During the Summer of 1791* (London, 1793).
Crane, Ralph J., 'Letters of Sir William Jones in the Dunedin Public Library', *Notes & Queries*, 39: 1 (March 1992), 66–7.
Craven, Elizabeth, *Memoirs of the Margravine of Anspach*, 2 vols (London, 1826).

Cozens-Hardy, Basil (ed.), *The Diary of Sylas Neville, 1767–1788* (Oxford, 1950).
Dalberg, Johann Friedrich von (trans.) *Gita-Govinda* (Erfurt, 1802).
A Discourse on the Impressing of Mariners; wherein Judge Foster's Argument is Considered and Answered (London, [1778]).
Douglas, Sylvester (ed.), *Reports of Cases Argued and Determined in the Court of King's Bench, in the Nineteenth, Twentieth, and Twenty First Years of George III*, 3rd edn (London, 1790).
Dow, Alexander, *The History of Hindustan* (London, 1768–72).
Erdman, David V. (ed.), *The Complete Poetry and Prose of William Blake* (New York, 1982).
Evans, D. Silvan (ed.), *Gwaith y Parchedig Evan Evans*, (Caernarfon, 1876).
Fay, Eliza, *Original Letters from India, 1779–1815*, ed. E.M. Forster (London, 1925).
Evans, Evan, *Some Specimens of the Poetry of the Antient Welsh Bards* (London, 1764).
Franklin, Michael J. (ed.), *Sir William Jones: Selected Poetical and Prose Works* (Cardiff, 1995).
——, '"I burn with a desire of seeing Shiraz": A New Letter from Sir William Jones to Harford Jones', *Review of English Studies*, N.S. 56: 227 (2005), 748–56.
Furber, Holden (ed.) *The Correspondence of Edmund Burke*, vol. 5 (Cambridge, 1978).
Ghose, M. M. (ed.), *Selections from the Writings of G.C. Ghose* (Calcutta, 1912).
Gleig, G. R. (ed.), *Memoirs of the Life of the Right Hon. Warren Hastings*, 3 vols (London, 1841).
Goethe, Johann Wolfgang von, *Werke*, Weimar ed. (W.A.) (Weimar, 1887–1912).
——, *Goethe: Begegnungen und Gespräche*, ed. Ernst Grumach and Renate Grumach (Berlin, 1985).
Greig, J. Y. T. (ed.), *The Letters of David Hume*, 2 vols (Oxford, 1932).
Hargrave, Francis, *An Argument in the Case of James Sommersett a Negro* (London, 1772).
Hawkins, Laetitia-Matilda, *Memoirs, Anecdotes, Facts, and Opinions*, 2 vols (London, 1824).
Hawkins, William, *Henry and Rosamond. A Tragedy* (London, 1749).
Herder, Johann Gottfried von, *Sämtliche Werke*, ed. Bernard Suphan, 33 vols (Leipzig, 1877–1913).
Holland, Lady Elizabeth, *Journal of Lady Elizabeth Holland* (London, 1908).
[Horsford, John], *A Collection of Poems Written in the East Indies By J—H—* (Calcutta, 1797).
Howell, T. B., *A Complete Collection of State Trials*, 21 vols (London, 1816).
Hume, David, *Political Discourses* (Edinburgh, 1752).
Isfahānī, Abū Ṭalēb Khān, *Dīvān-i Khvājah Ḥāfiẓ Shīrāzī adībāchah va qaṣāid. The Works of Hafez; with an account of his life and writings* (Calcutta, 1791).
Islam, Khurshidul and Ralph Russell, *Three Mughal Poets: Mir, Sauda, and Mir Hasan* (Delhi, 1991).

Jayadeva, *Love Song of the Dark Lord: Jayadeva's Gītagovinda*, trans. Barbara Stoler Miller (New York, 1977).
Jones, Lady Anna Maria, *The Poems of Anna Maria* (Calcutta, 1793).
—— (ed.), *The Works of Sir William Jones*, 6 vols (London, 1799).
—— (ed.), *The Works of Sir William Jones*, 13 vols (London, 1807).
Jones, Sir William, *Histoire de Nader Chah* (London, 1770).
——, *Kitab-i Shakaristan Dar Nahvi-i Zaban-i Parsi, Tasnif-i Yunus Uksfurdi, A Grammar of the Persian Language* (London, 1771).
——, *Dissertation sur la littérature orientale* (London, 1771).
——, *Lettre à Monsieur A*** du P**** (London, 1771).
——, *Poems, Consisting Chiefly of Translations from the Asiatick Languages* (Oxford, 1772).
——, *Poeseos Asiaticæ Commentariorum* (London, 1774).
A Speech on the Nomination of Candidates to Represent the County of Middlesex (1780).
——, *The Muse Recalled; an Ode on the Nuptials of Lord Viscount Althorp and Miss Lavinia Bingham* (Strawberry Hill: printed by Thomas Kirgate, 1781).
The Moallakát, or Seven Arabian Poems, which were Suspended on the Temple at Mecca (London, 1782).
——, *An Inquiry into the Legal Mode of Suppressing Riots. With a Constitutional Plan of Future Defence* (London, 1782).
——, *A Plan of National Defence* [London, 1782].
——, *A Speech of William Jones, Esq. to the Assembled Inhabitants of the counties of Middlesex and Surry, the cities of London and Westminster, and the borough of Southwark. XXVIII May, MDCCLXXXII* (London, 1782).
——, *The Principles of Government, in a Dialogue between a Scholar and a Peasant* (1782).
——, *A Discourse on the Institution of a Society [. . .] Delivered at Calcutta, January 15th, 1784: a Charge to the Grand Jury at Calcutta, December 4th, 1783: and a Hymn to Camdeo* (London, 1784).
——, *Sacontalá, or the Fatal Ring* (Calcutta, 1789).
——, *The Seasons: a Descriptive Poem by Cálidás, in the original Sanscrit* (Calcutta, 1792).
——, *Institutes of Hindu Law: or. The Ordinances of Menu* (Calcutta, 1794).
The Poetical Works of Sir William Jones, 2 vols (London, 1810).
Junius, ed. John Wade, 2 vols (London, 1865).
Kālidāsa, *The Recognition of Śakuntalā*, trans. W. J. Johnson (Oxford, 2001).
Knox, Vicesimus, *The Spirit of Despotism* (London, 1795).
Krummacher, F.A., *Parables*, trans. Frederic Shoberl (London, 1824).
Liberty and Property Preserved against Republicans and Levellers. A Collection of Tracts (London, 1793).
Linnaeus, Carl, *Linnaeus' Philosophia Botanica*, trans. Stephen Freer (Oxford, 2005).
Malone, Edmund (ed.), *The Works of Sir Joshua Reynolds*, 2nd edn, 3 vols (London, 1798).

Marshall, P. J. (ed.), *The Writings and Speeches of Edmund Burke:* V *India: Madras and Bengal* (Oxford, 1981).

——, *The Writings and Speeches of Edmund Burke,* VI *India: The Launching of the Hastings Impeachment, 1786–88* (Oxford, 1991).

Maurice, Thomas, *Memoirs of the Author of Indian Antiquities,* 3 vols (London, 1819).

Meadley, George Wilson (ed.), *Memoirs of William Paley, D.D.* (London, 1809).

Mitford, Revd. J. (ed.), *The Correspondence of Horace Walpole, Earl of Orford, and William Mason,* 2 vols (London, 1851), 2: 87.

Mojumder, Abu Taher, 'Three New Letters by Sir William Jones', *India Office Library and Records* (1981), 24–35.

Monier-Williams, Monier (ed. and trans.), *Śakuntalā, or Śakuntalā Recognised by the Ring* (Hertford, 1853).

Montagu, Lady Mary Wortley, *Turkish Embassy Letters,* ed. Malcolm Jack (London, 1993).

Montagu, Matthew (ed.), *The Letters of Mrs Elizabeth Montagu,* 4 vols (London, 1813).

Mustafā, Hājī, *Some Idea of the Civil & Criminal Courts of Justice at Moorshoodabad, in a Letter to Capt. John Hawkshaw* (Calcutta, 1789).

Nichols, John, *Literary Anecdotes of the Eighteenth Century,* 9 vols (London, 1812–15).

Owen, Hugh (ed.), *Additional Letters of the Morrises of Anglesey (1735–86),* 2 vols (London, 1947–9).

Paine, Thomas, *Rights of Man. Part the Second* (London, 1792).

The Parliamentary History of England (London, 1814).

The Parliamentary Register; or, History of the Proceedings and Debates of the House of Commons (London: Almon, 1778).

Parr, Samuel, *Works,* ed. John Johnstone, 8 vols (London, 1828)

Percy, Thomas, *Reliques of Ancient English Poetry,* 3 vols (London, 1765).

Piozzi, Hester Lynch, *Letters to and from the Late Samuel Johnson, LL.D.,* 2 vols (London, 1788).

Rajan, Chandra (ed. and trans.), *Kālidāsa: The Loom of Time* (New Delhi, 1989).

Ramsay, Sir Andrew Michael, 'A Discourse on Epic Poetry', in *The Adventures of Telemachus, the Son of Ulysses,* 2 vols (London, 1742).

Report of the Committee of Correspondence, confirmed by the Court of Directors [...] relative to Mr. Benfield ([London], 1781).

Roberts, William (ed.), *Memoirs of the Life and Correspondence of Mrs Hannah More,* 4 vols (London, 1835).

Rocher, Rosane, 'Alien and Empathic: The Indian Poems of N.B. Halhed', in *The Age of Partnership: Europeans in Asia before Dominion,* ed. Blair B. King and M. N. Pearson (Honolulu, 1979), 215–35.

——, 'Sir William Jones as a Satirist: An Ethic Epistle to the Second Earl Spencer', *Transactions of the Honourable Society of Cymmrodorion,* N.S. 11 (2005), 70–104.

Roth, Georges and Jean Varloot (eds), *Denis Diderot: Correspondance,* 16 vols (Paris, 1968).

Rousseau, Jean-Jacques, *Émile*, trans. Barbara Foxley (London, 1938).
Schlegel, August Wilhelm and Friedrich Schlegel (eds), *Athenäum, eine Zeitschrift*, 3 vols (Berlin, 1798–1800).
Schlegel, Friedrich, *Lectures on the History of Literature, Ancient and Modern*, 2 vols (Edinburgh, 1818).
——, *Friedrich Schlegels Briefe an seinen Bruder August Wilhelm*, ed. O. Walzel (Berlin, 1890).
Schmitz, L. Dora (trans.), *Correspondence between Schiller and Goethe* (London, 1909).
Scott, Geoffrey and Frederick A. Pottle (eds), *Private Papers of James Boswell*, 18 vols (New York, 1928–34).
Scott, Walter (ed.), *The Poetical Works of Anna Seward*, 3 vols (Edinburgh, 1810).
Seward, Anna, *Memoirs of the Life of Dr Darwin* (London, 1804).
Shah, Hasan, *The Nautch Girl*, trans. Qurratulain Hyder (Delhi, 1992).
Sharp, Granville, *An Address to the People of England: being the Protest of a Private Person against every Suspension of Law* (London, 1778).
——, *Memoirs of Granville Sharp, Esq*, 2 vols (London, 1828).
Shepherd, Richard, *An Essay on Education in a Letter to William Jones, Esq.* (London, 1782).
Shore, Charles John, Baron Teignmouth, *Memoir of the Life and Correspondence of John Lord Teignmouth*, 2 vols (London, 1843).
Sparks, Jared (ed.), *The Diplomatic Correspondence of the American Revolution*, 12 vols (Boston, 1829–30).
Spencer, A. (ed.), *Memoirs of William Hickey*, 4 vols (London, 1913–25).
Stukeley, William, *The Family Memoirs of the Rev. William Stukeley, MD*, Surtees Society, 73 (1882), 3 vols.
Sturt, Humphrey, *The Defence of Humphrey Sturt; Esquire, on a Charge Exhibited against him for Murder* (Calcutta, 1785).
Tabatabai, Ghulam Husain Khan, *A Translation of the Seïr Mutaqharin; or, View of Modern Times, being an History of India, from the Year 1118 to the Year 1195 (this year answers to the Christian year 1781–82)*, 3 vols (Calcutta, 1789 [1790]).
Thorpe, Lewis (trans.), *Giraldus Cambrensis: The Journey through Wales and The Description of Wales* (Harmondsworth, 1978).
Toynbee, Paget (ed.), *Satirical Poems Published Anonymously by William Mason with Notes by Horace Walpole* (Oxford, 1926).
Twining, Richard (ed.), *Selections from Papers of the Twining Family* (London, 1887).
Wharton, Francis (ed.), *The Revolutionary Diplomatic Correspondence of the United States*, 6 vols (Washington, 1889).
Wilkins, Charles (ed.), *The Bhăgvăt-Gēētā* (London, 1785).
Wilkinson, T. T., 'Mathematics and Mathematicians, the Journals of the late Reuben Burrow [pt 2]', *London, Edinburgh, and Dublin Philosophical Magazine*, 4th ser., 5 (1853), 514–22.
Wraxall, Sir Nathaniel, *Historical Memoirs of My Own Time*, 2 vols (London, 1815).
——, *Posthumous Memoirs of His Own Time*, 3 vols (London, 1836).

Zaidpuri, Ghŭlam Hussain Salim, *Riyazu-s-salatin* (1788), trans. Abdus Salam (Calcutta, 1902).

SECONDARY SOURCES

Abrams, M. H., *The Mirror and the Lamp: Romantic Theory and the Critical Tradition* (New York, 1953).

Ahmed, Akbar S., *Pakistan Society: Islam, Ethnicity and Leadership in South Asia* (Karachi, 1986).

Ahmad, Aziz, *Studies in Islamic Culture in the Indian Environment* (Oxford, 1964).

Alam, Muzaffar, 'Persian in Precolonial Hindustan', in *Literary Cultures in History*, ed. Pollock, 131–98.

Arberry, A. J., *Asiatic Jones* (London, 1946).

Ballinger, John, *The Bible in Wales: A Study in the History of the Welsh People* (London, 1906).

Barrell, John, *Imagining the King's Death: Figurative Treason, Fantasies of Regicide 1793–6* (Oxford, 2000).

Bayly, Christopher, *Empire and Information: Intelligence Gathering and Social Communication in India, 1780–1870* (Cambridge, 1997).

——, *The Birth of the Modern World 1780–1914* (Oxford, 2004).

Beeston, A. F. L. et al. (eds), *Arabic Literature to the End of the Umayyad Period* (Cambridge, 1983).

Beelaert, Anna Livia, 'Medical Imagery in the Description of the Seasons in Classical Persian Poetry', *Persica*, 14 (1990–92), 21–35.

Bhabha, Homi, *The Location of Culture* (London, 1994).

Blunt, Reginald (ed.), *Mrs Montagu 'Queen of the Blues': Her Letters and Friendships from 1762–1800*, 2 vols (London, 1923).

Calhoun, Craig (ed.), *Habermas and the Public Sphere* (Cambridge, MA, 1992).

Cannon, Garland, *The Life and Mind of Oriental Jones* (Cambridge, 1990).

Cannon, Garland and Michael J. Franklin, 'A Cymmrodor Claims Kin in Calcutta: An Assessment of Sir William Jones as Philologer, Polymath, and Pluralist', *Transactions of the Honourable Society of Cymmrodorion*, N.S. 11 (2005), 50–69.

Chakrabarti, Pratik, '"Neither of meate nor drinke, but what the Doctor alloweth": Medicine amidst War and Commerce in Eighteenth-Century Madras', *Bulletin of the History of Medicine*, 80: 1 (2006), 1–38.

Chatterjee, Kumkum, 'History as Self-Representation: The Recasting of a Political Tradition in Late Eighteenth-Century Eastern India', *Modern Asian Studies*, 32: 4, (1998), 913–48.

Chaudhuri, Sibadas (ed.), *Proceedings of the Asiatic Society*, vol. 1: *1784–1800*, (Calcutta, 1980), 351–67.

Clancy, Joseph P., *The Earliest Welsh Poetry* (London, 1970).

Cohen, Sheldon S., 'The Odyssey of Ebenezer Smith Platt', *Journal of American Studies*, 18: 2 (1984), 255–74.

Curley, Thomas M., *Sir Robert Chambers: Law, Literature and Empire in the Age of Johnson* (Madison, 1998).

Dalrymple, William, *White Mughals: Love and Betrayal in Eighteenth-Century India* (London, 2002).

Dasgupta, Atis, 'Early Trends of Anti-Colonial Peasant Resistance in Bengal', *Social Scientist*, 14: 4 (1986), 20–32.

David, Alun, 'Sir William Jones, Biblical Orientalism and Indian Scholarship', *Modern Asian Studies*, 30: 1 (1996), 173–84.

Derrett, J., *Duncan, Religion, Law and the State in India* (London, 1968).

Dhar, Niranjan, *Vedanta and the Bengal Renaissance* (Calcutta, 1977).

Drew, John, *India and the Romantic Imagination* (Delhi, 1987).

Dunster, Charles, *Considerations on Milton's Early Reading and the Prima Stamina of his Paradise Lost* ([London], 1800).

Erdman, David, *William Blake: Prophet against Empire*, 3rd edn (Princeton, 1977).

Faruqi, Shamsur Rahman, *Early Urdu Literary Culture and History* (New Delhi, 2001).

——, 'A Long History of Urdu Literary Culture, Part 1: Naming and Placing a Literary Culture', in *Literary Cultures in History: Reconstructions from South Asia*, ed. Sheldon Pollock (Berkeley, 2003), 805–63.

Franklin, Michael J. 'Accessing India: Orientalism, "Anti-Indianism" and the Rhetoric of Jones and Burke', in *Romanticism and Colonialism*, ed. Tim Fulford and Peter Kitson (Cambridge, 1998), 48–66.

——, 'The Building of Empire and the Building of Babel: Sir William Jones, Lord Byron, and their Productions of the Orient', in *Byron East and West*, ed. Martin Prorchazka (Prague, 2000), 63–78.

——, (ed.), *The European Discovery of India: Key Indological Sources of Romanticism*, 6 vols (London, 2001).

——, '"The Hastings Circle": Writers and Writing in Calcutta in the Last Quarter of the Eighteenth Century', in *Authorship, Commerce and the Public: Scenes of Writing, 1750–1850*, ed. Peter Garside, Caroline Franklin, and Emma Clery (Basingstoke, 2002), 186–202.

——, 'Cultural Possession, Imperial Control, and Comparative Religion: The Calcutta Perspectives of Sir William Jones and Nathaniel Brassey Halhed', *Yearbook of English Studies*, 32 (2002), 1–18.

Gerow, Edwin, 'Plot Structure and the Development of *Rasa* in the *Śakuntalā*', *Journal of the American Oriental Society*, Pt. 1, 99 (1979), 559–72; Pt. 2, 100 (1980), 267–82.

Gnoli, Raniero, *The Aesthetic Experience According to Abhinavagupta* (Varanasi, 1968).

Gombrich, Richard, *Theravada Buddhism: A Social History from Ancient Benares to Modern Colombo* (London, 1988).

Goodwin, Robert E., 'Aesthetic and Erotic Entrancement in the *Śakuntalā*', *Acta Orientalia Academiae Scientarium Hungaricae*, 43:1 (1989), 99–123.

Hale, Edward E., *Franklin in France*, 2 vols (Boston, 1888).

Holdsworth, W. S., *A History of English Law*, 17 vols (London, 1938).

Howard, John, *The State of the Prisons in England and Wales* (Warrington, 1777).

Hunter, W. W., *A Statistical Account of Bengal*, 20 vols (London, 1875–7).
Ibbetson, David, 'Sir William Jones as a Constitutional Lawyer', in *Sir William Jones, 1746–94, A Commemoration*, ed. Alexander Murray (Oxford, 1998), 19–42.
Ingalls, Daniel H. H., *Sanskrit Poetry* (Cambridge, MA, 1965).
Jones, Emyr Wyn (ed.), *Yr Anterliwt Goll: Barn ar Egwyddorion y Llywodraeth... Gan Fardd Anadnabyddus o Wynedd* (Aberystwyth, 1984).
——, *Diocesan Discord: A Family Affair, St Asaph 1779–1786* (Aberystwyth, 1988).
Karimi-Hakkak, Ahmad, 'Beyond Translation: Interactions between English and Persian Poetry', in *Iran and the Surrounding World*, ed. Nikki R. Keddie and Rudolph P. Matthee (Seattle and London, 2002), 36–60.
Kaye, W., *The Administration of the East India Company* (London, 1853).
Keith, A. B., *A History of Sanskrit Literature* (Oxford, 1920).
Kejariwal, O. P., *The Asiatic Society of Bengal and the Discovery of India's Past, 1784–1838* (Delhi, 1988).
Kenyon, George Thomas, *The Life of Lloyd, first Lord Kenyon* (London, 1873).
Khan, Gulfishan, *Indian Muslim Perceptions of the West* (Oxford, 1998).
——, 'Indo-Persian Scholarship and the Formation of Orientalism' (forthcoming).
Kopf, David, *British Orientalism and the Bengal Renaissance: The Dynamics of Indian Modernization 1773–1835* (Berkeley, 1969).
Lascelles, E. C. P., *Granville Sharp and the Freedom of Slaves in England* (Oxford, 1928).
Leask, Nigel, *British Romantic Writers and the East: Anxieties of Empire* (Cambridge, 1992).
Lee, Richard Henry, *Life of Arthur Lee, LL.D., Joint Commissioner of the United States to the Court of France*, 2 vols (Boston, 1829).
Lemmings, David, *Professors of the Law: Barristers and English Legal Culture in the Eighteenth Century* (Oxford, 2000).
Macpherson, W. C. (ed.), *Soldiering in India 1764–1787* (Edinburgh, 1928).
McGilvary, George, *Guardian of the East India Company: The Life of Laurence Sulivan* (London, 2006).
Maine, Sir Henry, *Village Communities in the East and West* (London, 1876).
Marshall, P. J., *The British Discovery of Hinduism in the Eighteenth Century* (Cambridge, 1970).
——, 'Warren Hastings as Scholar and Patron', in *Statesmen, Scholars and Merchants: Essays Presented to Dame Lucy Sutherland*, ed. Anne Whiteman et al. (Oxford, 1973), 242–62.
Mee, John, '"The Doom of Tyrants": William Blake, Richard "Citizen" Lee and the Millenarian Public Sphere', in *Blake, Politics, and History*, ed. Jackie DiSilvo et al. (New York and London, 1998), 97–114.
Mill, James, *History of British India* (1817), with notes by Horace Hayman Wilson, 6 vols (London, 1858).
Montriou, W. A., *Cases of Hindu Law Before H. M. Supreme Court* (Calcutta, 1853).
Morris, Henry, *The Life of Charles Grant* (London, 1904).

Moussa Mahmoud, Fatma, 'Sir William Jones and Mme Vaucluse', *Revue de Littérature Comparée*, 54 (1980), 5–16.
Mukherjee, S. N., *Sir William Jones: A Study in Eighteenth-Century British Attitudes to India* (Cambridge, 1968).
Müller, Max, *Chips from a German Workshop*, 4 vols (New York, 1876).
Naim, C. M., 'Transvestic Words?: The Rekhti in Urdu', *Annual of Urdu Studies*, 16: 1 (2001), 3–26.
Nārang, Gopi Chand, *Urdu Language and Literature* (New Delhi, 1991).
Niranjana, Tejaswini, *Siting Translation: History, Post-Structuralism, and the Colonial Context* (Berkeley, 1992).
O'Hanlon, Rosalind and David Washbrook, 'Histories in Transition: Approaches to the Study of Colonialism and Culture in India', *History Workshop Journal*, 32 (1991), 110–27.
Oldham, James, 'The Survival of Sir William Jones in American Jurisprudence', in *Objects of Enquiry: The Life, Contributions, and Influences of Sir William Jones*, ed. Garland Cannon and Kevin R. Brine (New York, 1995), 92–101.
Petievich, Carla, 'The Feminine and Cultural Syncretism in early Dakani Poetry', *Annual of Urdu Studies*, 8 (Winter 1993), 110–21.
Pratt, Mary Louise, *Imperial Eyes: Travel Writing and Transculturation* (London, 1992).
Rai, Amrit, *A House Divided: The Origin and Development of Hindi-Urdu* (New Dehli, 1991).
Raine, Kathleen, *Golgonooza, City of Imagination: last studies in William Blake* (New York, 1991).
Rajan. Rajeshwari Sunder, *The Scandal of the State: Women, Law, and Citizenship in Postcolonial India* (Durham and London, 2003).
Raychaudhuri, Tapan, *Europe Reconsidered: Perceptions of the West in Nineteenth-Century Bengal* (Oxford, 1988).
Rimius, Henry, *A Candid Narrative of the Rise and Progress of the Herrnhuters, commonly call'd Moravians, or, Unitas Fratrum*, 2nd edn (London, 1753).
Robb, Peter, *Clash of Cultures? An Englishman in Calcutta in the 1790s* (London, 1998).
Robbins, Helena H., *Our First Ambassador to China: an Account of the Life of George, Earl of Macartney* (London, 1908).
Rocher, Ludo and Rosane Rocher, *The Making of Western Indology: Henry Thomas Colebrooke and the East India Company* (London: Routledge, forthcoming).
Rocher, Rosane, *Orientalism, Poetry, and the Millennium: The Checkered Life of Nathaniel Brassey Halhed, 1751–1830* (Delhi, 1983).
——, 'Weaving Knowledge: Sir William Jones and Indian Pandits', in *Objects of Enquiry: The Life, Contributions, and Influences of Sir William Jones (1746–1794)*, ed. Garland Cannon and Kevin R. Brine (New York, 1995), 51–91.
Said, Edward, *Orientalism* (London, 1978).

Schuchard, Marsha Keith, *Why Mrs Blake Cried: William Blake and the Sexual Basis of Spiritual Vision* (London, 2006).
Schwab, Raymond, *The Oriental Renaissance: Europe's Rediscovery of India and the East, 1680–1880*, trans. Gene Patterson-Black and Victor Reinking (New York, 1984).
Scrafton, Luke, *Observations on Mr. Vansittart's Narrative* ([London], 1766).
Sen, Amartya, *Identity and Violence: The Illusion of Destiny* (London, 2006).
Shaffer, E. S., *'Kubla Khan' and 'The Fall of Jerusalem'* (Cambridge, 1975).
Shaw, Graham, *Printing in Calcutta* (London, 1981).
Shepperson, A. B., *John Paradise and Lucy Ludwell* (Richmond, VA, 1942).
Siegel, Lee, *Sacred and Profane Dimensions of Love in Indian Traditions as Exemplified in The Gītagovinda of Jayadeva* (Delhi, 1978).
Smith, J. T., *Nollekens and His Times*, 2 vols (London, 1828).
Solkin, David, *Richard Wilson: The Landscape of Reaction* (London, 1982).
Sparks, Jared, *The Life of Benjamin Franklin, containing The Autobiography* (Boston, 1856).
Tavakoli-Targhi, Mohamad, 'Orientalism's Genesis Amnesia', *Comparative Studies of South Asia, Africa and the Middle East*, 16: 1 (Spring 1996), 1–14.
Trautmann, Thomas, 'Indian Time: European Time', in *Time: Histories and Ethnologies*, ed. Diane Owen Hughes and Thomas Trautmann (Ann Arbor, MI, 1995), 167–97.
——, *Aryans and British India* (Berkeley, 1997).
Travers, Robert, *Ideology and Empire in Eighteenth-Century India* (Cambridge, 2007).
Varadpande, M. L., *History of Indian Theatre* (New Delhi, 2005).
Venkasawmy Row, T. A., *Indian Decisions (Old Series)*, vol 1: *Supreme Court Reports, Bengal* (Madras, 1911).
Vidyarthi, Abdul Haque, *Mohammad in World Scripture* (Lahore, 1940).
Viswanathan, Gauri, *Masks of Conquest: Literary Study and British Rule in India* (London, 1990).
Warton, Thomas, *The History of English Poetry*, 4 vols (London, 1774–81).
Wheeler, Kathleen M., *German Aesthetic and Literary Criticism* (Cambridge, 1984).
Willson, A. Leslie, *A Mythical Image: The Ideal of India in German Romanticism* (Durham, NC, 1964).
Woodfield, Ian, *Music of the Raj: A Social and Economic History of Music in late Eighteenth-century Anglo-Indian Society* (Oxford, 2000).
Woods, John A., 'The City of London and Impressment 1776–1777', *Proceedings of the Leeds Philosophical and Literary Society*, 8: 2 (1956), 111–27.

Index

Abdullah, Hājī 83
Abercromby, General Sir Robert 328
Abhinavagupta 265
Abrams, M. H. 87
Abu-Said Abil-Kheir 330
Adair, James 92, 103, 104
Adams, Dr William 166
Adina Masjid, Gaur 217
Advaita Vedānta 212, 258, 262, 273, 326, 354, 361
Agni, Vedic fire-god 18
Ahmad, Aziz 352, 355
Ahmed, Akbar S. 360
Ahmed, Shaikh 6, 7
Ahmuty, John 112
Ā'īn-i Akbarī 20
Aikin, John 283, 320
Aitken, James (John the Painter) 153–5
Akbar, Emperor Jalaluddin Muhammad 20, 63, 211, 235, 273, 352, 357, 360
Alam, Muzaffar 223
Alavi, Seema 223
Alcæus 85, 119, 177–9
Alcanzor and Zayda (Percy) 29
al-Din, Zayn 246
Alexander the Great 326, 357
al-Hamāsah (anthology of Bedouin poetry) 83
Allahabad, Treaty of (1765) 62
Alleyne, John 134, 138, 141, 153
Aloysia Sigea (Chorier) 248–9
Althorp Park 69
Alwi of Anjouan 6, 7, 295
American Declaration of Independence 130
American War of Independence 4, 6, 92, 138, 139, 142, 146, 147, 151, 152, 153–5, 156–7, 171, 174, 175, 181

Anacreon 71, 85
Anderson, James (agriculturalist) 257, 361
Anderson, Dr James (surgeon) 317
Andrometer 61
Aneurin 106
Angelo, Domenico 64, 170
Angelo, Henry 170
Anglesey (Ynys Môn) 43, 44, 45, 46, 59, 60, 61, 94, 100, 104–5, 187
Anglican/Methodist missions in Bengal 219
Anjouan 5–7
Anquetil-Duperron, Abraham-Hyacinthe 74–5, 107, 224
Arabian Nights 8, 251, 337 *see also* Galland
Arabic, linguistic relationship with Persian 62
Arabic algebra 222
Arberry, A J 313
Archilochus 85
Aristarchus of Samos 38
Aristotelian dramatic theory 260
Armenian nationalism 235, 236, 237
Aryabhata of Banaras 225
Aryans and Aryanism 39, 40
Ārzū, Sirāj al-Din 'Alī Khān 354–5
Ashurst, Sir William 159
Asiatick Miscellany, The (ed. Gladwin) 232–3, 234–5 *see also New Asiatic Miscellany*
Asiatick Researches 28, 29, 38, 206, 208, 209, 232, 235, 261, 317
  first volume, 1789 239–40
Asiatick Society of Bengal 18–19, 31, 36, 39, 42, 205–6, 207, 209–10, 212–13, 214, 215–17, 220, 221–7, 231–2, 234, 235, 241, 248, 272,

273, 309, 325, 326, 334, 335, 340, 345, 346
  and gender 241
Aśoca-tree 280, 361
Aśoka, Emperor 39, 356–7
  edicts 240, 357
Association Movement 164
astronomical tables, Brahmanic 222
Atticus 114
Audubon, Captain Jean 193
Aurangzeb, Emperor 226, 274, 343, 360–1
Ayeen Akbery, or, The Institutes of the Emperor Akbar (trans. Gladwin) 20
Ayurvedic medicine 226

Babri Masjid mosque, destruction of 333
Bacon, John 42
Bada Khan Ghazi 220
Bāfqi, Vahshi 325
Bahman 108
Baillie, William 221–2
Bailly, Jean-Sylvain 223
Baker, Sir George 146
Baker, David Erskine 53
Baker, Henry 53
Balfour, Francis 216
Banaras (Varanasi) 25–33, 217, 223, 225, 274, 287
  Brahmins of 223
  insurrection, 1781 341
Bancroft, Dr Edward 153, 154
Bande Mataram, anthem 286
Bangha, Imre 352
Banks, Sir Joseph 14, 55, 127, 129, 130, 131, 133, 168, 246
Banks, Sarah 133
Barbauld, Anna Lætitia 258–9, 320
Barber, Francis 134–5
Barker, Sir Robert 24
Barlow, George 19, 309
Barn ar Egwyddorion y Llywodraeth (Judgement on the Principles of Government) (Edwards) 202–3, 204
Barré, Colonel Isaac 168
Barry, James 182, 183
Barrington, Daines 120, 121, 199

Barrow, Isaac 274
Barry, James 182, 183
  The Phoenix or the Resurrection of Freedom 182
Bates, Joah 130, 139, 140 n.20
bathing and water 13, 356
Bathurst, Henry, second Earl Bathurst 151
'Battle of Argoed Llwyfain' (Taliesin) 109
Bayly, Christopher 65, 233
Bearcroft, Edward 92, 113, 114, 140, 200, 203
Beattie, James 78, 79–80, 85, 98
  The Minstrel 79
Beaumarchais, Pierre de 153, 158
  Le Barbier de Séville 158
Beaumaris 60
Beckford, William 125
  Vathek 78
Beecroft, Judith 258
Beefsteak Club 147, 196
Beethoven, Ludwig van 233
Belshazzar (Handel) 113
Benfield, Paul 184–5
Bengal Annual 4
Bengal famines 213
  1769–70 12, 291
  1788 291–2
Bengal Judiciary Bill 185–6
Bengal Renaissance 121, 272, 290, 340
Benn, John 33
Bennet, William 55
Bentinck, William Henry Cavendish, third duke of Portland 167
Berkeley, George 149
Bernier, François 226
Bertie, Willoughby, fourth earl of Abingdon 168
Bhabani, Rani 35
Bhabha, Homi 336
Bhagalpur 24, 25, 33, 246
Bhăgvăt-Gēētā (trans. Wilkins) 25, 213–14, 229, 215, 232
bhakti movement 244, 273, 276, 277, 279, 293, 334, 354
  poetry and devotion 230, 260, 280, 284
  song tradition 30–3

INDEX

Bhārata dynasty 262
Bhutan 25
Bhutan mission, Samuel Turner's 223, 247
Bhutto, Zulfikar Ali 361
Bibliothèque Nationale, Paris 261
Bicknell, John Laurens 156
Bill of Rights Society *see* Society of Gentlemen Supporters of the Bill of Rights
Bingham, Charles, Baron Lucan 181
Bingham, Margaret, countess of Lucan 180, 181
binomial theorem 222
Black Hole of Calcutta 102
Blackstone, Sir William 131, 184 n.32, 225, 307
Blake, William 108, 109, 169, 174, 182, 183–4, 231, 231 n.30
   The French Revolution 171
   All Religions are One 108
Blane, Sir Gilbert 247
Blaquière, W. C. 297–8, 297 n.15
Blechynden, Richard 327, 328–9
Bliss, Nathaniel 46
'Bloody Code' of law 115
Bloomfield, Robert *The Banks of the Wye* 103
Bodh Gaya cave 231
Bodleian Library, Oxford 62, 63, 74, 82, 83, 186
Booth, Nathaniel 167
Bopp, Franz 261
Boswell, James 131, 175, 330
Boughton, Sir Theodosius 116
Boughton Rouse, Sir Charles William 335
Bouton, Pierre 297–8
Bowdoin, James 193
box-clubs 196–7
Brahma 22, 228, 229, 245
Brahmans 34, 35, 108, 188, 223, 233, 234, 237, 238, 249, 250, 252, 271, 272, 273, 274, 275, 285, 288, 330, 355
Brāhmī language 240
Brand Hollis, Thomas 149
Brecht, Bertold 260
Brecon Priory 99
Brenan, Lieutenant Ambrose 290

Bristow, Emma [*née* Wrangham] 16
Brooke, William Augustus 347–8
Brougham, Henry Peter, first Baron Brougham and Vaux 111, 117
Brown, Lancelot 'Capability' 93, 148
Browne, Dr Richard 165
Bruce, James 337
Buddha, Gautama 361
   Fire Sermon 25
Buddhism 20, 25, 223, 334, 356, 360, 361
buffalo v. tiger contests 314–16
Buffon, Comte de 311, 312
Bughyat al-bahith (Ibn al-Mutaqqina) 186
Buildwas earthquake, 1773 92–3
Bulkeley, Richard 61
Buller, Sir Francis 200, 201
Burgoyne, General John 148
Burke, Edmund 20, 21, 83, 102, 148, 149, 155, 163, 164, 166, 169, 175, 182, 185–6, 194, 207, 235, 236, 294, 319–20
Burnett, James, Lord Monboddo *Of the Origin and Progress of Language* 47
Burney, Charles 177
Burrow, Reuben 45–6, 222–3
Butler, Charles *The Legality of Impressing Seamen* 127, 128, 144
Butler, Lady Eleanor 331
Butler, Marilyn 209
Byng, George 175
Byrom, John 46
Byron, George Gordon Noel, sixth Baron Byron 73, 78, 125, 284, 285

Cabala Club 46
Cadell, Thomas, the elder 143–4, 149
Caillaud, General John 5
calculus 44
Calcutta 9–24, 205–50, 251–86, 287–32
   Alipore 12–13, 14, 15, 22
   'Black Town' 297–8
   Botanic Garden 246
   Chandpal Ghat 10, 178
   Garden Reach, Ariśnagar 9, 57, 236, 244, 245, 246, 310, 311, 321, 325, 328, 349
   Madrasah 13
   St John's Church 219, 297 n.15

Calcutta (cont.)
    society and music-making 15–16, 241–2
    Supreme Council, Calcutta 15, 25–6, 163, 213, 294
    Supreme Court 1, 16–17, 150, 163, 215, 295–309, 329
    'White Town' 9
Caldecott, Thomas 241
Cambridge Platonism 213
Cambridge University 40, 51, 60, 94, 121, 130, 140, 167, 204
Camden, Charles Pratt, Earl 93, 133
Camden, Lady Elizabeth 93
Campbell, Thomas 284
Cannon, Garland 47–8, 153, 347
Cantopher, Manuel 239
Carmarthen circuit 92, 93–103, 111, 118, 142, 173, 302–3
Carnac, General John 66, 240
Caroline Matilda, Queen of Denmark 64, 65
Carter, Elizabeth 46, 76
Cartwright, Edmund 169
Cartwright, Major John 132, 173, 178, 190–1, 195
    Declaration of the Rights of Englishmen 164
    Give us our Rights! 190
caste system in India 188
catharsis, Aristotle's definition 265
Catholic Relief Bill (1778) 170
Caulfeild, James, first earl of Charlemont 190
Cavendish, Georgiana [née Spencer], Duchess of Devonshire 5, 69, 98, 158, 167, 168, 181, 194, 195, 241, 323
Cavendish, Lord Charles 45
Cavendish, Lord James 45
Cazim, Mohammed 232
Celtic Revival 59, 100, 110, 119, 121
Celticism 104–6
    Jones and 58–61, 109
Cemaes Assizes 104
Chait Singh, Raja of Banaras 215, 341–2
Chambers, Lady Frances 10, 14, 15–16, 242
Chambers, Sir Robert 10, 16, 17, 23, 56, 180, 207, 223, 296, 299, 302, 303, 304, 305, 306

Chambers, William 19, 35, 216, 219
Chandra, Krishna 35
Chandra, Raja Śiva 35, 238
Chandragupta, Maurya emperor 39, 356
Chapman, Charles 24, 220
Chapman, Mary 24
Chartist Circular, The 178
Chartist movement 204
Chateaubriand, François-René de 270
Chatterjee, Bankimchandra 290, 291
Chatterton, Thomas 131, 132
Chattopadhyay, Bankim 286
Chaucer, Geoffrey 44
Chaudhrani, Debi 290
chess 12, 26, 28–9, 33, 195
Child's Coffee-House 44
Chittagong 35, 113, 246, 314
Chomolhari peak 25
Christian VII of Denmark 64, 65, 66
chunam plaster 8, 13
Cicero 54, 55, 61, 69, 90, 91, 145, 147, 155, 176, 212
Cilgerran Castle 105
civil courts:
    chief (*sadr diwani adalats*) 17
    district (*diwani adalats*) 16–17
Clapham Sect 273
Clarke, Edward Daniel 121
Clevland, Augustus 24
Clive, Lady Margaret 222
Clive, Robert, first Baron Clive of Plassey 23, 42, 62–3, 149, 214, 336
Club of Honest Whigs 157, 177, 180
Coan, John 53–4
Coke, Thomas 219
Colebrooke, Sir George 66, 71, 208
Colebrooke, Henry Thomas 208, 323, 326, 340
Colebrooke, Robert Hyde 209
Coleridge, Samuel Taylor 58, 73, 78, 82, 131, 267, 284, 330 n.58
Collins, William *Persian Eclogues* 77
'common source' argument and the Greek and Indian zodiacs 224–5
comparative mythology 227, 228, 229
Confucius 206
    Shi-Ching 221
    Ta Hsüeh (Great Learning) 221

Confucius Sinarum Philosophus (trans. Couplet) 206
Conway, General Henry Seymour 186
Conway, Sir John 199
Cook, James 127
  second voyage 14
Cooper, Sir Grey 152
Coram, Thomas 49
Cornwallis, Charles, first Marquess Cornwallis, governor-general of India 209, 242, 299, 300, 316, 337, 340–1
Court of Chancery 95
Courtenay, Anne, Lady Cork 125, 148, 150
Courtenay, John 180
Courtenay, Kelland 125
Courtenay, William 'Kitty', 3rd Viscount 125
Courts of Great Sessions 95–8
  Select Committee reports on 95–6
Covent Garden 29, 98, 126, 131
Cowley, Hannah 244
Cox, James 221
Cox, John Henry 220, 221
Craven, Lady Elizabeth 75, 76, 148–19
Craven, William, 6th Baron 168
Crocodile, frigate 1, 4–5, 8, 10, 20, 205, 323
Croft, Sir Herbert 131–2
Croftes, Charles 314, 316
Crosby, Brass 132, 192
Crouch, Anna Maria 300
Curley, Thomas 304
Cuthbert, Richard 112
Cyrus, King of Persia 112–13
Cyrus (Metastasio) 113
Czartoryska, Princess Izabela 149
Czartoryski, Prince Adam 149, 239

Dabistan (Mohsanī Fani) 271, 343, 345, 349
dacoits 289–90, 294
Dafydd ap Gwilym 59, 119
Dai, Seedoo 297
Dalrymple, William 336
Dalton, John 325
Daniell, Thomas 221, 222
Darwin, Charles 48

The Descent of Man 37, 47
Origin of Species 47
Darwin, Erasmus 249, 283
Loves of Plants, The 249
Das, Bhavani 15
Das, Krishnaram 220
Das, Ram 15
Dashwood, Sir Francis 126
Data Sahib shrine atrocity 360
David, Alun 228
Davies, Sir John *Nosce Teipsum* 17
Davis, Samuel 223, 224, 225, 314, 325, 326, 330
Davy, William 134, 154
Day, Lady Benedicta 16
Day, Sir John 16, 313
Day, Thomas 156, 177, 180, 313
de Chézy, Antoine-Léonard 259, 261
de Lolme, John Louis 137–8
de Loutherbourg, Philippe 93
De Moivre, Abraham 46
  The Doctrine of Chances 45
de Rosario, Caesar 302
de Rozario, Kitty 298
De sacra poesi Hebraeorum (Lowth) 62
de Starck, Henry Savile 76
de Vaucluse, Anne Marie La Cépèdes de Fauques 75–6, 148
  Abbasai, histoire orientale 75
  Contes du sèrail, traduits du turc 75
  La Dernière guerre des bêtes 75
  History of the Marchioness de Pompadour 75
  Oriental Anecdotes 75
Declaration of the Rights of Englishmen (Cartwright) 164
Deh Majlis (Faz'li) 349
Della Cruscanism 244–5, 332
Demosthenes 156, 181
Derrett, J. Duncan 323
'Description of Assam, A' (trans. Vansittart) 232
devānagrī (language/'town-script' of the Gods) 269, 350, 350 n.29, 351
Devi Chaudhurani (Chatterjee) 290
Devi, Phoolan 290
Dhar, Niranjan 212–13
dharma (duty) 263, 264, 324, 356

Dickens, Charles *Barnaby Rudge* 136
Diderot, Denis 74, 147
Dilly, Charles 137, 177
Dilly, Edward 137
Dinefwr Castle 93, 94
Discourse on the Impressing of Mariners, A (attrib. Jones) 143–6
Divan Club 126
Dodd, Dr William 137
Dodsley, Robert 120
Dolben, Sir William 166, 167
Donellan, Captain John 'Diamond', poisoning trial 116, 117
Douglas, Sylvester 112, 159
Dow, Alexander *History of Hindustan* 65
Drake, John 297, 298
Dravidians 39
Drayton, Michael 110
Drew, John 231, 285
Druids and Druidic culture 45, 61, 105–6, 107, 108, 110, 120, 121, 173–4 *see also* Celticism
Dryden, John 54
Du Bartas, Guillaume 178
Duncan, Jonathan 223
Dundas, Henry, first Viscount Melville 325
Dunkin, James 303
Dunkin, Sir William 329
Dunning, John, Baron Ashburton 91, 92, 132, 133, 134, 138, 139, 140–1, 142, 148, 166, 168, 200
Dunster, Charles 178
Durgá, Hindu goddess 269, 288, 289, 316
Dutch republicanism 195
Dyer, William Charles 167
Dying Negro, The (Day and Bicknell) 156

East India Company (EIC) 40, 42, 62, 65, 76, 125, 149, 184, 309, 336, 342
  1772 plan 186
  army 30, 301
  Bengal Judiciary Bill 185–6
  Charter 163
  Charter renewal 354
  Court of Directors 5, 66, 213, 300
  and cultural responsibility 233
  Hastings' Orientalist project 19–21, 163, 186, 212–15, 351, 357
  informants 31, 62, 102, 238
  Judicature Act 186
  policy of non-interference in Hindu ritual 326
  and price control of foods 292–3
  Regulation 35 of the Judicial Plan 294
  and the Treaty of Allahabad (1765) 62–3
  'writers' 207–8
East Indiamen 5, 10, 12, 15, 63, 74, 215, 235, 266, 323, 328, 330, 331
East Indian slave trade 294–300
Edwards, Thomas (Twm o'r Nant) 202, 203, 204
Effects of Observation of India on Modern European Thought, The (lecture by Maine) 40
Eglwyswrw 104
Egyptian astronomy 225
Egyptian Campaign (Napoleonic, 1798–9) 261
Eichhorn, Johann Gottfried 88
Elegiac Sonnets (Smith) 245
el Tayib, Abdulla 84
Emin, Emin Joseph 235–7
Encyclopédie (Diderot) 147
Endeavour voyage 127
Enfield, William 245
English Constitution (de Lolme) 137–8
Enlightenment 21, 47, 256–7
  associational tendency 196–7
  experimental method 31, 53, 73, 76, 78, 81, 244, 284, 317, 355
  relativism 6, 74, 227, 273, 350
Ennius 155
'Epistle to Sir William Jones' (Horsford) 348
Eranda nut oil 226
Erdman, David 171
Erekle II of Georgia 235
Erskine, Thomas, first Baron 92, 200–2, 203
Essay on Man (Pope) 231
Essay on Woman (Wilkes) 126
Eton 54, 55

European cultural 'superiority' and Indo-European language 37
European Magazine 3, 178
Evans, Evan (Ieuan Brydydd Hir; Ieuan Fardd) 60, 109, 113, 119–21
  'Llys Ifor Hael' 119–20
  'Paraphrase of Psalm CXXXVII' 113
  Some Specimens of the Poetry of the Antient Welsh Bards 60, 84 n.36, 120
Exodus 3:14, *Bhagvadgītā* compared with 229
Ezra, Book of 112–13

Fakir-Sannyāsī rebellions 294
Falklands Islands Crisis 133, 135
Fani, Mohsen 274
Farhād va Shirin (Bāfqi) 325
Farhang-i Jahangiri (1608) (Inju) 63
Faruqi, Shamsur Rahman 351
Fatehpur Sikri 20
Fay, Eliza 208
feminine principle *see śakti* 30
Fénelon, François 258
Fielding, Henry 51, 51n
Fielding, William Basil Percy, Earl of Denbigh 129
Firdausī 71, 87, 108, 113, 311
  Shahnama 113
Firuz Shah 240, 357
Fishguard, French invasion 101
Fitzmaurice, Thomas 2, 199, 202, 203
Fleming, Dr John 246
Flintshire Association for Parliamentary Reform 199
Florence Miscellany, The (1785) 244
Foley, Richard 122
Folkes, Martin 46–7, 49
Foote, Samuel 146, 149
  The Cozeners 146
  The Nabob 149–50
Ford, Henry 165
Forms of Herkern, The (Balfour) 216
Forster, Georg 259, 266
Foster, Sir Michael 142, 145, 157
Foundling Hospital, London 49
Fowke, Francis 25–8, 217, 242, 287, 352
  'Heliophobia' 26–7

Fowke, Margaret 25, 26, 29, 30–1, 33–4, 217, 273, 287
Fox, Charles James 138, 148, 149, 163, 168, 174, 202
Francis, Philip 25, 149
Franco-American Treaties (1778) 152
Franklin, Benjamin 2, 3, 121, 138, 152, 153, 154, 155–6, 157–8, 161, 176, 177, 193, 194, 195
  annotations to Foster 157–8
  Autobiography 156
Free School Society 242
French East India Company 61
French invasion at Fishguard 101
French Revolution 197, 212

Galland, Antoine *Les Mille et une nuits* 61, 62, 251
Galli, Caterina 131
gambling 207
Gandhi, Mahatma 359
Ganges 9, 15, 18, 23, 25, 35, 108, 109, 223, 242, 244, 266, 302, 310, 355
Garrick, David 14
Gautier, Théophile 271
Gay, John *The Beggar's Opera* 126
Gaya 25, 231
General Insolvent Act 122
Genesis 38, 224, 227, 228
George III 1, 2, 14, 63, 65, 150, 151, 157, 187
Gerald of Wales 93
Gerow, Edwin 272
Ghose, Girish Chandra 358
Giardini, Felice 130
Gibbon, Edward 88, 185
Gifford, William 245
Gilchrist, Alexander 169
Gilchrist, John 232–3
  Dictionary English and Hindoostanee 351
Gilpin, William *Observations on the River Wye* 103
Gītagovinda (Jayadéva, trans. Jones) 266, 273, 275–84, 334, 345
  translation compared with Miller's 278, 281, 283
  translation compared with Siegel's 277, 278, 283

Gladwin, Francis 20, 210, 211, 212, 232–3, 235, 288–9, 309–10, 329, 345, 349, 351
Gluck, Christoph Willibald Ritter von
  Iphigénie en Tauride 158
Glynn, John 92, 132, 134, 142
Godhra riots 334
Gododdin, Y 60
Godwin, William 3, 244
Goethe, J. W. von 37, 88, 251–2, 259, 262, 267, 269, 283, 284
  Faust 260
  West-östlicher Divan 267
Golconda diamonds 34, 116
Goldsmith, Oliver 63, 88, 98, 132, 175
  She Stoops to Conquer 98
Gombrich, Richard 357
Goodwin, Robert 265
gopīs 22, 30–31, 32, 275–6, 278, 279, 311, 356
Gordon Riots, 1780 107, 169–72, 198
'Gorhoffedd' (Exulting Boast) (Gwalchmai ap Meilyr) 83–4
Gough, Richard 175
Govinda, Chinna 312
Gower, Granville Leveson-, 1st Earl Granville 98
Gower, Henrietta Elizabeth Leveson-, Countess Granville 98
Graham, Robert 159
Granard, Lady Georgiana Augusta 148
Grant, Charles 217–19, 220, 226, 292, 332
Grant, Jane 217, 219, 220
Granville, Mary (Mrs Delany) 107
Gravier, Charles, Comte de Vergennes 157, 195
Gray, Thomas 55, 60, 103, 120, 182
Greatheed, Bertie 244
Grecian Club 180
Greek zodiac, Indian compared 224–5
Grey, Charles 178
Griffin, Captain Daniel Fitzgerald 303, 304
Griffiths, Lieutenant, debt case 121–2
Griffiths, Mary, murder of 100
Griffiths, Ralph 177
Grigg, Susannah, trial 115
Grosvenor (East Indiaman) 10
Gwalchmai ap Meilyr 83

Gwenllian ferch (daughter of) Gruffydd 94

habeas corpus 138, 139, 140
  bill to suspend, 1777 138–9
Habermas, Jürgen 196
Hackman, James 131
Hadjee, Coja 336
Hāfiz 66, 71–3, 73–4, 85, 176, 213, 232, 260, 267, 274, 331, 345, 346
  ode presented to Jones 211–12
Haidar Ali of Mysore 8
Halhed, Helena [*née* Ribaut] 16
Halhed, Nathaniel Brassey 21, 208, 272, 287, 307
  A Code of Gentoo Laws 21, 307
Halley, Edmund 43, 45
Hamilton, Alexander 261
Hamilton, Charles 210, 226
Handel, George Frideric 107, 130, 140 n.20
  Belshazzar 113
  Jephtha 130
harams 7, 29, 263, 336
Harding, Luke 333–4
Hardy, Sir Charles 160
Hargrave, Francis 91, 134, 141, 154
Harington, John Herbert 31
Harris, John 44
Harrow school 54–7, 69
Harsha, Sri 248
Hartley, David (philosopher and physician) 258
Hartley, David (son of the above) 167
Hartley, Winchcombe Henry (half-brother of the above) 167
Hastings, Marian 12, 13, 208, 324
Hastings, Warren 9, 25–6, 206, 207, 208, 222, 287, 289, 311, 324, 325, 338–9, 341–2
  and Asiatick Society 209, 226, 272
  impeachment 102, 294, 319
  Jones relationship 12–13, 13–14
  and the Mughal rulers 15, 26
  Orientalist project in India 19–21, 163, 186, 212–15, 307, 351, 357
  papers 32

as patron 15, 214, 309
    Regulation 35 of the Judicial Plan 294
Hatton, Richard 158
Haverfordwest 97–8, 101, 121–2
    assizes 115–16, 117
    Castle 124
Hawkins, Henry 90–1
Hawkins, Sir John 56
Hawkins, Laetitia-Matilda 56, 90
Hawkins, William 178
    Henry and Rosamund 179
Haydn, Joseph 244
Hayley, William 183, 332
Heber, Reginald 310
Hebrew, as seminal language 38
Heine, Heinrich 270
Hell Fire Club 114, 125–6, 127, 196
Helvétius, Anne-Catherine de Ligniville 158
Henckel, Tilman 289, 290
henna 6, 270
Herder, Johann Gottfried von 59, 88, 259, 260
Hewson, Joseph 167
Hickey, William *The Memoirs of William Hickey* 303, 304
Hildegard of Bingen 276
Himalayas 25, 206, 288
Hindi language 8, 31, 32, 247, 273, 275, 280, 349, 350, 350 n.29, 352, 353, 355, 356
Hindu law 4, 34, 303, 306, 323, 325, 327
    Dāyabhāga school 308
    Mitākṣarā school 308
    see also Mānavadharmaśāstra
Hindu music *see* music, Indian
Hinduism 18, 20, 22, 31, 108–9, 212–3, 224, 228–31, 250, 251–2, 253, 258, 269 272–3, 275–84, 285, 287, 288, 289–90, 293, 321, 324
Hindustani songs 16, 30–3
Hiraṇyāṇḍa (cosmic egg of Brahma) 228
Hodges, William 9, 14, 15
Hodgson, William 177
Hogarth, William 49, 67
Holland, Lady Elizabeth 261
Hollanson, Jacob 299
Hollis, Thomas 149

Holwell, John Zephaniah *Interesting Historical Events* 101–2
Honourable Society of Cymmrodorion 48, 120, 130, 173
Hooker, Richard 273
Horace 54, 73–4, 106, 329
Horrebow, Peter 299–300
Horrebow, Sophia 300
Horseshoe Club 111–13
Horsford, Captain John 348
Howard, John 123
Howorth, Henry 92, 113, 114, 116, 138
Hugli River 8–9, 10, 12, 110, 241, 245, 295, 311
Hujwīrī, Data Ganj Bakhsh 360, 361
'human sacrifice', Chitpore 288, 289
Hume, David *Political Discourses* 128, 129
Humphrey, Ozias 221
Hunt, Professor Thomas 62, 63, 74–5
Hunter, John 116, 327
Husain, Mir Muhammed 345, 347
Hwfa ap Cynddelw, Lord of Llyslifon 58, 83
Hyde, John 16, 17, 22, 23, 25, 74, 207, 297–8, 299, 302, 303, 304, 305, 323, 329–30
Hyde, Mary 16
Hyde, Thomas 62
Hywel Dda 94

Ibbetson, David 303
Ibrahim Pasha 81
Ifor ap Llewelyn (Ifor Hael) 119–20
Iliad 276
imperialism, British 3, 19, 37, 39, 42, 65, 151, 210, 213, 215, 225, 233, 234, 259, 319, 320, 331, 339, 340, 341, 343, 356
Impey, Sir Elijah 9, 16–17
Impey, Lady Mary 15
impressment 127–8, 130, 133, 134–5, 135–6, 139, 152–3, 58–60
    Richard II statute 144
India
    confederacy in the Carnatic 15
    fauna 9, 15, 23, 129, 220, 247, 277, 310, 311–12, 317, 318, 352
    flora 16, 23, 24, 38, 209, 239, 245–9, 264, 280, 316, 321, 326, 361

India (*cont.*)
　creation myths 228–9, 230
　mathematics and astronomy 222–5
　medicine 226–7
　music 16, 22, 29, 346
　　ragas 22, 32
　　Sanskrit treatises 31
　science 8, 205, 210, 222–3, 224–5, 227, 240, 247, 248, 317, 325
　zodiac, Greek compared 224–5
Ingalls, Daniel 285
insolvent debtors 123
Isa-Upanisad (trans. Jones) 346
Isfahānī, Abū Talēb Khān 347
Ishky, Mirza Zainuddin 347
Islam 212
Islamic law 303
Islamic mysticism 213, 349 *see also* Sūfism
Ismat of Bokhara 345
I'tisam ud-Din, Shaikh 63, 66, 67

Jaan, Khanum 29–30
Jackson, Andrew 179
Jagannātha Tarkapañcānana 308, 321–2
　Vivādabhangārnava ('Oceans of resolutions of disputes') 323, 327
Jai Singh II, Raja 223
James, Thomas, Viscount Bulkeley 60
Jāmī 232
Janūb bint al-'Ajlan 81–2
Jay, John 193
Jayadeva 273, 274, 275, 276, 278, 280, 281, 283, 284, 334, 345
Jebb, Dr John 149, 192
Jefferson, Thomas 179, 193
Jehāngir, Mughal Emperor 63
Jena Romantics 179–80
Jenyns, Soame 180
Jephtha (Handel) 130
Jerningham, Edward 209
Jodrell, Richard Paul 180
John of Gaunt, 1st Duke of Lancaster 44
Johnson, Frances 'Begum' 242
Johnson, Joseph 183
Johnson, Nathaniel 46
Johnson, Richard, (friend of Jones) 18, 22, 24, 311, 346–7
Johnson, Richard, indigo planter 330

Johnson, Dr Samuel 1, 13, 43, 56, 87, 88, 120, 121, 134–5, 170, 180, 182, 188, 222, 306
Johnson, William J. 262 n.16, 268 n. 25, 270
Johnson, William 'Tally-Ho' 242
Jones, Lady Anna Maria [*née* Shipley] 58, 194, 195, 341
　botanical illustrator 246
　'botanical' strolls 23–4, 245–6
　Calcutta, first impressions 10–12
　Calcutta society and music making 15–16, 241–2
　delicate health in Calcutta 240–1
　editing Sir William's works 331–2
　Margaret Fowke friendship 33–4
　meeting the Hastings 12–13, 15
　pastoral farm and pets 311, 312
　poetry 244–5
　receiving news of Sir William's death 330–1
　returning home to England 321, 323
　voyage to Calcutta 1–9
Jones, David 96
Jones, Edward 109
Jones, Revd Griffith 48
Jones, Harford 360
Jones, Inigo 44
Jones, Mary (sister) 51, 54, 56–7, 90, 241
Jones, Mary [*née* Nix] (mother) 43, 49–51, 51–2, 52–3, 54
　death of 168
Jones, Mary, executed for shoplifting 135–7
Jones, Rhys 109
Jones, Rowland 110
Jones, William (father) 43–7, 48–52, 59, 60, 61
　and the Royal Society 43, 44, 45
　Analysis per Quantitatum Series, Fluxiones, ac Differentias 44
　New Compendium of the Whole Art of Navigation 44
　'The Practice of Interest' 45
　Synopsis Palmariorum Matheseos 44
　'Systems' of 'Ethicks', 'Politicks' and 'Economics' 51

INDEX

Jones, Sir William:
life:
earliest memories 43–4
comparative measurements with John Coan 53–4
early education 51–2
Harrow scholarship 54–7
oriental studies at University College, Oxford 61
elected fellow of University College Oxford 64
suspicious of unconstitutional authority 65, 66
Reynolds portrait 67, 68
dissatisfaction tutoring the Spencers 67–70
called to the bar 70–1, 88
Anquetil-Duperron, attack on 74–5
Madame de Vaucluse relationship 75–6
debut on the King's Bench 90–1
Carmarthen Circuit 92, 93–103, 110–13, 115–23, 124, 142, 173
Carmarthen Circuit balls 93, 98
Welsh language proficiency 96, 97
'Grand Vicar' soubriquet 112–13
Commissioner of Bankrupts appointment 151
Welsh tour 43, 57–8
Anglesey (Ynys Môn) 58, 59, 60–1
election to the Royal Society 88
Louis XVI interview 96, 96–7 n.5
Wye Valley 103–4
Cemaes Assizes 104
in Bath 147
visits to France 155–8, 176, 193
death of mother 168
Gordon Riots (1780) 169–72
'Indian scheme' canvassing 149–52, 154–5
Principles of Government seditious libel trial 199–202, 204
voyage to Calcutta 1–9
Hastings relationship 12–13, 13–14
Supreme Court, Calcutta 16–17
illness and convalescence in Benares 23–5, 217
Banaras (Benares) 25–33
Sundarbans expedition 220
Calcutta 9–19, 287–32
Cornwallis relationship 309–10
animals and hunting 311–17
as slave owner 7, 295, 327, 328, 337
devotion to Anna Maria 325
final illness and death 57, 327–9
political and constitutional ideas and campaigns:
and ancient Celtic liberties 94–5
and the American War of Independence 2, 174, 175
Celticism 58–61, 104–6, 109
and a civil militia 190–1, 192
as constitutional and civil rights lawyer 139
East India slave trade 299–300
East India slave trade and moral relativity 294, 295–6
extending suffrage 191–2, 198
impressment of mariners 124–5, 127–8, 130, 135–6, 152–3, 157–8, 164
Lockean theory of possessive individualism 191
London Tavern political address 191, 192
meritocracy and the class system 188–9
Mermaid Tavern political address 174–5
Oxford University parliamentary candidacy 165–8, 174
poetry of politics 177–84
as radical Whig 21, 118, 124–62, 164, 169, 174, 175
republican sentiments 164, 175, 176, 178–80, 186, 204
slavery and the African slave trade 29, 47, 174
and working class aspirations 198–9
scholarship and linguistic studies:
Arabic studies 62
Asiatick Researches 28, 29, 38, 206, 208, 209, 232, 235, 239–40, 261, 317
Asiatick Society of Bengal 18–19, 31, 36, 39, 42, 205–50, 272, 273, 309, 325, 326, 334, 335, 340, 345, 346
botany 245–50

Jones, Sir William: (*cont.*)
    comparative mythology 227, 228, 229
    concept of language evolution 37
    as cultural mediator/translator 252, 274–5, 277–8, 285–6
    Indo-European comparative grammar 36–7
    Indo-European language family concept 36–42, 47
    'Jonesian System' of phonetic transliteration 216
    Mosaic history and Indian antiquity 227–8
    Proto-Indo-European language 37, 48
    race and linguistic affinities 37, 39–42
    Romanticism and the lyric impulse 86–7
    Romanticism and Orientalism 72–3, 77–87
    Sanskrit studies 34–8, 238, 239, 343, 346, 359
    trials, cases and causes:
        'An assault with intent to ravish Mary Serraun' 297–8
        Ebenezer Smith Platt 138, 139, 140–1
        George Tyler v. *Fred. Deatker and Henrik Deatker* 303–4
        George Williams 115–16, 117
        Gunga Bissen will case 35–6
        Isaac Philips 101–2
        John Borthwick and sixteen Others 158–60
        John Millachip 139–41, 141–2, 141 n.23, 153, 160
        John Taylor v. *Philip Younge* 207
        Kissenpersand Tagore v. *Edward Maxwell & Thomas Motte* 305
        Kissnochurn Mullic v. *Ramnarain Mullick* 307
        Lieutenant Griffith 121–2
        Mary Jones 135–7
        Rex v. *Bakhtyar, and Saheb Ram* 301–2
        Rex v. *Humphrey Sturt Esq.* 295–6
        Rex v. *William Townsend Jones* 300–1
        Sommerset v. *Steuart* 91, 133, 134, 142
        Sree Ooday Cower v. *Mohhun Lall Busset* 307–8
        Susannah Grigg 115
    Works:
    Asiatick Society Discourses and Orientalist Researches
    2nd Anniversary Discourse 222, 227
    3rd Anniversary Discourse 'On the Hindus' 36, 38, 40, 273, 355
    6th Anniversary Discourse 'On the Persians' 345
    10th Anniversary Discourse 'On Asiatick History, civil and natural' 311, 355
    11th Anniversary Discourse 'On the Philosophy of the Asiaticks' 225, 262, 325
    'Botanical Observations on Select Indian Plants' 247–8, 264, 280, 326
    Design of a Treatise on the Plants of India', 'The 248
    'Dissertation on the Orthography of Asiatick Words in Roman Letters' 82
    Dissertation sur la littérature orientale 73–4
    Grammar of the Persian Language, A 71–3, 76, 82, 206, 260, 318
    Histoire de Nader Shah 65, 66
    Indian Game of Chess', 'The 29
    'Inscriptions on the Staff of Firuz Shah' 240, 357
    'On the Arts, Commonly Called Imitative' 86
    'On the Gods of Greece, Italy, and India' 173, 227–9, 273
    'On the Indian Game of Chess' 29
    'On the Loris, or Slowpaced Lemur' 312
    'On the Musical Modes of the Hindus' 31
    'On the Mystical Poetry of the Persians and Hindus' 273, 343, 349
    'On the Poetry of the Eastern Nations' 82–5, 85–6

'On the Spikenard of the
  Ancients' 247
Preliminary Discourse on the
  Institution of a Society', 'A
  18–19, 205–6, 209–11
'Remarks on the Island of Hinzuan or
  Johanna' 5–7
Seasons, The (Kālidāsa) 318–19
'Un traité sur la poësie orientale' 66
legal writings:
  'Charge to the Grand Jury' (1785)
    294–5
  Essay on the Law of Bailments,
    An 122, 185
  Institutes of Hindu Law: or the
    Ordinances of Menu 323, 325
  Mahomedan Law of Succession to the
    Property 122, 186
  Speeches of Isaeus Concerning the
    Law 122, 151, 155
  Vivādā-sārārnava ('Ocean of all
    disputes') 330
  Vivādabhangārnava ('Oceans of
    resolutions of disputes') 327
poetry:
  'Ad Musam' 89
  'Au Firmament' 332
  'Carmen ad Libertatem' 167–8
  'Caissa, or; The Game at Chess'
    29
  'Curious move at chess which was
    first shown to me by Sir William
    Jones at Benares' 28–9
  'Damsels of Cardigan' 106, 113
  Enchanted Fruit, or the Hindu Wife,
    The 233, 249–50
  'Ethick Epistle, An' 87–8
  'Fountain Nymph, The' 110–11
  'Hymn to Bhavani, The' 290–1
  'Hymn to Camdeo, A' 18, 19
  'Hymn to Durgá, A' 269, 287–8
  'Hymn to Gangá, A' 108
  'Hymn to Lacshmí, A' 273, 279,
    291–3, 350
  'Hymn to Náráyana, A' 229–31,
    232, 233, 273
  'Hymn to Súrya, A' 317
  'Hymns to Hindu Deities' 18, 108,
    233
  'In Answer to —'s
    Heliophobia' 27–8
  'Kneel to the goddess whom all men
    adore' 107–109, 173
  'Meleager' 55
  Muse Recalled, The 181–2
  Ode in Imitation of Callistratus,
    An 180, 194–5
  Ode in Imitation of Alcœus, An 119,
    177–80
  'On Seeing Miss *** Ride by Him,
    without Knowing Her' 107
  Oxford Circuit verses 113–14
  'Palace of Fortune, The' 77–8
  'Plassey-Plain' 23
  Poems, Consisting Chiefly of
    Translations from the Asiatick
    Languages 76–82, 85–6, 142
  Poeseos Asiaticæ
    Commentariorum 88–9, 143
  'Seven Fountains, An Eastern
    Allegory, The' 78
  'Solima, An Arabian Eclogue' 80–1
political writing and essays:
  Discourse on the Impressing of Mariners,
    A (attrib.) 143–6, 157
  'Fragment of Polybius, A' 155–6, 157
  Inquiry into the Legal Mode of
    Suppressing Riots, An 172–3
  Letter to a Patriot Senator, A 197–8
  Oration intended to have been spoken in
    the Theatre at Oxford 165
  A Plan of National Defence 190
  Principles of Government, The 2, 40,
    195–6, 199, 203–4
  Speech on the Nomination of
    Candidates 174
  A Speech to the Assembled Inhabitants
    of the counties of Middlesex and
    Surry, the cities of London and
    Westminster, and the borough of
    Southwark 191–2
translations:
  'The Gopy's Complaint' 32
  'The Gopy's Confession' (song
    translations) 32–3
  Gītagovinda (Jayadeva) 266, 273,
    275–84, 334, 345
  Isa-Upanisad 346

Jones, Sir William: (*cont.*)
'Lines from the Arabic' ('While sad suspense') 312
Moallakát, The 155, 185
'Persian Song of Hafiz, A' 82
Sacontalá; or, the Fatal Ring (Kālidāsa) 251–72
'Turkish Ode of Mesihi, A' 82
Jones, William (press gang victim) 135
Jordan, Barrett Bowen 101
Junction of two Seas, The (Prince Dāra Shikūh) 273–4
'Jungle Fever' 16
'Junius' letters 126
Jurrat, Qalandar Bakhsh 30

Kadamba tree 279–80
Kaempfer, Engelbert 211
Kahn, Ali Ibrahim 226, 240
Kālī, goddess 269, 281, 287, 288, 289–90
Kālidāsa:
  Shakespeare compared with 262; see also *Kumārasambhava; Ritusamhāra; Śakuntalā*
Kāma, Hindu god of love 18, 19, 263
Kashf-ul Mahjub (Hujwīrī) 361
Kasinath, pandit 34
Kashmir 78, 212, 222, 274, 285, 347, 354, 360
Kauffman, Angelica 56
Kaula, Śri Govardhana 35, 240, 307
Kenyon, Lloyd 114, 199, 204
Keppel, Augustus, Viscount Keppel, admiral and politician 168
Khān, 'Abd al-Qādir 347
Khan, Ali Ibrahim 25, 28, 34, 226, 240
Khan, Ataher Ali 231, 317
Khān, Tafazzul Husain 223
Khāqāni 227, 348
Khayyām, Omar 71, 348–9
Khosrow va Shirin (Nizāmī) 324–5
Khusrau, Amīr 38, 232, 333, 334, 348, 352–3, 354–6
King against John Borthwick and sixteen Others, The 158–60
King against Peter Horrebow for Manstealing or Kidnapping, The (1789) 299–300

Kirkpatrick, Captain William 232, 349, 350
Kissenpersand Tagore v. Edward Maxwell & Thomas Motte 305
Koenig, Johann Gerhard 246
Koh-i-noor diamond 65
Krishna 22, 31, 32, 220, 244, 245, 250, 273, 274, 275–6, 277, 278, 279, 280, 281, 283, 326, 356
Krishna-*bhakti* poets 32
Krishnagar 34–5, 314, 317, 320
Kshatriya caste 238
'Kubla Khan' (Coleridge) 284
Kühn, Sophie von 270
Kumārasambhava ('Birth of Kumara') (Kālidāsa) 269
Krummacher, Friedrich Adolph 271
Kyd, Captain Robert 209, 246

Ladies of Llangollen 331
Lafayette, Marquis de 193
Lakshmī, Hindu goddess 279, 280, 291–3
Lalla Rookh (Moore) 284
Lamartine, Alphonse de 271
Lambert, Captain 301
Langlès, Louis Mathieu 261
Langton, Bennet 176
Langton, George 176
Laudian Chair of Arabic, Oxford 62
Laurens, Henry 156, 194
Landor, Walter Savage 73, 78, 284
Law, Thomas 215–16, 290
Lawes, Henry 93
Laylī and Majnūn (Nizāmī) 274
Le Gentil, Guillaume 223, 224
Lebīd 83, 84
Lee, Arthur 152–3
Lee, William 152
Leibniz, Gottfried 44
Lemaistre, Stephen Charles 150
Lemmings, David 92
Lennox, Charles, Duke of Richmond 141 n.23, 170, 192, 198
Lennox, Charlotte 56
Leoni, Myer 130
Lewis, Thomas 133
Libel Act (1792) 202
Libertas Americana medal 2
Lindsey, Theophilus 149

linguistics
  beginnings as a science 38, 48
  Jones' concept of language
    evolution 37
Linley, Elizabeth 208
Linnaeus, Carl 246, 248
  sexual system 248–9
Livingston, Robert R. 193
Llanbabo parish 60, 188
Llandeilo 94
Llanddowror 48
Llanfechell 44
Llanfihangel Tre'r-Beirdd 43, 48, 105
Llanidan 104
Lloyd, Ann 107
Llywarch Hen 106
Locke, John 78, 93, 134, 165, 182, 191
Loll, Munnoo 35
London Corresponding Society
  (LCS) 179, 180 n.21
London Merchant, The (Lillo) 98
London Welsh society 45, 48, 118
Longinus 87
Louis XV 75
Louis XVI 96, 96–7n
Louisa of Prussia, Queen 271
Love and Madness (Croft) 131, 132
Love Epistles of Aristaenetus (trans. Halhed/
  Sheridan) 208
Lowth, Robert 62
Lucknow 15
Ludwell, Lucy 56
Lun Yu (Analects of Confucius) 221
Lyceums-fragment 65 (Schlegel) 177, 178–9
Lyon, John 64

Macartney, George, Earl 8, 15, 76
Macaulay, Catharine 132, 188
Macaulay, Thomas Babington 340, 358
Macpherson, Colonel Allan 342, 347,
  347 n.20
Macpherson, Governor-General Sir
  John 37, 236, 342
Mahābhārata 213, 249, 262, 263, 264,
  270, 324
Mahomet, Aumen 305–6
'maiden' assizes 98
Maine, Sir Henry 39
Majer, Friedrich 260–1, 284

Mānavadharmaśāstra (law-code of the
  School of Manu) 34, 35, 188,
  306–7, 308
Mancini-Mazarini, Louis-Jules Barbon,
  Duc de Nivernois 155, 158
Manners, Charles, fourth Duke of
  Rutland 128
Mansfield, James 140
Marmontel, Jean-François 158
Marshall, P. J. 228, 319
Martin, General 'Cupid' 56
Martin, Thomas 301
Marvell, Andrew 182
Maskelyne, Nevil 222
Masnaví (Rūmī) 274
Mason, William 168
Massachusetts minutemen 172
Maudsley, Thomas 329
Maurice, Thomas 132, 332
Maurya empire 39, 356
Maxwell, Edward 301
McGann, Jerome 233
Mee, John 183
Meiners, Christoph 74
Meninski, Franciscus à Mesgnien
  *Thesaurus Linguarum
  Orientalium* 66, 67
Meredith, Sir William 135–7
Merry, Robert (Della Crusca) 244
Mesīhī 82
Metastasio, Pietro Antonio Domenico
  Trapassi 113, 253, 332
Methodist Revival 118
Michaelis, Johann David 88, 239
Middleton, Colonel Richard 203
Miftāhi Kulūbu-l-Mubtadīn 347
Mill, James 286, 340, 358;
  The History of British India 358
Millachip, John, case 139–41, 141 n.23,
  141–2, 153, 160
Miller, Barbara 270, 275, 278
Milles, Thomas 92, 113, 168
Mills, Sir Thomas 12, 14
Milton, John 28, 54, 58, 69, 77, 165, 177,
  182, 183, 230
  Areopagitica 177
  Comus 93
  Paradise Lost 178
  Paradise Regained 54

Minnat, Mir Qamar ud-Din 347
'Minute on Education' (Macaulay) 358
Mīr Taqī 'Mīr 342
Mirabai 32
Mirza, Wahīd 352
Miśra, Śankara 283
Mohsanī Fani 343
moksha (self-release) 229
Molainville, Barthélemy d'Herbelot de 61, 75
Montagu, Basil 131
Montagu, Elizabeth 75, 76, 78–9, 80, 98, 125, 168, 180, 235, 236, 241
Montagu, John, fourth earl of Sandwich 8, 103, 114, 120, 124, 125–6, 127, 128, 129, 130, 131, 133, 139–40, 143, 150, 151, 161, 168
Montagu, Lady Mary Wortley 81
Montesquieu, Charles de Secondat, Baron 306
  Persian Letters 63
Moore, Thomas 73, 78, 284
Moravian Christianity 108, 109
Mordaunt, Anna Maria 64
Mordaunt, Charles, Earl of Peterborough 64
More, Hannah 1–2
Morgan, Mary 98, 99, 121
Morgan, Revd Dr Caesar 98
Morganwg, Iolo (Edward Williams) 119
Morland, Samuel 49
Morris, John 100
Morris, Lewis 58, 59, 106, 110, 119
Morris, Richard 48
Mosaic history 38, 47, 224, 227
Moser, Joseph 197
Mostyn, Sir Roger 43, 58, 59, 121, 122, 203
Mostyn Hall 57, 99
Motte, Thomas 301, 305
Muʿallaqāt (*Moallakát* in Jonesian transliteration) 83, 84, 87, 143, 155, 185, 238
Mubarak ud-Daula 339
Mughal empire and governance 3, 65, 66, 342–3, 350, 351, 351n, 32
Mukherjee, S. N. 272
Müller, Friedrich Max 358–9
Murray, Charles 4–5

Murray, Fanny 126
Murray, William, first earl of Mansfield 14, 91–2, 133, 134, 140, 141, 142, 144, 151, 170, 201
Murshidabad 12, 24, 291, 302, 337, 341–2
Muslim law 4, 122, 186, 210, 299, 303, 306, 308
Mustafā, Hājī (M. Raymond) 300, 335–42, 358

Nadir Shah 64–5, 66, 235, 317
Nágacésara tree 248
Naipaul, V. S. 357
Nandakumar, hanged for forgery 306
Napoleon Bonaparte 271
  Egyptian Campaign (1798–9) 261
Nārang, Gopi Chand 351
Nārāyana Purāna 32
Naubahār Zalīl 353–4
Nautical Almanack 222
Nayar, Mandira 333
Nazi Aryanism 40
Nehru, Jawaharlal *Discovery of India* 359
New Annual Register 164, 164 n.1, 245
New Asiatic Miscellany, The 345, 349–51, 350 n.28
Newdigate, Sir Roger 165
Newgate prison 169
Newton, Isaac 43, 44, 45, 47, 222, 225, 274, 325
Nichols, John 175
Nichols, Thomas 159
Nivernois, Duc de 155
Nix, Mary *see* Jones, Mary
Nizāmī 227, 324–5, 332
Nollekens, Joseph 56
North, Frederick, 2nd earl of Guilford [Lord North] 92, 112, 125, 127, 148, 151, 163, 165, 186, 187
Northern circuit 111
Novalis (Friedrich von Hardenberg) 270
Nuh sipihr (Khusrau) 355

'Ode to Spring' (Mesīhī) 82
'Of the Love of God' (Barrow) 274
Ogle, Thomas 256–7
O'Hanlon, Rosalind 408
Oldham, James 185
Omar Khayyām 71, 348–9

'On the Cure of the Elephantiasis' (Khan) 231
Oriental Field Sports (Williamson) 316
Origin of Language and Nations, The (Rowland Jones) 110
Origin of Species, The (Darwin) 47
Ormathwaite papers 26–8
Orme, Robert 5, 214
Onslow, George, first earl of Onslow 167
Ossian 78, 79, 84, 342
Othello (Shakespeare) 150
Othello (pet turtle) 310
Ovid 54, 59, 324
Owain, Prince of Gwynedd 83
Owenson, Sydney (Lady Morgan):
　The Missionary: An Indian Tale 285, 354
　The Wild Irish Girl 354
Oxford circuit 92–3, 103, 111, 115, 142

Pabo Post Prydain 60
Paine, Thomas 3, 196, 202
Paley, William 204
Palmer, Fyze Baksh 336
Palmer, Major William 158, 160, 223, 336
Pancha Ratha temples 216
pandits 18, 25, 34, 89, 222–6, 238, 240, 242, 248, 250, 270, 273, 302, 306, 307, 310, 315, 323, 330, 340
Paradise, John 7, 56, 155, 156, 158, 167, 189, 193
Parker, George, 2nd earl of Macclesfield 49, 52
Parker, Mary, Countess of Macclesfield 51
Parker, Thomas, 1st earl of Macclesfield 49
Parks, Frances 301
Parr, Samuel 55, 114, 173, 208, 310
Parsons, John 234, 320
Parsons, William 244
Pārvatī, goddess 269, 287–8
Paterson, John David 216
Pathak, Bhavani 290
patronage system 66, 67, 88, 125, 151, 154, 161, 166, 167, 183, 187
　ancient Welsh system 60, 119, 125
　and Indian scholarship and poetry 15, 214, 309, 346, 347–8

Peace of Amiens (1802) 261
Peace of Paris (1763) 155
Pennant, Thomas 202
Pepys, Sir William Weller 168
Percy, Thomas 29, 60, 120–1, 132
perjury 306
　Welsh/Indian comparison 97
Persian Eclogues (Collins) 77
Persian language 8
　relationship with Arabic 62
　similarities with Sanskrit 37–8
Persian Letters (Montesquieu) 63
Peterloo massacre (1819) 204
Petievich, Carla 353
Petty [*formerly* Fitzmaurice], William, 2nd earl of Shelburne and 1st marquess of Lansdowne 2, 69, 156, 157, 189, 190, 193–4, 195
Philipps, Richard, Baron Milford 98
Phillips, Isaac 101
Philosophia Botanica (Linnaeus) 246, 248
Phipps, Constantine John, Baron Mulgrave 129, 130, 132, 150
　A Voyage towards the North Pole 129
Picart, Bernard 219
Pigot, George, Baron Pigot 185
Pigot, Admiral Hugh 184
Pigs' Meat (journal) 178
Pindar 54, 85, 230, 237, 244
Piozzi, Hester Lynch Thrale 56, 57 n.14, 87, 170, 244
Pitt, William, first earl of Chatham [Pitt the elder] 236, 237
Pitt, William [Pitt the younger] 123, 128, 309
Plants of the Coast of Coromandel (Roxburgh) 246
Plassey, Battle of (1757) 23
Platt, Ebenezer Smith, case 138, 139, 140–1
Playfair, John 223
Plowden, Elizabeth 241
Plowden, Sophia 16, 241
Plumer, Thomas 111–12, 114
pluralism 286
　in Indian culture and religion 21, 294, 333–61
Pococke, Edward 62
　Aleppo manuscript 82, 83, 186
Pococke, Richard 126

'Poem of Tarafa, The' 238
Poems of Anna Maria, The (A. M. Jones) 244, 321
Poetics (Aristotle) 265
Poisson, Jeanne-Antionette (Madame de Pompadour) 75
Polier, Lieutenant-Colonel Antoine 240, 336
Pollard, Walter 132
Pollen, John 93
Poly-Olbion (Drayton) 110
Ponsonby [*née* Spencer], Henrietta Frances, countess of Bessborough 98
Ponsonby, Sarah 331
Pont de Vile, Antoine de Fériol, Comte de *La Somnambule* 149
Poore, Edward 93, 112, 113
Pope, Alexander 18, 54, 80–81, 90
possessive individualism, theory of 191
Pott, Percival 327
Powell, Charles 187–8
Powell, Sarah, murder 116 *see also* Williams, George, trial
Poyntz, Anna Maria 70
Poyntz, Isabella 125
Poyntz, William 125, 148, 150
prakriti (nature seen as female) 30, 32, 263, 275, 281, 290
Pratt, Mary 247
press warrants, legality of 142
Price, Richard 45, 69, 118, 158, 168–9, 177, 185, 253
Priestley, Joseph 69, 158, 177
Prime, Lady Hannah 56
Principia (Newton) 223
Prinsep, James 240
Prior, William 54
prisons, 18th century 122–3, 300, 305
Pritchard, Arthur 5, 25, 188–9, 192
Protestant Association 172
Proto Indo-European language, Jones hypothesis of 37
Psalms 113, 178
Ptolemy 247

Qissa Rangeen (Hasan Shah) 30
Queen Mab (Shelley) 78
'Quintuple Alliance' of radical reformers 191

Rādhā 32, 274, 275, 276, 277, 278, 279, 280–1, 282, 283, 326
Rādhākānta 248, 323, 357
Rādhā-Krishna cult 275, 276, 281
Rāgavibodha (Somanātha) 31
Ragonaut Chubdar 301–2
Rajan, Chandra 268
Rajan, Rajeshwari Sunder 290
Ram, Hari 293
Rāmachandra, pandit 34, 224
Rāmalocana, pandit 35, 240, 270
Rangpur peasant revolt, (1783) 293–4
rasa 244, 267, 275, 285
concept in theatre 264–5
Ray, Martha 130–1
Rāy-Mangala (Das) 220
Reconnaissance de Sacountala, La (de Chézy) 259
Recruitment Acts (1778, 1779) 128
Reeves, John 197
reincarnation, Hindu belief 253
'Rekhtah' language and poetry 350–2, 353–4
rēkhtī (genre in which male poet adopts a feminine voice) 353–4
Reports (Foster) 157
Reviczki, Count Charles 67, 75, 85
Rex v. Humphrey Sturt Esq. 295–6
Reynolds, Sir Joshua 14, 56, 67, 166, 182, 183, 195, 221
Rg Veda 317
Burial Hymn 326, 327
Rice, George 93
Richard II statute on 'impressment' 144
Richardson, John 67
Richmond, Charles Lennox, Duke of 192, 198
Rights of Man, The (Paine) 197, 202
Ritusamhāra (Kālidāsa) 318–19
Robertson, James 76
Robinson, Henry Crabbe 267
Robinson, Mary 'Perdita' 244
Rocher, Rosane 88 n.40, 208 n.6, 226
Rockingham-Shelburne coalition 187
Romanticism 40, 59, 72, 83, 86, 87, 105, 179, 206, 232, 233, 238, 244, 359
British 73, 78, 79, 82, 104, 169, 231, 244, 284, 285, 354
German 179, 259, 260, 266

Indophilia 260, 261, 263, 264, 272, 284, 320, 359
  and the lyric impulse 82, 86–7, 106, 275, 277, 284
  and Orientalism 72–3, 77–87, 206, 232, 233, 260, 284, 320
Rothman, Charles 327
rotten boroughs 138, 149, 164
Rousseau, Jean-Jacques 69–70, 106, 313
Roxburgh, Dr William 246, 361
Roy, Arundhati 359–60
Royal Society 43, 44, 45, 47, 88, 147, 206, 246, 247
  expedition (1768–71) 127
  and gender 241
Royal Society of Copenhagen 66, 88
Rūmī, Jalāl ud-Din 274, 349
Russell, Dr Patrick 246

Sabarmati Express atrocity (2002) 333
sabk-i Hindī, Indian style diction 352
Saʻdī 176, 213, 232, 311
  Bostan 85, 350
Safavid dynasty 65
Said, Edward 19, 39, 226, 261
sákti, feminine principle 30, 32, 263, 269, 275, 281, 285, 287, 290, 318, 354
Śakuntalā (Kālidāsa) 251–72, 276, 286, 308, 319, 334
  British Raj condemnation of 286
  Jones as cultural mediator/translator 256–60, 271–2,
  Jones's 'discovery' of 252–6
  Jones's translation compared with Rajan's 268–9, 269–70
  and Romanticism 263, 264
saltpetre trade 10, 24
Śankara 262
Sankhya philosophy 324
Sanskrit 18, 34, 89, 225, 226, 238, 239, 256, 261, 355, 359
  botanical names 247, 248
  culture 42, 112, 219, 247, 256, 260, 267, 269, 283, 285, 307, 319, 334
  dictionaries 248
  similarities with Persian 37–8, 355
Sappho 85, 86
Saratoga, British surrender 148
Sarman, Rādhākānta 240, 272

Sarman, Servōru 248
Sarum Missal, wedding liturgy 276
satī 326–7
Sauda 233
Saunders, Robert 247
Savile, Sir George 132, 167, 169–70
Sawbridge, James 192
Sawbridge, John 132
Schiller, Friedrich 270, 284
Schlegel, August Wilhelm 260–1
Schlegel, Friedrich 177, 178, 179, 260–1, 262, 267, 284
Schopenhauer, Arthur 260
Schubert, Franz 271
Schultens, Hendrik Albert 66, 91, 194, 195, 239
SCI *see* Society for Constitutional Information
Scott, Dr William 166
Scott, John 169
Scott Key, Francis 178
Scott-Waring, Major John 311
Scrafton, Luke 336
Seasons, The (Kālidāsa) 318–19, 334
Secker, Thomas, archbishop of Canterbury 219–20
Seïr Mutaqharin (Ghulam Husain) 335, 337, 339, 341–2, 343
Selden, John 165
Sen, Amartya 357
Sepoy Revolt (1857) 309, 358
Sermono, Śri Ramchurn 35
Serraun, Mary 297–8
Seven Years' War 236
Seward, Anna 249, 320
sexuality and eroticism in Indian literature 265–6, 267–8, 269–70, 275–84
Shāh 'Ālam, Mughal Emperor 62–3, 149, 342
Shah Jahān, Mughal Emperor 274
Shah, Hasan 30
Shaffer, Elinor 228
Shahrazâd 62, 256, 340
Shakespeare, Kālidāsa compared 262
Sharp, Granville 133, 134, 135, 139
Shelburne, Lord *see* Petty
Shelley, Percy 73, 78, 284–5, 361
  'Hymn to Intellectual Beauty' 231

Shelley, Percy (*cont.*)
   Prometheus Unbound 285, 361
   'Zeinab and Kathema' 285
Shepherd, Richard 69
Shepherd Fleets, Inc. v. Opryland USA, Inc. 185
Sheridan, Elizabeth 294
Sheridan, Richard Brinsley 55, 208, 351
Sherlocke, Martin 180
Shigurf Namah-i-Velaët (I'tisam ud-Din) 63
Shikūh, Dāra 212, 216, 343, 354, 360
   Majma 'al-bahrayn ('The Mingling of the Two Oceans') 212, 273–4, 343, 346
   Sirr-i Akbar ('The Great Secret') 224
Shikūh, Sulaimān 353–4
Shipley, Amelia 310
Shipley, Elizabeth 331
Shipley, Jonathan, bishop of St Asaph (Jones's father-in-law) 2, 58, 64, 88, 180, 330
Shipley, Penelope [*née* Yonge] 199
Shipley, William, dean of St Asaph (Jones's brother-in-law) 2, 7, 199, 201, 202, 203
Shore, John, Lord Teignmouth 44, 64, 205, 219, 273, 291, 293, 327, 328, 331, 336
Shuja ud-Daula, Nawab 223
Siegel, Lee 277, 278, 281 n.39, 283
Sikandar Shah, Sultan 217
Simonides 85
Simpson, Thomas 46
Singh, Raja Devi 293–4
Singh, Sooroup 302
Siraj ud-Daula, Nawab 23
Śiva 22, 25, 108–9, 263, 269, 281, 287, 288
slavery and slave trade 7, 35, 44, 133–4, 135, 142, 145, 156, 174, 193
   and the American cause 156
   Abyssinian females 337
   East Indian 299–300
Smith, Adam 161, 195, 292
Smith, Charlotte 245
Smith, Nathaniel 213
Smith, General Richard 'Nabob' 76, 102, 149, 150, 168, 186, 214
Smollett, Tobias *Roderick Random* 134

Society of Antient Britons 120
Society for Charitable Purposes 122, 128
Society for Constitutional Information (SCI) 132, 149, 178, 180, 189–90, 195, 197, 200, 202
Society for Effecting the Abolition of the Slave Trade 40, 257
Society for Promoting Christian Knowledge 48
Society of Gentlemen Supporters of the Bill of Rights 104, 132, 146
Solkin, David 100
Somanātha 31
Sommerset v. Steuart 133, 134, 142
Song of Solomon 86, 274, 276
Southey, Robert 73, 78, 131, 284, 285
   The Curse of Kehama 285
Speke, Peter 24
Spence, Thomas 178, 179
Spencer, George John, Viscount Althorp, later 2nd Earl Spencer 37, 61, 64, 69, 70, 88, 93, 140, 161, 177, 180, 237, 313, 331, 332
   parliamentary career 186–7
   Sir William's letters to 17, 57, 100, 102, 115, 124, 130, 143, 147, 252
Spencer, John, 1st Earl Spencer 64, 70
Spencer [*née* Poyntz], (Margaret) Georgiana, Countess Spencer 64, 67, 69, 70, 122, 125, 128, 142, 151, 155, 158, 167, 187–8, 192
Spencer [*née* Bingham], Lady Lavinia 180, 181
Spenser, Edmund 24, 274
'spikenard', Indian 246–7
Spinoza, Baruch 262
Srīmad Bhāgwatan 22
St Winifred's Well 58
Staël, Madame de (Baroness Anne Louise Germaine Staël-Holstein 284
Stapylton, Robert 133–4
Statham, Nicholas and Sir Robert Brooke *Les reports del cases en ley* 106
Stonehouse, John 350
Strahan, William 129
Stuart, Colonel Charles 'Hindoo' 311
Stukeley, Revd William 46–7, 126

Styles, Ann 135, 136
Sūfi poets and poetry 176, 221, 274, 275, 347, 349, 352
Sūfism 20, 212–13, 225, 274, 349, 350, 354, 361
  concept of *suhl-i kul* (peace with all) 211
Sulivan, Laurence 5, 151
Sumner, Robert 55
Sundarbans 246, 289
Sūrdās 32
Sūrya (Hindu sun god) 5, 23, 317–18, 319
Sūrya-siddhānta, astronomical manuscript 223
Swinton, Captain Archibald 63, 66
Sydney, Algernon 182
Sylvester, Josuah 178
syncretism 20, 21, 107, 173, 212, 220–21, 234, 258, 273–4, 340, 343, 350, 351, 354, 359, 360
  and Amīr Khusrau's poetry 356
  mythology, development of 227

Tabatabai, Ghulam Husain Khan 335, 339, 340, 341, 342, 343, 351, 358
Taliesin 59, 60, 105, 109
Tamāla blossoms 326
tapas, power accumulated through austerity 256
Tarafa 84, 238
Tarīkh-i Nādirī (Mahdī Khān Astarābādī) 64
Tasso, Torquato 271
Tate, Nahum *King Lear* (adaptation) 4
Tempest, The (Shakespeare) 264
Teresa of Avila 276
Tessier, Alexandre-Henri 148
Thackeray, Revd Dr Thomas 55
Theocritus 271
Thomson, James 177, 178, 182
Thornhill, Captain Cuthbert 337
Thornton, Major John 153
Thurlow, Edward, 1st Baron Thurlow 138, 140, 141, 152, 154, 186, 187
tigers, protection from 220–1
Tīpū Sultān 8, 209, 316, 347
Tiretta, Edward 328

Tlysau yr Hen Oesoedd (periodical) 59
Tooke, John Horne 132, 192
Tower of Babel 38, 47, 110
Townsend, James 132, 192
Townsend Jones, William case 300–1
trade unionism, roots in the box-clubs 197
Trautmann, Thomas 38, 224, 225, 227
Tribonian 309
'Trioedd Ynys Prydain' (Triads of the Isle of Britain) 60
Trivedi, Sarvoru Śarmā 330
tropical medicine 24, 226–7, 246, 268, 317–18
Tufton, Henry 121
Turk's Head Club 76, 88, 102, 121, 132, 148, 161, 166, 168, 175, 180, 196
Turner, George 167
Turner, Joseph Mallord William 93, 106
Turner, Samuel 223, 247
Twelve Views of Places in the Kingdom of Mysore (Kyd) 209
Twining, Thomas 310, 311, 312
Tyler, George 303
Tyler, Wat 44

Ullah, Sheriut 300
University College, Oxford 61, 63–4, 166, 189, 195
Upaniṣads 212, 224, 231, 274, 346
Urdu language and poetry 350–2, 353
Uri, Joannes 220
Ursa Major 325

Vali, Mohammed Vali 334, 350, 351, 352
Vallancey, Colonel Charles 354
Vansittart, Henry, governor of Bengal 126 n.1, 232, 336
Vansittart, Henry (son of the above) 232
Vansittart, Robert 103–4, 126 n. 1
varna dharma, purification rules 35
Varuna, Vedic god of the ocean 18
Vedantic philosophy 258, 262, 354, 260, 273
Vedas 212, 225, 346
Vesey, Elizabeth 1, 76, 167, 180, 241
Vidyarthi, Abdul Haque 35
Views of Calcutta (Baillie) 221–2
Vigo Bay, Battle of (1702) 44

Vināyaca 224
Virgil 54, 83, 324
Vishnu 22, 25, 42, 217, 228, 279, 293, 361 *see also* 'Hymn to Náráyena'
Vivādabhangārnava (Jagannātha) 323, 327
Vivādā-sārāmava (Jones/Trivedi) 330
Volney, Constantin-François Chasseboeuf, Comte de 261
Voltaire, François Arouet de 73, 102, 224
von Dahlberg, Johann Friedrich 284
von Görres, Johann Joseph 266

Wade, John 242, 300
Wahhabi Islam 360
Walker, Joseph Cooper 233
Wallace, Thomas 140
Walpole, Horace, 4th Earl of Orford 14, 70, 168, 180–1
Waltham Black Act 115
Warton, Joseph 148
Warton, Thomas 104
Washbrook, David 308
Washington, George 138
Watson, Captain 148
Wealth of Nations (Smith) 292
Wedderburn, Alexander 142
Wedgwood, Josiah 257
Welch, Anne 56–7, 57 n.14
Wellesley, Richard, Marquess Wellesley 212
Welsh bardism, decline in 119
Welsh Bible 48
Welsh language 109–10
  as indicator of cultural/moral inferiority 97
  translations in court 96
Wentworth, Charles Watson-, 2nd marquess of Rockingham 187, 193–4
Wesley, John 219
West, Benjamin 138
Whang Atong 21
Whatman, James 318
Whig party 45, 52, 64, 69, 137, 157, 165–7, 168, 177, 181, 187
whipping, as punishment 305–6
'White Town', Calcutta 9
Whitehead, William 109

White's Club, London 196
Wilberforce, William 219, 294
Wilkes, John 34, 114, 125–6, 132–3, 134, 137, 138, 143, 151, 152, 161, 168, 170–1, 174, 175, 180, 190, 197, 210, 212, 213–14, 215, 216, 231, 232, 239, 261, 272
  Essay on Woman 126
Wilkins, Charles 18, 210, 212, 319, 324
  Bhăgvăt-Gēētā (trans. Wilkins) 25, 213–14, 215, 232
Willes, Edward 160
Williams, David 118
Williams, John 'Bloom' 114
Williams, Moses 48
Williamson, Captain John 5, 6, 8, 12
Wilson, Horace Hayman 240, 327, 358
Wilson, Richard 99, 105
Wilton, Joseph 14, 56
Windus, Colonel Edward 139–40
Wollstonecraft, Mary 131, 256
Wombwell, John 337
women's rights 307–8
Wordsworth, William 79, 106, 131, 267
  Lyrical Ballads 82, 83, 86
Worsley, Sir Richard 167
Wraxall, Nathaniel 137, 180, 181
Wright, Patience 138
Wynn, Sir Watkin Williams 120, 130, 203
Wyvill, Christopher 149, 164

Yajurveda 306
Yeates, Thomas 189–90
Yonge, Sir George 246
Yorke, Philip, 1st Earl of Hardwicke 43, 49,
Yorke, Philip (great nephew of the above) 163
Yorkshire Association 164
Yugas (aeons) 224

Zaidpuri, Ghulām Hussain Salim 9–10
Zayn al-Din, Sheikh 15
Zend-Avesta (Anquetil-Duperron) 74, 224
Zia-ul-Haq, General Muhammad 361
Zoffany, Johan Joseph 12, 14, 15, 336
Zoroastrian Avesta 74
Zoroastrianism 108, 107–8